T0339991

Corporate Reputation and the News Media

This volume examines agenda-setting theory as it applies to the news media's influence on corporate reputation. It presents interdisciplinary, international, and empirical investigations examining the relationship between corporate reputation and the news media throughout the world. Providing coverage of more than 25 countries, contributors write about their local media and business communities, representing developed, emerging, and frontier markets—including Argentina, Brazil, Chile, China, Germany, Greece, Japan, Nigeria, Spain, and Turkey, among others. The chapters present primary and secondary research on various geo-political issues, the nature of the news media, the practice of public relations, and the role of public relations agencies in each of the various countries.

Each chapter is structured to consider two to three hypotheses in the country under discussion, including:

- the impact of media visibility on organizational prominence, top-of-mind awareness, and brand-name recognition;
- the impact of media favorability on the public's organizational images of these firms;
- in some cases, how media coverage of specific public issues and news topics relates to the associations people form of specific firms.

Contributors contextualize their findings in light of the geopolitical environment of their home countries, the nature of their media systems, and the relationship between business and the news media within their countries' borders.

Incorporating scholarship from a broad range of disciplines, including advertising, strategic management, business, political communication, and sociology, this volume has much to offer scholars and students examining business and the news media.

Craig E. Carroll (Ph.D., University of Texas at Austin) is Assistant Professor in the School of Journalism and Mass Communication at the University of North Carolina at Chapel Hill.

Communication Series
Jennings Bryant/Dolf Zillmann, General Editors

Corporate Reputation and the News Media

Agenda-Setting within Business News Coverage in Developed, Emerging, and Frontier Markets

Edited by
Craig E. Carroll

Routledge
Taylor & Francis Group

NEW YORK AND LONDON

First published 2011
by Routledge
711 Third Avenue, New York, NY 10017

Simultaneously published in the UK
by Routledge
2 Park Square, Milton Park, Abingdon, Oxon OX14 4RN

Routledge is an imprint of the Taylor & Francis Group, an informa business

© 2011 Taylor & Francis

Typeset in Sabon by EvS Communication Networx, Inc.

Library of Congress Cataloging in Publication Data
Corporate reputation and the news media : agenda-setting within business news coverage in developed, emerging, and frontier markets / edited by Craig E. Carroll. — 1st ed.
p. cm.
1. Corporate culture. 2. Mass media and business. I. Carroll, Craig E.
HD58.7.C6437 2010
659.2—dc22
2010002846

ISBN 13: 978-0-415-87153-2 (hbk)
ISBN 13: 978-0-415-87152-5 (pbk)
ISBN 13: 978-0-203-86858-4 (ebk)

This book is dedicated to
Maxwell McCombs, Charles J. Fombrun, and Cees B.M. van Riel:
Gentlemen, Scholars, and Intellectual Entrepreneurs.

Contents

PART III
Corporate Reputation and the News Media in Emerging and Frontier Markets   **241**

Foreword

Maxwell McCombs

In the decades since the seminal Chapel Hill study during the 1968 U.S. presidential election, agenda-setting theory has evolved from a narrowly focused theory of media effects to a broad theoretical map of the public opinion process that encompasses four distinct stages. These stages include the origins of the media agenda; the influence of this media agenda on the focus of public attention on both key topics and major aspects of these topics; the consequences of these two levels of agenda-setting effects on the public's attitudes and opinions; and the psychology of this process. For most of its intellectual history, agenda-setting theory has evolved primarily in a political communication setting, particularly in regard to public issues and political candidates. This is now changing.

In recent years agenda-setting theory has expanded to domains as diverse as professional sports, religion, and business. This latter area, and more specifically the agenda-setting influence of news coverage on corporate reputations, is the focus of this book whose chapters are a comprehensive and exciting opening gambit into this new domain. *Corporate Reputation and the News Media* is comprehensive in two distinct ways. It is geographically comprehensive with chapters examining the agenda-setting influence of business news coverage in more than two dozen countries. Every continent is represented here with a range of markets that extends from developed countries to frontier countries. And these markets are examined from a practical perspective as well as the broad theoretical perspective of agenda-setting. These dual perspectives buttress each other. The specifics of the outcomes in individual countries have greater value because this book replicates the agenda-setting process regarding corporate reputations across a vast international array of economic and business situations. In turn, the specifics from these different settings point the way to a more nuanced theoretical view of the contingent conditions for these agenda-setting effects.

In sum, this is a pioneering book in two important regards. In a global economy, *Corporate Reputation and the News Media* offers an international look at the impact of news coverage on public opinion about major corporations. In this new agenda-setting arena of corporate reputations, this volume maps the basic features of the agenda-setting process across a diverse business landscape. Simultaneously, it also makes an important theoretical contribution by bringing additional details to our intellectual maps of the agenda-setting process. *Corporate Reputation and the News Media* is an excellent contemporary example of Wilbur Schramm's repeated observation in the early days of communication research that there is nothing as practical as a good theory. In this instance, agenda-setting theory offers a succinct intellectual guide to the very practical matter of the influence of business news on corporate reputations.

Preface

Craig E. Carroll

In writing and editing this book, we are responding to the growing global interest in understanding the media's influence on corporate reputation. One of the primary motivators for this book was the spike in global interest about the influence of the news media on corporate reputation. This interest coincided with the 40th anniversary of the agenda-setting paradigm and the growth in the practice and scholarly interest in business news. In one sense, we wanted bring research on corporate reputation and the news media up-to-date with the rest of agenda-setting scholarship from political communication.

Politics, economic disparities, cultural differences, and ideology kept us apart, but our interest in the media's influence on corporate reputation brought us together. Within 2 hours of the original invitation by email, 70% of the chapter authors agreed to contribute chapters. The chapters were written thousands of miles apart, across many time zones and languages, and in some cases translated. Translators were used on chapters or raw materials, such as media texts and the articles for the literature review from Arabic, Spanish, Chinese, and Portuguese. I had the joy and privilege of meeting with many of the contributors in their home countries; when that was not possible, we convened at annual conferences of our respective fields.

Our contributors come from a number of networks: International Communication Association (ICA), Association for Educators in Journalism and Mass Communication (AEJMC), annual attendees of the Reputation Institute's International Conference on Corporate Reputation, Identity, and Competitiveness, and the Academy of Management. Additional scholars were found via referrals from Maxwell McCombs, Krishnamurthy Sriramesh, and Chris Roush.

Altogether, we included contributors from a wide range of disciplinary backgrounds for a project most closely related to journalism and public relations. These disciplines included organizational communication, management, marketing, economics, sociology, political science, and business journalism. For many of the chapter contributors, it was the first time for the collaborators to work together. And, they were doing so across disciplinary lines: business and journalism, political science and sociology, communication and information science, to name a few. We also have a wide range of generations in scholarship represented in the volume, from full professors who have been researching agenda-setting since close to the beginning, and young scholars recently completing their dissertations.

There were a number of issues that are worth more attention than I was able to give through this edited collection. Some of the changes we did not address fully include how satellite and cable TV, the Internet, corporate websites and online news media, or social media may have influenced our results. Simply, we needed to start somewhere. We now have directions for us to go with future research.

Some say that editing a book could be as much work as writing one and could produce the same effect. Not so with this volume! There is no way one person could have produced the wealth of knowledge generated within the same period of time. First off, I thank the chapter contributors for their patience, diligence, enthusiasm, and commitment to this project. I am lucky and blessed indeed to have such good colleagues to offer chapters. The chapter contributors were Peter Kjaer, Mette Morsing, Vilma Luoma-aho, Turo Uskali, Jouni Heinonen, Antti Ainamo, Roei Davidson, Nicolas Chazaud, Sabine Einwiller, Günter Bentele, Christine Landmeier, Eva Goutzamani, Stelios Zyglidopoulos, Philemon Banti-maroudis, Elena Dalpiaz, Davide Ravasi, Kenichi Ishii, Toshio Takeshita, May-May Meijer, Øyvind Ihlen, Peggy Simcic Brønn, Ángel Arrese, Manuel Baigorri, Magnus Fredriksson, Maria Grafström, Mark Eisenegger, Mario Schranz, Jörg Schneider, Federico Rey Lennon, Gonzalo Diego Peña, Ana de Castro Almeida, Dário Arantes Nunes, Leandro Batista, Magdalena Browne, Martin Kunc, LiFeng Deng, Kevin Keenan, Katja Koikkalainen, Heewon Cha, Sung-Un Yang, Serra Görpe, Erkan Yüksel, Olusanmi Amujo, Olutayo Otubanjo, Beatrice Lan-inhun, Daniel Adejo, Klement Podnar, Dejan Verčič, and Timothy Walters.

Thanks to Linda Bathgate who provided the commitment to this project from Routledge and the Series Editor Jennings Bryant. Also, Katherine Ghezzi, our Editorial Assistant on the project helped us stay on schedule, and was super organized throughout out this process.

Those who had a hand in helping me locate chapter contributors include Charles Fombrun, Max McCombs, Sherry Ferguson, Stelios Zyglidopoulos, Chris Roush, and Peter Kjaer.

Providing a home base from which to *launch* this project, Christos Pitelis at the Center for International Business and Management, Judge Business School, University of Cambridge, hosted me for a research leave. Thank you.

My appreciation for the candor and feedback from executives and students at Institute de Empressa's Marketing Management program in Madrid, Spain, and the University of Lugano's MSCom in Lugano, Italy, who read various chapters as a part of their course assignments.

I also thank the panelists and attendees at various conferences from whence the chapters had early opportunity for presenting their work: *International Communication Association* (Chicago, Illinois); annual conference on *Corporate Reputation, Identity, and Competitiveness* (BI School of Management, Oslo, Norway); the *Academy of Management* (Anaheim, California); *International Public Relations Research Conference* (Miami, Florida); the annual Agenda Setting conference organized by Media Tenor (Bonn, Germany). I also appreciate the opportunities to share the project with participants of the *European Associa-*

tion of Communication Directors (Brussels, Belgium) and the *European Center for Reputation Studies* (Rome, Italy).

From industry, I think Reid Walker, Katie Paine, Larry Gallo, Chip Griffin, and Ray Daley. I also appreciate the staff from the European Center for Reputation Studies, Lexis-Nexis Corporation, Harris Interactive, and Reputation Institute for their insights, feedback, inspiration, and resources supporting this project.

Special thanks to former students and research assistants who helped with a variety of logistics, tracking down references, finding translators, assisting with copy editing, and preparing the volume for publication: Laura Keller, Kelly Rebeck, Melita Garza, Liles Demmink, CC Glenn, and Rebecca Denison.

From the Observatory on Corporate Reputation I wish to thank: Marianna King, Stephanie Nobles, Josh Criscoe, Natalie Williams, Leslie Gray, Nell Huang, and Sun Young Lee.

Friends and mentors who provided guidance and counsel along the way: Rod Hart, Tom Goodnight, K. Sriramesh, Betteke van Ruler, Cees van Riel, Francesco Lurati, Sherry Ferguson, Clarke Caywood, James O'Rourke, IV, and David Deephouse. To my global friends and peers: Chantal, Eva, Guido, Joep, Johan, Klement, Laura, Mark, May-May, Sabine, Samuel, Stelios, Vilma, and Øyvind.

From UNC I thank: Dulcie Straughan, Don Shaw, Richard Cole, Jock Lauterer, Francesca Dillman Carpentier, Chris Roush, and Diego Garcia, and from USC: Sandy Green and Tom Goodnight.

To my dissertation committee from the University of Texas at Austin: Max McCombs, Chuck Whitney, Steve Reese, Rod Hart, and James Westphal.

Then finally, a special thanks again to Max McCombs, Charles Fombrun, and Cees van Riel, to whom this volume is dedicated.

Part I
Introduction

1 International Perspectives on Agenda-Setting Theory Applied to Business News

Craig E. Carroll

Introduction

For more than 40 years, the agenda-setting hypothesis—"While the news media may not be successful in telling the public what to think, they are quite successful in telling the public what to think about"—has been a cornerstone of political and mass communication research. The goal of this research has been to understand the news media's role in shaping public opinion (McCombs, 2004; McCombs & Shaw, 1972). In an examination of major milestones within the field of mass communication, Lowery and DeFleur (1995) noted that agenda-setting theory "has now become a well-trodden path in the research territory of the communication scholar" (p. 787). Dearing and Rogers (1996) noted that by the mid-1990s the agenda-setting research program had produced 350 scholarly publications. Slightly before the 40th anniversary of this program of research, McCombs (2004) listed over 400 empirical investigations that had been published using agenda setting as the framework for mass media and public opinion.

What is somewhat surprising is that for all of the research conducted during the first 30 years of the life of the agenda-setting program of research, many scholars missed a fundamental shift in the media's aggregate agenda: the rise of business news. With the creation of the Internet, and with average citizens becoming more savvy about investing in the stock market—and then losing their savings in economic crises—business news, in its many forms, has come to be an increasingly significant part of the media and public agenda.

The primary focus of agenda-setting theory applied to business news has been in the domain of corporate reputation (Carroll & McCombs, 2003), although considerable research has focused on the connection between media coverage and stock price or the general financial performance of firms (e.g., Deephouse, 2000). Corporate reputation is a concept with at least three dimensions. These dimensions include a firm's public prominence, its public esteem, and the series of qualities or attributes for which a firm is known. Corporate reputation has been a subject of considerable interest among scholars and practitioners because it is related to being able to increase market share, lower market costs, lower distribution costs, charge a premium, avoid overregulation, weather bad times, align employees, attract and retain talent, attract investors, gain access to new global markets, and have more favorable news coverage (Dowling, 2001; Jeffries-Fox Associates, 2000).

Global Interest in Corporate Reputation and the News Media

The present volume reflects the global spike of attention that agenda-setting theory applied to organizations has received from scholars around the world, particularly in the area of corporate reputation. The purpose of this edited volume is to examine three agenda-setting hypotheses in the context of the news media's influence on corporate reputation in developed, emerging, and frontier markets. Depending upon the level of research development in each country, each team of contributors is testing (or considering) two, or all three, of the following hypotheses in their home countries:

1. *The impact of firms' media salience on organizational prominence, top-of-mind awareness, or brand-name recognition.* For firms to acquire reputation, the public must first think about them (Carroll & McCombs, 2003). Adapting Cohen's (1963) well-known dictum about the media and politics to the study of firms, Carroll and McCombs argued that, while the news media may not be successful in telling the public what to think about a specific firm, they often succeed in telling the public which firms to think about. This level of "thinking about" is a firm's *public prominence* (Stocking, 1984).
2. *The impact of firms' media favorability on the public's images of or esteem for such firms.* A firm's public esteem is the degree to which the public likes, trusts, admires, and respects it. Without a base level of trust, admiration, and respect, individuals lack sufficient incentives to consider having a relationship with an organization, whether through employment, investing, product consumption, or social causes.
3. *The impact of issue coverage, news topics, or company attributes on the attributes people associate with firms.* Cognitive or substantive attributes are the series of qualities that a firm possesses or that are ascribed to it either implicitly or explicitly, constituting the third dimension of reputation. The question becomes not what is thought about these cognitive attributes, but which cognitive attributes are thought about at all.

The contributors then contextualize their findings in light of the geopolitical environment of their home countries, the nature of their media systems, and the relationship between business and the news media in their particular societies.

This edited volume contains interdisciplinary, international, and empirical investigations examining the relationship between corporate reputation and the news media throughout the world. Over 20 teams of researchers have been assembled to examine how companies are portrayed through their local (national) press. These countries represent developed, emerging, and frontier markets. The developed markets included in this volume are Denmark, Finland, France, Germany, Greece, Italy, Japan, the Netherlands, Norway, Spain, Sweden, Switzerland, and the United States. The emerging markets are Argentina, Brazil, Chile, China, Russia, and South Korea, and the frontier markets are Turkey, Nigeria, Slovenia, and the United Arab Emirates. The research presented in this volume will enhance national and international bodies of knowledge about the relationship between business and the news media. The chapters present additional primary and secondary research dealing with a variety of geopolitical issues, the nature of the news media, the practice of public relations, and the role of public relations agencies in each of the various countries.

Significance of This Volume

This volume is significant for a number of accomplishments:

First, *the project blends theory, research, and practice,* providing case studies and empirical investigations. We use agenda-setting theory to investigate the effects of the news media on public opinion (specifically, on corporate reputation). We also engage in historical and comparative work in order to contextualize these findings in light of structural and cultural differences in the practices of journalism and public relations in the different countries examined.

Second, *the project is interdisciplinary,* incorporating scholars from the fields of journalism, public relations, communication, advertising, strategic management, business ethics, business and society, political communication, and sociology.

Third, the project is *global and international in scope,* including empirical investigations on the practice of media relations in 24 countries around the world. Only five of our contributors are native English speakers. The book includes a number of "first" investigations of corporate reputation and media relations in various countries, including Chile, China, and Nigeria, among others. Other authors are seminal scholars in their home countries who review and translate knowledge published in their home countries for use by a much wider audience.

Then, finally, the chapters provide the state-of-the-art on research that examines the influence of the news media on corporate reputation. The data, methodologies, and findings vary from country to country depending on the level of research for that country. The methodologies in the chapters vary from literature reviews and secondary analysis of public opinion polls to the collection of original data, including interviews, focus groups, and surveys. Each chapter considers the application of agenda-setting theory from political communication to business communication.

Agenda-Setting Research Applied to Business News in Developed Markets

The first section of the book deals with agenda-setting research applied to organizations in developed markets. Table 1.1 provides a comparative overview of the data and methods used for each chapter.

In chapter 2, Peter Kjaer and Mette Morsing examine the first level and both dimensions of the second level of agenda setting applied to firms in Denmark.

Table 1.1 Data and Methods Used in Agenda-Setting Studies within Developed Markets

Country	Year	Methodology	Prominence	Attributes	Esteem	Number of Firms	Media	Media Time Frame	Public	Poll
Denmark	2006	media analysis & poll	√	√	√	42	4 largest daily newspapers		business leaders	Berlingske Nyheds-magsin's annual image ranking
Finland	2006	media analysis & poll	√	√	√	25	6 media outlets: main newspaper, economic newspaper, website, TV, and business weekly	1 week	business leaders	Arvopaperi
France	2004–2005	media analysis & poll	√			40	2 newspapers: general interest and business newspaper		business leaders	Datops
Greece	2000–2001	media analysis & poll	√		√	30	1 newspaper		General Public	Annual RQ Phase 1

Country	Years	Method				Number	Sources	Frequency	Audience	Survey
Italy	2000–2002	media analysis & poll	√	√	√	30	3 national newspapers	7 months	General Public	Annual RQ Phase 1 and 2
Japan	2003–2005	media analysis & poll	√		√	63 in one industry	4 national newspapers	2 years	General Public	Nikkei Corporate Image Survey
The Netherlands	1997–2000	media analysis & poll	√	√		8; 2 from 4 industries	five national dailies	3 years	General Public	TNS
Spain	2008	media analysis & poll	√	√		30	five national dailies	4 months	business leaders	Merco
Switzerland	2007–2009	media analysis & poll	√	√	√	39 largest Swiss firms	13 newspapers, business newspapers, public TV, news bulletins, weeklies, & political magazines	2 years	General Public	GfK
United States	1999-2000	media analysis & poll			√	30 firms	1 national newspaper	6 months	General Public	Annual Reputation Quotient Phase 1 & 2

They look at 140 firms ranked in the "Gold Image Study" as "Denmark's most prominent firms." The survey results are based on the evaluations of Danish business managers, who evaluate the firms on nine dimensions: responsibility, financial strength, innovation, communication, quality, leadership and management, employees, credibility, and competitiveness.

In chapter 3, Vilma Luoma-aho, Turo Uskali, Jouni Heinonen, and Antti Ainamo examine the first level and both dimensions of the second level of agenda setting applied to firms in Finland. They look at the status of 347 firms in 2006—the firms analyzed appeared in an average of 5 years of the general reputation ranking of the 100 biggest publicly traded Finnish firms.

In chapter 4, Roei Davidson and Nicolas Chazaud examine the first level of agenda setting applied to firms in France. They look at the 40 firms listed on the CAC index of large companies traded on the Paris stock exchange.

In chapter 5, Sabine Einwiller, Günter Bentele, and Christine Landmeier examine the first and the affective dimension of the second level of agenda setting applied to firms in Germany. They provide a descriptive study using data reported on by the Media Tenor Institute, which examined all companies that appeared in the politics and business sections of 15 media outlets. Einwiller et al. examine the agenda-setting hypothesis for the 10 best and the 10 worst cases, assuming that in these cases the agenda-setting effects would be most striking.

In chapter 6, Eva Goutzamani, Stelios Zyglidopoulos, and Philemon Bantimaroudis examine the first level of agenda setting applied to firms in Greece. They look at the 30 firms appearing in the Reputation Institute's Global RQ Project in Greece (see van Riel & Fombrun, 2002).

In chapter 7, Elena Dalpiaz and Davide Ravasi examine the first level of agenda setting applied to firms in Italy. They focus on the 33 firms appearing in the Reputation Institute's Global RQ Project in Italy (Ravasi, 2002).

In chapter 8, Kenichi Ishii and Toshio Takeshita examine the first level and both dimensions of the second level of agenda setting applied to firms in Japan. They also investigate corporate agenda setting through the use of advertising. Moreover, for the first level of agenda setting, they examine not only awareness of firms, but the amount of buzz generated through the number of messages posted to electronic bulletin boards about the company. They use corporate image data from the Nikkei Corporate Image rankings, which derive from a random sample of Japanese metropolitan areas. For the substantive attributes, they examine two: perceptions of managers and research and development activities.

In chapter 9, May-May Meijer examines the cognitive dimension of the second level of agenda setting. She looks at a variety of Dutch industries, including two firms each from the oil industry, the banking industry, the retail trade food industry, the transportation industry (the railways and the Amsterdam Schiphol Airport), and two professional sectors, the Dutch police and Dutch agriculture. She uses public opinion poll data gathered by TNS NIPO, a national representative sample made up of 1,000 households, all of which are provided with computers.

In chapter 10, Øyvind Ihlen and Peggy Simcic Brønn review the existing Norwegian literature about the first level and both dimensions of the second level of agenda setting. They document how the concept of reputation has become much more popular as a topic in the news media.

In chapter 11, Ángel Arrese and Manuel Baigorri examine the first level of agenda setting applied to firms in Spain. They study 30 firms ranked in the Merco reputation poll. Their study focuses on the agenda-setting effects of business news for business leaders, as their sample from Merco only includes executives, analysts, union members, and directors of consumer associations.

In chapter 12, Magnus Fredriksson and Maria Grafström review the state of Swedish literature about business news and media effects. In their review of the literature, they find only a small sample of studies applying agenda-setting theory.

In chapter 13, Mark Eisenegger, Mario Schranz, and Jörg Schneider examine the first and second levels of agenda setting applied to firms in Switzerland. They study 39 of the largest Swiss companies assessed by the general public. They examine 13 key Swiss media outlets, including both newspapers and television, using a representative poll of the public.

In chapter 14, I examine the first and the affective dimension of the second level of agenda setting applied to firms in the United States. I use the 2000 Harris Interactive Annual RQ, controlling for the previous year's scores from the inaugural year of the RQ. The general public nominated the sample of firms in the chapter study for having a good (or bad) reputation. The companies mentioned the most frequently were included in the study. The respondents were a random sample of the U.S. population over 18 years of age; the sample of media was *The New York Times*, which proved to be the only mainstream newspaper in the United States to give media attention to each of the firms in the sample.

Agenda-Setting Research Applied to Business News in Emerging and Frontier Markets

In the second half of the book, a series of researchers from emerging and frontier markets evaluates the state of agenda-setting research in their home countries. Countries are classified as emerging or frontier markets based on research by the FTSE Group, an independent company jointly owned by *The Financial Times* and the London Stock Exchange. The range of research in these chapters includes literature reviews, focus groups, personal interviews, and case studies—a much wider range of methodologies than that employed in the developed countries surveyed in the first half of the book (see Table 1.2).

In chapter 15, Federico Rey Lennon and Gonzalo Diego Peña report on one of the first, if not the first, studies on corporate reputation in Argentina. Using focus groups, they explore reputation through the concept of institutional credibility. Rather than focusing only on companies, they expanded their study to examine a variety of institutional forms, including the military, government, health care, and education. In their media analysis they examine media portrayals of national, multinational, and small to medium size enterprises (SMEs). They also conducted a telephone survey with 700 respondents to follow up on their focus groups, examining the credibility and power that each institution has

Table 1.2 Data and Methods Used in Agenda-Setting Studies within Emerging and Frontier Markets

Country	Year	Methodology	Prominence	Attributes	Esteem	Number of Firms	Media	Media Time Frame	Public	Poll
Argentina	2006	focus group, content analysis, & telephone survey		√	√	Political, economic, social and religious institutions	1 national newspaper	6 months	General Public	computer assisted telephone survey
Brazil	2005	media analysis & poll	√	√	√	2	1 influential economic newspaper, 1 regional mainstream paper	1 year	General Public	RepTrack
China	2002–2004	media analysis & poll	√	√	√	18-24 firms	2 newspapers	2 years	General Public	Beijing Horizon Research & Consultancy Group
Russia	1990–2007	media analysis & poll	√			top 3 from different time periods	2 leading business newspapers	17 years, 1 week a year	General Public	Ekspert; VCIOM Poll

Country	Year	Method			Sample	Media	Time period	Audience	Source
South Korea	2006	media analysis & poll	√	√	5	3 major news-papers	9 months	General Public	
Turkey	2004–2005	media analysis & poll	√		firms from 5 different sectors	18 national news-papers	2 years	Top managers	Capital magazine's 'Most Admired Companies' Gfk Research
Nigeria	2004–2005	in-depth interviews	√	√	25 banks	1 newspaper	18 months	consumers/investors	
Slovenia	2006		√		100 firms	major Slovenian media data provided by Pristop's clipping service, Kliping	1 year	general and business public	Agency Kline & Partner

in Argentina. Their study is significant for the multifaceted approach to establishing a platform for future reputation research.

In chapter 16, Ana Luisa de Castro Almeida, Dário Arantes Nunes, and Leandro Batista examine all three agenda-setting hypotheses in the context of two large Brazilian organizations that appear on the stock markets in the United States, Brazil, and Spain. They look at the most influential economic newspaper and a large regional newspaper for their media analysis. For their measure of reputation, Almeida et al. use the RepTrak™ Pulse which evaluated 20 companies, but Almeida et al. analyze two of them in more depth. The cognitive attributes the authors investigate include products/services, innovation, workplace, governance, citizenship, leadership, and performance.

In chapter 17, Magdalena Browne and Martin Kunc examine the first and second levels of agenda setting through a series of case studies in Chile. They examine Adimark/LaSegunda's "most respected firms" from 2002 to 2006 and the coverage of two main newspapers 4 months before the published rankings. Through these case studies, the authors focus on three Chilean holding companies—one concentrated mainly in pulp and paper manufacturing, one in energy and natural resources, and one in retail—and a fourth company that is a foreign global brand management corporation, one previously with a low profile in Chile that broke into the top five most recognized firms during the period under discussion.

In chapter 18, LiFeng Deng examines the first level and both dimensions of the second level of agenda setting applied to the firms identified as the most influential in China. He examines the overall awareness of multinational companies, their involvement in corporate social responsibility (CSR) activities, and corporate reputation rankings. For news coverage, he performs a content analysis of the *People's Daily* and *Economic Daily* over a period of one year preceding the poll of 1,252 respondents carried out by the Beijing Horizon Research and Consultancy Group. The number of companies ranged from 18 to 24, depending upon the hypothesis being examined.

In chapter 19, Kevin Keenan reviews the three agenda-setting hypotheses as applied to companies in Egypt. He approaches his research with a case study. He notes the paucity of business news in the country, and discusses how no Egyptian brands appeared in a recent consumer survey based on questions of brand familiarity, relevance, trust, and recommendation. The chapter helps illustrate the varying stages of progress that agenda-setting theory applied to business news has achieved around the world.

In chapter 20, Katja Koikkalainen examines the first level of agenda setting applied to companies in Russia. She examines the two leading Russian business newspapers, pointing out that in Russia the business press was reestablished after the collapse of the Soviet Union. Koikkalainen's chapter is unique because she does not specify the companies to be studied ahead of time, but simply relies on their frequent appearance on the front page of the business section.

In chapter 21, Heewon Cha and Sung-Un Yang examine the first and second levels of agenda setting applied to firms in South Korea. They also examine moderating variables that affect corporate reputation. They report on their study of five companies using a sample of three newspapers. The companies were selected because of their rank in various reputation surveys and the amount of news coverage they received. Their sample consists of about 400 residents in Seoul, South Korea's largest city. The survey content covers unaided and aided awareness of companies studied, evaluations of corporate attributes and companies, company-related information and involvement, issue-related information and involvement, and media credibility. Their study is one of the first agenda-setting studies to apply the research technique of unaided awareness to the study of firms.

In chapter 22, Serra Görpe and Erkan Yüksel examine the first level of agenda setting applied to firms in Turkey. They examined the "Most Admired Companies" of Turkey from five different sectors. This survey relies on the opinions of 1,350 top managers along 19 criteria. Görpe and Yüksel use a sample of 18 different national daily newspapers for their media analysis. The study is unique for the large sample of national newspapers that it employs.

In chapter 23, Olusanmi Amujo, Olutayo Otubanjo, Beatrice Laninhun, and Daniel Adejo examine the first level and both the cognitive and affective dimensions of the second level of agenda setting with investors and consumers in Nigeria. Given that this is the first study of agenda setting in Nigeria, the authors conduct qualitative research and use research questions rather than hypotheses. Semistructured interviews were conducted with 30 consumers/investors within the Lagos metropolis, the commercial and industrial capital of Nigeria. They examine news stories published in the *Financial Standard* on four critical industries in the Nigerian economy: banking, telecommunication, manufacturing, and aviation.

In chapter 24, Klement Podnar and Dejan Verčič examine the first level of agenda setting applied to firms in Slovenia. They use a list of the 100 companies mentioned most frequently in the major Slovenian media in 2006, which, they note, covers 98% of all business-related news in Slovenia. They use media data provided by Pristop's clipping service, Kliping. These data were combined with the rankings of the top 100 most reputable Slovenian companies in 2006, based on a representative sample of Slovenian general and business publics. Podnar and Verčič report that this is the only annual measurement of corporate reputation available in Slovenia.

In chapter 25, Timothy Walters, noting the paucity of research on agenda setting and of business news entirely in the United Arab Emirates, uses a case study that summarizes previous research. Walters conducts key word searches in both the *Gulf News*, the local English-language newspaper of record, and Google. Walters uses these figures as gross measures of the public's awareness, corporate attributes, and public perception of that attribute, because of the general absence of published public opinion about business more generally.

Then, in chapter 26, I summarize the state of research on agenda-setting theory as a theoretical framework for understanding the influence of the news media on corporate reputation in countries around the world. As previously mentioned, interest in agenda-setting theory applied to business news has spiked around the world; our goal in the present volume is to identify, summarize, and consolidate the state of knowledge in this growing field.

References

Carroll, C. E., & McCombs, M. E. (2003). Agenda-setting effects of business news on the public's images and opinions about major corporations. *Corporate Reputation Review, 6*(1), 36–46.

Cohen, B. C. (1963). *The press and foreign policy.* Princeton, NJ: Princeton University Press.

Dearing, J. W., & Rogers, E. (1996). *Agenda-setting.* Thousand Oaks, CA: Sage.

Deephouse, D. L. (2000). Media reputation as a strategic resource: An integration of mass communication and resource-based theories. *Journal of Management, 26*(6), 1091–1112.

Dowling, G. R. (2001). *Creating corporate reputations: Identity, image, and performance.* New York: Oxford University Press.

Golan, G., & Wanta, W. (2001). Second-level agenda setting in the New Hampshire primary: A comparison of coverage in three newspapers and public perceptions of candidates. *Journalism & Mass Communication Quarterly, 78*(2), 247–259.

Lowery, S. A., & DeFleur, M. L. (1995). *Milestones in mass communication research: Media effects* (3rd ed.). White Plains, NY: Longman.

McCombs, M. E. (2004). *Setting the agenda: The mass media and public opinion.* Cambridge, UK: Polity Press.

McCombs, M. E., & Shaw, D. L. (1972). The agenda-setting function of the mass media. *Public Opinion Quarterly, 36,* 176–187.

McCombs, M. E., Shaw, D. L., & Weaver, D. H. (1997). *Communication and democracy: Exploring the intellectual frontiers in agenda-setting.* Mahwah, NJ: Erlbaum.

Ravasi, D. (2002). Analyzing reputation in a cross-national setting. *Corporate Reputation Review, 4*(4), 354–361.

Stocking, S. H. (1984). Effect of public relations efforts on media visibility of organizations. *Journalism Quarterly, 62*(2), 358–366.

Van Riel, C. B. M., & Fombrun, C. J. (2002). Which firm is most visible in your country? An introduction to the special issue on the global RQ-project nominations. *Corporate Reputation Review, 4*(4), 296–302.

Part II

Corporate Reputation and the News Media in Developed Markets

2 Corporate Reputation and the News Media in Denmark

Peter Kjaer and Mette Morsing

In a small, high-trust country like Denmark with traditions of egalitarianism, participative management, and social-democratic politics, the corporate quest for social legitimacy has been tame (Greeness, 2003; cf. Hofsteede, 1994; Ingle-hart, Basanez, & Moreno, 1998). While Danish companies have always been concerned about the public's perceptions of them, historically they have not been exposed to the same criticism, skepticism, and anticorporate activism as companies in the United States (Marchand, 1998). The Danes generally trust corporations and their managers (Bibb & Kourdi, 2004, p. 11) and Danish companies have not had the urge to indulge in conspicuous corporate self-celebration. Only recently has corporate reputation become a key feature of Danish companies' strategic management; in the wake of globalization, Danish companies have realized the strategic importance of standing out from competitors and sensed the need to change from implicit, subtle communication to explicit, articulated communication strategies (Morsing & Beckmann, 2006).

A key contribution to the Danish debate on corporate reputation has been the linking of marketing oriented research with research on organizational culture and identity. This development has resulted in a focus on the dynamics between external presentations, public opinion, and perceptions, and changes in organizational culture. One path of research has emphasized the role of corporate branding in integrating internal and external communications, including reputation (Hatch & Schultz, 1997, 2000; Schultz, Antorini, & Csaba, 2006; Schultz, Hatch, & Larsen, 2000). Another path has pointed to the autocommunicative element of reputation management: that companies talk to themselves as they manage their reputations (Christensen, 1995, 1997). Yet another path focuses on the role of corporate social responsibility, reputation, and strategic management (Morsing, 2006; Morsing & Beckmann, 2006; Morsing, Midttun, & Palmås, 2007; Morsing & Schultz, 2006; Morsing & Thyssen, 2003).

To this end, a number of Danish companies have begun to engage in corporate reputation management with the ambition of "standing out" from the competition by publicizing what were once private, internal values. Jesper Kunde, a leading consultant in the Danish reputation area, praises the idea that strong corporate reputations are achieved by companies "speaking with one voice." In his book *Corporate Religion*, Kunde writes:

The company which has complete control of—and keeps in step with—its international organization can control both the organisation and the market with the aid of a strong Corporate Religion. A company's success depends simply on direction.... (p. 103)

A Corporate Religion ensures that all employees in a company share the same qualitative values.... (p. 98)

It might sound totalitarian, but with a clearly defined Corporate Religion, there is nobody who will have problems on the course because everybody's job is connected to the company's Corporate Religion. (Kunde, 2000, p. 103)

Researchers acknowledge that the pursuit for consistency, unity, and clarity which underpins mainstream reputation literature may lead to the development of rigid and inflexible organizations; they also suggest that a corporate obsession for developing a favorable reputation may lead to a reputation that is far from the actual reality of the organization's identity (Christensen & Morsing 2005; Christensen, Morsing, & Cheney, 2008).

Agenda-Setting Theory

Although theoretically informed use of the "agenda" concept has taken hold in political science and media studies since the mid-1990s, there were earlier attempts in Denmark to study agenda setting. In the field of election research, Siune and Borre (1975) compared the voters' agenda before and after a general election and showed how voters' ranking of issues was heavily influenced by radio and television coverage. However, research on the mass media remained a small niche within political science, and during the 1980s, research within Danish media studies departments increasingly moved toward more textually oriented approaches to mass media, and away from studies of political communication (Lund, 2001).

In the 1990s, there was renewed interest in the political role of the mass media and special interest in the agenda-setting role of the news media. Siune (1991) analyzed the European Community as a theme on the political agenda and the news media agenda, and showed how media campaigns were able to influence the public agenda—at least momentarily. This research was followed by a number of similar agenda-setting studies, exploring themes such as AIDS (Albæk, 1991), immigration (Togeby, 2004), and corporate social responsibility (Morsing & Langer, 2006). These studies showed that intense coverage in the news media clearly influenced the public agenda, but they also revealed how the public agenda showed remarkable stability from a long-term perspective. Further studies emphasized the relation between the news media agenda and the political agenda and suggested how media attention had an impact on policy making in relation to scandals or "single issues" by forcing politicians to act in the face of extreme media attention; for example, violence (Laursen, 2001), the environment (Lund, 2002), human rights (Pedersen & Kjaer, 2000), and health policy (Møller Pedersen, 2005).

In addition to studies of agenda-setting processes, Danish researchers have also begun to consider processes of agenda building—or institutionalization. Lund (2000) carried out a study of the news media agenda as the result of what was termed the "food chain of news making," which illustrated how news stories traveled between various media outlets in the course of a day or a week. Lund's study suggested that rather than seeing the news media agenda as the expression of particular interests or external influences, one should pay attention to routine selection and translation processes among a dispersed network of producers. In a somewhat similar vein, O. K. Pedersen et al. (2000) suggested that one consider the agenda as a political institution. Rather than using the agenda concept as a purely theoretical construct, it is also important to see how the position of the news media agenda and the relationship between the news media agenda and the political agenda have become institutionalized in recent decades in part as a result of the partial breakdown of established political governance structures and changes within the news media.

Business and the News Media

Research on the news media in Denmark has traditionally been preoccupied with political news, and media researchers have largely disregarded business and economic news, as well as media outlets that specialized in business journalism. Apart from a historical account of *Børsen*, the main business newspaper in Denmark (the Danish equivalent of the *Financial Times*; Fonsmark, 1996) and a number of smaller articles by practitioners on economic reporting and business journalism (e.g., Andersen, 1992), the field itself and its relationship to business was not examined until the late 1990s.

Kjaer and Pedersen (1999) provided an initial sketch of the business media in Demark in their study of the news media as a channel for the diffusion of management knowledge. Lund (2003) followed this study in a report to the Danish Newspaper Publishers' Association, which provided an account of themes, sources, and angles in business news content in Danish newspapers with national circulation. The study suggested that a large share of business news articles (41%) could be characterized as "service journalism" that passively reproduced stories originating from business sources or other media outlets, whereas an almost equal share was characterized as "routine journalism" involving some journalistic work but relying on just a single source.

Kjaer and Langer (2005) examined the institutional history of Danish business journalism. Their analysis relied on quantitative and qualitative data from four large newspapers and indicated that business news was characterized both by increased journalistic autonomy and ongoing negotiations with sources. The authors concluded that expansion of business journalism leads to new forms of problematization and conflict. In a subsequent study, Kjaer (2005) conducted an extensive quantitative analysis of economic content in two Danish dailies since 1960, revealing that the expansion of business and economic news triggered professionalization and popularization of the field. The analysis also suggested that business and economic coverage was increasingly being framed by a financial perspective on business (cf. Kjaer, 2006). Lastly, Larsen and Lin (2005) described the development of financial journalism on a global scale. Their book, primarily directed at practitioners, examined current trends in the financial press on the basis of interviews with leading editors and reporters, the majority of whom worked in the United States and Britain.

These attempts to describe the business media field have been complemented by a number of case studies focused on the interrelationship between business and the news media, and specifically how businesses may benefit from media coverage. Morsing (1999) studied how the media's enthusiastic coverage of organizational changes at Oticon (a Danish hearing aid manufacturer) influenced identity formation within the Oticon organization; she suggested that media coverage may have a *boomerang effect* that boosts aspects of organizational identity. In a later study, Morsing and Kristensen (2001) explored how the media sustained its ongoing mention of Oticon as "news" for 9 years by frequently identifying new features of the organization. Kjaergaard and Morsing (2006) followed with a 10-year longitudinal study analyzing the organizational impact of the iconic stability of Oticon's media reputation. From the perspective of discourse analysis, Chouliaraki (2006) studied the mediatization of suffering by examining how the media bring other people's misery into social life, and how organizations may strategically capitalize on this process.

Such case studies have also examined the interrelationship between business and the news media during periods of organizational scandal or crisis. Hedaa (1997) examined the coverage of an human resource-consultancy scandal in the news media and attempted to show how various journalists framed the story differently and how media pressure interfered with the consultancy process. Grolin (1999) studied the role of the news media in the coverage of the Brent Spar incident that involved Shell; he interpreted the controversy over the deep sea dumping of an oil rig as part of a "risk society" scenario that involves new challenges to corporate legitimacy and new forms of political organization in the face of media influence. In a later study, Backer (2001) interpreted the consumer boycotts related to the Brent Spar incident and similar controversies as outgrowths of the increased mediatization of business. Kjaer and Langer (2004) studied a scandal involving collusion between two airline companies (SAS and Maersk Air), and showed how the media coverage entailed shifting assignments of roles and responsibilities as the story evolved. Finally, an edited volume by Langer, Kjaer, and Horst (2009) presented a series of case studies of business–media encounters that ranged from cases concerning fraud and business ethics to cases involving innovation and consumer issues. In the same way, Chouliaraki and Morsing (2009) invited research and debate on the processes and linkages between media and corporations in their edited volume which focuses on identity construction in and between media and organizations as they are confronted on a daily basis in contemporary mediated society.

While all of these case studies and all of this theorizing considered the influence of media coverage on business, none of them explicitly used an agenda-setting approach. Lund's (2000, 2002) studies remain the only attempts by Danish researchers to apply an agenda-setting perspective in case studies about business and the news media (in examinations of two media scandals involving the *Dandy* case concerning a research contract between a Danish university and a large Danish chewing gum producer; and the *Riffelsyndikat* case concerning a large Danish corporation's actions during World War II). Both stories were seen as examples of investigative journalism where journalists actively engaged in agenda setting, albeit in close interaction with other actors in the field.

In sum, since the mid-1990s, business, media, and business–media relations has emerged as a research area in Denmark. However, this research has largely been preoccupied with the general status of the expanding field of business journalism and the political or organizational implications of the rise of the business press. Except for Lund's two qualitative case studies of *Dandy* and *Riffelsyndikatet*, researchers have not explored relations of agenda setting between media and business. A number of contributions, however, have mentioned and discussed the political role of the media (Chouliaraki, 2006; cf. Nielsen, 2001).

Hypotheses

Our review of existing research on corporate reputation, agenda setting, and the business media in Denmark suggests that, in recent years, each of these concepts has triggered a significant amount of research and even some original contributions to international debates. At the same time, research is lacking with respect to their interconnection in a Danish setting.

Inspired by Carroll and McCombs (2003), Deephouse (2000), and Pollock and Rindova (2003), we study empirically the relation between the media agenda and corporate reputation in Denmark. Carroll and McCombs (2003) formulated three hypotheses which allow us to carry out an initial assessment of the strength of the media–reputation connection in addition to examining how the relationship is affected by contextual factors.

> *Hypothesis 1.* There is a positive correlation between a company's position on the news media agenda and the level of public awareness of that particular firm.
> *Hypothesis 2.* The news media's ranking of a particular company's attributes (such as finance, management, or human resources) correlates positively with the public's ranking of those attributes.
> *Hypothesis 3.* There is a positive correlation between the degree to which companies are described in a positive light by the news media and the degree to which their reputations are perceived to be positive.

Taken together, these hypotheses indicate the degree to which the news media agenda may affect corporate reputation, and suggest that the cognitive and affective aspects of agenda setting are related to the awareness and evaluative aspects of corporate reputation. Obviously, a more exact nature of this relationship cannot be ascertained without also considering some key contextual factors. Factors at a national or industry level influence both the nature of agenda setting and the dynamics of corporate reputation. Consequently, such factors will be considered, beginning with the nature of the corporate reputation landscape in Denmark.

Case Study: The Danish Corporate Reputation Landscape

The Danish corporate reputation field has expanded since 2000. During that period, we have witnessed a move from merely occasional measurements of reputation in opinion polls toward a general interest in reputation, visibility, and management of legitimacy, not only among companies, but also among such entities as schools, hospitals, and public authorities. Four national reputation rankings have developed in Denmark, in addition to more specialized rankings focused on issues (such as "best place to work" in particular industries). Three of the national reputation rankings are produced by the news media in collaboration with consulting agencies, while the fourth is produced solely by a consulting agency. In the mid-1990s, Denmark's weekly business magazine (*Berlingske Nyhedsmagasin*) and the country's daily business newspaper (*Børsen*) both introduced a systematic measurement and ranking of corporate reputation. *Mandag Morgen*, the weekly magazine on politics and business, launched its MediaMonitor in 2001, which carried out "communication audits" of selected firms and organizations based on a broad range of aspects including "communicative performance."

In 2000 the Reputation Institute launched its Reputation Quotient Index in Denmark. The Reputation Institute's system of ranking is unique in that it surveys respondents from the general population to achieve a broader picture of reputations of a large sample of firms (as opposed to only assessing managers' opinions of other companies). Individual firms can then purchase further analyses of their reputation data; for example, in relation to particular stakeholder groups. The internationally benchmarked Reputation Quotient Index is one important indication of the increasing professionalization and commercialization of the Danish reputation ranking landscape.

Companies not selected for participation in annual reputation rankings call news media editorial offices to complain, which is a symptom of burgeoning corporate interest in reputation rankings. At companies like Tryg and TDC, participation in many reputation rankings each year has become the norm, and managers report that a lower than expected ranking will lead to organizational changes. Indeed, some companies now include achieving better ranking positions as part of their annual goals.

Since rankings are based on surveys or interviews during which respondents express their *perceptions* of certain corporations, influencing others' perceptions becomes a central task for reputation management. Denmark's small size and subsequent potential for word of mouth communication creates a ripe environment for influencing those perceptions. Similarly, Denmark is a tightly networked society where companies seek negotiation and consensus rather than conflicts between employer and employee organizations, and thus the public's *perceptions* of other companies are often built on experience and firsthand knowledge of collaborating with the company (Kristensen, 1999). Such networking helps temper the tone of corporate coverage in the news media and ensures stability in the reputations of Danish companies (Schultz, Mouritsen, & Gabrielsen, 2001). Accordingly, corporate scandals are very rare in the Danish reputation landscape.

The Danish Media System

The Danish media system belongs to what Hallin and Mancini (2004) described as the "Democratic Corporatist Model," which is characterized by a long history of press freedom combined with a strong party press. Thus the mass media have played an important role in the process of modernization and democratization in Denmark and historically there have been several ties between the news media and the field of politics. Although the structure of the news media has changed profoundly over the last 20 to 30 years, the news media are still widely considered as important social and political institutions (cf. Medieudvalget, 1995; Togeby, Andersen, Christiansen, Jørgensen, & Vallgårda, 2003).

The Danish press dates back to the state regulated commercial press of the 18th century, but the real birth of a modern political press occurred between 1880 and 1920 (Thomsen, 1972). During this period Denmark experienced remarkable newspaper expansion as political actors engaged in the creation of local newspaper outlets related to each of the four leading political parties. By World War I, each provincial town had three or four local newspapers that became important vehicles for democratization. The party press was not controlled by national party organizations but was organized as locally based networks of newspapers and editors associated with a particular party interest. Each party press network established a joint news service which constituted a labor market that aligned journalists and editors within a party network,

Alongside the party press, a more apolitical and news-oriented press began to develop after 1905 when the large Copenhagen daily *Politiken* adopted a new "omnibus" format that was gradually copied by other national newspapers (Søllinge, 1998). After World War II, local monopolies emerged as the party press came under increasing pressure because production costs soared, and competition increased in the newspaper field (Søllinge & Thomsen, 1991). Newspapers began to downplay their party affiliations in order to cater to larger, more politically diverse local audiences; soon national media institutions were established. The news services of Danish radio and television were granted editorial autonomy in 1964. In 1988 a second, semicommercial national television channel was established, and the Radio Council that supervised public radio and television in Denmark was replaced by a board of governors that reflected professional expertise rather than political affiliation. Additionally, the state-sponsored Danish School of Journalism was established, further severing journalistic education from the networks of party news outlets. Finally, as a result of a series of political investigations regarding the development and organization of the news media, the state established a number of financial subsidy schemes to assist in restructuring the national press structure (Kjaer, 2000).

As formal linkages between political parties, the state, and the news media have been gradually loosened, media access has become a hotly debated topic. In general, politicians have maintained informal relationships with journalists and editors, but competition for access has intensified. This has strengthened the role of journalists as gatekeepers of the news through their use of professional news judgment, but it has also intensified attempts by politicians and organizational actors to manage access by nursing relationships to particular journalists and media, offering news stories and exclusives (Lund, 2005). Several studies have emphasized how media access is a negotiated process subject to strategic interaction between journalists, politicians, and organizations (Lund, 2005; Pedersen, Kjaer, Esmark, Horst, & Carlsen, 2000).

News Values and Organizational Newsworthiness in Denmark

A number of conventional handbooks exist for journalists describing particular values as central in Danish journalism (e.g., Kramhøft, 2000; Mogensen, 2000). Most of these manuals emphasize novelty, relevance, conflict, identification, and sensation. However, such propositions about news values are rarely grounded in concrete observations or broader debates and simply refer to conventions that are taken for granted in the field. Several observers have attempted to infer news values from news content by emphasizing variation in the types of content deemed fit to print or broadcast; that is, the degree to which conflicts are emphasized (Hjarvard, 1995; Pedersen et al., 2000; Søllinge, 1999). While such analyses have been useful as indicators of overall orientations in actual content, they are indirect indicators of how journalists and editors decide on what issues and events to cover.

Few researchers have studied how news judgments are practiced in concrete news organizations. One recent exception is Schultz (2006), who studied work processes in television newsrooms and found support for the use of the five conventional news values. However, as Schultz stressed, news values and news judgments are always used relationally: news values reflect the assessment of news leads and the dynamic nature of which news producers are focused on a story. Because news judgments are relational and tied to the position and interaction of news producers, Schultz also found that exclusivity had become a news value, perhaps due to increased competition in the news media field, where exclusive stories become a way for journalists to improve their position within news organizations and increase their market value.

No systematic studies of the news values pertaining to reporting on organizations and corporations in Denmark have been carried out. In their study of work practices at the business desk of a Danish daily, Kjaer and Langer (2003) found that journalists applied standard news values: but those values were applied differently to different types of content; stories for the regular business pages emphasized the current, relevant, and conflict-laden issues, whereas stories for special supplements and weekend editions emphasized "identification." In terms of relevance, they found that the newspaper prioritized companies based on financial assets in terms of stock value (publicly traded firms were clearly prioritized) and number of employees.

In a recent conversation, Tomas Munkshof, *Berlingske Nyhedsmagasin*'s business news editor, commented on the impact of "family" and "democracy" on relevancy in the Danish business press. Munkshof believes there is a tendency to favor national and family owned corporate icons, as well as companies that are publicly traded and thus of potential interest to the public, their potential shareholders. "These types of companies are overrepresented in the media in relation to their importance," says Munkshoff. Furthermore, he argues that "audience preferences" now serve as another criterion of relevance for selecting and presenting news. Customers' influence on the definition of news will have tremendous implications on the development of the media. Such trends are of great importance to understand the development of the Danish media system.

The Danish Public Relations Industry

Public relations is a post-World War II phenomenon in Denmark. The first professional association (the Danish Public Relations Club) was established in 1961 as an attempt to bring together early practitioners in the field, and to suggest that public relations encompassed more than simply the drafting of press releases and handling press contacts (Madsen, 2001). However, public relations work did not gain proper foothold until the 1980s, when an increasing number of firms began to establish PR functions and specialized consultancy firms began to emerge. Early practitioners typically had a background in journalism, but the establishment of a university level program in public relations in 1986 led to expansion and professionalization of the field, especially during the 1990s (Blach, 2006), when public relations functions also expanded in the public sector and in the so-called third sector (Pedersen et al., 2000). Indeed, the Danish Communication Association (DKF) has grown from 850 members in early 2000 (PLS Rambøl, 2000) to 2,300 in 2006 (*Berlingske Tidende*, 2006), and it is believed that two-thirds of all practitioners in the field are members (Kristensen, 2004). Denmark's business association for public relations firms (BPRV) organizes 30 public relations firms (www.bprv.dk) and indicates the emergence of a broader subfield of professional consultancies, though the overall size of the industry is still a matter of some disagreement (Kristensen, 2004).

Two surveys of Danish communication professionals have been carried out in recent years, painting a picture of the growing field of public relations and its professionals. The early survey (PLS Rambøl, 2000) showed that more than two-thirds of the respondents (communication professionals and DKF members) had academic backgrounds, and about half worked in the private sector as consultants or in communication functions in corporations. Almost 50% worked in independently organized communication departments while only about 15% worked in other departments. A later survey (Kristensen, 2005) emphasized the media relations of communication professionals and showed that about 40% of the respondents worked in the private sector. Respondents emphasized media handling as a key task and suggested that direct interactions with journalists were important to actively influence the media agenda. The study also showed that practitioners saw the field as having experienced expansion and professionalization in recent years.

Research Methodology

The Media Data   *Berlingske Tidende*, *Jyllands-Posten*, *Politiken*, and *Børsen*, the four largest Danish dailies in terms of circulation, share an almost equal readership and are similar in terms of overall format. *Berlingske Tidende* and *Jyllands-Posten* are conservative and liberal newspapers, respectively with a strong emphasis on business and a probusiness orientation. *Politiken* is social liberal in tone and is more consumer-oriented in its business coverage. All three newspapers (and *Jyllands-Posten* in particular) have featured in-depth critical stories on business issues. *Børsen* is a specialized business newspaper with a clear probusiness position, but it has also published critical business stories. Taken together, our sample covers about 50% of the daily circulation of the 10 largest newspapers in Denmark.

The media data were retrieved from Observer Ltd., a multinational news monitoring agency. Observer provided data on the 2005 media coverage of the 50 largest Danish companies. However, the Observer data only include information about overall media coverage and the positive/neutral versus negative news angles. It does not contain data about thematic emphases. We are thus only able to test Hypotheses 1 and 3 and as such we have chosen to discuss Hypothesis 2 on the basis of what we know from other Danish sources.

Public Opinion Data   We have chosen *Berlingske Nyhedsmagasin*'s (BNY) annual image ranking because it represents the oldest and most comprehensive analysis in terms of number of companies and issues involved; competing rankings do not embrace the same number of ranked companies.

Each year, the Instituttet for Opinionsanalyse (IFO) conducts the BNY Gold Image Study, which ranks 140 companies in Denmark and is published in *Berlingske Nyhedsmagasin*. The companies included in the study are described as "Denmark's prominent companies" and are selected by the BNY staff based on their internal "journalistic criteria of relevance." The results of the survey are based on evaluations by 2,937 Danish business managers, who responded to questions about their overall knowledge of selected firms, evaluated the importance of nine image parameters (responsibility, financial strength, innovation, communication, quality, leadership/management, employees, credibility, and competitiveness), and assessed the companies' performance on these parameters. The image ranking of a company is a weighted combination of the awareness score, performance on the nine image parameters, and the perceived importance of those parameters. BNY also provides individual rankings on awareness, overall image (for the sample as a whole and for particular industries), and performance on individual parameters.[1] Rankings are published in May, which means that the survey and data analysis is carried out the early months of the year in question. We have therefore selected the 2006 data for the correlation analysis with the media data for 2005 on the assumption that the 2006 data would give a more accurate depiction of possible image effects of the media coverage in the preceding year.

Data Analysis

While much research has investigated corporate reputation and media in general in Denmark, and some research has emerged on business news and agenda setting, no systematic study of the relations between the areas have been carried out. Yet, it is often assumed by researchers and practitioners that positive linkages exist between a strong reputation, positive media attention, and agenda setting. Carroll and McCombs (2003) have encouraged more systematic study of the relations. In the following, we present our findings from the Danish case study of the relationship between news media coverage of businesses and public opinion about those businesses.

Results

Hypothesis 1   In relation to Hypothesis 1, we found a statistically significant ($p < 0.001$) positive correlation (Spearman's rho 0.79) between the amount of media coverage and the respondents' awareness of that firm. Figure 2.1 plots the distribution of the 42 sample firms.

The figure shows that the 10 companies highest on the media agenda are among the 15 best known companies in the BNY sample, while the 10 least known companies are among those receiving the least media coverage. Interestingly, there

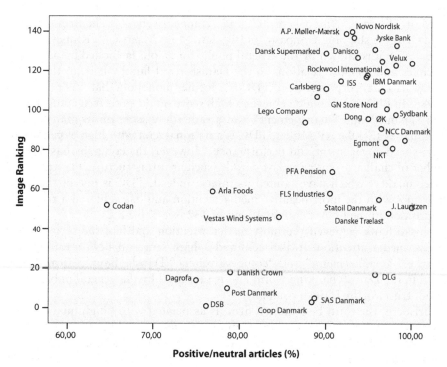

Figure 2.1   Media coverage and awareness

Table 2.1 Firms That Achieve Most Media Mention and Firms that
Are Most Well Known

Observer	Berlingske Nyhedsmagasin
1. Danske Bank	1. AP Møller – Maersk
2. AP Møller – Maersk	2. TDC
3. TDC	3. Carlsberg

is a small group of well-known companies—such as Falck (rescue and security), Danfoss (thermostats), and Lego (toys)—that did not receive a lot of media coverage in 2005. There were no cases of companies receiving high levels of media coverage but maintaining low levels of awareness.

Hypothesis 2   In testing the second hypothesis, we found that that the two (of three) firms achieving most media attention are also the best known companies in Denmark. Table 2.1 illustrates the ranking.

AP Møller (Maersk) (shipping) and TDC (telecommunications) were among the three most mentioned and the two best known firms in 2005. Moreover, Danske Bank (banking) was the most mentioned and Carlsberg (brewery) was the third best known company.

On BNY's ranking, AP Møller achieves a high score on perceived competences on "finance," "management," and "competitiveness." The firm runs the world's largest shipping company and is chaired by Maersk McKinney Møller (born 1913); it is known by the general public for its old-fashioned management principles and its close relations to the Danish royal family. It is, in the truest sense, a national corporate icon. TDC is a former monopoly that was privatized in 1986. In BNY's ranking it achieves a high score on the perceived competences of its "finance" and "management" and a rather low score on its management of "employees." Like AP Møller, TDC is a national icon with high expectations for its social engagement and performance. However, the company has faced a number of challenges over the last decade (such as infrastructure, taxation, and service quality) which have tainted its image; indeed, TDC is one of the three companies with the most negative media mention and has achieved a relatively low position in the BNY ranking: 49 out of 132 (see Table 2.2).

Danske Bank achieved the most media attention and had the second most positive media attention. It also achieved a high score on BNY's ranking on "finance," "management," and "competitiveness." Danske Bank is firmly positioned in the Danish banking world and is perceived by the general public to be a solid, trustworthy Danish company.

Carlsberg, the third best known firm, is associated with "high quality" and "responsibility" on BNY's ranking. Among the general public it is particularly known for its products and the history of its founder, I. P. Jacobsen.

What characterizes all these firms is that they are "local heroes." AP Møller is *the* Danish company to invest in, Danske Bank is *the* bank that handles the

Table 2.2 Companies with Most Negative Media Attention Related to Their Reputation

Top 3 in negative reporting in media (more than 10% negative articles) (Observer)	Position in BNY's ranking for the firms with most negative media mention
1. DSB	DSB 121 (out of 132)
2. Arla Foods	Arla Foods 62 (out of 132)
3. TDC	TDC 49 (out of 132)

Danes' money, TDC is responsible for the Danes' telecommunication, and Carlsberg for the Danes' beer consumption. All four firms are "Danish" and international companies highly present in the Danish corporate landscape.

Hypothesis 3   In relation to Hypothesis 3, we found a statistically significant (*p* = 0.015) positive correlation (Spearman's rho 0.376) between the share of positive/neutral coverage of a firm and its overall ranking in terms of image. However, the correlation is somewhat weaker than the correlation found between news coverage and awareness.

Figure 2.2 illustrates how the position of many firms in the BNY ranking seems to be related to their share of positive/neutral media coverage (i.e., the relative absence of negative angles).

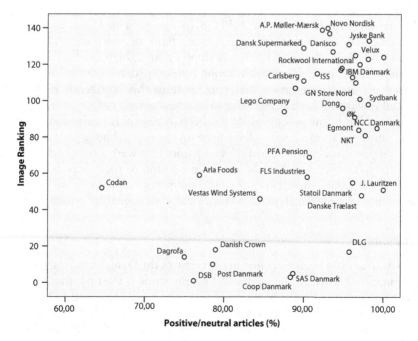

Figure 2.2 Corporate reputation and positive media coverage

For many of these companies, highly positive media coverage (defined by less than 10% negative reports) coincides with high image rankings (top 40). Similarly, companies that experience highly negative media coverage obtain a low image ranking. However, there is an outlying group of firms that receive positive news coverage but remain in the bottom half of the image ranking. This likely mirrors either low levels of overall media coverage or low awareness scores in the BNY survey.

Discussion: Media Effects   Media coverage is closely related to corporate reputation. There is a strong, positive correlation between position on the media agenda and overall public awareness. Anecdotal evidence also suggests that for companies with the highest awareness rankings, media coverage of particular corporate attributes (e.g., finance, management, or quality) correlates with respondents' rankings of those attributes for those companies. Finally, we found some support for the claim that positive media coverage is correlated with positive public image (although we also found a number of divergent cases). Though the analysis suggests that a correlation exists, we are unable to determine whether changes in corporate reputation are directly affected by media agenda setting, or whether there are intervening variables or even reverse causation. One important intervening variable may have to do with the status of particular companies.

Company Variations

The findings indicate a subset of companies of particular importance to the media–national icons which are believed to represent products and identities of particular consumer concern (e.g., private banking, telecommunications) or national pride (e.g., the world's largest shipping firm, high quality brewery) for the Danes. To be sure, Denmark's strong economy, deregulation, reforms, and increased private consumption may contribute to this apparently national-oriented and inward-looking perspective in business news.

As the field of business journalism has been increasingly professionalized, corporate communication activities have been on the rise. Although we do not have data to support the claim, some of the companies that were mentioned most often seem to be overrepresented in the media in relation to their importance (based on their stock value, annual turnover, or number of employees); we believe that these companies are also those that strategically manage their reputations.

Limitations

Until now, there has been no coherent overview of the Danish landscape of corporate reputation related to the media. While our study is the first attempt to present such an outline, it is based on preliminary findings that need to be explored and expanded in future research. Our data are limited in that the hypotheses were tested on only 42 firms. Also, use of the Observer data precluded us from considering which dimensions or attributes of firms were covered. Similarly, the BNY data only concerned a sample of business leaders, and not a broader sample of the Danish public. To be sure, a more thorough testing of the hypotheses would have required additional empirical data and perhaps an analysis of variation over time; such a longitudinal study would allow us to detect long-term stability and changes in the patterns of media coverage and corporate reputations. Yet despite these limitations, we believe that this study will be the first in an ongoing stream of research on the relations between corporate reputations and media in Denmark.

Conclusions

Our findings highlight a positive relation between media coverage and corporate reputations, but we still lack the answer to the "chicken or the egg" question: is it media coverage that leads reputations, or the other way around? We need to more fully understand causal relationships between degrees of awareness and media coverage. Is it the news media that drive reputations? Or do corporate communication activities drive the news media? More research is needed to better understand these relationships.

Notes

We did not have access to the original IFO data but only to the data published in BNY. Access to the original data is only possible on payment of a fee. Our description of the IFO methodology is based on an interview with editor Tomas Munksgaard Hoff at BNY, and information provided by IFO on their webpage (http://www.ifo-analyser.dk/) and in the BNY special issue on the image study.

We sincerely thank the Danish Strategic Council for Research for support to the research.

References

Albæk, E. (1991). Den politiske dagsorden—en skraldespand? [The political agenda—a garbage can?]. AIDS som illustrativt case. *Politica, 23*(4), 396–417

Andersen, V. (1992). Fra tallerkenrækkeperspektiv til verdenshorisont [From plate-rack to world horisont]. *Samfundsøkonomen, 1,* 31–37.

Backer, L. (2001). The mediated transparent society. *Corporate Reputation Review, 4*(3), 235–251.

Berlingske Tidende. (2006, March 14). 3rd section, 17

Bibb, S., & Kourdi, J. (2004). *Trust matters: For organisational and personal success.* London: Palgrave Macmillan.

Blach, T. (2006, June 1). Veje hertil og herfra [Roads to and from here]. Retrieved from http://www.kommunikationsforening.dk

Carroll, C. E., & McCombs, M. (2003). Agenda-setting effects of business news on the public's images and opinions about major corporations. *Corporation Reputation Review, 6*(1), 36–46.

Chouliaraki, L. (2006). *The mediation of suffering.* London: Sage

Chouliaraki, L., & Morsing, M. (Eds.). (2009). *Media, organization and identity.* London: Palgrave Macmillan.

Christensen, L. T. (1995). Når virksomheden taler med sig selv: Auto-kommunikativ ledelse. *Ledelse i dag*, 4(20), 32–42.

Christensen, L. T. (1997). Marketing as auto-communication. *Consumption, Markets & Culture*, 1(3), 197–227.

Christensen, L. T., & Morsing, M. (2005). *Bagom corporate communication* [Going behind corporate communication]. Copenhagen, Denmark: Samfundslitteratur.

Christensen, L. T., Morsing, M., & Cheney, G. (2008). *Corporate communications: Convention, complexity and critique.* London: Sage.

Deephouse, D. L. (2000). Media reputation as a strategic resource: An integration of mass communication and resource-based theories. *Journal of Management*, 26(6), 1091–1112.

Fonsmark, H. (1996). *Børsens Danmarkshistorie 1896–1996* [Børsen's history of Denmark]. Copenhagen, Denmark: Børsens.

Greenness, T. (2003). Scandinavian managers on Scandinavian management. *International Journal of Value-Based Management*, 16, 9–21.

Grolin, J. (1999). Brent Spar i risikosamfundet [Brent Spar in risk society]. In K. Nielsen, A. Greve, F. Hansson, & K. Rasborg (Eds.), *Risiko, politik og miljø i det moderne samfund* (pp. 264–292). Copenhagen, Denmark: Forlaget Sociologi.

Hallin, D. C., & Mancini, P. (2004). *Comparing media systems.* Cambridge, UK: Cambridge University Press.

Hatch, M. J., & Schultz, M. (1997). Relations between organizational culture, identity and image. *European Journal of Marketing*, 31(5), 356–365.

Hatch, M. J., & Schultz, M. (2000). Scaling the Tower of Babel: Relational differences between identity, image, and culture in organizations. In M. Schultz, M. J. Hatch, & M. H. Larsen (Eds.), *The expressive organization: Linking identity, reputation and the corporate brand* (pp. 11–35). Oxford, UK: Oxford University Press.

Hedaa, L. (1997). *Sat ud af spillet* [Placed out of the game]. Copenhagen, Denmark: Samfundslitteratur.

Hjarvard, S. (1995). *Nyhedsmediernes rolle i det politiske demokrati* [The role of news media in the political democracy]. Copenhagen, Denmark: Statsministeriets medieudvalg.

Hofstede, G. (1994). *Cultures and organizations: Software of the mind.* London: HarperCollins.

Inglehart, R., Basanez, M., & Moreno, A. (1998). *Human values and beliefs: A cross-cultural sourcebook.* Ann Arbor: University of Michigan.

Kjaer, P. (2000). Forestillinger om politik og journalistik: et historisk blik [Perceptions of politics and journalism] (pp. 87–144). In O.K. Pedersen & P. Kjaer (Eds.), *Politisk journalistik.* Århus, Denmark: Ajour.

Kjaer, P (2005). *The evolution of business news in Denmark 1960–2000: Context and content* (CBP Working Paper). Copenhagen, Denmark: Copenhagen Business School.

Kjaer, P. (2006). Business news and the definition of business and society. In M. Morsing & S. C. Beckmann (Eds.), *Strategic CSR Communication* (pp. 83–105). Copenhagen, Denmark: Djoef.

Kjaer, P., & Langer, R. (2003, July 3–5). *The negotiation of business news: A study of journalist–source interaction.* Paper presented at the 19th EGOS Conference, subtheme 14: "Organizing Power and Authority in a Fluid Society," Copenhagen, Denmark.

Kjaer, P., & Langer, R. (2004). Virksomhed og politik i en mediestorm. En analyse af SAS-Mærsk kartelsagen [Company and politics in a media storm: an analysis of the

SAS-Maersk cartel case] (pp. 29–56). In C. Frankel (Ed.), *Den politiske virksomhed* . Frederiksberg, Denmark: Samfundslitteratur.

Kjaer, P., & Langer, R. (2005). Infused with news value: Management, managerial knowledge and the institutionalization of business news. *Scandinavian Journal of Management, 21*(2), 209–233.

Kjaer, P., & Pedersen, J. S. (1999). Northern case: Denmark. In J. L. Alvarez, C. Mazza, & J. Mur (Eds.), *The management publishing industry in Europe* (CEMP Working Paper No. 99/4, 35–57). Barcelona: IESE Business School.

Kjaergaard, A., & Morsing, M. (2006, July 6–8). *Captured by the image in the mirror: A longitudinal analysis of the dynamics of corporate and organisational identity.* Paper presented at the European Group on Organization Studies (EGOS), Bergen.

Kramhøft, P. (2000). *Journalistik med omtanke* [Journalism with concern]. Århus: Ajour.

Kristensen, N. N. (2004). Den journalistiske udfordring [The journalistic challenges]. *Nordicom Information, 4*, 51–68.

Kristensen, N. N. (2005). *Kommunikationsbranchens medierelationer—Professionelle netværk, kommunikationsfaglige perspektiver og mediedemokratiske konsekvenser* [The communication industry's media relations—Professional networks, communication professional perspectives and media democratic implications]. (Modinet Working Paper no. 19). Retrieved from http://ww.modinet.dk

Kristensen, P. H. (1999). Strategies in a volatile world. In P. Karnøe, P. H. Kristensen, & P. H. Andersen (Eds.), *Mobilizing resources and generating competencies: The remarkable success of small and medium-sized enterprises in the Danish business system* (pp. 259–296). Copenhagen, Denmark: Handelshøjskolens Forlag.

Kunde, J. (2000). *Corporate religion: Building a strong company through personality and corporate soul.* London: Prentice-Hall.

Langer, R., Kjaer, P., & Horst, M. (Eds.). (2009). *Produktiv journalistik. Virksomheder—Medier-Markeder.* Copenhagen, Denmark: Handelshøjskolens Forlag.

Larsen, P. L., & Lin, X. (2005). *Nyheder til salg: Den globale revolution i finanspressen* [The global revolution in the finance press]. Copenhagen, Denmark: Børsens Forlag.

Laursen, S. (2001). *Vold på dagsordenen: Medierne og den politiske proces* [Violence on the agenda: the media and the political process]. Aarhus, Denmark: Aarhus Universitetsforlag.

Lund, A. B. (2000). *Først med det sidste—En nyhedsuge i Danmark* [Follow latest news —a week with news in Denmark]. Århus, Denmark: Ajour.

Lund, A. B. (2001). *Forskning om medier og demokrati: Tre aktuelle interviewundersøgelser* [Research on media and democracy: three recent interview investigations]. Danske Dagblades Forenings debatserie, nr. 16.

Lund, A. B. (2002). *Den redigerende magt—Nyhedsinstitutionens politiske indflydelse* [The editing power — News institutions' political influence]. Aarhus, Denmark: Aarhus Universitetsforlag.

Lund, A. B. (2003). *Erhvervsstoffet mellem journalist og virksomhed* [Corporate news between journalist and company]. Odense, Denmark: Syddansk Universitet Odense.

Lund, A. B. (2005). Strategisk brug af kommunikation—Ledelsesretorik, offentlighedsarbejde og nichepleje [Strategic use of communication—Leadership rhetorics, public service and niche management]. In Busch, T., Vanebo, J. O., Hansen, K. K., & Johnsen, E. (Eds.): *Modernisering av offentlig sektor.* Oslo, Sweden: Universitetsforlaget

Madsen, M. (2001). *Færdig med fyrre* [This is it]. Retrieved from http://www.kommunikationsforening.dk

Marchand, R. (1998). *Creating the corporate soul: The rise of public relations and corporate imagery in American big business*. Berkeley: University of California Press.

Medieudvalget. (1995). *Betænkning om medierne i demokratiet* [Note about media in democracy]. Copenhagen, Denmark: Statsministeriet betænkning Report no. 1320.

Mogensen, K. (2000). *Arven: Journalistikkens traditioner, normer og begreber* [The heritage: traditions, norms and concepts in journalism]. Copenhagen, Denmark: Samfundslitteratur.

Morsing, M. (1999). The media boomerang: The media's role in changing identity by changing image. *Corporate Reputation Review, 2*(2), 116–136.

Morsing, M. (2006). Strategic CSR communication: The challenge of telling others how good you are. In J. Jonker & M. C. Witte (Eds.), *Management models for CSR: A Comprehensive overview* (pp. 237–245). Heidelberg: Springer Verlag.

Morsing, M., & Beckmann, S. C. (2006). (Eds.). *Strategic CSR communication*. Copenhagen, Denmark: Djoef.

Morsing, M., & Kristensen, J. (2001). The question of coherency in corporate branding: Over time and across stakeholders. *Journal of Communication Management, 6*(1), 24–40.

Morsing, M., & Langer, R. (2006, April 21–22). CSR-communication in the business press: Advantages of strategic ambiguity. In K. Podnar & Z. Jančiĉ (Eds.), *Contemporary issues in corporate and marketing communications: Towards a socially responsible future: Proceedings of the 11th International CMC conference on corporate and marketing communications* (pp. 26–34). Ljubljana, Slovenia: Fakulteta Za drubenevede.

Morsing, M., Midttun, A., & Palmås, K. (2007). Corporate social responsibility in Scandinavia: A turn towards the business case? In S. May, G. Cheney, & J. Roper (Eds.), *The debate over corporate social responsibility* (pp. 87–104). London: Oxford University Press.

Morsing, M., & Schultz, M. (2006). Corporate social responsibility communication: Stakeholder information, response and involvement strategies. *Business Ethics: A European Review, 15*(4), 323–338

Morsing, M., & Thyssen, C. (Eds.). (2003). *Corporate values and responsibility: The case of Denmark*. Copenhagen, Denmark: Samfundslitteratur.

Møller Pedersen, K. (2005). *Sundhedspolitik* [Health policy]. Odense, Denmark: Syddansk Universitetsforlag.

Nielsen, M. F. (Ed.). (2001). *Profil og offentlighed: Public relations for viderekomne* [Profile and public]. Frederiksberg, Denmark: Samfundslitteratur.

Pedersen, O. K., Kjaer, P., Esmark, A., Horst, M., & Carlsen, E. M. (Eds.). (2000). *Politisk journalistik* [Political journalism]. Århus, Denmark: Forlaget Ajour.

PLS Rambøl Management. (2000, March). *Dansk Kommunikationsforening Medlemsundersøgelse* [Danish Communication Assocation survey]. Copenhagen, Denmark: Author.

Pollock, T. G., & Rindova, V. P. (2003). Media legitimation effects in the market for initial public offerings. *Academy of Management Journal, 46*(5), 631–642.

Schultz, I. (2006). *Bag nyhederne* [Behind the news]. Copenhagen, Denmark: Samfundslitteratur.

Schultz, M., Antorini, Y. M., & Casaba, F. (2006). *Corporate branding: Purpose/people/process*. Copenhagen, Denmark: Copenhagen Business School Press.

Schultz, M., Hatch, M. J., & Larsen, M. H. (2000). *The expressive organization. Linking identity, reputation and the corporate brand*. Oxford, UK: Oxford University Press.

Schultz, M., Mouritsen, J., & Gabrielsen, G. (2001). Sticky reputation—Analyzing a ranking system. *Corporate Reputation Review,* 4(1), 24–41.

Siune, K. (1991). *EF på dagsordenen* [EU on the Agenda]. Aarhus, Denmark: Politica.

Siune, K., & Borre, O. (1975). Setting the agenda for a Danish election. *Journal of Communication, 25,* 212–246.

Søllinge, J. D. (1998). *Danish newspapers: Structure and developments.* Gothenburg, Sweden: Nordicom.

Søllinge. J. D. (1999). Historien om den politiske journalistik: Et drama i flere akter uden slutning [The story about political journalism]. In E. M. P. Carlsen, P. Kjaer, & O. K. Pedersen (Eds.), *Magt og fortælling: Hvad er politisk journalistik* (pp. 76–95). Aarhus, Denmark: CFJE.

Søllinge, J. D., & Thomsen, N. (1991). *De danske aviser 1634–1991* (3 vols.) [The Danish newspapers]. Odense, Denmark: Odense Universitetsforlag

Thomsen, N. (1972). *Dagbladskonkurrencen* [The competition among the dailies]. Copenhagen, Denmark: Universitetsforlaget.

Togeby, L. (2004). *Man har et standpunkt: om stabilitet og forandring i befolkningens holdninger* [One has a point of view: About stability and change in public opinion]. Aarhus, Denmark: Aarhus Universitetsforlag.

Togeby, L., Andersen, J. G., Christiansen, P. M., Jørgensen, T. B., & Vallgårda, S. (2003). *Magt og demokrati i Danmark: Hovedresultater fra Magtudredningen* [Power and democracy in Denmark: Main results from the Power Investigation]. Aarhus, Denmark: Aarhus Universitetsforlag.

3 Corporate Reputation and the News Media in Finland

Vilma Luoma-aho, Turo Uskali,
Jouni Heinonen, and Antti Ainamo

For several reasons Finland makes an interesting case study through which to study the news media's role in the creation of public images and opinions (Carroll & McCombs, 2003). First, the news media in Finland is dominated by one major newspaper (cf. Ainamo, 2003), and one may ask whether there is a consensus in public opinion due to this homogeneity (for opposing views, see Moring, 2005). Second, Finland is a relatively small country (5 million inhabitants) for both business and media, and it could be speculated that the news media's effects are less visible than in larger countries (where diffusion of news occurs directly via social contact). Third, Finland has been a breeding ground for cutting-edge innovations and successful companies or communities, which could guide both the field of journalism and the media in Finland in general toward increased internationalization as global media outlets balance the agenda-setting capabilities of national outlets. Finally, Finland's long tradition of democracy and its active membership in the European Union provide potential for business news to flow from the country, not merely into it.

The structure of the chapter is as follows. First, there is a brief overview of the corporate sphere and the national news media in Finland. Second, extant literature on the news media and communication theory, with a particular focus on agenda-setting theory and reputation management is reviewed. The methodology and data collected are described and discussed. Finally, a conclusion is reached on corporate reputation and the news media in Finland, and implications and directions are provided for further inquiry.

The Corporate Sphere and the National News Media in Finland

Research has found that the development of the corporate sphere and national news media in Finland have been strongly connected to development, and, more precisely, in its geopolitical position (Ainamo, Tienari, & Vaara, 2006). Finland is a relatively young country, but since it declared its independence in 1917 development has been rapid, so that the country has developed from a newly independent democracy into a strong welfare state and the liberal economic democracy it is today (Castells & Himanen, 2002). The Finns made a quick and remarkable transformation from a farm–forest economy to a diversified modern industrial economy, which has one of the highest per capita incomes in Western Europe (e.g., Hobsbawm, 1994). The state was the main financer of many corporations and organizations formed after the world wars, and it produced large state-owned enterprises and monopolies which are quite rare elsewhere in Western Europe; however, neoliberal thinking has prompted the privatization of many state-owned monopolies, and thus state control of commerce is weakening (Alapuro, 1989; Jokinen & Saaristo, 2002; Määttä & Ojala, 1999; Ojala, Eloranta, & Jalava, 2006).

In comparison to the other European countries, the Finnish news media is politically a rather homogenous entity (Ojala & Uskali, 2005). This consensus is almost imprinted in the history of the nation-state. Until the late 20th century, almost all the newspapers were mouthpieces of national political parties. With polarization of the country's politics in the first decades of the 20th century, *Helsingin Sanomat* (HS; Helsinki Messages or News) was among the first to declare independence from party connections in the early 1930s. During the 1980s, the major regional newspapers followed *Helsingin Sanomat*'s example.

The opening of the financial markets in the 1990s helped financial and business news bloom (Ainamo et al., 2006; cf. Tainio, Huolman, Pulkkinen, Ali-Yrkkö, & Ylä-Anttila, 2003). The Finnish news media entered into a new stock market era, which prompted some newly public companies to adopt new roles and processes due to business-oriented thinking (e.g., Ainamo, 2005). Several companies faced ownership struggles when investors attempted to "conquer the corners" by purchasing strategically important portions of media stocks (Salokangas, 2003). In the 1990s, the country's worst economic depression since its independence led to restructuring of the media landscape and an era of media conglomerates began: A concentration of the Finnish media industry emerged in 1997 and 1998 with the formation of SanomaWSOY and Alma Media. One large and established daily newspaper, *Uusi Suomi*, was closed by Alma Media, and several other newspapers changed owners; and many of them (about 80%) were merged into chains owned by SanomaWSOY, Alma Media, and Väli-Suomen Media (Ainamo, 2005; Jyrkiäinen & Savisaari, 2003; Luostarinen & Uskali, 2006; Tommila & Salokangas, 1998).

Today, Finland is transparent (Transparency International, 2005, 2008), without corruption (Eurobarometer, 2009), and there is free public debate, which has prompted some to describe the country's climate for corporate activity as "open" (Luoma-aho, 2005). The Finnish economy (which is tied to the euro) is a stable small market; Finnish companies are almost all listed on the Helsinki stock exchange, and thus available for media analysis. Finally, Finland has been called the most Americanized country in Europe (Heinonen & Pantzar, 2002) due to its quick adoption of U.S. produced food, television, and film; however, the nation retains its distinctive national traits such as its extensive welfare state, a high level of technological development, and the popularity of newspapers (Castells & Himanen, 2002; Luoma-aho, 2005). Finland is a leader in globalization in multiple arenas, including journalism and the news media. This chapter discusses corporate reputation and the news media in Finland through systematic inquiry and propositions articulated on the basis of a current literature review.

Review of the Literature

Corporate Reputation in Finland

Reputation is a growing area of interest in Finland's corporate and academic spheres, as is agenda setting and its effect on the public's views of major business organizations. Most of the work on reputation in Finland has been published in Finnish (Aula & Heinonen, 2002; Karvonen, 1997, 1999, 2000), but more recent studies are in English (Aula & Mantere, 2008; Luoma-aho, 2005; Luoma-aho & Nordfors, 2009).

Although Finland has been included in international comparisons such as the Reputation Quotient and RepTrak (Fombrun, Gardberg, & Sever, 2000), it is only recently that reputation has become a trendy topic among Finnish scholars. The dominant point of view in Finland has traditionally been the U.S. approach to corporate reputation, and Fombruns studies are particularly well known (1996; Fombrun et al., 2000; Fombrun & van Riel, 2003; van Riel & Fombrun, 2007). Karvonen's book on imagology (1997) was one of the first works by a Finn on corporate reputation, and it defined corporate reputation as the combination of actions and impressions which are derived from the visions, values, ethics, image, and strategies of organizational actors (2000). Lehtonen (2000) sees reputation as the sum of stakeholder trust in the success of the corporation, and Luoma-aho (2005, p. 142) argues that "trust turns into reputation as present turns into past." Luoma-aho also links reputation with legitimacy and considers reputation as a form of intangible capital (2006). To her, reputation is based first and foremost on past deeds and is formed whether the corporation wants it or not. Aula and Heinonen (2002) argue that reputation should be divorced from the concepts of image or brand, and that cultural understanding should play a role in researching and measuring reputation. Aula and Heinonen define reputation as the sum of the stories told, and see these factors of reputation as a publicly announced, evaluative set of statements about the corporation, available simultaneously, at least in principle, to all potential audiences.

As for Finnish studies on reputation, Aula and Heinonen studied reputation in Finland[1] (in collaboration with the communications consultancy Pohjoisranta and the investors periodical *Arvopaperi*) mirroring the *Fortune* Most Admired Studies and Reputation Quotient of Fombrun et al. (2000). Their resulting "wheel of reputation" displays six factors for reputation that are particularly Finnish: (a) corporate culture and leadership; (b) products and services; (c) operational dynamics; (d) public image; (e) social responsibility; and (f) excellence. Of these, they argue that corporate culture and leadership are the most important factors for Finnish corporations. Additionally, Finns look to the monthly periodical *Maine* (Reputation), which in 2000 began focusing on corporations and the challenges of maintaining reputation.

Finnish research on reputation has also extended to state enterprises and organizations, which remain major players in Finland's reputation landscape due to the universal welfare system. Tarvainen (2002) compared the reputation of business organizations to the reputation of public sector organizations and reported fundamental differences in opinions of both economic performance and basic organizational functions. Luoma-aho (2005) designed a reputation barometer for state-owned organizations and argued that a neutral reputation is preferable to ensure critical operating distance (2007). Finland's municipalities have also developed their own reputation barometer (see Pohjoisranta & Finnish Association of Municipalities (Pohjoisranta, 2004) for a cross-sectional study of the local reputations of Finnish municipalities).

To be sure, Finnish organizations which actively practice reputation management integrate reputation into the very core of business processes and strategic management (Heinonen, 2006). However, such organizations are the exception and not the rule because reputation management as it is practiced in other countries is not yet the trend in Finland. Currently, the Finnish approach to reputation focuses more on managerial and leadership issues rather than on communications and PR.

Agenda-Setting Theory

Agenda-setting theory has been translated into Finnish as *päiväjärjestysmalli*; that is, "the day-order model" (e.g., Aula, 1996; Luostarinen & Uskali, 2006). Although the theory itself is well-known among Finnish scholars, agenda setting has not become a popular topic for research in Finland. What little research has been done has been published in Finnish for a limited audience, including studies on the news media's discussion of EU-related topics and the process that took place when Finland joined the EU (Aula, 1996; Heikkilä, 1993; Tapper, 1994). Later studies have examined reputation and organizational visibility in the media, but were limited in scope to one organization, a particular city (Harinen, 2003), or to a specific medium, such as letters to the editor (Laitio, 2006). More recently, Luostarinen and Uskali (2006) used agenda-setting theory when studying the topics that appeared as front page news in the leading Finnish daily (*Helsingin Sanomat*) from 1980 to 2000. Their study showed that political and foreign news dominated front pages in Finland until 1993, when financial and business news began to appear on the front pages more often.

Luostarinen and Uskali (2006) conclude that journalists in Finland find it difficult to detect new topics or frames to replace the old ones. This is paradoxical because news is supposed to provide something *new* to the reader, viewer, or listener. This work by Luostarinen and Uskali is of importance also in other parts of the world; often journalists and the media are conservative about changing their style or subject matter or the discourse in which they participate.

To summarize agenda-setting theory and basic research in the Finnish context, it is clear that for the most part it has been applied to studies of political communication, journalistic traditions, and mass communication. The studies have been limited to specific issues and major changes, such as Finland joining the European Union, and news reporting on the event. Previous studies have found general trends in reporting and style. These studies are mostly written in Finnish, and only a few have been translated. Newer trends include media visibility and corporate reputation. There is a rise in interest regarding agenda setting as a central theory or topic for bachelor's and master's theses, hence the next few years may see many new contributions on the topic. This chapter, however, is the first of its kind to focus on agenda setting and individual business organizations in a Finnish context.

Business and the News Media

Business and the news media is a comparatively new field of study in Finland (Heikkilä, 2001); this is due in part to Finnish business media taking an increasingly greater role over the past 30 years (Ainamo et al., 2006; Huovila, 2003; Mikkonen 1998; Ojala & Uskali, 2005; Uskali, 2005). The media business sphere is still developing; there are now two economic dailies and two daily economic news broadcasts. There are also several online news services that focus on business news, from international players like Reuters and Bloomberg, as well as investors' magazines and several economic periodicals. Online services and chats of economic dailies have become important debate forums for business issues. Some examples include the Web sites of *Arvopaperi* online and *Kauppalehti* online, which are very popular among small investors.

There is a clear distinction between advertising and news in Finland. There are clear national policies regarding advertising content that it must be clearly distinguishable from newspaper articles. The main media outlets and the traditional media honor these principles to a great degree. As for research on the relationship between the different media in Finland, some interesting studies have been carried out. Herkman (2005) applied the political economy frame for his studies on intermedia relations in Finnish television and the afternoon papers. In brief, the research demonstrated how corporate interests influenced the commercial popular media. Herkman also argued that though the Finnish media were supported by political parties and other institutions until the 1980s, the political press has now turned to privately owned and commercially produced media. To some degree, the "strong journalism" (Heikkilä, 2001) of investigative reporters or the civic society agenda has been replaced by the professional ethos of PR practitioners or content producers who work for corporations.

While research on the history of Finnish business journalism has begun (Ainamo et al., 2006; Huovila, 2003; Mikkonen, 1998; Uskali, 2005), a pronounced research gap exists in agenda setting and corporate reputation. To contribute to filling these research gaps, we approach agenda-setting theory on three levels of analysis in the next section of this chapter. In order to synthesize the foregoing literature review and the research gaps identified in the literature, seminal data are also provided.

Hypothesis 1: Awareness: First Level Agenda Setting: Media Visibility and Top-of-Mind Awareness

Media visibility of corporations and top-of-mind awareness have been studied in Finland mostly in marketing research and as studies of individual corporations. Suhonen (1986) and Ainamo (1996) studied the small yet reputable design house Marimekko, touching also upon questions of its reputation. Students in journalism have applied agenda setting on a small scale to specific topics, such as feminism (Toivanen, 2000), local elections (Rosenblad, 1992), or reputation. Studies and monitoring of corporate visibility are quite common in praxis, but scientific research is still lacking and mainly focused on a very limited topic.

Hypothesis 2: Associations: Second Level, Substantive Agenda Setting: Media Associations and Corporate Associations

Miettinen's (1980) seminal study has analyzed the topics of news stories and the contents of news articles in Finnish newspapers. Some studies used content analysis as a method for understanding the news flows in Finland in the context of foreign news (Kivikuru & Pietiläinen, 1998; Uskali, 2003). So far the most comprehensive study on the content of Finnish dailies has been published by the Finnish Newspaper Association. It indicates for instance that the economy as a journalistic topic emerged strongly only during the 1990s (Statistics Finland, 2006a). Ainamo (1997) and Ainamo et al. (2006) point to the coevolution of Nokia's role in the Finnish economy and the development of business journalism but include no content analysis in their study. Table 3.1 sums up the content

Table 3.1 Contents of Dailies Years 1991–2004

Editorial material % of space	1991	1992	1994	1996	1998	2000	2002	2004
Articles	5.3	5.7	5.1	5.1	5.1	4.5	4.6	4.2
Culture	6.3	6.8	6.1	6.8	6.8	7	6.1	5.8
Home news	33.6	33.9	33.4	31.6	31.6	30.4	26.5	25.9
Main circulation area						19.9	15.7	15.4
Other areas						10.5	10.8	11.4
International news	7.6	6.7	7.3	6.5	6.3	6.2	6.4	6
Economy	8.4	8	8	8.1	7.8	9.9	9.2	9.2
Sports	14.4	14.8	14.8	14.7	13.9	13.6	13.2	13.8
Entertainment	11	10.4	11.1	13.7	13.8	13.6	19.4	20.7
Letters to the Editor	2.4	2.6	2.6	2.5	2.5	2.7	2.4	2.7
Cartoons	2.9	2.9	2.6	3.3	2.5	2.4	2.2	2.1
R & TV pages	8.2	8.3	9	7.7	9.7	9.6	9.5	9.6
Total	100	100	100	100	100	100	126	126.8
Breakdown of total registered space**								
Editorial material	64.9	71.6	70.8	69.1	70.9	68.5	70	66
Advertisements	35.1	28.4	29.2	30.9	29.1	31.5	30	34
Total	100	100	100	100	100	100	100	100

Note. Source: Statistics Finland 2006a (* Based on one-week samples of dailies. (Week 47.) Breakdown of material calculated on the basis of total space. ** Total registered space is the combined space taken up by editorial material and advertisements. In addition, there remains "empty space" which is taken up by headings in the advertisement section as well as space left between stories, pictures, and advertisements (in 2004 the figure for empty space was 6 %).)

of the Finnish dailies. The shift is toward increased entertainment and content provision: there is a visible increase in the amount of advertisements as well as a decrease in the editorial material over the observation period of 1991 to 2004. This trend, however, seems to be global and hence not typical only of Finland.

Hypothesis 3: Image: Third Level, Affective Agenda Setting: Valence and Organizational Image

The impact of news reporting on corporate reputation and the ways that reputation affects media coverage are new topics for Finns. Studies that have been carried out have consisted mainly of traditional media analyses. However, Ainamo et al. (2006) and Ojala and Uskali (2005) found that the power of the business press began to grow in the 1980s. In the RepMap studies (Aula & Heinonen, 2000; Heinonen, 2006) media coverage has been one of the factors in developing the dimension of public image. In these studies the correlation of the public image to reputation was found to be statistically significant between the years 2001 and 2005. Next, the focus is on the case study, the corporate reputation, and the news media in Finland.

Case Study: Corporate Reputation in Finland

Finland is one of the least corrupt countries in the world, and high priority is placed on telling the truth and being honest (cf. Drori, Meyer, and Hwang, 2006; Transparency International, 2005). The corporate reputation landscape in Finland is, in international terms, still quite naïve and to a large degree deeds oriented (cf. Luoma-aho, 2005). In-house communication departments are still the norm in most Finnish corporations because of a belief that external consultants cannot have a sufficiently intimate knowledge of the corporation. In other words, everything that has approached "image creation" has traditionally been regarded as questionable. Corporate annual reports and even brochures have mainly stated decisions made by the proper authorities according to appropriate mechanisms of governance, concrete actions, numbers certified by outside auditors, and past deeds.

Lately, however, there has been a change. Intangible assets are gaining more ground and corporations as well as the media are interested in their "triple bottom line" and reputation. This is especially apparent in the various reputation and brand listings that have appeared within the last decade. Unlike general opinion polls, many of the new rankings concentrate on specific issues, such as brand value or financial wealth. Also newer aspects, such as corporate social responsibility have become central topics of listings.

National reputation listings mostly include Finnish companies. Certain transnational companies are mentioned if they also have a presence in Finland. This may be due to the limited size of the markets, but also traditional news values come into play, and proximity is an important criterion (Galtung & Ruge, 1965). The Helsinki Stock Exchange does not list many transnational companies. The best known companies in reputation research have been the big conglomerates, such as Nokia, Kone, UPM-Kymmene, Amer Sports, and Stora Enso, all of which have their head offices in Helsinki, the governmental, regional, and business center of Finland. Those corporations that are also large players in the domestic market, often also in the consumer sector, such as Nokia (telecom), TeliaSonera (telecom), SanomaWSOY (the media), Kesko (retail), Stockmann (retail), Finnair (airline), and Sampo (banking and insurance) rank high in both visibility and esteem. Nokia is the leader in several areas; for example, in 2004 the media intelligence company Observer reported on media coverage of Nokia, which yielded about 22,000 stories. After Nokia, the most reported on companies were Telia-Sonera, UPM-Kymmene, Stora Enso, and Finnair. From the data analyzed in 2004, two-thirds of all the coverage was considered neutral, 22% was positive, and 19% negative. The total number of stories was almost 200,000 (Barber & Odean, 2006; Hulbert, 2003). The average Finnish citizen will be familiar with most of these corporations at least by name. When business journalism and the business media were still underdeveloped, these corporations were the topics of much criticism. After the fall of the Soviet Union, they have increasingly become the topic of positive news (Ainamo et al., 2006).

Media Systems

The current media system or landscape in Finland is very liberal and free-ranging, including blogs, the Internet, digital television, and traditional daily newspapers. There has been a drastic change from the closed market of the Finnish media system before the 1980s. Finland and other Nordic countries top the Reporters Without Borders annual Index on Press Freedom. In fact, the top 10 countries of well established and robust press freedom were all European: Sweden came in 12th, the United States was 44th, after a fall of over 20 places within the last few years (Reporters Without Borders, 2006).

Newspapers have always been, and still are, considered the single most important news media for Finns. Each day newspapers reach over 80% of Finns, making them the medium with the second best coverage in Finland. Television, however, is overall the leading medium, as it is in most countries. What makes the Finnish case exceptional, however, is that Finland is the leading country in the EU in terms of aggregate newspaper circulation relative to the population (Jyrkiäinen & Savisaari, 2003). Most of the biggest newspapers are still published in broadsheet format in Finland, which differs from the general trend toward smaller formats (Finnish Newspaper Association, 2010; World Press Trends, 2005, p. 294).

Newspapers' most important strength is the fact that readers regard them as "reliable" and believe they benefit from the information and advertisements which newspapers contain. More than 80% of the Finns trust the veracity of the news in their newspapers either very much or somewhat. The affiliated newspapers had an aggregate circulation of about 3.2 million in 2005 (Finnish Newspapers Association, 2006), but the circulation has been declining since 1990 (Statistics Finland, 2006).

In the ownership structure there has been a trend toward newspaper chains. Through takeovers and mergers the market share of the biggest media houses has increased from the 1980s. The publishing of dailies is concentrated in three newspaper chains: SanomaWSOY Corporation, Alma Media Group, and Inter-mediate-Finland Media (Väli-Suomen Media) (Jyrkiäinen, 2000). The media landscape is at the moment under rapid change mainly due to digitization of media content and especially a new, increasingly popular medium: the Internet.

Finns are almost 100% literate and well educated, and interested in differ-ent types of media. Since the deregulation of economy and society began in the 1980s, the variety of available media has vastly increased. For electronic media such as radio and television, the years 1985, 1993, and 1997 were important turning points in the Finnish market. The first licenses for commercial local radio stations were issued in 1985, right after deregulation began. In 1993, the commercial television station MTV3 Finland started full service operation on its own channel. The first nationwide commercial radio station, Radio Nova, began operation in 1997, and the second commercial national television network, Chan-nel Four (Nelonen) began broadcasting later the same year. These moves largely broke the state monopoly of the public service broadcasting service, Yleisradio (YLE; General Radio) (Jyrkiäinen 2000). Table 3.2 sums up the time Finns spend with different media. Table 3.2 shows the importance of television and radio as well as newspapers.

Table 3.2 shows how television is the leading medium in Finland in terms of time spent. This trend is global, but what is different is the high status of radio

Table 3.2 The Average Time Finns Spend Each Day with Different Media

Time spent with mass media 2004	All	Sex		Age			
Population 12+	min /day	Female	Male	24–Dec	25–44	45–59	60–
Magazines	33	32	35	29	28	37	44
Newspapers	48	44	53	25	41	61	79
Free papers	10	10	10	8	9	11	16
Direct advertising	2	2	2	2	2	2	1
Books	29	37	21	55	20	22	27
Print media total	122	124	120	119	99	132	167
TV	207	201	213	184	186	221	273
Radio	169	160	179	122	181	194	158
Video & DVD	11	11	11	20	12	6	8
Phonograms	18	17	20	39	20	8	3
Internet	33	24	41	48	39	24	7
Electronic and recorded media total	438	413	463	414	437	453	449
Total	560	537	583	532	536	585	617

Note. The data come from a survey involving some 2 550 persons aged 12–69 years, with a response rate of 53 per cent.
Source: TNS Gallup Group/Statistics Finland 2006b

and newspapers in Finland. Age matters as well; with increasing age television consumption increases yet Internet consumption declines. Sex shows some minor differences as well: Finnish men tend to read more newspapers, whereas women read more books. Men are also bigger consumers of all radio, TV, and the Internet, but overall the differences are not that drastic. Finns are quite a homogenous people in relation to the universal welfare system, so income and class differences are not significant factors in media outreach or media consumption.

News Values

News values in Finland are much the same as in other Western European countries. The traditional 12 news criteria (frequency, threshold, unambiguity, meaningfulness, consonance, unexpectedness, continuity, composition, references to élite nations and élite persons, personalization, and negativity) made by Galtung and Ruge (1965) are still valid with one addition: entertainment (Uskali, 2002).

The geographical and historical developments have provided Finns with their own news culture and its particular flavors, and most significant of all is the tradition of self-censorship. As an example, during the Cold War Finnish media were not able to openly criticize Finnish foreign policy or the Soviet Union (Salminen, 1999). Today, the climate is very different, and as noted above, there is considered to be a free press in Finland. The processes of self-censorship, however, still apply on some levels. The mechanisms of self-censorship could still be used with sensitive topics, for instance in business news.

Organizational Newsworthiness

What makes the news in Finland does not differ that much from what makes the news in other countries. For international news, Finnish news organizations depend greatly on international news agencies, although the largest media companies have their own foreign correspondents in capitals around the world. Naturally Finnish news media are more interested in Finnish companies; Nokia's performance is of higher importance than for instance Samsung's, although Samsung's activities are also reported on by Finnish journalists because they are of importance; mobile phone makers as a whole spark interest. Also, major Scandinavian forest products companies and other public firms mentioned above almost automatically receive publicity in major news outlets whenever there is new information about them. Furthermore, when these companies listed on the stock exchange announce their annual or quarterly reports, it is always news. It is true that all financial information published by these companies is strictly regulated by stock exchange laws. However, Finnish business journalism, as is true in other countries, is concentrated on monitoring the actions of public companies. In addition, the boom in business journalism since the 1980s was linked with the rise of the number of stock investors in Finland (Uskali, 2005). The Finnish government has high visibility and access to news media, especially during occasions such as the recent changes in the welfare state.

Public Relations

As noted above, Finland's small population, which is spread over vast distances has enabled it to become the innovation center for communication technologies (Lehtonen, 2004). The Internet is much used in various communication contexts and almost all corporations whether listed or not, have their own online or wireless services, which provide access for cell phone users who wish to buy a tram ticket to online conferences. Huovila (1998) estimates that up to 80% of the material published in the famously much-read Finnish newspapers comes, in one form or another, from the Internet.

Public relations in Finland is a term with a bad reputation and one that has been misused. *Corporate communications* is the preferred term. There is, however, a long history of information providing (tiedottaminen) and publicity (julkisuustyö) that fall into the category of public relations. Although Finland is closely following global trends, there is still an abiding assumption that communication is mostly about information provision, and new ideas of relationship management or joint discourse have yet to become firmly established in daily corporate practices. Most of the top management of Finnish corporations does not see PR or communications as a strategic function. A study by ProCom (association of Finnish communications professionals) and VTL (association of the Finnish communications consultancies) in 2002 indicates that only one in 10 among top management sees communications as a vital part of strategic management. Communication and PR are considered mainly as support functions, which do not have the contemporary connotation of relationship management.

In Finland, only 56% of communications and PR professionals in 2002 were official members of the management group. This is interesting, given that public relations (or "informing") in Finland dates back to the early 20th century, when German-style professional associations were the vogue. Public relations in Finland began as advertising and counseling, and wartime propaganda was practiced during the two world wars. After the wars, PR practitioners were hired as propagandists in the public sector, where they faced new demands such as standards for ethical behavior and learning public relations practices. Information grew as an area of interest, and PR clubs and associations have been established since the 1940s. One of the best known is Tiedotusmiehet (Information Men) established in 1947. The focus has shifted since from state affairs to the corporate world, and the club has been renamed and changed into what it is today, ProCom, the public relations association of Finland (Lehtonen, 2004; Pietilä, 1987). Among the important changes affecting the development of PR in Finland was the introduction of electronic media in the 1950s, which brought an increase in advertising and public awareness, and in 1986 the Chernobyl nuclear power plant accident in Finland's neighbor, Ukraine, which emphasized the importance of access to information and led to several government agencies as well as large corporations establishing information or communication units as well as hiring information officers.

The size of the commercial PR market in Finland was around €40 million in 2005. Fee income growth has been for many years approximately 15%, but in the last few years it has dropped to 5%. The demand for integrated communications services has led to the situation where advertising agencies have focused on building up PR departments or teams to provide media relations for their clients. In Finland there are many PR agencies, most of them very small with only two or three employees. The biggest agencies employ around 30 people. Only a few international communication corporations have entered the Finnish market. There are only a few agencies that focus on strategic communications and reputation management, but public affairs is a growing area of PR agencies. Outsourcing PR and communications still takes place at very low levels, but it is growing steadily. The communication and advertising agencies and offices also provide media related services, which are the most common service bought from the PR agencies.

Research Methodology

Choice of News Media   The focus of this study was on print, though electronic media were also analyzed. This study used media content analysis of six selected types of media most popular as news sources in Finland: The main newspaper, *Helsingin Sanomat*, the main economic newspaper *Kauppalehti*, the Web site of the main mass media in Finland, Yleisradio at www.yle.fi, the main YLE TV1 news broadcast at 8:30 p.m. and the main news agency in Finland, STT (via leading business weekly *Talouselämä*, 2006). The data were collected during the first week of August 2006 to ensure that it was up-to-date and ensure quality as well as in terms of time to match the prepublication period of the reputation barometer in the fall of 2006. The data were collected for one week because of time as well as resource constraints, and hence represent a mere peek into the news media agenda setting in Finland. It does, however, provide some guidelines and ideas of the content and style of Finnish news media reporting on corporations.

Media Systems   Media access, media control, and media outreach (Sriramesh & Verčič, 2003) in Finland follow the typical traits of other developed democracies. As noted previously, there freedom of the press to a high degree, and there are many different media available which enjoy public support (both economic and intellectual). The media in Finland reach almost everybody. The general trend is toward ever increasing power of the digitized media, especially for the younger generation. Moreover, illiteracy is almost nonexistent in Finland, and there is vast access to media because the principles of the universal welfare state still guide Finland. With the introduction of the new digital TV, there has even been discussion of whether the government should provide each citizen with a digital receiver box.

There is very little propagandistic or manipulative guidance of the press in Finland, but the different newspapers have their own political emphases. The political parties have lately been accused of isomorphism and watering down their ideologies to suit the masses, and hence these differences are not very visible in the daily news. The larger media houses are often privately owned big corporations consisting of print and electronic media. The public sector in Finland also provides its own programs and channels without advertising. Corporations have access to the media both via advertising as well as reporting based on press releases. With the increased pressures of real-time media, corporate press releases have gained power as a source for news. Corruption of journalists, is, however, very rare.

Public Opinion Polls   There are several rankings of corporations published in Finland annually. Moreover, the Finnish Gallup Poll and the consumer ombudsman do their own listings and rankings of different products and services. The public opinion polls are well known and established, but they do not target corporate reputation. The respondents for the existing reputation polls are often specific groups such as investors, analysts, or readers of some specific magazine. The most influential for corporate reputation and the news media are the general reputation ranking of the 100 biggest publicly traded Finnish companies by communications consultancy Pohjoisranta published in *Arvopaperi* (Bond/Stock) and the top 300 brands published in *Markkinointi & Mainonta* (Marketing & Advertising). Some others include the top 500 companies in Finland measuring net sales by the periodical *Talouselämä* (Economic Life) and the brand-tracking by MTV3 (a commercial TV channel).

Data Analysis

The data collected were analyzed both qualitatively and quantitatively. Altogether 347 companies were reported on during the observation period of one week in August 2006. These were chosen to match the national characteristics of news reporting and to ensure applicable results for the hypotheses. To ensure results for Hypothesis 1 regarding media visibility, the number of mentions of each corporation and organization were recorded. To ensure answers to Hypotheses 2 and 3, each story was briefly content analyzed and coded into four "tone of writing/mentioning" groups. These four groups were positive tone mention, negative tone mention, neutral tone mention, and mixed tone mention. The positive group included the stories reporting only favorable aspects for the corporation, whereas the stories coded negative consisted of only unpleasant and unfavorable aspects of the corporations. Those stories, which mainly consisted of facts or mentions that had neither positive or negative tones attached, were coded as neutral, and the stories with both positive and negative or neutral tones were coded as mixed. Within one story, each corporation was reported once, counting the overall tone of the article. Some of the references to different corporations were within one story, but the tone of the reporting on the various corporations mentioned often differed.

For comparison, these listings were compared with the general reputation ranking of 100 of the biggest publicly traded Finnish companies published in the periodical *Arvopaperi*. More precisely, the list chosen was an average of 5 years of barometers published in *Arvopaperi*, so the reputation rankings form a stable ground for the media analysis. This ranking can be viewed below in Table 3.3.

Table 3.3 A Comparison of the Reputation Barometer Rankings and the Mentions within the Media Data Collected in the Study

	Arvopaperi/Pohjoisranta Barometer 5 year average ranking (2001–2005)	*Mediadata collected N = 5 media, 768 mentions (week 31, 2006)*
1	Nokia	23 mentions
2	Marimekko	1 mention
3	Kone	4 mentions
4	SanomaWSOY	9 mentions
5	Sampo	1 mention
6	F-Secure	9 mentions
7	UPM-Kymmene	4 mentions
8	Stockmann	3 mentions
9	Amer Sports	0 mentions
10	Finnair	4 mentions
11	Ponsse	0 mentions
12	Stora Enso	6 mentions
13	Fortum	6 mentions
14	Nokian Tyres	0 mentions
15	Technopolis	1 mention
16	Elcoteq	3 mentions
17	TietoEnator	4 mentions
18	Alma Media	2 mentions
19	Kesko	18 mentions
20	YIT-group	4 mentions

Results

Hypothesis 1: Media Visibility The Finnish data collected seemed to support the media visibility hypothesis, because those companies that were extensively reported on also ranked quite high on the reputation ranking lists. This was, however, only true for the larger companies. The reporting on smaller companies with good reputations was mainly within broader stories and not stories on the specific corporations; that is, the smaller companies were mentioned as good examples. There was a tendency of one newspaper to print multiple stories on one corporation when the topic was timely, for example, when there was an increase or decrease in stock value. There would be the stock news presented in a neutral or factual way enumerating which stock dropped in value and by how much.

There were altogether 768 different references during the measuring period in August 2006, dealing with and reporting on 347 corporations. Several references were one time only, but the focus here is on the corporations that were mentioned most often. Most of the companies reported on were Finnish, 21 of the top 25. The top 25 most reported companies represented very different areas of expertise from telecommunications to the metal industry and media and consumer goods. The most mentioned companies were Nokia, Wärtsilä, Kesko, European Central Bank, Toyota, NesteOil, SOK, Raisio, KCI Konecranes, Finnlines, F-Secure, Metso, SanomaWSOY, Bella-veneet, Volkswagen, Electrobit, Hartwall, MTV3, Fortum, TeliaSonera, Ford, Fortum, Microsoft, M-Real, and Stora Enso. All of these received six or more mentions in the five media studied within the observation period. Table 3.3 compares these mentions to the reputation barometer of the periodical *Arvopaperi* and communications consultancy Pohjoisranta, and reports the publicity and number of mentions of the 20 top companies.

The most mentions received were Nokia (mobile communications), Kesko (retail), and Fortum (energy). These companies are also very present in the daily lives of Finns through their phones, shopping, and energy consumption. Of these companies, it is mainly Nokia that is visible abroad. Hence Hypothesis 1 was partly confirmed: Reporting and ranking on the reputation barometer in the case of larger corporations were related, but with the smaller corporations this was not the case.

Hypothesis 2: Organizational News Topics   Hypothesis 2 was treated as a matter of content in the study. Most mentions and stories were fact related and neutral. The emphasis was on financial performance or merger/buyout decisions and news, which could have also resulted from the type of media chosen (news media and business news). Stories covering employees, executives, as well as products and services were present in the bigger stories presented in a somewhat list-like style, mainly for the purpose of providing background information. The companies with most mentions were also publicly traded companies listed on the Helsinki Stock Exchange, so about half of the stories on the most mentioned companies were mentions of their stock, reports on whether their price had gone up or down, and possible reasons for the activity. Such was the case with Nokia, KCI Konecranes, F-Secure, and Kone, for example. Smaller corporations with a good reputation (Marimekko, Technopolis) were mostly mentioned within other stories as examples of good image or brand management, but were not discussed for their own sake.

Smaller corporations that make it into the top stories are often mentioned as part of a larger story on the field or state of the art. The smaller corporations that made it into the top stories did so mostly because of similar issues that had risen on the agenda. One such example is the reporting on boats after a fire in a large Finnish boat factory, Bella-veneet. Due to this incident, as well as the extremely warm weather in Finland that week, many of the observed topics included boats, sailing, and other issue-related topics. The foreign corporations received slightly more negative coverage in stories than the domestic ones, but this was probably due to the news criteria. Also, there was less reporting on foreign companies than on domestic ones. Hence Hypothesis 2 was not entirely met: the content of the stories were mostly fact based and mostly affected by news criteria, and did

Tone of mentions of corporations in
Finnish newsmedia (N=894)

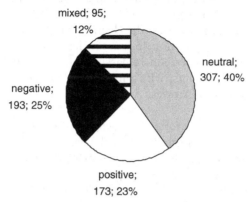

Figure 3.1 The tone of mentions of the corporations measured in the study

not include to a significant degree the traits or the content of the corporations or information relating to their reputation.

Hypothesis 3: Image   The image of the stories reported was mostly neutral. In fact, out of the 894 mentions analyzed, 40% were neutral mentions. There was an almost equal amount of positive reporting (23%) and negative reporting (25%), whereas mixed mentions were only 12%. Figure 3.1 describes this division. These trends seem to be quite general and global, and reflect perhaps the fact-based culture and maybe also the traditional role of the Finnish news media as reporters of facts (see Luoma-aho, 2005). The divide was very similar among the different types of media as well, though the nature of the electronic media restricted the amount of stories and mentions, hence making the print media the provider of the majority of the main data. Moreover, the electronic media (TV, Internet) were somewhat more negative in all their reports. The short time-span of the study and limited space provide for only chosen stories, which often seem to be negative.

The best reputed companies seem to form two groups in Finland: good reputation and and a lot of publicity and good reputation and very little publicity. The nature of the products and services the corporations provide also makes a difference in the number of stories. For example, the larger providers of general goods such as food (Kesko) or mobile communications (Nokia) get more extensive coverage than the equally well reputed textile designer (Marimekko) or the forest machinery manufacturer (Ponsse). Those corporations that are more tangible to the media through the visibility of their products and services seem to receive more coverage.

Discussion

Media Effects of Business News Coverage   The media in Finland report on very different corporations varying in both size and type. Naturally the type of media and time of year also affect their choice of stories to cover. In the case of corporate reputation, the most fruitful media seem to be the business newspapers and Web sites. The overall tone of reporting in Finland is quite neutral—40% of the mentions were neutral. Print media were able to provide more detail and more mixed, positive, and negative stories; the electronic media were mostly negative. Moreover, mentioning a corporation does not include a full story: over half of the stories analyzed in the study were mere passing references within other articles, pointing out examples and facts, which may not affect corporate reputation to the same extent as would full stories.

Local, National, vs. Transnational Companies　The news reported and the barometer compared were not totally alike: the barometer only included Finnish publicly listed corporations, whereas the news media data collected included listed, nonlisted, national, and foreign corporations. The number of news articles and mentions of foreign corporations within the Finnish media were, however, surprisingly small: out of the top 24 most reported corporations (reported 6 or more times), only 5 were foreign and all the others were Finnish. The Finnish corporate landscape is still quite small; the Helsinki Stock Exchange mainly lists only Finnish companies. The few mentions of transnational and foreign companies that did meet the news criteria of the Finnish news media were mostly negative in tone.

Media Systems: Media Access, Media Outreach, Media Control　The media system in Finland is tricky yet ideal for corporate reputation formation in the news media: the freedom of journalists, the pluralistic political system, the high media saturation and outreach, as well as the lack of media control contribute to a fruitful ground for public relations. Moreover, with the increasing pressures of real-time news reporting, the corporate press releases play an increasing role. The role of PR varies among different types of journalists; sometimes professional, more qualified, and older journalists try to avoid using press releases, and instead seek news by their own scoops. The demand for scoops, journalists´ and news organizations' own news, is high in Finnish news media, because the media are considered important and reach almost everybody.

"What Is News?"　News in Finland is quite fact based, and not as narrative as it is in the United States. The lead sentence contains the most important piece of news, and the rest of the story includes more facts based on several mainly authoritative sources. During the Cold War international and domestic politics ruled as news topics, but since the collapse of communism economics has played a more important role in news. Violent and surprising events, such as crimes and accidents have always been among the most watched in news. Also sports, especially motor sports like Formula 1 and World Rally Championships and ice hockey have reached big audiences (Luostarinen & Uskali, 2006). Overall, the news in Finland is quite similar to news in other countries, with a national accent and an emphasis on local news.

Findings and the Practice of Public Relations in Finland The findings show a possible chance for increased public relations activities in the near future for corporations in Finland: much of the reporting on corporations was for the most part fact based, and hence the role of news sources is important. Also the role of practitioners within the corporations is an area of development, and the replacement of functional PR activities with strategic planning and reputation management is a trend of the future.

Finland remains a rather reliable and fact-based country, where levels of social capital and generalized trust are high (Luoma-aho, 2005). This is visible also in the news reporting and formation of reputation; for example, the amount of neutral stories and mentions—40% of the stories analyzed contained neither bad nor good associations, but were mere factual statements about the corporation. The role of news sources is, however, on the increase in Finland. The Internet has become a central source of information, and is hence used by both journalists and public relations practitioners and corporations.

Limitations of the Study The study was the first of its kind to measure corporate reputation and the news media. The biggest limitation includes the sample: the news media data were collected for the period of one week in August 2006, and only from the five different media chosen for the study. That period of data collection was chosen to work with the end of the summer holidays and match the time of the reputation barometer data collection. The stories analyzed did still partially represent a summer holiday mentality. This was apparent in detailed reporting of certain topics such as sailing and boats, while not covering others, such as international mergers as closely. The chosen media could also be questioned as to whether they represent the whole scope of news reporting in Finland. Other limitations of the study include the level of detail in analysis because the approach was more quantitative than qualitative, to ensure an overall impression of the present situation. Due to the size of the data, there was an emphasis on testing Hypotheses 1 and 3, while focusing less on Hypothesis 2. This led to the results being more generalizable, yet limited in detail. However, the sample included several different and the most popular and credible media in Finland, as well as several different days and times, so as a result the data can be considered applicable and valid for the analysis.

Conclusions

Agenda-setting theory is one of the leading theories of communications research in the Western world. In part because of the peculiarities of the Finnish case, there has been a dearth of studies on corporate reputation and the news media in Finland. In this chapter, agenda-setting theory has been applied to inquire into the field of the media and journalism, on one hand, and the reputation rankings of business organizations with the media, on the other hand.

This chapter can be said to be the first of its kind in that no previous study in Finland has ever explicitly compared communications and PR practices of business organizations and the reputation rankings of these business organizations. The present study has reviewed and synthesized the research literature on the Finnish news media, as well as reporting findings on the content of the corporations with the best reputations and the content of their coverage in the news. The chapter also opens up interesting new directions for research and practice in other countries.

Global Corporate Reputation

The evidence presented in this chapter supports suggestions across disciplines that Finnish companies have become more international and perhaps more "Western," as the Finnish news media have increased their reporting on the Western global economy. This trend, however, is far from being dominant. The Finnish news media still focus mostly on Finnish corporations listed on the Helsinki Stock Exchange. On the whole, the Finnish news media appear to assume that their Finnish audience will find reports on local events and developments and Finnish business organizations more interesting than those of events far away or relating to Finnish subsidiaries of multinational corporations. These trends may be explained simply by proximity. Another explanation may be that reports and stories on foreign and transnational corporations appear less prevalent because the media are historically not free of nationalism (Ainamo et al., 2006; Dacin, 1997). If so, foreign business organizations would be well advised to behave as did all business organizations during the Cold War (cf. Ainamo et al., 2006); that is, to try to stay away from the front page because "no news is good news." A third explanation would be that there may be a time lag before the global network economy can ever make what is geographically distant appear emotionally and ideologically proximate for audiences or, indeed, the representatives of the media. Further research is needed to provide understanding on why and how multinational corporations, on the whole, appear strangely absent from the front and business pages of Finnish periodicals, as our analysis would appear to suggest.

Public Relations

Public relations practitioners in Finland are not always recognized as members of a distinct profession. The practices of reputation management as well as outsourcing into public relations agencies are both becoming more popular, but inhouse corporate communications departments remain the center of activity. Longitudinal research is required to identify signs of stability or change and to uncover the underlying mechanisms for such developments. On the basis of our analysis, corporate reputations are not discussed in detail in the news media because they still concentrate to a great degree on the larger agenda and follow the national news criteria. This could, however, be subject to change as the corporate field in Finland becomes more internationalized and as the news media continue to fragment to serve specific publics and needs brought by the global expansion of the Internet (Miel & Faris, 2008).

Organizations

On the basis of our analysis, Finland would appear to have a rather high degree of successful business and economic activity because most Finnish business organizations are reported upon in the media only in a positive light. It is obvious that almost all of the corporations that are reported upon are quite large in size. Only one innovative, rather small firm (Marimekko) with a relatively good international reputation for its size appears to be an exception, though it is often only mentioned as an example, not the focus of the article. If a comparison were to be made between the first set of corporations with the second set, it can be speculated that those predominantly large and international Finnish corporations that show a high level of innovation and ability to change are the ones with the best reputation. Such is most clearly the case with the top corporation of the present study, Nokia.

The Media Effects of Agenda Setting

Though there are several other significant players in the formation of reputation, news reporting seems to be an important factor. Whether the influence of corporate reputation affects the news media or vice versa, is not clear. Most important appears nonetheless to be the news media's ability to keep corporations in the spotlight for mass audiences by reporting on their activities (Carroll & McCombs, 2003). Corporations with a poor reputation tend subsequently to continue on that track. We have addressed in this chapter also a claim common among laypeople; that is, whether a company is in the spotlight in a negative or positive way does not matter because publicity and visibility matter. In both cases, the audience gets information about the very existence of the company, and it is argued that this is seen also, for example, in stock markets (Tainio et al., 2003). The more a company is covered by the media the more people buy its stocks; the direction of causality on this issue remains unclear.

Organizational Newsworthiness

Newsworthiness depends on many factors. In Finland, proximity is one important issue because the distances are vast and Finns sometimes feel isolated from the rest of the world. However, because the country is small and greatly dependent on foreign trade, multinational corporations receive some space in the media as well. Some Nordic traits must also be taken into consideration, such as the importance of leadership and the importance of facts over impressions. For listed companies, all their actions are more or less newsworthy, but for unlisted corporations, the traditional news criteria still apply.

Using the News Media for Evaluating Corporate Reputation

Though news reporting and reputation are in many ways linked, there are certain problems when the news media evaluates corporate reputation. Reputation can be seen as a broader phenomenon than just a media related issue, involving various stakeholder relationships, not all of them manageable through the media (Luoma-aho, 2005). According to Aula and Heinonen (2002), corporate culture and leadership are the most important factors in building sustainable corporate reputation in Finland, which would imply that managers and leaders ought to be placed in a central role. From this perspective, just analyzing reputations from the media may not be enough for understanding the various stakeholder expectations. However, the present study serves as a starting point for future study on agenda setting and the corporate reputation. The present study may not be the final word on the news media as influencers or factors in the formation of corporate reputation but it does provide a start.

Note

1. Communications consultancy Pohjoisranta and Professor Pekka Aula conducted a research project in 2000 and 2001 through which they discovered the composition of reputation in Finland. The research had three phases. In Phase 1 the focus was on defining the phenomenon of reputation. Five hundred and sixty-five respondents on the Internet panel assessed which organizations or companies were most valued and why they were most valued. The result was 3,267 reputation related evaluative statements. In Phase 2 these evaluative statements were content analyzed by qualitative research methods using AtlasTi-software. All 3,267 statements were categorized in 212 families of statements and after the following recategorization the amount of the evaluative categories was reduced to 84. Phase 3 was implemented with 84 questions about reputation. Seven hundred and twenty-two respondents answered the questionnaire. The data were analyzed by using factor analyses and demonstrated the structure of reputation in Finland. The corporate reputation is a six-dimensional phenomenon composed of 24 qualitative attributes. Pohjoisranta has used the same method for demonstrating the elements or dimensions of reputation in Latvia in 2003 and in Sweden in 2006. The main conclusion from the research is that reputation has a lot of characteristics that are culturally driven. The method was also used in analyzing the drivers of reputation of municipalities and cities in 2003.

References

Ainamo, A. (1996). *Industrial design and business performance: A case study of a Finnish fashion firm.* Helsinki, Finland: Helsinki School of Economics.

Ainamo, A. (1998). Evolution of the Finnish system of innovation: The contribution of Nokia. In B. Fynes & S. Ennis (Eds.), *Competing from the periphery: Core issues in international* business (pp. 423–439). London: Oaktree Press (Original work published 1997)

Ainamo, A. (2003). Small step for insiders, great leap for outsiders: The case of the "Tiger Leap of SanomaWSOY." In P. Mannio, E. Vaara, & P. Ylä-Anttila (Eds.), *Our path abroad: Exploring post-war internationationalization of Finnish corporations* (pp. 315–330). Helsinki, Finland: Taloustieto,

Ainamo, A. (2005). SanomaWSOY:n synty, kehitys ja muuntautuminen myös kansainväliseksi toimijaksi. In J. Ojala & T. Uskali (Eds.), *Mediajättien aika: Uusia heikkoja signaaleja etsimässä* [Time of the media giants: Looking for the weak signals] (pp. 183–211). Helsinki, Finland: Infor.

Ainamo, A., Tienari, J., & Vaara, E. (2006). Between West and East: A social history of business journalism in Cold War Finland. *Human Relations, 59*(5), 611–636.

Alapuro, R. (1989). The intelligentsia, the state and the nation. In M. Engman & D. Kirby (Eds.), *Finland: People, nation, state* (pp. 147–165). London, UK: Hurst.

Aula, P. (1996). Mediasta verkkoihin, detaljeista metateemoihin: Kansalaisten mediakäsitykset ja viestintäverkot. In U. M. Kivikuru (Ed.), *Kansa euromyllyssä; Journalismi, kampanjat ja kansalaisten mediamaisema Suomen EU-jäsenyysprosessissa* [The People in the European Mix; Journalism, campaigns & citizen view of the media In the EU-membership process] (pp. 215–227). Helsinki, Finland: Helsinki University Press.

Aula, P., & Heinonen, J. (2002). *Maine: Menestystekijä* [Reputation, the success factor]. Helsinki: WSOY.

Aula, P., & Mantere, S. (2008). *Strategic reputation management.* New York: Routledge.

Barber, B. M., & Odean, T. (2006). *All that glitters: The effect of attention and news on the buying behavior of individual and institutional investors.* Paper presented at the EFA Moscow Meetings. Retrieved from http://ssrn.com/abstract=460660

Carroll, C., & McCombs, M. (2003). Agenda setting effects of business news on the public's images and opinions of reputations of major corporations. *Corporate Reputation Review, 6*(1), 36–46.

Castells, M., & Himanen, P. (2002). *The information society and the welfare state: The Finnish model.* Oxford, UK: Oxford University Press.

Dacin, T. (1997). Isomorphism in context: The power and prescription of institutional norms. *Academy of Management Journal, 40*, 46–81.

Drori, G., Meyer, J., & Hwang, H. (Eds.). (2006). *Globalization and organization.* New York: Oxford University Press.

Eurobarometer. (2009). Discrimination in the EU in 2009, Special Eurobarometer 317, European Commission. Retrieved from http://ec.europa.eu/public_opinion/archives/eb_special_en.htm

Finnish Newspaper Association. (2010). Facts about newspapers in Finland. Retrieved from http://www.sanomalehdet.fi

Fombrun, C. J. (1996). *Reputation: Realizing value from the corporate image.* Boston. MA: Harvard Business School Press.

Fombrun, C. J., Gardberg, N. A., & Sever, J. M. (2000). The reputation quotient: A multi-stakeholder measure of corporate reputation. *The Journal of Brand Management, 7*(4), 241–255.

Fombrun, C., & van Riel, C. (2003). *Fame and fortune: How successful companies build winning reputations.* Upper Saddle River, NJ: Prentice-Hall.

Galtung, J., & Ruge, M. H. (1965). The structure of foreign news: The presentation of Congo, Cuba and Cyprus crises in four Norwegian newspapers. *Journal of Peace Research, 1*, 64–91.

Harinen, A. (2003). *"Joensuun taudin" medialogiikka: kuinka ilon kaupungista tuli valtakunnan lehdistössä rasismin ja pelon tyyssija?* ["Joensuu syndrome" medialogic: How a city of joy turned into a ghetto of racism and fear?]. Unpublished master's thesis, Faculty of Humanities, University of Jyväskylä, Finland.

Heikkilä, H. (1993). Monimutkaiseen päiväjärjestykseen julkisuuden taistelevat agendat ja median politisoituminen EY-kysymyksessä [Toward a complicated agenda, the fighting agenda and media politification in the EY-questions]. *Tiedotustutkimus, 16*(4), 33–43.

Heikkilä, H. (2001). *Ohut ja vankka journalismi: Kansalaisuus suomalaisen uutisjournalismin käytännöissä 1990-luvulla* [Thin and strong journalism: Citizenship in

Finnish news journalism practices in the 1990s]. Tampere, Finland: Tampere University Press.

Heinonen, J. (2006). *Mainejohtaja* [Reputation leader]. Juva, Finland: WSOY.

Heinonen V., & Pantzar, M. (2002). Little America: The modernization of the Finnish consumer society in the 1950s and 1960s. In M. Kipping & N. Tiratsoo (Eds.), *Americanisation in 20th century Europe: Business, culture, politics* (Vol. 2). Lille, France: Centre de Recherche sur l'Histoire de l'Europe du Nord-Ouest, Université Charles de Gaulle.

Herkman, J. (2005). *Kaupallisen television ja iltapäivälehtien avoliitto: Median markkinoituminen ja televisioituminen* [The open marriage of commercial tv and yellow press: The marketization and televization of media]. Tampere, Finland: Vastapaino.

Hobsbawm, E. (1994). *Age of extremes: The short 20th century, 1914–1994.* London, UK: Michael Joseph/Pelham.

Hulbert, M. (2003, December 14). Strategies, good news? Buy! Bad news? Buy anyhow! *New York Times.* Retrieved from http://www.nytimes.com

Huovila, T. (1998). Digitaalisuus yhdistää välineominaisuuksia uutisessa [Digital technique makes the news media characteristics uniform]. In T. Perko & R. Salokangas (Eds.), *Kymmenen kysymystä journalismista* [Ten questions about journalism] (pp. 225–249). Jyväskylä, Finland: Atena-Kustannus.

Huovila, T. (2003). *Tiedolla korkoa: Suomalaista talousjournalismia 1900-luvulla* [Gaining interest with information: Finnish economic journalism in the 1900s]. Helsinki, Finland: Infor.

Jokinen, K., & Saaristo, K. (2002). *Suomalainen yhteiskunt* [The Finnish Society]. Porvoo, Finland: WSOY.

Jyrkiäinen, J. (2000). The Finnish media landscape. *European Journalism Center.* Retrieved from http://www.ejc.nl/jr/emland/finland.html

Jyrkiäinen, J., & Savisaari, E. (2003): Sanomalehdistön nykytila. In K. Nordenstreng & O. Wiio (Eds.), *Suomen mediamaisema* [The current state of the press. In Finland's Media scenery] (pp. 62–76). Helsinki, Finland: WSOY .

Karvonen, E. (1997). *Imagologia: Imagon teorioiden esittelyä, analyysia, kritiikkiä. Akateeminen väitöskirja* [Imagology: Some theories of the public image presented, analyzed and criticized]. Unpublished doctoral dissertation, Acta Universitatis Tamperensis 544, Tampere, Finland Tampereen yliopisto..

Karvonen, E. (1999, January 8–9). *Maine kulttuurisena käsitteenä.* A paper presented at the Communication Colloquium, Helsinki.

Karvonen, E. (2000) Imagon rakennusta vai maineen hallintaa? [Building and image or managing reputation?] In P. Aula & S. Hakala (Eds.), *Kolmet kasvot: Näkökulmia organisaatioviestintään* [Three faces: Views on organizational communication]. Helsinki, Finland: Loki-Kirjat.

Kauppalehti [Economic newspaper]. Retrieved from http://www.kauppalehti.fi

Kivikuru, U., & Pietiläinen, J. (1998). *Uutisia yli rajojen: Ulkomaanuutisten maisema Suomessa* [News over boarders: The foreign news perspectives in Finland]. Helsinki, Finland: Palmenia Publications.

Laitio, H. (2006). *Helsingin kaupungin liikennelaitoksen (HKL) maine mielipidekirjoituksissa* [The reputation of HKL (Helsinki transportation office) in letters to the editor]. Unpublished master's thesis, Faculty of Humanities, University of Jyväskylä, Finland.

Lehtonen, J. (2000). Toimiva viestintä. Yrityksen aineetonta pääomaa [Good communication: An intangible asset of corporations]. In P. Aula & S. Hakala (Eds.), *Kolmet kasvot: Näkökulmia organisaatioviestintään* [Three faces: Views on organizational communication] (pp. 187–210). Helsinki, Finland: Loki-Kirjat.

Lehtonen, J. (2004). Finland. National profile. In B. van Ruler & D. Verčič (Eds.), *Public relations and communication management in Europe: A nation-by-nation introduction to public relations theory and practice* (pp. 107–119). Berlin, Germany: Mouton de Gruyter.

Luoma-aho, V. (2005). Faith-holders as social capital of Finnish public organizations. *Studies in Humanities, 42*. Retrieved from http://urn.fi/URN:ISBN:951-39-2262-6

Luoma-aho, V. (2006). Intangibles of public organizations: Trust and reputation. In V. Luoma-aho & S. Peltola (Eds.), *Public organizations in the communication society* (Publications of the Department of Communication, No. 29). Jyväskylä, Finland: University of Jyväskylä.

Luoma-aho, V. (2007). Neutral reputation and public sector organizations. *Corporate Reputation Review, 10*(2), 124–143.

Luoma-aho, V., & Nordfors, D. (2009). Attention and reputation in the innovation economy. *Innovation Journalism, 6*(2). Retrieved from http://www.innovationjournalism.org/archive/injo-6-2.pdf

Luostarinen, H., & Uskali, T. (2006). Suomalainen journalismi ja yhteiskunnan muutos [Finnish journalism and societal change]. In R. Heiskala & E. Luhtakallio (Eds.), *Uusi jako: Miten Suomesta tuli kilpailukyky yhteiskunta* [New deal: How Finland became a competitive society] (pp. 179–201). Helsinki, Finland: Gaudeamus.

Määttä, S., & Ojala, T. (1999). *Tasapainoisen onnistumisen haaste: Johtaminen julkisella sektorilla* [The balanced success challenge: Management in the public sector]. Hallinnon kehittämiskeskus, valtiovarainministeriö. Helsinki, Finland: Edita.

Miel, P. & Faris, R. (2008). *News and information as digital media come of age.* Overview 2008, The Berkman Center for Internet & Society at Harvard University. Retrieved from: http://cyber.law.harvard.edu/sites/cyber.law.harvard.edu/files/Overview_MR.pdf

Miettinen, J. (1980). *Sanomalehtien lukeminen. Maakuntien ykköslehtien lukijoiden kiinnostus sekä väline- ja sisältökäyttö.* [Reading newspapers: Reader's interest, their use as a tool and content in the case of major local newspapers]. Espoo, Finland: Weilin & Göös.

Mikkonen, A. (1998). *Rahavallan rakkikoirat: Taloustoimittajien yhdistys.* [The watchdogs of money: The Association of Financial Journalists]. Helsinki, Finland:

Moring, T. (2005). Joukkoviestintävälineet Suomen poliittisessa järjestelmässä [Mass communication In the Finnish political system]. Lecture. Retrieved from http://www.valt.helsinki.fi/vol/spj/electures/Moring.htm

Ojala, J., Eloranta, J., & Jalava, J. (2006). *The road to prosperity: An economic history of Finland.* Helsinki, Finland: SKS.

Ojala, J., & Uskali, T. (2005). Mediakentän muutos pitkällä aikavälillä: uutiskirjeistä internetiin [The change in the media industry: From newsletters to the Internet]. In J. Ojala & T. Uskali (Eds.), *Mediajättien aika: Uusia heikkoja signaaleja etsimässä* [The era of media giants: The search for new weak signals] (pp.121–161). Helsinki, Finland: Infor.

Pietilä, J. (1987). Neljä etappia, viisi epookkia: Eli suomalaisen tiedotuksen vuosikymmenet [Four stages, five eras: The decades of public information in Finland]. *Tiedottaja, 8*(5–6), 4–6.

Pohjoisranta (2004) Viestintätoimisto Pohjoisrannan RepMap kuntamainemittaristo, Aula, P. & Heinonen, J.: Selvitys kuntamainetekijöistä. Suomen Kuntaliitto & Viestintätoimisto Pohjoisranta. (In Finnish: Pohjoisranta & Finnish Association of Munic-

ipalities, RepMap Municipality Reputation Barometer) Retrieved from: http://hosted.
kuntaliitto.fi/int

Pohjoisranta Oy. (2001–2005). RepMap-mainetutkimusaineisto [RepMap-reputation
data]. Unpublished. Communication Consultancy Pohjoistranta.

ProCom & VTL. (2002). Tutkimus johdon viestintäasenteista [Unpublished study on
managements' attitudes toward communication].

ProCom. (2005). Yhteisöviestintätutkimus [Corporate communications study]. Retrieved
from http://www.procom.fi/dman/Document.phx/~public/Julkiset+dokumentit/Yhte
isoviestintatutkimus2005?cmd=download#search=%22Procom%20yhteis%C3%B6v
iestint%C3%A4tutkimus%22

Reporters Without Borders. (2006). North Korea, Eritrea and Turkmenistan are
the world's "black holes" for news. Retrieved from http://www.rsf.org/rubrique.
php3?id_rubrique=554>

van Riel, C., & Fombrun, C. (2007) *Essentials of corporate communication*. London:
Routledge.

Rosenblad, L. (1992). *EG-kampanjen i kommunalvalet 1992* [EG-campaign in the com-
munal elections in 1992]. Unpublished master's thesis, Faculty of Social Sciences, University of Helsinki.

Salminen, E. (1999). *Silenced media: The propaganda war between Russia and the West
in Northern Europe*. London, UK: Palgrave Macmillan.

Salokangas, R. (2003). "Ankarat käskyt kohtalon." Vaasa Oy, Vaasa-lehti ja Pohjalainen
kohtaavat lehtimarkkinoiden muutoksen ["Fierce orders of Fate," Vaasa Magazine
and the newspaper Pohjalainen meet the change in markets]. Vaasa Oy Publications:
Vaasa.

Sriramesh, K., & Verčič, D. (2003). A theoretical framework for global public relations
Research and practice. In K. Sriramesh & D. Verčič (Eds.), *The global public relations
handbook: Theory, research, and practice* (pp. 1–19). Mahwah, NJ: Erlbaum.

Statistics Finland. (2006a). Culture and the media. Retrieved from http://www.stat.fi/
tup/suoluk/suoluk_kulttuuri_en.html#Newspaper

Statistics Finland. (2006b). Mass media market 2000–2004. Retrieved from http://www.
stat.fi/til/jvie/2004/jvie_2004_2006-03-09_tie_001_en.html

Suhonen, P. (1986). *Marimekko-ilmiö* [The Marimekko phenomenon]. Helsinki, Finland: Marimekko/Taideteolline museo.

Tainio, R., Huolman, M., Pulkkinen, M., Ali-Yrkkö, J., & Ylä-Anttila, P. (2003). Global investors meet local managers: Shareholder value in the Finnish context. In M-L.
Djelic & S. Quack (Eds.), *Globalization and institutions: Redefining the rules of the
economic game* (pp. 37–56). Cheltenham, UK: Edward Elgar .

Talouselämä. (2006). Top 500 companies in Finland. Retrieved from http://www.talou-
selama.fi/te500list_eng.te

Tapper, H. (1994). EU as a salvation for the Finnish economy? Does the media discourse
meet the people? *Interim Report, 2*, 38–44.

Tarvainen, V. (2002). *Valvoo, neuvoo, tietää: Julkisen organisaation stakeholdereiden
käsityksiä maineesta. Case Säteilyturvakeskus. Pro gradu –työ, viestintätieteiden lai-
tos, Jyväskylän yliopisto.* [Regulates, advises, knows: Public organization's stakeholders' views on reputation: Case of radiation and nuclear safety authority]. Unpublished
Master's Thesis, Department of Communication, University of Jyväskylä, Finland.

Toivanen, K. (2000). Feminismi Suomalaisen valtavirtajournalismin uutisissa [Feminism
in the mass media in Finland]. Unpublished Master's thesis, Department of Communication, University of Jyväskylä, Jyväskylä, Finland. Retrieved from http://selene.lib.
jyu.fi:8080/gradu/f/ktoivanen.pdf

Tommila, P., & Salokangas, R. (1998). *Sanomia kaikille: Suomen lehdistön historia* [News for all: The history of the Finnish press]. Helsinki, Finland: Edita.

Transparency International Corruption Index. (2008). Corruption Perception Index. Retrieved from http://www.transparency.org/policy_research/surveys_indices/cpi/2008

Transparency International Corruption Perceptions Index (2005). Retrieved from http://www.transparency.org/policy_research/surveys_indices/cpi/2005

Uskali, T. (2002) Kriittisyys: Nykyjournalismin selkäranka, viisi käytännön neuvoa hyvän journalismin lisäämiseksi [Criticism: The spine of modern journalism, five practical tips to increase good journalism]. In T. Perko, R. Salokangas, & H. Luostarinen (Eds.), *Median varjoss* [In the shadow of the media] (pp. 30–47). Jyväskylän yliopisto, Finland: Media instituutti.

Uskali, T. (2003). "Älä kirjoita itseäsi ulos," suomalaisen Moskovan-kirjeenvaihtajuuden alkutaival 1957–1975. ["Do not write yourself out," the beginning of the Finnish Moscow correspondence in 1957–1975]. Jyväskylän yliopisto: Jyväskylä.

Uskali, T. (2005). Talousjournalismin historia, rajat ja tulevaisuus [The history, boundaries and future of financial journalism]. In J. Ojala & T. Uskali (Eds.), *Mediajättien aika: Uusia heikkoja signaaleja etsimässä* [The era of media giants: The search for new weak signals] (pp. 27–54). Helsinki, Finland: Infor.

World Press Trends. (2005). *World Association of Newspapers.* Paris: ZenithOptimedia.

4 Corporate Reputation and the News Media in France

Roei Davidson and Nicolas Chazaud

Introduction

This chapter considers the agenda-setting capacities of the French media with regard to corporate reputation. It uses public opinion data gathered in late 2004 and content analysis to test a variant of the basic agenda-setting hypothesis, namely, that the number of mentions of French firms in the French press will be positively related to the ease with which the public can form an opinion of those firms, in other words, assign a reputation to them. This chapter also considers whether other information sources related to a firm's business model, most importantly the existence of a retail relationship with the consumer, play a part in setting the public's corporate reputation agenda. We find evidence supporting the agenda-setting power of the press. Finally, the chapter uncovers suggestive evidence regarding the similarity of business news reporting across business and mainstream newspapers.

Literature Review

Corporate Reputation

Unlike many other countries, French media have not regularly published annual reputation rankings. Nevertheless, some studies have measured related concepts in the French context (Fombrun, 2007). A 2007 survey (TNS-Sofres, 2007) measuring confidence in French companies found that, in comparison to 1993, confidence in corporations had not collapsed. In fact, it had risen, while confidence in executives had decreased. Small companies enjoyed much more confidence from the public than did large companies.

Corporate social responsibility (CSR) is a reputation-related field where data and research is plentiful, though not publicly available. It has been argued that the high salience of CSR in France and its particular construction is conditioned by three unique factors: the strong role of the state, the mistrust of private actors, and skepticism regarding the reality of corporate transparency. These factors, though weakened in recent years, continue to exert significant influence.

A product of the 1970s, French CSR reporting and rating emanated from legislation mandating that companies issue an annual report (*bilan social*) that focused on labor relations. This report, though submitted to both a government agency and to a workers' council is not published publicly.[1] In the 1990s, private agencies were established that specialized in social ratings, selling their products to private clients. Consequently, the state is directly involved in cultivating CSR. Additionally, labor relations are the prevailing concern of CSR at the expense of other domains such as the environment. Ironically, this *social* ranking process produces private reputation-related indicators (Antal & Sobczak, 2007; Igalens & Gond, 2005).

The primacy of work relations is vital in shaping opinions of corporations (TNS-Sofres, 2007). Outsourcing and layoffs were found to be two factors affecting public confidence in corporations. A global comparison of CSR perceptions suggests that the French are more supportive of socially responsible companies than are Americans. French respondents assigned the most importance to legal social responsibilities, followed by ethical, philanthropic, and economic responsibilities; in the United States, economic considerations were the most important (Maignan, 2001).

The French mistrust of private actors is evident in a comparative Franco-American analysis of attitudes toward corporations and the economy (World Values Survey [WVS], 2006). Confidence in major companies is somewhat higher in the United States than in France, though a more striking difference appears when comparing attitudes toward competition. Americans are more likely to support competition: 28.6% of U.S. respondents and only 16.1% of French respondents believe competition is good.[2] These results suggest that, overall, corporate reputation indicators should be relatively low in France.

Many elite French consider American corporations, especially those operating in cultural industries, to be a threat to French cultural integrity. Scholars have noted that the roots of Franco-American animosity stem from both countries' universalist ambitions to shape the world in their own image (Bourdieu, 1992; Hoffman, 2000). For example, Disney's decision to launch an amusement park on French soil was met with derision in the French press. French intellectuals expressed their fear that the institution of Disney, symbolizing America, represented an attempt to colonize French culture, believing it would both destroy the social and ecological fabric of nearby communities and infringe on French workers' rights. Nonetheless, this less than glowing portrayal of Disney by the French press was not embraced by the broader French society, many members of which flocked to the park (Forman, 1998). The growing French acceptance of mega-brands like Disney indicates that foreign companies may no longer suffer from a significant "reputation deficit" in France.

Additionally, the Disney case suggests (see also Burt & Sparks, 2002) that firms who have a direct retail relationship with their consumers through which they can convey an image independent of the press can bypass, to an extent, the media agenda-setting process.

Agenda Setting

French agenda-setting literature primarily discusses political issues. Favre (1999a, 1999b) described how interest groups with few resources try to affect public opinion by influencing the media agenda. Through an exploratory project, he studied how governmental work (defined as the government's decision-making process about public policies) could follow a "general" agenda without interacting with the media agenda. Neveu (1998) integrated agenda-setting theory into a larger overview of the relationships between media and politics in the French literature. He argues that Blumer, Cayrol, and Thoveron (1978) were the first to introduce agenda-setting theory in French political science. Their fundamental paper was the first French systematic study about the influence of television, but also introduced theories into the French communication research field, including uses and gratifications and agenda setting. Cayrol and coauthors highlighted the growing importance of television in French electoral campaigns for the voters and the candidates, as well as the limits of its influence on final decisions.

Champagne (1990) focused on public opinion issues through a critical perspective drawn from Bourdieu's work. Rejecting the claim that there is a "public space," he described the existence of intermediary groups that select information according to their own rules. A qualitative analysis of the development of nuclear power plants in France in the 1970s suggests that the mass media had a central role in making this issue a political issue debated not only by technical experts, but also by grass-root organizations and labor unions. Survey data suggest that following the increase in mass media coverage, the French public became more aware of the subject, although the evidence is not clear cut (Garraud, 1979).

Another study examined the salience of topics in both the French media and campaign messages during the 1986 legislative election campaign, analyzing the importance French voters assigned to topics without strictly adopting a traditional agenda-setting methodology (Missika & Bregman, 1987). The study found only a limited relationship between the salience of topics in the media (print and television) and the importance attributed to them by voters. On the other hand, party campaign messages broadcast on television were more closely related to their importance in the minds of voters. No studies examining agenda setting in corporate contexts have been found.

Business and the News Media

The relationship between the news media and French business has been examined frequently, though from a critical perspective focusing more on the effect business institutions have on media institutions than vice versa. Bourdieu (2005) argued that French journalism became steadily commercialized in the late 20th century. The autonomy the French press had enjoyed was replaced by a commitment to commercial criteria in news making. The 2007 French presidential election highlighted these problems: At the time, a number of journalists and politicians denounced the relationships between influential media outlets and big companies (Santi, 2007).

The development of a business press in France illustrates the increased commercialization of French journalism. Business publications appeared in the 19th century and depended on commercial backers (Gille, 1959). Following World War II, business weeklies, dailies, and business sections in newspapers materialized in France. Early on, many companies lacked public relations mechanisms, forcing the French business press to rely on governmental sources. The media also viewed itself as responsible for educating the general public about economic realities (Riutort, 2000).

Since then, both business and mainstream publications have produced business news directed at an audience of business people and consumers and less at the general public. The social aspects of business have been neglected in economic coverage (Duval, 2000).[3] Institutionally, business media have depended on the commercial sector. The growing reliance on advertising revenue reflects this trend (Duval, 2005). The purchase of *Les Echos*, the highest circulating business newspaper in France, by the French luxury products group LVMH, which, at the time, already owned the other French business newspaper *La Tribune*, is an example of the growing dependence of the French business media on the corporate sector (Philippon, 2007; Santi, 2007).[4] This position suggests that companies are welcomed into the French journalistic sphere, and that, as a result, the agenda set by the media originates from corporate circles.

Media System

The French state shapes both the French economy and the media system, though the state has intervened less with the media sphere than the economy in recent decades. The French state views itself as the custodian of France's cultural heritage, justifying the state's protectionist cultural policies, including quotas for French content on television and radio (Becker & Ory, 2002; Collard, 2000). Until the 1980s, the French state either maintained direct (through ownership) or indirect control of most electronic media in France (Browne, 1999; Lamizet, 1996). Print media were highly politicized through their affiliation with political parties and figures (Hallin & Mancini, 2004, chap. 5).

In the last two decades, a key public channel was privatized, reducing the state's media control. Media regulation has endured periodic, often ritualistic reform, frequently circling back to the status quo. Such incessant reform is a continuing indicator of the state's media involvement. French commercialized television news has mirrored developments in the United States by transforming itself into a blend of news and entertainment, with increasing personalization of political news by focusing on politicians and the anchors who deliver the news (Bourdon, 1994, pp. 302–330). Such mimicry is clear when comparing guests on French and American political talk shows (Darras, 2005).

Due to low advertising revenue, the French national press, concentrated in Paris, is more dependent than the American press on direct income from newsstand newspaper sales. The French state also supports the press in several ways (Albert, 2004). Newspapers traditionally expressed a political orientation that was often coupled with an unequivocal affiliation with a political party, though this tendency has begun to weaken (d'Almeda & Delporte, 2003; Martin, 1997). Newspapers that exhibit a strong political identity have suffered greatly. Simultaneously, the French electorate has become less confident in its party system and membership has declined (see Worms, 2002, p. 182 on the French party system).

Although Sriramesh and Verčič (2003) believe capitalist control results in a net increase in press freedom, the French media system does not support this trend; in France, one mode of powerful external control, the government, has been gradually replaced by another, commercial organizations. While political actors perhaps have lost some media access, in turn, corporate actors have gained media access. Even so, a comparative content analysis of French and American news demonstrates that French news presents a wider diversity of viewpoints and assigns more coverage to civil society (Benson & Hallin, 2005). Consequently, social activists might be expected to have significant access to the media in France.

Because of France's high literacy rate and the developed technological ability of the media to deliver messages, the two structural factors which might constrain media outreach, according to Sriramesh and Verčič (2003), are not relevant in France.[5] In comparison to other countries, French national newspaper circulation is low, declining steadily since the 1970s. National papers have suffered exceptional circulation decreases, while regional newspapers and magazines maintain a relatively high market share.

On average, the French spend more time listening to the radio and watching television than reading print media. To counteract this trend, the media grant significant space to covering television, giving it added reach (Albert, 2004, pp. 116–117).[6] However, French opinion leaders who identify themselves as influencing their peers in specific consumer categories, are heavy consumers of magazines, newspapers, and the Internet. The latter medium is especially important for leaders in telecommunication services, Internet, financial products, and travel (Vernette & Flores, 2004), categories that arguably have a special affinity for corporate reputation. Thus, the reach of magazines, newspapers, and the Internet is elevated among opinion leaders, allowing these media to potentially have increased agenda-setting capacities both directly and through interpersonal networks.

News Values

A series of Franco-American comparative studies (Benson, 2005; Benson & Hallin, 2005; Benson & Saguy, 2005) argues that, although the French news media is commercialized, it exhibits a contextual orientation, often stressing social rather than individual aspects. These studies compared the coverage of various social issues such as sexual harassment and immigration rather than economic issues, for the differences in the coverage of economic issues are narrower. French business and popular newspapers show the same tendency to focus on discrete events as their American counterparts, while prestigious newspapers remain differentiated. The slighter differences could be explained by the global nature of the objects being covered (e.g., multinational corporations) (Davidson, 2007).

Organizational Newsworthiness

Little has been written about organizational newsworthiness in France; however, a brief consideration of the nature of the French political economy may enable us to extrapolate which aspects of organizational life receive significant coverage by the French media. From World War II to the 1960s, the French economy operated in accordance with *le modèle Français,* whereby the state plays a central role in managing the economy either through ownership or through cooperation with the corporate and labor sectors. This centralized model, rooted in the French monarchy, gradually disintegrated after the 1960s; however, *le modèle Français,* as an ideal, remains strong (Gauchon, 2002). To ease the social transition to a more market-oriented economy, the state expanded social services, creating a "social anesthesia state" (Levy, 2005, p. 181). Given the continuing importance of the state and the stress it puts on social services, it is possible that state–corporate and labor relations would be deemed especially newsworthy in France.

Less concerned with the content of the news, French journalism enjoys delivering news with stylistic excellence and critical argumentation (Neveu, 2004). This suggests that the whole concept of "newsworthiness," characterized by the objective quest for facts, is culturally bound by American notions of journalism. In a tradition where the worth of journalistic output is a function of how well it is written and not necessarily of the external object it depicts, newsworthiness loses significance. Nevertheless, as Neveu notes, French journalism has emulated American journalistic traditions, suggesting that some of the news values that guide American journalism—drama, conflict, deviance, and importance—might guide French business coverage as well.

Public Relations

Public relations, which surfaced in France after the First World War, became more salient after the Second World War. The first companies to employ PR methods were active in the oil industry. Initially, many practitioners were trained according to American methods. In fact, the prominence of foreign actors in this field remains high; many French agencies are affiliated to or directly owned by multinational advertising or PR companies (SYNTEC, 2006b).

By the end of the 20th century, French public relations were increasingly subsumed under the label of corporate or organizational communication. Professionals in this field have attempted to position themselves as strategic consultants, instead of merely technicians implementing executive decisions. The French term *relations publiques* denotes a broader phenomenon than the English *public relations* does. Such terminology permits practitioners more public legitimacy for their activities.

Though marred by a low response rate, a 2000 survey of top French companies suggests that more than half of companies have separate communication departments. In comparison to other developed communication markets, it seems that more French companies prefer to manage their communication activities internally. Another study, published in 1999, suggests that, despite the broader label of corporate communication, practitioners primarily engaged in press relations, modeling the core of Anglophone PR practices. The government plays an active role in corporate communications, providing an official definition of public relations in the 1960s. In the 1990s, the French government placed regulatory limits on alcohol advertising in the realm of alcohol and nonethical advertising practices (Carayol, 2004).

Recent research by the French public relations trade organization SYNTEC-RP provides a snapshot of the industry (SYNTEC, 2006a). Based on responses from over 400 French companies, the overall annual communication market in France is estimated at €31.8 billion, €17.5 billion of which is spent on nonadvertising communication. Almost 15% of the nonadvertising budget is spent on media relations, while 30% of media relations expenditure is outsourced to external organizations. Furthermore, the survey found that media relations expenditure was related to client characteristics. Manufacturing companies invest a larger proportion of their communication budget in media relations than their counterparts in the service industry. A second report (SYNTEC, 2006b) suggests that the three most prominent industrial sectors from which clients originate are telecommunications and technology, energy and heavy industries, and food and agriculture.[7]

Research Methodology

The study conducted a media content analysis of French newspapers and secondary analysis of a corporate reputation poll from late 2004 and early 2005 (Datops, 2005).

Content Analysis

The content analysis is based on a sample of articles from *Le Figaro* and *Les Echos*. *Le Figaro* is a conservative newspaper that publishes a daily economics section. *Les Echos* is the highest circulation business daily in France. Given the study's focus on corporate reputation, and the public opinion sample of French executives used in this study, it is appropriate to sample content from dailies that cater to such an audience.

The analysis was limited to a 2-month period which preceded the public opinion survey data collection. This period was chosen based on previous agenda-setting research showing that public opinion salience at a given point in time is most sensitive to the media's agenda-setting power in the preceding 6 to 8 weeks (Winter & Eyal, 1981).

Public Opinion Poll

The Datops survey, completed from late 2004 to early 2005, sampled 300 French executives. The sample, with both a majority of male respondents and respondents from the Paris area, is commensurate with the centrality of Paris in the French economy (see Tables 4.1 and 4.2 for further demographic details regarding the survey's composition). Administered by mail and via the Internet, the survey focused on the reputation of companies included in the CAC40 index of large companies traded on the Paris stock exchange. Consequently, the survey does not examine corporate reputation in France as a whole, but analyzes the reputation of large publicly traded companies, mostly French, many with a multinational presence. While the CAC40 is not representative of the French corporate domain as a whole, it includes many significant French publicly traded companies operat-

Table 4.1 Datops 2005 Sample:
Geographical Location

Paris Area	61%
Rest of France	33%
Overseas workers	7%

Table 4.2 Datops 2005 Sample: Gender and Age

Men	< 30 years old	14,5%
	from 30 to 44 years old	38,6%
	from 45 to 59 years old	20,8%
	> 59 years old	9,7%
Women	< 30 years old	4,8%
	from 30 to 44 years old	6,8%
	from 45 to 59 years old	4,3%
	> 59 years old	0,5%

ing in various sectors including service and industrial. The survey included both closed and open-ended questions that asked participants to rate the reputation of the companies and to elicit responses regarding companies with the most positive and negative reputations overall and with regards to specific domains such as products or employment (Datops, 2005).

Hypothesis

The main agenda-setting hypothesis examines whether a relationship exists between the salience of a company in the news and the salience of a company's reputation. The former was operationalized using an article count of company mentions in *Les Echos* and *Le Figaro* archived in the non-English collection of Lexis-Nexis.[8] Reputation salience was measured by the percentage of the sample that could assign a reputation grade to a given company. This measure approximates reputation salience: the more salient a reputation is in an individual's mind, the easier it should be for an individual to grade the company either negatively or positively. The relationship between the two variables was then measured using a Pearson correlation.

In addition, a consumer's direct experience with a company can affect a company's reputation. Companies with a direct retail presence, whereby consumers learn about the company by using its services or buying its products under the company name, have the ability to affect corporate reputation (Burt & Sparks, 2002). Therefore, a dummy variable was constructed, scored "1" for companies that operate directly with the general consuming public in France under the company name and "0" for all others. In addition, anecdotal evidence suggests that financial and consulting company names often appear in a supporting role when their analysts serve as sources in stories on other companies. These mentions should not materially contribute to an individual's capacity to construct a company's reputation. Companies operating in the consulting or financial sectors were scored as "1" and all others as "0." Both variables were coded by two independent coders, attaining acceptable levels of reliability.[9] The specified model, including media salience, retail presence, and operation in the consulting or financial sectors was tested using OLS regression with reputation salience as the dependent variable.

Results

The results confirm the hypothesis by suggesting that a relationship exists between the media salience of a company and its salience in the minds of the public. The number of company mentions in *Les Echos* and *Le Figaro* is moderately correlated with the ability of the respondents to assign a reputation grade to a company. The relationship is stronger for the business daily *Les Echos* ($r = .41$, $p < .01$) than it is for the general daily *Le Figaro* ($r = .36$, $p < .05$).

The moderate correlations suggest the presence of extraneous factors. An OLS regression of reputation salience on media salience, retail presence, and consulting and financial operations reveals that, in the case of *Les Echos*, media salience, as measured by the number of articles where a company is mentioned, has an effect on reputation salience that grazes conventional significance ($p < .06$) even when controlling for additional factors (see Table 4.3). Roughly speaking, an addition of 40 articles regarding a company increases the public's capacity to assign a reputation grade to that company by 1%.

One additional factor, retail presence, is found to be strongly significant. The coefficient indicates that a retail presence has a positive impact on reputation salience. As hypothesized, operating in the consulting or financial domain has a negative effect on reputation salience; however, this effect is not significant. A similar pattern is unearthed when examining the relationship between mentions in *Le Figaro* and reputation salience (see Table 4.4). Nevertheless, the impact of mentions in *Le Figaro*, when retail presence and operation in the consulting or financial domains is controlled for, does not approach statistical significance ($p < .15$).

There is a strong and highly significant correlation between the salience of companies in the two newspapers ($r = .85$, $p < .001$). For every five articles on a

Table 4.3 OLS Regression of Reputation Salience on Media Salience in *Les Echos*, Retail Presence and Consulting and Financial Operations

Variable	B	SE B	β
Articles in Les Echos	.024†	0.012	0.246
Retail presence	7.028*	1.422	0.608
Consulting/financial operations	-1.767	1.78	-0.119
Intercept	79.777*	1.256	

Note. $R^2 = .51$; n=40; Retail presence (Yes = 1); Consulting/financial operation (Yes = 1); †p<.10; *p<.001.

Table 4.4 OLS Regression of Reputation Salience on Media Salience in *Le Figaro*, Retail Presence and Consulting and Financial Operations

Variable	B	SE B	β
Articles in Le Figaro	0.028	0.019	0.185
Retail presence	7.239*	1.45	0.626
Consulting/financial operations	-1.22	1.789	-0.082
Intercept	79.890*	1.356	

Note. R^2 = .49; n=40; Retail presence (Yes = 1); Consulting/financial operation (Yes = 1); *p<.001.

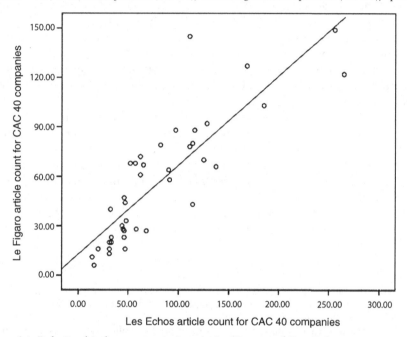

Figure 4.1 Relationship between mentions in *Le Figaro* and *Les Echos*

given company in the business daily, there are approximately three articles in the general daily (see Figure 4.1).

Discussion

Modest evidence was found for the agenda-setting capacities of the French press with regard to French firms' corporate reputation. Firms mentioned frequently in the press were also more easily assigned a reputation grade by the sample of respondents. In other words, the more salient a company was in the press, the more salient it was in the public's mind. There are indications that the French business newspaper's capacity to set the agenda for business executives is stronger than that of its mainstream counterpart. Nevertheless, the methodological design cannot establish causality.

The analysis also suggests that channels other than the press may shape the public's agenda regarding corporations. Regarding corporate reputation, companies that have a direct retail presence under the company name are more salient in the French public's mind than companies that do not have a retail presence. Thus, a company's salience is driven by an individual's experience with a company. The analysis suggests that an additional 7% of the public can form an opinion about a firm's reputation when it has a retail presence. Therefore when testing media agenda-setting effects factors in addition to the press should be modeled.

Finally, *Le Figaro* and *Les Echos* have a very similar agenda (though the absolute amount of coverage is consistently higher in the business daily). In terms of the salience of corporations in the two outlets, the newspapers are homogenous, and therefore do not contribute significantly to a pluralist media environment. In fact, cross-outlet similarity was found in the first agenda-setting study (McCombs & Shaw, 1972). The similarity between *Le Figaro* and *Les Echos* supports previous evidence of similarity between business newspapers and mainstream newspapers in institutional terms in France (Duval, 2000) and in framing terms in the United States (Davidson, 2007).

In France, like many developed economies, a shift has occurred toward a greater reliance on market mechanisms. This transformation reallocates financial risk from collective institutions to individuals (Hacker, 2004), making business news consumed by individuals of much greater importance for their financial well-being. Given this, the consistent indicators of homogeneity in the provision of business news should be seen as a problematic state of affairs, and some thought should be put into enhancing business news pluralism to better serve a public that is increasingly dependent on such information.

Notes

1. Further proof of the enduring importance of the French state as an initiator in the corporate field is a 2001 law that mandated publicly traded companies to include CSR information in their annual reports.
2. The aversion toward competition is also reflected in policy circles. As an example, we can cite the efforts made by the French delegation during the June 2007 European Union summit in Brussels to remove the clause enshrining "free and undistorted competition" in the negotiated simplified treaty (*The Economist*, 2007).
3. An awareness of this problem perhaps motivated the former French economy minister, Thierry Breton, to form a committee that would explore various mechanisms the government might set up to ensure accessible diffusion of economic information. The very creation of this committee reflects the enduring statist orientation of French society (Ministère de l'Économie, des finances et de l'industrie, 2006)
4. Because of antitrust regulations, in 2007 LVMH sold *La Tribune* to NextradioTV, the owner of BFM and other radio stations.
5. Television ownership is slightly higher than the world average and tracks the average for the G7 (group of seven industrialized economies) average. The strength of the French telecommunication industry and infrastructure is evident in the higher rates of broadband Internet penetration (26% in 2007) in comparison to both the G7 (23%) and the world as a whole (7%) (Economist Intelligence Unit, 2007).
6. On the face of it this suggests any agenda-setting analysis should focus on the electronic media. However, the national printed press has more extensive corporate sector coverage and a readership that is probably more heavily drawn from that sector and fits well with the sample on which the reputation data we used is based.

7. Note that this finding could be the simple result of the size of these industrial sectors in the French economy and not a sign of relatively high expenditures in these sectors.
8. In cases where the company name had other ambiguous connotations (e.g., Carrefour is both the name of the well-known French retailer and is the French word for *crossroads*), the raw word count was manually filtered. In addition, routine stock exchange announcements which appeared in *Les Echos* and included any of the CAC40 firms were excluded from the count, given that they cannot be considered to be editorial content.
9. Simple intercoder agreement on retail was 90% and Cohen's κ (a reliability measure that takes into account chance agreement) was .80. Simple intercoder agreement for the finance-consulting variable was 95% and Cohen's κ equaled .83. One of the authors, who has less exposure to the French corporate domain, used Hoover's, a database of corporate profiles, as an aid. The two coders (the authors) discussed the few cases of disagreement and coded the companies jointly.

References

Albert, P. (2004). *La Presse Française* (Rev. ed.) [The French press]. Paris: La documentation Française.

Antal, A. B., & Sobczak, A. (2007). Corporate social responsibility in France: A mix of national traditions and international influences. *Business and Society, 46*(1), 9–32.

Becker, J.-J., & Ory, P. (2003). *Crises et Alternances 1974–2000* (Rev. ed.) [Crises and Alternations 1974–2000]. Paris: Edition du Seuil.

Benson, R. (2005). Mapping field variation: Journalism in France and the United States. In R. Benson & E. Neveu (Eds.), *Bourdieu and the journalistic field* (pp. 85–112). Cambridge, UK: Polity.

Benson, R., & Hallin, D. (2005, May 26–30). *How states, markets and globalization shape the news: The French and American national press, 1965–1997.* Paper presented at the ICA annual meeting, New York City.

Benson, R., & Saguy, A. C. (2005). Constructing social problems in an age of globalization: A French-American comparison. *American Sociological Review, 70*(2), 233–259.

Blumer, J., Cayrol, R., & Thoveron, G. (1978). *La télévision fait-elle l'élection?* [Does television make the election ?] Paris: Presses de la *FNSP*.

Bourdieu, P. (1992). Deux imperialismes de l'universel [Two universalistic imperialisms]. In C. Faure & T. Bishop (Eds.), *L'Amerique des Francais* (pp. 148–155). Paris: Editions F. Bourin.

Bourdieu, P. (2005). The political field, the social science field, and the journalistic field. In R. Benson & E. Neveu (Eds.), *Bourdieu and the journalistic field* (pp. 29–47). Cambridge, UK: Polity.

Bourdon, J. (1994). *Haute fidélité: Pouvoir et télévision 1935–1994* [High fidelity: Power and television 1935–1994]. Paris: Editions du Seuil.

Browne, D. R. (1999). *Electronic media and industrialized nations: A comparative approach.* Ames: Iowa State University Press.

Burt, S. L., & Sparks, L. (2002). Corporate branding, retailing, and retail internationalization. *Corporate Reputation Review, 5*(2–3), 194–212.

Carayol, V. (2004). France. In B. Van Ruler & D. Vercic (Eds.), *Public relations and communication management in Europe* (pp. 135–151). Berlin, Germany: Mouton de Gruyter.

Champagne, P. (1990). *Faire l'opinion: Le nouveau jeu politique* [Opinion making: The new political game]. Paris: Editions de Minuit.

Collard, S. (2000). French cultural policy: The special role of the state. In W. Kidd & S. Reynolds (Eds.), *Contemporary French cultural studies* (pp. 38–50). London: Arnold.

d'Almeda, F., & Delporte, C. (2003). *Histoire des médias en France de la Grande Guerre á nos jours* [A history of the French media from World War I to the present]. Paris: Flammarion.

Darras, E. (2005). Media consecration of the political order. In R. Benson & E. Neveu (Eds.), *Bourdieu and the journalistic field* (pp. 156–173). Cambridge, UK: Polity.

Datops. (2005). *Reputation: Notation 2005 des entreprises du CAC40, etude Datops/Observatoire de la Reputation* [Reputation: The 2005 ranking of CAC 40 firms]. Paris: Datops/Observatoire de la Reputation.

Davidson, R. (2007). *Just a few rotten apples? The social construction of corporate scandals in France and the United States* (Unpublished doctoral dissertation). University of Michigan, Ann Arbor, MI.

Duval, J. (2000). Concessions et conversions á l'économie: Le journalisme économique en France depuis les années 80 [Concessions and conversions to the economy: Economic journalism in France over the past 80 years]. *Actes de la recherche en sciences sociales* (131-132), 56-75.

Duval, J. (2005). Economic journalism in France. In R. Benson & E. Neveu (Eds.), *Bourdieu and the journalistic field* (pp. 135–155). Cambridge. UK: Polity.

The Economist. (2007, June 28). France's hyperactive president—The Sarko show. 46.

Economist Intelligence Unit. (2007). Market indicators and forecasts [Database].

Favre, P. (1999a). La manifestation de rue entre espace privé et espace public [Street demonstrations between private space and public spaces]. In E. Neveu & B. François (Eds.), *Espaces publics mosaïques*. (pp. 135–152). Rennes, France: PU Rennes.

Favre, P. (1999b). Travail gouvernemental et agenda generalisé [Governmental work and generalized agenda]. In J. Gerstlé (Ed.), *Les effets d'information en politique* (pp. 143–174). Paris: L'Harmattan.

Fombrun, C. J. (2007). List of lists: A compilation of international corporate reputation ratings. *Corporate Reputation Review, 10*(2), 144–153.

Forman, J. (1998). Corporate image and the establishment of Euro Disney: Mickey Mouse and the French press. *Technical Communication Quarterly, 7*(3), 247–258.

Garraud, P. (1979). Politique électro-nucléaire et mobilisation: La tentative de constitution d'un enjeu [Nuclear electricity policy and mobilization: The attempt to structure an issue]. *Revue française de science politique, 29*(3), 448–474.

Gauchon, P. (2002). *Le modéle Français depuis 1945* [The French model since 1945]. Paris: Presses Universitaires de France.

Gille, B. (1959). Etat de la presse économique et financière en France [The state of the economic and financial press in France]. *Histoire des Entreprises, 4*, 58–76.

Hacker, J. S. (2004). Privatizing risk without privatizing the welfare state: The hidden politics of social policy retrenchment in the United States. *American Political Science Review, 98*(2), 243–260.

Hallin, D. C., & Mancini, P. (2004). *Comparing media systems: Three models of media and politics*. New York: Cambridge University Press.

Hoffmann, S. (2000). Deux universalismes en conflit [Two universals in conflict]. *La revue Tocqueville, 21*(1), 67–71.

Igalens, J., & Gond, J.-P. (2005). Measuring corporate social performance in France: A critical empirical analysis of ARESE data. *Journal of Business Ethics, 56*, 131–148.

Lamizet, B. (1996). The media in France. In A. Weymouth & B. Lamizet (Eds.), *Markets and myths: Forces for change in Western Europe* (pp. 173–205). London: Longman.

Levy, J. (2005). Economic policy and policy-making. In A. Cole, P. L. Gales, & J. Levy (Eds.), *Developments in French politics* (Vol. 3, pp. 170–194). London: Palgrave MacMillan.

Maignan, I. (2001). Consumers' perceptions of corporate social responsibilities: A cross-cultural comparison. *Journal of Business Ethics, 30,* 57–72.

Martin, M. (1997). *Médias et Journalistes de la République* [The media and journalists of the republic]. Paris: Odile Jacob.

McCombs, M. E., & Shaw, D. L. (1972). The agenda-setting function of mass media. *Public Opinion Quarterly, 36,* 176–187.

Ministere de l'economie des finances et de l'industrie. (2006, September 9). Installation du conseil pour la diffusion de la culture economique (CODICE) [Establishment of a committee for the diffusion of economic culture]. Retrieved February 14, 2008, from http://www.finances.gouv.fr/presse/dossiers_de_presse/ministre/codice/som_conf060904.php

Missika, J.-L., & Bregman, D. (1987). On framing the campaign: Mass media roles in negotiating the meaning of the vote. *European Journal of Communication, 2,* 289–309.

Neveu, E. (1998). Media and politics in French political science. *European Journal of Political Research, 33*(4), 439–458.

Neveu, E. (2004). *Sociologie du journalisme* [The sociology of journalism]. Paris: Editions La Decouverte.

Philippon, T. (2007, July 2). Des medias independants, condition d'une bonne gouvernance des enterprises [Independent media: a condition for good governance of firms]. *Les Echos,* p. 15.

Riutort, P. (2000). Le journalisme au service de l'économie: Les conditions d'émergence de l'information économique en France á partir des années 50 [Journalism in the service of the economy: Conditions for the emergence of economic information in France over the past 50 years]. *Actes de la recherche en sciences sociales, 131–132,* 41–55.

Santi, P. (2007, June 29). Le forum des sociétés de journalistes demande á rencontrer Nicolas Sarkozy [The forum of journalists request to meet Nicolas Sarkozy]. *Le Monde,* p. 16.

Sriramesh, K., & Verčič, D. (2003). A theoretical framework for global public relations research and practice. In K. Sriramesh & D. Verčič (Eds.), *The global public relations handbook: Theory, research and practice* (pp. 1–19). Mahwah, NJ: Erlbaum.

SYNTEC. (2006a). *Business and public relations in France: A pattern for growth—Research summary.* Retrieved February 18, 2010, from http://www.syntec-rp.fr/docs/document/62/DOSSIER%20PRESSE%20SYNTEC%20Ang.pdf

SYNTEC. (2006b). *Enquette annuelle: Activité des agences en 2005.* Retrieved February 18, 2010, from http://www.syntec-rp.com/docs/document/63/R%C3%A9sultats%20RP_2005vs%20site.pdf

TNS-Sofres. (2007). *Etude top com corporate 2007.* Paris: Département Stratégies d'Opinion.

Vernette, E., & Flores, L. (2004). Communiquer avec les leaders d'opinion en marketing: Comment et dans quel medias? [Communication with marketing opinion leaders: How and in which media]. *Decision Marketing, 35,* 23–37.

Winter, J. P., & Eyal, C. H. (1981). Agenda setting for the civil rights issue. *Public Opinion Quarterly, 45*(3), 376–383.

World Values Survey (WVS). (2006). World Values Survey online data analysis (1981–2004). http://www.jdsurvey.net/bdasepjds/wvsevs/WVSAnalize.jsp

Worms, J.-P. (2002). France: Old and new civic and social ties in France. In R. D. Putnam (Ed.), *Democracies in flux: The evolution of social capital in contemporary society* (pp. 137–188). New York: Oxford University Press.

5 Corporate Reputation and the News Media in Germany

Sabine Einwiller, Günter Bentele, and Christine Landmeier

"Daimler, Siemens, Porsche, Lufthansa, SAP. In the international arena German companies have an excellent reputation. They represent 'Made in Germany,' known as a seal of quality the world over. They represent innovation, quality and cutting-edge technology."[1] With this statement the German Federal Foreign Office presents the German economy to the outside world on the home page of its Web site, "Facts about Germany." This prominently placed self-portrayal indicates that the country's government recognizes that corporate reputation is a valuable asset and serves as a good selling point for Germany, which is the world's third largest economy and a large scale exporter of goods.

Interest in corporate reputation has grown in Germany since 2000 and it has been developed in the world of business and the news media as well as in academia. Ten years ago, Dunbar and Schwalbach noted that "[r]ecently ... German managers have come to recognize corporate reputation as something that is distinct, significant and important even though it remains an intangible asset" (2000, p. 115). Surveys show that this notion has stabilized. In a survey conducted in 2003 among members of management, marketing, and corporate communication in German companies, Wiedmann and Buxel (2005) found that two thirds of the respondents attached high or very high importance to reputation management, and three quarters of the respondents indicated that the achievement of reputation objectives was the direct responsibility of top management. A more recent study conducted in 2008 among the heads of communication of the 400 largest corporations in Germany, Austria, and Switzerland revealed that reputation is considered one of the most important intangible assets of a firm. Furthermore, 88% of the survey participants expressed the opinion that corporate communication has a strong impact on a company's reputation (Nix, Schnöring, & Siegert, 2009).

Discussions on corporate reputation in German academia, but also in business and the media, circle largely around the construct's structure and measurement as well as opportunities to analyze its potential impact on corporate value and performance. The latter aspect, in particular, is intensely discussed in the context of communication controlling (see Liehr, Peters, & Zerfass, 2009), and an effort is made to substantiate the business case for corporate communication.[2] Thus, discussions and research on corporate reputation in Germany have a strong business and management focus. Most researchers apply a definition of corporate reputation as stakeholders' perceptions and evaluations of a company on a variety of attributes and dimensions. Although there are differing viewpoints on the nature of these attributes and dimensions and on how they are measured (e.g., Helm, 2005; Schwaiger, 2004; Walsh & Beatty, 2007b), there is general agreement that reputation is a construct that resides in the minds of a company's stakeholders.

Although the role of the media in the development of corporate reputation is emphasized by international and also by German scholars (e.g., Carroll & McCombs, 2003; Deephouse, 2000; Eccles, Newquist, & Schatz, 2007; Eisenegger, 2005), there have been only a few attempts to integrate media content and stakeholder data in order to analyze media effects on corporate reputation (Einwiller, Carroll, & Korn, 2010; Media Tenor, 2006). This is despite the fact that media effects research has a long tradition in Germany (see Schenk, 2007) and research on agenda-setting theory has received considerable attention from German scholars in this field (e.g., Brosius & Kepplinger, 1990, 1995; Huck, Quiring, & Brosius, 2009; Hügel, Degenhardt, & Weiss, 1989; Schönbach, 1982). Agenda-setting research has focused on sociopolitical issues and events and has also covered economic issues. Corporate reputation, however, has been largely ignored.

In this chapter we bring together the German research strands on corporate reputation and agenda-setting. First, we will describe some national characteristics of the economy and corporate sphere, the media system, and public relations. We then provide an introduction to corporate reputation research in Germany and a summary of the agenda-setting research that has been conducted in this country. Finally, we will outline the research on corporate reputation and the news media in Germany before reaching some final conclusions and proposing questions for future research.

National Characteristics

Economy and Corporate Sphere

Germany is the world's third largest economy and the largest economy in Europe. With an area of 356,790 square kilometers and nearly 82 million inhabitants it is also the country with the largest population in Central Europe. Many multinational corporations have their headquarters in Germany, and 15 were ranked among the top 100 in *Fortune* magazine's 2009 ranking of the world's 500 largest companies (Volkswagen, Allianz, Daimler, E.on, Siemens, Metro, Deutsche Post, BASF, Deutsche Telekom, Deutsche Bank, ThyssenKrupp, BMW, RWE, Munich Re, Robert Bosch).[3]

Some of those multinational players regularly appear among *Fortune* magazine's list of the world's most admired companies (WOMAC). In 2009, BMW ranked number one in motor vehicles and BASF achieved the top position in chemicals while Henkel was ranked second in soaps and cosmetics.[4] There are also German surveys that regularly measure the reputation of large firms in the country. Since 1987 the business magazine *Manager Magazin* has conducted a yearly survey, "Image Profile," among German CEOs and business executives which is similar to *Fortune*'s WOMAC study. For the fifth year in a row, Porsche was number 1 in terms of reputation, followed directly by its competitors BMW (no. 2) and Audi (no. 3).[5] The annual RepTrak™ study by the Reputation Institute, an online survey of the general public that measures the reputations of 600 of the world's largest corporations in 29 countries, has also been conducted in Germany. The 2009 results show, that Lufthansa is held in the highest esteem by the German public, followed by Volkswagen and Robert Bosch. Interestingly, a comparison of the German ratings with those of other countries indicates that Germans evaluate "their" firms rather critically. The reputation score of the best German firm, Lufthansa, is only in the midfield of the overall worldwide ranking of companies (Lufthansa ranks 53, Volkswagen 66, and Robert Bosch 110).[6] This indicates that in comparison to the citizens of other countries, Germans are rather critical toward corporations and reluctant to make positive appraisals, true to the saying that "not grumping is sufficient praise" (Wiedmann, 2007).

Apart from the large corporations that appear in the image and reputation rankings, the corporate sphere in Germany also comprises numerous small and medium-sized enterprises (SMEs) that are world market leaders. These are firms with annual sales of below €50 million and a payroll of less than €500,000. Some 99.7% of all companies in Germany are SMEs and around 70% of all employees work in this type of firm. In fact, this ratio is very similar in most countries. Since SMEs generally lack important news factors (e.g., prominence), media coverage on SMEs is low compared to the coverage of large multinational corporations. Thus, when looking at corporate reputation and the news media, we have to bear in mind that we are for the most part considering large corporations that make up less than 1% of most developed countries' corporate landscape.

The German Media System[7]

The German constitution (*Grundgesetz*) guarantees freedom of the press and freedom of reporting on radio and television. There is no censorship (*Grundgesetz*, article 5, 1st paragraph). The mass media in Germany are assigned a "service function," which includes three main tasks: to encourage the development of public opinion, to control the legislature, the government, and their executive institutions, as well as the legal authorities (judiciary), and to mediate between citizens and state institutions (Branahl, 2000). At the same time, mass media are economic entities that have to be regulated. One regulatory element is media diversity, which means that preferential treatment is deliberately granted to the print media because the diversity of the print media market ensures the liberal development of opinions or external pluralism (Papier & Möller, 1999). In addition, media monopolies can be legally prevented (Pürer & Raabe, 1996).

Until the mid-1980s, the German media system was strictly divided into the privately owned print media market and the publicly held broadcasting market. Due to the development of cable and satellite broadcasting, a "dual broadcasting system" was introduced in the mid-1980s, which is now characterized by public and commercial broadcasting operating side by side (Stuiber, 1998).

Public and commercial broadcasting are subject to different legal regulations. Public broadcasting, which is financed by license fees to ensure independence from state budgets, has to serve the greater public good and provide audiences with information, sports, entertainment, and culture. It has an integrating function because it articulates the interests of minorities and encourages interaction between different spheres of interest (Hesse, 1999). For this reason, public broadcasting pursues a pluralistic concept which means that every program has to reflect the actual diversity of the society. Commercial broadcasting, on the other hand, which faces less stringent constitutional demands does not receive any funding from license fees but is dependent on advertising revenues.

The emergence of a commercial broadcasting market came with greater opportunities for companies and their public relations to be recognized by the media and to select media outlets for their advertising. The increasing number of radio and TV stations led to an increase in journalistic activities and therefore more public relations activities. Also, it became easier to reach specific publics because of the large number of specialized media. However, at the same time, because of increased audience fragmentation it became more difficult to reach the entire population via traditional media relations activities.

In 2005, Germans spent an average of 28 minutes each day reading newspapers (Fritz & Klingler, 2006). However, numbers are declining: In 2001, 84% of the population claimed to read a newspaper several times a week compared to 78% in 2006. This decline is particularly pronounced in the age group 20 to 29 (2001: 73%; 2006: 64%), which is partly due to an ever increasing use of the Internet (Gerhards & Klingler, 2007). Data from 2008 (ARD/ZDF, 2008) reveal that TV is the medium used most by the overall population in Germany: People spent 225 minutes per day on average watching television, followed by radio (186 minutes), and the Internet (58 minutes). However, amongst 14- to 19 year-olds the Internet is the most popular medium (120 minutes daily use) followed by television (100 minutes) and radio (97 minutes). In 2008, 65.8% of all Germans (14 years and older) were using the Internet. In the age group 14 to 29 nearly everybody was online (96%) and among those between 60 and 79, 29% were surfing the Web in 2008. "Silver surfers" (60+) showed the highest growth rate (11% compared to 2007). The Internet is mainly used for information searches despite the growing attractiveness of multimedia applications: 62% claimed to use the Internet mainly to gather information compared to 19% who put entertainment first (van Eimeren & Frees, 2008).

These data on the use of the media in Germany show that the Internet plays an increasingly important role in research. This suggests that the Internet is also becoming more important for gaining awareness and forming perceptions of corporations. While television and newspapers are still central sources of information, the younger generation is gathering much of its information online meaning that corporations have to increase their communication activities on the Internet. In this context, audience fragmentation as well as audience specialization (i.e., the extent to which users limit their news consumption to specific topics driven by underlying motives of interest), are just some of the new challenges for public relations (Tewskbury, 2005).

News Value in Germany

Ruhrmann and colleagues (Ruhrmann, Woelke, Maier, & Diehlmann, 2003; Maier, Ruhrmann, & Stengel, 2008) analyzed the development of news value in German television news between 1992 and 2007. A central finding of the study is a significant discrepancy in the coverage of nonpolitical topics between public and commercial broadcasting. While the large public broadcasters ARD and ZDF include only 36% (ARD) and 41% (ZDF) nonpolitical topics in their news programs, this percentage jumps to 65% (RTL) and 80% (Kabel1, RTL2) in the news programs of commercial channels. For commercial broadcasting, this percentage has shown a continuous decline since 1995 meaning that the news on the commercial television channels has become increasingly apolitical over the years. The study furthermore revealed differences in the news factors and thus in the selection criteria applied by public and private broadcasting. While public broadcasting channels prefer to report about influential persons and well-known groups or personalities, commercial channels choose topics or events in which moving images are more important than the spoken word.

Scholars have come to the conclusion that TV news programs are increasingly oriented toward sensationalism and emotional content, because increasing numbers of viewers were watching news over the course of the study period, covering all topic areas and channels. The visual illustration of emotions is particularly striking for international and apolitical events (Maier et al., 2009). Although this can be shown for public and commercial broadcasters, it is stronger for the latter because they spend more airtime on covering nonpolitical events and issues than public broadcasting does.

An online survey of news editors in television, radio, the print media, online, and news agencies shed more light on the role of news values from a journalistic perspective (Ruhrmann & Göbbel, 2007). Journalists judged the scope of news values, German involvement in a particular story, negative and positive consequences, surprise, and controversy as being of particular importance; visualization, visual depiction of emotions, and availability of pictures gained in importance according to survey participants (see also Diehlmann, 2003). At the time of the survey (early 2007), social and economic topics were considered particularly relevant as well as international conflicts and climate and energy problems. Journalists also mentioned a continuing trend toward tabloidization of news while political topics were losing ground.

The above-cited findings imply that times are shaping up well for corporations to be newsworthy because nonpolitical events and issues are covered to a greater extent than was once the case. This increase in corporate newsworthiness should be more pronounced in commercial as compared to public broadcasting. The findings furthermore indicate that corporate newsworthiness can be enhanced by providing good visual materials coupled, ideally, with some emotional content.

Public Relations in Germany[8]

Following an earlier definition by J. Grunig and Hunt (1984), Bentele defines public relations as the management of information and communication processes between organizations on the one side and their internal and external environments (publics) on the other side. Public relations serves the functions of information, communication, persuasion, image building, continual building of trust, management of conflicts, and the generation of social consensus. (Bentele, 1997, p. 22)

Public relations has been a growing industry in Germany since the end of the 1980s. One indicator for this growth is an increase in the number of PR agencies. This is coupled with, and is to a great extent generated by the boom in marketed media which began with the introduction of the commercial media market described above. The total number of full-time public relations practitioners in Germany is estimated to be about 40,000, of which around 40% work in corporate public relations, 20% in organizations such as associations, clubs, churches, and unions, another 20% in institutions (e.g., political administration at the national, regional, and local level, the courts), and another 20% work in public relations firms (Bentele, 1998). The lion's share of the daily work of a public relations practitioner is allocated to media relations (press reports, press conferences, organizing talks with journalists). Bentele, Grosskurth, and Seidenglanz (2009) show that 64% of more than 2000 spokesmen and communication managers, who were asked in a very recent study, are active in media relations, 24% in other areas.

As stated in the introduction, reputation is considered one of the most important intangible assets of a company and corporate communication is believed to have a strong impact on the firm's reputation (Nix et al., 2009). Therefore, the necessity of "communication management" and the need to employ well-qualified academics are mainly unquestioned, though not yet recognized universally in the country. The bigger an enterprise the more readily public relations is accepted by the organization as an independent function, preferably combined with other communication functions (Bruhn & Boenigk, 1999; Haedrich, Jenner, Olavarria, & Possekel, 1994). Haedrich's survey among managers further revealed that 71% defined public relations as a management function and 26% described it as a line function. Thirty-three percent ranked public relations at the top of the corporate hierarchy, 54% ranked it at the second level (i.e. directly under the executive level), 12% ranked it at the third level, and only 1% assigned public relations a lower position.

Corporate Reputation Research in Germany

Definitions of Corporate Reputation

The first scholarly work on the reputation construct in Germany can be found in the economics literature. Within the context of principal agent theory, Spremann (1988) argued that reputation is built when the diligence and predictability of an agent (e.g., a company) is disseminated to potential principals (e.g., customers), and Picot, Reichwald, and Wigand (2001) defined reputation as public information on the trustworthiness of an agent.

Current discussions on corporate reputation in Germany are dominated by scholars from marketing, public relations, and management. Definitions of the construct as stakeholder perceptions are influenced by definitions provided by Fombrun and colleagues (Fombrun, 1996; Fombrun & Rindova, 1996 cited in Fombrun & Van Riel, 1997), who described reputation as a set of collective beliefs or a collective representation about a firm's past actions and results. Wiedmann (Wiedmann, Fombrun, & Van Riel, 2007), who is the director of the Reputation Institute in Germany, defines corporate reputation based on Fombrun as the sum of perceptions and evaluations of a company by its relevant stakeholders including, and this is a new definition, the specific potentials for support (e.g., purchase, word-of-mouth, defense against criticism). Helm (2007a), another German marketing scholar, argues that reputation results from stakeholders' perceptions of the firm's ability and willingness to perform according to stakeholders' needs, and Schwaiger (2004) conceptualizes reputation as an attitudinal construct, where attitude denotes subjective, emotional, and cognitive based mindsets. Similarly, Walsh and Beatty (2007) argue that consumer-based corporate reputation is associated with thoughts and feelings, which can lead to behaviors toward a firm, and therefore is a customer attitude.

Conceptualization of Corporate Reputation

Reputation is often conceptualized as consisting of various dimensions that are made up of a variety of attributes or beliefs. The reputation quotient (RQ) has six dimensions or "pillars" of corporate reputation: products and services, vision and leadership, workplace environment, social responsibility, financial performance, and emotional appeal (Fombrun, Gardberg, & Sever, 2000). In an attempt to validate the RQ for Germany, Walsh and Wiedmann (2004) conducted a qualitative study that, apart from confirming those six dimensions, gave rise to four new reputation dimensions: fairness, sympathy, transparency, and perceived customer orientation. These extra dimensions were, however, not included in the RepTrak™ Pulse Germany study in 2007; Walsh and Wiedmann's extension of the RQ model for Germany came up with four consequences of reputation: Loyalty, trust, word of mouth, and satisfaction.

Based on qualitative and thorough quantitative research in the consumer context, Walsh and Beatty (2007) developed an instrument to measure customer-based reputation consisting of five dimensions: Customer orientation, good employer, reliable and financially strong, product and service quality, and social and environmental responsibility. Using structural equation modeling on customer survey data, Walsh, Mitchell, Jackson, and Beatty (2009) applied the model to examine the impact of customer satisfaction and trust on corporate reputation, as well as how corporate reputation affects customer loyalty and word of mouth behavior.

Like Walsh and colleagues, Schwaiger (Schwaiger, 2004; Schwaiger & Cannon, 2004) conducted qualitative and quantitative research to conceptualize corporate reputation and came up with a two-dimensional solution of corporate reputation. In Schwaiger's structural model, reputation consists of two latent constructs, a cognitive one (competence) and an affective one (sympathy). These two constructs of reputation are measured reflectively while their antecedents (responsibility, attractiveness, quality, and performance) are conceptualized formatively. Schwaiger found that performance aspects drive competence but dampen sympathy, whereas responsibility items have a positive impact on sympathy and a negative impact on competence.

The discussion concerning formative or reflective measurement of reputation is ongoing in reputation research. In reflective measurement, the researcher assumes that the observable indicators are reflections of the unidimensional construct; formative indicators, on the other hand, are thought to form and represent different dimensions of the construct (Chin & Newsted, 1999). The challenge in formative measurement is to consider all possible indicators of a construct because "failure to consider all facets...will lead to an exclusion of relevant indicators" (Diamantopoulos & Winklhofer, 2001, p. 271). Helm (2005) argues that reputation should be measured formatively, because indicators like quality of management and treatment of employees lead to reputation and not the other way around. Since Helm conceptualizes reputation as one construct with 10 indicators, this approach certainly makes sense. If different reputation dimensions are measured separately, each consisting of various underlying indicators, reflective measurement can also be argued for.

Helm analyzed the role of corporate reputation in determining satisfaction and loyalty in consumers (Helm, 2006) and in investors (Helm, 2007b) and finds a significant effect of corporate reputation on loyalty in both studies. In order to build supplier reputation in industrial markets, Helm furthermore stresses the role of customer reference relationships and word-of-mouth communication about diverse facets of the firm's conduct (Helm, 2007a).

Corporate Reputation in Germany: Findings from Reputation Ranking Studies

Schwalbach and colleagues (Dunbar & Schwalbach, 2000; Schwalbach, 2004) analyzed the results over time of the "Image Profile" study published by *Manager Magazin* since 1987. In this survey, senior managers rate the overall reputation of the 100 biggest German companies and rate at least 20 companies in their particular industry on the following five attributes: management quality, innovativeness, communication ability, environmental orientation, and financial and economic stability (ratings are from 0 "very good" to 10 "very bad"). However, for the analyses Dunbar and Schwalbach (2000) only used the overall ratings executives gave for the years 1988, 1990, 1992, 1994, 1996, and 1998.

The authors found that the reputation level of companies fluctuates over time. Only four corporations (BMW, Bosch, Daimler-Benz, and Siemens, 9% of the sample) were able to maintain a high reputation level over more than 10 years, and seven firms either clustered in the poor reputation group or deviated from it only once and then returned (equaling about 22% of the sample). Although no systematic media content analyses were conducted, the authors express the assumption that "[m]edia visibility may have been the driving force behind many temporary movements in reputation status" (Dunbar & Schwalbach, 2000, p. 118). To support this assumption, they give examples like the involvement of Deutsche Bank in the Schneider real estate bankruptcy as a likely cause for the bank's reputation slump in 1994, or Shell's Brent Spar crisis that may have precipitated the fall in Deutsche Shell's reputation in 1996. The analyses furthermore revealed that reputation fluctuates between industry sectors with automobile firms having the best reputation. Also, larger firm size and more concentrated ownership was positively related to reputation.

Wiedmann (2002) analyzed the results of Phase 1 of the reputation quotient (RQ) study in 2001 that measured top-of-mind awareness of companies with the best and worst reputation in Germany. The study revealed that a total of 27% of all votes were cast for the top five companies, while the top 10 received 40% of all votes. This indicates that the general public is unable to think of very many top companies when asked to do so spontaneously. Interestingly, no truly foreign company could be found on the top 10 list and all top five companies can be classified as technology companies (3 automobile companies, 1 telecommunications, 1 technology). The author concludes on the basis of the polling data that the following factors play an important role for top-of-mind awareness of firms in Germany: "media presence and general public presence, relevance to individual experience and ties to spheres that the public values in general, such as fascinating technology, economic success, quality and social responsibility" (Wiedmann, 2002, p. 353).

Agenda-Setting Research in Germany

Agenda-setting theory constitutes an important theoretical foundation when discussing corporate reputation and the news media (Carroll & McCombs 2003). Before describing the still very limited research on corporate reputation and the news media in this country, we give a selective overview of the extensive research on agenda-setting conducted in Germany. Research has mainly focused on the theory's first-level hypothesis, namely, that the salience of issues or objects on the news agenda influences their salience on the public agenda, and on sociopolitical and economic issues.

Agenda-Setting Research on Social and Political Issues

Brosius and Kepplinger (1990) analyzed the agenda-setting function of TV news using weekly surveys on problem awareness of the public regarding 16 issues and a content analysis of the main television news shows in Germany in 1986. The authors showed that although the public generally reacted to media coverage with corresponding increases and declines of problem awareness, the media sometimes also reacted to problem awareness by counterbalancing the public opinion trend. Reanalyzing the same data, Brosius and Kepplinger (1995) found evidence for their assumption that coverage of and concern about new issues will remove old issues from the agenda. Although they do not find evidence for so called "killer" issues within the media agenda, they identified some killer issues in the public agenda. Coverage of these issues increased public concern about them and decreased concerns about other issues. The authors called these cross-issue agenda-setting effects "second order effects."

Hügel, Degenhardt, and Weiss (1989) tested contingent conditions of political agenda-setting (need for orientation, interpersonal communication, issue-specific sensitivity) against direct exposure and content effects of newspapers and television. The findings are based on a secondary analysis of survey data from 1980 and content analysis data on the national election campaign in West Germany (TV and newspapers September-October 1980). A series of structural equation models revealed no media effects for an "obtrusive" issue (social security).[9] Instead, issue sensitivity emerged as the only predictor of awareness of this issue. The authors furthermore found that for an "unobtrusive" issue (foreign affairs), media agenda-setting was shaped by interpersonal political communication. Newspaper agenda-setting was found to be highly dependent on interpersonal communication about politics, while television agenda-setting had low levels of dependence in that area.

Rössler (1999) showed how interpersonal communication, egocentric networks, and mass media shape individuals' perception of political issues by combining three data sets: a representative survey among German citizens, a snowball survey among the interaction partners of these interviewees, and a content analysis of different media (newspaper, TV, radio). Whereas the aggregate-level analysis showed the usually high correspondence between media and societal agenda, the individual-level comparison of whole issue agendas indicated mutual dependencies, with the personal agenda leading the individual media agenda more frequently. Rössler and Schenk (2000) analyzed the same data over a period that included German reunification in 1989, and found pronounced media effects for respondents with a high need for orientation concerning political issues.

The role of interpersonal communication in the agenda-setting process, particularly for nonusers, was examined by Krause and Gehrau (2007). Their models confirm the agenda-setting effect: The media agenda affects the public agenda at later points in time, but the public agenda does not have an effect on the later media agenda. In addition, there are indirect effects on people who seldom watch TV news. Although media input has no direct immediate effect on those people, there is a significant effect some days later, which the authors interpret as a consequence of interpersonal communication.

Tiele and Scherer (2004) integrated schema theory into the agenda-setting model and examined the influence of cognitive schemas on the perception of political issues presented in the media during the German federal elections of 2002. By means of a quasi-experimental design the authors showed that recipients pay more attention to political issues already clearly anchored in their issue schemas, and remember those issues better than others.

Stressing the importance of perceptual components in the conceived process of media influence, Huck et al. (2009) presented a theoretical model of agenda-setting effects. Starting with third-person perceptions, they argue that part of the agenda-setting function of the mass media is to inform recipients about what other people believe to be important.

Agenda-Setting Research on Economic Issues

Research by the Institut für Demoskopie Allensbach (IFD) revealed an inter-relationship between the assessment of the economic state published by German public TV channels (media data by Media Tenor) and individual optimism among citizens in Germany (survey data by IFD). The findings indicate that the media climate determines people's mood concerning optimism or pessimism toward the future (Anonymous, 2004). Findings by Wörsdörfer (2005) confirm this correlation.

Brettschneider (2000), who compared survey data with different types of media data, showed that people's estimation of the economic climate in Germany corresponds with the economic reality presented by the media. He argued that the limited aspects of economy covered by the media represent only a very small and quite "virtual" detail of reality. This detail, however, appears quite real to members of the public and influences their perception of the country's economic state.

Quiring (2004) conducted research to analyze which specific aspects of TV coverage on economic issues influence voters' attitudes that are relevant for their election decision. He found that, on the one hand, the economic coverage directed people's attention toward certain economic developments and thereby raised their interest and awareness for such problems. On the other hand, economic news shaped people's perception of the country's economic future as well as the political candidates' and the parties' competence directly. In most cases individual experience was rare and the crucial information originated directly from the media. Quiring concluded that the media influence could partly explain the electoral outcome in 1998. Conducting elaborate correlations with official statistics, he furthermore revealed that the picture the media presented of the economy was far more negative than statistics during this time suggested.

Research by Bachl (2009) generated further evidence for the media's influence on people's perception of economic climate. By analyzing three types of data—print and TV data from 1998–2007 (provided by Media Tenor); survey data (provided by GfK); and official statistics—Bachl showed that media statements on general economic development influence the public's prognostic and retrospective perception of the economic situation, the prognostic estimation of their own financial situation, and their prediction of the unemployment rate. As the unemployment rate is the one aspect of the economic situation that is covered continuously and most frequently by the media (see also Brettschneider, 2000), changes in this parameter had a remarkable impact on people's estimation of the general economic situation in Germany.

These findings all point in the same direction: The media create a picture of the economic situation and this media reality influences people's perception of the economic state of the country. Early research by Kepplinger and Roth (1978) showed that media coverage on economic issues can even have an impact on people's behavior. During the oil crisis of 1973 and 1974 the objective reality was that the oil supply for Germany was available and safe; however, a content analysis of daily newspapers showed a tendency to present the oil supply as poor and insufficient. Surveys revealed that people were worried about the security of the oil supply and sales of oil took an atypical course. Kepplinger and Roth concluded that the media had enticed people to buy oil ahead, which in turn caused delivery problems and the impression of a supply crisis.

Finally, Scheufele and Haas (2008) examined the relationship between news coverage on stocks of selected German corporations and their stock prices and trading volumes. The analyzed media content comprised print media, special TV programs, and Internet Web sites reporting on stocks and investing. The time series analyses showed that media coverage can only under certain conditions moderately influence trading volume. This is the case, for example, when media reports are comprehensive and uniform and a large portion of the stocks of the respective company are held by retail investors. Stock prices, on the other hand, were hardly influenced but only reflected what the media reported.

Corporate Reputation and the News Media in Germany

Media visibility and media coverage are frequently mentioned as important factors that influence corporate reputation. Although agenda-setting research has flourished in Germany, as shown by the brief overview given above, its application to corporate reputation is still in its infancy. In the studies on corporate reputation, media effects on corporate reputation were, if at all, assumed and derived from unsystematic observations (e.g., Dunbar & Schwalbach, 2000; Wiedmann, 2002). In the following, we present two studies conducted in Germany that deal with news media influences on corporate reputation, notably with the second-level hypothesis stating that the salience and valence of company attributes on the media agenda is related to the salience and valence of those attributes on the public agenda (Carroll & McCombs, 2003).

Exploring Corporate Agenda-Setting: A Descriptive Study

The institute Media Tenor examined the question of whether the agenda-setting approach can be applied to corporate reputation management (Media Tenor, 2006). The survey data of the "2006 Image Profile" by *Manager Magazin* were compared with media content data collected by Media Tenor. The media sample was chosen to include coverage on all companies in the politics and business sections of 15 opinion forming German media from April 1 until September 30, thus comprising media coverage of the six months prior to and during the interviews that take place in September and October before the publication of the "Image Profile." The 10 firms with the best and worst reputation in the "2006 Image Profile," as well as those with the strongest image gain and loss compared to the "2004 Image Profile," were analyzed on the assumption that agenda-setting effects would be particularly striking in these cases.

Data analysis relied on descriptive statistics on the overall assessment of selected firms (from 0 "very good" to 10 "very bad") and the amount of coverage (number of reports) as well as its overall assessment (positive to negative valence of reports). Furthermore, survey results of the "2004 Image Profile" were used to calculate image losses and gains. More elaborate statistical analyses like correlations were not reported.

The descriptive analyses, however, revealed some indication of agenda-setting. They show that all 10 companies with a very good overall reputation received positive overall coverage prior to the survey and eight of those had increased their share of positive media assessments compared to the previous year. For 6 out of the 10 negatively rated companies in the survey the media assessments were negative, two were balanced evenly between positive and negative, and two received slightly positive coverage. Furthermore, for the "image flops"—changes in media assessment for companies, compared to the year before, were more volatile than for the "image tops." Concerning media presence, the authors find that low media presence is more pronounced for companies with weak reputations than for those with strong reputations, and that a company's media assessment is more volatile when media presence is low. The authors assume that "a broader media presence can contribute to an improved reputation, even if it is partly negative" (Media Tenor, 2006, p. 34). Although the study hints at some interesting effects of agenda setting, it remains difficult to draw scientifically valuable conclusions without any kind of statistical analyses.

Contingent Conditions of Agenda-Setting Effects on Corporate Reputation

A point of criticism in previous research is the dependence on overall assessments of corporate reputation and/or media coverage, assuming and testing uniform effects of the news media's influence on corporate reputation. However, as outlined above, there is wide agreement that reputation is composed of various dimensions and attributes. Furthermore, various agenda-setting studies reveal that agenda-setting effects are dependent on contingent conditions (e.g., Hügel et al., 1989).

In a study conducted in the context of the German automobile industry (the research subject was a large automobile company), Einwiller et al. (2010) analyzed whether media effects for certain dimensions of corporate reputation are more strongly pronounced than for other dimensions. Specifically, a second level agenda-setting effect of media valence on corporate reputation was expected for such reputation dimensions that are difficult to directly experience or observe and for which the news media is the main source of information (e.g., social responsibility); Demers, Craff, Choi, and Pessin (1989) speak of "unobtrusive" issues, but not for those that could easily be observed and personally experienced (e.g., products of a car company). Furthermore, need for orientation concerning the different dimensions, that is, whether stakeholders are at all interested in finding out about a firm's performance on a respective dimension, was also expected to moderate the effect.

In order to test the hypothesis on contingent conditions affecting the degree of the media influence, Einwiller et al. (2010) developed an integrated measurement instrument to gauge media coverage and stakeholder evaluations on the same dimensions of reputation. The dimensions were: products and services, innovativeness, social and environmental responsibility, management quality and strategy, financial performance, and emotional appeal (this dimension was not measured by media content analysis); they were measured by means of 29 indicators on a scale from 1 "completely disagree" to 7 "completely agree." The survey was conducted in November and December of 2003 and used a volunteer convenience sample of 295 university students taken from seven major regional and geographically distributed German universities. Media content data of 20 print media titles that survey respondents claimed to use most frequently to gather information on business corporations and business topics were provided by PRIME Research, an international communication research firm, and covered a time span of 11 months just prior to the survey.

The survey revealed that stakeholders attach different levels of importance to the different dimensions of the firm's reputation, and structural equation modeling showed that those dimensions that the student respondents considered most important (e.g., products and services and social and environmental responsibility) had a significant direct or indirect effect on their emotions and behavioral intentions (applying for a job, purchasing a product). In contrast, dimensions that were regarded as not very important (e.g., management quality and strategy and financial performance) impacted neither directly nor indirectly on emotions and intentions to apply or purchase.

To test the hypothesized contingent effects, the news reports and the survey data were linked. Because the media usage of each respondent was recorded in the survey, news reports could be matched with the survey responses according to respondents' individual media usage. Specifically, for each respondent, the media tone coding (from -3 "very negative" to +3 "very positive") of the print medium he or she used most frequently was inserted into the individual datasets. Correlations between evaluated reputation dimensions and media tone on the same dimensions revealed a significant relationship between coverage on the dimension "social and environmental responsibility" and the evaluation of the firm thereon (Rho = .20). Also, media tone on "social and environmental responsibility" was significantly and positively related to stakeholders' "emotional appeal" (Rho = .24). The correlations between the dimensions that were either not important to respondents ("management quality and strategy" and "financial performance") or can easily be inspected or experienced ("products and services") were nonsignificant. The authors concluded that media dependency enhanced the likelihood that media coverage on the firm's responsible behavior altered stakeholders' evaluations on this dimension.

The results of this study show the need to evaluate news media's influence on corporate reputation in a differentiated manner. If corporate reputation is conceptualized as a multidimensional construct and if media cover the firm on different dimensions (which they do), analyzing the interrelationships between those different dimensions is a more fruitful approach than testing an overall media effect on an overarching reputation construct. However, there are various limitations to this study including its restriction to one firm and industry sector, one type of media (print: newspapers and magazines), and one stakeholder group (university students).

Conclusions

Corporate reputation is considered an important intangible asset by managers and has received increased attention from scholars in the fields of marketing, public relations, and management in Germany. And, as the introductory quote shows, the international reputation of the country's large firms is considered by the government to be a positive contributor to Germany's economy.

German scholars have defined reputation as a multidimensional construct that resides as perceptions or attitudes in the minds of a firm's stakeholders. As has been shown in the regular surveys published by the business magazine *Manager Magazin*, by *Fortune* magazine's world's most admired companies, as well as by the RepTrak™ study of the Reputation Institute, technology companies, and in particular automobile manufacturers, are held in the highest esteem by the managers or members of the public who were interviewed. Also, it is the home grown company that generally ranks among the top players; few foreign firms make Germany's most admired lists.

While the role of the media in corporate reputation is acknowledged, research on the interrelationship of business news and corporate reputation in general and in the context of agenda-setting theory is scarce. This is despite the fact that agenda-setting theory has not only received considerable attention by communication scholars in Germany but was also conducted at a highly sophisticated level in this country. Against the background of previous research on agenda setting and on corporate reputation, scholarly work on the role of business news coverage in a company's reputation can and should be advanced further. The following questions may guide further research on corporate reputation and the news media:

- What are the individual characteristics that influence the role of media coverage on the different attributes of the firm in the formation of corporate reputation (on different reputation dimensions; e.g., prior knowledge about and need for orientation concerning the firm and its attributes, level of involvement, prior attitudes, stereotypes of firms and sectors, belonging to a certain stakeholder group, such as employee, customer, investor)?
- What are the company characteristics that influence the role of media coverage (on the different attributes of the firm) in the formation of corporate reputation (on different reputation dimensions) e.g., company size, a company's country of origin, industry sector?
- What are the media characteristics that influence the role of media coverage in the formation of corporate reputation (e.g., reputation of the source, type of media—print, online, TV, radio)?
- How do people integrate information about companies from different (media) sources in the formation of corporate reputation?
- What role does interpersonal communication play concerning the role of media coverage in the formation of corporate reputation?
- What role do certain news factors play concerning the role of media coverage in the formation of corporate reputation (e.g., personalization, elite persons, such as the firm's CEO, negativity)?

- To what extent does the reputation of a company influence media coverage of that company?

The use of elaborate methodological instruments and designs are required if those research questions are to be analyzed. Specifically, questions concerning the relationship between attribute news coverage and the evaluation by corporate audiences require surveys and media analyses to be harmonized; that is, they should measure identical attributes and dimensions of corporate reputation. Furthermore, the role of different information sources like media and interpersonal communication in the formation of corporate reputation requires data collection on different levels. The studies and ideas on corporate reputation and the news media presented in this chapter represent only a small building block in this research field. However, we hope that they will serve as an inspiration and trigger for more research on the role of the news media in the development of corporate reputation which will result in interesting theoretical and also practical insights on this topic.

Notes

1. German Federal Foreign Office. Retrieved from http://www.tatsachen-ueber-deutschland.de/en/wirtschaft.html
2. See http://www.communicationcontrolling.de
3. http://money.cnn.com/magazines/fortune/global500/2009/index.html
4. http://money.cnn.com/magazines/fortune/mostadmired/2009/index.html
5. http://www.manager-magazin.de/unternehmen/imageprofile/0,2828,530173,00.html
6. http://www.reputationinstitute.com/knowledge-center/global-pulse
7. This paragraph is partly based on Bentele and Wehmeier (2003).
8. Ibid.
9. Issues are obtrusive when most members of the public have dealt with them directly. Issues are unobtrusive if audience members have not had direct experience with the issue (Demers et al., 1989).

References

Anonymous. (2004). Fernsehen bestimmt die Stimmung [Television determines the sentiment]. *MT Forschungsbericht, 140,* 48–50.

ARD/ZDF. (2008, August 1). ARD/ZDF-Onlinestudie. Press release. Frankfurt/Main. Retrieved from http://www.unternehmen.zdf.de/uploads/media/ARD-ZDF-Online-studie_2008_03.pdf

Bachl, M. (2009, May 21–25). Economic news coverage and economic perceptions. In *Proceedings of the 59th Annual Conference of the International Communication Association,* Chicago, IL.

Bentele, G. (1997). PR-Historiographie und funktional-integrative Schichtung: Ein neuer Ansatz zur PR-Geschichtsschreibung [PR historiography and functional-integral stratification. A new approach on PR historiography]. In P. Szyszka (Ed.), *Auf der Suche nach Identität. PR-Geschichte als Theoriebaustein* (pp. 137–169). Berlin, Germany: Vistas.

Bentele, G. (1998). *Berufsfeld PR* [The PR-profession]. Berlin, Germany: PR Kolleg, Loseblattwerk.

Bentele, G., Großkurth, L., & Seidenglanz, R. (2009). *Profession Pressesprecher 2009: Vermessung eines Berufsstandes* [Profession press officer 2009: Determination of a profession]. Berlin, Germany: Helios.

Bentele, G., & Wehmeier, S. (2003). Public relations in Germany. In K. Sriramesh & D. Verčič (Eds.), *International public relations* (pp. 199–221). Mahawah, NJ: Erlbaum.

Branahl, U. (2000). *Medienrecht: Eine Einführung* [Media law: An introduction] (3rd ed.). Wiesbaden, Germany: Westdeutscher Verlag.

Brettschneider, F. (2000). Reality bytes: Wie die Medienberichterstattung die Wahrnehmung der Wirtschaftslage beeinflusst [Reality bytes: How media coverage influences the perception of the economic climate]. In J. Falter, O. W. Gabriel, & H. Rattinger (Eds.), *Wirklich ein Volk? Die politischen Orientierungen von Ost- und Westdeutschen im Vergleich* (pp. 539–569). Opladen, Germany: Leske & Budrich.

Brosius, H.-B., & Kepplinger, H. M. (1990). The agenda-setting function of television news: Static and dynamic news. *Communication Research, 17,* 183–211.

Brosius, H.-B., & Kepplinger, H. M. (1995). Killer and victim issues: Issue competition in the agenda-setting process of German television. *International Journal of Public Opinion Research, 7,* 211–231.

Bruhn, M. & Boenigk, M. (1999). *Integrierte Kommunikation. Entwicklungsstand in Unternehmen* [Integrated communication]. Wiesbaden, Germany: Gabler.

Carroll, C. E., & McCombs, M. (2003). Agenda-setting effects of business news on the public's images and opinions about major corporations. *Corporate Reputation Review, 6,* 36–46.

Chin, W. W., & Newsted, P. R. (1999). Structural equation modeling analysis with small samples using partial least squares. In R. H. Hoyle & H. Rick (Eds.), *Statistical strategies for small sample research* (pp. 307–341). Thousand Oaks, CA: Sage.

Deephouse, D. L. (2000). Media reputation as a strategic resource: An integration of mass communication and resource-based theories. *Journal of Management, 26,* 1091–1112.

Demers, D. P., Craff, D., Choi, Y.-H., & Pessin, B. M. (1989). Issue obtrusiveness and the agenda-setting effects of national network news. *Communication Research, 16,* 793–812.

Diamantopoulos, A., & Winklhofer, H. M. (2001). Index construction with formative indicators: An alternative to scale development. *Journal of Marketing Research, 38,* 269–277.

Diehlmann, N. (2003). Journalisten und Fernsehnachrichten [Journalists and TV-news]. In G. Ruhrmann, J. Woelhe, M. Maier, & N. Diehlmann (Eds.), *Der Wert von Nachrichten im deutschen Fernsehen: Ein Modell zur Validierung von Nachrichtenfaktoren* (pp. 99–144). Opladen, Germany: Westdeutscher Verlag.

Dunbar, R. L., & Schwalbach, J. (2000). Corporate reputation and performance in Germany. *Corporate Reputation Review, 3,* 115–123.

Eccles, R. G., Newquist, S. C., & Schatz, R. (2007, February). Reputation and its risks. *Harvard Business Review,* 104–114.

Einwiller, S., Carroll, C. E., & Korn, K. (2010). Under what conditions do the news media influence corporate reputation? The roles of media dependency and need for orientation. *Corporate Reputation Review, 12,* 299–315.

Eisenegger, M. (2005). *Reputation in der Mediengesellschaft: Konstitution—Issues monitoring–Issues management* [Reputation in media society: Constitution–issues monitoring–issues management]. Wiesbaden, Germany: VS Verlag.

Fombrun, C. J. (1996). *Reputation: Realizing value from the corporate image*. Boston, MA: Harvard Business School Press.

Fombrun, C. J., Gardberg, N., & Sever, J. (2000). The reputation quotient: A multi-stakeholder measure of corporate reputation. *The Journal of Brand Management, 7,* 241–255.

Fombrun, C. J., & Van Riel, C. (1997). The reputational landscape. *Corporate Reputation Review, 1,* 5–13.

Fritz, I. & Klingler, W. (2006). Medienzeitbudgets und Tagesablaufverhalten [Media time budgets and behavior of daily routine]. *Media Perspektiven, 4,* 222–234.

Gerhards, M., & Klingler, W. (2007). Mediennutzung in der Zukunft [Media use in the future]. *Media Perspektiven, 6,* 295–309.

Grunig, J. E., & Hunt, T. (1984). *Managing public relations*. New York: Holt, Rinehart & Winston.

Haedrich, G., Jenner, T., Olavarria, M., & Possekel, S. (1994). *Aktueller Stand und Entwicklungen der Öffentlichkeitsarbeit in deutschen Unternehmen—Ergebnisse einer empirischen Untersuchung* [Current situation and developments of Public Relations in German businesses — Results of an empirical study]. Berlin, Germany: Institut für Marketing, Lehrstuhl für Konsumgüter- und Dienstleistungs-Marketing.

Helm, S. (2005). Designing a formative measure for corporate reputation. *Corporate Reputation Review, 8,* 95–109.

Helm, S. (2006). Exploring the impact of corporate reputation on consumer satisfaction and loyalty. *Journal of Customer Behaviour, 5,* 59–80.

Helm, S. (2007a). One reputation or many? Comparing stakeholders' perceptions of corporate reputation. *Corporate Communications: An International Journal, 12,* 238–254.

Helm, S. (2007b). The role of corporate reputation in determining investor satisfaction and loyalty. *Corporate Reputation Review, 10,* 22–37.

Hesse, A. (1999). *Rundfunkrecht* [Broadcasting law]. München: Vahlen.

Huck, I., Quiring, O., & Brosius, H.-B. (2009). Perceptual phenomena in the agenda-setting process. *International Journal of Public Opinion Research, 21,* 139–164.

Hügel, R., Degenhardt, W., & Weiss, H.-J. (1989). Structural equation models for the analysis of the agenda-setting process. *European Journal of Communication, 4,* 191–210.

Kepplinger, H. M., & Roth, H. (1978). Kommunikation in der Ölkrise des Winters 1973/74: Ein Paradigma für Wirkungsstudien [Communication during the oil crisis in the winter of 1973/74: A paradigm for effects studies]. *Publizistik, 23,* 337–356.

Krause, B., & Gehrau, V. (2007). Das Paradox der Medienwirkung auf Nichtnutzer: Eine Zeitreihenanalyse auf Tagesbasis zu den kurzfristigen Agenda-Setting-Effekten von Fernsehnachrichten [The paradox of media effects on non-users: A time series analysis on the short-term agenda setting effects of TV-news]. *Publizistik, 52,* 191–209.

Liehr, K., Peters, P., & Zerfass, A. (2009). Reputationsmessung: Grundlagen und Verfahren [Reputation measurement: Fundamentals and procedures]. Document No. 1. Retrieved from http://www.Communicationcontrolling.de. Berlin, Leipzig, Germany: DPRG, Universität Leipzig.

Maier, M., Ruhrmann, G., & Stengel, K. (2008). *Der Wert von Nachrichten im deutschen Fernsehen. Inhaltsanalyse von TV-Nachrichten im Jahr 2007* [The value of news in German television. Content analysis of TV-news in 2007]. Duesseldorf, Germany: Landesanstalt für Medien Nordrhein-Westfalen (LfM).

Media Tenor. (2006). Corporate agenda-setting. *Media Tenor Journal, 1,* 29–34.

Nix, P., Schnöring, S., & Siegert, G. (2009, January). Den guten Ruf professionell managen [Managing the good reputation professionally]. *Harvard Business Manager*, (1), 8–11.

Papier, H.-J., & Möller, J. (1999). Presse- und Rundfunkrecht [Press and broadcasting law]. In J. Wilke (Ed.), *Mediengeschichte der Bundesrepublik Deutschland* (pp. 449–468). Bonn, Germany: Bundeszentrale für politische Bildung.

Picot, A., Reichwald, R., & Wigand, R. (2001). *Die grenzenlose Unternehmung: Information, Organisation und Management: Lehrbuch zur Unternehmensführung im Informationszeitalter* (4th ed.) Informationszeitalter [The boundless corporation: Information, organization and management: A textbook for corporate management in the information age]. Wiesbaden, Germany: Gabler.

Pürer, H. & Raabe, J. (1996). *Medien in Deutschland: Presse* [Media in Germany: Press] (Vol. 1, 2nd ed.). Konstanz, Germany: UVK Medien.

Quiring, O. (2004). *Wirtschaftsberichterstattung und Wahlen* [Business coverage and elections]. Konstanz, Germany: UVK.

Rössler, P. (1999). The individual agenda-designing process: How interpersonal communication, egocentric networks, and mass media shape the perception of political issues by individuals. *Communication Research, 26*, 666–700.

Rössler, P., & Schenk, M. (2000). Cognitive bonding and the German reunification: Agenda-setting and persuasion effects of mass media. *International Journal of Public Opinion Research, 12*, 29–47.

Ruhrmann, G., & Göbbel, R. (2007). *Veränderung der Nachrichtenfaktoren und Auswirkungen auf die journalistische Praxis in Deutschland: Abschlussbericht für netzwerk recherche e.V* [Changes in news factors and impacts on the journalistic practice in Germany: Final report for netzwerk recherche e.V.].

Ruhrmann, G., Woelke, J., Maier, M., & Diehlmann, N. (2003). *Der Wert von Nachrichten im deutschen Fernsehen*. Opladen, Germany: Leske & Budrich.

Schenk, M. (2007). *Medienwirkungsforschung* [Media effects research] (3rd ed.). Tübingen, Germany: Mohr Siebeck.

Scheufele, B., & Haas, A. (2008). *Medien und Aktien: Theoretische und empirische Modellierung der Rolle der Berichterstattung für das Börsengeschehen* [Media and stocks: Theoretical and empirical modelling of the role of news coverage for what is happening on the stock exchange]. Wiesbaden, Germany: Verlag für Sozialwissenschaften.

Schönbach, K. (1982). "The Issues of the Sixties": Elektronische Inhaltsanalyse und die langfristige Beobachtung von Agenda-Setting Wirkungen der Massenmedien [The issues of the sixties: Electronic content analysis and the long-term monitoring of agenda setting effects of mass media]. *Publizistik, 27*, 129–140.

Schwaiger, M. (2004). Components and parameters of corporate reputation—An empirical study. *Schmalenbach Business Review, 56*, 46–71.

Schwaiger, M., & Cannon, H. M. (2004). Unternehmensreputation—Bestandsaufnahme und Messkonzepte [Corporate reputation—Inventory taking and measurement concepts]. *Jahrbuch der Absatz- und Verbrauchswirtschaft, 50*, 237–261.

Schwalbach, J. (2004). Reputation. In G. Schreyögg & A. Werder (Eds.), *Handwörterbuch Unternehmensführung und Organisation* (4th ed., pp. 1262–1270). Stuttgart, Germany: Schäffer-Poeschel.

Spremann, K. (1988). Reputation, Garantie, Information [Reputation, guarantee, information]. *Zeitschrift für Betriebswirtschaft, 58*, 613–629.

Stuiber, H.-W. (1998). *Medien in Deutschland: Vol. 2. Rundfunk* [Media in Germany]. Konstanz, Germany: UKV Medien.

Tewskbury, D. (2005). The seeds of audience fragmentation: Specialization in the use of online news sites. *Journal of Broadcasting & Electronic Media, 49*, 332–348.

Tiele, A., & Scherer, H. (2004). Die Agenda—ein Konstrukt des Rezipienten. Die Bedeutung kognitiver Informationsverarbeitung im Agenda-Setting-Prozess [The agenda—a construct of the recipient. The meaning of cognitive information processing in the agenda setting process]. *Publizistik, 49,* 439–453.

Van Eimeren, B., & Frees, B. (2008). Ergebnisse der ARD/ZDF-Onlinestudie 2008. Internetverbreitung: Größter Zuwachs bei Silver-Surfern [Results of the ARD/ZDF online study 2008. Internet reach: Silver-surfers show largest growth]. *Media Perspektiven, 7,* 330–344.

Walsh, G.. & Beatty, S. E. (2007). Customer-based corporate reputation of a service firm: Scale development and validation. *Journal of the Academy of Marketing Science, 35,* 127–143.

Walsh, G., Mitchell, V.-W., Jackson, P. R., & Beatty, S. E. (2009). Examining the antecedents and consequences of corporate reputation: A customer perspective. *British Journal of Management, 20,* 187–203.

Walsh, G. & Wiedmann, K.-P. (2004). A conceptualization of corporate reputation in Germany: An evaluation and extension of the RQ. *Corporate Reputation Review, 6,* 304–312.

Wiedmann, K.-P. (2002). Analyzing the German corporate reputation landscape. *Corporate Reputation Review, 4,* 337–353.

Wiedmann, K.-P. (2007, June 26). Zentrale Ergebnisse der Studie RepTrak™ Pulse Germany 2007 [Central findings of the RepTrak™ Pulse Germany, 2007]. Press release. University of Hannover and Reputation Institute, Hannover, Germany.

Wiedmann, K.-P., & Buxel, H. (2005). Corporate reputation management in Germany: Results of an empirical study. *Corporate Reputation Review, 8,* 145–163.

Wiedmann, K.-P., Fombrun, C. J., & Van Riel, C. B. M. (2007). Reputationsanalyse mit dem Reputation Quotient [Reputation anaylsis with the reputation quotient]. In M.Piwinger & A. Zerfass (Eds.), *Handbuch Unternehmenskommunikation* (pp. 321–337). Wiesbaden, Germany: Gabler.

Wörsdörfer, S. (2005). Wie die Wirtschaftsberichterstattung der Medien das Konsumentenvertrauen lenkt: Empirische Evidenzen für Deutschland 1995–2005 [How media coverage of the economy guides consumer trust: Empirical evidence for Germany 1995–2005]. *Wirtschaft im Wandel, 11,* 338–344.

6 Corporate Reputation and the News Media in Greece

Eva Goutzamani, Stelios C. Zyglidopoulos, and Philemon Bantimaroudis

Introduction

Since the early 1970s, agenda-setting theory has been one of the most influential paradigms in the field of mass communication. Over 350 studies have been conducted worldwide, which have generated data that support the theory's central hypothesis: media sets the public agenda, telling people "what to think about" (Cohen, 1963, p. 120). This study applies agenda-setting theory to the field of corporate reputation. As scholars discover significant applications of agenda-setting theory in the corporate world, the salience of corporate institutions has been scrutinized in international markets.

The current research assembles evidence of salience drawn from both Greek media content as well as the corporate environment. Greek scholars have seldom been concerned with either agenda-setting or corporate reputation research. As a result, the combination of these concepts is noteworthy because it intends to fill a void in the literature of both the Greek media and Greek corporate research.

Similar projects conducted in the United States and elsewhere in Europe have yielded significant relationships between the media agenda and public salience of corporations. The current project aims to investigate the validity of this relationship in the Greek corporate environment. Initial findings reveal that the transfer of salience is subject to cultural factors, such as the element of cynicism, and thereby subsequent data are needed to clarify the role of agenda-setting functions in Greece.

Agenda-Setting Theory and Corporate Reputation

Agenda-setting theory has been applied to different settings, though studies primarily emphasize elections and public policy issues. In their seminal study, McCombs and Shaw (1972) discovered significant correlations between the media agenda and the public agenda, arguing that the media attribute relative importance to issues or political figures which, in turn, are perceived as "important" by the public. This process became known as "the transfer of salience." McCombs and Shaw operationally defined media prominence in terms of the volume of coverage that different issues received. On the other hand, the public was asked to rank issues according to their perceived importance.

This ground-breaking research provided basic conceptual tools about how the media attribute importance to certain issues, also known as "objects." Consequently researchers around the world began to examine different variables that explain media's influence on the dependent variable, public salience. Researchers discovered that not all issues have the same chance of influencing the media agenda. Researchers categorize issues as either obtrusive or unobtrusive. Obtrusive issues have a greater possibility of becoming salient (Zucker, 1978). Experimental evidence has demonstrated television's ability to set agendas (Iyengar, Peters, & Kinder, 1982), while other researchers have demonstrated intermedia agenda-setting possibilities of newspapers (Reese & Danielian, 1989). Agenda-setting theory has various applications in the context of politics and campaign coverage. Shaw and Martin (1992) suggest that the media agenda serves as a consensus builder in a democratic society; however, Sumpter and Tankard (1994) argue that the media cover elections as "horse races," and in the process destroy issues relevancy.

As agenda-setting theory develops, researchers have found various levels of media influence over the public's agenda. Studies have examined the effects of second-level agenda-setting, signifying researchers' attention to particular attributes or frames of issues or personalities. The result of these studies has been to contribute to a general understanding not only of the existence of a transfer of salience from the media to the public, but also the mechanisms that allow media salience to be transferred to the public. Second-level agenda setting also investigates the ability of particular attributes to contribute to public salience as well as how attributes interact with one another to achieve public salience. This attribute–frame analysis reveals not only what audiences think about, but also how they think about issues presented by the media (Ghanem, 1997). The evolution of agenda-setting theory veers in various directions as thematic topics and examples chosen by scholars increase significantly, applying the theory to the field of politics and public policy in addition to examining corporate and cultural factors.

Scholars have applied the agenda-setting model to the field of corporate reputation (e.g., Carroll & McCombs, 2003), examining whether media visibility of corporations contributes to specific public perceptions of those companies. Similarly, Deephouse (2000) argued that "media coverage is a reasonable indicator of the public's knowledge and opinions about firms within a few months of the publication date" (2000, p. 1096). Additionally, Fombrun and Shanley (1990) suggested that "the media themselves act not only as vehicles for advertising and mirrors of reality reflecting firms' actions, but also as active agents shaping information through editorials and feature articles" (1990, p. 240). Studies by Carroll and McCombs (2003) and Carroll (2004) paved the way toward a corporate example of agenda setting, arguing that agenda setting was not solely applicable to political communications, but that it could also be applied to corporate reputation. Carroll (2004) expanded the scope of this work by examining how certain attributes contribute to public salience of corporate entities. Confirmation of the effects of first- and second-level agenda-setting theory has been found.

Agenda Setting in Greece

Although the first- and second-level agenda-setting hypothesis has been tested in different cultural and ethnic settings, very little such research has been conducted in Greece. Various reasons are found for this void in agenda-setting research. First, the field of mass communication is relatively new in Greece: the first university departments were not established until the early 1990s. In consequence, paradigms such as agenda setting, gatekeeping, and framing, models that have received significant attention from international scholars, have been largely neglected by Greek scholars.

Nonetheless, some Greek research exists that relates to these theoretical terrains. For example, Harris, Kolovos, and Lock (2001) and Kenterelidou (2005) investigated media coverage of political candidates, demonstrating that media coverage is related to candidate preferences and voting patterns. Zaharopoulos (1989) dealt with the coverage of U.S. issues by the Greek media, arguing that the Greek media cover the U.S. extensively:

> They give an indication of a superpower whose relations with other nations... and its domestic, political and defense issues do in fact affect the rest of the world. They also give a good indication of the tremendous cultural as well as technological leadership of the United States. Also shown is the obvious importance to Greece of such topics as U.S.–Greek relations, U.S.–Turkish relations and the activities of Americans of Greek descent. (Zaharopoulos, 1989, p. 189)

Additionally, Zaharopoulos (1990) finds similar results while analyzing Greek media coverage of the 1988 U.S. presidential election. He finds that "the obvious newsworthiness to the Greeks of the Dukakis candidacy played a role in the selection of news elements over which the local gatekeepers had control" (Zaharopoulos, 1990, p. 194).

Furthermore, Roberts and Bantimaroudis (1997) examined the gatekeeping practices of 25 newspaper editors representing elite Athenian newspapers. One of the central research questions dealt with media influences to which Athenian newspaper editors are subject.

> The study found that Greek editors rely on Greek sources, such as the Athenian Press Agency, more than they rely on foreign sources. Nevertheless, European influences are not negligible. The European editions of Time, Newsweek, and the French Le Monde and TV-5 appeared to be quite influential. (Roberts & Bantimaroudis, 1997, p. 72)

Although most of the above research projects do not constitute agenda-setting research, nevertheless they represent empirical work involving the nature of media salience and the factors that affect it.

Greek Cultural Factors and Media Ownership

Although agenda-setting theory is applied to different national and cultural settings, it does not preclude country-specific variables. In fact, researchers have demonstrated significant differences between institutions in Greece and corresponding Western institutions. Factors such as media ownership influence the nature of media content. Scholars recognize that the Greek media market is small, displaying an excess of supply over demand, with a great number of newspapers, TV stations, and magazines. For example, "the ratio of daily newspaper copies per 2000 inhabitants in 1996 was 590 for Norway, 445 for Sweden and 331 for Britain, while it was only 153 for Greece" (Papatheodorou & Machin, 2003, p. 35).

Journalism practices in Greece deviate from those of Western organizations (Papathanassopoulos, 1999; Zaharopoulos & Paraschos, 1993), as organizational interests supersede journalistic values. Survey data demonstrate public perceptions that media owners determine issue prominence (Papathanassopoulos, 2001). Moreover, the majority of Greek journalists are underpaid, insecure about their jobs, and thus in no position to exercise any kind of professional autonomy. Greek media owners, engaging in different business ventures including telecommunications, shipping, and oil refining, use their media power to promote their interests and to exert pressure on government officials (Hallin & Papathanassopoulos, 2002; Papathanassopoulos 1999; Papatheodorou & Machin, 2003). Greek media openly display partisan affiliations, using a colorful and excessive language that is deemed unacceptable by journalists in the Western world (Zaharopoulos & Paraschos, 1993). Diamandouros (1997) argued "the Greek media are widely perceived as playing too pervasive and negative a role in the country's politics" (p. 36).

State influences on media content are not negligible. There is widespread belief that political elites maintain a vague regulatory media role which they use to ward off unwanted attacks (Papathanassopoulos, 1999). Furthermore, the Greek economy is characterized by a great number of state-owned enterprises. Therefore it is reasonable to expect that the reputation of these enterprises often becomes a political matter reflecting on the government's ability and policy agenda.

The above discussion of agenda-setting theory with respect to corporate reputation, the peculiarities of the Greek media environment, and the relative lack of research involving the link between agenda setting and corporate reputation, influenced this study's primary hypothesis. Previous agenda-setting research in Greece has demonstrated that media coverage is related to candidate recognition, therefore this study expected to find similar results regarding the reputations of corporations. At the same time, it was anticipated that cultural factors might play an important role in the way that agenda-setting phenomena unfold in Greece. For example, given the highly politicized media environment of Greece it would not be unlikely to find that the Greek public has developed a certain level of cynicism, arguably not present in other national settings. Overall, it was hypothesized that Greek media should influence the public agenda in terms of corporate salience.

Method

Data Sources

To investigate the agenda-setting phenomenon in Greece, two sources of data were utilized. First, in order to measure the media salience variables, the authors relied on the Greek newspaper Ta Nea, one of the most significant Greek dailies, which has an electronic database of its publications dating back to 2000, the first year in which reputation data for major Greek companies became available. Second, to measure the corporate reputations of the most visible Greek companies, the authors drew on the Global Reputation Quotient Project (RQ Project). The project, carried out in 12 European countries (including Greece), drew the participation of over 12,000 members of the public in the fall of 2000, and was reported in Van Riel and Fombrun (2002). Instead of rating a fixed group of firms, "the RQ method solicits the general public's nominations of best and worst companies" (Van Riel & Fombrun, 2002, p. 297), and thus identifies the top 30 most visible companies for further assessment.

Media Salience Variables

With respect to the exposure that a particular company (from the 30 most visible companies identified in the RQ survey) received in the news, the authors measured two aspects of exposure: visibility and tone. Visibility was measured by counting the number of times the company name appeared in content during two distinct time periods: January to August 2000, and August 2000 to January 2001. Extracting data from these two periods allowed the researchers to examine media content from the period before and after the RQ survey.

Tone, the overall mood expressed toward a company in an article, was measured based on a content analysis of news articles during the relevant periods. The articles were classified according to their title as positive (favorable), negative (unfavorable), neutral, or not applicable. Two coders were used for this process, coding a total of 4,033 articles. The interrater reliability was measured through the Holsti test, which achieved a value of 0.98, significantly above the 0.80 limit considered as adequate in such cases.

An article was classified as portraying a company favorably when it made references to the company's products and services in a favorable way, rising stock prices, expansion, entry into international markets, or a merger with another company. On the other hand, an article was classified as portraying a company unfavorably if it referred to a company's products and services in an unfavorable way, to falling stock prices, losing ground in the market, unethical behavior, lawsuits, complaints, or government investigations. Articles were deemed as neutral when the company was mentioned in the title, but it was portrayed in neither a favorable nor an unfavorable manner. For example, certain events pertaining to a company were simply reported, such as the gathering of stockholders or the presence of a company representative at a public event. When a company was not mentioned in the title, the article was classified as not applicable and was excluded from the measuring of tone.

Reputation Variables

Corporate reputation, the primary dependent variable, was measured in three ways, in accordance with the 2000 Reputation Institute survey (Van Riel & Fombrun, 2002). First, the authors measured the familiarity of a company by the number of respondents who nominated it as having the best or worst reputation. Second, the authors used as an indicator of the firm's good reputation the percentage of respondents who nominated the company as having the best reputation out of all the respondents who nominated the same company. Third, in a similar manner, they used as an indicator of the firm's bad reputation the percentage of respondents who nominated the company as having the worst reputation from all the respondents who nominated the same company.

A Pearson-product correlation evaluated both the impact that prior media attention variables had on the reputation variables and the impact that the reputation variables had on subsequent media attention variables. The Pearson coefficient was deemed an appropriate measure because the data were at the interval level and the distribution approaches normality. The relationships assessed were linear in nature.

Findings

Only negative reputation, when correlated with newspaper coverage, yields positive relationships which are statistically significant. In some cases, best reputation companies correlated with media coverage yield reverse relationships. Specifically, company reputation variables are correlated with four indicators of media visibility: overall coverage, positive coverage, negative coverage, and a neutral coverage indicator. All correlations are reported in Tables 6.1 and 6.2, describing the relationships for the years 2000 and 2001, respectively.

For data from the year 2000, the companies' worst reputation indicator is positively correlated with the overall coverage (.519), the positive coverage (.662), and the neutral coverage (.721). These correlations are statistically significant (p < .01). The companies' best reputation indicator displays a reverse relationship with the newspaper's overall coverage (-.35), the positive coverage (-.50), and the neutral coverage (-.623). These correlations are statistically significant (p < .05).

For data from the year 2001, the companies' worst reputation is positively correlated with the overall newspaper coverage (.477), the positive coverage (.557), the negative coverage (.611), and the neutral coverage (.672). On the other hand,

Table 6.1 Correlation between Nomination and Media Visibility in 2000

Corporate Reputation	Overall Coverage	Positive Tone	Negative Tone	Neutral Tone
Best Reputation	-0.356	-0.506	-0.151	-0.623
Sig.	0.054	0.007	0.451	0.004
Worst Reputation	0.519	0.662	0.3	0.721
Sig.	0.003	0	0.129	0

Table 6.2 Correlation between Nomination and Media Visibility in 2001

Corporate Reputation	Overall Coverage	Positive Tone	Negative Tone	Neutral Tone
Best Reputation	-0.356	-0.506	-0.151	-0.623
Sig.	0.054	0.007	0.451	0.004
Worst Reputation	0.519	0.662	0.3	0.721
Sig.	0.003	0	0.129	0

the companies' best reputation indicator displays a reverse relationship with the newspaper's overall coverage (-.310), the positive coverage (-.384), the negative coverage (-.463), and the neutral coverage (-.519). These relationships are statistically significant at least at the 0.05 levels except one, which approaches significance at the 0.09 level.

Discussion

Despite its international attention, agenda-setting theory has been understudied in Greece. Various reasons can be cited for this theoretical gap in media scholarship, in part because the Greek media field is relatively young and underdeveloped. There is no doubt that the Greek agenda-setting literature needs further development in the context of political communication, so that data are generated to explain not only the transfer of salience from the media to the public, but also the cultural factors that intervene in this relationship. Greece stands at the crossroads between East and West, and in terms of how media institutions and the public interact in Balkan societies, researchers may discover significant differences from what has been discovered in the United States, Germany, and Spain. Preliminary research demonstrates that the cultural factor merits further investigation.

Regarding the field of corporate reputation, more data are needed to evaluate media and public salience, namely more survey data that assess corporate reputation and more media analysis, drawn from multiple sources and different kinds of media, both print and electronic. Despite the limitations, the data from this study yield some interesting discoveries and raise new questions. First, positive company reputation displays a reverse relationship to the coverage of the newspaper Ta Nea for both periods of data. Although the implications of this discovery are not clear, it confirms a widespread notion that the agenda-setting process in the context of Greek society is subject to culture-specific factors that affect the transfer of salience process. Although media salience and public salience display a statistically significant relationship, the dynamics of this relationship need further clarification. For example, do public relations initiatives for the enhancement of corporate images yield meaningful results when compared to similar campaigns undertaken in other Western markets? Answering this foundational question is significant as business executives consider budget planning for such endeavors. Some critical comparisons between the Greek market and similar European markets can reveal the extent of the effectiveness of such image promotion ventures in Greece. The current findings imply that extensive media visibility does not necessarily lead to a better corporate reputation; in fact the opposite may be true.

Second, the worst company reputation is positively correlated to media coverage, producing relatively strong relationships. This relationship applies to all media indicators for both time periods under examination. This is consistent with Greece's other social indicators as one of the most fear filled, pessimistic, negative societies in the European Union. Does this mean that primarily negative coverage influences the public agenda in Greece? If yes, this is consistent with experimental agenda-setting research at the second level, which has demonstrated that negative attribute salience of political candidates produced higher public salience (Kiousis, Bantimaroudis, & Ban, 1999). However, this particular trend seems to be affecting Greek society in a more pronounced manner as cynicism surrounds not only the core of politics but also the business world. Scholars need to assess influences both at the first and second level, so this finding needs careful examination, which might reveal particular cultural attributes that explain the transfer of salience. If this finding applies to corporate reputation, Greek corporations or companies active in the Greek market need to consider factors that affect negative news reaching the media and how they manage crises. It seems that scandals, corruption, and mismanagement, despite their international news value, attract more attention in the Greek environment. This spiral of cynicism may be affecting different institutions' ability to reach the public through various news recycling mechanisms.

The current study represents an initial effort to assess corporate agenda-setting influences in Greece. As different cultural attributes are investigated, the agenda-setting theory can be further enriched to provide insights about our multicultural world and the movement of salience among complex institutions and their publics. Certainly, more data are needed to investigate these relationships in detail and to produce results that can be generalized, especially in Greece.

References

Carroll, C. (2004). *How the mass media influence perceptions of corporate reputation: Exploring agenda setting effects within business news coverage.* (Unpublished doctoral dissertation). University of Texas, Austin.

Carroll, C., & McCombs, M. (2003). Agenda setting effects of business news on the public's images and opinions of major corporations. *Corporate Reputation Review, 16*(1), 36–46.

Cohen, B. (1963). *The press and foreign policy.* Princeton, NJ: Princeton University Press.

Deephouse, D. L. (2000). Media reputation as a strategic resource: An integration of mass communication and resource-based theories. *Journal of Management, 26*(6), 1091–1112.

Diamandouros, N. P. (1997). Greek politics and society in the 1990s. In T. A. Graham & K. Nicolaidis (Eds.), *The Greek paradox: Promise versus performance* (pp. 23–38). Cambridge, MA: MIT Press.

Fombrun, C., & Shanley, M. (1990). What's in a name? Reputation building and corporate strategy. *Academy of Management Review, 33*(2), 233–258

Ghanem, S. (1997). Filling in the tapestry: The second level of agenda setting. In M. McCombs, D. Shaw, & D. Weaver (Eds.), *Communication and democracy* (pp. 3–14). Mahwah, NJ: Erlbaum.

Hallin, D. C., & Papathanassopoulos, S. (2002). Political clientilism and the media: Southern Europe and Latin America in comparative perspective. *Media, Culture & Society, 24*, 175–195.

Harris, P., Kolovos, I., & Lock, A., (2001). Who sets the agenda? An analysis of agenda setting and press coverage in the 1999 Greek European elections. *European Journal of Marketing, 35*(9–10), 1117–1135.

Iyengar, S., Peters, M. D., & Kinder, D. R. (1982). Experimental demonstrations of the "not-so-minimal" consequences of television news programs. *American Political Science Review, 76*, 848–858.

Kenterelidou, C. (2005). *Public political communication and media: The case of contemporary Greece* (Unpublished doctoral dissertation). Department of Journalism and Mass Communication, Aristotle University, Thessaloniki, Greece.

Kiousis, S., Bantimaroudis, P., & Ban, H. (1999). Candidate image attributes: Experiments on the substantive dimension of second level agenda setting. *Communication Research, 26*(4), 414–428.

McCombs, M., & Shaw, D. (1972). The agenda setting function of the mass media. *Public Opinion Quarterly, 36*, 176–187.

Papathanassopoulos, S. (1999). The effects of media commercialization on journalism and politics in Greece. *The Communication Review, 3*(4), 379–402.

Papathanassopoulos, S. (2001). Media commercialization and journalism in Greece. *European Journal of Communication, 16*(4), 505–521.

Papatheodorou, F., & Machin, D. (2003). The umbilical cord that was never cut. *European Journal of Communication, 18*(1), 31–54.

Reese, S. D., & Danielian, L. J. (1989). Intermedia influence and the drug issue: Convergence on cocaine. In P. J. Shoemaker (Ed.), *Communication campaigns about drugs: Government, media and the public* (pp. 29–45). Hillsdale, NJ: Erlbaum.

Roberts, M., & Bantimaroudis, P. (1997). Gatekeepers in international news: The Greek media. *The Harvard International Journal of Press/Politics, 2*(2), 62–76.

Shaw, D. L., & Martin, S. E. (1992). The function of mass media agenda setting. *Journalism Quarterly, 69*(4), 902–920

Sumpter, R., & Tankard, J. W. (1994). The spin doctor: An alternative model of public relations. *Public Relations Review, 20*, 19–27.

Van Riel, C. B. M., & Fombrun, C. J. (2002). Which firm is most visible in your country? An introduction to the special issue on the global RQ-project nominations. *Corporate Reputation Review, 4*(4), 296–302.

Zaharopoulos, T. (1989). The image of the U.S. in the Greek press. *Journalism Quarterly, 66*, 188–193.

Zaharopoulos, T. (1990). Cultural proximity in international news coverage: 1988 U.S. presidential campaign in the Greek press. *Journalism Quarterly, 67*, 190–194.

Zaharopoulos, T., & Paraschos, E. M. (1993). *Mass media in Greece, power politics and privatization*. Westport, CT: Praeger.

Zucker, H. M. (1978). The variable nature of news media influence. In B. D. Ruben (Ed.), *Communication yearbook* (Vol. 2, pp. 225–240). New Brunswick, NJ: Transaction.

7 Corporate Reputation and the News Media in Italy[1]

Elena Dalpiaz and Davide Ravasi

In communication studies, agenda-setting theory suggests that media coverage and content tend to influence what members of the public think about in general, and in particular how they feel about a company's corporate image and reputation.

The aim of this chapter is threefold. First, it will review how the Italian literature has applied agenda-setting theory in various academic fields. Second, it will analyze both the characteristics of the news values at work in Italy and the main features of the media system, in terms of outreach, access, and control (Sriramesh & Verčič, 2003). Third, it will report results from an empirical test of hypotheses suggested by agenda-setting theory carried out in an Italian setting. Our study investigated the relationships between the magnitude and valence of media coverage of 33 large companies, and the top-of-mind awareness and image of the same companies held by a random sample of the Italian population. Moreover, a qualitative analysis of media content explored the extent to which the public image of two large Italian firms mirrors themes covered or emphasized by the popular press.

Results from this study do not seem to support the hypothesis that higher media visibility is correlated to higher top-of-mind awareness, which conversely appears to be more related to the degree to which companies advertise. However, a significant and robust correlation is found between media valence and corporate image. Finally, the qualitative comparison between media associations and corporate associations seems to indicate that the influence of media may be stronger when respondents do not have a direct experience of the company and its products.

Review of the Literature

Corporate Reputation in Italy

The Italian literature on corporate reputation is characterized by a twofold analytic attitude. On the one hand, organizational and communication studies generally tend to apply existing frameworks, with rare attempts to improve our general understanding of the concept; on the other hand, some economic studies endeavor to propose and test new hypotheses.

Research belonging to the first group (Nelli & Bensi, 2003; Ravasi & Gabbioneta, 2004; Romenti, 2005) is rooted in the theories developed by international scholars because authors tend to frame the topic of corporate reputation by integrating seminal studies in the U.S. and northern European tradition (Dowling, 1986; Fombrun, 1996; Fombrun & Shanley, 1990) with the most recent developments in the field.

To our knowledge, only a few studies published in Italy try to shed new light on the construct of corporate reputation (Cameran & Livatino, 2005; Ravasi & Gabbioneta, 2004). The large majority of works are either practice-oriented books or teaching manuals (Invernizzi, 2005; Nelli & Bensi, 2003; Romenti, 2005). The purpose of these publications is to present state-of-the-art research about corporate reputation rather than to explore new domains.

Conversely, the economic literature on the topic is published mainly in academic journals, and it attempts to spot new implications and peculiarities of reputation in specific settings. For instance, Nicola Doni (2005) shows in the context of public contracts the potentially negative effects of rules for awarding contracts that, as happens in Italy, neglect a company's reputation. Vincenzo Scoppa (1999) proposes a model based on repeated game theory and self-enforcing implicit mechanisms in which the agent's reputation helps enforce agency contracts.

Agenda-Setting Theory

In Italy, agenda-setting theory has been mainly applied within political studies and mass communication studies. In addition to thorough reviews of the influence of the media on public perceptions (Bentivoglio, 1994; Mancini & Marini, 2006), numerous empirical applications of the agenda-setting framework to Italian political campaigns have been published in specialized journals such as *Comunicazione Politica*.

Some studies (Mancini, 2002; Marini, 2002) have compared the hierarchy of contents proposed by TV and the press with the hierarchy of issues perceived by the general public during the 2001 electoral campaign. The findings empirically corroborate the hypothesis of the influence exerted by the media on the salience of the issues in the public agenda.

Mazzoleni (2002) suggests that some research in the field seems to shed new light on the possibility of testing empirically the causal influence of the media on the salience of the attributes of issues. In fact, findings from research on the relationship between media coverage during the 2001 electoral campaign and the vote subsequently expressed support for the hypothesized causal relationship (Sani, 2002; Testa, Loera, & Ricolfi, 2002).

Some evidence from psychology seems to move in the same direction. Applications of prospect theory to political decisions such as voting have shown that the possible solutions invoked by the media strongly influence individual views and decisions about that issue (Legrenzi & Girotto, 1996). However, scholars tend to stress that the "mediatization" of politics does not yet imply the supremacy of the media over politics (Mazzoleni & Schulz, 1999). In the current situation, political institutions are dependent upon and shaped by the media because of their ability to diffuse contents and messages to the greater public and because of their power to set the political issues at the center of the public debate. However, since political institutions maintain control over both political processes and functions, mass media cannot usurp political functions.

The reviewed literature seems not to have recently applied the agenda-setting theory in a business context. This conclusion is reinforced by interviews carried out with influential academicians and practitioners, who unanimously concurred in claiming the paucity, if not the absence of recent agenda-setting research in the business context.

Business and the News Media

No research that applies agenda-setting theory to the relationship between business and news media has been carried out in Italy in recent times.

This relationship was discussed within books that dealt in more general terms with corporate communication, in which the importance of the media for the organization is emphasized with respect to both the transmission of advertising messages and the diffusion of news about the firm. These contributions seem to adopt the overarching approaches of "image building" (Montericcio, 2006) or "reputation management" (Cocco & Romenti, 2005; Nelli & Bensi, 2003). This work may be grouped into two broad categories. Some contributions mention image or reputation as a taken-for-granted desirable goal for organizations to pursue. Public relations practices are placed at the center of the analysis of relationships with news media and are described as fundamental for the purpose of building and delivering a good image and reputation (Cocco & Romenti, 2005; Montericcio, 2006; Spantigati, 2001). Other studies propose thorough discussions about organizational image or reputation: fundamental concepts are soundly reviewed and integrated with contributions from the literature, and the use of numerous instruments is proposed to evaluate the communication activity either generically intended (Romenti, 2005) or specifically aimed at managing the news media (Nelli & Benzi, 2003).

Case Study

Corporate Reputation in Italy

In Italy, most corporate reputation rankings are not publicly available. In fact, they are mainly commissioned by organizations or trade associations and performed by ample multiclient market-based research or market research firms such as Doxa, Demoskopea, or AC Nielsen. Hence, findings tend to circulate only among clients.

A notable exception is the Reputation Quotient (RQ) study, carried out in 2002, based on a methodology jointly developed by Harris Interactive and the Reputation Institute (Fombrun, Gardberg & Sever, 2000). Based on the survey of a representative sample of the Italian population, 20 "highly visible" companies have been ranked across six dimensions of reputation (i.e., emotional appeal, vision and leadership, financial performance, products and services, workplace environment, and social responsibility) eventually combined in the RQ. Results from this multiclient research have been published in academic and practitioner-oriented reviews, such as the *Corporate Reputation Review* (Ravasi, 2002) and *Economia & Management* (Ravasi & Gabbioneta, 2004).

La Repubblica, a national daily, publishes a yearly ranking of the best-known universities in Italy. However, the variety and typology of criteria used for the poll (e.g., teaching quality, productivity, attraction, and influence) does not qualify it as a proper reputation ranking.

A publicly available ranking, which we may consider as a proxy for a list of the most reputed institutions in the nation, is the Edelman Trust Barometer. It reports each year on the results of a survey of 150 Italian opinion leaders that aims at capturing the degree of trust in national organizations and institutions. In 2006, the mass media turned out to be the least trusted institution in Italy, while the 10 most trusted organizations in the country were all multinational companies and NGOs: Sony, WWF, Samsung, Microsoft, Amnesty International, Greenpeace, Nissan, Johnson & Johnson, Kraft, and Ford.

Media System

To describe the Italian media system, we can apply the framework suggested in Sriramesh and Verčič (2003), which suggests analyzing the press and TV system across three main dimensions: media control, media outreach, and access.

Media Control

The media control dimension refers to influence over the editorial content of the media. Sriramesh and Verčič (2003) seem to suggest that this dimension is effectively captured by the relative degree of press independence; hence it may be fruitfully captured by the ranking presented by Freedom House, a nonpartisan organization that supports the expansion of political and economic freedom worldwide. According to this source, Italy is the only Western European country having a "partly free" press (Freedom House, 2006). The reasons provided for this categorization are twofold but intertwined.

First, the ownership structure of both print and TV media in Italy is considered too concentrated in privately held industrial conglomerates that force their influence on politics. Hallin and Mancini (2004) interpret the twofold increase of the coverage of political news in the Italian print media from 1976 to 1996 as a possible expression of political parties' influence on the media.

Second, Freedom House considers the laws that are intended to deal with the high concentration and conflict of interest in the media sector (the Gasparri Act and Frattini Act in 2004) as inadequate to ensure the independence of editorial content.

As we write, in the broadcasting media industry, a single company (Mediaset), which is controlled by the political leader Silvio Berlusconi, owns three of the six most important channels in the country and two minor radio stations. The remaining three channels are controlled by RAI, the state-owned network, whose editorial content is subject to political influence. In fact, almost every change in the governing coalition is mirrored in the replacement of the direc-

Table 7.1 Italian TVBroadcasters: Revenues (million euros) and Market Share in 2005 (%)

Broadcaster		Revenues		Market share
		2004	2005	
RAI	Total	2,545	2,570	37.5
	Advertising	1,040	1,056	
	Subscription fee	1,474	1,483	
	Agreements	31	31	
RTI (gruppo Mediaset)	Total	2,157	2,264	33
	Advertising	2,157	2,228	
	Pay-offers	-	36	
Sky Italia	Total	1,125	1,450	21.2
	Advertising	58	84	
	Pay-offers	1,067	1,366	
Telecom Italia Media (Gruppo la 7)	Total	113	137	2
	Advertising	113	128	
	Pay-offers	-	-	
Fastweb	Total	27	27	0.4
	Pay-offers	27	27	
Others	Total	392	403	5.9
	Advertising	377	388	
	Agreements	15	15	

Source: Il sistema delle comunicazioni nel mondo, in Europa e in Italia. In *Relazione annuale sull'attività svolta e sui programmi di lavoro* (2006, June). Autorità per le Garanzie nelle Comunicazioni. Retrieved from http://www.agcom.it/rel_06/index.htm

tor of TG1, the most important news program in the country in terms of audience (*La Repubblica*, 2006). In 2005, RAI and Mediaset together accounted for 70.5% of total broadcast revenues (Table 7.1). Their combined share of the advertising revenues, however, is estimated to be around 85%.

The print media situation is different. Data on national and interregional editions of newspapers in 2005 show a higher number of relevant players (Autorità per le Garanzie nelle Comunicazioni, 2006): RCS Mediagroup (18.66%), Gruppo Editoriale l'Espresso (13.20%), Caltagirone Editoriale (8.90%), and the Monti Group (6.39%). Nonetheless, many of these groups are directly or indirectly controlled by industrial families that do not hide their political affiliation and support for particular political parties. Table 7.2 shows circulation data of the most important dailies in Italy.

Media Outreach

To describe the extent of the reach of the media, we will rely on data about consumption of newspapers and radio programs.

Table 7.2 Italian Daily Newspapers: Circulation without Free Newspapers, 2005 (%)

Newspaper	Owner	Net circulation
Corriere della Sera	R.C.S. Editori s.p.a.	9.61
La Repubblica	Gruppo Editoriale l'Espresso s.p.a.	7.78
La Gazzetta dello Sport	R.C.S. Editori s.p.a.	6.20*
Il Sole 24 Ore	Il Sole 24 Ore s.p.a.	4.83**
La Stampa	Editrice La Stampa s.p.a.	4.82
Corriere dello Sport Stadio	Corriere dello Sport s.p.a.	4.58*
IL Messaggero	IL Messaggero s.p.a.	3.61
Il Giornale	Società Europea di Edizioni s.p.a.	3.51
Il Resto del Carlino	Poligrafici Editoriali s.p.a.	2.43
TuttoSport	Nuova Editoriale Sportiva s.r.l	2.19**

* Sports; ** Business and Finance.
Source: Il sistema delle comunicazioni nel mondo, in Europa e in Italia. In *Relazione annuale sull'attività svolta e sui programmi di lavoro* (2006, June). Autorità per le Garanzie nelle Comunicazioni. Retrieved from http://www.agcom.it/rel_06/index.htm

According to the Annual Report of the Autorità per le Garanzie nelle Telecomunicazioni (2006)—the national authority on media and telecommunication—business and sport newspapers in 2004 sold on average 453,000 and 783,000 daily copies, respectively, whereas the top 10 newspapers sold daily on average 2,685,000 copies in the same year. This relatively low circulation of newspapers in the country is the result of a trend over the past few years. In fact, the yearly diffusion of dailies has dropped from 2,114 million copies in 1997 to 2,080 million copies in 2004 (Autorità per le Garanzie nelle Comunicazioni, 2006).

However, radio audience has increased in recent times. In 2005, about 37 million listeners were recorded every day, corresponding to 72% of Italian population aged 11 and older on an average day (which is defined as the 24 hours before the interview) (Autorità per le Garanzie nelle Comunicazioni, 2006).

Considered overall and despite the limited reach and decline in the sale of dailies, data about consumption of media products support the idea that exposure to messages conveyed by print, TV, and radio is consistently high throughout the 58.5 million inhabitants of Italy (Istat, 2004).

Media Access

Access to the media system seems to differ according to the relative size of the organization that wants to spread its message. On the one hand, large organizations gain access to the general or specialized media through their press/investor relations office. On the other hand, medium and small-sized organizations resort to public relation agencies or specialized professionals that act as intermediaries in the relationship with the media, and these operators also take on the sticky issues that large firms outsource to them.

News Values

The characteristics of news values at work in Italy have been deeply analyzed in particular by Carlo Sorrentino (1995, 2002, 2006) within the framework of the well-known five criteria proposed by Wolf (1985), namely (a) the content of the news, (b) the product, (c) the medium, (d) the competitors, and (e) the public. Distinguishing aspects were identified regarding the first two criteria.

The Content of the News

Criteria about the content of news pertain to both the importance of a given event and the interest that it may generate. Both importance and interest relate to the following variables: (a) type of subjects involved in the event (e.g., persons who are either famous or have public positions or are involved in events at the center of the public debate); (b) geographical proximity of the place of the happening to the area of news circulation; (c) number of persons involved in the event; (d) possibility of related developments.

In the aforementioned books, Sorrentino identifies two features of Italian news values. First, persons whom the media focus on for a long period of time are likely to be placed at the center of news about subsequent events that are both related and unrelated. For example, the bribery scandal commonly referred to as *Tangentopoli* ("Bribesville"), which destabilized the Italian political and economic system during the 1990s, brought magistrates to the center of all the news about the scandal. Subsequently, magistrates have become central in unrelated news and in almost all reporting of legal issues in the media.

Second, the geographic proximity criterion, according to which local news should be prominent in the local media, is partly derogated in the Italian regional press. Sorrentino considers the local information as scant when compared to that of other European countries or North America. The reason for the actual prominence devoted to national level issues goes back to the period after World War II when the local press were engaged in building the Italian national identity through giving more prominence to news of national interest (Sorrentino, 2002).

The News Product

Criteria about the product regard the ease of fitting a given piece of news in a given press format. In particular, the balance of the news in Italy is such that within the same press format hard news (i.e., related to important events) coexists with soft news (i.e., related to curiosities or entertaining events). The distinction between the tabloid press (devoted to soft news) and the elite press (focused on hard news) does not exist in Italy (Murialdi, 1984). Moreover, this so-called *hybrid* national press (Bechelloni, 1995) has recently seen a shift in the balance of news as the soft, light news has increased at the expense of the hard news (Bechelloni, 2002).

Organizational Newsworthiness

In the absence of specific literature on what makes organizations newsworthy in Italy, we collected informal opinions from relevant scholars or professionals in the field of public relations and journalism.

The newsworthiness of organizations is said not to differ from the newsworthiness of any event: in both instances, the exceptional nature of the story involves a subject. However, particular patterns seem to underlie and guide the (orchestrated) visibility of firms in the media.

Until recently, many large firms (e.g., Enel, Telecom, etc.) had no interest in improving their image or in increasing their visibility in the media because they were monopolies or were privately owned, often by the State itself. After the liberalization of the utility and telecommunication sectors, the substantial increase in the number of IPOs, and the increase in media attention to issues of corporate social responsibility, this attitude seems to have changed. Nowadays, public relations professionals do for organizations what the "spin doctors" do for individuals. Through thoughtful plans and management, they attempt to orchestrate the organizations' appearance to the media in order to avoid unwanted mental associations with relatable facts, figures, or persons. For example, at the time of the Parmalat milk scandal, Barilla, a leading company in the food industry, which was headquartered in the same city as the collapsed firm, took care to disappear from the media.

Opposite behavior is found from firms that attempt to gain visibility in the media regardless of the context or the valence of the news with which they are associated. In a personal conversation, Toni Muzi Falconi, a prominent public relations expert, referred to these organizations as affected by a "visibility syndrome."

Public Relations

The historical and present scenario of the Italian public relations industry has been thoroughly analyzed by Muzi Falconi and Kodilja (2003). Given the availability of public data thereafter, we will present facts and figures that relate to this industry integrating the aforementioned study with partial data provided from two of the most important associations in the field (Assorel and FERPI).

There were an estimated 70,000 public relations practitioners in Italy in 2003: 40,000 were in the public administration sector; 10,000 in the private sector; 5,000 in the third sector; and 10,000 operating as consultants and professionals (Muzi Falconi, 2004).

According to Assorel estimates, there are 74 large public relations agencies (i.e., those employing at least five operators and reporting yearly revenues above €400,000), 49 of which are affiliated with the association they represent. Extending the definition of a large agency to include those with more than three employees, the estimate increases to about 130 agencies. Data for the sole Assorel affiliated agencies (Assorel, 2005) show an increase in revenues from €65 million in 1997 to €125 million in 2005, with a significant growth of the revenues per employee (from €80,000 in 1997 to €115,000 in 2005) due to the increased employment in the sector. More than 60% of the revenues are generated from relations with the media, product communication, and institutional communication.

The Italian public relations sector is currently evolving in regard to its relationship with the media. This process is accompanied by the salient debate about the need for an ethics code that informs communication activity. The FERPI's report (2006) on socially responsible communication revealed the existence of a large gap between judgments of public relations professionals and citizens about the meaning of responsible communication. PR practitioners refer basically to things like adherence to codes of conduct, respect for consumers, and truth, while citizens refer to practical aspects that are not mentioned by practitioners, such as promotion of socially responsible behaviors and promotion of fund raising for society. Moreover, as noted by Muzi Falconi (2006a), citizens particularly stress the importance of "telling *all* the truth," which implies a richness of meanings with respect to the "truth telling" manifested by practitioners.

The FERPI's report also shows that only 6% of public relations professionals apply the professional ethics code, just 13% think it is useful, and a mere 29% even know it exists in the first place. These attitudes may partly explain results contained in the same report: 91% of Italian citizens believe that organizational communication is just a little responsible or not at all responsible.

One of the reasons for the state of the public relations sector may relate to what some practitioners call the "membership culture." The Italian attitude of developing personal networks between public relations managers and the media shapes the professional relationships between the sectors. The intertwining of both personal and professional interests sometimes results in communications that lack clarity, transparency, and correctness.

On top of this, it is a widely acknowledged (mal)practice of organizational communicators to outsource the transmission of sticky information to external public relations operators so as to pass the news to the media without citing the source (Muzi Falconi, 2006b). In this way eventual responsibility for the truth of the content cannot be traced back to the original source.

To halt this practice and hence improve the image of organizational communication in the eyes of the relevant public, some communicators and editors have recently acknowledged the problem and offered a solution. Among those who propose guidelines to inform the debate for a shared solution, Muzi Falconi (2006c) suggests the following criteria as fundamental to shaping responsible communications with journalists: transparency, truthfulness, clarity, completeness, timeliness, relevance, and correct facts. Since the debate is in its earliest phase, specification of these criteria, different attitudes toward them, eventual acceptance, and common sharing of criteria, as well as involvement of journalism professionals have yet to emerge.

Research Methodology

The present study relies on a combination of quantitative and qualitative data to investigate the three general hypotheses common to all other studies in this collective work:

Hypothesis 1. The more frequent the appearance of a company in the media (media visibility), the higher the top-of-mind awareness of the company among the general population.

Hypothesis 2. The higher the prominence in the media of a certain theme relating to a given company (media associations), the higher the prominence of the same theme in the way the company is perceived by the general population (corporate associations).

Hypothesis 3. The more favorable is the content of news about a company (media valence), the more favorable the perception of that company among the general population (corporate reputation).

More specifically, Hypothesis 1 and Hypothesis 3 were tested using quantitative data gathered between 2000 and 2002 in the course of the RQ study mentioned earlier; whereas, in the absence of large scale quantitative data, the relation between media associations and corporate associations hypothesized in Hypothesis 2 were investigated through content analysis of article titles.

Sample　Our study was carried out on three different subsamples following the relative availability of data about corporate awareness, associations, and reputation, collected at various stages of the RQ Italy study (Ravasi & Gabbioneta, 2004).

In Italy, the RQ study was conducted in two phases. During the first phase, more than 1,000 randomly selected respondents were contacted by telephone and asked to name one or two firms with good or bad reputations, or companies with which they were familiar. Overall, 598 valid company and brand names were collected, for a total of 2,083 "nominations." Several entries, however, had to be excluded from the analysis because they referred to commercial brands and not companies. Furthermore, most companies were mentioned only once or twice. Eventually, we decided to retain 33 companies that were mentioned at least 10 times; below this threshold, the number of mentions decreased rapidly and more commercial brands appeared in the list. For each of the selected companies, data collected at this stage allowed us to measure the relative top-of-mind awareness and to build a rough indicator of its perceived image. Hence, we used data from this subsample to test Hypotheses 1 and 3.

During the second phase of the study, a smaller sample of 20 companies was selected for further investigation.[2] The criteria we used for the selection were the following: (a) selected companies had legal, organizational, and physical autonomy (e.g., Tim and Ferrari were included even though they were part of larger business groups; i.e., Telecom and Fiat) and (b) were "nationals" (i.e., they had been founded and developed in the country, even if some of them [Galbani and Omnitel] had been acquired by foreign investors). For each of these companies, more extensive data were collected.

In March 2002, a telephone questionnaire was administered to a random sample of the Italian population. The representativeness of the sample was guaranteed by the use of the computer assisted telephone interview (CATI) methodology for data collection. The sample was composed of 3,000 people between 18 and 65 years old. None of the interviewed citizens had participated in the nomination phase of the study. The questionnaire was composed of five sections and was designed to gather extensive data for the purpose of investigating how each company was perceived by the general public (see Fombrun & Van Riel, 2004; Ravasi & Gabbioneta, 2004). Parts of these data were used to build another measure of organizational image to be used in testing Hypothesis 3.

Six of the 20 companies in the second subsample helped fund the research. For these companies, respondents were asked in addition to mention the very first thing that came to mind when they thought about the company. These free associations were used to explore the relationship implied in Hypothesis 2 on two firms about which there were a reasonable number of published articles.

Data Collection and Measures   The source of data was twofold. Data about the dependent variables in the hypotheses were collected in the course of the RQ study. Data about the independent variables as well as control variables were collected through an archival research tapping several sources.

Dependent Variables

We defined *top-of-mind awareness* as the total number of mentions collected in the first round of the RQ for the sample of 33 firms where individuals were required to name the first one or two firms they could think of.

Corporate associations were measured through a categorization of free associations collected in the second round of the RQ study for the subsample of six Italian firms, along six dimensions of reputation identified in previous studies: emotional appeal, vision and leadership, financial performance, products and services, workplace environment, and social responsibility (Fombrun, Gardberg, & Sever, 2000).

Finally, we built two measures of *corporate reputation*. The first was constructed as the relative percentage of positive mentions over total mentions in the nomination phase of the RQ study for the sample of 33 firms. The second used, for the subsample of 20 Italian firms, three questions included in the questionnaire administered in the second phase ("I like company A"; "I trust company A"; "I respect and admire company A") combined into a single scale, Emotional Appeal (Fombrun, Gardberg, & Sever, 2000). Since such a measure taps the extent of liking, trust, and esteem for a given firm, it seems to capture appropriately the overall reputation of the firm.

Independent Measures

In order to measure media-related variables (media visibility, media valence, and media associations), content analysis was performed on article titles published in three leading Italian newspapers: *Il Corriere della Sera*, *La Repubblica* (the most popular newspapers), and *Il Sole 24 Ore*, the most widely distributed business newspaper (see Table 7.2).

Our test of Hypothesis 1 required us to measure the *media visibility* of each of the 33 companies, for which data about top-of-mind awareness were available. As a proxy for company media visibility, we used the total number of articles published in the three selected newspapers in which the company name appeared in the title. We assumed that names in titles stick out clearly, and hence may be encoded in the memories of even those readers that browse through the newspaper more than is the case with names that appear in the text of an article. We limited the search to articles published in the seven months before the beginning of the nomination phase of the RQ study (September 2000); that is, those articles published from February 1, 2000 to September 1, 2000. In this way, we allowed for a lag of some months, which is defined as the time between the publication date and the actual acknowledgment of the topic by the public. We collected an initial sample of 13,797 articles,[3] from which we dropped articles with the following characteristics: (a) the company name was contained only in the subheading rather than in the main heading; (b) the name of homonymous firms (e.g.: Ferrari is also the name of a winery) or persons (e.g., the actress Isabella Ferrari) with no relation to the company; (c) brief news on stock exchange trends. We finally retained 2,669 articles in which the name of the company was present in the title, regardless of the syntactical role of the word (i.e., names as subject, object, and indirect references were retained) and regardless of whether it referred to the firm's products, services, founders, or managers.

In order to explore empirical support for Hypothesis 2, we measured *media association* (i.e., what the media refer to when talking about firms) through content-analyzing articles published in the 6 months before the collection of data about corporate image in the second phase of the RQ study (from September 1, 2001 to March 1, 2002). While data gathered in the course of the RQ study allowed us to track corporate associations for six companies, we could collect a reasonable amount of articles (i.e., more than 15) for only two companies; hence our final sample included only Eni and Enel, for which we were able to collect 40 and 106 articles, respectively. Content analysis followed the same criterion described above for corporate associations. The content of the article was inferred from the title and categorized following the six dimensions of corporate reputation that composed the RQ index. For example, a positive reference to managers' expertise in either tapping market opportunities or setting clear plans of development was coded as an association with vision and leadership. Articles were categorized separately by the two authors and a comparison of results displayed substantial agreement. As data about corporate associations were collected among the general population, and articles from the specialized financial press gave overwhelming emphasis to financial and business topics, we carried out our final analysis only on articles published in *Corriere della Sera* and *Repubblica*, excluding *Il Sole 24 Ore*.

Finally, testing Hypothesis 3 required us to measure the *valence of media articles* for each of the 33 companies in the sample. The valence of articles was inferred from the valence of titles. It does not seem unreasonable to assume that the tone of article texts mirrors the tone of their titles. Article titles were coded separately by the two authors, who previously agreed on the codification protocol (interrater agreement of 90%). We coded as positive those articles in which the title either made reference to positive events per se (e.g., growth in revenue), quoted sentences with positive content (e.g., someone's positive opinion toward the firm or its products and services), or contained words of positive valence (e.g., conquest, success). We operationalized the media positive valence of a firm with the percentage of positive articles about that firm. For testing the relation with the first measure of corporate image (i.e., the percentage of positive mentions for the sample of 33 firms), we used the same articles as for testing Hypothesis 1, whereas for the second measure (i.e., emotional appeal of the sample of 20 Italian companies), we retrieved articles published in the three dailies from September 2001 to March 2002.

Control Variables

In order to account for the possible influence of other variables on top-of-mind associations (Van Riel, 2002) and corporate reputation (Fombrun & Shanley, 1990), we included control variables. In the case of Hypothesis 1 (media visibility and top-of-mind awareness), we controlled for the company's *age* (years from foundation to 2000); *size* (measured as the natural logarithm of sales in 1999, in thousands of euros; for foreign firms, we considered data relating to Italian subsidiaries); and *advertising expenses* (in 1999, the year before the survey, in thousands of euros). These controls were chosen because it is not unreasonable to assume that people may be more aware of firms that are large, have been around for a long time, and advertise heavily (Van Riel, 2002). In the case of Hypothesis 3 (media valence and reputation), we controlled for *advertising expenses* (in 1999 and in 2000 for testing the first and second measure of reputation, respectively) and for *size* (in 1999 and in 2000 for testing the first and second measure of reputation, respectively). Advertising conveys messages aimed at building favorable product or company images, and firm size may be interpreted as a sign of success and respectability, hence leading to a favorable corporate reputation (Fombrun & Shanley, 1990).

Data Analysis

In order to test Hypothesis 1, we used both OLS and negative binomial regression. This type of regression is more efficient than OLS to estimate models in which the dependent variable is a nonnegative count variable. When the variance of the data is high, however, OLS is acceptable.

In order to test Hypothesis 3 we built two models using two alternative measures for the dependent variable (i.e., corporate reputation). First, for the sample of the 33 firms, we performed a hierarchical OLS regression of the percentage of positive articles (measuring media valence) on the percentage of positive mentions (measuring corporate reputation). Second, for the subsample of the 20 Italian firms, we performed another hierarchical OLS regression of the percentage of positive articles on the emotional appeal score.

Finally, in order to explore potential support for Hypothesis 2, we qualitatively confronted the frequency of the different categories of media and corporate associations about the only two companies for which we could gather sufficient data: Eni and Enel.

We first organized corporate associations reported by individuals in two main categories: descriptive and evaluative. Descriptive associations included simple definitions of the firm's businesses, activities, and products. Evaluative associations contained valenced mentions of firms, which in turn have been exploded into mentions of products and services, leadership of managers and market vision, socially responsible conduct, financial performance, and any mentions that denoted emotional responses. A residual category included a heterogeneous array of responses that could not fit into the main categories.

Media associations were also divided into descriptive and evaluative categories, according to whether they provided any valenced reference to the firm. The evaluative associations were then analyzed in terms of the reference to the six dimensions.

Results and Discussion

Table 7.3 shows descriptive statistics of the variables involved in testing Hypothesis 1. Although OLS regression is less efficient for fitting nonnegative count data, the high variance of the dependent variable (2143.57) allowed using also such a model. Hence, before running the more appropriate negative binomial model, we analyzed data with the OLS regression. As shown in Table 7.4, the only variable that appears to correlate with the number of mentions is the advertising cost. The other variables, including the measure for company media visibility, are not statistically significant.

Then, we ran a negative binomial regression to check whether these results are consistent also with the more appropriate model for estimating these data. As shown in the second panel of Table 7.4, the overall regression is significant ($p < .00$), although it explains very little variance of the data (Pseudo $R^2 = .08$). The number of total articles, which measures media visibility, is not significantly correlated with the number of total mentions ($p < .64$), suggesting that citizen awareness of firms does not covary with a higher visibility of firms in the press news. Hence, Hypothesis 1 does not seem to be supported. Nor does top-of-mind awareness covary with the firm's age, suggesting that the time a firm has been in the market does not seem to significantly affect people's (top-of-mind) awareness of the company. Advertising is not the only significant variable, however, and it differs from the results of the OLS regression ($p < .01$); but also, the firm's sales

Table 7.3 Media Visibility and Top-of-Mind Awareness: Descriptive Statistics

Variables	Mean	s.d	1	2	3	4
1. Total mentions	31.48	46.29				
2. Total articles	80.87	83.78	0.39			
3. Advertising	34900.55	44218.82	0.39	0.09		
4. Age	126.78	314.14	-0.07	0.08	-0.05	
5. Sales (ln)	14.94	1.28	0.45	0.55	0.17	0.09

Table 7.4 Media Visibility and Top-of-Mind Awareness: Results from OLS Regression and Negative Binomial Regression

Variables	OLS	Negative Binomial
Total articles	0.11	0
	-0.11	0
Advertising	.00*	.00**
	0	0
Sales (ln)	11.2	.27**
	-7.38	-0.12
Age	-0.01	0
	-0.02	0
F-value	3.31**	
Adjusted R2	0.24	
LR Chi2 (4)		23.58***
Pseudo R2		0.087

Standard errors in parenthesis: * p < .10; ** p < .05; *** P < .01.

appear to covary significantly with total mentions ($p < .02$). However, only the firm's size has a positive effect on awareness (beta = .27), which suggests that being bigger increases the likelihood of high awareness to a greater extent than larger investments in advertising (the coefficient of which is about 0).

The interpretation of these results, which seem to contradict the classical tenet of agenda-setting theory, has to be done with caution for two reasons. First, the number of observations (30, rather than 33, due to some missing values) may be too small to generalize the results. Future studies should endeavor to extend these exploratory findings by considering larger samples. Second, we considered only news which appeared in the press. Discussion about the Italian media system showed that there is a decrease in the distribution of newspapers in Italy and that their reach is less than TV and radio. Hence, it may be the case that the public's awareness of companies covaries less with press articles than with TV or radio news. Incidentally, a large portion of the advertising budget, which seems to be the main covariate of corporate awareness, is spent on TV commercials. Based on these results, future research may want to broaden the arrays of media analyzed, since top-of-mind awareness of firms may be influenced in different ways by media other than newspapers.

Moreover, results from this exploratory study may suffer from other limitations that future research should try to address. First, a problem of spurious correlation might arise if we suspect that an unobservable variable reflecting a deeper underlying set of perceptions at societal level influences both the independent variable (i.e., media visibility) and the dependent variable (i.e., top-of-mind awareness). However, the news-making criteria we have discussed above support the assumption that the decision to write an article about a given firm is not correlated with what may affect people's awareness of the firm (although their interest in the firm may reasonably be influenced by the same variables). In fact, journalists use objective criteria (e.g., content and news product) to decide what events to report about a given firm according to what may reasonably influence public interest in the firm—though not the public's awareness of it (i.e., unless news has been reported by the media, geographic distance hinders knowledge of it).

Second, the sample selection may bias the result. In fact, we considered as an dependent variable only articles about firms that have been mentioned in the survey. If the number of articles is believed to have also a slope effect on awareness (i.e., that the beta coefficients differ across articles regarding firms that have been mentioned and those that have not), we should run the two-step Heckman procedure to address this issue. However, we did not expect that people's awareness of mentioned firms varies with the number of articles about other (i.e., not mentioned) firms. Hence, the relevance of the sample selection bias is reduced greatly. Nonetheless, future studies that will go beyond simple exploratory research should try to analyze the relationship with top-of-mind awareness of the media visibility of a random sample of firms that have not been mentioned.

Analysis of associations between media and corporations suggests that having direct experience and knowledge of the company and its products may affect the extent to which people think of a particular topic when thinking of a particular firm, and thus mirror attitudes in the media. We present findings for the two firms under analysis (i.e., Eni and Enel) separately, because the different characteristics of the firms' products and activities may explain some of the observed differences in the themes that people associated with these companies. Although they are both multiutility firms, consumers have a more direct experience of products and services offered by Enel rather than those offered by Eni. Enel is the dominant producer and seller of electricity in Italy, and it also distributes natural gas; the company name is very well known because it appears on all utilities bills. Conversely, people may have a less direct experience with the Eni name because it labels very few products or services that might be purchased by the general public. In fact, some products (gasoline and diesel) are branded with a different name (Agip), and some of the products that Eni now offers (gas under the name Italgas and electricity under the name Enipower) are less widely distributed than those of Enel, which previously had a monopoly of the electricity markets. Moreover, Eni is in the business of engineering and construction (Snamprogetti and Saipem) and in the petrochemical industry (Polimeri Europa), with which the vast majority of the population may not have any direct experience. This might suggest that the themes that individuals associate with Eni may be more mediated by the press than their associations to Enel, for which they have much more direct experience with the firm's name and products.

As shown in Figure 7.1, the themes that the media evoke about Eni are largely evaluative (77%) in the sense that they contain a valenced reference to one of the six dimensions of corporate reputation (financial performance, products and services, vision and leadership, workplace environment, emotional appeal, and social responsibility). In particular, more than half of the themes covered in the two dailies with reference to Eni are in regard to the financial performance of the

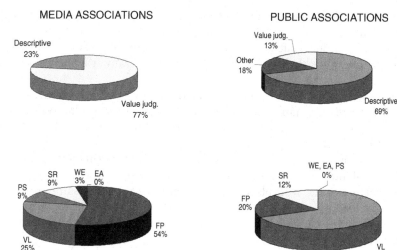

FP: financial performance; VL: vision and leadership; PS: products and services; SR: social responsibility; WE: workplace environment; EA: emotional appeal.

Figure 7.1 Media associations and public associations for Eni

company, and one quarter regard the long-term vision and leadership ability of its managers. Few judgments are made with reference to products and services, and to matters of responsibility toward communities and the environment. Very few associations regard Eni as a place to work and none contain any emotional reference to the firm.

Unlike those portrayed by the media, the top-of-mind associations made by the interviewed people are more descriptive (69%) than evaluative (13%). The category "other" includes both the answers of those who cannot come up with any theme to associate with Eni and words that have unclear relationships with the firm (e.g., *cartoons, fire,* etc.). The evaluative judgments partly mirror the main themes covered by the press, at least in terms of the categories of themes people described. Paralleling the media predisposition, themes about company vision and managers' leadership (e.g. "well-managed company"; "leader in oil production") as well as financial performance topics (e.g. "safe investment") are the most cited among the public. However, the relative frequency presents a reverse order among the public with respect to that of the press: 58% for vision and leadership among the public versus 25% in the press, and 20% for financial performance among the public versus 54% in the press. The frequency of concern for topics about social responsibility is similar to the frequency in the press (12% and 9%, respectively), even though Eni's activities (oil refining, construction of extraction plants, etc.) have a very high environmental impact. Moreover, individual responses parallel the press in the lack of emotional appeal.

Overall, these qualitative findings seem to show a reflection of the main themes covered by the press in the themes that people associated with Eni. A possible explanation for this may be the fact that the general public lacks either direct experience with Eni's products and services (many services such as plant construction are not purchased by the general population), or are not aware of Eni (many common products such as gasoline are not branded with the Eni name). Hence people likely cue their knowledge about the company from other sources, such as the press.

As shown in Figure 7.2, the themes that the press associates with Enel are more evaluative (81%) than descriptive (19%). Among the evaluative associations, the frequency of the different themes about Enel is more balanced than those about Eni. Forty-one percent of articles are devoted to topics related to the firm's vision and its leaders. Associations with financial performance are also frequent (21%). Mentions of products and services, socially responsible activities, and topics related to the workplace environment have about the same frequency that they have for Eni (13%, 9%, and 1%, respectively). However, the press does associate Enel with topics that have some emotional appeal and this does differ from the press response to Eni.

The themes that the public associates with Enel are more descriptive (65%) than evaluative (30%). Among the evaluative associations, the great majority of themes have to do with Enel's products and services (e.g., "very expensive bill"; "good service") that are mostly neglected by the press. On the contrary, only few associations (9% of the total) are made to topics of vision and leadership by citizens, even though the press gives those aspects prominent attention (41% of the total articles). Also, topics on financial performance are neglected by the public (just 4% of the total), despite rather high frequency in the press (21%). We observe similar frequency in the topics that involve emotional appeal (e.g., "If Enel did not exist, what would I do?"); that is, 13% and 15% of the public and media associations, respectively. The general reversal of prominence in the

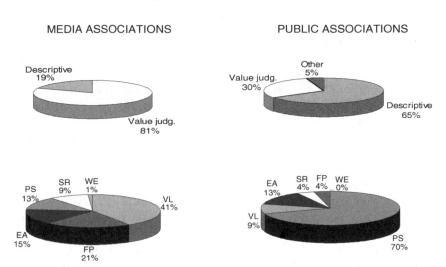

MEDIA ASSOCIATIONS   PUBLIC ASSOCIATIONS

FP: financial performance; VL: vision and leadership; PS: products and services; SR: social responsibility; WE: workplace environment; EA: emotional appeal.

Figure 7.2 Media associations and public associations for Enel

themes associated to Enel among the public with respect to what is portrayed in the press suggest that direct experience of the firm's products and services may play a role in influencing what to think of when thinking of the firm.

Overall, these findings seem to suggest that a correlation between media associations and public associations about a firm exists when people cue topics on the firms primarily through the media because of lack of direct experience. However, when a direct experience is possible, media do not seem able to influence the prominence of the topics most thought of, which are inferred from other sources. Since these findings are based on a qualitative analysis of just two firms they cannot be generalized and further investigation is thus needed to validate the explanation proposed here.

In regard to Hypothesis 3, we present findings for the two models separately. The OLS regression of media valence on the percentage of positive mentions as dependent variable explains just 10% of the variance of the data. However, as shown in Table 7.5, adding media valence as an independent variable slightly improves the ability of the model to explain the variance of the data. Media valence, measured as the percentage of positive articles regarding the firms, is just slightly significant ($p < .08$) and each percentage increase in positive articles is correlated with an increase in corporate image by about 55%. Although the result is not striking, it corroborates the hypothesis that media positive valence about firms correlates with the positive image held by people about the firms. Increasing advertising expense is not associated with improved valence of a firm's image ($p < .92$). Although results from testing Hypothesis 1 showed that it does strongly correlate with top-of-mind awareness, this result now adds the factor that advertising does not appear to affect the valence of the corporate image. In other words, while heavy advertising seems to positively affect the extent to which a company is remembered it does not necessarily lead to positive impressions about it. Sales correlate with image ($p < .07$), although negatively. With caution, we may interpret this result as an outcome of negative experiences with

Table 7.5 Media Valence and Corporate Image: OLS Regression Results

Variables	Image as percentage of positive mentions		Image as emotional appeal	
	Model 1	Model 2	Model 1	Model 2
Sales (ln)	-5.81*	-6.37*	-1.64	-1.19
	-3.49	-3.37	-1.35	-0.752
Advertising	5.03E-06	8.85E-06	0	-3.51E-07
	0	0	0	0
Percentage positive articles		.55*		.42***
		-0.31		-0.07
F-value	1.41	2.09	1.13	14.11***
Adjusted R2	0.028	0.1	0.015	0.69

Standard errors in parenthesis: *p < .10; ** p < .05; *** p < .01

products and services of some large firms in our small sample (e.g., Poste Italiane, Ferrovie dello Stato) that may affect the likelihood of thinking favorably about those companies.

Overall, this model provides some support for the hypothesis that the corporate image held by the public covaries with the firm's image conveyed by the media through the valence of the news. Further, and stronger, support was found in the second model.

The OLS regression of media valence on firm image measured as the emotional appeal score on the subsample of 20 Italian firms explains a large part of the variability of the data (adjusted R^2 = .69) and it is strongly significant (p < . 00). Adding media valence as regressor (i.e., percentage of positive articles published between March 2001 and February 2002) greatly improves the explanatory power of the model (Table 7.5), and it is the only variable which significantly correlates with people emotional appeal about firms (p < .00). These results seem to support the idea that the valence of articles about a given firm covaries significantly with the emotional appeal about the firm. Surprisingly, advertising expense does not significantly influence the creation of positive emotions about a given firm. As shown in model 1 of the second panel of Table 7.5, the lack of effect of advertising on corporate emotional appeal persists when the percentage of positive articles is not included in the model. Nor is firm size associated significantly with emotional appeal.

Overall, findings that come from both sets of regressions in which corporate image has been differently operationalized, seems to support the hypothesis that positive media valence is correlated with the reputation of firms among the general public. Although the emotional appeal about firms seems to covary neither with advertising intensity nor with firm's size, the percentage of positive mentions is correlated with a firm's sales. However, these results must be interpreted with the same caution we have discussed for the study testing Hypothesis 1. First, the small number of firms in the samples (33 for the first regression and 20 for the second) does not allow generalizing of the results. Hence, future studies should investigate these relations with more ample samples. Second, since we have considered only articles from the press, these results should be corroborated by analyzing also the relation with corporate image of news coming from media with further reach. Moreover, the studies for testing Hypothesis 3 have some limitations. First, a possible endogeneity problem may be an issue. An unobservable general predisposition of people (both the public and the journalists) may affect the valence of the firm's image and the valence of the articles. This general predisposition is not captured by the models herewith proposed, and it would need more fine-grained data that future research might endeavor to collect and analyze. Second, a potential sample selection problem might deserve future considerations, for similar reasons as those proposed in discussing findings of Hypothesis 1. However, also in this context, we would not expect that positive mentions or the emotional appeal for a given firm would vary with positive articles about the firms that were not mentioned. If this assumption seems reasonable, sample selection should not affect the present findings.

Conclusions

The characteristics of the Italian media system we discussed in this chapter seem to provide only partial support to the tenet of the agenda-setting theory that top-of-mind awareness, image, and topics that the public associates to organizations may be correlated with the visibility, the valence, and the themes that news media associated with them. We tested the three hypotheses of the agenda-setting theory on a random sample of 1,000 and 3,000 individuals for three samples of conveniently selected 33, 20, and two firms, analyzing the articles of the three leading Italian newspapers in selected periods. These exploratory analyses suggested the following: First, results from a negative binomial regression do not support the hypothesis that top-of-mind awareness is correlated with company visibility in the media. Conversely, it seems that the public's awareness relates only to company visibility derived from advertising expenditures. Second, findings from the qualitative analysis of the frequency of the press and people topics seem to suggest that the themes the public associates with firms mirror those proposed by the press only for firms for which it has mainly a mediated knowledge. Conversely, when individuals have a direct knowledge of a given firm (e.g., because the company's name is visible on the products or services people buy), the frequency of specific themes associated with that firm does not mirror the attention devoted to them by the press. Finally, results from two OLS regressions suggest that the reputation of the company among the public seems to be correlated with the positive valence displayed in the articles. The correlation between media valence and corporate reputation is stronger when the latter is measured in terms of emotional appeal.

We have indicated above in our discussion of results for each hypothesis limitations in the results that derive from this exploratory study. Especially relevant is the consideration that the ideas that these results suggest may be dependent upon the type of media we have analyzed. The extent of the reach of different media in Italy does indeed support the consideration that print news is less likely to be correlated with the public's perceptions of firms than news on TV. Hence, in addition to alleviating the other indicated limitations, future research should endeavor to broaden the types of media to analyze.

Notes

1. This chapter was written based on research partly carried out on the early 2000s. All statements about the media situation in Italy are based on data relating to 2006 or before.
2. The size of the second subsample was determined by the amount of funds required to cover the costs of such large scale rating of companies.
3. This high number is due to the fact that the electronic archive of *Corriere della Sera* does not allow restricting the search to titles. Hence, the outcome of the search by name also includes articles where the company name appears in the full text. Once this material was sorted it produced a list by relevance; articles in which the name is displayed in titles are listed first.

References

Assorel. (2005). *L'andamento del mercato delle relazioni pubbliche in Italia: settori mer-ceologici, aree professionali* [The trend in the market for public relations in Italy: sectors, professional areas]. Retrieved from http://www.assorel.it/download/classifica/analisi_mercato_2005.pdf

Autorità per le Garanzie delle Comunicazioni. (2006). *Il sistema delle comunicazioni nel mondo, in Europa* [The communication system in the world and in Europe]. Retrieved from http://www.agcom.it

Bechelloni, G. (1995). *Giornalismo o post giornalismo? Studi per pensare il modello italiano.* [Journalism or post-journalism? Studies to conceive the Italian model]. Naples, Italy: Liguori.

Bechelloni, G. (2002). La bomba mediatica. [The mediatic bomb]. *Doc, 1,* 23–25.

Bentivoglio, S. (1994). *Mediare la realtà. Mass media, sistema politico ed opinione pubblica* [Mediating reality: mass media, political system, and public opinion]. Milan, Italy: Angeli.

Cameran, M., & Livatino, M. (2005). *La reputazione delle società di revisione operanti in Italia: Premium price, criteri di selezione e opinioni dei clienti* [Reputation of auditing companies in Italy: Price premium, selection criteria, and clients' opinions]. Milan, Italy: EGEA.

Cocco, R. & Romenti, S. (2005). La gestione delle relazioni con i media [The management of media relations]. In E. Invernizzi (Ed.), *Manuale di relazioni pubbliche: Le tecniche e i servizi di base* (pp. 259-302). Milan, Italy: McGraw-Hill.

Doni, N. (2005). L'affidamento mediante gara di contratti pubblici: l'importanza della reputazione [Public service auctions: the importance of reputation]. *Politica Economica, 307–355.*

Dowling, G. R. (1986). Managing your corporate images. *Industrial Marketing Management, 15.*

FERPI. (2006). Rapporto FERPI sulla comunicazione socialmente responsabile. Comunicatori d'impresa, stakeholder e cittadini [FERPI report on social responsible communication: Corporate comunicators, stakeholders, citizens]. Retrieved from http://www.ferpi.it/ferpi/novita/notizie_ferpi/notizie_ferpi/lo-scorso-4-luglio-a-milano-ferpi-ha-presentato-il-rapporto-2006-sulla-comunicazione-socialmente-responsabile-per-chi-lavesse-persoeccolo-qua/notizia_ferpi/36026/11

Fombrun, C. J. (1996). *Reputation: Realizing value from corporate image.* Cambridge, MA: Harvard Business School Press.

Fombrun, C. J., Gardberg, N., & Sever, J. (2000). The reputation quotient: A multistakeholder measure of corporate reputation. *Journal of Brand Management, 7*(4), 241–255.

Fombrun, C. J., & Shanley, M. (1990). What's in a name? Reputation building and corporate strategy. *Academy of Management Journal, 33*(2), 233–258.

Fombrun, C. J., & Van Riel, C. B. M. (2004). *Fame and fortune: How successful companies build winning reputations.* Upper Saddle River, NJ: Financial Times Prentice-Hall.

Freedom House. (2006, July). Freedom of the press 2006: Country draft. Retrieved from http://www.freedomhouse.org/uploads/PFS/DraftCountryReportsForPR27April06.pdf

Hallin, D. C., & Mancini, P. (2004). *Modelli di giornalismo: Mass media e politica nelle democrazie occidentali* [Journalism models: mass media and politics in Western democracies]. Bari, Italy: Gius. Laterza & Figli.

Invernizzi, E. (2005), *Manuale di relazioni pubbliche: Le tecniche e i servizi di base.* Milan, Italy: McGraw-Hill.

Istat. (2004). Approfondimenti [Insights]. Retrieved from http://www.istat.it/dati/catalo go/20050912_00/01poplazione.pdf

La Repubblica. (2006, September 13). Direttori nel tritacarne del potere è la maledizione del Tg1. Retrieved from http://ricerca.repubblica.it/repubblica/archivio/repubblica/2006/09/13/direttori-nel-tritacarne-del-potere-la-maledizione.html

Legrenzi, P. & Girotto, V. (1996). *Psicologia politica* [Political pshychology]. Milan, Italy: Cortina.

Mancini, P. (2002). Agenda dei media e agenda degli elettori [Media agenda and voters agenda]. *Comunicazione Politica* 3(1), 31–50.

Marini, R. (2002). L'agenda della campagna elettorale "lunga" 2000–2001 [The agenda of the "long" electoral campaign 2000–2001]. *Comunicazione Politica, 1,* 81–101.

Mancini, P. , & Marini, R. (2006). *Le comunicazioni di massa: Teorie, contenuti ed effetti* [Mass communication: Theories, content, and consequences]. Rome, Italy: Carocci.

Mazzoleni, G. (2002). Una campagna elettorale speciale e un'influenza mediatica speciale [A special electoral campaign and a special media influence]. *Comunicazione Politica,* 3(1), 5–8 .

Mazzoleni, G., & Schulz, W. (1999). Mediatization of politics: A challenge for democracy? *Political Communication,* 16(3), 247–261.

Montericcio, M. (2006). *L'immagine d'impresa e la sua gestione; Come si analizza-come si valuta- come si costruisce* [Corporate image and its management: how to analyze, value, and build it]. Milan, Italy: Franco Angeli.

Murialdi, P. (1984). Breve storia del "Corriere della Sera" e della "Repubblica" [Brief history of "Corriere della Sera" and "Repubblica"]. In M. Livolsi (Ed.), *La fabbrica delle notizie.* Milan, Italy: Franco Angeli.

Muzi Falconi, T. (2004). *Governare le relazioni: Obiettivi, strumenti e modelli delle relazioni pubbliche* [Relations management: Goals, tools, and models of public relations]. Milan, Italy: Il Sole 24 Ore.

Muzi Falconi, T. (2006a). Opinioni e commenti [Opinions and comments]. Retrieved from http://www.ferpi.it/news_leggi.asp?ID=42681

Muzi Falconi, T. (2006b). Off the record...E' questo il ruolo strategico delle relazioni con i media? [Off the record: strategic role of media relations?]. Retrieved from http://www.ferpi.it/news_leggi.asp?ID=41291

Muzi Falconi, T. (2006c). Relazioni con i media: ripartire? Ma da quali basi? Seconda puntata della nostra riflessione [Media relations: start again? How? Second appointment]. Retrieved from http://www.ferpi.it/news_leggi.asp?ID=41828

Muzi Falconi, T., & R. Kodilja (2003). Italy. In B. Van Ruler & D. Verčič (Eds.), *Public relations and communication management in Europe: A nation by nation introduction to public relations theory and practice* (pp. 227-244). Berlin, Germany: Mouton de Gruyter.

Nelli, R. P., & Bensi, P. (2003). *L'impresa e la sua reputazione. L'evoluzione della media coverage analysis* [Corporate reputation: Evolution of the media coverage analysis]. Milan, Italy: Vita e Pensiero.

Ravasi, D. (2002). Analyzing reputation in a cross-national setting. *Corporate Reputation Review, 4,* 354–361.

Ravasi, D., & Gabbioneta, C. (2004). Le componenti della reputazione aziendale: Indicazioni dalla ricerca RQ Italy [Corporate reputation components: results from the RQ research in Italy]. *Economia & Management, 3,* 77–100.

Romenti, S. (2005). *Valutare i risultati della comunicazione: Modelli e strumenti per misurare la qualità delle relazioni e della reputazione* [Assess communication results: models and tools to measure the quality of relations and reputation]. Milan, Italy: FrancoAngeli.

Sani, G. (2002). L'oroscopo del marziano: Comunico ergo sum? [The Martian's horoscope: Comunico ergo sum?]. *Comunicazione Politica*, 1, 122–126.

Scoppa, V. (1999). Un modello con contratti di agenzia "self enforcing" e reputazione dell'impresa [A model with self-enforcing agency contracts, and corporate reputation]. *Rivista Italiana degli Economisti*, 1, 37–72.

Sorrentino, C. (1995). *I percorsi della notizia: La stampa quotidiana italiana fra politica e mercato* [News path: Italian daily news between politics and market]. Bologna, Italy: Baskerville.

Sorrentino, C. (2002). *Il giornalismo: Cos'è e come funziona* [Journalism: What it is and how it works]. Rome, Italy: Carocci.

Sorrentino, C. (2006). Newsmaking. In P. Mancini & R.Marini (Eds.), *Le comunicazioni di massa: Teorie, contenuti, effetti* (pp. 137–165). Rome, Italy: Carocci.

Spantigati, F. (2001). *I fondamenti della comunicazione; Come usare l'informazione per centrare gli obbiettivi* [The basis of communication: How to use communication to achieve objectives]. Milan, Italy: FrancoAngeli.

Sriramesh, K., & Verčič, D. (2003). *The global public relation handbook: Theory, research and practice*. Mahwah, NJ: Erlbaum.

Testa, S., Loera, B., & Ricolfi, L. (2002). Sorpasso? Il ruolo della televisione nelle elezioni politiche del 2001 [Overtaking? TV role in 2001 Italian political election]. *Comunicazione Politica*, 3, 101–115 .

Van Riel, C. B. M (2002). The Netherlands: Top of mind awareness of corporate brands among the Dutch public. *Corporate Reputation Review*, 4(4), 362–373.

Wolf, M. (1985). *Teorie della comunicazione di massa* [Theory of mass communication]. Milan, Italy: Bompiani.

8 Corporate Reputation and the News Media in Japan

Kenichi Ishii and Toshio Takeshita

As interest in corporate social responsibility grows, Japanese entrepreneurs have become increasingly interested in corporate reputation. However, only a few studies in Japan have focused on the relationship between the news media and corporate reputation. Seeking to fill this void, this study discusses corporate reputation, business news, and mass media in Japan, examining the effects of the media on corporate reputation from an agenda-setting perspective.

Corporate Reputation in Japan

In Japan, some management researchers have only recently begun to study corporate reputation as an intangible asset. For example, Sakurai (2005, p. 41) discussed the significance of corporate reputation for corporate finance, estimating that Shimadzu Corp. earned ¥10 billion as a result of a reputation boost when employee Koichi Tanaka was awarded the Nobel Prize for Chemistry in 2002. In contrast, Sakurai estimated that Mitsubishi Motors Corp. lost ¥164 billion after the major automaker failed to report customer complaints to the Ministry of Transport.

Agenda-Setting Research in Japan

Japan's agenda-setting research began in the late 1970s. Okada (1979) was the first to extensively discuss the concept in a textbook on mass communication. The first empirical test of the agenda-setting hypothesis was conducted by Maeda (1978) in a study examining the correlations between the audience agenda and the perceived media agenda. Since the 1980s, most of the empirical tests of the media's agenda-setting role have been conducted in a political context, using political issues for the items on the media and public's agendas (Takeshita, 1993). Findings often reveal that agenda-setting effects seem to occur under contingent conditions (e.g., high levels of news exposure, political interest, or need for orientation) (Takeshita, 1983, 1993). Also, data show that newspapers have a stronger agenda-setting effect in Japan than does television news.

A strong association between the media and public agendas does not prove that media actively and independently determine the public's agenda. Some scholars believe that mainstream news media in Japan are not an active agenda setter but passively reflect what their sources, the political elite, use the press to publicize (Ishikawa, 1990; Krauss & Lambert, 2002). Ishikawa (1990, 1995) cites two reasons for the media's passivity: the presence of *kisha clubs* (press clubs) as a unique news-gathering system in Japan and the professional norms of *fuhen futo* (impartiality). The former facilitate and make more economic the tasks of news gathering, but also facilitate close relations between news sources and reporters. Some criticize the press club system, referring to the clubs as "information cartels" (e.g., Freeman, 2000). The Japanese norms of impartiality act to scare journalists from raising political issues for fear of being seen as partisan.

In 1990 second-level agenda-setting research emerged in Japan. Takeshita and Mikami (1995) conducted a simultaneous test of both first- and second-level agenda-setting effects using the 1993 general election. At the first level, a high level of attentiveness to election news corresponded with a voter being more likely to regard the primary election issue as most important. At the second level of agenda-setting, a high level of attentiveness to election news was associated with a voter being more likely to see the primary issue from the same perspective as was dominant in the news. An experimental study by Ogawa (2001) examined how agenda-setting interacts with framing. He showed that agenda-setting effects are dependent not only on dominance, but also on how an issue is framed in news stories.

Thus far, Japan's agenda-setting research has primarily focused on public affairs, neglecting the study of economic news and advertising. However, Tokinoya (1983) tried to detect agenda-setting effects of TV advertisements.

Business and the News Media

Though previous studies have focused on business and the news media, the agenda-setting theory has not been applied to this topic in Japan. In regards to Japan's "bubble economy," Takahashi (1998) pointed out that editorials in major newspapers presented inconsistent views on economic policy in the 1990s. Sugita (2002) also argued that major newspapers fostered the bubble economy by stimulating readers' interest in investment. Ishii (1994) showed that, based on a content analysis of markets in the bubble economy period, stock market news increased significantly when the market prices decreased. On the other hand, when stock prices increased, news decreased. These results demonstrate that Japanese business news had a biased and inconsistent pattern during the bubble economy period.

Case Study of Corporate Reputation Research in Japan

Despite the scarcity of academic studies on public corporations, several corporate rankings related to corporate reputation are published in Japan. The *Nikkei Corporate Image Survey* rankings, published yearly since 1990, include data from 31 items, including company awareness, advertising awareness, familiarity with and intention to buy shares, from over 1,000 leading companies. Several employment agencies in Japan publish job rankings for graduating university students. The *Nikkei Finance Organizations Ranking*, published yearly since 2004, bases its survey in the metropolitan area and includes several indexes about customer satisfaction.

Media Systems

Media Control   The Japanese constitution guarantees freedom of speech and freedom of publication. Under the free competition regime, all major media are privately owned, with the exception of NHK, the Japan Broadcasting Corporation. Nevertheless, the government has enacted several regulations concerning the media that have led to a closed market structure. The five national newspapers, *Yomiuri, Asahi, Mainichi, Nikkei,* and *Sankei,* comprise 53.3% of the total circulation (51.4 million) of morning newspapers in Japan (Dentsu Soken, 2004; Nihon Shinbun Kyokai, 2009a). Systems such as home delivery and price-stabilized merchandise have preserved the closed market. All but 5% (94.6%) of newspapers are home-delivered by delivery agents as of 2008 (Nihon Shinbun Kyokai, 2009a) and Japanese law prevents newspapers and distributors from offering discounted subscription rates. As a result, the top three major national newspapers and 11 local newspapers are sold at the same price for a monthly subscription (Nihon Shinbun Kyokai, 2005).

Four nationwide commercial TV broadcasting networks, Nippon TV, TBS, TV Asahi, and TV Tokyo, control the domestic market. Three of these four major TV stations, combined with Fuji TV, form a business alliance with the major newspapers. In addition, two large agencies, Dentsu and Hakuhodo, dominate the advertising market, handling 42.7% of the TV advertisements in Japan (Dentsu Soken, 2004). The closed market structure in the Japanese mass media has remained stable since 1960.

Media Outreach   Japan is a homogeneous nation in terms of media outreach. TV and radio broadcasting services are available nationwide except for some remote islands. The personal Internet use rate is 75.3% (Ministry of Internal Affairs and Communications, 2009). Digital broadcasting service emerged in three major cities in 2003, and should replace analog broadcasting nationwide by 2011. Despite the recent advent of various new media, TV broadcasting holds a dominant position with regard to media access. According to a Japan World Internet Project (2005) survey an individual averaged TV viewing time of 180.3 minutes per day, while the average time spent on reading newspapers was only 26.1 minutes.[1]

Japan's newspaper diffusion rate (65% of individuals read newspapers) is second only to Norway (Shibayama, 2006). However, most Japanese read newspapers for social columns and domestic political issues, not for business news When asked, "What stories do you usually read in the newspaper?" only 30.0% of the respondents chose business news, while about half of them chose social columns (50.8%) and domestic political issues (50.0%) (World Internet Project Japan, 2005).

Media Access As described previously, the *kisha club* (press club) acts as gatekeeper between the media and corporations in Japan. According to Shibayama (2006), there are about 900 press clubs in Japan, available only to the 145 member companies of Japan's Press Association. Seventy percent of news reports in major newspapers and 90% of news reports in local newspapers are released to the press clubs (Shibayama, 2006). The system supports the monopolistic control over news information by the major news media. In most major governmental, political, and business organizations, press clubs regulate access to and presentation of the news. In response to a 2003 European Community request to open the press club system because it prevented foreign and nonmainstream reporters from attending many press briefings and getting official press releases, Japan's Press Association retorted, "The kisha club is a voluntary institution for news-gathering and news-reporting activities made up of journalists who regularly collect news from public institutions and other sources" (Nihon Shinbun Kyokai, 2009b).

News Values

Because of Japan's media system, news values have been critically debated in connection with the unique characteristics of Japan's media system. Takahashi (1998) points out three problems of Japanese economic news reporting (p. 129): dependence on government authorized information; witch-hunt scandals; and lack of political and philosophical grounds. Major newspapers traditionally emphasize impartiality and political neutrality. The *Asahi* credo begins with the words "to be impartial and unbiased" (*Asahi Shimbun*, 2006b). Previous studies examined the homogeneity of news agendas in the Japanese newspapers. Zhang (2000) addressed the issue that, based on a content analysis of news stories from 1998, the two main newspapers, *Yomiuri* and *Asahi*, exhibit similar news agendas. Likewise, Hagiwara (2001) demonstrated a striking similarity among three major newspapers' news topics, as compared with TV news programs. Despite a highly competitive newspaper market, the Japanese press lacks diversity of news reports and demonstrates homogenous opinions (Westney, 1996). In opposition to the homogeneous news agendas of major media, minor media, such as magazines, books, and the Internet, exhibit autonomy for they are not members of the press clubs, and often engage in government criticism to a greater extent than the major media. For example, a magazine article prompted the resignation of former Prime Minister Kakuei Tanaka in 1974. Major media reporters, though aware of the prime minister's transgressions, would not report the alleged wrongdoing (Shibayama, 2006, p. 121).

Public Relations

U.S. General Douglas MacArthur introduced the concept of public relations to Japan in 1947 (Inoue, 2003); however, this concept is understood in a different way from the U.S. concept. Many Japanese believe that media relations activities are the core of public relations, necessitating a healthy relationship between the media and public relations practitioners (Inoue, 2003, p. 78). A Keizai Koho

Center survey (Japan Institute for Social and Economic Affairs, 2002)[2] found that Japanese companies' most important public is the press (48.3%), followed by shareholders and investors (14.5%), customers (13.6%), consumers (10.3%), finance analysts (4.3%), the local community (3.1%), and employers (2.9%). This result indicates that major Japanese companies value media relations. In response to consumers' ability to self-publish, Japanese companies now pay more attention to their reputation on the Internet. Gossip and rumors about companies are rampant on popular Web sites such as *ni-channeru* (2ch.net). To meet these demands, researchers have developed an automatic weblog monitoring system to measure opinions on the Internet (Okumura, Nanno, Fujiki, & Suzuki, 2004).

Hypotheses

Considering the Japanese media's homogeneity, major media are expected to significantly influence the public's awareness and image of companies.

First-Level Agenda-Setting: Media Visibility and Top-of-Mind Awareness   First-level agenda-setting is concerned with the salience of objects, in this case, the focal companies. Considering the key role of newspapers in business news, this study defines news media as the major Japanese newspapers. Newspapers were chosen because TV programs rarely report on focal companies, and because previous studies show that newspapers have a stronger agenda-setting effect than television (Takeshita, 1983). This study also considers advertising because it influences company awareness. Thus, the following two hypotheses were proposed:

Hypothesis 1a. The amount of news coverage about a company will be positively correlated with the level of awareness of the company.
Hypothesis 1b. The amount of advertising for a company will be positively correlated with the level of awareness of the company. Additionally, this study explored the relationship between the Internet and news coverage about a company:
Hypothesis 1c. The amount of news coverage about a company will be positively correlated with the number of messages posted on an electronic bulletin board about the company.

Second-Level, Substantive Agenda-Setting: Media Associations and Corporate Association   Substantive agenda-setting effects refer to the relationship between media and the public regarding cognitive attributes of objects. Carroll and McCombs (2003) listed a number of attributes that were found in previous reputation surveys; however, due to the lack of available data in Japan, only one attribute, research and development activity (R&D activity), was examined. Despite an enormous number of new products in the market, only some of them are reported in the news media. Thus, the following hypothesis was proposed:

Hypothesis 2. The amount of news coverage about new products will be associated with the perception of strong research and development activities of the company.

Second-Level, Affective Agenda-Setting: Valence and Organizational Image   Affective agenda-setting effects denote the relationship between the media and the public regarding evaluative attributes of the objects. First, a general hypothesis was proposed.

> *Hypothesis 3a.* A positive description of a company in the newspapers will be associated with company preference.

Both business leadership and the CEO's reputation are important attributes for corporate reputation (Carroll & McCombs, 2003). In effect, management is critical to building corporate reputation. Thus, we hypothesized links between the evaluation of corporate managers and news coverage about managers as well as between news coverage of CEOs and the image of a CEO.

> *Hypothesis 3b.* The amount of positive news coverage about managers will be associated with a better evaluation of managers of focal companies.
> *Hypothesis 3c.* The amount of news coverage about CEOs will be associated with a better image of the CEOs.

Methods

Three types of data were employed in this study: survey data (published corporate rankings), media data, and financial data. Fifty-eight leading food companies based in Japan were chosen as the focal companies. Since the survey data are based on a questionnaire completed by citizens, companies with widely marketed products, such as food companies, seemed more appropriate as a research target. Additionally, using companies from one industry eliminates differences between industries such as advertising spends or company sales.

Published Corporate Image Data   This study used data from the 2004 and 2005 *Nikkei Corporate Image Rankings*. Respondents between the ages of 18 and 69 were selected from a random sample of residents in Japanese metropolitan areas. To test the agenda-setting hypotheses, four series of rankings, including *corporate awareness, corporate preference, good manager perception,* and *perceived strong R&D activity,* were chosen from the published data. *Corporate awareness,* defined as the average response to questions about the awareness of companies, was scored on a 4-point scale based on increasing company awareness. Scored dichotomously, *corporate preference* was defined as the average response to a question concerning the likeability of a company. With regard to substantive attributes, two variables, *good manager perception* and *perceived strong R&D activity,* were operationalized. *Good manager perception* was scored as a percentage of responses to the statement: "the manager of the company is excellent." *Perceived strong R&D activity* was scored as a percentage of responses to the statement: "the company has strong research and new product development activity."

Content Analysis of News Articles   Media coverage about the focal companies in four major national newspapers (*Yomiuri, Asahi, Mainichi,* and *Nikkei*) was analyzed for the period from September 20, 2003 to September 20, 2005. Content was analyzed either electronically or by coders. Relevant news articles in which the focal companies were mentioned were retrieved from the database *Nikkei telecom 21*. Of the retrieved data, news articles with specified keywords (names of the CEOs of focal companies and "new product") were selected. Two independent coders analyzed a total of 323 articles with an interrater reliability of 0.764 (N = 219) and 0.620 for description of the focal companies and their managers, respectively (N = 213). Due to the time limitation, only major pages[3] in *Asahi* were analyzed. Coders were requested to rate the description of the focal company and its managers based on a 5-point Likert-type scale (with "1" meaning very negative and "5"meaning very positive). The *corporate description* score was defined as the average of the descriptions about the focal company. Likewise, the *management description* score was defined as the average of the descriptions of managers.[4]

Messages on the Internet   Messages on the BBS Web sites for the focal companies in *Yahoo! Japan* were analyzed for the period from September 2003 through September 2005.[5] *Finance data*. Sales and advertising expenditures were collected from existing data (Nikkei Advertising Research Institute, 2005).

Results

Table 8.1 summarizes descriptive statistics of the main variables in this study. Of the examined news articles from the *Asahi*, 44 (20.1%) of the articles were positive, 27 (12.3%) were negative, and 148 (67.6%) were neutral in terms of the description of the company. With regard to the description of managers, 59 (27.7%) were positive, 51 (23.9%) were negative, and 103 (48.4%) were neutral. Positive stories outnumbered negative stories about the focal companies. Negative news stories center on a few illegal acts involving the focal companies such as evading customs duties on imported pork, while positive news stories include a variety of topics such as new products, disaster recovery assistance, and eco-friendly activities.

Media Visibility

Corporate awareness was compared with the amount of advertising and the amount of coverage of the companies. The regression model was applied to the pooled data from 2004 and 2005. Table 8.2 indicates that advertising expenses significantly and positively correlate with awareness of the focal companies, while the number of news stories is not significantly correlated with corporate awareness. Hence, Hypothesis 1b is supported, while Hypothesis 1a is not supported. Interestingly, the estimated parameters suggest that an effect of one news article is equivalent to ¥0.696 million[6] expenditures (approximately U.S.$5.9 million) on advertising, albeit not being statistically significant.

Table 8.1 Descriptive Statistics of the Main Variables

	n	M	SD	Correlations								
				2	3	4	5	6	7	8	9	10
Finance variables												
1 Sales amount (a)	76	259	269	.89***	.44***	.39***	.60***	.57***	.40***	.04	-.07	.48***
2. Amount of advertising (a)	76	8.61	9.34		.40***	.46***	.70***	.68***	.47***	.07	.05	.42***
Public variables												
3. Awareness score	106	2.1	0.45			.93***	.26*	.33**	.30**	.00	-.03	.26*
4. Preference (%)	117	69.9	17.1				.30**	.45***	.27**	.04	.02	.11
5. Good manager perception (%)	75	4.4	2					.76***	.24*	.11	.13	.41**
6. Perceived strong R & D (%)	81	19.6	5.8						.35**			.32*
Media variables												
7. N of news stories	114	390	879							-.10	-.13	.16
8. Corporate description	118	3	0.26								.74***	.01
9. Manager description	118	3	0.38									.04
10. N of BBS messages	66	413	373									

Note. a: one billion yen. * p<.05, ** p<.01, *** p<.001

Table 8.2 Regression Estimation: Variables Predicting the Public Awareness and BBS Messages of the Focal Companies

	Public awareness (N=69)		Number of BBS messages (N=64)	
	Estimated parameters	t-value	Estimated parameters	t-value
Number of articles about the companies	0.000005112	0.228	0.02516	0.515
Amount of advertising expenses	0.007344	3.321**	16.91	3.36**
Constant	2.142		228.801	
R-square	0.182		0.182	

Note. N=62. **p<.01

Corporate News Topics

To test the relationship between the perception of *strong R&D activity* and the number of articles about new products, a regression model was applied. Table 8.3 indicates that, contradictory to the hypothesis, only the amount of advertising is significantly correlated with the perception of strong R&D activities. Therefore, Hypothesis 2 is not supported.

Corporate Image

To measure the effects of corporate image on the preference for a focal company, the regression model was employed. Table 8.4 indicates that only advertising is significantly correlated with a preference for the focal company. Negating Hypothesis 3a, corporate image in the newspaper is not associated with the public's preferences. In order to test the effects of news coverage with CEO names, the perception of good managers was regressed. Table 8.4 indicates that, after controlling for total amount of coverage about the focal companies, both the fre-

Table 8.3 Regression Estimation: Variables Predicting Perceived Strong R&D Activity

	Estimated parameters	t-value
Number of news articles	-0.000975	-1.3848
Amount of advertising	0.298	2.045*
Frequencies of new products	0.062	1.222
Constant	16.733	
R-square	0.502	

Note. N=55. *p<.05

Table 8.4 Variables Predicting Preference for the Companies and the Perception of Good Manager

	Corporate preference for the focal companies (N=75)		Perception of good manager (N=50)	
	Estimated parameters	t-value	Estimated parameters	t-value
Number of news articles	-0.0007305	-0.459	-0.000194	-0.807
Amount of advertising	0.579	3.999**	0.0569	1.524
Corporate description score	-1.26	-0.289		
Frequencies of CEO names			0.092	3.277**
Manager description score			1.229	2.082*
Constant	73.892		-0.319	
R-square	0.215		0.606	

Note. * p<0.05, ** p<0.01.

quency of CEO names and the manager description score in the newspapers are significantly correlated with the good manager score, supporting both Hypothesis 3b and Hypothesis 3c.

Discussion and Conclusions

Findings showed that advertising is more influential than news reports. A large advertising spend has a stronger influence on the public's awareness of the focal company than do news reports. It is important to note that the amount of advertising is strongly correlated with the sales amount. In general, a larger sales amount means that consumers are more likely to buy or see the company's products. Since the sales amount was not included as an independent variable in the regression models due to high multicollinearity, the estimated effects of the advertising may involve the effect of the sales amount.

Four hypotheses were tested regarding second-level agenda-setting effects. The findings revealed that both a positive description of company management and the frequencies of CEO names in newspapers led to better evaluation of the management of the focal companies. This result suggests that the status conferral function of the mass media (McCombs & Shaw, 1977) also applies to business news. Nevertheless, other hypotheses regarding agenda-setting effects were not supported. Only the amount of advertising was found to have a significant effect on the preference for the companies and the perception of strong R&D activities.

Despite the dominant position and low diversity of news reporting of Japanese major newspapers, news media do not have a strong agenda-setting effect on public awareness and attitudes about companies. These results suggest that, aside from the major news media, small media including magazines, books, and the Internet occupy a position of influence. The low diversity of news reports in Japanese major media may be balanced by such small media, which cover companies from a different viewpoint. A future study should consider the effects of these smaller media. Methodologically, this study has some limitations. First, the number of the focal companies is small because only food companies were considered. Second, aggregate data were employed in the analysis. A future study should test the hypotheses using individual-level data regarding more companies in different types of industries.

Notes

1. These averages were computed based on the total population, giving nonusers the value of zero.
2. The survey was conducted in 2002. A total of 484 large companies responded; of them, 81% are listed on the stock market (Keizai Koho Center, 2006).
3. Only articles on the front page, the first social column page, and the business news pages are considered. The front and first social column pages were most often accessed by readers. According to a survey by *Asahi Shimbun* (2006a), the readership rate is 88.2%, 87.1%, and 66.9%, for the front page, the first social column page, and the business news pages respectively.
4. The variable is defined for every fiscal year. If there is no news item about a company, a value of 3 (neutral) is given to the variable.
5. Companies listed on the stock market are considered in this analysis, because only these companies have BBS Web sites in Yahoo! Japan.
6. This is computed as 0.000005112/0.007344*1000=0.696.

References

Asahi Shimbun. (2006a). Asahi Shimbun koukokukyoku webusaito [Web site of the AD section of the *Asahi Shimbun*]. Retrieved from http://adv.asahi.com/2006/rs-page/index.html

Asahi Shimbun. (2006b). The *Asahi Shimbun* credo. Retrieved from http://www.asahi.com/shimbun/honsya/e/e-credo.html

Carroll, C. E., & McCombs, M. (2003). Agenda-setting effects of business news on the public's images and opinions about major corporations, *Corporate Reputation Review*, 6(1), 36–46.

Dentsu Soken [Dentsu Communication Institute Inc.]. (2004). *Joho media hakusyo 2005* [Information media white paper 2005]. Tokyo, Japan: Diamond.

Freeman, L. A. (2000). *Closing the shop: Information cartels and Japan's mass media.* Princeton, NJ: Princeton University Press.

Hagiwara, S. (2001). Nyusu bangumi no naiyo to keishiki [The content and form of news programs]. In S. Hagiwara (Ed.), *Henyosuru media to nyusu hodo* (pp. 67–114). Tokyo, Japan: Maruzen.

Inoue, T. (2003). An overview of public relations in Japan and self-correction concept. In K. Sriramesh & D. Verčič (Eds.), *The global public relations handbook: Theory, research, and practice* (pp. 68–85) Mahwah, NJ: Erlbaum.

Ishii, K. (1994). Keizai doko to syohi ishiki [Economic trends and consumer psychology]. In H. Akuto (Ed.), *Syohi kodo no syakai sinrigaku* (pp. 230–248). Tokyo, Japan: Fukumura Syoten.

Ishikawa, M. (1990). Media: Kenryoku heno eikyoryoku to kenryoku karano eikyoryoku [Media's impact: "To the powers that be" to "from the powers that be"]. *Leviathan*, 7, 30–48.

Ishikawa, M. (1995, February). Gidai-settei no hitsuyosei [Calling for agenda setting by the media]. *Shimbun Kenkyu*, 27–30.

Japan World Internet Project. (2005). Internet Usage in Japan—Survey Report 2005. Tokyo, Japan: Communications Research Laboratory.

Keizai Koho Center. (2006). Dai 8kai kigyo no ishiki jittai chosa houkokusyo [The 8th survey report on current status and awareness of public relations]. Retrieved from http://www.kkc.or.jp/pub/index.html

Krauss, E. S., & Lambert, P. (2002). The press and reform in Japan. *Harvard International Journal of Press/Politics*, 7(1), 57–78.

Maeda, T. (1978). Kodokushi to seiji-ishiki [Newspaper subscription and political consciousness]. *Hogaku-Kenkyu*, 51(5), 311–338.

McCombs, M. E., & Shaw, D. L. (1977). The agenda-setting function of the press. In D. L. Shaw & M. E. McCombs (Eds.), *The emergence of American political issues: The agenda-setting function of the press* (pp. 1–18). St. Paul, MN: West.

Ministry of Internal Affairs and Communications. (2009). Heisei 20nen Tsusin Doukou Chosa no Gaiyou [Overview of 2008 Telecommunication Survey]. Retrieved from http://www.soumu.go.jp/main_content/000016027.pdf

Nihon Shinbun Kyokai [Japan Newspaper Publishers and Editors Association]. (2005). *Nihon sinbun nenkan '05–'06* [Japan Newspaper Annual '05–'06]. Tokyo, Japan: Dentsu.

Nihon Shinbun Kyokai [Japan Newspaper Publishers and Editors Association]. (2009a). Circulation. Retrieved from http://www.pressnet.or.jp/english/index.htm

Nihon Shinbun Kyokai [Japan Newspaper Publishers and Editors Association]. (2009b). Kisha Club Guidelines. Retrieved from http://www.pressnet.or.jp/english/index.htm

Nikkei Advertising Research Institute. (2005). Yuuryoku kigyo no koukoku sendenhi [AD spending of leading Japanese corporations 2005]. Tokyo, Japan: Nikkei Advertising Research Institute.

Ogawa, T. (2001). Framing and agenda setting function: A comparative study between "objective fragmentary information" and "influential forecast information." *Keio Communication Review*, 23, 71–86.

Okada, N. (1979). Seiji [Politics]. In Z. Hayakawa, A. Fujitake, O. Nakano, H. Kitamura, & N. Okada (Eds.), *Masu-komyunikeishon nyumon* (pp. 147–171). Tokyo, Japan: Yuhikaku.

Okumura, M., Nanno, T., Fujiki, T., & Suzuki, Y. (2004). Automatic collection and monitoring of Japanese weblogs. *FIT2004* (7K-6). Retrieved from http://www.lr.pi.titech.ac.jp/blogwatcher/paper/fit2004.pdf

Sakurai, M. (2005). *Koporeito repyuteisyon* [Corporate reputation]. Tokyo, Japan: Chuokeizai.

Shibayama, T. (2006). *Nihon kata media shisutemu no kobo* [The rise and fall of the Japanese media system]. Kyoto, Japan: Minerva Shobo.

Sugita, S. (2002). Nihon no baburu to masu media [The bubble economy and mass media in Japan]. In M. Muramatsu & M. Okuno (Eds.), *Heisei baburu no kenkyuu (jyou)*. Tokyo, Japan: Toyokeizaishinposha.

Takahashi, F. (1998). *Keizai Hodo* [Economic news reporting]. Tokyo, Japan: Chuokoron.

Takeshita, T. (1983). Media gidai-settei kasetsu no jisshoteki-kento [An empirical examination of the media agenda-setting hypothesis]. *Todai Shimbun-Kenkyujo Kiyo, 31*, 101–143.

Takeshita, T. (1993). Agenda-setting effects of the press in a Japanese local election. *Studies of Broadcasting*, *29*, 194–216.

Takeshita, T., & Mikami, S. (1995). How did mass media influence the voters' choice in the 1993 general election in Japan? A study of agenda-setting. *Keio Communication Review*, *17*, 27–41.

Tokinoya, H. (1983). Gidai-settei riron ni yoru kokoku-koka no kenkyu [Agenda-setting theory and advertising effects]. In *16th Josei-Kenkyu-shu* (pp. 75–87). Tokyo, Japan: Yoshida Hideo Memorial Foundation.

Westney, D. E. (1996). Mass media as business organizations: A U.S.-Japanese comparison. In S. J. Pharr & E. S. Krauss (Eds.), *Media and politics in Japan* (pp. 47–88). Honolulu: University of Hawaii Press.

World Internet Project Japan. (2005). *Internet usage trends in Japan: Survey report 2005*. Tokyo, Japan: The National Institute of Information and Communications Technology.

Zhang, N. (2000). Nyusu hodo niokeru media kan no kyosinsei no kensyo [A test of inter-media consonance in news reporting]. *Masu Komyunikeisyon Kenkyuu*, *56*, 130–144.

9 Corporate Reputation and the News Media in the Netherlands

May-May Meijer

This chapter examines how media coverage in the Netherlands affects the public's perceptions of companies. Fombrun and Shanley (1990) conducted a pioneer study in this field which examined the impact of a wide range of variables on reputation (such as the amount of news, the tone of news, profitability, charitable giving). Findings from this study regarding the amount and tone of news recur in two other studies on the effects of news on reputation (Verčič, 2000; Wartick, 1992) and in a study on the effects of news on return on average assets (Deephouse, 2000).

Further studies (Carroll, 2004; Carroll & McCombs, 2003; Meijer & Kleinnijenhuis, 2006) examine the effects of issue-related news on corporate reputation. Organizations deal with issues such as the environment, employee diversity, profits, and product quality. Issue-related news enables experts and others to evaluate companies on the basis of issue performance; for example, to make informed decisions about purchasing products or selling stock warrants. The omnipresence of issues for organizations clarifies why, according to an overview (Botan & Taylor, 2004), issues management may be the foremost tool in public relations. Therefore, the effects of issue-related news on corporate reputation deserve attention. The agenda-setting theory (McCombs & Shaw, 1972) has been investigated widely with fairly robust results in the field of political communication, so it is logical to use this theory to investigate the effects of news on corporate reputation.

Review of the Literature

Corporate Reputation in the Netherlands

Academic corporate reputation research in the Netherlands has been driven by Van Riel et al. (Fombrun & Van Riel, 1997; Van Riel, 1997, 2001; Van Riel & Fombrun, 2002; Van Riel, Stroeker, & Maathuis, 1998). Van Riel is editor-in-chief of the *Corporate Reputation Review*, which he launched together with his American coeditor-in-chief Charles Fombrun. Increased publication in international peer-reviewed journals, along with Fombrun and Van Riel's collaboration, has made possible a study of the Dutch viewpoint of the concept of corporate reputation.

Meijer (2005) has noted that there are several definitions of the term *corporate reputation* (Dowling 1994; Fombrun, 1996; Maathuis, 1999). Different points of view exist regarding whether corporate reputation is an aggregated concept or whether it is possible to measure corporate reputation on the individual level. Fombrun (1996) argued that corporate reputation is an aggregated concept: the overall evaluation of several corporate images that exist among different stakeholders. More specifically, Fombrun portrayed corporate reputation as the overall evaluation of the customer image, community image, investor image, and employee image. In contrast, Dowling (1994) focused on the individual level. He used the terms *corporate reputation* and *corporate image* to describe the total beliefs and feelings an individual may hold about an organization.

Meijer (2005) proposes that corporate reputation be applied on the individual level. She uses the term *corporate reputation* to refer to the overall evaluation (usually in terms of good or bad) of an individual's mental associations regarding a company.

Agenda-Setting Theory

The agenda-setting concept is described in the Netherlands in both political communication studies (De Vreese, 2004; De Vreese & Boomgaarden, 2006; Kleinnijenhuis and Rietberg, 1995; Peter, 2003) and also in corporate communication research (Meijer 2005; Meijer & Kleinnijenhuis, 2006).

Peter (2003) tested the first level of agenda-setting effect, focusing on the issue of European integration. His study focused on the connection between exposure to news about the European Union (EU) by individuals and the nature of elite opinion on European integration at the country level. Content analysis was performed and survey data from 14 EU member states were linked at the individual level. Peter's (2003) results showed that more media coverage about the EU did not automatically increase the perceived importance of European integration. There was, however, a correlation between exposure to news about the EU and the nature of elite opinion. The more EU stories that respondents watched in countries in which political elites disagreed about European integration, the more important they considered European integration to be.

In addition to the media agenda and the public agenda, Kleinnijenhuis and Rietberg (1995) also focus on the political party agenda. The authors describe three models: the bottom up agenda-setting model (the political agenda responds to the public agenda); the top-down agenda-setting model (the political agenda sets the media agenda, which in turn sets the public agenda); and the mediacracy model (both the public and the political agenda are influenced by the media agenda). The research method consisted of linking three different types of data from 1980 to 1986: European Manifestos to measure the political agenda, content analysis of political-economic news to measure the media agenda, and data on public concern to measure the public agenda. Six economic issues were focused upon in these datasets: taxes and premiums, leveling of incomes, real wages, GNP, inflation, and social security expenditures. The numbers from these issues, published in the Netherlands by the Central Office of Statistics, were used as a control variable. Kleinnijenhuis and Rietberg (2005) found that the top-down model and the bottom-up model were confirmed. The model of mediacracy was rejected; the media agenda does not reflect the public agenda.

To our knowledge, Meijer's (2005) dissertation, which was supervised by Kleinnijnenhuis, is the first study in the Netherlands to apply agenda-setting theory to business. The data from the dissertation will be used in this chapter.

Business and the News Media

Several studies have examined the relationship between business and the news media in the Netherlands (Hoeken & Renkema, 1997; Van Lunenburg, 2001). Hoeken and Renkema (1997) studied the effects of negative publicity on corporate image. Their study showed that negative publicity worsens corporate image. After 2 weeks, the damage was still there.

Van Lunenburg (1999) investigated whether the type of industry influences media visibility and tone of news about 25 large Dutch companies, which are listed on the Amsterdam Stock Exchange. Content analysis was used to analyze the news in five national newspapers. Van Lunenburg found that newspapers were significantly more negative about business activity in the transport sector (airline KLM, Nedloyd) and hardware sector (companies such as Philips and Telecom company KPN). The newspapers were significantly more positive about financial companies than about companies from other industries. The transport sector, the hardware sector, and the financial sector received the most media attention of the industries tracked. As suggested by Van Lunenburg (1999), further research needs to include the size of the company and should take into account the number of press reports that were released by the companies as well, which may influence the amount of media coverage. Based on this dataset Van Lunenburg (2001) investigated whether there are differences between the five national newspapers in reporting about the 25 companies. She found that the newspapers differ little in their reporting about the companies.

The first level of agenda setting deals with the salience of an issue or an organization (Carroll & McCombs, 2003). If there is a lot of news about the environment and respondents mention the environment as one of the most important problems facing the world today, this indicates a first-level agenda-setting effect. This hypothesis will not be tested in this chapter.

The second level of agenda setting deals with the *attributes* of the issue or the organization concerned (Carroll & McCombs, 2003). If Shell is repeatedly in the news with its pollution of the environment and respondents associate the actor "Shell" with the attribute "environment," a second-level agenda-setting effect is said to be present. Or to put it simply: in the case of the first level of agenda setting, only one actor or issue is involved, whereas in the case of the second level of agenda setting, *the attributes* of that actor or issue are involved as well. Carroll and McCombs (2003) distinguished between the substantive and affective second level of agenda setting. In the case of substantive agenda setting the effects of the prominence of attributes in the news on the relative salience of these attributes are studied. This hypothesis can be formulated as follows:

Hypothesis 1: The greater the amount of news devoted to particular attributes of a company, the more people will define the company by these attributes.

Carroll and McCombs (2003) focused on the effects of the tone of the attributes in the news on how the public will perceive that attribute for evaluative agenda setting. This hypothesis will not be tested in the present study.

Case Study

Corporate Reputation in the Netherlands

The Netherlands is part of the Global Reputation Quotient (RQ) project, which is described by Van Riel and Fombrun (2002). The RQ is a standardized measurement instrument that is used to track the reputations of companies. The RQ consists of six dimensions: emotional appeal, products and services, vision and leadership, workplace environment, social and environmental responsibility, and financial performance (see Fombrun, Gardberg, & Sever, 2000 for a more detailed description of the development of the RQ). Since 2001, the Dutch RQ data have been gathered annually by commercial research agency Blauw in the Netherlands and published in the Dutch business magazine *Incompany 500*. The Dutch transnational company Philips has the best reputation, followed by the Dutch airline KLM, and the Dutch transnational company TNT (Smit, 2006, p. 15). Van Riel and Fombrun (2002) state that the RQ methodology is the first standardized measurement instrument to be systematically carried out on a global scale (United States, Canada, Australia, South Africa, and 12 European countries). The nominations for the most visible companies in 13 countries are presented in the same issue of the *Corporate Reputation Review*.

Media Systems

Sriramesh (1999) describes three factors (media control, media outreach, and media access) that can be used by public relations professionals in order to design their media relations strategy. In this section these three factors are described and applied to the situation in the Netherlands. Sriramesh and Verčič (2003) postulate that in order to maintain a good relationship with the media, public relations professionals need to understand who *controls* the media organizations in a country and whether such control extends to editorial content. The Dutch media are free and independent. Nevertheless, after the Second World War discussions began about "press concentration" (De Bakker & Scholten, 2003). De Bakker and Scholten distinguish three different forms of concentration: editorial concentration (the mergers of editorships); public concentration (the public divides itself disproportionately over several newspapers); and concentration of publishers (mergers of publishers). As is stated by De Bakker and Scholten, journalists regard editorial concentration and concentration of publishers with suspicion. Concentration of publishers is seen as a forerunner to the loss of editorial independence. This could affect the quality of the societal debate by reducing the number of individual voices taking part in it. However, De Bakker and Scholten (2003) note that a concentration of editorships may result in greater diversity of opinions among the remaining newspapers.

The media outreach in the Netherlands will focus on the circulation numbers of the national newspapers and the viewer rating of Dutch television news. De Bakker and Scholten (2003) estimated that the national newspapers reach approximately 64% of Dutch households. These figures do not take into account that some households read more than one newspaper or share a newspaper. De Bakker and Scholten indicate that the coverage percentage of 64% has been declining since the mid-1970s. The circulation numbers of the leading national newspapers in the Netherlands are as follows: *De Telegraaf* (15.6%), *ADN Dagbladen* (12.3%), *de Volkskrant* (5.5%), *NRC Handelsblad* (3.7%), *Trouw* (2.3%), *Refomatorisch Dagblad* (1.8%), *Nederlands Dagblad* (1.6%), and *Het Financieele Dagblad* (0.9%). *ADN Dagbladen* has a 56-page national section with 8 pages of regional news. There are two free national newspapers distributed at railway stations: *Metro* (12.3%) and *Spits* (12.7%). Subscriptions to daily newspapers are responsible for 85% of the total circulation (De Bakker & Scholten, 2003). This makes the Netherlands a suitable country for testing the effects of media coverage in a real-life situation.

The Netherlands has a dual broadcasting system for television and radio, which consists of a public and a commercial system. There are three public television channels, which are financed primarily by the state and to a smaller extent by advertising revenues. The seven largest commercial television channels are owned by the Holland Media Group (RTL 4, RTL 5, RTL 7, and RTL 8) or by the Scandinavian Broadcasting System (SBS 6, Net 5, Veronica). The public national broadcasting company's 8:00 p.m. NOS news usually has the highest viewer ratings of all news shows. After that come the 7:30 p.m. news on the commercial channel RTL 4 and the commercial news show *Hart van Nederland* with the highest viewer ratings. Hart van Nederland is a news show with a specific national and regional character.

Media access is defined as the extent to which various segments of a society can approach the media to disseminate messages they deem important (Shriramesh, 1999). Compared to other countries, media access in the Netherlands seems to be good. The NGO Reporters without Borders presented its Press Freedom Index 2006 on October 23, 2006. Freedom of expression is highest in the press of the Netherlands, Ireland, Iceland, and Finland.

Research Methodology

This study used media content analysis and poll data from 1998, 1999, and 2000. Bearing in mind the generalizability of the results, it was decided to examine industrial companies, with two companies from each industry: the oil industry (Shell and British Petroleum); the banking industry (ABN Amro and the

Rabobank); the retail trade food industry (Albert Heijn and Super de Boer); the transport industry (Dutch Railways and Amsterdam Airport Schiphol); and two professional sectors, the Dutch Police and Dutch Agriculture. Two focal companies from each industry were selected in order to make sure that, in general, they were coping with similar issues, such as economic development, environmental problems, consumers, and stakeholders. Large organizations and professional sectors were selected in order to ensure enough news was generated about the companies to study news effects.

Content Analysis The coders coded the frequency of news about the various issues. For each of the industries, a list of issues was compiled. Examples of issues in the case of Shell and BP are profit, mergers, and the environment (news about sustainable products). Of the companies tracked, Schiphol and the Dutch police received the most media attention,[1] whereas BP and Super de Boer received the least media attention.[2]

Choice of News Media Media coverage of the tracked companies in newspapers and on television was analyzed for the period from July 24, 1997 to July 22, 2000. This period was selected in agreement with public opinion polling data; all the media coverage from the year preceding the poll was analyzed. The newspaper articles were selected from the five largest Dutch daily newspapers: *De Telegraaf, Algemeen Dagblad, NRC Handelsblad, Trouw,* and *de Volkskrant.* Of television news, broadcasts of the public broadcasting company NOS and the commercial channel RTL 4 were analyzed.

The relevant articles were retrieved from electronic newspaper archives (Lexis-Nexis, Nederlandse Persdatabank). The key terms used to retrieve the articles contained the name, and, if available, the abbreviation of the focal company. This resulted in 9,285 articles. The *headlines* of all articles were analyzed. A weight factor was used to take into account the position of the article in the publication (the page number)[3] and the magnitude of the article (see appendix).

Data about news broadcasts by the public broadcasting company NOS and the commercial channel RTL 4 were gathered in cooperation with both organizations, which have archives with transcriptions of spoken text). In the case of television news, the transcriptions were analyzed, whereas in the case of print news, only headlines were coded. A total of 2,225 news items were analyzed. A weight factor was used to take into account the importance of items within a news item (see appendix).

Public Opinion Polls A market research agency, TNS NIPO, conducted a survey with respect to the tracked companies and sectors among their representative sample of respondents. The data were gathered by using the NIPO Telepanel. This is a national representative panel made up of approximately 1,000 households, all of which are provided with computers. The respondents received and returned the questionnaires via a modem. To prevent the respondents from finding the questions tedious, they were required to fill out the questions for only six organizations (and not for all 10).

The panel surveys were conducted in the summer of three consecutive years from 1998 to 2000. Not all respondents took part in each of the three waves: 606 respondents took part once; 306 respondents took part twice; and 446 respondents took part three times. This resulted in approximately 830 respondents for the cross-sectional tests per company. For the models with a lagged dependent variable (autoregressive models), approximately 280 respondents per company were available. This number is considerably lower because respondents have to participate at least twice in consecutive years to be included in the autoregressive models.

Data Analysis

The focus of the empirical part of this chapter will be on the second level of agenda-setting hypothesis. The more attention a medium devotes to an issue in the context of organizational news, the higher the likelihood that this issue will become a salient association with an organization in the minds of the users of that medium. In this study the term *corporate associations* is used to refer to an individual's beliefs about a company (Brown & Dacin, 1997). The salience of corporate associations was measured by asking the respondents to choose their two most salient associations from a checklist consisting of 12 substantive potential associations and the categories "Don't know" and "Other." The checklist for each of the organizations consisted of issues related to the core business of an organization (e.g., gasoline stations in the case of oil companies, diversity of products in the case of supermarkets); economic performance criteria (e.g., profits, prices, efficiency); and a few societal issues (e.g., the environment). Items that were on opposite sides of one association, such as efficiency and inefficiency, were offered as two different associations to the respondents. Such related items, as well as associations that were mentioned infrequently, were recoded afterwards, after which 8 to 10 associations remained for each organization, with the police (5) and agriculture (6) as exceptions. The salience of corporate associations is a binary variable. The value "0" was assigned if a certain association was not salient, the value "1" was assigned if a certain association was salient.

In accordance with the second-level agenda-setting hypothesis, it is expected that if respondents are asked what they think of when they think about an organization, they will mention associations (issues) that are mentioned in the media. This results in the following equation:

$$\text{Salience}_{i, a, t, o} = b_0 + b1 \, (\text{Freq. of issues television news}_a) + b2 \, (\text{Freq. of issues print news}_a) + e_i$$

Because the dependent variable is dichotomous, logistic regression was used.

Results

It appears from Table 9.1 that the amount of news about a certain issue influences the salience of that issue. This means that the more Shell was in the news

Table 9.1 Logistic Regression Analysis of the Frequency of Issue News on Issue Salience

Predictors (variable names)	Cross-sectional		Autoregressive	
	B	Odds Ratio	B	Odds Ratio
Frequency of issues television news	.01***	1.01	.01***	1.01
Frequency of issues print news	.01***	1.01	0.006	1.01
Salience issue, t-1			-2.54***	12.61
Constant	-2.28***		-2.81***	
Nagelkerke R2	0.03		0.22	
N	118,893		41,697	

Note. Cell entries are unstandardized regression coefficients and odds ratios from binary logistic regression. For BP, no significant media effects were found. General issues were not included in the models.

in relation to the issue "environment," the more respondents associated Shell with the "environment." This was the case for both television news about a certain issue (*B* television news = .01, odds ratio = 1.01) and for print news about a certain issue (*B* print news = .01, odds ratio = 1.01) in the cross-sectional model. In the pooled model, only the effect of television news remained significant after controlling for the lagged salient association.

Separate models were made per organization (these models are not shown in Table 9.1). These models were in agreement with the results that were found in the pooled model. It appeared that television news about issues had a positive influence on the salience of association for the models of eight organizations, while issue news in the print media was significant in the predicted direction in models of six organizations. Remarkably, in the case of the supermarkets and the agricultural sector, a negative effect of the amount of news on the salience of an issue was also found. In the case of Albert Heijn and the agricultural sector, these effects disappeared in the autoregressive model. In the case of Super de Boer, this effect remained in the autoregressive model.

Conclusions

This study showed that theories from the field of political communication apply in a business communication context, as was already argued by Carroll and McCombs (2003). Meijer's (2005) dissertation, which was supervised by Kleinnijenhuis, is the first study in the Netherlands to apply agenda setting to business. In applying a second level of agenda setting, this study focused on the different issues with which the companies were associated with in the news. This is what McCombs, Llamas, Lopez-Escobar, and Rey (1997) and McCombs, Lopez-Escobar, and Llamas (2000) refer to as the "substantive (or cognitive)" dimension of the attribute agenda. The substantive aspects of political candidates include their issues positions, perceived qualifications, personality, and integrity. In the Netherlands, studies focused on the first and the second level of agenda setting are scarce; more studies in this field should be conducted. The Netherlands is a suitable country for testing the effects of media coverage in a real-life situation. As noted above, subscriptions to daily newspapers are responsible for 85% of the total circulation here (De Bakker & Scholten, 2003).

In addition, future studies on issue ownership in a business context may focus on the question of which issues should be downplayed or emphasized to enhance the corporate reputation of specific firms. Studies that cross the borders of the subdisciplines of communication science (political communication, public relations, organizational communication, interpersonal communication) may add to the understanding of communication phenomena in each subdiscipline.

Notes

1. Schiphol $n_{issues, 1998} = 768$, $n_{issues, 1999} = 520$, $n_{issues, 2000} = 282$; Dutch police $n_{issues, 1998} = 495$, $n_{issues, 1999} = 477$, $n_{issues, 2000} = 307$.
2. BP $n_{issues, 1998} = 7$, $n_{issues, 1999} = 53$, $n_{issues, 2000} = 9$; Super de Boer $n_{issues, 1998} = 30$, $n_{issues, 1999} = 2$, $n_{issues, 2000} = 6$

References

Botan, C. H., & Taylor, M. (2004). Public relations: State of the field. *Journal of Communication, 54*(4), 645–661.

Brown, T. J., & Dacin, P. A. (1997). The company and the product: Corporate association and consumer product responses. *Journal of Marketing*, 61, 68–84.

Carroll, C. E. (2004). *How the mass media influence perceptions of corporate reputation: Exploring agenda-setting effects within business news coverage.* Unpublished doctoral dissertation, The University of Texas at Austin, Austin, Texas.

Carroll, C. E., & McCombs, M. E. (2003). Agenda-setting effects of business news on the public's images and opinions about major corporations. *Corporate Reputation Review, 6*(1), 36–46.

De Bakker, P., & Scholten, O. (2003). *Communicatiekaart van Nederland* [Communication map of the Netherlands]. Alphen aan de Rijn, The Netherlands: Kluwer.

Deephouse, D. L. (2000). Media reputation as a strategic resource: An integration of mass communication and resource-based theories. *Journal of Management, 26*(6), 1091–1112.

De Vreese, C. H. (2004). The effects of frames in political television news on issue interpretation and frame salience. *Journalism and Mass Communication Quarterly, 81*(1), 36–47.

De Vreese, C. H., & Boomgaarden, H. G. (2006). Media message flows and interpersonal communication: The conditional nature of effects on public opinion. *Communication Research, 33*(1), 19–37.

Dowling, G. R. (1994). *Corporate reputations: Strategies for developing the corporate brand.* London: Kogan Page.

Fombrun, C. J. (1996). *Reputation: Realizing value from the corporate image.* Boston, MA: Harvard Business Schoool Press.

Fombrun, C. J., Gardberg, N. A., & Sever, J. M. (2000). The Reputation Quotient SM: A multi-stakeholder measure of corporate reputation. *The Journal of Brand Management, 7*(4), 241–255.

Fombrun, C. J., & Van Riel, C. B. M. (1997). The reputational landscape. *Corporate Reputation Review, 1*(1–2), 5–13.

Fombrun, C. J., & Shanley, M. (1990). What's in a name? Reputation building and corporate strategy. *Academy of Management Journal, 33*(2), 233–258.

Hoeken, H., & Renkema, J. (1997). Negatief in het nieuws. Een experimenteel onderzoek naar de invloed van negatieve publiciteit op het bedrijfsimago [Negative in the news: An experimental study of the influence of negative publicity on corporate image]. *Tijdschrift voor Communicatiewetenschap, 25,* 98–115.

Hoeken, H., & Renkema, J. (2000). Can corrections repair the damage to a corporate image caused by negative publicity? *Corporate Reputation Review: an international journal, 2*(1), 52–61..

Kleinnijenhuis, J., & Rietberg, E. M. (1995). Parties, media, the public and the economy: Patterns of societal agenda-setting. *European Journal of Political Research,* 95–118.

Maathuis, O. J. M. (1999). *Corporate branding: the value of the corporate brand to customers and managers.* (Unpublished doctoral dissertation). Erasmus University, Rotterdam, the Netherlands.

McCombs, M., Llamas, J. P., Lopez-Escobar, E., & Rey, F. (1997). Candidate images in Spanish elections: second-level agenda-setting effects. *Journalism & Mass Communication Quarterly, 74*(4), 703–717.

McCombs, M., Lopez-Escobar, E., & Llamas, J. P. (2000). Setting the agenda of attributes in the 1996 Spanish general election. *Journal of Communication, 50*(2), 77–92.

McCombs, M. E., & Shaw, D. L. (1972). The agenda-setting function of the mass media. *Public Opinion Quarterly, 36,* 176–187.

Meijer, M. M. (2005). *Does success breed success? Effects of news and advertising on corporate reputation.* Amsterdam, the Netherlands: Aksant.

Meijer, M. M., & Kleinnijenhuis, J. (2006). Issue news and corporate reputation: Applying the theories of agenda setting and issue ownership in the field of business communication. *Journal of Communication, 56,* 543–559.

Peter, J. (2003). Country characteristics as contingent conditions of agenda setting: The moderating influence of polarized elite opinion. *Communication Research, 30*(6), 683–712.

Smit, R. (2006, May 17). Nederlandse consument vertrouwt bank: Philips komt als beste uit reputatieonderzoek, energieaanbieder Oxxio als slechtste [Dutch consumer trust bank: Philips comes out best of reputation study, energy supplier Oxxio worst]. *Het Financieele Dagblad,* 15.

Sriramesh, K., & Vercic, D. (2003). *The global public relations handbook,* Mahwah NJ: Erlbaum.

Van Lunenburg, M. (1999). Berichtgeving over bedrijven: Inhoudsanalyse van berichten over vijfentwintig grote ondernemingen in Nederland [Media coverage about companies: Content analysis of articles about twenty five large companies in the Netherlands]. *Tijdschrift voor Communicatiewetenschap, 27*(2), 152–166.

Van Lunenburg, M. (2001). Vijf dagbladen: een gezicht! Hoe pluriform zijn Nederlandse dagbladen in hun berichtgeving over Nederlandse bedrijven? [Five newspapers: one look! How diverse are Dutch newspapers in their coverage of Dutch companies?]. *Tijdschrift voor Communicatiewetenschap, 29*(3), 168–185.

Van Riel, C. B. M. (1997). *Identiteit en imago: Grondslagen van corporate communication* [Identity and image: Foundations of corporate communication]. (2nd ed.). Schoonhoven, the Netherlands: Academic Service.

Van Riel, C. B. M. (2001). Corporate communication: Het managen van reputatie [Corporate communication: The management of reputation]. Alphen aan den Rijn, The Netherlands: Kluwer.

Van Riel, C. B. M. & Fombrun, C. J. (2002). Special issue on the global RQ-project: The nominations phase. *Corporate Reputation Review, 4*(4), 296–302.

Van Riel, C. B. M., Stroeker, N. E., & Maathuis, O. J. M. (1998). Measuring corporate images. *Corporate Reputation Review, 1*(4), 313–326.

Verčič, D. (2000). *Trust in organizations: A study of the relations between media coverage, public perceptions and profitability.* Unpublished doctoral dissertation, The London School of Economics and Political Science, London.

Wartick, S. L. (1992). The relationship between intense media exposure and change in corporate reputation. *Business & Society, 31*(1), 33–49.

Appendix: *The Weight Factor to Weight the News*

There are two weight factors for newspaper articles: one weight factor takes into account the page number of the article, and another weight factor takes into account the total number of words in the article. An article on the front page is assigned the value "2." The articles on pages 2 and 3 are assigned the same weight factor, namely 0.91 (which is 1/ln (page number) in the case of even page numbers, and 1/ln(page number +1) in the case of uneven page numbers). It was assumed that the economic section is important for people with an interest in news about companies. While the economic section usually starts on page 11, page 11 is assigned the same value as an article on page 3 in the case of news about companies. The weight factor, which is composed of the number of words, is a linear weight factor that is topped off at the top and at the bottom. The two weight factors are multiplied and divided by 2 (the weight factor of the page number and the weight factor of the number of words have the same weight in the total weight factor).

The weight factor of television news is based on the viewer ratings of a random week in the middle of the research period. The eight o'clock evening news, which is watched most often, was assigned the maximum value of "2." The newscast watched the least was assigned the minimum value of "0.5."

The "total" weight factor of newspaper and television news is applied in such a way that before and after weighting the dataset consisted of approximately the same number of assertions. This is done by first calculating the sum of the weight factor. Subsequently, the sum of the weight factor is divided by the original number of assertions. That outcome is multiplied by the weight factor. After multiplication, the sum of the new weight factor equals the original number of assertions.

10 Corporate Reputation and the News Media in Norway

Øyvind Ihlen and Peggy Simcic Brønn

Since the time of the Vikings, reputation has been of great concern to Norwegians. The following stanza from *The Poetic Edda* illustrates this concern (1996):

> Cattle die, kinsmen die
> the self must also die;
> I know one thing that never dies:
> the reputation of each dead man.

Though little empirical research has been conducted on the effect of the media on corporate reputation in Norway, there is an increasing interest in the concept. Many studies could not find any strong media effect on corporate reputation, but one experimental study indicated that media influenced the attributes that individuals assigned to a company.

Agenda Setting

Many people believe they "know" a business or a business leader based on what is presented in the news. Conversely, many businesses and business leaders believe their images are a result of media coverage, thus believing that any negative images are the media's fault. For public relations practitioners, attaining media coverage is a major objective. To a practitioner, if a firm or individual is of interest to the media, then they must be interesting and relevant news. Additionally, journalists, theoretically, are nonbiased, so that what they write is "truth" and is thus more credible than a company's statements about itself. Research on the credibility of information sources support practitioners beliefs, demonstrating that business media, magazines in particular, rate as the most credible source for company news (Edelman, 2009). In contrast, the credibility of a company's own communications department in 2009 was rated half as credible as it was in 2008. Further, company spokespersons such as CEOs and CFOs are ranked even lower, steadily falling in recent years.

It is interesting to study agenda-setting theory in the context of image/reputation and the media. Walter Lippmann (1922/2004) stated that people experience reality through pictures in their heads, pictures that are often "placed" in one's head by the media. According to early agenda-setting theory researchers

McCombs and Shaw (1972/1997) mass media "set the agenda" by highlighting certain issues. They believed that the media do not tell us *what* to think, but rather what to think *about*. Or, as formulated by Bernard C. Cohen: "[The press] may not be successful much of the time in telling people what to think, but it is stunningly successful in telling its readers what to think about" (Cohen, 1963, p. 13).

Two basic assumptions behind most agenda-setting research are that the press and the media do not reflect reality; they filter and shape it, and media concentration on a few issues and subjects leads the public to perceive those issues as more important than other issues. Consequently, the media are seen as having a gate-keeping function, selecting what is important and what is not. Other concepts include priming, the idea that media draw attention to some aspects of political life and not others, and framing, the presentation of information in a way that guides its interpretation. Thus, it is easy to understand corporations' concerns with how they are portrayed in the media and what effect this may have on their reputation. As noted by Argenti (1998), the rise of interest in business by the public has never been greater as the public has become more aware of the impact of business on their lives. This statement raises the question of whether consumers are more aware of corporations and corporate behavior due to their own interests or whether the media is "setting the agenda." Additionally, it is important to determine if and how reputation rankings influence the public's opinion of firms.

Norway and the Media

Norway, a small country with 4.8 million inhabitants, is a strong welfare state with low levels of conflict. In this and the two following sections, we describe the situation in Norway in regard to the media, corporate reputation, and the practice of public relations.

The Norwegian media market is described in several English language publications (see Carlsson & Harrie, 2001; Harrie, 2003), and national statistics can also be found at the Web site MedieNorge (http://medienorge.uib.no/). Here we will concentrate on the landscapes of newspapers, television/radio, and ownership structures.

Newspapers

Since the Second World War, Norwegian newspapers have boasted high circulation numbers. The average Norwegian household buys 1.5 newspapers each day (Høst, 1998). During most of the 1990s, the total daily circulation was approximately 3.1 million (Høst 2000, as cited in Østbye, 2001). Given that Norway only has a population of 4.8 million, this is quite a large number. In 2008, 68% of the population had read a newspaper, a decrease from 84% in 1991 (http://medienorge.uib.no/, accessed June 26, 2009). The Norwegian press structure has been unique, with local papers, strong regional papers, and the national press. In total about 220 titles are published (Østbye, 2001). Historically, political par-

Table 10.1 Circulation Figures of the Five Largest Norwegian Newspapers 2008

Name	Circulation	Owner
VG	284,414	Schibsted
Aftenposten Morgen	247,556	Schibsted
Aften	124,807	Schibsted
Dagbladet	123,383	Orkla Media
Bergens Tidende	85,825	Mediehuset Bergens Tidende

Note. Source: http://medienorge.uib.no/, accessed June 26, 2009

ties have owned the Norwegian papers, but this system crumbled during the 1960s (Høyer, 1995). Today, three large owners dominate the market: Schibsted, A-pressen, and Orkla Media. The 2008 circulation figures of the five largest newspapers are listed in Table 10.1.

Television and Radio

Until 1981, the government-owned Norwegian Broadcasting System (NRK), funded through TV license fees, monopolized television and radio services. In the early 1990s, the commercial television station TV2 and the radio station P4 were granted concessions. Later the television stations TV Norge and TV3 began broadcasting. The Swedish company MTG, the principal owner of TV3 has fought for the past few years for its national concession with Kanal24. NRK maintained dominance, holding three of four nationwide stations (Harrie, 2003). In 2008, 80% of the population watched television daily. Table 10.2 illustrates the market share of each station, as well as names of the owners (http://medienorge.uib.no/ accessed June 26, 2009).

Ownership and Regulation

The NRK monopoly was ended in 1981, and since that time Norwegian politicians have been concerned that there has been a tendency toward ownership concentration. This tendency has fostered new regulatory bodies (The Media Ownership Authority) and new legislation (The Media Ownership Act) with the aim of ensuring freedom of expression and continued media access.

Table 10.2 Market Shares of Norwegian Television Stations 2008

Name	Share	Owner
NRK	32	Publicly owned
TV2	25	A-pressen, Egmont
TV Norge	8	ProSiebenSat1
TV3	6	MTG
NRK2	3	Publicly owned

Note. Source: www.tns-gallup.no/medier, accessed June 26, 2009)

Dual leadership has been the tradition in Norwegian newspapers, with a general manager handling finances, administration, and technology, while the editor-in-chief maintains sole responsibility for the content. Owners could influence overall editorial policy, but were expected to refrain from daily editorial leadership. After the year 2000, this structure changed in some newspapers giving way to a unified management system. This transformation was vigorously debated (Østbye, 2001). In 2006, another debate arose when Orkla Media was sold to Mecom, a British investment company.

News Values

Starting in the 1960s, the party press structure began to fall apart, and in the 1990s, new commercial television stations were established. The largest circulation newspapers had previously demonstrated an outspoken party affiliation with corresponding news values; they relied on similar journalistic news ideology. Now all the news media are owned by investors and publishing companies, and are run on business terms. In other words, the news media have become profit-making institutions. The conditions for the government-owned broadcasting stations have also changed and they now wish to compete with commercial stations in order to preserve their legitimacy as publicly funded through license fees (Allern, 2001b).

Norwegian tabloid newspapers uniquely serve a mixture of hard-hitting news, political journalism, and celebrity gossip, setting them apart from, for instance, their German counterpart *The Bild-Zeitung* or the British newspaper *The Sun*. A content analysis of 10 Norwegian newspapers revealed that the typical Norwegian newspaper was an informative, regional, or local paper that carried a wide mixture of content in each issue. The analysis concluded that the Norwegian press, in general, was serious and focused on issues of social importance. At the same time, however, the analysis pointed out that few nonpowerful sources were used; a preference for elites and patriarchal values was found (Allern, 2001b). Studies of business news have documented the same elite orientation (Slaatta, 2003).

An analysis of the NRK and TV2 television news indicated that the former covered political news from an idealized citizen perspective, while the latter adopted a consumer perspective. TV2 emphasized crime more than NRK, and on the whole it was suggested that the two stations had developed their own news perspectives, representing existing traits found in the Northern European news culture (Waldahl, Andersen, & Rønning, 2002).

Corporate Reputation in Norway

In Norway, the concept of corporate reputation has become considerably more popular over the last few years (Brønn & Ihlen, 2009), demonstrated by a rise of image or reputation measurements and rankings published by the media, often in cooperation with private research agencies. This growth arguably started with the MMI-*Aftenposten* (now Synovate) image survey and has expanded to include others such as *Best Place to Work in Norway, Firms with the Most Women on the Board, the Top Ten Hotels, the Most Preferred Place to Work by Students, the Top 10 Leaders, the Best Liked Sport Club.* In 2003, the Reputation Quotient (RQ) methodology (see for instance, Fombrun, Gardberg, & Sever, 2000) was introduced, receiving a great deal of media coverage from the Norwegian business press. The RQ instrument is based on attributes as defined by the agenda-setting theory, including the six dimensions of financial success, vision and leadership, product performance, corporate social responsibility, workplace environment, and emotional appeal, which includes the concept of trust. The older instrument, MMI, uses four attributes: quality of information, environmental and ethical position, financial performance, and overall perception of the firm.

A simple word search of reputation on the web-based news archive *Retriever A-tekst* illustrates the increased interest in the topic (see Figure 10.1). Mentions of reputation were relatively stable from 1995 until 2003, but nearly tripled within the 5 years after the Reputation Institute introduced its annual reputation rankings in Norway in 2003. The increase in the media's coverage of reputation may have begun as a result of the first survey released that year by the country's leading business daily *Dagens Næringsliv* (Ottesen, 2006).

The word *reputation* is most often translated as the Norwegian *omdømme*. At the same time, a textual analysis of the Internet sites of Norwegian public relations agencies, as well as citations from the professional press, showed a striking tendency: The English word *image* was often used synonymously with reputation, or *omdømme* (Moen, 2005). In other words, the analysis indicated that the agencies were not abreast of the scholarly debate on the differences between identity, image, and reputation.

Little academic research has been conducted on the topic of reputation in Norway. Currently, three articles have been published in scholarly journals, and

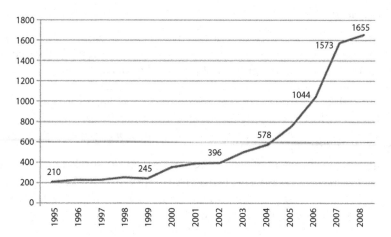

Figure 10.1 Frequency of the word reputation ("Omdømme") in Norwegian news media 1995–2008

at least 12 master's theses or doctoral dissertations have been generated on the subject of reputation or image between 2000 and 2009. The first published article, a theoretical critique of the RQ, suggested Data Envelopment Analysis as an alternative approach to investigating organizational reputation (Brønn & Brønn, 2005). The authors believe their approach leads to an assessment of the internal operational aspects of reputation, thereby assisting managers in better utilizing this strategic resource.

The second study compared the reputations of the most visible Scandinavian companies as ranked by the RQ method (Apéria, Brønn, & Schultz, 2004). This study showed surprising results, given that Scandinavian countries are often treated as a homogenous region. The study indicated, for instance, that the top five Norwegian companies enjoyed lower reputational scores than top-ranked Swedish and Danish companies. Nonetheless, some similarities were found among the countries: emotional appeal was the most important driver, the visible companies often had a local heritage, and treatment of employees and of the environment was seen as the most important aspect of corporate social responsibility. The third article (Brønn, 2007) suggested that instead of measuring reputation, organizations should be measuring relationship outcomes. The author argues that relationships form the basis for building good reputations, but are overlooked in literature.

At least three books were published in Norwegian on the subject in the years 2007 to 2009. The first book was written by a public relations consultant and also published by the author's firm (Apeland, 2007). The most recent book, by Brønn and Ihlen (2009), resulted from the need for Norwegian public relations and management professionals to have a book that would help them understand the subject of corporate reputation in their native language and that had academic weight. The third book (Ihlen, 2007) explores communication and reputation in one specific industry, the Norwegian oil industry.

Public Relations

The industrialization of Norway presented both organizations and the public alike with some of the same challenges that were witnessed in the United States and, in the modern sense, the growth of public relations in Norway is a phenomenon of the post-Second World War period. This influence was important for Norwegian public relations and still continues to be. The first book on public relations was, in fact, called *Public Relations in the U.S.A.* (Apeland, 1960). Additionally, the professionalization of the field in Norway has largely followed American trends (Klasson, 1998).

The huge public sector in Norway has had a profound influence on the development of the field. It is often posited that a special cooperative atmosphere dominated the rebuilding process after the Second World War. In addition to the development of the social democratic tradition in the country, this atmosphere contributed to close relations between business interests and the government. For example, in 1949, the Prime Minister participated in the inaugural meeting of the Norwegian Public Relations Club, the first professional PR organization, and "spoke in confidence on hot Norwegian issues for two hours" (Mørk, 1994, p. 10).

The first president of the Norwegian Public Relations Club had been head of the Norwegian Information Service in America during the Second World War, and was inspired by the development of the public relations field there. An interesting adaptation to the Norwegian context was that public relations, as acknowledged by the club, should be applied for "the good of society," rather than economic profit. For the first eight years, the club did not, in fact, allow membership from the private sector (Mørk, 1994). Later, the Club changed its name to the Norwegian Information Association.

In 1999, the Norwegian Information Association merged with the Forum for Public Information, the public relations organization exclusively for practitioners in the public sector. The new organization adopted the name of Norwegian Communication Association (NCA), which has over 3,000 members, 62% of whom are women and 50% of whom have an education in public relations, communication, or media studies (www.kommunikasjonsforeningen.no).

Public relations agencies are organized in the Norwegian Public Relations Consultants Association (NIR), which currently (2009) includes 24 members. The largest member agency is Burson-Marsteller. Still, some of the bigger agencies are not members of NIR. For example, Geelmuyden-Kiese, recognized as one of the largest agencies in Norway, is not a member. About 10 years ago, the importance of the agencies increased: several new ones were established, often through mergers with international or other Nordic agencies. It may be deduced in a qualified way that more or less all the larger companies and public institutions use or have used an agency, either on a regular or ad hoc basis.

Prior to the turn of the 21st century, little independent or comprehensive research was conducted concerning the public relations profession in Norway. One exception involves research conducted in the late 1990s that explored the strategic orientation of Norwegian communication directors (Brønn, 2000). This research examined the roles of directors, their educational backgrounds, and their reporting lines. Brønn concluded that directors were not strategically oriented and they carried out predominantly tactical roles. Additionally, Brønn found that only 2 out of 102 respondents had an education in communication, and reporting lines were somewhat blurred.

In the past decade, at least 84 master's theses or doctoral dissertations have been produced concerning public relations and organizational or corporate communication, a figure three times the number produced in the 1990s. The establishment of the Center for Corporate Communication at the Norwegian School of Management has fostered research momentum. The Center's first project replicated the Corporate Communication International benchmark study of practices and trends. This study demonstrated that Norwegian communication executives today hold a higher level of education in more relevant areas than they did 10 years ago with more than 60% of executives holding advanced degrees. Further, approximately 80% indicate that they report to the CEO. However, Ihlen and Rakkenes (2009) claim that the "profession still has a way to go in terms of developing methodologies and raising the ethical bar. As for now, however,

Norwegian consultants are doing brisk business trading on their networks, common sense analysis, and operational experience" (p. 485).

Public Relations and the Media

In 1997, the Norwegian TV program Brennpunkt (Burning Point) aired a program titled *Behind the News* (Bak nyhetene). The position of the program was that anyone (read corporation) with enough money could gain media space. The program gave examples of public relations agencies' influence on the political process through lobbying. Criticism of the program emerged from both the media and academics. Some believed the program presented public relations as a manipulative process. Public relations agencies defended themselves by declaring their actions contributed to the strengthening of the democratic process by helping those without political connections and knowledge about the media present their arguments (NRK, 1997).

Further disapproval concerned the fact that the media used material from public relations agencies and businesses without revealing their sources (Allern, 1997; NRK, 1997). The main point was that these "mysterious sources" thrived in the dark of anonymity and couldn't stand the light of day. As a result, the media improved their own guidelines for ethical practices in the "Vær Varsom Plakat " (Be careful guidelines). In addition, as a consequence of this debate, 150 public relations practitioners were expelled from the Norwegian Press Club in 1997; no longer welcome as members because their titles did not conform to the new membership rules (Ottosen, 2004).

The relationship between journalists and communication or public relations consultants in Norway is a continued subject of letters to the editor by both journalists and consultants. For example, the national newspaper *Aftenposten*'s cultural editor warned that the financial crisis in the media industry should not deter journalists from "digging out their own news" (Hvattum, 2009). The editor advised journalists not to lower their credibility by depending on speculative sources such as messages from media advisors in the pay of business. On the contrary, according to the leader of a public relations agency, it is the media themselves that tear down their credibility by constantly worrying about the increase in media advisors (Bonvik, 2009). The leader of the Norwegian Press Club believes that the presence of more information advisors and public relations practitioners than journalists, and the fact that these people are becoming more professional in their efforts to reach the media, reveals the level of resources individuals in institutions with power are willing to employ to influence public debate through the media (Bisgaard, 2008).

Agenda-Setting Research in Norway

Based on the background of public relations, the media, corporate reputation and the agenda-setting theory in Norway, the authors examined three main hypotheses concerning the three levels of agenda-setting theory.

Hypothesis 1: Level 1, agenda setting: Media visibility and top-of-mind awareness.

Hypothesis 2: Level 2, substantive agenda-setting: Media associations and corporate associations.

Hypothesis 3: Level 2, affective agenda-setting: Valence and organizational issues.

Research questions were analyzed by way of a literature review and secondary data from sources such as *Retriever A-Tekst*, the database of Norwegian media, the Norwegian search engines Kvasir and Sesam, and the library database Bibsys.

Hypothesis 1: Level 1 Agenda Setting: Media Visibility and Top-of-Mind Awareness

Several Norwegian media researchers have written about the agenda-setting hypothesis (e.g., Mathiesen, 1993; Waldahl, 1999), but very few empirical studies have been conducted. Among the exceptions are two studies in political science and one in mass communication:

One political science study focused on the 1993 election in Norway, but found little support for the agenda-setting hypothesis. The voter's agenda seemed to be established well before the media began its election coverage, and "to the extent that the media agenda deviated from the initial voter agenda, this was not reflected among the voters" (Aardal, 1999, p. 532).

One master's thesis indicated how the media agenda influenced the political agenda in the Norwegian parliament (the *Storting*). The media were shown to be more important than the voters' agenda, but not as important as the agenda of the political parties themselves. Media importance was heightened during elections (Thesen, 2004).

A third study conducted in mass communication was founded on a simple two-step methodology. First, environmental interest expressed in public opinion polls from a 20-year period (1977, 1981, 1985, 1993, and 1997) was compared to environmental coverage in three central newspapers (Ihlen, 2001). The study demonstrated a certain covariation between the two data categories. However, when the newspaper dataset was compared with two measures for "environmental friendly attitudes," no such covariation was found. Thus, the study supported some findings from first-level agenda-setting literature, but little regarding the second level. The author, however, labeled the publication a pilot study, presented several methodological caveats, and discussed the relationship between the media and the public as a transactional process. That is, both the media and the public are seen as influencing agendas, for the public also influences media content (Dalton, Beck, Huckfeldt, & Koetzle, 1998).

A modest increase in interest in the relationship between business reputation and media visibility has been seen in Norway primarily in the form of master's theses. Some have chosen to examine the correlation between a firm's media investment and its influence on public opinion in addition to how firms can optimize internal processes in order to prevent negative media coverage. The greatest research interest has focused on the impact of media coverage on Norway's image from their hosting of the Winter Olympic Games in 1994 (NORDICOM, n.d.).

Some nonempirical evidence for top-of-mind awareness being linked to media coverage has been found. For instance, the Swedish firm Ikea, consistently ranked among the top three of the Reputation Institute's best liked firms in Norway for 4 years in a row, was not really on the reputation radar of Norwegians before 2004. The most visible firms are nominated by Norwegians in response to the question of which corporation they believed held the best or worst reputation. In 2003, the first year the Reputation Institute carried out its survey in Norway, Ikea was not listed in the top 20 most visible firms. Yet, only one year later, Ikea was ranked number 1, and since then has scored in the top positions.

In 2003 only 600 mentions were found in the press about Ikea (*Retriever A-tekst*). This figure nearly doubled by 2005, including coverage from both national and local papers. Not all coverage was positive, but a preliminary analysis revealed most coverage to be positive. A combination of visibility plus a genuine liking for the firm seemed to resonate with people.

Hypothesis 2: Level 2 Substantive Agenda-Setting: Media Associations and Corporate Associations

Second-level agenda-setting concerns the attributes that media assign to corporations and their impact on public perceptions. For example, McCombs and colleagues (1997) found significant correlations between political candidate attributes as presented in newspaper advertisements and media coverage and public perceptions of candidate attributes.

A few studies have been conducted on the media relations of Norwegian corporations, as well as the influence of public relations agencies (e.g., Allern, 1997, 2001a). These studies, in Norwegian, have mainly been of a qualitative character and focused on the potential for critical journalism despite the growing public relations industry. For instance, some commentators point to how resource-drained news desks often resort to using news subsidies in the form of information from public relations practitioners. The relationship between the media and their sources is sometimes negotiation based; at other times the media only serve as ambassadors for business interests.

One extensive study of expanding Norwegian business journalism demonstrated that during the period 1980 to 2005, new journalism developed through four stages, becoming the largest single category in the Norwegian news media. First, business weeklies and monthlies like *Kapital* and *Økonomisk Rapport* were established. Afterwards, specialized business dailies like *Dagens Næringsliv* and *Finansavisen* were published, and in a somewhat overlapping third stage, the expansion of business news took place in mainstream dailies. The fourth notable stage witnessed the expansion of the same type of journalism on digital platforms (Slaatta, 2003).

The same study confirmed the increasing focus on persons in business journalism. The coverage is typically ambivalent; media exhibit admiration for power and money, but at the same time, chastise the "excessive consumption" of the rich and famous. This tendency was particularly notable in the popular press that wanted to personalize the economic players. The business sources express frustration over what they feel are unpredictable journalists with viewpoints that differ from case to case, story to story, and that sometimes take on roles as actors in the economic arena themselves (Slaatta, 2003).

The Norwegian research findings referenced above provide ambiguous answers regarding the substantive agenda-setting hypothesis. The findings do point to increased coverage of business, the ways business is covered, and an increased interest in reputation measurement. Still, it is not possible to draw links between these datasets.

Hypothesis 3: Level 2 Affective Agenda-Setting: Valence and Organizational Issues

The affective level of agenda setting recognizes that the media may convey feelings and tone, in particular positive, negative, neutral, or mixed tones (Carroll & McCombs, 2003). These researchers proposed that positive media coverage of organizational attributes impact the public perception of that organization.

No specific data exist on organizational newsworthiness in Norway, but given the growth of business news and subsequent reputation instrument measurements, it seems likely that the large Norwegian corporations enjoy a high degree of newsworthiness. However, given the media's preference for conflict and negative news, it could be hypothesized that only the biggest companies are newsworthy in themselves. For instance, positive financial results of Statoil and Hydro are considered newsworthy, since this has a direct impact on the majority of the audience. Positive financial results from smaller companies are less likely to be covered. However, Norwegian business news coverage appears to be more negative than positive. From 2004 to 2006, for example, several Norwegian businesses experienced crises caused by corruption, food poisoning, strikes, and overbudgeting. Media coverage and focus on reputation issues in Norway have been substantial, and as a result, the general trust in business seems to be low among Norwegians.

The Reputation Quotient survey includes corporations in its survey as derived from a polling of a representative sample of the Norwegian public. Respondents are asked to name one firm that they believe has the worst reputation and one that has the best reputation. One of the authors (Brønn) of this chapter is the academic representative working with the RQ in Norway and as such has experience with the media's interest in the results. Suffice it to say, the firms with the worst reputations are more interesting as news than those with the best.

Study: Linking Media Coverage and Reputation

An examination of the Norwegian media's influence on public perceptions was conducted by Hval in 2002. This study, based on how a firm's top management was portrayed in the media, analyzed Det Norske Veritas, a Norwegian consultancy with about 300 offices in 100 countries. The company offers services for managing risks in four major industries: maritime, oil and gas, process, and transportation (www.dnv.no). The company, established in 1864, is fairly well-known in Norway, partly because of its participation in a corporate misconduct crisis in 2002.

Hval's (2002) study aimed to determine if media coverage of a CEO influenced an organization's image, and thus ultimately reflected on its corporate brand value. A sample of 200 participants was used, most of whom were students at the Norwegian School of Management between the ages of 20 and 24. After being divided into two equal groups, respondents were asked to answer a questionnaire concerning a news article on Det Norske Veritas and its CEO. Half of respondents were presented with a positive article, while the other half were given a negative one. The negative article was published in the financial daily, *Finansavisen,* in April 2002 (Jacobsen, 2002), and revealed that the then chair of the board had secured a compensation deal for the president and CEO of the company, a procedure that was in violation of Norwegian law because it was not mentioned in the Annual Report as mandated.

The positive story was published in the daily *Aftenposten* in March 2001 (De Lange, 2001). This story described how Veritas and its president and CEO, the same individual in the negative story, took decisive action to force out 85 ships that did not meet the standard requirement for being awarded a Veritas classification. In order to emphasize the tone in each article, irrelevant information was removed from both stories. A pretest questionnaire confirmed these edits (Hval, 2002).

The data underwent a correlation analysis, a factor analysis, and then a discriminant analysis. The analyses implied a correlation exists between the portrayal of a top leader by the media and the resulting perceptions of the general public. The factor analysis revealed four primary factors that impacted perceptions: the current image of the firm held by the respondents, knowledge of the firm, the credibility of the media, and the influence of the top leader portrayed in the media. All factors but credibility of the media were found to be significant (Hval, 2002).

A RepTrak results analysis from 2009 also revealed some interesting tendencies. Of the 29 firms with good to excellent reputations, six scored highest on leadership. In other words, respondents ranked the leaders of these firms higher than the firms' products and services and other attributes. Each of these firms has a highly visible leader: Norwegian, Aker, Olav Thon Gruppen, Choice, Microsoft, and Kiwi. Both the airline firm Norwegian and the hotel chain Choice use their leaders for company profiling.

The question is whether obtaining a rating of leaders that is higher than ratings for products and services is a sustainable strategy. Adjusting the ratings for the firms so that leadership received a score in line with how people felt about the corporations regarding their other qualities, resulted in Norwegian dropping five places and Choice dropping 10 in the ranking. This corresponds to other research indicating that Norwegian has declining customer satisfaction and Choice has hard competition in both customer satisfaction and loyalty.

While there is a lack of research in Norway regarding agenda-setting research, this study does support the second-level affective agenda-setting hypothesis, in particular that media coverage of leaders influences individuals' perceptions of organizations. This research also indicates that, while blaming the media for negative impressions seems naïve, some truth to the notion exists.

Conclusion

Research on corporate reputation and the news media, still in its infancy in Norway, is steadily growing. This chapter has presented a short overview and given some insights into how corporate reputation is understood in Norway. The chapter has also pointed out some peculiarities of the Norwegian media systems, business news, and public relations industry. It is argued that media coverage has an influence on the public's opinion, an influence that was illustrated by a study where respondents were exposed to negative and positive news coverage of a particular company. Regarding other aspects of the agenda-setting hypotheses, however, caution should be taken as to interpreting their influence, as the research is rather inconclusive.

References

Aardal, B. (1999). Issue voting and the political agenda: A spiral of silence? In M. Narud & T. Aalberg (Eds.), *Challenges to representative democracy: Parties, voters and public opinion* (pp. 327–354). Bergen, Norway: Fagbokforlaget.

Allern, S. (1997). *Når kildene byr opp til dans* [When the sources ask for a dance]. Oslo, Norway: Pax Forlag.

Allern, S. (2001a). Kildene og mediemakten. In M. Eide (Ed.), *Til dagsorden! Journalistikk, makt og demokrati* [To the agenda! Journalism, power and democracy] (pp. 273–303). Oslo, Norway: Gyldendal Akademisk.

Allern, S. (2001b). *Nyhetsverdier: Om markedsorientering og journalistikk i ti norske aviser* [News values: On the market orientation and journalism in ten Norwegian newspapers]. Kristiansand, Norway: IJ-forlaget.

Apeland, N. M. (1960). *Public relations i USA* [Public relations in the U.S.A.]. Oslo, Norway: Gyldendal.

Apeland, N. M. (2007). *Det gode selskap: Omdømmebygging i praksis* [The good firm: Practical reputation building]. Oslo, Norway: Hippocampus.

Apéria, T., Brønn, P. S., & Schultz, M. (2004). A reputation analysis of the most visible companies in the Scandinavian countries. *Corporate Reputation Review, 7*(3), 218–230.

Argenti, P. A. (1998). *Corporate communication* (2nd ed.). Boston, MA: McGraw-Hill.

Bisgaard, A. B. (2008). Maktmennesker er selvopptatt [Power people are self-absorbed]. *Kampanje, 3,* 24.

Bonvik, Ø. (2009, February 18). Å spare bort troverdighet [Saving away credibility]. *Nationen*, p. 28.

Brønn, C., & Brønn, P. S. (2005). Reputation and organizational efficiency: A data envelopment analysis study. *Corporate Reputation Review, 8*(1), 45–58.

Brønn, P. S. (2000). *Measuring the strategic orientation of communication directors.* (Unpublished doctoral dissertation). Reading, UK: Henley Management College.

Brønn, P. S. (2007). Relationship outcomes as determinants of reputation. *Corporate Communications: An International Journal, 12*(4), 376–393.

Brønn, P. S., & Ihlen, Ø. (2009). *Åpen eller innadvendt: Omdømmebygging for organisasjoner* [Open or introspective: Reputation building for organizations]. Oslo, Norway: Gyldendal.

Carlsson, U., & Harrie, E. (Eds.). (2001). *Media trends 2001 in Denmark, Finland, Iceland, Norway and Sweden: Vol. 6. Nordic media trends.* Göteborg, Sweden: NORDICOM.

Carroll, C. E., & McCombs, M. E. (2003). Agenda-setting effects of business news on the public's images and opinions about major corporations. *Corporate Reputation Review, 6*(1), 36–46.

Cohen, B. C. (1963). *The press and foreign policy.* Princeton, NJ: Princeton University Press.

Dalton, R. J., Beck, P. A., Huckfeldt, R., & Koetzle, W. (1998). A test of media-centered agenda setting: Newspaper content and public interests in a presidential election. *Political Communication, 15*, 463–481.

De Lange, G. (2001). Veritas kaster ut rustholker [Veritas forces rust hulks out]. *Aftenposten*, p. 50.

Edelman. (2009). *Annual Edelman trust barometer.* New York: Author.

Fombrun, C. J., Gardberg, N. A., & Sever, J. M. (2000). The Reputation Quotient: A multi-stakeholder measure of corporate reputation. *Journal of Brand Management, 7*(4), 241–255.

Harrie, E. (2003). *The Nordic media market: Vol. 7. Nordic media trends.* Göteborg, Sweden: NORDICOM.

Hval, N. (2002). *Toppleders atferd eksponert av media: En studie av bedrifters image og merkestyrke* [The action of CEOs exposed by the media: A study of the image and brand strength of companies]. (Unpublished Sivilmarkedsføreroppgave). The Norwegian School of Management, Oslo.

Hvattum, T. (2009, July 16). Agurktid i en krisetid [Cucumber days in times of crisis]. *Aftenposten*, p. 9.

Høst, S. (1998). *Daglig mediebruk* [Daily media use]. Oslo, Norway: Pax Forlag.

Høyer, S. (1995). *Pressen mellom teknologi og samfunn: Norske og internasjonale perspektiver på pressehistorien fra Gutenberg til vår tid* [The press between technology and society: Norwegian and international perspectives on the press history from Gutenberg to our time]. Oslo, Norway: Universitetsforlaget.

Ihlen, Ø. (2001). Medier, miljø og påvirkning [Media, environmental issues, and effects]. *Tidsskrift for samfunnsforskning, 42*(1), 65–88.

Ihlen, Ø. (2007). *Petroleumsparadiset: Norsk oljeindustris strategiske kommunikasjon og omdømmebygging* [The petroleum paradise: The strategic communication and reputation management of the Norwegian oil industry]. Oslo, Norway: Unipub.

Ihlen, Ø., & Rakkenes, K. (2009). Public relations in Norway: Communication in a small welfare state. In K. Sriramesh & D. Verčič (Eds.), *The global public relations handbook: Theory, research, and practice* (rev. ed., pp. 466–487). New York: Routledge.

Jacobsen, S. (2002, April 20). Toppsjefer brøt loven [CEOs in violation with the law]. *Finansavisen*. Retrieved from http://www.hegnar.no/bors/finans/article178831.ece

Klasson, P. (1998). *Public relations som profesjonaliseringsprosjekt: Utviklingstrekk ved den norske informasjonsbransjen 1960-1998* [Public relations as a project of professionalization: The development of the Norwegian public relations sector 1960–1998]. Unpublished master's thesis, University of Bergen, Bergen, Norway.

Lippmann, W. (2004). *Public opinion*. Mineola, NY: Dover. (Original work published 1922)

Mathiesen, T. (1993). *Makt og medier: En innføring i mediesosiologi* [Power and media: An introduction to media sociology] (2nd ed.). Oslo, Norway: Pax.

McCombs, M. E., Llams, J. P., Lopez-Escobar, E., & Rey, F. (1997). Candidate images in Spanish elections: Second-level agenda-setting effects. *Journalism & Mass Communication Quarterly, 74*, 703–716.

McCombs, M. E., & Shaw, D. L. (1997). The agenda-setting function of the mass media. In O. Boyd-Barrett & C. Newbold (Eds.), *Approaches to media: A reader* (pp. 153–163). London: Arnold. (Original work published 1972)

Moen, L.-M. W. (2005). *Corporate image, corporate reputation: Konseptstudium* [Conceptual study]. Norwegian School of Management, Oslo.

Mørk, E. (1994). *Et slag med halen: Informasjonsforeningens historie 1949–1994* [Wagging the tail: The Information Association's history 1949–1994]. Oslo, Norway: Informasjonsforeningen.

Norwegian Broadcasting System (NRK). (1997, January 7). Brennpunkt: Bak nyhetene [Brennpunkt: Behind the news].

NORDICOM (n.d.). http://www.nordicom.gi.se

Østbye, H. (2001). The Norwegian media landscape: Structure, economy and consumption. In U. Carlsson & E. Harrie (Eds.), *Media trends 2001 in Denmark, Finland, Iceland, Norway and Sweden: Vol. 6. Nordic media trends* (pp. 239–247). Göteborg, Sweden: NORDICOM.

Ottesen, G. (2006, May 31). Tommelen ned for næringslivet [Thumbs down for business]. *Dagens Næringsliv*, p. 1.

Ottosen, R. (2004). *I journalistikkens grenseland: Journalistrollen mellom marked og idealer* [In the borderland of journalism: The journalist role between market and ideals]. Kristiansand, Norway: IJ-forlaget.

The Poetic Edda (1996 trans.). (C. Larrington, Trans.). Oxford, UK: Oxford University Press.

Slaatta, T. (2003). *Den norske medieorden: Posisjoner og privilegier* [The Norwegian media order: Positions and privileges]. Oslo, Norway: Gyldendal Akademisk.

Thesen, G. (2004). *Parti, velgere, media og politikk: Innflytelse på Stortingets dagsorden gjennom representasjon og agandasetting i 1985–2001* Unpublished master's thesis, University of Bergen, Bergen, Norway.

Waldahl, R. (1999). *Mediepåvirkning* [The Media's Influence] (2nd ed.). Oslo, Norway: Ad Notam Gyldendal.

Waldahl, R., Andersen, M. B., & Rønning, H. (2002). *Nyheter først og fremst: Norske tv-nyheter: Myter og realiteter* [News first and foremost: Norwegian television news: Myths and realities]. Oslo, Norway: Universitetsforlaget.

11 Corporate Reputation and the News Media in Spain

Ángel Arrese and Manuel Baigorri

Introduction

It is only comparatively recently that there has been any interest in corporate reputation and its relationship to the media. There is a lack of tradition in Spain compared to other countries in three key fields that relate to reputation and the media: corporate communication, business journalism, and public relations.

The almost four decades of Franco's dictatorship set Spain apart from the international arena in many aspects of public life. Despite greater openness in commerce and the ongoing process of liberalization that has continued since the 1960s, it wasn't until the 1970s that the necessary conditions existed in the new democratic system that followed Franco's death for full development of a vast number of activities to take place.

Guillén (1989) reminds us that within the business field, the democratic transition gave a new importance to the entrepreneurial class and to private enterprise, which could no longer look to the state for protection and had to make a case for its legitimacy to the public. In order for that to happen, an essential period of redefinition had to take place, and indeed lasted until the 1980s, during which time the business world had to redefine its own social function and its identity (Flores, 2000). From then on, the importance of such institutions as the stock market or the privatization of companies that had previously been state owned, boosted the interest of businesspeople and companies in corporate communication. At the same time, with the emergence of some multinationals, many Spanish companies became active in countries other than Spain, a trend that eventually would lead to more transparency in the markets (Guillén, 2005).

Until the late 1980s, unlike other European countries, there had been no Spanish media that specialized in economic and business issues. The first economic daily, *Cinco Días*, was launched in 1978, and it was another decade or more before there was further activity in that field. In the United States and Europe, where some business dailies were almost a hundred years old, the boost in business and economic publications had taken place in the 1950s and 1960s (Arrese, 2002).

Finally, within the public relations field, there was not a truly professional sector until the 1970s. As Rodríguez Salcedo (2004) has noted, with a few exceptions, between 1960 and 1975 the public relations field was almost nonexistent.

But the peculiarities that can be found today in Spain related to the management of corporate reputation and their connection to media activity, cannot only be attributed to the effects of the dictatorship. Historically and culturally speaking, there has been a mistrust on the part of the Spanish general public toward companies and businesspeople, and some commentators would extend this to the whole area of economic activities. De Miguel (2003) has analyzed this attitude of mistrust as it was found amongst Spanish academicians, especially during the 20th century. But its ancient and deep roots must also be acknowledged, based on an idealistic worldview, which is characteristic of Spanish history and culture (Álvarez & Merchán, 1994). It is significant that the most influential Spanish school of economic thought in history, the Salamanca School, active in the 16th century, was somewhat hostile to commercial and financial activities (Melé, 1999). It is also striking that there is a stereotype about corruption and lack of transparency (Heywood, 1997; Wattley-Ames, 1999), a cliché that in the business field nurtures without a doubt "suspicion" of public opinion regarding company profits and the enrichment of businesspeople (Argandoña, 1999).

Nowadays, in a global context, perhaps those peculiarities may be expressed covertly, but that does not mean that they do not exist. The next two examples are illustrative for the purpose of this work.

As an institution, the corporation does not seem to have in general the same reputation that it enjoys in other countries. A survey of Spanish citizens asked "whether the private property of businesses should increase related to the public"; only 24% supported that statement (1–4 on a scale of 9). In similar but diverse cultures, such as the United States or Germany, the positive answer reached 68% and 56%, respectively. Regarding the question about the positive or negative effects of competition, key in the functioning of markets, 49% of Spaniards valued it as basically good, against 71% of Americans and 64% of Germans (*World Values Survey*, 2000).[1]

The Spanish general public does not have much interest in media coverage of economic and business issues. A European Union survey found that only 18% of the Spanish population had a high interest in news about those issues, a figure that is admittedly higher than Italy (17%) and Portugal (5%). But the average for the 27 countries of the Union was 28%, with Sweden and Finland interest levels upwards of 40% (Eurobarometer, 2007).

These introductory ideas give some idea of the situation in Spain vis-à-vis corporate reputation and its link with media activity.

Corporate Reputation

Barnett, Jermier, and Lafferty (2006) have asserted that there are at least three different conceptual focuses in defining the term *corporate reputation*: reputation as an asset (*asset*), as a group of concepts and perceptions (*awareness*), and as a judgment or opinion (*assessment*).

With such a variety of focuses, Barnett et al. propose a definition of corporate reputation as "observers' collective judgments of a corporation based on assessments of the financial, social and environmental impacts attributed to the corporation over time" (p. 34). This definition provides a useful focus for the present work, and is somewhat in contrast with other definitions that are focused on economics.

Spain has a diversity of perspectives. In the last few years, there has been a movement away from elaborated concepts of identity analysis and corporate image (*awareness*) to analyzing corporate reputation as an asset (*asset*), relating it to real rather than perceived behavior on the part of organizations. Of course, some more conventional definitions have been followed, such as those proposed a decade ago by Fombrun and Van Riel (Fombrun, 1996; Fombrun & Van Riel, 1997).

Justo Villafañe, one of the first Spanish authors since the late nineties to analyze this concept in any depth, defines corporate reputation as "the acknowledgment that the stakeholders of a company have of its corporate behavior with clients, employees, shareholders if they exist, and the community in general" (Villafañe, 2000, 2003, p. 193). To this author, the key for the conceptual delimitation of reputation is its distinction from the concept of corporate image, and hence the emphasis on the substance of reputation in terms of its reflecting a company's development over an extended period of time. Key to that vision is the knowledge dimension (*awareness*) and the real value (*asset*), compared with those aspects that are based more on opinion or are more subjective (*assessment*).

From a more economic perspective, focusing on the contractual dimension of reputation, and on its informational content, De la Fuente and De Quevedo (2003) work with a concept that not only takes into account the perceptual aspects, but also companies' level of transparency when communicating with their stakeholders. In later works, these authors have also shown a special interest in delimiting the frontiers of the concept of corporate reputation with another concept that is close to it, corporate social performance (CSP), trying in the process to clarify the perceptual dimensions (subjective) of the descriptive dimensions (objective) related to a corporation's behavior (De Quevedo, De la Fuente, & Delgado, 2007). Eventually, this research has been oriented to define the value of reputation as an asset that is able to generate future economic return (De Quevedo, 2003).

A third theoretical example, in this case from the perspective of knowledge management, is a proposal by the corporate reputation team of Deloitte Spain. The key term here is *prestige*, which derives from the appropriate management of intellectual capital. It is a proposal that has to do more with the previous focus on the role of opinion in defining reputation (Zabala et. al., 2005).

None of these theoretical approaches gives special emphasis to the importance of media coverage to confirm the status of reputation. Implicitly, the media are identified as a category of stakeholders, but it is not visibility in the media that has special importance, in the sense that was given originally by Fombrun and Shanley (1990), or the one that other authors have proposed, especially Deephouse (2000). In some more recent theoretical revisions, such as the one proposed by Martín Castro, Navas, and López (2006), evaluation by the media relates to social reputation ("insights and perceptions of other stakeholders who are more distant from day by day business activities than investors and the community in a wider sense," p. 367), but they are not even quoted explicitly.

In conclusion, there has been little interest amongst Spanish academics in analyzing the links between corporate reputation and media coverage.

Media Visibility and the Theory of Agenda Setting

The academic studies on media coverage in Spain have focused on the analysis of political and social issues, with few if any on economic and business issues. But there is a tradition of research on agenda setting, especially in the political communication field.

In the mid-1990s, a team of researchers from the University of Navarra's Public Communication Department (Pamplona), conducted by Esteban López-Escobar, began work to validate agenda-setting theory in Spain. In close collaboration with Maxwell McCombs, they analyzed the influence of the media agenda on the population of Pamplona regarding the local and regional elections that took place in 1995. That was the first study that confirmed that agenda-setting theory could usefully be applied to Spanish media and audiences (Canel, Llamas, & Rey, 1996).

A few months before, the journal *Comunicación y Sociedad* had published the pioneer work of McCombs and Evatt (1995) about the second level of agenda setting. Its theoretical and practical implications were challenged as a consequence of the local elections (López-Escobar, McCombs, & Rey, 1996), as well as other aspects related to the interrelation of agendas between the different media covering the campaign (López-Escobar, Llamas & Rey, 1996).

This research verified, in the case of Spain, the basic thesis of agenda setting both on its first and second level. The confirmation of the agenda's second level thesis had a very special importance; namely, that the media not only communicate the prominence of issues, but also their aspects, attributes, and features. The empirical work on the second level represented a theoretical breakthrough in the field.

The relevance of all this research and its discoveries was shown in the publication of several works on these issues in some prestigious international journals: about the second level of the agenda (McCombs, Llamas, López-Escobar & Rey, 1997; McCombs, López-Escobar, & Llamas, 2000); about the interrelation between the media's agenda and advertising (López-Escobar, Llamas, McCombs & Rey, 1998); and on the correlation between the media's effective agenda and the popular consensus about some characteristics of the candidates during the electoral period (López-Escobar & Llamas, 1998). McCombs highlighted the importance that all these contributions would have in his seminal paper, "New Frontiers in Agenda Setting: Agendas of Attributes and Frames" (1997).

These pioneer works were followed by a proliferation of studies that focus on some particular aspects of agenda setting, whether in the context of political campaigns or increasingly about other current issues (López-Escobar, 2007). Thus, in the field of electoral studies, Semetko and Canel (1997) analyzed the influence-conditioning of the creation of the informative agenda on television during the 1996 general elections; Vara (2001) also focused on the relationship between building the agenda and its transmission to the public during the local Pamplona elections in 1999; Martín, López-Escobar, McCombs, and Tolsá (2000) studied the interrelation of agendas within the media, with special emphasis on the role of radio, in order to get a better understanding of some aspects related to how the second level of agenda setting works.

Outside the political field, there were studies by Martín (2000, 2004) about health care issues and gender-based violence; Igartua, Muñiz, Otero, and M. De la Fuente (2007) and Mena (2008) wrote on immigration. Rodríguez-Díaz (2004) expanded the possibilities of using agenda theory in relation to education. Agenda setting has been used to try and understand events such as the terrorist attack in Madrid on March 11, 2004, in which almost 200 people died, and which preceded by 3 days the general elections that were held on March 14 (Benavides et. al., 2006; García Galera, 2006; Sampedro et. al., 2006).

However, there is no such abundance of research on economic and business issues, although there is some isolated work, such as one regarding the advent of the Euro (Micu & Geana, 2004). More specifically, there are no academic works about corporations' visibility in the media, a field that had already been referenced. In fact, the only exception is a recent study by Capriotti (2007), which will be commented on later, and which makes partial use of agenda-setting theory.

Business and Media

Unlike other Western European countries, the Spanish media's interest in business coverage dates at best to the 1970s (Arrese, 2007). During that decade, when the first oil crisis took place, most of the attention in the media went to macroeconomic and labor issues, which led to the founding of the economic daily *Cinco Días* (1978). Business information was tightly controlled by corporations, and focused almost exclusively on the stock market. Moreover, journalism at the time, especially in the economic and business area, was hardly professional, which guaranteed that media coverage of corporations was limited to publishing companies' press releases (Del Río, 2000, pp. 24–27).

This situation did not improve consistently until the late 1980s. Indeed, according to a survey made in 1984 by ALEF, labor information continued to be of most interest to the general public, and in terms of business, only information related to banks generated significant interest (Muñoz Alonso, 1984). During the same time period, Pedro Cases, of the daily newspaper *El País*, talked about the lack of transparency of private companies about their dealings, which was in marked contrast to the transparency of public companies whose shares were traded on the stock exchange (Cases, 1985, p. 195).

Some events would change this situation during the second half of the decade. The entrance of Spain into the European Union in 1986, some well-known financial operations, the development and modernization of Madrid's stock exchange, and some privatizations of industries previously government run, definitively boosted business. Specialized media were launched at this time, such as *Expansión* (1986) and *La Gaceta de los Negocios* (1989).

This activity accelerated during the 1990s, and two points are important here: first, media coverage has been highly influenced by the experience of the print media; second, to a great degree, business information has focused on companies that are obliged to follow a degree of transparency because their shares are traded on stock exchange. However, a lack of transparency continues to exist in a good number of privately held companies, because Spain is a country where the family enterprise, both small and medium size, plays a crucial role in the economy (De la Cruz & Cabrera, 2005).

Nowadays, the information related to business exists in a context of increasing professionalization, both in the media and corporations. This practical development, though, has not generated much specific research. Some professional associations such as Asociación de Periodistas de Información Económica (APIE; [The Association of Economic Publications]) or Asociación de Directivos de la Comunicación (DIRCOM; [The Association of Communication Directors]) have shown interest in studying the relationship between business and the media (Estudio de Comunicación, 2006). They have been responsible for media professionals researching corporate communication practices. DIRCOM publishes a report on the state of communication in Spain which deals with practical rather than theoretical issues.

However, Capriotti (2007), following Carroll and McCombs (2003), has analyzed the media coverage of 35 companies using the main benchmark of Madrid's stock market, the IBEX-35. His study focuses on a content analysis of the main dailies—*El País*, *El Mundo*, *ABC*, and *La Vanguardia*—but the analysis is a very limited one. The main conclusions from the research are: (1) related to the first level of agenda setting, a small group of eight companies gets a disproportionate amount of attention from the media (55.4% of all published articles); and (2) 27 companies that have less visibility make up the other 44.6%. The second level of the agenda has a predominance of economic issues and attributes (95.7% of the news) compared with social issues, which amount to 4.3% of coverage.

There is a great need for more of this kind of research, which would counterbalance the rankings of corporate reputation which have been developed in Spain over the past few years, and which in general do not take into account media coverage.

Rankings and Ratings of Corporate Reputation

Since 2000, when Van Riel and Fombrun (2002) carried out their first test of the Reputation Quotient (RQ), which included a survey of Spain, there have been several initiatives to evaluate reputation, social responsibility, and other intangible corporate assets. However, the one that has been most promising is the "Monitor Empresarial de Reputación Corporativa" (Merco [Corporate Reputation Business Monitor]).

Merco was born in 2000 from some university research undertaken by Justo Villafañe, who is the main Spanish expert in this field. The first study was carried out in 2001 and since then it has taken place annually under the supervision of Villafañe & Associates. The Spanish ranking was built from six different variables: (1) economic and financial outcomes; (2) product-service quality; (3) corporate culture and labor quality; (4) ethics and social corporate responsibility; (5) global dimension and international presence; and (6) innovation. One thousand executives of companies with more than €50 million in sales are surveyed. This led to a reputational ranking, which is evaluated again by a sample composed of almost 50 experts (financial analysts, union leaders, editorial leaders, etc.). Finally, the main data for each company are verified through an analysis of public documents and executive interviews. The final outcome is a report on almost 100 Spanish companies with the best corporate reputation.

During the eight editions of Merco, 18 companies have been listed among the top 10 (see Table 11.1), information that sheds some light on the reliability of this study. In the last few years, besides Merco-rated companies, this consultancy, using a similar methodology, has developed other studies on entrepreneurial leaders, brands, and the labor environment (MercoLeaders, MercoBrands, MercoPeople).

Merco was inspired by the *Fortune* magazine ranking of the most admired companies, as has been the case with other reports published by the media (*El País, Actualidad Económica*, etc.), which are similar to the ones in other countries (Fombrun, 1998, 2007). Among them, the list of the best companies to work

Table 11.1 Top Ten in Merco (2001–2008)

Rank	2001	2002	2003	2004	2005	2006	2007	2008
1	El Corte Inglés	El Corte Inglés	El Corte Inglés	El Corte Inglés	El Corte Inglés	El Corte Inglés	El Corte Inglés	Inditex
2	BBVA	BBVA	Inditex	Inditex	Inditex	Tele-fónica	Inditex	Tele-fónica
3	Repsol	Tele-fónica	Tele-fónica	Tele-fónica	Tele-fónica	Inditex	Tele-fónica	El Corte Inglés
4	Tele-fónica	Repsol	Repsol	Repsol	Repsol	Repsol	Repsol	Repsol
5	BSCH (*)	Inditex	BBVA	BBVA	BBVA	BBVA	BBVA	Santander
6	Bank-inter	SCH	SCH	San-tander	San-tander	San-tander	San-tander	La Caixa
7	Endesa	Banco Popular	Banco Popular	La Caixa	La Caixa	La Caixa	La Caixa	BBVA
8	Inditex	Endesa	Endesa	Banco Popular	Iber-drola	Iberd-rola	Iber-drola	Iber-drola
9	Mapfre	La Caixa	Bank-inter	Endesa	Iberia	Siemens	Endesa	Mer-cadona
10	La Caixa	Bank-inter	Gas Natural	Iberia	Endesa	Iberia	Fer-rovial	Acciona

(*) Banco Santander Central Hispano, later Santander.
Source: Villafañe & Asociados. www.villafane.com

for has been very popular during the last few years (www.greatplacetowork.es), as has been the case with other occasional studies of promising companies or responsible businesses that act responsibly toward the environment. However, none of them has reached the level of influence of the lists published by *Fortune* or the *Financial Times*.

From the perspective of methodology and operational issues, in 2005 the Corporate Reputational Forum (fRC) began work with the Reputational Institute's RepTrack® system, a new development from the analysis model RQ. In contrast to the tool created by Fombrun, this one does not provide an average of the 20 variables analyzed in the RQ model, but it does give a value to each of them. Moreover, RepTrack is not a specific study, but a continuing one, and it can be applied to different stakeholders and also be used to analyze public opinion. The fRC, representative in Spain of the Reputation Institute, does not publish the listings of the analysis outcomes, which are used by its partners, some 10 big Spanish corporations. Some of them, like Telefónica, have undertaken their own reputational analysis and developed their own management model, the integrated model of corporate reputation (MIRC) (Rodríguez Carrasco, 2004).

The Ipsos Key Audience Research (KAR) instrument was introduced into Spain in late 2006. Initially, the research focused on the analysis of opinions from a sample of economic and business journalists, but in 2008 other audiences were added (analysts, politicians, academicians, and business leaders).

In all the cited works, the vast majority of companies appearing in the rankings are Spanish, although some foreign businesses are always well positioned. As an example, Merco 2008 pointed out that 30 out of 100 companies on its list are from other countries (three of them, Vodafone, IBM, and Microsoft, are among the top 20).

Frequently, the publication of the outcomes of these studies has some sort of echo in the media, most often in the specialized ones (Merco, for example, was associated with the economic daily *Cinco Días* in order to provide more visibility to its conclusions). The country's broadcasting media, which are the most influential, pay more attention to spectacular rankings, such as the *Forbes* list of the world's wealthiest people.

The Media System

In 2004, Villafañe & Asociados studied Spanish CEOs' evaluation of reputation management. One of the issues analyzed related to the most influential stakeholders: after the clients, 88.1%, came the print media with 73.3%, very far from the broadcast media (9.9%), and other stakeholders (financial analysts [30.7%], shareholders [28.7%]) (Villafañe & Asociados, 2004). This mirrors the situation in most countries, though in Spain it is shown more acutely (Edelman, 2007).

Unlike central and northern European countries, when considering general news the Spanish media system is clearly dominated by the broadcast media. Both television and the radio are the main sources of information for the vast majority of the population. The average Spaniard spends about 3½ hours a day watching television, and almost 2 hours listening to the radio: 90% in the case of television, and 55% for radio. Both have a very different and competitive variety of offerings (national and regional channels, public and private, free and subscription based, etc.). However, in spite of this variety amongst the broadcast media, there is very little business and economic information. According to a study of the main free TV channels, business and economic issues accounted for 3% of the news programs on prime time (AIDEKA, 2005, p. 18). Moreover, business and economic TV programs are almost nonexistent; the Intereconomía channel has a very tiny audience. This situation is in clear contrast to that in other countries (Arrese, 2002, pp. 256–264).

Penetration of the press is very low compared with other European countries and way below the European average (WAN, 2008). About 140 newspapers sell around 4.2 million copies daily, which means around 100 issues for each 1,000 inhabitants. Forty-one percent of the population reads the press regularly and 51% read magazines (mostly celebrity magazines) (AIMC, 2008). The two largest papers in terms of circulation are *El País* (440,000) and *El Mundo* (340,000), followed closely by the sports paper *Marca* (315,000). Regarding magazines, there are six celebrity publications (*Hola* being the best known) and two TV guides within the top 10 titles in terms of circulation.

During the last decade, the most significant trend in the Spanish press market has been the extraordinary success of the free press. More than 4 million copies are distributed daily of four titles, *Metro, 20 Minutos, Qué!* and *ADN*, which is similar to the total circulation of the paid press. These publications have little interest in business news although in 2006 a free title that specialized in those issues (*Negocios*) was launched and is having some success.

It is not unusual, given this context, that the most valued business information, both in quantity and quality is concentrated in just a few titles, especially in the main news dailies and in the specialized press. The audience for most of these publications is business executives and other decision makers and opinion leaders in the economic and business areas, all of them key audiences when it comes to evaluating corporate reputations. As is shown by the latest European Business Readership Survey (EBRS),[2] five titles—*El País, El Mundo, ABC, Expansión,* and *Cinco Días*—accumulate a big chunk of this public's reading in Spain (see Table 11.2).

To serve those audiences, the development of the Spanish economic press during the last few decades has played an important role in improving the level of business information. Three veteran newspapers, *Expansión, Cinco Días,* and *La Gaceta de los Negocios,* and a new one launched in 2005, *El Economista,* reach about 300,000 readers daily, although with a somewhat small circulation of 125,000. This is in fact one of the problems of the media: its atomization. Even though *Expansión* has been the leader for many years, with a circulation of 60,000, it has neither the market power nor the influence on public opinion that similar publications have in their respective countries, such as *The Wall Street Journal, Financial Times,* or *Il Sole 24 Ore.* On the other hand, the intense market development of daily newspapers has interfered with the potential growth of business magazines. There are some successful publications, such as *Actualidad Económica, Emprendedores,* and *Capital,* but their market penetration and

Table 11.2 Spanish Business Men Readership (2006)

Universe: 23.930/Sample: 549			
Title	Type of publication	Average Issue Readership	%
El País	General Daily	14,589	61
El Mundo	General Daily	11,591	48
ABC	General Daily	5,685	24
Expansión	Business Daily	13,047	55
Cinco Días	Business Daily	7,141	30
La Gaceta de los Negocios	Business Daily	4,367	18
Actualidad Económica	Business Weekly	9,465	40
Capital	Business Monthly	5,199	22
Dinero	Business Monthly	5,882	25
Emprendedores	Business Monthly	6,738	28

Source: European Business Readership Survey, 2006.

their importance are much less than that of similar titles in such countries as the United States, France, or Germany. To some extent, this somewhat fragile journalism structure is a result of the relatively brief existence of the economic and business information sector, and of its accelerated growth almost from scratch since the 1980s.

The main quality dailies and business newspapers also dominate the specialized audience on the Internet. Although the net penetration in Spain could clearly be improved—in 2008, about 26.2% of the population used it on a daily basis—the positioning of the most important media outlets is very good. Regarding the public to which we are referring (businesspeople and decision maker, who are more active Internet users than the average), the online versions of those dailies are very important (Mindshare, 2004).

Professional Values and Practices

The period of political change that occurred during the 1970s was also a turning point in the professionalization of journalism. The end of censorship and the excitement related to current political news in those years made it essential for professional journalists to rapidly update their standards (Humanes, 1998). Spanish journalism grew in influence and prestige. Other characteristics are also derived from this period: hiring of journalists increased; there was somewhat of a trend to mix information and rumor; and, with the exception of sports, political journalism predominated.

Some studies undertaken during the 1990s tried to evaluate changes in the professional profile of journalists as a consequence of the democratization of the country (Canel & Piqué, 1998; Canel, Sánchez Aranda, & Rodríguez, 2000; Diezhandino, Bezunartea, & Coca, 1994; Ortega & Humanes, 2000). In general, some significant changes were noticed in the professional paradigm, such as the move from an ideological–partisan focus to one that was more adversarial and nonpartisan; there was a change from journalists being "servants of the system" to being "servants of the audience" (Canel & Piqué, 1998, p. 318). There remained, however, some problems of inadequate professional standards; a lack of a clear definition on the work tasks and on ethical responsibilities; and the need for a more comprehensive understanding of the role of the media in a democratic society (Ortega & Humanes, 2000). As a consequence, there were some professional attitudes which were quite in contrast to those of other journalism cultures. For example (see Table 11.3), the use of private and public (official) documents without the owners' permission was a practice mostly avoided by Spanish journalists, whereas only a minority of other countries saw a problem in using such material.[3]

During the last few years, the professional consciousness of Spanish journalists (at least in the field of political information) does not differ a great deal from that of other European countries (Sanders & Canel, 2006); Spanish journalists have similar educational levels to their colleagues elsewhere (Sanders, Hanna, Berganza, & Sánchez Aranda, 2008).

The professionalization of journalists in the economic and business information field has followed a similar path to the one described so far for journalists in general. In fact, there have been great advances related to the two main challenges for journalists who specialize in those fields: the deontological and that of education. Where there is perhaps more work to do is on developing the craft of a more incisive journalism, which rather than being led by official sources depends more on its own research and topics.[4] This is not always easy in an industry where traditionally there has been a high staff turnover, with very young and frequently quite inexperienced people working in newsrooms (Del Río, 2000, pp. 47–54). Moreover, in the early 21st century, the economics and business media, not only in Spain but also in other countries, face some structural challenges (business, technology, and advertising related, among others). This makes it even

Table 11.3 Unacceptable Journalistic Practices

% of journalists that consider that practice wrong			
	Break confidentiality	*Pay for the news*	*Use official documents without permission*	*Use private documents without permission*
Germany	90%	59%	89%	46%
France	96%	64%	88%	31%
United Kingdom	91%	35%	51%	14%
Finland	61%	38%	61%	28%
United States	95%	80%	52%	18%
Spain	97%	79%	92%	63%

Source: Sánchez Aranda & Rodríguez, 1999, 108.

harder to achieve vigorous business journalism that is free of conflicts of interest (Arrese, 2008).

The tensions derived from those structural challenges are shown in very diverse forms, some of them in direct relation with other informative tasks. One of them is the decreasing number and variety of the sources used in order to develop information. In an analysis done in 2005 about the use of sources in five mainstream newspapers (*El País, El Mundo, ABC, La Vanguardia,* and *La Razón*) it was concluded that almost two thirds of the sources used in those publications were from newswires, official sources, or sources with particular interest in the story; almost half of the news only quoted one source; and there was an excessive number of sources insufficiently documented ("La batalla de las fuentes," 2005).

News stories about corporations focus on those companies that are forced by law to make a big chunk of official information public. Also, those that have strong communication strategies, or are multinationals, generate bigger global attention via wire stories or the main international media. Similarly, as pointed out by Capriotti (2007), that "official" predominance is related to the heavy weight that media coverage has on the hard issues: earnings releases, business operations; against the soft issues of social action, labor issues, or marketing.

In this configuration of the news agenda around businesses, the communication departments of big companies have become more important along with the public relations consultants that work for them. Like the media, the PR industry also has gone through an intense development and professionalization process in Spain.

Public Relations and Corporate Communication

Public relations activities in Spain had an initial professional boost during the 1960s after the economic liberalization begun by Franco starting in 1959, and thanks to the arrival of international companies in the domestic market (Noguero i Grau, 1994). However, the industry truly took off during the 1980s, as a consequence of the economic prosperity that occurred in the country after Spain joined the European Union in 1986, and continued through the magic year of 1992, with the celebration of the Olympic Games in Barcelona and the World Exhibition in Seville (Josephs & Josephs, 1992).

Between 1981 and 1989, the number of public relations agencies increased from 9 to 85. In fact, during that decade 14 of the 17 biggest existing agencies in 1992 were created (Wilson & Saura, 2003). This led to the creation of a new professional association in 1991, ADECEC, which brought together existing associations established during the 1960s. During the same period, there was a parallel development of the departments and communications directors of the great corporations and institutions, which in 1992 created its professional association, DIRCOM.

Modernization of the PR industry has been underlined by the role of multinational companies (Burson-Marsteller, Hill & Knowlton, Sandwick, etc.), but both in the academic field as well as in the professional one great efforts have been made to align the Spanish corporate communication system with that of the most developed countries (Míguez González, 2007). However, a traditional conception of public relations has not yet been set aside; that is, the use of uni-directional models that Grunig and Hunt (1984) commented on, which focus on the management of media relations (Arceo, 2004, p. 300), and cannot therefore deal with the real exigencies of the market.

During the last few years, the complexity of corporate communication activities has increased at the same time that these activities are perceived as being more relevant. According to an ADECEC study (2004) of the 500 biggest Spanish companies, 88.6% have an internal communication department, 49% work with one or more external consultant agencies, and 18% collaborate with experts. The integration of these activities, internal and external, is oriented to develop communication plans with three main goals: the improvement of corporate reputation (85%), the increment of brand knowledge (83%), and the achievement of some impact in the media (79%). On the other hand, according to this survey, the systems used to evaluate the results of the campaigns are basically these: how to gauge the impact of those actions on the media (82%); the analysis of whether sales have increased or decreased (41%); and image auditing (40%). Similar conclusions, especially related to the importance of media relations (8.8 points out of 10) were drawn in a study undertaken at about the same time by DIRCOM from a total of 1,000 big corporations (DIRCOM, 2005, p. 43).

It is understood that with those priorities the volume of the organizations' activities directed to the media (press releases, press conferences, events, etc.) has grown considerably. According to the study *Journalists, Companies and Institutions*, about 140 press releases from companies and institutions arrive every day in the newsroom of a national media outlet (Estudio de Comunicación, 2006, pp. 18–19). In the case of economic and business media, that number may be even bigger. Nonetheless, in some fields such as financial communication, the complexity of relations between journalists and sources, and market sensitivity to news published by the media, make it more critical that there be a "control" function regarding content, highlighting some of the commented features so far related to corporate communication in general (Gutiérrez, 2006).

All in all, the media system we have just described, as well as the development of corporate communications within organizations, are influenced by the still developing professionalization, a result of the big political and economic changes that have happened in Spain during the last three decades. On the other hand, it cannot be forgotten that the Spanish case fits well in the media model known as "plural polarized" (Mediterranean), according to the media typology system of Hallin and Manzini (2004). This is a model in which the press plays a smaller role, where the media are quite aligned politically speaking, there is some predominance of editorial journalism, there are some clear opportunities for greater professionalization of the newsmakers, and often the media are manipulated. Of course, those characteristics are especially relevant within political journalism, but as has been seen in this work, they can also have some specific influence on economic and business journalism.

Media Visibility and Corporate Reputation: An Empirical Analysis

Carroll and McCombs (2003) suggest five propositions that should be verified in order to evaluate the effects of the media agenda on the relationship with corporate reputation. In this short empirical endeavor, for the case of Spain, we will deal only with the first proposition, which is around the first level of agenda setting: "the amount of news coverage that a firm receives in the news media is positively related to the public's awareness of the firm" (p. 39).

In fact, this media visibility or exposure was the first to be considered in the work of Fombrun and Shanley (1990), which concluded that there was not a positive relationship between media exposure and reputation. Later on, that media visibility has been the basis of more complex concepts, such as "media reputation" (Deephouse, 2000).

For this study, the cited hypothesis from Carroll and McCombs (2003) is reformulated as: "the amount of news coverage that a firm receives *in the key news media for businessmen* is positively related to the *businessmen's evaluations of the corporate reputation of firms*."

The simplicity of the analysis that is pursued here (correlations between the quantity of news and indexes of corporate reputation using a sample of companies) is compensated for with the study of a specific audience: businesspeople, decision makers, and opinion leaders within the business community. This is in contrast with other studies undertaken, along the lines of Reputation Quotient (RQ), which take the public in general as their base, used later in order to be confronted with the informative coverage of a very generic sample of media (often quite small). This concentration on a very specific and special target, that of the business community, follows the line of analysis of communication effects and processes on "rational audiences" and elite groups, proposed by Aeron Davis in some works (Davis, 2000, 2003, 2006). Thus, the reduced focus adjusts very well to the peculiarities that have been commented on in previous epigraphs regarding the media system and business and economic information in Spain. Therefore, using the company sample, we will study the companies at the top of the Merco ranking.

The empirical analysis uses two sources of data: the ranking of the Merco study 2008, especially the value related to the first 30 companies; and the amount of news about those companies published in five national dailies (*El País, El Mundo, ABC, Expansión,* and *Cinco Días*), which have most of their business audience in Spain; that also includes the audience profile that constitutes the base for the elaboration of Merco.[5]

Merco 2008 carried out the fieldwork between October 2007 and January 2008, which was also the period for news content analysis. But in this case it was decided to extend the period to half a year, between July 1st and December 31st of 2007 in order to show news coverage over a longer time line, which enabled a more vigorous frame of the surveyors' opinions, in order to take into account the most recent corporate behavior.

Lexis-Nexis Academic was used to quantify the amount of news that was used—it provides the complete texts of the print editions of the five media analyzed. Only those articles that quoted the company's name in a headline were chosen, with the goal of having a clearer view of the relevance and visibility of each corporation. In order to eliminate the texts that used the names of some companies as generic terms—*telefónica* and *popular* as adjectives, or *Santander* as a city—all the headlines were analyzed in order to verify the news content. Although the number of stories that quote the company in the headline is an incomplete measure of its visibility compared with other more complex methods (see Kiousis, 2004), it is enough for the exploratory approximation described here. Table 11.4 shows data from Merco 2008 related to the two variables for the 30 companies with better reputations.

Without taking into account other variables of control common in this kind of study (e.g., Fombrun & Shanley, 1990; Van Riel, 2002; Zyglidopoulos & Georgiadis, 2006), when analyzing the data related to the 30 leading companies listed by Merco, it is possible to assert that a significant correlation exists ($r = 0.55$, $p < 0.01$) between the corporate reputation index and the media coverage.

This generally positive relationship could be qualified even more if two features of the media and companies analyzed are taken into account: on the media front, its general or specialized nature (general newspapers: *El País*, *El Mundo*, and *ABC*; economic newspapers: *Expansión* and *Cinco Días*); on the companies front, if they are publicly listed or not on the Madrid Stock Exchange (18 public companies; 12 private companies).

Table 11.5 shows the correlations with the total of the sample and with the relationships within the qualified subsamples.

The data show that the higher correlations were obtained within the economic press and the companies whose shares trade on the stock exchange, which proves some of the ideas shown in this chapter about the print media and about the extra visibility of public companies, as well as other conclusions of earlier contributions about the media prominence of some corporations (e.g., Van Riel, 2002).

From a more qualitative point of view, it could be asserted that the general correlation between the reputation index and the media coverage improves significantly if some "special cases" are excluded from the sample, such as the ones explained next. More precisely, the correlation reached an $r = 0.91$, $p < 0.01$, if five companies with special circumstances are excluded: Inditex, El Corte Inglés, Mercadona, Endesa, and Gas Natural.

The first three (Inditex, El Corte Inglés, and Mercadona) are companies with significantly small media coverage, compared with their high reputation. This is the case of companies that have unconventional communication strategies. Inditex (parent company of the Zara brand), is a case in point: its international visibility is bigger than its reputation in Spain, in spite of having its shares traded on the Madrid Stock Exchange and the fact that Zara is a very popular brand. Inditex has almost nonexistent publicity, and its founder Amancio Ortega has played things close to the chest to an almost legendary degree. Something similar happens with El Corte Inglés, although in this case the company is one of the biggest advertisers in the country. It is also one of the biggest companies in Spain, though it is not publicly traded, and it has maintained a remote tone toward the

Table 11.4 Reputation and Media Visibility: Top 30 Merco 2008

| | Merco 2008 | General Newspapers | | | Total General | Business Newspapers | | Total Business | Total |
		El País	El Mundo	ABC		Expan-sión	Cinco Días		
Inditex	10,000	10	4	9	23	28	59	87	110
Telefónica	9,756	129	89	202	420	159	238	397	817
El Corte Inglés	9,618	12	13	47	72	22	29	51	123
Repsol	8,554	54	34	90	178	79	84	163	341
Gruop Santander	8,408	95	53	110	258	82	114	196	454
La Caixa	8,245	51	30	117	198	63	48	111	309
BBVA	7,909	46	52	107	205	104	157	261	466
Iberdrola	7,462	69	40	116	225	135	93	228	453
Merca-dona	6,154	2	5	10	17	4	3	7	24
Acciona	5,079	33	29	74	136	52	70	122	258
Caja Madrid	5,042	20	30	62	112	62	64	126	238
Ferrovial	4,751	20	11	20	51	48	58	106	157
Mapfre	4,741	12	5	12	29	26	25	51	80
Vodafone	4,726	14	16	24	54	33	33	66	120
Bankinter	4,385	22	9	14	45	41	44	85	130
Indra	4,344	6	1	3	10	23	20	43	53
IBM	4,286	1	2	3	6	5	21	26	32
Gas Natural	4,261	37	24	80	141	54	63	117	258
Microsoft	4,218	24	6	28	58	30	57	87	145
Siemens	4,129	9	10	31	50	23	14	37	87
ACS	4,080	18	14	27	59	41	47	88	147
Endesa	4,073	129	61	162	352	95	128	223	575
Banco Popular	4,022	12	16	32	60	28	31	59	119
Abertis	3,945	26	5	15	46	63	65	128	174
Novartis	3,911	3	2	2	7	4	6	10	17
Accentur	3,911	0	0	0	0	6	2	8	8
MRW	3,886	0	1	0	1	0	1	1	2
Gamesa	3,885	5	1	2	8	12	32	44	52
Nestlé	3,851	3	0	4	7	8	4	12	19
Cepsa	3,762	17	3	16	36	10	16	26	62

Table 11.5 Correlations between General and Business Newspapers

		Total	General	Business
Pearson correlation	Merco 2008	0,55**	0,53**	0,56**
Sig. (unilateral)		0.0007	0.0012	0.0006
N		30	30	30
Pearson correlation	Merco 2008	0,58**	0,51*	0,64**
Sig. (unilateral)	Stock Market	0.0058	0.0149	0.0020
N		18	18	18

*p<0.05, **p<0.01

media. Finally, Mercadona has recently appeared in the Merco, and its business system also focuses on an intense relationship with its clients while maintaining a low institutional profile. It is worth noticing that the three companies work hard on detail sales, and their reputation and the prestige of their business model has been built from direct and intense contact with millions of clients at the point of sale.

Regarding the other two companies (Endesa and Gas Natural), the opposite happens: they have disproportionately high media coverage. After a deep analysis of that coverage, it is evident that it corresponds to an extraordinary moment in those companies' lives. There was continual front page coverage during the second half of 2007 of the controversial acquisition of Endesa, the biggest electric company in Spain, in which several businesses participated, included some foreign consortiums and Gas Natural. Because of its political and business implications, it has been one of the most commented on business affairs by the media. Besides, Endesa was shown as a company that was to be bought by foreigners, and consequently, somehow seen as a "loser" amid the highly competitive environment of the global markets. This is shown clearly in Merco 2008, where it ranked 23 whereas in previous years it had appeared amongst the top 10.

Other companies whose special behavior would deserve individual analysis are the foreign companies, which as it has been explained have little importance when compared with Spanish companies with the best reputation. In the sample of the 30 companies analyzed, six are foreign companies (Vodafone, IBM, Microsoft, Siemens, Novartis, Accenture, and Nestlé). Three of them, Vodafone, Microsoft, and Siemens have a quite balanced relationship between the reputation index and media coverage, whereas the rest have very low visibility in terms of the reputation index (see Table 11.4).

There is no doubt that this empirical approach to the relationship between corporate reputation and media visibility has significant limitations. The conclusions reached could be generalized for a variety of reasons: The size of the cohort and the criteria used to choose the sample, which focused on the companies with the best reputation, and the undertaking of a simple analysis of correlations—without taking into account the variables of control—such as the use of a media visibility gage as simple as the number of stories. At the same time, to compensate for those drawbacks, the results are of great interest if they are analyzed from the perspective of the study of companies, audiences, and media that are of crucial importance to public opinion as it relates to corporate and business issues. In that field, the clear positive relationship between corporate reputation and journalism coverage, at least in Spain, may have important theoretical and practical implications.

Conclusions

In this chapter we have contextualized the recent interest in corporate reputation issues in Spain, and analyzed its relationship to corporate coverage by the media.

In the case of Spain, this relationship must be understood in the context of a business sector and journalism markets that have developed in an accelerated way during the last two decades. In contrast to what happens in other countries, where the relationship between the media and business has a long tradition, in Spain the brevity of this trend has important consequences, which are added to a traditional disinterest in business and economic issues on the part of the general public.

One of the clearest consequences of this situation is that news about business is relegated to a great extent to specialized fields where concepts such as the corporate reputation function. This is clearly seen in two of the topics studied in this work. On the one hand, there is the lack of attention that business issues receive in the mass media, especially the broadcast ones, which at the same time are where most of the population gain information about current issues. On the other hand, companies have been too focused on their own fields of interest, those of the business world, and that is also reflected in the studies about corporate reputation undertaken in this country. All of them gage corporate reputation via executives, specialists, and expert opinion, underestimating the significance of an evaluation that could be made by the general public.

The second idea, which is derived from the previous one, is that the analysis of the role that could be played by the media on the configuration of corporate reputation from the agenda-setting perspective requires a focus on some particular media platforms (especially print), a few specific audiences (especially the executive public), and a limited number of companies (giving special weight to those that are publicly traded). It is in such a concentrated universe of interests where the interrelation between visibility and reputation could be correctly evaluated.

From those two basic ideas, the exploratory empirical analysis offered at the end of this chapter, although it could be further developed, confirms that in the case of Spain there is a high correlation between the level of media visibility and the corporate reputation index of the main Spanish companies, which means the accomplishment of the agenda-setting hypothesis in this field, at least at its most basic level. Moreover, the study suggests that the logic focus explained in this chapter, and which is coherent with the thesis about the functioning of elite audiences (Davis, 2003), works when isolating the companies' visibility in the most specialized media, and when isolating likewise those that because they are publicly traded companies require more intense media and corporate communication management.

Notes

1. Representative samples for comparison: Germany West (1999); Spain (2000); United States (1999).
2. The European Business Readership Survey (EBRS) is the only pan-European survey that is published regularly and with enough methodological consistency so as to analyze readership habits of European executives and business people since 1973. This survey, normally biannual, offers audience data from almost 300 publications in 17 different countries, and its use is very common within the media planning of international campaigns targeted to this segment of the market. The audience profile that is analyzed is that of high-level executives from medium and large business organizations, defined by both the number of employees and sales volume (EBRS, 2006).
3. In order for this data to be better understood, it cannot be forgotten that in 2008 Spain was among the few European countries that did not have specific legislation covering access to public information.
4. According to the macro survey carried out amongst journalists in 1997 at the University of Navarra's Public Communication Department, the economic journalists declared much more than those in other fields of news that the daily news agenda was very predetermined (81% against 65%), and that the public relations agencies were a very useful source of information (78% against 39%) (for a description of the survey, see Sánchez Aranda & Rodríguez, 1999).
5. The sample of Merco 2008 interviews comprised 1,250 executives who answered a general survey, and five samples of experts who evaluated different aspects of the first 100 companies, 100 analysts who evaluated the financial and economic results; 88 union members who evaluated the quality of a workplace; 78 directors of consumer associations who evaluated the commercial quality; and 55 opinion leaders who shared their opinions on the reputation of 100 business leaders.

References

ADECEC. (2004). *La Comunicación y las Relaciones Públicas. Radiografía del Sector 2004* [Communication and Public Relations. Industry Analysis 2004]. Madrid: Ediciones Pirámide.

AIDEKA. (2005). *Estudio comparativo de los informativos de TVE, Antena 3 y Telecinco* [A comparative study of television news programmes in TVE, Antena 3 and Telecinco]. Madrid, Spain: Asociación para la investigación y desarrollo de la cultura audiovisual (AIDEKA).

AIMC. (2008). *Marco General de Medios en España 2008* [Spanish Media General Survey 2008]. Madrid: Asociación para la Investigación de Medios de Comunicación (AIMC).

Álvarez, J. L., & Merchán, C. C. (1994). From escapism to resented conformity: Market economics and modern organizations in Spanish literature. In B. Czarniawska-Joerges & P. Guillet de Monthoux (Eds.), *Good novels, better managment: Reading organizational realities in fiction* (pp. 175–198). Abingdon, UK: Harwood.

Arceo, A. (2004). Public relations in Spain: An introduction. *Public Relations Review, 30,* 293–302.

Argandoña, A. (1999). Business ethics in Spain. *Journal of Business Ethics, 22,* 155–173.

Arrese, A. (2002). *Prensa económica: De la Lloyd's List al wsj.com* [Economic and financial press: From the Lloyd's List to the wsj.com]. Pamplona, Spain: Eunsa.

Arrese, A. (2007). Prensa económica y financiera en España. Apuntes para una historia reciente [Economic and financial press in Spain. Notes for a contemporary history]. In J. J. Fernández (Ed.), *Prensa especializada actual: Doce calas* [Specialized Press. Twelve studies] (pp. 1–36). Madrid, Spain: McGraw-Hill.

Arrese, A. (2008, April 7–9). *Desafíos estructurales de la prensa económica* [Structural challenges for the economic and financial press]. Paper presented at the 4th Congreso Internacional de Prensa y Periodismo Especializado. Guadalajara, Spain.

Barnett, M. L., Jermier, J. M., & Lafferty, B. A. (2006). Corporate reputation: The definitional landscape. *Corporate Reputation Review, 9*(1), 23–38.

Benavides, J., Canel, M. J., Echart, N., Jerez, A., Luengo, O., Sampedro, V. et al. (2006). Agendas electorales y agendas de la prensa de referencia: La cobertura de la campaña de 2004 en los diarios de difusión estatal [Electoral and press agendas:. The coverage of the 2004 elections in the main national newspapers]. In A. Vara, J. Virgili, E. Jiménez, & M. Díaz (Eds.), *Cobertura informativa del 11-M* [News coverage of the 11-M Madrid train bombing] (pp. 73–81). Pamplona, Spain: Eunsa.

Canel, M. J., Llamas, J. P., & Rey, F. (1996). El primer nivel del efecto agenda-setting en la información local: Los "problemas más importantes" de la ciudad de Pamplona [The first level of agenda-setting effects in local news: The "most important problems" of the city of Pamplona]. *Comunicación y Sociedad, 9*(1–2), 17–37.

Canel, M. J., & Piqué, A. M. (1998). Journalists in emerging democracies: The case of Spain. In D. H. Weaver (Ed.), *The global journalist: News people around the world* (pp. 299–319). Creskill, NJ: Hampton Press.

Canel, M. J., Sánchez Aranda, J. J., & Rodríguez, R. (2000). *Opiniones y actitudes: Periodistas al descubierto* [Opinions and Attitudes: Journalists at a glance]. Madrid, Spain: Centro de Investigaciones Sociológicas.

Capriotti, P. (2007). La Responsabilidad Social Corporativa de las empresas españolas en los medios de comunicación. [Media coverage of corporate social responsability of spanish companies]. *Zer: Revista de Estudios de Comunicación, 23*, 61–74.

Carroll, C. E., & McCombs, M. (2003). Agenda-setting effects of business news on the public's images and opinions about major corporations. *Corporate Reputation Review, 6*(1), 36–46.

Cases, P. (1985). Las empresas [The companies]. In *Informar de Economía* [To inform about the economy] (pp. 193–196). Madrid, Spain: APIE/Banco de Santander.

Davis, A. (2000). Public relations, business news and the reproduction of corporate elite power. *Journalism, 1*(3), 282–304.

Davis, A. (2003). Whither mass media and power? Evidence for a critical elite theory alternative. *Media, Culture and Society, 25*, 669–690.

Davis, A. (2006). Media effects and the question of the rational audience: Lessons from the financial markets. *Media, Culture & Society, 28*(4), 603–625.

Deephouse, D. L. (2000). Media reputation as a strategic resource: An integration of mass communication and resource-based theories. *Journal of Management, 26*(6), 1.091–1.112.

De la Cruz, M., & Cabrera, K. (2005). Corporate social responsibility and family business in Spain. *Journal of Business Ethics, 56*, 27–41.

De la Fuente, J. M., & De Quevedo, E. (2003). The concept and measurement of corporate reputation: An application to Spanish financial intermediaries. *Corporate Reputation Review, 5*(4), 280–301.

Del Río, R. (2000). *La profesionalización de la información económica en España* [The professionalization of business news in Spain]. Madrid, Spain: APIE.

De Miguel, A. (2003). *Las ideas económicas de los intelectuales españoles* [The economic ideas of spanish intellectuals]. Madrid, Spain: Instituto de Estudios Económicos.

De Quevedo, E. (2003). *Reputación y creación de valor: Una relación circular* [Reputation and value creation. A circular relationship]. Madrid, Spain: Thompson/Paraninfo.

De Quevedo, E., De la Fuente, J. M., & Delgado, J. B. (2007). Corporate social performance and corporate reputation: Two interwoven perspectives. *Corporate Reputation Review, 10*(1), 60–72.

Diezhandino, P., Bezunartea, O., & Coca, C. (1994). *La élite de los periodistas* [The elite of the journalism profession]. Bilbao, Spain: Universidad del País Vasco.

DIRCOM. (2005). *El estado de la comunicación en España 2004* (2nd ed.) [The state of the communication industry in Spain 2004]. Madrid, Spain: Asociación de Directivos de la Comunicación (DIRCOM).

Edelman. (2007). *Edelman trust barometer, 2008*. New York: Author.

Estudio de Comunicación. (2006). *Periodistas, empresas e instituciones: Claves de una relación necesaria* [Journalists, companies and institutions: Keys for a relationship]. Madrid, Spain: Estudio de Comunicación/Demométrica/APIE.

Eurobarometer. (2007, December). *Scientific research in the media: Special Eurobarometer, 282*. Brussels, Belgium: European Commission.

European Business Readership Survey 2006. (2006). London: Ipsos-RSL.

Flores Andrade, A. (2000). Los empresarios y la transición a la democracia en España [Businessmen and the political transition to democray in Spain]. *Estudios Sociológicos, 18*(54), 695–726.

Fombrun, C. (1996). *Reputation: Realizing values from the corporate image*. Boston, MA: Harvard Business School Press.

Fombrun, C. (1998). Indices of corporate reputation: An analysis of media rankings and social monitor's ratings. *Corporate Reputation Review, 1*(4), 327–340.

Fombrun, C. (2007). List of lists: A compilation of international corporate reputation ratings. *Corporate Reputation Review, 10*(2), 144–153.

Fombrun, C., & Shanley, M. (1990). What's in a name? Reputation building and corporate strategy. *Academy of Management Journal, 33*(2), 233–258.

Fombrun, C., & Van Riel, C. (1997). The reputational landscape. *Corporate Reputation Review, 1*(1–2), 5–13.

García Galera, C. (Ed.). (2006). *Audiencia infantil e información sobre terrorismo: Los medios ante el 11-M.* [Young audiences and news about terrorism. The media coverage of 11-M]. Madrid, Spain: CIE Dossat.

Guillén, M. F. (1989). *La profesión de economista: El auge de economistas, ejecutivos y empresarios en España* [The economist profession: The rise of economists, managers and businessmen in Spain]. Barcelona, Spain: Ariel.

Guillén, M. F. (2005). *The rise of Spanish multinationals*. Cambridge, UK: Cambridge University Press.

Gutiérrez, E. (2006). *Comunicación institucional financiera* [Financial corporate communication]. Pamplona, Spain: Eunsa.

Grunig, J. & Hunt, T. (1984). *Managing public relations*. New York: Rinehart & Winston.

Hallin, D., & Manzini, P. (2004). *Comparing media systems: Three models of media and politics*. Cambridge, UK: Cambridge University Press.

Heywood, P. (1997). From dictatorship to democracy: Changing forms of corruption in Spain. In D. Della Porta & Y. Mény (Eds.), *Democracy and corruption in Europe* (pp. 65–84). London: Continuum.

Humanes, M. L. (1998). La profesión periodística en España [The journalist profession in Spain]. *Zer. Revista de Estudios de Comunicación, 4*, 265–278.

Igartua, J. J., Muñiz, C., Otero, J. A., & De la Fuente, M. (2007). El tratamiento informativo de la inmigración en los medios de comunicación españoles: Un análisis de contenido desde la Teoría del Framing [News coverage of immigration issues in the spanish media: A content analysis based on framing theory]. *Estudios sobre el Mensaje Periodístico, 13*, 91–110.

Josephs, R., & Josephs, J. (1992, May). Spain gains world attention as public relations comes of age. *Public Relations Journal, 48*(5), 18–22.

Kiousis, S. (2004). Explicating media salience: A factor analysis of New York Times issue coverage during the 2000 U.S. presidential election. *Journal of Communication, 54*(1), 71–87.

La batalla de las fuentes. (2005, December). *Cuadernos de Periodistas*, 13–22.

López-Escobar, E. (2007). Una contribución a la investigación sobre los efectos de agenda setting de los medios de comunicación [A contribution to the research on agenda setting effects of the mass media] [Special issue]. *Sphera Pública, 1*, 195–213.

López-Escobar, E., & Llamas, J. P. (1998). Agenda setting and community consensus: First and second level effects. *International Journal of Public Opinion Research, 10*(4), 335–348.

López-Escobar, E., Llamas, J. P., McCombs, M. & Rey, F. (1998). Two levels of agenda setting among advertising and news in the 1995 Spanish elections. *Political Communication, 15*, 225–238.

López-Escobar, E., Llamas, J. P., & Rey, F. (1996). La agenda entre medios: Primero y segundo nivel [Inter-media agenda: first and second level]. *Comunicación y Sociedad, 9*(1–2), 67–90.

López-Escobar, E., McCombs, M., & Rey, F. (1996). La imagen de los candidatos: El segundo nivel de la agenda setting [The candidate image: The second level of the agenda setting]. *Comunicación y Sociedad, 9*(1–2), 36–66.

Martín Castro, G., Navas López, J. E., & López Sáez, P. (2006). Business and social reputation: Exploring the concept and main dimensions of corporate reputation. *Journal of Business Ethics, 63*, 361–370.

Martín, M. (2000). *Information, action and reaction: The agenda setting process for anorexia and other eating disorders in Spain.* Paper presented at the Joint Meeting of the World Association for Public Opinion Research and the American Association for Public Opinion Research, Portland, OR.

Martín, M. (2004). *Breaking the silence ceiling: How gender violence became a social problem in Spain through media and politics.* Paper presented at the 2nd International Symposium, Communication in the Millennium, Istanbul, Turkey.

Martín, M., López-Escobar, E., McCombs, M., & Tolsá, A. (2000). *Framing political leaders' images and the second level inter-media agenda-setting: The role played by radio in Spain.* Paper presented at the Joint Meeting of the World Association for Public Opinion Research and the American Association for Public Opinion Research, Portland, OR.

McCombs, M. (1997). New frontiers in agenda setting: Agendas of attributes and frames. *Mass Communication Review, 24*(1–2), 32–52.

McCombs, M., & Evatt, D. (1995). Los temas y los aspectos: Explorando una nueva dimensión de la agenda setting [Issues and aspects: Exploring the second level of the agenda setting]. *Comunicación y Sociedad, 8*(1), 7–32.

McCombs, M., Llamas, J. P., López-Escobar, E., & Rey, F. (1997). Candidate images in Spanish elections: Second-level agenda setting effects. *Journalism and Mass Communication Quarterly, 74*(4), 703–717.

McCombs, M, López-Escobar, E., & Llamas, J. P. (2000, Spring). Setting the agenda of attributes in the 1996 Spanish general election. *Journal of Communication, 50*(2), 77–92.

Melé, D. (1999). Early business ethics in Spain: The Salamanca School (1526–1614). *Journal of Business Ethics, 22,* 175–189.

Mena, N. (2008). *Immigration agenda setting in Spain: When news-worthy events play a role in how and when public opinion and politicians consider immigration to be an important social issue.* Paper presented at the 6th International Symposium, Communication in the Millennium, Istanbul, Turkey.

Micu, A., & Geana, M. V. (2004). *The multifaceted euro: An agenda setting study on attitudes towards the euro in France, Spain and Great Britain.* Paper presented at the Annual Meeting of the International Communication Association (ICA), New Orleans, LA. Retrieved from http://www.allacademic.com/ meta/p112595_index.html

Míguez González, M. I. (2007). Aproximación a la investigación y a la situación de las relaciones públicas en Europa: Estudio comparativo entre el caso español y el alemán [An approximation to the research and to the state of public relations in Europe: A comparative study between the spanish and german case]. *Revista Latina de Comunicación Social 62.* Retrieved from http://www.ull.es/publicaciones/latina/200715Miguez.htm

Mindshare. (2004). *Estudio directivos 2004* [Businessmen Survey 2004]. Madrid: Author.

Muñoz Alonso, A. (1984). Información económica y opinión pública [Economic information and public opinion]. In *Actas de las Terceras Jornadas de Información Económica* (pp. 11–21). Bilbao, Spain: APIE/Banco de Bilbao.

Noguero i Grau, A. (1994). La historia de las relaciones públicas en España: 1954–1990 [History of public relations in Spain: 1954–1990]. *Revista Universitaria de Publicidad y Relaciones Públicas, 1,* 67–90.

Ortega, F., & Humanes, M. L. (2000). *Algo más que periodistas: Sociología de una profesión* [Something more than journalists: The sociology of a profession]. Madrid, Spain: Ariel.

PR Week, & Burson Marsteller. (2007, November 12). CEO survey 2007. *PRWeek.* Retrieved from: http://www.beckersf.com/press/prweek_nov07.pdf

Rodríguez Carrasco, J. M. (2004). Percepción y medida en la reputación empresarial [Business reputation: perception and measurement]. *Economía Industrial, 357,* 117–131.

Rodríguez Díaz, R. (2004). *Teoría de la Agenda-Setting. Aplicación a la enseñanza universitaria* [Agenda setting theory. An application to higher education]. Madrid, Spain: OBETS Editorial.

Rodríguez Salcedo, N. (2004). *Evolución histórica de las Relaciones Públicas en Europa: S.A.E. de RP y el desarrollo de la profesión en España (1960–1975)* [Historical evolution of public relations in Europe: S.A.E. and the professional development of public relations in Spain (1960-1975)]. Unpublished doctoral dissertation, School of Communication, University of Navarra, Pamplona.

Sampedro, V., Luengo, O., Jerez, A., Saperas, E., Benavides, J., Canel, M. J., et al. (2006). Agendas electorales y televisivas. La cobertura de la campaña de marzo de 2004 en las televisiones públicas y privadas [Electoral and tv news agendas. The coverage of the 2004 campaign in private and state owned televisions]. In A. Vara, J. Virgili, E. Jiménez, & M. Díaz, *Cobertura informativa del 11-M* (pp. 203–237). Pamplona, Spain: Eunsa.

Sánchez Aranda, J. J., & Rodríguez, R. (1999). Profesionalidad y ética. El caso de los periodistas españoles [Professionalism and ethics. The case of spanish journalists]. *Comunicación y Sociedad, 12*(2), 93–114.

Sanders, K., & Canel, M. J. (2006). A scribbling tribe: Reporting political scandal in Britain and Spain. *Journalism, 7*(4), 453–476.

Sanders, K., Hanna, M., Berganza, M. R., & Sánchez Aranda, J. J. (2008). Becoming journalists: A comparison of the professional attitudes and values of British and Spanish journalism students. *European Journal of Communication, 23*(2), 133–152.

Semetko, H., & Canel, M. J. (1997). Agenda-senders vs. agenda-setters: Television in Spain's 1996 election campaign. *Political Communication, 14,* 459–479.

Van Riel, C. (2002). Top of mind awareness of corporate brands among the Dutch public. *Corporate Reputation Review, 4*(4), 362–373.

Van Riel, C., & Fombrun, C. (2002). Introduction: Which company is most visible in your country? [Special issue]. *Corporate Reputation Review, 4*(4), 296–302.

Vara, A. (2001). *La influencia de los partidos políticos en la construcción de la agenda mediática y el rol de los periodistas como mediadores sociales* [The influence of political parties in the building of media agendas and the role of journalists as social intermediaries]. Unpublished doctoral dissertation, School of Communication, University of Navarra, Pamplona, Spain.

Villafañe, J. (2000). La reputación corporativa [The corporate reputation]. In J. Villafañe (Ed.), *El Estado de la Publicidad y el Corporate en España* (pp. 161–194). Madrid,Spain: Pirámide.

Villafañe, J. (2003). *La buena reputación: Claves del valor intangible de las empresas* [The good reputation. Keys of a company intangible value]. Madrid, Spain: Pirámide.

Villafañe & Asociados. (2004). Cómo valoran la reputación los CEO españoles [How spanish CEOs value reputation]. Retrieved from www.reputacioncorporativa.org/ ator/media/documento/Cómo_valoran_la_reputación_los_CEO_españoles. Pdf

Wattley-Ames, H. (1999). *Spain is different.* Boston, MA: Intercultural Press.

Wilson, D. J., & Saura, P. (2003). Public relations and the new golden age in Spain: A confluence of democracy, economic development and the media. *Public Relations Review, 29,* 125–143.

World Association of Newspapers (WAN). (2008). *World press trends, 2008.* Paris: Author.

World Values Survey. (2000). Tilburg, Netherlands: The European Values Study Foundation and World Values Survey Association. Retrieved from http://www.worldvalues-survey.org/

Zabala, I., Panadero, G., Gallardo, M. L., Sánchez-Galindo, M., Tena, I., & Villalba, I. (2005). Corporate reputation in professional services firms: Reputation management based on intellectual capital management. *Corporate Reputation Review, 8*(1), 59–71.

Zyglidopoulos, S. C., & Georgiadis, A. P. (2006). *Media visibility as a driver of corporate social performance* (Working Paper Series 16). Cambridge, UK: Cambridge Judge Business School.

12 Corporate Reputation and the News Media in Sweden

Magnus Fredriksson and Maria Grafström

This chapter examines how the news media in Sweden affect the public's perceptions of companies. The news media's attention toward the corporate life has increased significantly over the last few decades. In concert with this development, corporate communication has become more sophisticated. The public relations industry is established, and *corporate reputation* has become an important term both within the business community and in research. In Sweden, the relationship between news media and companies is often understood and discussed from the perspective of trust, and consequently trust has also become an important dimension of corporate reputation.

The chapter first presents the national traits of Sweden, followed by a literature review of extant research in Sweden on corporate reputation, agenda-setting theory, and the relationship between business and the news media. This is followed by an outline of data showing trust as a key dimension of corporate reputation in Sweden. The chapter ends with research conclusions and a discussion.

Expansion of Swedish Business News

The history of the news media and their relationship with corporate life is relatively short in Sweden (Grafström, 2006). Whereas business news media have increased rapidly over the last few decades, media's coverage of companies was almost nonexistent as late as the early 1960s. During the 1960s and 1970s, the current prominent Swedish business newspapers were founded, and the subsequent decades showed significant increases in the number of publications relating to business and economics (Figure 12.1). During the 1980s and 1990s, specialized news media grew and general news media, whether newspapers, radio, television, or the Internet, increasingly began to increase their coverage of Swedish corporate life (Djerf-Pierre & Weibull, 2001; Grafström, 2006; Lindqvist, 2001; Severinsson & Nilsson, 2000).

Against the background of an increase in business news over the last few decades, interest in news media and agenda-setting theory concerning business has also become very active. Swedish research on corporate reputation and the relationship between business and news media is, however, nascent. But in concert with the recent rise over the past few decades and the popularization of business journalism, the media have become important agenda setters for major corporations and their activities in Sweden (Carroll & McCombs, 2003; Pallas, & Strannegård, 2010; Petrelius Karlberg, 2007; Sahlin-Andersson & Engwall, 2002). Today's business journalism plays a salient role in the Swedish corporate world.

The Swedish Model

According to the annual ratings of the World Economic Forum, Sweden is the world's fourth most competitive economy (Global Competitiveness Report, 2009–2010). In Sweden, the relationship between corporations and other institutional actors has been built on "the Swedish model," an extensive compromise defining the responsibilities of the state and the industrial and commercial world. Olof Petersson (1991) points toward this model as a framework within which the Social Democrats could reform and better implement the welfare state. In turn, the industrial and commercial world was given autonomy and support to develop industrial renewal using rational and internationally compatible production. The compromise limited the responsibilities of corporations to the economy and the workplace. It also limited the number of groups that had the right to put forward claims on corporations. Apart from stakeholders with economic interests, the only legitimate interests were those posed by employees and their representatives (trade unions). In this matter Sweden has a history of central negotiations and national agreements between trade unions and employers' associations rather than legal construction and formulation of the rules for the labor market.

The notion of the Swedish model is in itself vague and it contains several contradictions within it. It is therefore better to describe the concept as a prototype

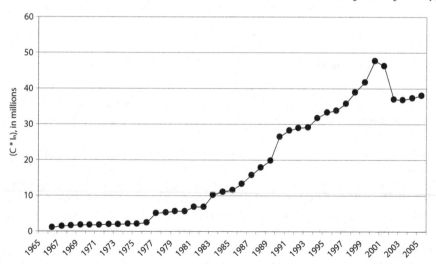

Figure 12.1 Circulation development of the Swedish business press between 1965 and 2005. The graph includes circulation and number of issues for Affärsvärlden, Veckans affärer, Dagens Industri, and Finanstidningen, where *C= Circulation per issue* and *LN = Number of Issues.*

with a number of distinctive features—a coherent idea with general applicability. Some of the more central ideas incorporated in the Swedish model are a culture of understanding built on corporatism and a drive for collective agreements at a national level. The public sector is given a dominant position and by the use of social engineering (legitimized by science and powered by practical issues) it works for collective solutions in areas such as health care, education, child care, and social welfare. The underpinning is a universal system giving all citizens the same benefits irrespective of their needs. It is also a system where individual solutions (insurance or agreements between the individual and the employer) and philanthropic initiatives are counteracted on ideological grounds.

The foundations for the social structure, a capitalist economy and the welfare state have been thoroughly transformed. According to Ulrich Beck (1994) and Anthony Giddens (1996) urbanization, globalization, individualization, and the transition into a late, reflexive modernity have transformed many of the properties of the industrial society. Traditional forms (order, class, gender roles, the family, etc.) have been replaced by new social forms (fragmentation, individualization, reflexivity, etc.), and in Sweden we can see the transition of the Swedish model. Internal factors (expansion of the public sector, increasing intrusion by the state in the industrial and commercial world, the breakdown of central negotiations, an increasing tension between public authorities and popularly elected officials, etc.) and external factors (new forms of production, environmental issues, globalization, increasing heterogeneity, political instability, economic crises, etc.) have created new forms of relationships between work, capital, and new frames of reference when individuals interact with authorities, corporations, and their political and trade union representatives. There is a clear expansion in the number of stakeholders making demands on corporations (Micheletti & Stolle, 2003, pp. 105–108).

Agenda-Setting Theory

Swedish research on mass media and audience has been dominated by a uses and gratifications perspective, and as a consequence there are only two major works published on agenda-setting theory. In *Mäktiga massmedier* (Powerful Mass Media), Kent Asp (1986) studies the election campaigns before the referendum concerning nuclear power in Sweden in 1980. He focuses on the presence of the issue and actors in major Swedish news media and analyzes the range, the representation, and the quality of the news content. The second study presents the results from two surveys (one before the referendum and one after) concerning the knowledge, perception, values, and actions of the Swedish public that are related to the matter. The results show a clear relationship between the agenda of news media and public opinion.

Bengt Johansson (1998) follows the tradition in his work *Nyheter mitt ibland oss* (News Among Us) where he concentrates on the importance of local news media as an agenda-setting agent regarding people's knowledge and attitudes toward the actors, issues, and practices of local politics. The results confirm the theory of agenda setting. In addition to these major works there are additional works where agenda-setting theory plays a minor role (e.g., Bennulf, 1994; Nord, 1995).

Business and the News Media

In line with the above discussion, research on the influence of the news media on business in Sweden is nascent and studies explicitly using agenda-setting theory within the field are nonexistent. Extant research in this area has mainly focused on media from a corporate governance perspective. The news media have been conceptualized as carriers of management ideas, participating in creating, shaping, and circulating ideas and practices that relate to corporate behavior (Buhr & Grafström, 2007; Engwall & Sahlin, 2007; Sahlin-Andersson & Engwall, 2002). In this way, the media participate in creating new conditions for corporations. One consequence is the "mediatization of corporate leadership," which has been investigated by Petrelius Karlberg (2007, 2008). Another Swedish study from 1990 concluded that corporate leaders have "stepped into the limelight, alternatively been brought out by journalism" (Hvitfelt & Malmström, 1990, p. 48).

Swedish studies in the area also show that corporations increasingly build relationships with and learn to handle news media. Today, corporations plan and organize their media relations and activities in communication departments (Pallas, 2007). Often, these departments are populated by people trained in communications or by former journalists. A Swedish study on production of business—how quarterly reports were transformed into business news—proves that the work of business news reporters and corporate communication personnel are highly interrelated and dependent on one another (Grafström, Grünberg, Pallas, & Windell, 2006). It is shown that values and norms guiding business news production permeate not only editorial offices, but also the work of corporate information departments. In addition, former journalists often populate information departments, further strengthening the idea of common understanding among business and the news media (Grafström & Pallas, 2007).

A recent stream of literature has paid attention to news media and their relationship with the business world from the perspective of innovative systems (e.g., Nordfors, 2004; Nordfors, Kreiss, & Sandred, 2005; Nordfors & Ventresca, 2006). The concept of "innovation journalism" is defined as "journalism about innovation, i.e. the market introduction of inventions, for example commercialization of emerging technologies" (Nordfors, 2004, p. 3). The aim is to overcome the oft-made distinctions between business and technology in journalistic publications (Nordfors et al., 2005, p. 6) and to set issues about innovation systems on the (business) journalistic agenda.

Coming back to agenda-setting theory, the first hypothesis concerns media attention and public awareness (Carroll & McCombs, 2003; McCombs, 2004). In order to be prominent in the public consciousness, corporations need to gain attention through media content. Whereas a few studies show the visibility of corporations in the Swedish news media (Apéria, Brönn, & Schultz, 2004), none has explicitly examined the relationship between media visibility and the public awareness of corporations. The second level of agenda-setting theory—substantive attributes—proposes that organizational attributes that gain attention in media and organizational attributes that are prominent in public awareness are positively related. In addition, the third hypothesis (second level—affective— agenda setting) suggests a positive correlation between positive (negative) presentation of attributes in the media and positive (negative) perceptions about the same attributes by the public. Research in Sweden on these two second-level agenda-setting hypotheses about corporations is still absent.

Corporate Reputation

Even though the interest has increased significantly over the last few years, research on business and media is still nascent in Sweden. Much of the emerging Swedish corporate reputation discourse is influenced and shaped by the American tradition within the field. The only existing peer-reviewed article on corporate reputation in Sweden (Apéria et al., 2004) uses the framework of Fombrun, Gardberg, and Sever (2000) in order to measure reputational dimensions, such as emotional appeal, products and services, workplace environment, financial performance, vision and leadership, and social responsibility. In 2004, the first Reputation Quotient (RQ) was carried out in Sweden (Apéria et al., 2004) within the framework of the Reputation Institute global project (Van Riel & Fombrun, 2002). The project was initiated in the United States in 1999, and today includes members all over the world.

In the wake of recent corporate scandals in Sweden, research is emerging about how and to what extent corporate reputation decreases in such situations and if a bad reputation is contagious among corporations. A study of the Swedish insurance company Skandia, Jonsson, Greve, and Fujiwara-Greve (2007) shows how corporate deviance leads to legitimacy loss for organizations that resemble the offending organization. Even though research about the concept of corporate reputation has been scarce in Sweden, other streams of studies have examined closely related concepts, such as organizational image (e.g., Czarniawska, 2000) and corporate brand (Melin, 1999).

In the RQ study from 2004, the Swedish furniture retailer, Ikea, was the best known company in Sweden (Apéria et al., 2004). RQ data from 2006 ranks Ikea as having the fourth best corporate reputation worldwide (Reputation Institute, 2006). According to the RQ study in 2004, in addition to Ikea, other retailing firms with direct consumer relations gained relatively high reputational scores: ICA, Coop, McDonald's, and Systembolaget. The majority of the most visible companies in Sweden have a local heritage, even though the current ownership may be more international. Exceptions were Microsoft, McDonald's, and Nokia. Moreover, state-owned or former state-owned corporations gained low reputational scores among the Swedish public. Emotional appeal was the main driver of corporate reputation in Sweden, a trait that has proved to be pan-Scandinavian, and which is interpreted by Apéria et al. (2004, p. 227) as "Scandinavians want to feel good about a company and to trust, admire and respect it."

Over the last few years, other types of annual media rankings have emerged in Sweden. Since 1998, the media analyst corporation Infopaq (formerly Cision) has published quarterly reports ranking the most visible corporations in the Swedish media (Näringslivsbarometern [The Business Barometer]). The Swedish business press also presents rankings and lists on the visibility of corporate leaders and how they handle the media (see e.g., *Affärsvärlden*, 2006).

The Swedish Media System

The Swedish media system has gone through extensive changes following the consequences of globalization, commercialization, technological development, deregulation, and the concentration of ownership. It is a system that combines libertarian ideology and the ideology of social responsibility. The former situation describes the market for printed media and the latter the market for broadcast media. In recent times broadcast media has begun to develop a libertarian ideology.

Freedom of the press has had a strong position in the constitution ever since it was formulated in 1766. The act provides anonymity for those who give journalists information, and it is only the editor who can be charged for any offense resulting from publication. There is a right of free establishment, so that anyone may launch a magazine or newspaper, although this is not valid for radio and television. These are regulated by general agreements between the media organizations and the state, which control the allocation of different types of content and state the importance of balanced and impartial news reports (Hadenius & Weibull, 2003). A study of "cash for news coverage" shows that there is very little likelihood that news sources would be able to bribe Swedish journalists in order to publish or not publish information (Kruckeberg & Tsetsura, 2003).

Newspapers

Historically there has been a close link between political parties and newspapers, and for a long time most publications were owned or controlled by political organizations. Today nearly all are run as commercial organizations even if most newspapers claim a party signature (55% nonsocialist, 18% socialist, and 27% other) (Hadenius & Weibull, 2003).

The Swedish market for newspapers has two significant features: (1) newspapers are first and foremost local/regional, there are only two quality papers, two tabloids, and one business paper that are regarded as national papers; (2) almost all newspapers are sold by subscription and delivered to the home each day, only the tabloids are the exception to this.

There are about 160 newspapers on the Swedish market with a total distribution of 4.2 million copies and a revenue of SKr18 billion (approx. $2.5 billion) in 1999. They could be divided into four different segments: (1) the metropolitan morning papers/quality papers (25%); (2) the metropolitan evening papers/tabloids (20%); (3) the regional and local morning papers (45%); (4) newspapers published once or twice a week (10%). Figures in parentheses are the share of total circulation (Hadenius & Weibull, 2004).

Newspapers traditionally function as an information base, and are read by all social groups. Eighty-one percent of the population read a newspaper on an average day. This makes the consumption of newspapers in Sweden equal to Finland but somewhat less than Norway (Nordicom, 2006).

Broadcasting

Sveriges Radio (the public service radio broadcaster in Sweden) was given a monopoly in 1925 when radio was introduced in Sweden, following the European tradition of public service. The same was valid for television when it was established in 1956. In 1986, satellite channels were permitted and the first channel with programs in Swedish (TV3) was introduced via satellite in 1987. It was followed by others and in 1992, the first commercial terrestrial TV channel (TV4) was launched followed by commercial radio stations in 1993. Today there are four realms of broadcast media in Sweden: (1) public service, (2) private national, (3) satellite and cable, and (4) community radio (Hadenius & Weibull, 2004).

As a result of digitization, established actors introduce new TV channels and new actors also establish TV channels, and as a result there has been a dramatic increase in the supply of TV programs in Swedish. The consumption of television and radio has been rather stable for the last 15 years (.29). On an average day television is consumed by 86% of the population and radio by 74%. The public service channels dominate both markets (Sundin, 2006).

News Values

On a comprehensive level, the development of news values in Sweden has gone through four stages (Djerf-Pierre & Weibull, 2001). During the first stage (from 1925 to 1945), journalism was seen as a tool for *enlightenment* and national cohesion guided by political interests during a turbulent time. This stage was followed by a period of *mirroring* (from 1945 to 1965) where the focus shifted toward a preference for objective news: balancing the interests between politics and the public. This balance allowed the news producers to avoid conflicts. During the third period (from 1965 to 1985) of *investigation,* conflict and questioning had great driving force as journalism moved toward professionalism. News media functioned as critics of the state of society based on an ideal of scrutiny. The principle of the journalist as the public's attorney has been replaced by a new ideal: the journalist as an *interpreter.* The fourth and current period (from 1985 to present) is driven by decentralization, and commercialization has increased the market orientation and the will to satisfy the audience. What we can see is a popularization, a will to touch, engage, and recount everyday experiences for audiences, and a division into new subgenres, new formats, and hybrids of those.

Organizational Newsworthiness

Swedish business news content focuses on the activities of the stock exchange and individual public companies, which constitute "the hub" of subject matter for contemporary business journalism (Bjur, 2006; Haglund & Englund, 2001). Studies of business news content show that issues concerning the macroeconomy, the labor market, and consumerism receive minor attention on the business news pages; whereas news about business and companies dominate (Bjur, 2006; Kjaer, Erkama, & Grafström, 2007). Corporate news is presented largely from the point of view of individual companies. Articles about the stock exchange, whether they are about individual companies or overall trends in quotations, are also frequent business news items (Bjur, 2006; see also Haglund & Englund, 2001).

Contemporary business news increasingly portrays individual companies through their corporate leaders, whose leadership skills, strategies, and corporate vision are discussed. Moreover, their private lives have become an issue of interest to the media: What do they do on their vacations? What are their family situations? What are their opinions on various public issues? In this way, the business press has given the corporate world its own celebrities. In Sweden, one of the most visible corporate celebrities is Carl-Henrik Svanberg, former CEO of the Swedish telecommunication company Ericsson. During his time at Ericsson, Svanberg was rated the best CEO in Sweden in the area of communication, which means that he had the highest media visibility among Sweden's CEOs (*Affärsvärlden* 2006, February 7; Observer 2005). He personifies Ericsson in the media even to the extent that his name replaces the company name in headlines and texts. In her research, Petrelius Karlberg (2007, 2008) defines this development as the "mediatization" of corporate leaders.

Hence, much of today's Swedish business news popularizes the subject and focuses on individuals, scandals, and even gossip from the corporate world. Photographs and other types of graphics are frequently used and have become important features of business journalism (Bjur, 2006; Grafström et al., 2006; Kjaer et al., 2007), a development that also has been described as "business" becoming "show business" (Petrelius Karlberg, 2007).

Public Relations

Sweden has one of the largest concentrations of public relations practitioners per capita. There are more than 4,500 practitioners among a population of approximately 9 million (Flodin, 2004).

To a great extent, the history of public relations in Sweden follows the development of the public sector and the emergence of powerful special interests. There are early examples of public relations in the business sector but it wasn't until the 1980s that there was a clear expansion in this area. In the beginning the development of public relations in the public sector was miniscule, but during the 1960s public communication became a question of great political interest following the development of the Swedish model and other structural changes. Overall there were three transformations leading to this political interest (SOU, 1984):

1. *An increase in the size of the public sector.* During the 1960s there was an exceptional expansion in the public sector.
2. *A decrease in the number of local government entities.* In order to finance expansion, local government had to increase the number of inhabitants that came under a particular local government. During the period from 1952 to 1984 the number of municipalities decreased from 2,500 to 284. This change led to increased distance between politicians/civil servants and the public. It also meant decreased numbers of politicians, and in turn it became harder for citizens to have personal contact with the politicians who were supposed to represent their interests.
3. *A decrease in the number of daily newspapers.* During the same period there was a drastic decrease in the number of newspapers. As a consequence the area of distribution increased and there were increasing difficulties in obtaining information about local matters because newspapers had to cover a larger area than had previously been the case. Consequently, there was an increasing need for new ways to disseminate public information.

The development of communicative strategies in the public sector has continued. Today the state is the dominant buyer of public relations services and advertising in Sweden. A combined 2,005 governmental departments, public civil service departments, and other public organizations invested SKr2.1 billion ($300 million) in communication. The downfall of the welfare state and a legitimization crisis has changed the prerequisites and aim of the investments. The center of attention has turned from information to (re)presentation (Fredriksson, 2009).

The expansion of corporate public relations had its beginning in the early 1980s, and it showed a vigorous growth in the 1990s. First and foremost it is an expansion of the consultancy business, which could be explained by several factors (Flodin, 2004). Two of the more important aspects are economic growth and adjustments to market liberalization. Other factors are Swedish membership in the European Union (1995), changes in the Swedish media system, and more general issues such as globalization and individualization (Flodin, 2004; Larsson, 2005). Today, public relations is a practice with vast significance for the social, political, cultural, and economical development of the Swedish society.

The Swedish public relations industry is represented by three different bodies organizing practitioners and consult agencies: Sveriges informationsförening (Swedish Public Relations Association, SPRA; www.sverigesinformationsforening.se) with 4,600 individual members; *Precis* (The Association of Public Relations Consultancies in Sweden; www.precis.se) with 39 member companies; and Svenska PR-företagen (The Public Relations Agencies of Sweden; www.prforetagen.se) with 22 member companies.

Trust as a Key Dimension of Corporate Reputation

Corporate scandals in Sweden have paved the way for an intensified corporate governance debate and have had a negative impact on the public's impression of the corporate world. The Skandia management scandal that began in autumn

2003 (Jonsson & Buhr, 2007) has colored the corporate governance debate in Sweden. ABB also received bad press due to a scandal over the former management, and the alcohol retailer Systembolaget was involved in yet another scandal.

In the wake of corporate scandals and high incentive systems, the issue of corporate trust has received increased attention in Swedish public discourse and has been the focus of much discussion. Among other initiatives the Swedish government appointed a commission, Förtroendekommissionen (The Commission of Trust), to analyze the need for measures to secure public trust in corporations. In this chapter, we therefore focus on how Swedish news media participate in creating corporate reputation, here understood from the perspective of trust.

There are several examples of recurrent surveys of public trust in corporations, and three of the main ones are Förtroendebarometern (The Barometer of Trust), the SOM survey, and Forskningsgruppen för Samhälls- och Informationsstudier's survey (The Research Group for Society and Information Studies; SFI). They all differ somewhat from one another as some of them focus on brands/single corporations and others have an institutional focus. In this chapter, we focus on the first two surveys.

Förtroendebarometern is an annual survey conducted by MedieAkademin[1] (The Media Academy), which examines the Swedish population's trust in institutions, authorities, nongovernmental organizations, mass media, and corporations/brands. It began in 1997, and the numbers of actors included in the study vary. Some are included every year, others make less frequent appearances. In 2006, 31 actors were included of which 16 where corporations/brands.[2] The results are presented in Table 12.1.

Following the results of Förtroendebarometern it becomes clear that the results presented in Apéria et al. (2004), and discussed earlier in this chapter, have a wide reach. The most trusted companies are those with a clear national heritage, such as Ikea, Volvo, Ericsson, and Saab. In this range we also find the public service corporations (SR, SVT) and the quality press (Dagens Nyheter). At the next level we find state-owned, or formerly state-owned corporations (Posten, TeliaSonera), which are followed by corporations which are highly visible in the popular culture (TV3, Kanal 5, Aftonbladet, CocaCola). In the end we find Skandia as one of the more mistrusted corporations in Sweden.

The results presented in the survey from 2006 follow the results presented in earlier studies. There are some variations between individual corporations but the order of precedence of the categories is stable.

A second study that focuses on trust is the annual survey from the SOM Institute.[3] In this material there are no examples of individual corporations, only institutions and aggregates of organizations, and one of these aggregates is "large corporations." The results from 2005 show a minor increase in trust for this category in comparison with 2004, but it is still clear that people in general dissociate themselves from corporate actors compared to "healthcare," "universities," "the police," and "radio/TV," which are the four most trusted actors in this rank (Holmberg & Weibull, 2006, p. 69).

Table 12.1 The Swedish Public's Trust in Corporations

1.	IKEA	80	17.	Riksdagen	35
2.	SR	76	18.	Telia Sonera	33
3.	Universitet/högskolor	75	19.	Socialdemokraterna	32
4.	SVT	72	20.	Facket	32
5.	Volvo	69	21.	Dagspressen	31
6.	Småföretagen	62	22.	Moderaterna	30
7.	Riksbanken	61	23.	TV3	28
8.	Ericsson	59	24.	Kanal 5	28
9.	TV4	58	25.	Aftonbladet	25
10.	SAAB	57	26.	Coca Cola	22
11.	Dagens Nyheter	56	27.	EU-kommissionen	21
12.	Radio/TV	52	28.	Folkpartiet	21
13.	AstraZeneca	47	29.	Skandia	18
14.	Svenska kyrkan	46	30.	Partierna	16
15.	Storföretagen	38	31.	Sverigedemokraterna	4
16.	Posten	38			

Note. The figures are the percentage of the respondents answering the question "How much confidence do you have in the way the following institutions/business do their job?" with the answer "very much" or "fairly much"

The material from the SOM Institute was used as a foundation for the work of the Commission of Trust. In the study, a large number of structural and individual factors were used to investigate the reasons behind the decreasing trust in Swedish corporations. Examples of individual factors were gender, education, political orientation, interest in trading shares, and media use. Among the structural factors we find the number of unemployed individuals, the number of bankruptcies, the development of GDP, and media coverage of corporate life.

Following the analyses presented in this work, it becomes clear that there are individual differences when it comes to trust, but they are permanent when there is a change in public opinion. For example, individuals with a right-wing orientation tend to trust corporate actors more compared to left-wing oriented individuals, but when trust increases in the former the latter show the same pattern.

Among the institutional factors there are two with a clear correlation to the public's trust in "large corporations," the development of GDP and media coverage. The relation has a negative bias; that is, the decrease in trust is more extensive when the GDP and media coverage are negative compared to the increase in trust when the two factors show a positive development. These results are supported by a recent study in Sweden about Skandia and how negative visibility in media coverage significantly decreased its reputation (Jonsson & Buhr, 2007). The results show that not only the company at hand, in this case Skandia, but also other companies in the same industry, as well as organizations with similar names, were negatively affected by the negative media coverage.

Even though there are no clear correlations between media use and trust, Holmberg and Weibull (2004, pp. 39–41) point toward the importance of media information in their final analysis. They emphasize the importance of mass media as a direct or indirect source of information for individuals. Results from a recent study on the behavior of investors in the Swedish market for mutual funds shows that the financial media play a prominent role in shaping the same market (Jonsson & Buhr, 2007). At the same time we should be careful before we blame the mass media for the decreasing trust the public shows in corporate life. Holmberg and Weibull (2004) point toward the many national and international corporate scandals in which mass media function as mediators and agenda setters rather than as a scandalmongers.

Concluding Discussion

This chapter has outlined extant literature on corporate reputation in relation to news media and agenda-setting theory in Sweden. Over the last few decades, there has been a drastic increase in the news media's attention to corporate life in Sweden. In concert with this development, the number and size of corporate communication departments has grown, and the public relations industry has been established. During recent years, researchers have awakened, and increasing numbers of studies within the field have emerged.

Hence, researchers' attention to the relationship between the news media and corporations is relatively nascent in Sweden, and the paucity of research about corporate reputation makes it an important future area of investigation. On the other hand, the literature review presents a stream of work about reputation, though mainly from the perspective of the concept of trust. Swedish research and surveys about corporate life and the Swedish public suggest trust to be a key dimension for corporate reputation.

Notes

1. Medieakademin is a foundation established in 1997 by Göteborg University, Forsman & Bodenfors (advertising agency), *Göteborgs-Posten* (local newspaper), and TNS Gallup. Its aim is to deepen the public debate on society, politics, and culture. For further information see http://www.medieakademin.se
2. The survey includes 778 telephone interviews with respondents aged 16 to 74 years of age, and the work was completed by TNS Gallup between October 17 and 26, 2006.
3. The SOM Institute is a research center at Göteborg University studying Society, Opinion, and Media (SOM). The institute is jointly managed by the Department of Journalism and Mass Communication, the Department of Political Science, and the School of Public Administration. Since 1986, the SOM Institute has carried out a nationwide survey in which people are asked questions about politics, society, their use of media, public service, the environment, risks, new media technology, and their leisure-time activities. The 2005 Riks–SOM survey has been mailed to 6,000 randomly selected individuals between the ages of 15 and 85. For further information see http://www.som.gu.se/english.htm

References

Affärsvärlden, 2006, Svanberg bäst i test [Svanberg best in test]. Retrived February 7, 2006, from http://www.affarsvarlden.se/hem/nyheter/article270654.ece

Apéria, T., Brönn, P. S., & Schultz, M. (2004). A reputation analysis of the most visible companies in the Scandinavian countries. *Corporate Reputation Review*, 7(3), 218–230.

Asp, K. (1986). *Mäktiga massmedier: Studier i politisk opinionsbildning* [Powerful massmedia. Studies of the formation of political opinion]. Stockholm, Sweden: Förlaget Akademilitteratur AB.

Beck, U. (1994). The reinvention of politics: Towards a theory of reflexive modernization. In U. Beck, A. Giddens, & S. Lash (Eds.), *Reflexive modernization: Politics, tradition and aesthetics in the modern social order* (pp. 1–55). Cambridge, UK: Polity Press.

Bennulf, M. (1994). *Miljöopinionen i Sverige* [The opinion on environmental issues in Sweden]. Lund, Sweden: Dialogos.

Bjur, J. (2006). *De goda nyheternas journalistik: En kartläggning av ekonomijournalistik i lokal och nationell morgonpress* [The journalism of good news: Mapping business journalism in local and national dailies]. Stockholm, Sweden: SNS Medieforum.

Buhr, H., & Grafström, M. (2007). The making of meaning in the media: Corporate social responsibility in the financial times. In F. den Hond, F. G. A. de Bakker, & P. Neergaard (Eds.), *Managing corporate social responsibility in action: Talking, doing and measuring* (pp. 15–32). Farnham, UK: Ashgate.

Carroll, C. E., & McCombs, M. (2003). Agenda-setting effects of business news on the public's images and opinions about major corporations. *Corporate Reputation Review*, 6(1), 36–46.

Czarniawska, B. (2000). The European capital of the 2000s: On image construction and modeling. *Corporate Reputation Review*, 3(3), 202–217.

Djerf-Pierre, M., & Weibull, L. (2001). *Spegla, granska, tolka. Aktualitetsjournalistik i svensk radio och TV under 1900-talet* [Mirroring, scrutinizing, and interpreting: "Up-to-dateness" journalism in Swedish radio and TV during the 20th century]. Stockholm, Sweden: Prisma.

Engwall, L., & Sahlin, K. (2007). Corporate governance and the media: From agency theory to edited corporations. In P. Kjaer & T. Slaatta (Eds.), *Mediating business: The expansion of business journalism in the Nordic countries* (pp. 265–284). Copenhagen: CBS Press.

Fombrun, C., Gardberg, N. A., & Sever, J. (2000). The reputation quotient: A multistakeholder measure of corporate reputation. *Corporate Reputation Review*, 7(4), 241–155.

Fredriksson, M. (2009). On Beck: Risk and sub-politics in reflexive modernity. In Ø. Ihlen, B. v. Ruler, & M. Fredriksson (Eds.), *Public relations and social theory key figures and concepts* (pp. 21–42). London: Routledge.

Grafström, M. (2006). *The development of Swedish business journalism: Historical roots of an organisational field* (Unpublished doctoral dissertation). Uppsala University, Uppsala, Sweden.

Grafström, M., Grünberg, J., Pallas, J., & Windell, K. (2006). *Ekonominyhetens väg: Från kvartalsrapporter till ekonominyheter* [The route of a business news story: From quarterly reports to business news]. Stockholm, Sweden: SNS Medieforum.

Grafström, M., & Pallas, J. (2007). Negotiation of business news. In P. Kjaer & T. Slaatta (Eds.), *Mediating business: The expansion of business journalism in the Nordic countries* (pp. 217–234). Copenhagen Business Press, Copenhangen.

Hadenius, S., & Weibull, L. (2004). *Massmedier: En bok om press, radio och TV* [Mass-media: A book about press, radio and TV] (8th ed.). Stockholm, Sweden: Bonniers.

Haglund, L., & Englund, L. (2001). *Från jämförpriser till börskriser. En kvantitativ kartläggning av ekonomi- och konsumentjournalistiken i svenska medier år 2000* [From cost-per-unit price to stock exchange crises: A quantitative mapping business and consumer journalism in Swedish media the year of 2000] (Report no. 2). Stockholm: Stiftelsen Institutet för Mediestudier.

Holmberg, S., & Weibull, L. (2004). Förtroende för näringslivet. [Trust in Trade and Industry]. In *SOU:2004:47 Näringslivet och förtroendet*. Retrieved from http://www.regeringen.se/sb/d/361/a/20445

Holmberg, S., & Weibull, L. (2006). Flagnande förtroende. [Decreasing Trust. In S. Holmberg & L. Weibull (Eds.), *Du stora nya värld. Trettiofyra kapitel om politik, medier och samhälle* [A grand new world: Thirty-four chapters about politics, media and society] (pp. 65–84). Gothenburg, Sweden: SOM Institute.

Hvitfelt, H., & Malmström, T. (1990). *Ekonomi och arbetsmarknad: Journalistik i förändring* [Economy and labour-market: Journalism in transition] (No. 4). Stockholm, Sweden: Svensk Informations Mediecenter.

Johansson, B. (1998). *Nyheter mitt ibland oss: Kommunala nyheter, personlig erfarenhet och lokal opinionsbildning* [News among us: News about local governments, personal experiences and the formation of local opinions]. Göteborg, Sweden: Institutionen för journalistik och masskommunikation Göteborgs universitet.

Jonsson, S., & Buhr, H. (2010). *The limits of media effects: Field positions and cultural change in a mutual fund market.* Unpublished Manuscript. Uppsala University, Uppsala.

Jonsson, S., Greve, H. R., & Fujiwara-Greve, T. (2009). Undeserved loss: The spread of legitimacy loss to innocent organizations in response to reported corporate deviance. *Administrative Science Quarterly, 54*(2), 195–228.

Kjaer, P., Erkama, N., & Grafström, M. (2007). Transforming business news content: A comparative analysis. In P. Kjaer & T. Slaatta (Eds.), *Mediating business: The expansion of business journalism in the Nordic countries* (pp. 131–158). Copenhagen, Denmark: CBS Press.

Kruckeberg, D., & Tsetsura, K. (2003). *A composite index by country of variables related to the likelihood of the existence of "cash for news coverage."* Gainesville, FL: Institute for Public Relations.

Larsson, L. (2005). *Opinionsmakarna: En studie om PR-konsulter, journalistik och demokrati* [The Opinion Makers: A Study of PR-Consultants, Journalism and Democracy]. Lund, Sweden: Studentlitteratur.

Lindqvist, M. (2001). *Is i magen. Om ekonomins kolonisering av vardagen* [Keep cool: On the colonialization of economy in everyday life]. Stockholm, Sweden: Natur och Kultur.

McCombs, M. (2004). *Setting the agenda: The mass media and public opinion.* Cambridge, UK: Polity Press.

Melin, L. (1999). *Varumärkesstrategi* [Brand strategy]. Malmö: Liber.

Micheletti, M., & Stolle, D. (2003). Politiska konsumenter: Marknaden som arena för politiska val [The Market as Arena for Political Decisions]. In S. Holmberg & L. Weibull (Eds.), *Ju mer vi är tillsammans: Tjugosju kapitel om politik medier och demokrati* [The more we are together: Twenty-seven chapters about politics, media and democracy] (pp. 103–116). Gothenburg, Sweden: SOM Institute.

Nord, L. (1995). Sundsvalls politiska dagordning [Sundsvall's Political Agenda]. In G. Bostedt (Ed.), *Mitt i opinionen* (pp. 49–62). Sundsvall, Sweden: KVC Förlag.

Nordfors, D. A. (2004). The role of journalism in innovation systems. *Innovation Journalism, 1*(7), 1–18.

Nordfors, D. A., Kreiss, D. R., & Sandred, J. (2005). Introducing an innovation journalism index: Benchmarking the Swedish market. *Innovation Journalism, 2*(5), 3–23.

Nordfors, D. A., & Ventresca, M. J. (2006). Innovation journalism: Towards research on the interplay of journalism in innovation ecosystems. *Innovation Journalism, 3*(2), 1–18.

Nordicom. (2006). *Nordicom-Sveriges Mediebarometer 2005* [The Media Barometer of Nordicom-Sverige 2005]. Göteborg, Sweden: Nordicom-Sverige, Göteborg University.

Observer. (2005). Observers näringslivsbarometer [Observer's corporate barometer]/. Stockholm.

Pallas, J. (2007). *Talking organizations: Corporate media work and negotiation of local practice.* Unpublished doctoral thesis. Department of Business Studies. Uppsala, Uppsala University.

Pallas, J., & Strannegård, L. (Eds.). (2010). *Företag och medier* [Corporations and media]. Malmö: Liber.

Petersson, O. (1991). *Demokrati och makt i Sverige: Huvudrapport från maktutredningen* [Democracy and power in Sweden: Main report from the governmental report on power]. Stockholm, Sweden: Allmänna förlaget.

Petrelius Karlberg, P. (2007). *Den medialiserade direktören* [The mediatized corporate leader]. Unpublished doctoral thesis, Stockholm, Stockholm School of Economics, EFI.

Petrelius, Karlberg, P. (2008). *VD under press — Om medialiseringen av näringslivets ledare* [CEO under press — on mediatization of corporate leaders]. Forskning i fickformat [pocket-size research]. Stockholm: EFI och Öhrlings PricewaterhouseCoopers.

Reputation Institute. (2006). *The global RepTrak 200: The world's best corporate reputations 2006.* New York: Reputation Institute.

Sahlin-Andersson, K., & Engwall, L. (2002). Carriers, flows, and sources of management knowledge. In K. Sahlin-Andersson & L. Engwall (Eds.), *The expansion of management knowledge. carriers, flows, and sources* (pp. 3–32). Stanford, CA: Stanford University Press.

Severinsson, R., & Nilsson, Å. (2000). Dagspressens innehåll [The content of the daily press]. In I. Wadbring & L. Weibull (Eds.), *TRYCKT. 20 kapitel om dagstidningar i början av 2000-talet* [PRINTED. 20 chapters about daily newspaper in the beginning of the 21th century] (pp. 43–56). Göteborg, Sweden: Dagspresskollegiet, Institutionen för Journalistik och masskommunikation, Göteborg University.

Sundin, S. (2006). *Den svenska mediemarknaden 2006* [The Swedish media market 2006]. Göteborg, Sweden: Nordicom-Sverige, Göteborg University.

Van Riel, C., & Fombrun, C. (2002). Introduction: Which company is most visible in your country? [Special issue]. *Corporate Reputation Review, 4*(4), 296–302.

13 Corporate Reputation and the News Media in Switzerland

Mark Eisenegger, Mario Schranz, and Jörg Schneider

This chapter examines the relationship between *media reputation*—defined as the overall evaluation of a company presented in the media (Deephouse, 2000)—and the *corporate reputation* of the 39 largest Swiss companies amongst the general public. This lends our study a pioneering character, because research into agenda setting in Switzerland has hitherto found application only within the context of political communication. There has so far been a lack of studies in the field of business communication. Our study will examine both first- and second-level agenda-setting effects (Carroll, 2004; Carroll & McCombs, 2003; McCombs & Shaw, 1972). It draws on data from a comprehensive content analysis on coverage of corporations in 13 key Swiss media (newspapers, television) as well as on a representative opinion poll among the general public. Both the content analysis of the media and the opinion poll covered the awareness (salience of the company), the issue involvement, as well as the evaluation of these companies in order to examine first- and second-level agenda-setting effects. Among other things, the study confirms a significant effect of awareness and evaluation (positive/negative) of the analyzed companies in the media on their corporate reputation. However, a strong agenda-setting effect is also seen when the media cover these companies on crisislike occasions that generate a high intensity of reporting. Before describing the results of the empirical studies, the chapter gives an overview of Swiss research into reputation and agenda setting.

Literature Review: Corporate Reputation

In Switzerland, scientific research into reputation is pursued mainly at the Universities of Zurich, Fribourg, and St. Gallen. Whereas the institutes in Zurich and Fribourg are oriented to communication science and have supplemented their empirical work by presenting an autonomous, three-dimensional reputation concept (Eisenegger, 2005; Eisenegger & Imhof, 2008; Ingenhoff, 2007), the corporate reputation research in St. Gallen focuses on the importance of reputation to business management as a value-added factor (Fieseler, Hoffmann, & Christian, 2008).

A fundamental aspect of Eisenegger's approach (University of Zurich) is its deconstruction of reputation into three components: the functional, social, and expressive reputation (Eisenegger & Imhof, 2008). Functional reputation reflects how well actors (persons, organizations) satisfy the performance expectation of their respective *function* systems; that is, to what extent they fulfill or disappoint their role expectations. If a company's operations prove to be profitable, these actors have a positive functional reputation. *Social reputation* describes the corporate reputation in terms of social expectations, and *expressive reputation* refers to the affect (sympathy, emotional appeal) emanating from the company to its various stakeholder groups. The innovative feature of this three-dimensional approach to reputation is that it may be applied to any type of organization (companies, parties, NGOs etc.) and individuals (managers, politicians, scientists, etc.), also outside the economic sphere.

In contrast to Zurich and Fribourg, the institute in St. Gallen operates with the approach to reputation pioneered by the Reputation Institute (Fombrun, 1996). In 2006 the Reputation Institute, Switzerland for the first time published its annual reputation ranking of the 15 leading Swiss companies.

Agenda Setting

Swiss research into agenda setting has hitherto focused on political communication only. Even less than in an international context, in Switzerland the hypotheses of agenda-setting research have so far found very little application in the sector of business communication.

In the sector of research into political communication, Bonfadelli, Dahinden, and Leonarz (2002, 2007) found indications of second-level agenda-setting effects in an analysis of the change in media reporting and the perception of genetic engineering in Switzerland. As predicted by the consonance model, they showed that respondents pointedly select media contents that conform to their preconceived opinions. This study therefore confirmed that media reporting primarily fulfills an agenda-setting function by reinforcing the opinions already held by the respondents (Bonfadelli et al., 2002, p. 124). The individual dispositions of agenda-setting effects are also examined by Matthes (2005, 2008). His results showed that the individual need for orientation (NFO) leads to an increase in the perceived media salience of specific issues, and by doing so promotes the first-level agenda-setting function of the news media. As regards second-level agenda setting, Matthes showed that the NFO has no influence on the perceived media salience of affective issue attributes. He concluded that the need for orientation of the respondents explains the extent of information seeking, but not the affective tone of the information that individuals are looking for (Matthes, 2008, p. 440). Selb presented another agenda-setting study in the field of political communication. It showed that the extent to which a party is associated by the population with topics that have a high salience in media reporting is decisive for electoral success (Selb, 2003).

Business and the News Media

The relationship between business and the news media was examined in Switzerland primarily in connection with questions of media change. This research, stemming from Jürgen Habermas's study of the *structural transformation of the public sphere* (Habermas, 1976/1990) shows that a fundamental change has occurred in Switzerland since the 1970s, as the media quickly loosened their ties to political and other intermediaries (such as parties, unions etc.), which resulted in an increasingly commercialized media system oriented toward market criteria (Imhof, 2003; Jarren, 1994; Lucht & Udris, 2009). Parallel to the emergence of a commercialized media system, we can observe an increase in media concentration in Switzerland that experienced its greatest intensity in the 1970s and 1990s. In the 1970s, important mergers took place between media organizations whose political and ideological affiliations had previously been opposed. From the 1980s on, the Swiss media market has been increasingly dominated by a few leading media corporations (Publigroupe, SRG, SSR Idée, Suisse Ringier, Tamedia, and Edipresse).

Research into the changes in the media system shows that since the 1960s, business news has gained in importance parallel to the commercialization of the Swiss media system. Thus, the more the media orient themselves toward criteria of business success, the more do business topics move into the forefront of media reporting and the volume of the business sections expands (Eisenegger & Vonwil, 2004; Einwiller, Lehmann, Winistörfer, Ingenhoff, & Sommer, 2008). A tremendous growth in the volume of business news can therefore be observed in the last three decades in Switzerland, no less than in the United States (Carroll & McCombs, 2003, p. 36). This change has not only affected the extent of business reporting, but also the logic of reporting about companies. Thus, a trend has become apparent toward an increasing focus on corporate scandals and personalities (Eisenegger & Imhof, 2008; Schranz, 2007). The reporting on corporate scandals has increased in parallel with the tendency to increasingly push key company executives (CEOs, chairmen) into the limelight. All in all, the research findings from Switzerland show that not only has business news increased greatly in volume but there is a greater tendency to subject companies to more critical examination than had previously been the case.

Corporate Reputation in Switzerland

The fact that the reputation of Swiss companies is also seen increasingly as a relevant factor in corporate success is shown not least by the recent growth in publication of reputation rankings by private and university institutions. The two market research institutes, Gfk Switzerland and the Reputation Institute, have been publishing annual reputation rankings of the leading Swiss companies independently of each other since 1984 and 2006, respectively. The Center for Research on the Public Sphere and Society (FÖG) of the University of Zurich has developed a Media Reputation Index (MRI) and has published studies regularly since 1998 on the reputation of both business and political organizations in the media.

The results of these studies show that the following corporate groups regularly dominate the media and public agenda: first, large Swiss multinationals (UBS, Credit Suisse, Nestlé, Novartis, Roche, ABB, Swiss Re, Zurich Insurance); second, companies owned partially or wholly by the state (SBB, Post, Swisscom, cantonal banks); and third, cooperative companies with strong social commitment (Migros, Co-op, and Raiffeisenbanks). Therefore, the main objects of reputation formation in Switzerland are Swiss companies with a high international profile or retailers with an extensive network of branches at regional and local levels. In contrast, transnational foreign companies located in Switzerland attract only minor attention.

The types of company found regularly in the front ranks of all these studies are firms such as Migros, Coop, and the Raiffeisen banks, which indicates the great importance of social responsibility as a reputation driver in Switzerland. As regards the large Swiss multinationals, the various rankings assign the best reputation values to those that are successful in business; that is, show a positive functional business reputation and whose social reputation has not been tarnished by scandals. An interesting finding of Swiss reputation research is thus that only smaller companies with a regional scope of operations gain sustained reputation benefits from CSR issues, which tend merely to represent a risky hygiene factor for the large companies operating on a transnational level.

In view of the global economic turmoil triggered by the subprime crisis, media focus on the financial and bank sectors increased greatly in the years 2008 and 2009. The available rankings show that the reputations of the two large banks, UBS and Credit Suisse, have suffered greatly, while financial institutes with a stronger orientation to the home market such as the Raiffeisen and cantonal banks have benefitted from this development to emerge from the crisis as winners. This indicates a marked effect of Swiss reputation trends: the contrast of reputation winners and losers in connection with salient issues (currently, the financial crisis) is making an emphatically strong impact on the logic of assigning corporate reputation.

The Swiss Media System

The peculiarities of the Swiss media system have been described in various papers in national and international publications (Blum, 2003; Bonfadelli, 2008; Künzler, 2009; Meier, 2004; Puppis, 2009). The Swiss media system is characterized by (small) local and decentralized structures. Switzerland is a small federal country (7.5 million inhabitants) divided up into 26 cantons, and at a lower level into about 3,000 municipalities, which are the smallest political units. Across this political structure, the country comprises four linguistic regions in which German, French, Italian, and Rhaeto-Romanic, respectively, are spoken. These small structures have given rise to an extraordinary diversity of press products concentrated in the respective linguistic regions. To what extent these regions are cut off from each other is still a controversial and largely open question. Those authors who stress this segmentation are referring specifically to the strong linguistic regional anchorage of the media infrastructures (Blum, 2003; Kriesi, Matteo, Sciarini, & Wernli, 1996; Meier & Schanne, 1994). However, other voices contest segmentation on the level of content and thus stress the high agreement of media content (especially regarding issue salience) across these linguistic regions (Tresch, 2008). Against this background, then, it must be assumed that regional linguistic differences refer less to the first-level agenda setting (issue salience) than to the second level in the form of various attributions and framings of the treated issues. However, reliable information on the differences in terms of agenda setting in the country's various linguistic regions is still missing.

The newspaper with the highest circulation in Switzerland (apart from the free dailies) is the tabloid *Blick* (circulation 2008, 231,000, Ringier Verlag), followed by *Tages-Anzeiger* (214,000, Tamedia). The *Neue Zürcher Zeitung*, known internationally as a quality newspaper thanks to its comprehensive foreign reporting, has a circulation of 143,000. In recent years, various free newspapers have gained massively in importance in Switzerland. Thus, the leading free paper *20 Minuten* reached a circulation of 530,000 in 2008, greatly exceeding the paid-for newspapers mentioned above.

Whereas the Swiss population shows a marked preference for print media, it is a laggard as regards watching TV, and it is in the midrange by European standards in listening to the radio. Generally, also in an international comparison, Switzerland achieves high and above-average *media outreach* (Sriramesh & Verčič, 2003), especially due to the high use of print and online media. With a view to *media access*, the commercialization of the Swiss media that began in the 1960s has increased the opportunities for civic groups (NGOs, social movements, consumer organizations, etc.) to have access to the media, as they successfully adapt to the new media logics. This can be shown particularly clearly by analyzing the media reporting on mass layoffs by individual companies: the proportion of civic groups that have expressed critical views in the media in response to such events has increased noticeably (Schranz, 2007).

Public Relations

Swiss PR research shows little autonomy and is not well developed in terms of theory, and especially of empirical research into PR practices (Röttger, 2004). There is little reliable information on this vocational field or the history of Swiss PR. Indeed, this field was not examined comprehensively and systematically until a 2003 study (Röttger, Hoffmann, & Jarren, 2003). The study covered comparative research by PR communicators into the subsystems of politics and business and showed various degrees of professionalism for the various organizations (headed by PR agencies and NGOs).

The Swiss market for PR agencies is comparatively small and comprises only a few large agencies (BPRA [Association of Public Relations Agencies in Switzerland] statistics on the Swiss PR agency market, 2008). Farmer Consulting is the largest Swiss PR agency with 58 employees and a net income of CHF14.5 million in 2008. The influence of foreign PR agencies on public communications in Switzerland has remained low up to the present (Löffler, 2000). With the exception of Burson-Marsteller, the third largest agency in Switzerland, no other major foreign agency has so far become established in the country. On the whole, the few available research findings indicate that Swiss PR is characterized significantly more strongly by corporate communication departments than by specialized PR agencies.

Apart from research into the vocational field, there is still much less information on the influence of PR on the logic of media reporting. Hitherto, only one study has examined the influence of PR (especially media broadcasts) on media reporting. It concluded that the influence of public relations in Switzerland is relatively large, the media handle large parts of it, especially corporate PR, but produce little of their own research (Grossenbacher, 1989, 2006).

Hypotheses and Analysis

Hypothesis 1. A positive correlation exists between the salience of a company in the media and the company's salience among the public.

Hypothesis 2. A positive correlation exists between media reputation and corporate reputation. The more positive media coverage is for a particular company, the more positively will members of the public perceive that company. Conversely, the more negative that media coverage is for a particular company, the more negatively will members of the public perceive that company.

Hypothesis 3. The strength of the correlation between media reputation and corporate reputation is directly proportional to the degree to which the media reputation of a company is determined by salient issues. A particularly strong and negative influence becomes apparent from issues linked to crises. The more a company is involved in salient, crisislike issues by the media, the more negative is the effect on its corporate reputation.

Research Methodology

This study will for the first time apply research into agenda setting to the sector of business communication in Switzerland. Both first- and second-level agenda-setting hypotheses will be examined (Carroll, 2004; Carroll & McCombs, 2003). First-level agenda-setting effects will be considered by capturing how the salience of the analyzed companies in the media influences the awareness of these companies amongst the general public. Furthermore the effect of media reputation on corporate reputation will be examined. Media reputation was defined by Deephouse as "the overall evaluation of the firm presented in the media resulting from the stream of media stories about the firm" (Deephouse, 2000, p. 1097). The correlation of media and corporate reputation thus allows us to examine second-level agenda-setting effects in the evaluative dimension. Finally, second-level agenda-setting effects will also be examined in the substantive dimension. Here, our interest focuses on the impact on corporate reputation resulting from the involvement of the companies in issues that are widely and intensively discussed in the media. In agreement with Meijer and Kleinnijenhuis (2006) and Botan and Tayler (2004), it is expected that media coverage of companies in connection with salient issues such as the current financial crisis will strengthen the effect of media coverage on corporate reputation. Our study combines a comprehensive content analysis of the leading Swiss media with a representative public opinion poll carried out together with the market research institute GfK Switzerland.

Content Analysis

The content analysis is based on determining the media reputation of the 39 largest Swiss companies during the period from April 2007 to March 2009 in 13 leading Swiss media. Critical factors for determining the size of a company were its turnover and number of employees in Switzerland. All Swiss companies listed on the stock exchange and appearing on the Swiss Market Index (SMI) were also included in the survey. Accordingly, the most significant Swiss business sectors such as banking, insurance, pharmaceuticals, telecommunications, as well as manufacturing, food, and retail appeared in our analysis. The content analysis examined how frequently the media reported on specific companies, in which thematic contexts (issues) the companies were covered, and how the companies were evaluated. The recorded evaluations (positive, negative, neutral, mixed) allowed us to build a Media Reputation Index (MRI) (Eisenegger & Imhof, 2008, p. 136). It was calculated on the basis of all evaluations made of the companies in the media reports in a specific period. The MRI can assume maximum values of +100 (completely positive reporting about the company) and −100 (completely negative reporting). All in all, 46,000 media articles were analyzed in this study.

For the content analysis, a sample of 13 key Swiss opinion-forming media was examined. It covered both key print media as well as newscasts by public service broadcasters. The opinion-forming dailies *Blick* (circulation, 231,000), *Tages-Anzeiger* (214,000), *Neue Zürcher Zeitung* (143,000), and *Le Temps* (46,000) were included. From the business press, the publications *Handelszeitung* (45,000), *Finanz und Wirtschaft* (35,000), and *Cash* daily (112,000) were selected. For Swiss television, which is clearly dominated by the public service broadcaster SRG, the two main (German-speaking) news programs *Tagessschau* and *10vor10* were analyzed. Finally, the weeklies *Sonntagszeitung* (202,000), *Sonntagsblick* (262,000), *NZZ am Sonntag* (126,000), and the political magazines *Weltwoche* (85,000), leaning to the right, and *Wochenzeitung* (14,000), with clear affiliations to the left, were included.

Public Opinion Poll

The survey data were drawn from a representative public opinion poll carried out annually in the spring by the market research institute GfK: it asked how respondents would evaluate each of those 39 largest Swiss companies also examined in our content analysis (provided respondents would recognize a company at all). For this article, we worked with poll data from the years 2008 and 2009. The poll was carried out by means of computer aided web interview (CAWI). The sample for the 2009 survey covered 3,331 respondents (2008: 3,446 respondents). Both the recognition and corporate reputation of the various companies were determined within the scope of this poll. Working together with the market research institute, we were able to influence the conceptual design of the questionnaire. Among other things, the corporate reputation was operationalized on the basis of the three-dimensional reputations theory of Eisenegger (Eisenegger & Imhof, 2008, p. 127). The measurement of corporate reputation thus entailed functional (business success, quality of products and services), social (ecological and social responsibility) as well as emotional (sympathy, emotional appeal) poll items. A formative PLS estimation was used to form a corporate reputation index on a scale from *Correlation of media reputation and the corporate reputation* 100 to +100 exactly like the Media Reputation Index.

The range of data from 2007 to 2009 for the content analysis and 2008 to 2009 for the opinion poll allowed not only agenda-setting effects to be determined statistically but also to be compared over two periods. The period of the content analysis refers to the 12 months before the polls conducted in April 2008 and May 2009.

Data Analysis

To determine the tonality of issue involvement, the companies were classified according to the following categories: companies that received a negative rating in salient issues (variable value: *Correlation of media reputation and the corporate reputation* 1), companies not involved in any salient issues or not evaluated in this context (0), and companies that received a positive rating in salient issues (+1).

Spearman rank order correlations were calculated to determine the relationship between the salience of the companies in the media and the company's salience in public perceptions (Hypothesis 1) as well as between media reputation and corporate reputation (Hypothesis 2). A structural equation model (SEM) with standardized regression weights on the basis of a maximum likelihood estimation was calculated for the analysis of the effect of salience in the media, media reputation, and issue involvement on corporate reputation (Hypothesis 3).

Results

The test of Hypothesis 1 shows a significant correlation between the salience of a company in the media and the company's salience in public perceptions (r_s = .50, p <.001). However, only a midstrength first-level agenda-setting effect was found. This may be explained by the selection of the companies; that is, this study was limited exclusively to traditional Swiss companies with high awareness. The company sample consequently shows little scatter with respect to awareness, which is reflected in a merely midstrength correlation.

A similarly strong correlation (r_s = .52, p <.001) was found for the relationship between media reputation and corporate reputation (Hypothesis 2). A positive media reputation is consequently associated with a positive corporate reputation, whereas a negative media reputation correlates with a negative corporate reputation (see Figure 13.1). A significant second-level agenda-setting effect was thus found with respect to the evaluative dimension

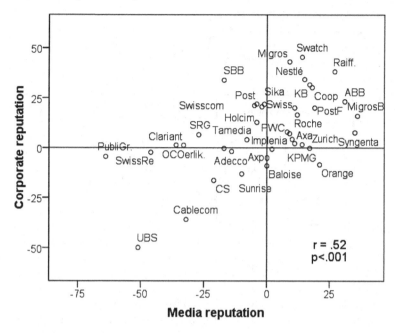

Figure 13.1 Correlation of media reputation and the corporate reputation

With the aid of a structural equation model, the effects of a company's involvement in salient issues in the media (Hypothesis 3), its salience in the media, as well as its media reputation on its corporate reputation can be determined in a more refined way (ML estimation,

Chi-square = 1.233 (df = 1, p =.267), RMSEA = .078).

An initial correlation of the poll results on corporate reputation in 2008 and 2009 shows that the values remain relatively stable (r_s = .94, p <.001). The changes in corporate reputation between the years 2008 and 2009 can nevertheless be unequivocally modeled as agenda-setting effects. Across the board, a 54% change in corporate reputation from 2008 to 2009 can be explained with our model. See Figure 13.2. However, this change is not due so much to the absolute media coverage of a given company in a particular year, but rather to the rise and fall of the media reporting from one year to the next. An increase in a company's media salience thus significantly reduces its corporate reputation (β = −.28, p <.05).

In addition, this increase in coverage shows a negative correlation with the tonality of issue involvement (r = −..46, p <.01). This means that the increasing coverage of a company relates greatly to its media involvement in salient and sensitive issues (such as scandals or crises). However, not only the salience of a company in the media depends strongly on its involvement in media issues. The involvement of a company in salient media issues has an even greater effect on the change in corporate reputation. Consequently, a main finding of this study is that a change in corporate reputation depends less on the pure salience of a company

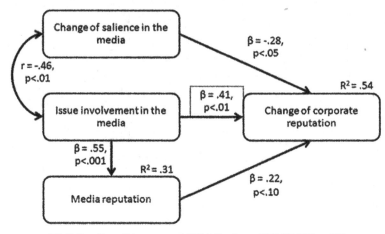

ML-Estimation, Chi-square = 1.233 (df = 1, p=.267), RMSEA = .078

Figure 13.2 Structural equation model

in the media than on whether it is involved by the media in issues that are intensively and emotionally debated. The tonality with which the company is treated within the scope of such issues has a strong effect on the change in corporate reputation ($\beta = .41, p < .01$). This means that a positive treatment of the company within the scope of such an issue promotes reputation gains, whereas a negative involvement leads to reputation losses. Referred to the current financial crisis, which represents the issue with the highest salience in our study, this means that companies which were strongly involved in this issue by the media and were treated in a negative way as instigators of the crisis suffered the greatest losses in corporate reputation. By the same token, those companies that could be seen in a positive light in connection with the crisis in the financial markets showed a positive growth regarding corporate reputation.

Discussion and Conclusion

This study tested for the first time in Switzerland first- and second-level agenda-setting hypotheses in the context of business communication. It confirmed some of the established findings of international agenda-setting research. However, new types of correlation were also found.

First, in agreement with other studies (Carroll, 2004, p. 87), a significant first-level agenda-setting effect was confirmed. Thus the salience of a company in the media showed a significant correlation with the Swiss population's awareness of it.

Second, this study tested second-level agenda-setting hypotheses in both the substantive and evaluative dimensions. Here too, a significant correlation was shown between media reputation—defined as the "overall evaluation of a firm presented in the media" (Deephouse, 2000, p. 1091)—and corporate reputation. The confirmation of such an evaluative agenda-setting effect is in agreement with the findings of Fombrun and Shanley (1990), Wartick (1992), and Carroll (2004). However, our results additionally show that the changing salience of a company in the media has an even greater effect on the change in corporate reputation than the effect of media reputation on the corporate reputation itself. In other words, the sheer change (increase or decline) in a company's media coverage explains the change in corporate reputation better than the explanatory variable of media reputation. In this context, a negative correlation could also be found between increasing media coverage and corporate reputation: the greater the salience of a company in the media, the more does its corporate reputation change in a negative direction. Therefore, high media salience is associated with increased reputation risks. This finding agrees with the Fombrun and Shanley study (1990), which also found that intensive media visibility has a negative effect on a company's reputation regardless of whether that news coverage is favorable or unfavorable. The significant correlation between a company's salience in the media and corporate reputation shows that first- and second-level agenda-setting variables should be better interlinked in future research. As this study shows, first-level agenda-setting variables such as a company's media salience have a direct effect on its evaluation by the public, a factor usually examined within the scope of second-level hypotheses.

Third, a main finding of this study is that a company's involvement in issues that are intensively and emotionally discussed in the media has the strongest influence on changes in corporate reputation. This effect proves to be even stronger than the effects of the two other variables in our models: media reputation and change of media coverage on corporate reputation. It therefore seems to be the case that public awareness of a company depends strongly on whether it is involved in salient issues by the media and that this issue involvement strikingly influences corporate reputation. The central influence of media issues on corporate reputation was also shown by Meijer and Kleinnijenhuis (2006). Their study focuses on the effects of issue ownership: this thesis assumes that stakeholders attest a good corporate reputation to companies associated positively with an issue discussed in the media—for instance as problem solvers or mitigators. Moreover, Meijer and Kleinnijenhuis particularly stress a *positive* issue-owner effect. Our study can also show this positive effect. Thus, in connection with the crisis in the financial markets hotly debated in the media, we showed that the small regional banks in particular enjoyed a reputation bonus because their business models, in contrast to those of the large banks, were deemed to be sustainable and less subject to risks.

However, our study also shows a *negative* issue-owner effect that is significantly more important in explaining the change in corporate reputation than the positive effect. This negative issue-owner effect results from a company being associated in a strongly negative way with an issue, for example as the direct cause of the crisis. Accordingly, our study showed that the large Swiss banks were among those companies who suffered the largest (negative) fluctuations in corporate reputation from 2008 to 2009 because the media involved them most strongly in the issue of the financial crisis and lambasted them as instigators of the crisis.

Like all studies, this one also has its limitations. First, it should be noted that during the period of the study in the years 2008 to 2009 the financial crisis strongly dominated the Swiss media agenda. In order to further confirm the effect of issue involvement on the change in corporate reputation, it would be of interest to include in the study periods that are dominated less strongly by such crisis issues. A second limitation refers to the selection of the companies. In order to adequately check first-level agenda-setting effects, the study basis should be extended beyond the traditional companies considered here to include companies with a lesser degree of recognition that results from a long history of gradual growth.

References

BPRA (Bund der Public Relations Agenturen der Schweiz) [Association of Public Relations Agencies in Switzerland]. (2008). Statistics on the Swiss PR agency market. Retrieved from http://www.bpra.ch/files/Marktstatistik_1728.pdf

Blum, R. (2003). Medienstrukturen der Schweiz [Media Structures in Switzerland]. In G. Bentele, H.-B. Brosius, & O. Jarren (Eds.), *Öffentliche Kommunikation: Handbuch Kommunikations- und Medienwissenschaft* (pp. 366–381). Wiesbaden, Germany: Westdeutscher Verlag.

Bonfadelli, H. (2008). Switzerland: Media system. In W. Donsbach (Ed.), *International encyclopedia of communication* (pp. 2092–2096). Oxford, UK: Blackwell.

Bonfadelli, H., Dahinden, U., & Leonarz, M. (2002). Biotechnology in Switzerland high on the public agenda, but only moderate support. *Public Understanding of Science*, 11(2), 113–130.

Bonfadelli, H., Dahinden, U., & Leonarz, M. (2007). Mass media and public perceptions of read and green biotechnology: A case study from Switzerland. In D. Brossard, J. Shanahan, & T. C. Nesbitt (Eds.), *The media, the public and agricultural biotechnology* (pp. 97–125). Wallingford, UK: CABI.

Botan, C. H., & Taylor, M. (2004). Public relations: State of the field. *Journal of Communication, 54*, 645–661.

Carroll, C. E. (2004). *How the mass media influence perceptions of corporate reputation: Exploring agenda-setting effects within business news coverage* (Unpublished doctoral dissertation). The University of Texas, Austin.

Carroll, C. E., & McCombs, M. E. (2003). Agenda-setting effects of business news on the public's images and opinions about major corporations. *Corporate Reputation Review, 6*(1), 36–46.

Deephouse, D. L. (2000). Media reputation as a strategic resource: An integration of mass communication and resource-based theories. *Journal of Management, 26*(6), 1091–1112.

Einwiller, S., Lehmann, D., Winistörfer, N., Ingenhoff, D., & Sommer, K. (2008). *Wirtschaftsberichterstattung in den Fernseh- und Radionachrichten: Erfüllen die Nachrichtensendungen den Service Public?* [Economic Reporting in TV- and Radio News: Does the News Satisfy the Public Service?]. Eine Untersuchung durchgeführt mit Unterstützung des Bundesamtes für Kommunikation (BAKOM) [An Investigation Supported by the Federal Office for Communication]. (Study Report). University of Applied Science Olten and University of Fribourg, Switzerland.

Eisenegger, M. (2005). *Reputation in der Mediengesellschaft: Konstitution, issues monitoring, issues management* [Reputation in the media society. Constitution, issues monitoring, issues management]. Wiesbaden, Germany: VS Verlag für Sozialwissenschaften.

Eisenegger, M., & Imhof, K. (2008). The true, the good and the beautiful: Reputation management in the media society. In A. Zerfass, B. van Ruler, & K. Sriramesh (Eds.), *Public relations research: European and international perspectives and innovations* (pp. 125–146). Wiesbaden, Germany: VS Verlag für Sozialwissenschaften.

Eisenegger, M., & Vonwil, M. (2004). Die Wirtschaft im Bann der Öffentlichkeit. Ursachen und empirische Evidenzen für die erhöhte öffentliche Exponiertheit ökonomischer Organisationen seit den 90er Jahren [The economy under the public spell. Causes and empirical evidencies for an increased exposure of economic organisations since the 1990s]. *Medienwissenschaft Schweiz, 2*, 80–89.

Fieseler, C., Hoffmann, C., & Christian, P. (2008). Linking corporate reputation and journalistic perception in capital markets. *Studies in Communication Sciences, 8*(1), 115–133.

Fombrun, C. J. (1996). *Reputation. realizing value from the corporate image.* Boston, MA: Harvard Business School Press.

Fombrun, C. J., & Shanley, M. (1990). What's in a name? Reputation building and corporate strategy. *Academy of Management Journal, 33*, 233–258.

Grossenbacher, R. (1989). *Die Medienmacher: Eine empirische Untersuchung zur Beziehung zwischen Public Relations und Medien in der Schweiz* [The media makers. An empirical investigation of the relationship between public relations and the media in Switzerland]. Solothurn, Switzerland: Vogt-Schild.

Grossenbacher, R. (2006). *Politische Öffentlichkeitsarbeit in regionalen Medien: Ein Forschungsprojekt der Publicom AG* [Political public relations in the regional media: An investigation of the Publicum Corporation]. Kilchberg, Switzerland: Publicom.

Habermas, J. (1990). Strukturwandel der Öffentlichkeit. Untersuchungen zu einer Kategorie der bürgerlichen Gesellschaft [The structural transformation of the public sphere: An inquiry into a category of bourgeois society]. In H.-U. Wehler (Ed.), *Moderne deutsche Sozialgeschichte* (pp. 197–221). Cologne, Germany: Kiepenheuer & Witsch. (Original work published 1976)

Imhof, K. (2003). Wandel der Gesellschaft im Licht öffentlicher Kommunikation [Social change in the focus of public communication]. In M. Behmer, F. Krotz, & C. Winter (Eds.), *Medienentwicklung und gesellschaftlicher Wandel: Beiträge zu einer theoretischen und empirischen Herausforderung* (pp. 153–182). Wiesbaden, Germany: Westdeutscher Verlag.

Ingenhoff, D. (2007). Integrated Reputation Management System (IReMS). Ein integriertes analyseinstrument zur messung und steuerung von werttreibern der reputation [An integrated analysis tool to measure and to control reputation drivers]. *PR-Magzin, 7*, 55–62.

Jarren, O. (1994). Medien-Gewinne und Institutionen-Verluste? Zum Wandel des intermediären Systems in der Mediengesellschaft: Theoretische Anmerkungen zum Bedeutungszuwachs elektronischer Medien in der politischen Kommunikation [Media gains and institution-losses? The change of the intermediate system in media society: Theoretical notes to the increasing importance of electronic media in political communication]. In O. Jarren (Ed.), *Politische Kommunikation in Hörfunk und Fernsehen* (pp. 23–35). Opladen, Germany: Leske & Budrich.

Kriesi, H., Matteo, G., Sciarini, P., & Wernli, B. (1996). *Problèmes de compréhension entre les communautés linguistiques en Suisse* [Comprehension problems between the speech communities in Switzerland]. Bern, Switzerland: Bundesamt für Statistik.

Künzler, M. (2009). Switzerland: Desire for diversity without regulation: A paradoxical case? *International Communication Gazette, 71*(1–2), 67–76.

Löffler, J. (2000). Wird der Schweizer PR-Markt gobaler? *Marketing & Kommunikation, 1*, 52–53.

Lucht, J., & Udris, L. (2009, May 21-25). *Transformation of media structures and media content. A diachronic analysis of five European countries.* Paper presented at the Annual meeting of the International Communication Association (Political Communication Division), Chicago, IL.

Matthes, J. (2005). The need for orientation towards news media: Revising and validating a classic concept. *International Journal of Public Opinion Research, 18*(4), 422–444.

Matthes, J. (2008). Need for orientation as a predictor of agenda-setting effects: Causal evidence from a two-wave panel study. *International Journal of Public Opinion Research, 20*(4), 440–453.

McCombs, M. E., & Shaw, D. L. (1972). The agenda-setting function of mass media. *Public Opinion Quarterly, 36*, 176–187.

Meier, W. A. (2004). Switzerland. In M. Kelly, G. Mazzoleni, & D. McQuail (Eds.), *The media in Europe: The Euromedia handbook* (pp. 249–261). Thousand Oaks, CA: Sage.

Meier, W. A., & Schanne, M. (1994). *Medien-"Landschaft" Schweiz* [Media-landscape Switzerland]. Zürich, Switzerland: Pro Helvetia.

Meijer, M. M., & Kleinnijenhuis, J. (2006). Issue news and corporate reputation: Applying the theories of agenda setting and issue ownership in the field of business communication. *Journal of Communication, 56*, 543–559.

Puppis, M. (2009). Media regulation in small states. *International Communication Gazette, 71*(1–2), 7–17.

Röttger, U. (2004). Public relations in Switzerland. In B. Van Ruler & D. Verčič (Eds.), *Public relations and communication management in Europe: A nation-by-nation introduction to public relations theory and practice* (pp. 425–440). New York: Mouton de Gruyter.

Röttger, U., Hoffmann, J., & Jarren, O. (2003). *Public relations in der Schweiz: Eine empirische Studie zum Berufsfeld Öffentlichkeitsarbeit: (Vol. 16)* [Public relations in Switzerland: An empirical study to the vocational field public relations]. *Forschungsfeld Kommunikation.* Konstanz, Germany: UVK.

Schranz, M. (2007). *Wirtschaft zwischen Profit und Moral: Die gesellschaftliche Verantwortung von Unternehmen im Rahmen der öffentlichen Kommunikation* [The economy between profit and morality: The corporate social responsibility in the public discourse]. Wiesbaden, Germany: VS Verlag für Sozialwissenschaften.

Selb, P. (2003). *Agenda-Setting Prozesse im Zürcher Wahlkampf zu den National- und Ständeratswahlen 1999* [Agenda-setting-processes during the election campaign in Zurich concerning elections of the parliament 1999]. Unpublished doctoral dissertation, University of Zürich, Switzerland.

Sriramesh, K., & Verčič, D. (Eds.) (2003). *The global public relations handbook: Theory, research, and practice.* Mahwah, NJ: Erlbaum.

Tresch, A. (2008). *Öffentlichkeit und Sprachenvielfalt: Medienvermittelte Kommunikation zur Europapolitik in der Deutsch- und Westschweiz: Vol. 1* [The public and language diversity: Media-imparted communication relating to European politics in the German- and French-speaking part of Switzerland]. *Studien zur Schweizer Politik, 1.* Baden-Baden, Germany: Nomos.

Wartick, S. L. (1992). The relationship between intense media exposure and change in corporate reputation. *Business & Society, 31*(1), 33–49.

14 Corporate Reputation and the News Media in the United States

Craig E. Carroll

Scholars have long recognized the interdisciplinary nature of the concept of corporate reputation. Just about every major social science discipline (e.g., economics, management, marketing, psychology, sociology) has enjoyed some facet of interest and contribution (Fombrun & Van Riel, 1997). Mass communication is often considered to be a latecomer to the study (Carroll, 2004). As this chapter will show, seeds of mass communication research can be found in the concept's early American history. This chapter will briefly explore some of these influences and then provide an empirical test of the agenda-setting function of the news media as it is applied to organizations in the United States.

History of Research on Image, Reputation, and the News Media in the United States

Some of the earliest influences on corporate reputation research in the United States can be found in management and marketing journals. The earliest empirical studies on image—a precursor to the reputation concept—appeared in the *Harvard Business Review* (Eells, 1959), *California Management Review* (Martineau, 1958), and the *Journal of Marketing* (Spector, 1961). Meijer (2004) speculates on why research on the influence of the news media on corporate reputation has come so late. She attributes it to its roots in management and marketing research where the emphasis at the time was on the concept of image itself rather than antecedents or consequences. Moreover, there was no media research going on at the time in the fields of management and marketing.

At the time, during the 1950s and 1960s, concomitant research within mass communication was dominated by Klapper's (1960) minimal effects theory, which was heavily influenced by Lazarsfeld, Berelson, and Gaudet (1944) and Berlson, Lazarsfeld, and McPhee (1954). Lazarsfeld and Berlson were from the field of political communication, and focused on the role of media in American elections, with one adaptation to the world of business (Dahl, Haire, & Lazarsfeld, 1959).

The first work on image (still as a precursor to reputation) with implications for journalism and mass communication, was written by Daniel Boorstein, former librarian of the U.S. Library of Congress. Boorstin, who wrote *The Image: A Guide to Pseudo-Events in America*, used the term *image* as a signification of the "graphical revolution" where much of what the public knows becomes mediated through the graphic interfaces, such as advertising, the news media, or other third parties. Boorstin attributes his source of inspiration to Walter Lippmann, who used image to describe the "pictures in our heads" of the world outside of our direct experience.

Stone, Dunphy, and Bernstein (1966) are considered by some to be the first to suggest investigating the effects of news coverage on corporate image. Stone is also the first to suggest comparing the images presented through the mass media with the images received and discussed by audiences through the use of surveys. This methodology was later applied in the first agenda-setting study, which was published in 1972 (i.e., McCombs & Shaw, 1972).

Nearly 15 years went by before others considered investigating the role of media in business. One of the first studies was a master's thesis at Syracuse University under the direction of Maxwell McCombs. As McCombs recalls,

> During a three-year period when the Standard & Poor 500 stock market index increased 2.3 per cent, the stocks of fifty-four companies featured in *Fortune* magazine increased 3.6 per cent. Companies receiving favorable coverage increased the most, 4.7 per cent, but any escalation in the salience of these companies resulted in some increase, 1.9 per cent with negative coverage and 1.7 per cent with neutral coverage. (McCombs, Lopez-Escobar, & Llamas, 2000, pp. 132–133)

The focus of this early study was primarily on financial effects not reputation; nevertheless it did introduce business to agenda-setting studies.

In industry, it was not long before *Fortune* magazine opened a special issue with a cover story devoted to the most admired corporations in the United States. The methodology *Fortune* used was not scientific, nor was there the intent to have an annual issue devoted to reputation, but sales of the special issue prompted the editors to codify the methodology and to pursue this new marketing opportunity (Deephouse, 2000).

Scholarly research on business ethics and the relationship between business and society is where *Fortune* magazine's special issue held primary interest. Scholars interested in corporate social performance and business ethics were starved for measures that could help validate some of their interests. In the domain of corporate strategy, Fombrun and Shanley (1990) opened the door for the use of the *Fortune* measures in scholarly research. They also reopened the door for media studies by examining the role of news coverage in the construction of *Fortune's* reputation rankings for the most admired companies in America. Their focus was on a variety of forces contributing to reputation, the media being just one. Fombrun and Shanley used research from economics and sociology as the basis for their tests, even though they were formulated consistently with agenda-setting theory. To the surprise of agenda-setting scholars, they found that the greater the volume of news coverage, the worse the firm's reputation. They found no support for their hypothesis that a more positive tone of news reports contributed to a more positive reputation, nor that there was an interaction effect between tone and volume.

In a separate study 2 years later, Wartick (1992) investigated the effects of news coverage on corporate reputation, also using *Fortune* magazine's list of the most admired companies in America. He found no relationship when aggregating the results to the level of the overall set of firms (29 U.S. firms); however, when he divided his sample into subgroups based on their reputation scores, he found effects. He found that for companies with "good" or "average" reputations, more media coverage was related to larger, positive changes in reputation. Companies with "poor" reputations that received negative coverage had diminished reputations.

In the Fombrun and Shanley (1990) and Wartick (1990) studies, the dependent variable, corporate reputation, was taken from the published reputation rankings found within *Fortune* magazine's annual listing of corporate reputation. One limitation that many scholars have noted about using the *Fortune* ratings is that the respondents are CEOs, executives, and analysts evaluating other firms in their industry. Thus, to some degree, there is a vested interest in not having the reputations venture too far from the norm.

Fombrun later goes on to develop his own measure of reputation, the Harris-Fombrun Reputation Quotient, recently completing its 10th year in the field. This study reports on data from the first 2 years of data collection from the annual reputation quotient study. The benefit of the annual RQ and others like it, such as the Reputation Institute's Reputation Pulse, is that they contain random samples of the population from the countries where they are drawn.

Firms' Media Visibility and Public Prominence

Carroll and McCombs (2003) argued that for firms to acquire a reputation, the public must first think about them. They adapted Cohen's (1963) well-known dictum about the study of firms, arguing that, while the news media may not be successful in telling the public what to think about a specific firm, they often succeed in telling the public which firms to think about. This level of "thinking about" is an organization's public prominence (Stocking, 1985, p. 450), which some scholars have identified as a dimension of corporate reputation (Rindova, Williamson, Petkova, & Sever, 2005). An organization's public prominence refers to the degree to which it receives large-scale collective recognition and public attention and is salient in the minds of stakeholders (Rindova et al., 2005). It involves the sorting out of one organization amidst a sea of organizations competing for attention. Rindova et al. (2005) found that higher degrees of public prominence afforded firms the ability to charge premium prices for their products and services. An organization's public prominence differs from its familiarity in that organizations may be publicly prominent even though individuals may not be personally familiar with them. When people lack first-hand knowledge of an organization and thus are operating under conditions of uncertainty, they rely on others, such as the news media, for data, even if most of the data they receive are general, nonspecific impressions; as a result, some organizations may receive a disproportionate amount of public attention.

So far, no investigations of agenda setting have used an organization's public prominence as a reflection of public salience; instead, corporate reputation is commonly used as a global variable. At least three investigations have examined the effects of media salience on corporate reputation. Fombrun and Shanley (1990) examined firms listed in *Fortune* magazine's "most admired" rating and found that the sheer volume of media attention to the 292 U.S. firms correlated negatively with their reputations, independent of specific firm attributes or news topics discussed. Also using the *Fortune* ratings, Wartick (1992) found a positive relationship between news attention and reputation, but only for firms with "average" reputations, not for those with "good" or "poor" reputations. Most recently, Kiousis, Mitrook, Wu, and Seltzer (2006) used a representative sample of the general public rather than the business elites who contribute the *Fortune* most admired companies ratings—a better test of agenda-setting theory because it captured public opinion—and found no effect at the first level. All three studies used corporate reputation as a global variable, and the data in all three studies contained aggregate scores with different corporate reputation attributes (financial performance, social responsibility, and executive leadership).

One explanation for the relative paucity of evidence for agenda-setting effects at the first level is that for the first level of agenda setting an isolated dimension of the global variable reputation may serve as a better operationalization of public salience than the global variable as a whole. Following Carroll and McCombs' (2003) first proposal about agenda setting related to organizations, an organization's media salience should relate to its prominence in the minds of the public, rather than directly to its reputation. Based on the first level of agenda-setting theory, therefore, the following hypothesis is proposed for testing in the United States:

Hypothesis 1: A firm's media visibility is positively related to its public prominence.

Firms' Media Favorability and Public Esteem

Organizational public esteem is the degree to which the public likes, trusts, admires, and respects an organization. This study offers it as a second dimension of corporate reputation, with other dimensions being organizational prominence and attributes of quality (Rindova et al., 2005). Organizational public esteem is a fundamental concern for organizations because without a base level of trust, admiration, and respect, individuals lack sufficient incentives to consider relationships with organizations, whether through employment, investing, product consumption, or social causes. An organization's public esteem may even affect an individual's desire to get to know the people who work there.

Attribute agenda setting is the most prevalent theoretical perspective for describing the relationship between firms' media favorability and their public esteem. Using this theory, McCombs and colleagues (e.g., McCombs, 1997; McCombs, Llamas, Lopez-Escobar, & Federico, 1997; McCombs et al., 2000) have articulated two dimensions of attributes: the cognitive and the affective. Assessments of the affective dimension recognize that news stories and public survey responses convey not only descriptions of objects but also feelings and tone about the objects described (McCombs, Shaw, & Weaver, 1997; McCombs et al., 2000). McCombs, Llamas, Lopez-Escobar, & Rey (1997) found a close correspondence between the affective descriptions of the attributes of political candidates and the audience's descriptions of those candidates during the 1996 Spanish general election. Others have reported similar results (Becker & McCombs, 1978; Golan & Wanta, 2001; Kiousis, Bantimaroudis, & Ban, 1999; Weaver, Graber, McCombs, & Eyal, 1981).

The affective dimension with a firm as the focal object can be termed a firm's focal media favorability. Several studies across disciplines have established a relationship between firms' focal media favorability and their financial performance (Deephouse, 2000; Fombrun & Shanley, 1990; Kiousis, Popescu, & Mitrook. 2007; Wartick, 1992).

In contrast, the results of studies seeking a link between focal media favorability and the public's opinion about publicly traded firms are mixed (Fombrun & Shanley, 1990; Kiousis et al., 2007). One explanation for the mixed findings is that previous research has failed to break corporate reputation into its relative dimensions. The present study proposes that firms' media favorability should relate more to one specific dimension of reputation—public esteem—rather than to the global variable. Thus, for the portrayal of the firm, the following relationship is proposed for firms in the United States:

Hypothesis 2: A firm's media favorability is positively related to its public esteem.

Methods

This study used content analysis and a secondary analysis of the Annual Reputation Quotient (RQ) 2000 (Alsop, 2001; Fombrun, Gardberg, & Sever, 2000), an annual public opinion poll on corporate reputation which Harris Interactive has conducted each year since 1999.

The present study evaluates the public's perceptions of the most prominent firms in the United States across a number of cognitive attributes and one affective attribute. This study used the earliest Annual RQ data available at the individual level of analysis in order to control for alternative explanations. For the past 10 years, Annual RQ scores have been published in the media, making it possible that the media's reporting on firms' reputation ratings, rankings, and scores may influence the public's esteem for these firms more than the media's routine news reporting. Previous secondary research using the Annual RQ (e.g., Kiousis et al., 2007) has only had access to the published, aggregate rankings that are published in news reports, much like the annual ratings in *Fortune* magazine. Kiousis et al. used the Annual RQ for 2005, the 7th year of the Annual RQ. By this time, the results of the Annual RQ had become routinely released to the media. Little attempt has been made to delineate the differences between firms' news coverage about issues and events in which they may find themselves intertwined, and news coverage devoted to these firms that focuses on their published reputation scores.

Sample of Firms

The present study only includes U.S.-based publicly traded firms nominated during both of the first 2 years of the Annual RQ, reducing the sample from 30 to 26 firms. For Hypothesis 1, respondents were asked to nominate two firms they felt had the best overall reputation and two firms they felt had the worst overall reputation. The nominations were open ended and were used to construct the list of firms for testing Hypothesis 2. The companies with the most total nominations were considered to be the most prominent firms and those with fewer nominations to be less prominent. Gardberg and Fombrun (2002) found that the original 30 companies accounted for almost 90% of all U.S. nominations in 1999.

For Hypothesis 2, the study used the rating phase from the Annual RQ phase two. The dates of data collection were September 27 through October 17, 2000). Table 14.1 provides the demographic information on the firms included in this study.

Respondents

The Annual RQ was conducted in two phases: a nomination phase (August 10 to September 11, 2000) and a rating phase (September 27 and October 17, 2000).

Table 14.1 Demographics of Annual RQ Firms Studied

Firms	Ticker	Industry Categorization	Metropolitan Area	Founded	Revenue	Assets
Apple Computer, Inc.	AAPL	Technology	San Francisco, CA	1976	786	6,803
Anheuser-Busch	BUD	Food & Beverage	St. Louis, MO	1852	1,552	13,085
Dell Computer Corporation	DELL	Technology	Austin, TX	1983	2,177	13,435
The Walt Disney Company	DIS	Conglomerate	Los Angeles, CA	1923	-158	45,027
Ford Motor Company	F	Transportation	Detroit, MI	1903	3,467	284,421
FedEx Corporation	FDX	Transportation	Memphis, TN	1973	584	13,340
General Electric Company	GE	Conglomerate	New York, NY	1892	12,735	437,006
General Motors	GM	Transportation	Detroit, MI	1908	4,452	303,100
Gateway, Inc.	GTW	Technology	San Diego, CA	1985	241	4,153

Firms	Ticker	Industry Categorization	Metropolitan Area	Founded	Revenue	Assets
Hewlett-Packard Company	HWP	Technology	San Francisco, CA	1938	408	32,584
IBM	IBM	Technology	New York, NY	1911	8,093	88,349
Intel Corporation	INTC	Technology	San Francisco, CA	1968	10,535	47,945
Johnson & Johnson	JNJ	Consumer	New York, NY	1885	4,800	31,321
Kmart Corporation	KM	Consumer	Detroit, MI	1897	-244	14,630
The Coca-Cola Company	KO	Food & Beverage	Atlanta, GA	1886	2,177	20,834
Southwest Airlines Co.	LUV	Transportation	Dallas-Fort Worth, TX	1967	603	6,670
McDonald's Corporation	MCD	Food & Beverage	Chicago, IL	1948	1,977	21,684
Philip Morris Companies	MO	Food & Beverage	New York, NY	1847	8,510	79,067
Microsoft Corporation	MSFT	Technology	Seattle, WA	1979	7,346	59,257
Maytag Corporation	MYG	Consumer	Des Moines, IA	1907	201	2,669
NIKE, Inc.	NKE	Consumer	Portland, OR	1962	590	5,820
Procter & Gamble	PG	Consumer	Cincinnati, OH	1837	2,922	34,387
Sears, Roebuck and Co.	S	Consumer	Chicago, IL		1,343	36,899
AT&T Corp.	T	Technology	New York, NY		4,669	242,223
Target Corporation	TGT	Consumer	Minneapolis, MN		1,264	19,490
WorldCom Group	WCOM	Technology	Jackson, MS		4,153	85,893
Wal-Mart Stores, Inc.	WMT	Consumer	Fayetteville, AR		6,295	78,130

Note. Industry categories are dummy coded with the media industry as the reference group. Metropolitan area is recoded as the dummy variable regional proximity, with New York City as the reference group. Founding is recoded as age. Revenue and assets are reported in millions of U.S. dollars.

In the first phase, Harris Interactive conducted 4,651 online interviews and 1,010 telephone interviews throughout the United States. The online interviews were obtained from random invitations drawn from the company's Harris Poll Online (HPOL) panel of more than 7 million people and the resulting sample was representative of the U.S. adult general public. Telephone interviews were conducted in conjunction with the regular Harris Poll (Gardberg & Fombrun, 2002, p. 385).

Harris Interactive then constructed a list of companies named most often by the respondents in the first phase. Harris Interactive deleted wholly owned subsidiaries, brands, telecommunications service providers, and media companies. Harris Interactive weighted all data using demographic variables (age, sex, education, race, ethnicity, household income, and region) to project findings to the U.S. adult population (Alsop, 2001). An average of 710 respondents from the Annual RQ Phase 2 rated each firm on the attribute overall emotional appeal. Table 14.2 lists the number of respondents per firm for 1999 and 2000.

Sample of News Content

News articles mentioning any of the focal firms' ticker symbols during the 6 months prior to the rating phase of the Annual RQ 2000 were downloaded from *The New York Times* using the Lexis-Nexis database. The date range was April 15, 2000, through September 26, 2000.[1]

In political communication research, scholars use *The New York Times* to represent the national media environment due to its intermedia agenda-setting power and the strong relationship that exists between it and other national and local news sources, including television networks and Internet Web sites (Dearing & Rogers, 1996; Reese & Danielian, 1989; Tan & Weaver, 2007). As Gans (2005) argued,

> The *Times* is treated as the professional setter of standards.... When editors and producers are uncertain about a selection decision, they will check whether, where, and how the *Times* has covered the story; and story selectors see to it that many of the *Times*' front-page stories find their way into television programs and magazines. (p. 180)

The *Wall Street Journal* was not used because the present study's sample was of the general public; moreover, this study was concerned with general interest news rather than business news. As a further corroboration of the validity of using the *Times* as a proxy for other media outlets, Coombs and Holladay's (2009) investigation of the differences between print and television found that these two types of media produced similar effects on corporate reputation. Table 14.2 lists the number of articles per firm. The average number of articles per firm was 93.

Measures

Dependent Variable For Hypothesis 1, the dependent variable, *firms' public prominence* (Rindova et al., 2005), was measured by the number of nominations

Table 14.2 Number of News Articles and Respondents per Firm

Company	Public Prominence, Previous Year	Public Prominence	Advertising Expend.	Corporate Salience	Media Salience
Anheuser-Busch Inc.	4	57	703.6	30	2
Apple Computer Inc.	8	120	213.8	20	1
AT&T Corp.	29	421	1,430.60	671	30
Coca-Cola Co.	10	192	867.2	149	8
Dell Computer	19	136	305.6	328	0
FedEx	9	31	140.6	359	3
Ford Motor Co.	25	775	2,111.10	532	84
Gateway Inc.	20	122	307.8	118	2
General Electric Co.	23	397	1,111.10	406	15
General Motors Co.	20	482	4,118.40	255	23
Hewlett-Packard Co.	16	134	817.8	365	1
IBM	30	363	1,130.90	1,558	15
Intel Corp.	9	95	617	722	6
Kmart Corp.	12	162	477.4	114	3
Maytag Corp.	3	34	181.4	45	2
McDonald's Corp.	15	189	1,203.80	110	2
Microsoft Corp.	114	1,085	588.5	4,896	145
NIKE Inc.	14	215	591.3	60	7
Philip Morris Cos.	10	520	2,527.30	65	0
Procter & Gamble	30	398	2,694.00	118	11
Sears & Roebuck	31	410	1,460.20	164	4
Southwest Airlines	13	83	137.8	62	1
Target Corp.	4	75	791.1	126	0
Wal-Mart	86	832	457	112	4
Walt Disney Co.	38	233	1,545.20	325	9
WorldCom Group	5	82	1,109.40	324	16

*Advertising expenditures are reported in millions of U.S. dollars.

the firms received from the first phase of the Annual Reputation Quotient conducted by Harris Interactive and the Reputation Institute. Rindova et al. (2005) identified the nomination process used by the RQ as a suitable measure of firms' public prominence.

For Hypothesis 2, the dependent variable, *firms' public esteem*, was measured using the three-item affective attribute measure from the Annual RQ 2000. The three items concerned the public's degree of trust, admiration, and respect for the firms evaluated. The questions used a scale from 0 to 10, where "0" represented a bad feeling and "10" represented maximal trust, admiration, and respect. A weighted average was computed for each of the three questions based on the number of respondents who answered at each level. Once the weighted average was computed for each of the three questions, the mean was used as the score for the firms' public esteem.

Independent Variables   For Hypothesis 1, the independent variable, media visibility, was measured by the count of news articles with significant mentions of the publicly traded firms in the news content of three prominent sections of *The New York Times*, according to the "ticker" field attached to the documents. A significant mention of a firm was defined as a firm receiving 90% or higher from the Lexis-Nexis algorithms that machine-coded the articles for mentions of the firm.

The three sections of the *Times* analyzed were the main front page, the front page of the business section, and the editorial pages (editorials, letters to the editor, and columns). One factor (eigen = 3.3, % variance = 97.3) of media salience (Kiousis, 2004) emerged from a principal axis factor analysis with direct Oblimin rotation of the three content sections—front page (0.92), front page of the business section (0.84), and editorial pages (0.87).

The control variable, *firms' news release salience*, was measured using the number of wire-issued news releases for each firm occurring from May 1 to July 31, 2000—the 4 months preceding the Annual RQ 2000 nomination phase. Wire-issued news releases from PR Newswire and Businesswire were downloaded from Lexis-Nexis. These wire services are the primary vehicles by which *Fortune* 500 companies' submit their news releases to the press.

The firms' advertising expenditures (expressed in millions of dollars) were a control variable and were downloaded from *Advertising Age*'s Top 200 Advertisers archive in the Lexis-Nexis database. All of the firms in this study fell within the Top 200 Advertisers. Advertising expenditures were included in the analysis because previous research (Carter & Dukerich, 1998; Fombrun & Shanley, 1990) has determined that paid publicity in the form of advertising has a direct effect on public prominence. The firms' public relations expenditures were not available. As Kim (2000, 2001) has noted, firms have not disclosed their public relations expenses because this information has traditionally been considered proprietary. Future research should find ways to overcome this limitation.

For Hypothesis 2, firms' *media favorability* was measured using human coders. The term *core media favorability* was chosen because the firm was the object of analysis in each news article. For the firms' core media favorability, each firm appearing in the same article received a unique score based on its portrayal, as determined by the human coders. For this variable, two types of screening were done. First, human coders screened each article for its relevance to the firms in the study. Articles not relevant to the firms were eliminated from the sample. Second, if an article remained in the sample, only passages whose content directly related to the portrayal of a firm were analyzed. Each focal firm appearing in the same article received a unique score based on its portrayal.

The degree of a firm's favorability was coded categorically as favorable, neutral, mixed, or unfavorable. Media content coded "favorable" referred to the focal firm with an evaluative tone of admiration, respect, or trust. Conversely, media content coded "unfavorable" referred to the focal firm with an evaluative tone as unworthy of admiration, respect, or trust. "Neutral" was defined as the absence of both favorable and unfavorable evaluations of the firm. "Mixed" was defined as the presence of both favorable and unfavorable evaluations of the firm. "Neutral" and "mixed" were combined to enable the calculation of the Janis-Fadner coefficient (Deephouse, 2000; Pollock & Rindova, 2003).

Six undergraduate coders from a large West Coast university were trained on content analysis. The coders received extensive training prior to coding the sampled articles. Scott's Pi (π) with the Potter and Levine-Donnerstein (1999) correction formula were used to calculate coder reliability. Assessment of the news articles began after coders reached a reliability of .80 or higher for every variable. The following are the Scott's Pi estimates for each variable: relevance (yes or no) (.92), unfavorable (.85), mixed (.84), neutral (.88), and favorable (.86). Because the unit of analysis was the firm, two firms within an article could receive different scores depending upon how each was portrayed. If two focal firms appeared in the same news article, they were coded by different coders.

After coding was completed, a 10% sample was pulled for examining intercoder reliability. Holsti's reliability was calculated for each pair of coders; the results were at an acceptable level of reliability, ranging from .77 to .87 for each pair of coders.

From the manual coding, a Janis–Fadner coefficient of imbalance (Janis & Fadner, 1965)—a method used in media research to assess the degree of media favorability (Deephouse, 2000; Pollock & Rindova, 2003)—was computed. The coefficient measured the relative proportion of articles that had a favorable tenor versus an unfavorable tenor for each year. The coefficient has many useful properties, including (1) a meaningful zero point when a firm had an equal number of favorable and unfavorable articles; (2) a decrease in the coefficient when the number of articles increased; and (3) an increase in the coefficient when the number of favorable tenor articles increased. The coefficient of media imbalance is produced when f is the number of positive articles about a firm, u is the number of unfavorable articles about it, and v is the total volume of articles; if $f > u$, then $(f^2 - fu) / \text{total}^2$; if $f = u$, then 0; if $u > f$, then $(fu - u^2) / \text{total}^2$.

Data Analysis

Tabachnick and Fidell (2003) recommend a minimum of five cases for each variable included using regression analysis; this study met that ratio. While the case-to-variable ratio is low, the numbers of news articles, news releases, and members of the public undergirding the cases aggregated to the level of the firm are large. Because of the autocorrelation existing between the firms' Annual RQ 1999 and 2000 prominence scores, all the variables were regressed individually onto 1999 prominence scores and the residuals were obtained.

The 2000 prominence score residuals were regressed onto all other residuals. The parameter estimates obtained doing this and doing the multiple regression model in which the 2000 prominence scores were regressed onto all variables— including the 1999 prominence scores—were identical; what differed was the R-square. Typically R-square is computed by $SS(model)/(SS(model)+SS(error))$, where SS stands for sum-of-squares. The model is analogous to $(SS(model) - SS(Prominence\ 1999)) / (SS(model) + SS(error) - SS(Prominence\ 1999))$. In both the numerator and the denominator, the effect of Prominence 1999 was removed. The same result is obtained using $(R^2(model) - R^2(Prominence\ 1999)/ (1-R^2(Prominence\ 1999))$.

Results

This study examined the relationships between two dimensions of corporate reputation and media visibility and favorability for firms within the United States., The articles coded for the firms' media visibility and media favorability came from *The New York Times*, the newspaper with the widest organizational news hole for mainstream news. Media visibility was represented by the volume of news articles about each firm. Media favorability was represented by the tone of the news articles for how each firm was portrayed within them. The news articles were aggregated to the firm level of analysis.

Hypothesis 1 predicted a positive relationship between the firms' media salience and their public prominence. Table 14.3 provides the descriptive statistics and partial correlations controlling for firms' previous levels of prominence. The results show that firms' media visibility was significant after partialing out the effects from the firms' existing levels of prominence. A firm's degree of media visibility ($\beta = .705, p = .002$) had a significant effect on its public prominence (see Table 14.4). Hypothesis 1, therefore, was supported.

Hypothesis 2 asserted a positive relationship between the salience of the firm's focal media favorability and its level of public esteem. Hypothesis 2 was supported ($.55, p < 0.03$).

Discussion

The present study focused on the effects of firms' media visibility and media favorability for firms appearing in the nomination phase of Harris Interactive's

Table 14.3 Descriptive Statistics and Partial Correlations Controlling for Firms' Previous Levels of Prominence

	Mean	S.D.	1	2	3
1 Firms' Public Prominence	293.8	270			
2 Ad Expenditures	10,630.10	933.8	.681**		
3 Wire Issued News Release Salience	462.9	960	-0.016	-0.11	
4 Firms' Media Salience	15.2	31.4	.459*	0.189	.719**

$*p < .05.$ $**p < .01.$

Table 14.4 Regression Analysis Examining Firms' Media Salience Controlling for Firms' Previous Levels of Prominence

Block Order Entry	Variables	β	Increment to R2
1	Advertising Expenditures	.655**	.429**
2	News Release Salience	0.048	0.002
3	Media Salience	.705**	.204**
	Total R² (%)		.635**
	Total Adjusted R² (%)		.588**

Note. Betas are for the final model in which all variables are entered into the model. The last column indicates the increment to variance explained associated with the variable or block of variables listed, after accounting for variance due to prior block of variables in the model. N= 27.
*p < .05. **p < .01.

Annual Reputation Quotient study, in which a random sample of the U.S. population nominates firms as having the best or worst reputation. To assess the change in media salience from one year to the next, the analysis controlled for the firms' levels of public prominence in the previous year. The study identified all news releases and news articles about these firms in PR Newswire, Business Newswire, and *The New York Times* over the same 6-month period for 2 years in a row in which the firms appeared.

Since it is likely that firms' existing levels of public prominence make some more newsworthy than others, the present study controlled for these levels. Taking into account a firm's existing level of public prominence, the change in the firm's media salience contributed to the firm's rise or fall in prominence in the subsequent year. Traditional agenda-setting effects in the context of news about firms were hypothesized and supported—namely, that firms' media salience is related to their public prominence.

The data for this study were collected pre-9/11 and pre-Enron. Some may view the data as irrelevant in light of recent corporate scandals. Yet public scandals involving firms occur on a regular basis. The question is whether more recent scandals have altered the relationships between firms' media visibility and their public levels of prominence or their media favorability and their levels of public esteem, since the present study's focus was on the theoretical relationship between media portrayals of firms and their levels of public esteem.

This particular data set has advantages because it was collected before the Annual RQ's top-level data were institutionalized through the media. This study looked at the first 2 years of the Annual RQ, now in its 11th year of regular reporting. Thus, this study was able to assess the relationships without the confounding that occurs when researchers cannot decipher when audiences who evaluate corporate reputations have been influenced by the news media's reporting on firms' day-to-day behaviors or by the news media's publishing of the top-level reputation rankings that now occur on a yearly basis. That is, one complication of using more recent aggregated data is that it raises the possibility that the news media's publishing of a firm's reputation scores may influence the firms' public prominence or esteem rather than the news media's reporting on the firms themselves.

For people who follow the day's news but who have nothing to do with a firm (through product purchases, investing, or boycotting), their esteem for the firms evaluated may ebb and flow with day-to-day media reporting, different polls, and the ways questions are asked. It is possible that uninvolved participants in the Annual RQ survey answered questions positively or negatively only because they felt obligated to give an answer to an interviewer even if they had never really thought about the firm before. The selection criteria Harris Interactive used for assigning respondents to specific firms should have minimized this possibility. That is, respondents had to be at least somewhat familiar with the firms in order to evaluate them for the survey, although their specific knowledge about particular attributes may have been limited.

Some may conclude that public relations professionals should concentrate on influencing organizational behaviors and performance that directly affects publics with a relationship with the firm and pay less attention to influencing media coverage of the firm that affects only those who pay little attention to it. Nevertheless, negative media coverage might discourage people who know nothing about a firm or have no relationship with it from pursuing a relationship (Deephouse, 2000).

The present study only examined firms' appearance on the newspaper's front page, the front page of the business section, and editorials and columns. This study did not examine, for instance, other pages of the business section; nor did it examine advertorials published in the mix of these pages. Some firms not included in this study appeared routinely in these other pages, and thus would have had higher levels of media salience if these pages were included. These firms, however, did not appear in the Reputation Quotient's annual study. This finding provides some indication that firms are able to sustain routine news coverage without being subject to greater levels of public awareness. As Gardberg and Fombrun (2002) observe, these 26 firms were among the 30 that captured close to 90% of the nominations from a random sample of the U.S. population. Since the firms in the sample were all highly prominent, it is likely that their public relations practitioners were experienced and media savvy (Reese, 1990; Sheafer, 2001) and had strong relationships with the news media.

Clearly, not all firms wish to achieve publicity or public prominence; indeed, many firms invest in public relations in order to stay out of the press. Kiousis and Wu (2008) found that many countries employed public relations counsel precisely for this reason and that these countries enjoyed a lower volume of negative press articles as a result. Researchers should therefore avoid interpreting public prominence as a goal for all organizations or generalizing the present results to all organizations pending further research on other organizational contexts. Whether low levels of salience are a result of firms' public relations efforts aimed at keeping them out of the press, a reflection of media gatekeeping, or a product of media bias remains a subject for future exploration. That some firms are not highly salient in the public sphere does not mean that their activities and interests are not of concern to the public. Future research should begin theorizing about this field of firms' public and media visibility for the relative effects they have on the public sphere.

The present study contributes to the broad field of communication in several ways. First, the study breaks down corporate reputation into multiple dimensions and offers two new measures for the first two dimensions which have not been used concomitantly in previous research. Second, the study partials out the effects of firms' existing levels of prominence, allowing for closer examination of the contribution of firms' media salience to their change in prominence.

Note

1. The "ticker" document segment accompanying the news articles identified a firm's presence in the article if it received a 50% or higher score from the Lexis-Nexis algorithms that machine coded the articles for a firm's presence. The "ticker" document segment is an encoded topical index term produced and maintained by Lexis-Nexis for identifying relevant firm content. Each firm's ticker was the stock exchange symbol designated by firms on the stock-exchange markets. This paper used encoded topical index terms generated by Lexis-Nexis bibliographers who catalogue topical index terms for subjects (or issue topics), public persons, publicly-traded companies, and organizations. These terms are attached to news stories for Lexis-Nexis premier customers, but are not available with standard academic subscriptions. The scores are computed from frequency counts of keywords found in the document divided by the number of words in the document; they measure the salience of the subject for the article. A 90% score indicates that the story has a major reference to a particular term, while 50% indicates a weak, passing reference. Any story with no relevant keywords for a given topic—low enough to fall below 50%—receives no score for that topical index term. A full list of the topical index terms is available online at http://www.lexisnexis.com/infopro/products/index/. Those used for this study were current as of May 14, 2004.

Bibliography

Alsop, R. (2001, February 7). Survey rates companies' reputations, and many are found wanting. *The Wall Street Journal*, p. B1.

Alsop, R. (2003, February 12). Scandal-filled year takes toll on firms' good names. *The Wall Street Journal*, p. B1.

Arpan, L. M., & Pompper, D. (2003). Stormy weather: Testing "stealing thunder" as a crisis communication strategy to improve communication flow between organizations and journalists. *Public Relations Review, 29*, 291–308.

Arpan, L.M., & Roskos-Ewoldsen, D. R. (2005). Stealing thunder: An analysis of the effects of proactive disclosure of crisis information. *Public Relations Review, 31*, 425–433.

Atwood, L. E., Sohn, A. B., & Sohn, H. (1978). Daily newspaper contributions to community discussion. *Journalism Quarterly, 55*, 570–576.

Baron, R. M., & Kenny, D. A. (1986). The moderator-mediator variable distinction in social psychological research: Conceptual, strategic, and statistical considerations. *Journal of Personality and Social Psychology, 51*(6), 1173–1182.

Becker, L. B., & McCombs, M. E. (1978). The role of the press in determining voter reactions to presidential primaries. *Human Communication Research, 4*(4), 301–307.

Berelson, G., Lazarsfeld, P. F., & McPhee, W. (1954). *Voting.* Chicago, IL: University of Chicago Press.

Berger, B. K. (2001). Private issues and public policy: Locating the corporate agenda within agenda-setting theory. *Journal of Public Relations Research, 13*(2), 91–126.

Boorstin, D. J. (1961). *The image: A guide to pseudo-events in America.* New York: Harper & Row.

Buley, J. (1995). Evaluating exploratory factor analysis: Which initial-extraction techniques provide the best factor fidelity? *Human Communication Research, 21*(4), 478–493.

Carroll, C. E. (2004). *How the mass media influence perceptions of corporate reputation: Exploring agenda-setting effects within business news coverage* (Unpublished doctoral dissertation). The University of Texas, Austi, TX, USA.

Carroll, C. E., & McCombs, M. E. (2003). Agenda-setting effects of business news on the public's images and opinions about major corporations. *Corporate Reputation Review, 6*(1), 36–46.

Carter, S. M., & Dukerich, J. M. (1998). Corporate responses to changes in reputation. *Corporate Reputation Review, 1*(1–2), 250–270.

Cohen, B. C. (1963). *The press and foreign policy.* Princeton, NJ: Princeton University Press

Coombs, W. T., & Holladay, S. J. (2002). Helping crisis managers protect reputational assets: Initial tests of the situational crisis communication theory. *Management Communication Quarterly, 16,* 165–186.

Coombs, W. T., & Holladay, S. J. (2009). Further explorations of post-crisis communication: Effects of media and response strategies on perceptions and intentions. *Public Relations Review, 35*(1), 1–9.

Curtin, P. A. (1999). Reevaluating public relations information subsidies: Market-driven journalism and agenda-building theory and practice. *Journal of Public Relations Research, 11*(1), 53–90.

Dahl, R. Mason Haire, A., & Lazarsfeld, P. F. (1959). *Social science research on business: Product and potential.* New York: Columbia University Press.

Dearing, J. W., & Rogers, E. M. (1996). *Agenda setting.* Thousand Oaks, CA: Sage.

Deephouse, D. L. (2000). Media reputation as a strategic resource: An integration of mass communication and resource-based theories. *Journal of Management, 26*(6), 1091–1112.

Eells, R. (1959). The corporate image in public relations. *California Management Review, 1*(4), 15–23.

Fombrun, C. J. (1998). Indices of corporate reputation: An analysis of media rankings and social monitors' ratings. *Corporate Reputation Review, 1*(4), 327–340.

Fombrun, C. J., Gardberg, N. A., & Sever, J. M. (2000). The Reputation Quotient: A multi-stakeholder measure of corporate reputation. *Journal of Brand Management, 7*(4), 241–255.

Fombrun, C. J., & Shanley, M. (1990). What's in a name? Reputation building and corporate strategy. *Academy of Management Journal, 33*(2), 233–258.

Fombrun, C. J., & Van Riel, C. B. M. (1997). The reputational landscape. *Corporate Reputation Review, 1*(1–2), 5–13.

Gans, H. J. (2005). *Deciding what's news: A study of CBS Evening News, NBC Nightly News, Newsweek, and Time.* Evanston, IL: Northwestern University Press.

Gardberg, N. A., & Fombrun, C. J. (2002). USA: For better or worse: The most media visible American corporate reputations. *Corporate Reputation Review, 4*(4), 385–391.

Golan, G., & Wanta, W. (2001). Second-level agenda setting in the New Hampshire primary: A comparison of coverage in three newspapers and public perception of candidates. *Journalism and Mass Communication Quarterly, 78*(2), 247–259.

Hong, S. Y. (2008). The relationship between newsworthiness and publication of news releases in the media. *Public Relations Review, 37*(4), 297–299.

Janis, I. L., & Fadner, R. (1965). The coefficient of imbalance. In H. D. Lasswell, N. Leites, & Associates (Eds.), *Language of politics* (pp. 153–169). Cambridge, MA: MIT Press.

Kim, Y. (2000). Measuring the bottom-line impact of corporate public relations. *Journalism & Mass Communication Quarterly, 77*(2), 273–291.

Kim, Y. (2001). Measuring the economic value of public relations. *Journal of Public Relations Research, 13*(1), 3–26.

Kiousis, S. (2004). Explicating media salience: A factor analysis of New York Times issue coverage during the 2000 U.S. presidential election. *Journal of Communication, 54*(1), 71–87.

Kiousis, S. (2005). Compelling arguments and attitude strength: Exploring the impact of second-level agenda setting on public opinion of presidential candidate images. *The Harvard International Journal of Press/Politics, 10*(2), 3–27.

Kiousis, S., Bantimaroudis, P., & Ban, H. (1999). Candidate image attributes: Experiments on the substantive dimension of second-level agenda setting. *Communication Research, 26*(4), 414–428.

Kiousis, S., Mitrook, M., Wu, X., & Seltzer, T. (2006). First- and second-level agenda-building and agenda-setting effects: Exploring the linkages among candidate news releases, media coverage, and public opinion during the 2002 Florida Gubernatorial Election. *Journal of Public Relations Research, 18*(3), 265–285.

Kiousis, S., Popescu, C., & Mitrook, M. (2007). Understanding influence on corporate reputation: An examination of public relations efforts, media coverage, public opinion, and financial performance from an agenda-building and agenda-setting perspective. *Journal of Public Relations Research, 19*(2), 147–165.

Kiousis, S., & Wu, X. (2008). International agenda-building and agenda-setting exploring the influence of public relations counsel on U.S. news media and public perceptions of foreign nations. *International Communication Gazette, 70*(1), 58–75.

Klapper, J. T. (1960). *The effects of mass communication.* New York: Free Press.

Lazarsfeld, P. F., Berelson, B., & Gaudet, H. (1944). *The people's choice: How the voter makes up his mind in a presidential campaign* (3rd ed.). New York: Duell, Sloan & Pearce.

Lazarsfeld, P. F., & Merton, R. K. (1960). Mass communication, popular taste, and organized social action. In W. Schramm (Ed.), *Mass communication* (2nd ed., pp. 497–498). Urbana: University of Illinois Press.

Martineau, P. (1958). Sharper focus for the corporate image. *Harvard Business Review, 36*(6), 49–58.

McCombs, M. E. (1997). New frontiers in agenda-setting: Agendas of attributes and frames. *Mass Communication Review, 24*(1&2), 32–52.

McCombs, M. E., Lopez-Escobar, E., & Llamas, J. P. (2000). Setting the agenda of attributes in the 1996 Spanish general election. *Journal of Communication, 50*(2), 77–92.

McCombs, M. E., Llamas, J. P., Lopez-Escobar, E., & Federico, R. (1997). Candidate images in Spanish elections: Second level agenda-setting effects. *Journalism and Mass Communication Quarterly, 74*(4), 703–717.

McCombs, M. E., & Shaw, D. L. (1972). The agenda-setting function of mass media. *Public Opinion Quarterly, 36*(2), 167–187.

McCombs, M. E., & Shaw, D. L. (1993). The evolution of agenda-setting research: Twenty-five years in the marketplace of ideas. *Journal of Communication, 43*(2), 58–67.

McCombs, M., Shaw, D. L., & Weaver, D. (Eds.). (1997). *Communication and democracy: Exploring the intellectual frontiers in agenda-setting theory.* Mahwah, NJ: Erlbaum.

Meijer, M. (2004). *Does success breed success? Effects of news and advertising on corporate reputation.* Amsterdam, the Netherlands: Aksant.

Meijer, M., & Kleinnijenhuis, J. (2006a). The effects of issue news on corporate reputation: Applying the theories of agenda setting and issue ownership in the field of business communication. *Journal of Communication, 56*(4), 543–559.

Meijer, M., & Kleinnijenhuis, J. (2006b). News and corporate reputation: Empirical findings from the Netherlands. *Public Relations Review, 32*(4), 341–348.

Park, D. J., & Berger, B. K. (2004). The presentation of CEOs in the press, 1990–2000: Increasing salience, positive valence, and a focus on competency and personal dimensions of image. *Journal of Public Relations Research, 16*(1), 93–125.

Park, H. S., Dailey, R., & Lemus, D. (2002). The use of exploratory factor analysis and principal components analysis in communication research. *Human Communication Research, 28*(4), 562–577.

Pollock, T. G., & Rindova, V. P. (2003). Media legitimation effects in the market for initial public offerings. *Academy of Management Journal, 46*(5), 631–642.

Potter, W. J., & Levine-Donnerstein D. (1999). Rethinking validity and reliability in content analysis. *Journal of Applied Communication Research, 27*(3), 258–284.

Reese, S. D. (1990). Setting the media's agenda: A power balance perspective. *Communication Yearbook 14* (pp. 309–340). New Brunswick, NJ: International Communication Association.

Reese, S. D., & Danielian, L. H. (1989). Intermedia influence and the drug issue: Converging on cocaine. In P. J. Shoemaker (Ed.), *Communication campaigns about drugs: Government, media, and the public* (pp. 29–46). Hillsdale, NJ: Erlbaum.

Rindova, V. P., Williamson, I. O., Petkova, A. P., & Sever, J. M. (2005). Being good or being known: An empirical examination of the dimensions, antecedents, and consequences of organizational reputation. *Academy of Management Journal, 48*(6), 1033–1049.

Roberts, P. W., & Dowling, G. R. (2002). Corporate reputation and sustained superior financial performance. *Strategic Management Journal, 23*(12), 1077–1093.

Sheafer, T. (2001). Charismatic skill and media legitimacy: An actor-centered approach to understanding the political communication competition. *Communication Research, 28*(6), 711–636.

Shoemaker, P. J., & Reese, S. D. (1996). *Mediating the message: Theories of influences on mass media content.* White Plains, NY: Longman.

Shoemaker, P. J., Tankard, J. W., Jr., & Lasorsa, D. L. (2004). *How to build social science theories.* Thousand Oaks, CA: Sage.

Spector, A. J. (1961, October). Basic dimensions of the corporate image. *Journal of Marketing, 25,* 47–51.

Shrout, P. E., & Bolger, N. (2002). Mediation in experimental and nonexperimental studies: New procedures and recommendations. *Psychological Methods, 7*(4), 422–445.

Stocking, S. H. (1985). Effect of public relations efforts on media visibility of organizations. *Journal Quarterly, 62*(2), 358–366.

Stone, P. J., Dunphy, D. C., & Bernstein, A. (1966). The analysis of product image. In *The general inquirer: A computer approach to content analysis* (pp. 619–627). Cambridge: MIT Press.

Swisher, K., & Reese, S. D. (1992). The smoking and health issue in newspapers: Influence of regional economies, the Tobacco Institute, and news objectivity. *Journalism Quarterly, 69*(4), 987–1000.

Tabachnick, B. G., & Fidell, L. S. (2003). *Using multivariate statistics* (4th ed.). New York: HarperCollins College.

Tan, Y., & Weaver, E. (2007). Agenda-setting effects among the media, the public, and Congress, 1946–2004. *Journalism & Mass Communication Quarterly, 84*(4), 729–744.

Van Riel, C. B. M., & Fombrun, C. J. (2002). Which company is most visible in your country? An introduction to the special issue on the global RQ-project nominations. *Corporate Reputation Review, 4*(4), 296–302.

Wartick, S. L. (1992). The relationship between intense media exposure and change in corporate reputation. *Business & Society, 31*(1), 33–49.

Weaver, D. H., Graber, D. A., McCombs, M. E., & Eyal, C. H. (1981). *Media agenda-setting in a presidential election: Issues, images and interest.* New York: Praeger.

Yoon, Y. (2005). Legitimacy, public relations, and media access: Proposing and testing a media access model. *Communication Research, 32*(6), 762–793.

Part III

Corporate Reputation and the News Media in Emerging and Frontier Markets

15 Corporate Reputation and the News Media in Argentina

Federico Rey Lennon and Gonzalo Diego Peña

In today's market, where consumer cynicism remains at high levels, sensitive companies are acknowledging the importance of their own corporate reputations as a corporate asset. Prestige or an organization's reputation arises from the comparison of organizational characteristics in the public mind, based upon experience and knowledge, and comparing these characteristics to what each individual considers specific values and behaviors in these organizations (Rey Lennon & Bartoli Piñero, 2007). Thus defined, reputation does not represent an institutional image. It is a concept far more complex. Reputation represents the public's valuation or appraisal of that specific image. Reputation is therefore a quality that stakeholders give to an organization. It is built upon perceptions of previous and future institutional performance (for this reason the strategic vision a company has of its own business is of great importance); this global perception describes the attraction an organization produces at different public levels when it is compared with a competitor. The stakeholders' perception is corporate reputation. Reputation is vital because it is capable of conditioning attitudes toward an organization, and consequently it is a valuable corporate asset. However, reputation is not part of a communication campaign. It is a value built on planning and effective management over a period of time.

Agenda-Setting Theory

Argentina was a pioneer in the study of agenda-setting theory in Latin America. Federico Rey Lennon first researched the subject in 1977 when he studied the legislative elections in the Buenos Aires metropolitan area (Rey Lennon, 1998/2000). It was a typical agenda-setting study in a political campaign context and was divided into two parts. The first part dealt with the first level of agenda-setting theory ("most important problem"), and the second analyzed the image of political candidates in the mass media agenda using categories developed for second-level agenda-setting studies made in Pamplona, Spain (Canel, Llamas, & Rey, 1996; McCombs, López-Escobar, Llamas, & Rey Lennon, 1997, 1998). Maxwell McCombs (2004, pp. 15–16), when referring to Rey Lennon's work (1998), pointed out, "corruption was prominent on both the public and media agendas throughout the fall, always ranking first or second." It considered that as election day came near, "the correspondence between the two agendas—public and media—for the top four issues soared to +0.80, an increase that suggested considerable learning from the news media in the closing weeks of the election campaign."

After this pioneer work by Rey Lennon (1997), two additional studies followed under his tutorship: one by Alicia Casermeiro de Pereson (2004) and the other by Ramon Monteiro (2006). The first is a study conducted in Buenos Aires during a primary election held in 1988 to select the presidential candidate for a major coalition. In this case, the study analyzed both first-level and second-level agenda-setting theory following the guidelines of previous studies (Pamplona and Buenos Aires). This valuable research by Casermeiro de Pereson included print and TV news agendas.

Ramon Monteiro's work (2006) was the first study of its kind conducted in Argentina outside the city of Buenos Aires. In this case, Monteiro analyzed the influence of the local TV news in the city of Rio Cuarto, a middle size district in the Province of Cordoba located in the center of Argentina. It was a single issue study (the issue was unemployment) in a nonelectoral context including first- and second-level agenda-setting theory.

Institutional Credibility

Institutional credibility was a relevant issue in the study of public opinion. In the country and abroad, surveys were carried out regularly to measure and characterize those institutions that offer higher or lower credibility. Examples of systematic measurements may be found in TNS Gallup, IPSOS Mora y Araujo, Analogías, or the Latinobarómetro Corporation, dedicated annually since 1995, to measure the degree of institutional trust or confidence in 18 Latin American countries. Information obtained from these investigations of public opinion represented a value input for the state and civil society. In the above mentioned cases, the approach of this phenomenon was based on quantitative techniques aimed at proposing a statistics dimension regarding the degree of institutional credibility that public opinion holds at a given time. These studies generate the publication of rankings in institutional credibility from TV, radio, and print media. Likewise, institutional credibility was one of the six key attributes Fombrun, Gardberg, and Server (2000) identified through focus groups as the attribute agenda of corporate reputation. Although the relationship between institutional credibility and the media was without a doubt of vital importance to understanding how the reputation of a company was built in the mind of the stakeholders, there are no studies in Argentina that have applied the methodology exposed here.

Case Study: Corporate Reputation in Argentina

In the Argentine corporate community the concept of corporate reputation is relatively new. During the 1990s, it began to appear in academic literature and the specialized press. Also, in those years the press began to publish relevance rankings of "image" or "credibility," which today are mainly known as prestige or corporate reputation rankings. There are three rankings that are particularly relevant in business, those managed and published by *Mercado* and *Apertura*

Table 15.1 Corporate-Prestige Ranking One Decade (1994–2004)

1. Coca Cola	Large Multinational Co.
2. Repsol YPF	Large Multinational Co.
3. Arcor	Large National Co.
4. Unilever	Large Multinational Co.
5. Techint	Large National Co.
6. Perez Companc	Large National Co.
7. American Express	Large Multinational Co.
8. Mastellone Bros.	Large National Co.
9. Cervecería Quilmes	Large Multinational Co.
10. Mercedes Benz	Large Multinational Co.

Notes. CEOP (Centro de Estudios de Opinión Pública) presented in 2004 the corporate prestige ranking "of the decade". The CEOP is the institute of opinion research which annually makes for the newspaper Clarín the corporate prestige rankings and brand image. Repsol YPGF was a State oil company privatized in the 90s. Cerverceria Quilmes was national until the year 2004 in which it was bought by AmBev, a Belgium company proprietary of Brahma.

magazines and the Centro de Estudios de la Opinión Pública (CEOP), which the daily *Clarín* publishes annually (CEOP, 2005a, 2005b). The *Clarín* ranking, because of the importance of the media, is considered to have greater impact on stakeholders than other instruments.

Basically the three rankings are based on quantitative surveys of directors and managers of the most important companies in Argentina. They measure the opinion of "experts," not of public opinion in general. In the case of corporate prestige, the CEOP/*Clarín* ranking has the most effect on directors/general managers, middle management, and headquarters. The effective sample of interviewed people for all editions of the study has increased from 350 in 1995 to 490 in 2006. An analysis of the rankings over the last 10 years shows that the first 10 positions are held by large national and multinational companies.

Nevertheless, it is interesting to emphasize that between 2003 and 2006 the top ranking was held by the Argentine company ARCOR, the world leader in caramel manufacturing and sales. ARCOR is one of the few Argentine companies that managed to operate globally without losing its national character. In that period, the two companies below ARCOR in the ranking were large and multinational (Repsol YPF and Coca-Cola in 2003 and 2006; Repsol YPF and Unilever in 2004 and 2005).

Media Systems in Argentina

There was a strong trend in the 1990s toward concentration, development of multimedia groups, and investment of foreign capital in the Argentine media business (and in general in the communications sector). Some of these foreign companies included the Telefónica Group (Spain), Hicks Group, Recoletos (and Pearson Group), Prime (Australia), Cisneros (Venezuela), Globo (Brazil), Televisa (Mexico),

Rupert Murdoch's News Corporation, Goldman Sachs, and others. This investment of foreign capital sometimes took the form of the outright purchase of local media and in other cases in businesses in which local groups also invested. The mergers and acquisitions involved in this process date from the 2000.

There is a generalized perception that Argentina has been permissive regarding foreign investors in the local media as well as throughout the communication industry. Nevertheless, evidence shows that this was a worldwide phenomenon, in spite of the restrictions that, for example, countries of Western Europe have imposed. In the present globalized world, with huge financial flows that are transferred between countries without effective government controls, the communication business in Argentina was not an exception to what was happening throughout the global economy.

Why are mass media bought (and sold) in Argentina? Cost reduction appears to have been a major cause of this activity. Almost all the innovations in the communication field entail the application of end technologies, which involve major investment.

The emergent countries of Latin America had economic growth in the 1990s, which made them of interest to investors. For example, it is typical to witness the formation of strategic alliances between large international companies and multimedia groups in a region for the purpose of exploiting the promising digital television market.

As the global village described by McLuhan becomes a fact, competition becomes implacable. The fight to capture audiences does not have borders (satellite TV is an example of this), and survival depends on the capacity of the companies to be victorious on the technological front and the media content front, which will soon be the most important one.

Some data can help to make sense of the media system in Argentina. Since the late 1990s, newspapers and magazines have been losing audience. Newspapers, which previously were read by 34% of the population dropped to only 21% of the population. Similarly, magazines fell to 40% of the population from 53%. In this same period television viewers increased by 32%.

The circulation numbers of the two mainly dailies showed that both lost audience (see Table 15.2).

Public Relations in Argentina

In Latin America, Brazil is the public relations pioneer with the creation early in 1914 of the Sao Paulo Tramway Light and Power Company's PR department.

Table 15.2 Main Newspaper Circulation in Argentina

Main Newspapers Circulation / Argentina		Clarín	La Nación
Monday to Saturday	2000	457.698	159.953
	2005	346.695	143.843
Sunday	2000	844.24	242.511
	2005	787.845	258.839

On the other hand, in Argentina, the first PR professionals emerged in the 1940s and were associated with the arrival of large foreign companies, particularly American companies such as Ford Motors, General Motors, Exxon, and Ducilo and European companies such as Shell, Fiat, and Olivetti.

Through the mid-1950s and early 1960s, public relations was viewed as a professional task. These years show a marked growth of multinational companies in Argentina, mainly in the oil and automotive industries. At the same time the development of independent professionals began, including such pioneering PR consulting firms as Opinion S.A. (partner of the American group McCann Erickson); A & C—Analysts and Consultants—and Asesoramiento Empresario Institucional.

The Argentine Association of Public Relations was created in 1958. A group of professionals left the Association and created the Argentine Professional Circle in June 1961. This association opened the first PR School in 1962, which was the first to grant a technical degree.

In 1964, the Universidad Argentina de la Empresa (UADE) began the first PR academic degree course. One year later, in 1965, the first graduates then went on to create the Graduate College. The 1970s were marked by permanent political and social conflict and growing trade union activism. At that time, the big issue in public opinion was that private entrepreneurship and multinationals' management were viewed as the source of all evil. Multinational executives from companies such as Ford and Exxon were attacked and kidnapped. Crisis communication and media training of spokespersons expanded dramatically during this time.

In the late 1970s, PR actions expanded to include support for schools, health care, patronage, and donations to nonprofit entities. Also, banks began to incorporate PR positions into management. In 1976, a coup d'état brought a new military government. The dictators changed the relationship between companies and the state once again. This situation promoted the development of company lobbyists who tried to intervene with the military government. The dictatorship caused an economic crisis in national industry, which generated an expansion of PR freelance work and was the seed for later development of PR consulting firms.

The return to democracy in 1983 meant demands for more information and an expansion in the PR industry. In 1989, the two existing professional entities merged and create the Public Relations Professional Council of the Argentine Republic.

The 1990s brought the internationalization of the corporate world and the Argentine privatization of public services companies. Globalization meant the arrival of international consultants in a way that has now been consolidated. Burson-Marsteller (1995), Hill & Knowlton (1996), Edelman (1997), and Porter Novelli (1998) opened offices in Argentina at that time.

The privatization of most public service companies and the need to manage the public and along with particular interest in public opinion generated the further expansion of the profession in Argentina. The new century has marked the climax of this process of PR globalization and local development.

Research Methodology

This investigation aimed at generating a value input to analyze institutional credibility, starting from a qualitative approach. At this point, it was convenient to
refer briefly to the main differences observed between quantitative and qualitative studies. According to Soler (1997, p. 26), "the most relevant characteristics
in qualitative studies are their understanding of the framework, the availability
of data at a deep level and their interest in factual description. From a statistics
standpoint, however, qualitative studies are not representative of the universe
studied and, therefore, may not be considered of a general nature."

In this case, the focus group technique was applied in order to understand what
associations and meanings were related to institutional credibility. This exploratory analysis was carried out with the intention of supplementing the quantitative research in the second part of the investigation. The second part used media
content analysis and public opinion poll data to analyze the relationship between
the credibility of companies in the sampled population and the way in which the
media report on companies. Both investigations, qualitative and quantitative, were
carried out on residents of the main urban clusters of Argentina in August 2005.

Objectives   This work sought to characterize the concept of institutional
credibility under which public opinion operates today; to trace a qualitative
mapping of the main components on which institutional credibility is articulated
at present; to survey institutions of high and low credibility; and to establish the
reasons for higher and lower institutional credibility considering the practices (of
communication and journalism) on which they are based.

Focus Groups   The first part of the research focused on qualitative analysis
of public opinion. Four focus groups from the Metropolitan Buenos Aires area
(AMBA) were organized and segmented based upon their gender, age, and
socioeconomic level.

Prior to initiation of the focus groups, each participant filled out a questionnaire indicating institutions with higher or lower credibility. The material
obtained was later used by the focus group coordinator as input for further
group discussion. Some of the issues discussed in the groups were the concept of
institutional credibility and which institutions have higher or lower credibility.
An analysis of the following institutions was sought during these focus groups:

Political: The President of Argentina, Ministers of the National Government;
    House of Representatives, the Senate, the judiciary, political parties;
Labor: trade unions;
Business: small and medium corporations, large national companies, large
    multinational companies;
Other: nongovernment organizations (NGOs); mass media;
Religious groups: Roman Catholic Church;
Military and law enforcement: armed forces; the police;
Education: national state universities, private universities, public schools,
    private schools;
Healthcare: public and private hospitals.

These institutions were chosen based upon contributions of quantitative studies made at present by TNS Gallup, CEOP, and Latino barómetro operating together with ICOS contributions on this issue. Each focus group was made up of five or six persons and was observed for 60 minutes on average in a Gesell Chamber located in Buenos Aires City.

The second part of the study focused upon content analysis of the main newspaper of the country, *Clarín*. There were many reasons to choose this newspaper. It is a multimedia member of the biggest group in Argentina which puts *Clarín* into a situation where it is in an intermedia agenda setting. Second, it is the most widely read newspaper in the country, with national distribution, and with readers from all socioeconomic levels represented by the sample in the focus groups and the opinion survey. As Stempel (1991) found, most consumers and stakeholders affirmed that they acquired information about corporations and industries from the print media more than from TV or radio. This study dealt with how the general public constructed the credibility of these institutions in their minds, and unlike many of the indexes and studies on corporate reputation it was not a study of the business elite's opinions. For that reason it seemed to us more pertinent to use a mass medium and not an economic newspaper aimed at a more select public. On the other hand, the corporate public relations departments and PR consultants in Argentina considered *Clarín* as an informative source and an agenda setter. One final reason to choose this medium, although not the least important, *Clarín* was the newspaper that, along with CEOP, had the most important ranking of company reputation in the country.

For content analysis, a random sample of the news was extracted based upon the inclusion of the following keywords in either the body or holder: *companies; multinational companies; large companies and small and medium corporations.* The news was analyzed in the period between February 1 and July 31, 2005. There were 228 analyzed news articles.

Public Opinion Poll   For this investigation a sample survey was used. The unit of analysis was residents in the survey location, more than 18 years old, both sexes, of all socioeconomic levels. The collection technique was telephone surveys assisted by computer (CATI) with a structured questionnaire. The questions were open, closed, multiple, simple alternatives, and opinion scales. The sample consisted of 700 cases with an error: +/- 3.77% and a 95.5% confidence interval. The locations were the cities of Buenos Aires and Greater Buenos Aires; Mendoza; Comodoro Rivadavia; Neuquén-Confluencia; Rosario; Córdoba; Tucumán; and Resistencia-Corrientes.

Data Analysis and Results: Qualitative Analysis of Public Opinion

According to the different issues dealt with by each group the results of the investigation are organized in two parts: (1) the concept of institutional credibility; (2) institutions with higher or lower credibility.

On the Concept of Institutional Credibility   The concept of credibility is a complex notion for all participants. It operates via multiple associations that also refer to different levels. From the results obtained, it is possible to establish the main elements on which the concept of credibility is based. In this case, the interest is focused on public opinion perceptions organized at two levels as a result of focus group analysis:

- *Primary (Basic) Level*   In this level, "the hard core," the main values on which institutional credibility is based, are established. If these attributes are satisfied, all those related to the secondary level, with a higher degree of probability will follow.
- *Secondary Level*   These values also represent important components for the perception of institutional credibility provided previous validation of the elements belonging to the basic level is made.

The following list of values for each of the above levels follows:

Primary Level is found where structural values of institutional credibility are located. Within it, credibility as a concept is associated with four main values:

- *Efficiency:* The institution must reach its objectives or goals and try to avoid deceiving the community.
- *Power:* According to participants, every institution presents a certain degree of power.
- *Transparency:* Each institution must be clear in its performance, showing coherence between what is said and what is done. Transparency is also associated to the capacity each institution offers when information is requested by the stakeholders.
- *Coherence:* Express the coherence between what the institution said and what it has done; refer to the fulfillment of the institutional promise.

Secondary Level is articulated according to the following attributes:

- *Satisfaction:* It corresponds to public opinion expectancy for each institution.
- *Public interest or general concern:* All institutions are asked, beyond their specificity, to care about general welfare, imposing themselves beyond group or private interests that could be inserted in the organization and are expressed as "general" or common to all citizens, when (their actions) are really shared by a certain group.
- *Institutional nearness or proximity* concerned with the participants' everyday life. This component contributes to institutional identification, as well as to its objectives, decisions, methodology, and actions.

Perception of institutional credibility condenses institutional performance in each of the above values and attributes. It may be observed from our analysis that participants do not match symmetrically (in relevance/importance) the weight of each attribute. On the contrary, according to the specificity between the origin and institutional objectives, participants will match the elements/components in a different order (ranking) of importance.

In consequence, a ranking of values and attributes related to institutional credibility articulated by participants is presented:

Primary (basic) level
• Efficiency
• Power
• Transparency
• Coherence
Secondary level
• Satisfaction
• Public interest/General concern
• Nearness/Proximity

Institutions with Higher or Lower Credibility It is important to point out the interrelation observed between the perceptions of credibility and institutional power. For participants, that an institution may show high credibility does not imply it exercises wide power. Small and medium size companies represent the most symbolic case aligned with this statement. In our chart, this group of companies is perceived as holding the highest credibility, but it is clear that the power they have is clearly more limited than the power held by large national and multinational companies. Nongovernmental organizations, schools, hospitals, and universities share this asymmetric performance: all represent high credibility amongst the general public, but the perception is that they have limited power. The Catholic Church, the president, ministers of the national administration, and the mass media, on the other side, are placed in the quadrant of high credibility simultaneously with a perception of high power.

Transversal analysis of credibility and power perceptions make possible the construction of the following matrix (see Table 15.3).

Table 15.3 Institutional Positioning Chart

Credibility Perception	Power Perception		
	High	*Medium*	*Low*
High	• Roman Catholic Church • The President • Mass Media • Ministers of the National Administration		• Small and Medium Corporations • NGOs (Third Sector) • Schools (Private & Public) • Hospitals (Private & Public) • Universities (Private & Public)
Medium	• Large national companies	• Police	• Armed Forces
Low	• The Judiciary • Large multinational companies • House of Representatives • The Senate • Political Parties	• Unions	

Table 15.4 Attributes/Affective Dimension

Attributes	Negative	Neutral	Positive	Total	%
Economic development	4	9	29	42	18,4
Agro	0	3	18	21	9,2
Public services corporation (privatized)	13	3	2	18	7,9
New techs	2	7	9	18	7,9
Management & corporate governance	4	11	1	16	7,0
Human resources	4	5	4	13	5,7
Government control	10	1	1	12	5,3
Exportation	0	4	8	12	5,3
Finance	0	5	7	12	5,3
Government aid	1	7	3	11	4,8
Remunerations	4	4	2	10	4,4
Ethics	7	0	0	7	3,1
Security	4	2	1	7	3,1
Energy	2	3	1	6	2,6
Taxes	4	2	0	6	2,6
Inflation	3	2	0	5	2,2
Environment	2	0	3	5	2,2
Others foreign markets	0	3	0	3	1,3
Mercosur	0	0	2	2	0,9
Devaluation	1	0	0	1	0,4
Reputation rankings	0	1	0	1	0,4
Total	65	72	91	228	100

Quantitative Analysis of Public Opinion and the Press: Media Agenda   The most important data of the content analysis of *Clarín* (February to July 2005) can be observed in the following tables. In the first place it is interesting to note that more than half of the news about companies (58.7%) discusses those of national origin, small, medium, or large size. Barely 19.3% talk exclusively about multinational companies. Most of the news that referred to large national and multinational companies (which represent 21.9% of the total news), are about general information on aspects of management or national policies that apply to big corporations. Regarding the affective dimension of the news that referred to companies, in general the coverage by *Clarín* displays a balance: 4 out of 10 contain positive news (39.9%); in second place comes neutral news (31.6%); and in the last place negative news (28.5%).

There are two issues in the corporate news agenda that take up 27.6% of the total: economic development and agriculture. Economic development includes news about the development and growth of the Argentine economy and corpora-

Table 15.5 Actors/Affective Dimension

	Negative	Neutral	Positive	Total
Large multinational Co.	20	12	12	44
Large national Co.	26	30	25	81
Large national & multinational Co.	14	17	19	50
Small & medium Co.	5	13	35	53
Total	65	72	91	228

tions, specially emphasizing the recovery after the 2001 and 2002 economic crises. So this is news that gives positive coverage to companies as engines of change whose activities directly affect the economy. The agriculture issue includes information about this mighty sector of the Argentine economy, and in this case there is no news with negative affective valuation.

If we now analyze the affective valuation of corporate news we see that big multinational and also large national companies are more frequently discussed with a negative slant. This is more remarkable if we compare them with small and medium corporations which only receive 9.4% of negative valuations and the biggest percentage of positive valuations (66%).

Public Opinion Agenda   We now center our analysis on the data produced by the public opinion survey. Here we worked on two questions, the first of which referred to the spontaneous evaluation of institutions with greater credibility in Argentina, a similar question to the one addressed in the qualitative study. The data are forceful and clearly corroborate the tendencies glimpsed in focus groups.

The second question was about the perception of the power that each institution has in the public space. The survey also corroborates the tendency observed in focus groups.

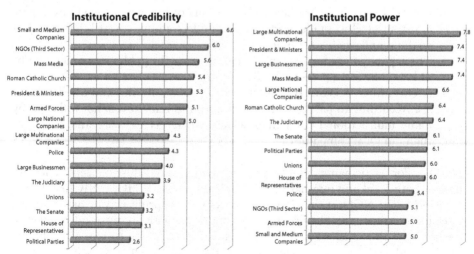

Figure 15.1 Institutional credibility and institutional power

Discussion

Qualitative Research: *Main Drivers that Explain Higher or Lower Corporate Credibility* From the participants' standpoint, to characterize different practices helps to achieve a certain degree of credibility, and it is a task that requires a special analysis of each institution. Relevant actions are related to their own institutional specificity and also the practices adopted by each institution during the past year. In consequence, a detailed individual institutional analysis is made in order to present the main drivers explaining higher or lower current credibility.

Small and Medium Corporate Executives Participants considered the business spectrum to have medium to low credibility with the exception of the owners of medium and small size companies, which presented high credibility and trust levels. There is a certain amount of nationalism at work here, and an acknowledgment of the prowess of the self-made man. Argentina's 2001 to 2002 crisis stirred up profound nationalism in public opinion. During the nineties, international companies occupied a leading role in terms of credibility perception. During the institutional and economic crisis of 2001 this scenario was fractured. Since 2002, small and medium corporations and large national companies acquired (or regained) credibility in the public view and quite rapidly pushed foreign organizations into second place.

The banking and financial services industry constitutes a leading case in relation to this subject. During the period of the Argentine Currency Board system ("Convertibility"—1991–2001) the international element was a key attribute of credibility. After the currency devaluation, the situation changed due to reassessment of the performance or the local origin of that organization.

The three most relevant factors articulating small and medium corporations' credibility are:

- Closeness/proximity to the everyday events of life, which generates in participants a feeling of identification and understanding toward the owners of medium and small size companies.
- The capacity to generate employment, because the public views lack of jobs as being the main problem in the country.
- A corporate decision to remain in the country during and after the crisis. According to participants, the decision to remain was not followed by many multinational companies which had larger capacity and resources than did local companies.

NGOs For participants, NGOs represent a wide and diffuse concept. They are part of both local and international organizations (i.e. WHO, UNICEF, etc.) or CARITAS (the NGO of the Catholic Church) as nonprofit private associations. Greenpeace constitutes the first top ranking NGO with an outstanding level of credibility. To be concerned about the general welfare, not to aim at profitable results, and working independently from the government, represent the main drivers on which institutional credibility of NGOs is based.

Mass Media For participants, the level of credibility reached is supplemented with the high power of perception the media possesses nowadays. In relation to types of media, higher credibility is present in printed material in general but more specifically in newspapers. Radio occupies second place while TV ranks third.

Large National and International Companies As mentioned previously, the 2001 crisis produced a relevant change in the credibility of these institutions (see Figure 15.2).

During the nineties, international banks that included the attribute of "internationality" as a differentiated factor in their communications and their image constitute the group that is most responsible for contributing to the decrease in credibility of international companies. Their performance during the 2001 financial crisis best exemplifies this situation. At that point, national companies began to gain credibility in public opinion. The capacity to generate employment—a concern that preoccupies the general public—is the first action that contributes to credibility. As a member of the focus group stated, "During the crisis, small and medium corporations could not leave. They had to take strong action. Many of them could not survive in the marketplace. But some should be honored for their efforts to stay in business without dismissing employees."

Quantitative Research

As we previously indicated when presenting data from the public opinion survey, the quantitative results confirm the observations of the qualitative focus groups around the division today in Argentine public opinion regarding credibility and institutional power. The Spearman rank correlation between both agendas is very high:

$$+.9571 \ (N = 14; \ p < = 0.7638).$$

As mentioned before, an institution may show high credibility but that does not imply that it has widespread power. The banking and financial sector has an

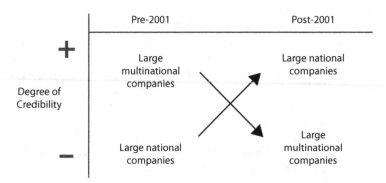

Figure 15.2 Shifts in degrees of credibility for large national and multinational companies

important place amongst multinational companies and their loss of credibility, and it has reduced the credibility of foreign capital in Argentine public opinion. Multinational companies with lower to middle levels of credibility are at the same time still considered to be powerful institutional actors.

An analysis of financial institutions by the IPSOS group in its work *Argentines DC 2004: After the Corralito... Facing 2004* noted in relation to the banks: "Hostility and lack of trust on the part of public opinion towards banking and financial activities." The Argentine press named *corralito* or the *corral effect* a restriction on removal of bound, cash flows and accounts savings imposed by the government of Fernando de la Rúa in December 2001. The government knows that the street's perception of risk can be fatal to the financial system. Rumors of a bank's insolvency can quickly become a self-fulfilling prophecy. Pursuing these restrictions the corral effect aimed at avoiding the output of money from the banks, trying to prevent a wave of panic and the collapse of the Argentine financial system. The report maintains:

- It is difficult to see the corral effect as a historical fact.
- There is an attitude between caution and resignation because a bank is an essential institution.
- Although the satisfaction indicators have been improved, they are far from excellence indexes, nevertheless it is more a reputation problem than one of quality of service.
- Banks do not constitute an exception. Argentina has been in the process of economic recovery since the year 2003 and the necessity for an injection of external capital was essential (in order for production capacity to be maintained) if the economic process was to be sustained beyond the "bounce effect." But public opinion is immersed in a cycle of demand-distrust.

Multinational corporations must collaborate with national development, with productive investments that generate new jobs, but there is still distrust of their "true" intentions. Thus, public relations professionals in these organizations have the complex challenge of operating in this tense situation to design and implement concrete actions that deactivate or at least, limit the feelings of distrust that are produced by corporate decisions.

In terms of corporate reputation, the last five years has witnessed the small and medium corporations effect. These corporations registered during the nineties when they had limited levels of institutional credibility. This paradigm broke with the devaluation of the currency in 2001. From that moment, public credibility ratings for this type of company have increased to a remarkable degree. Today, this category is at the top of the institutional credibility ranking with an average of 6.6 points.

Nevertheless, the actual benefits derived from a positive public rating are limited. In terms of institutional power, this category ranks at the bottom. Small and medium corporations are in a cycle of valuation-impotence: They have public credibility but they have difficulty in increasing their power.

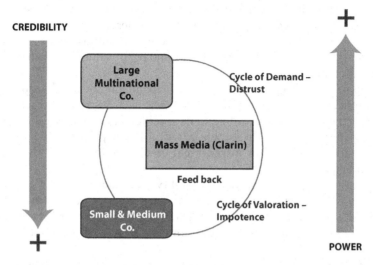

Figure 15.3 Present situation of institutional credibility and power

And where are the media while this happens? The mass media collaborate in the perpetuation of this situation. As we noted previously, *Clarín*—Argentina's leading newspaper—has a different way of dealing with news about small and medium corporations than it has in regard to multinationals, according to results of the content analysis that we made. The data are eloquent. While 66% of the news that referred to small and medium corporations is framed in a positive dimension, only 27.2% of the news covers multinationals and 30.8% of the news covers large national companies.

At this point, the complexities of this scenario experience a qualitative jump. The cycle of demand-distrust, specific to the relationship between public opinion and the multinational companies, intersects with the highly positive valuation—with strong affect—of the small and medium companies. Clearly, in the positive valuation of the small and medium companies the media do not remain neutral. On the contrary, they feed this new cycle.

Conclusions

This exploratory research has described the current scenario of the Argentine crisis as a profound crisis in values which has affected the society. In our research, participants reflected that they are going through a period of redefinition. It is a period during which some values now have new meaning compared to a few years ago when public opinion supported their perception of the future.

This crisis in values seems to participants that they want a different future than they had once envisaged. And here institutions and institutional credibility are seen as key communication links between institutions and public opinion. The manifestation of institutional credibility is a necessary factor to thinking about the viability of a different future. Without institutional credibility the future cannot be determined.

For participants, credibility rests upon a series of seven basic values: efficiency, power, transparency, coherence, satisfaction, general concern, and nearness/proximity with everyday life. Actions and communications adopted by institutions (as practices) operating within this boundary of values strengthen the level of perceived credibility.

It is important to keep in mind that participants do not weigh symmetrically (in importance) each element. On the contrary, each institution reaches a mix, evaluated in a special way according to its specificity and objectives. In this case, a quantitative study may help establish, with further precision the weight corresponding to the concept of institutional credibility in each of the attributes mentioned before.

On the other hand, institutional credibility is characterized in the perception of power as an independent variable. As an example, it is possible to establish a comparison between the high credibility found today in owners of medium size and small companies matching at the same time their own low perception of power.

From a different perspective, the media appear as special participants. They constitute a relevant institution which, at the same time, represents an important channel through which participants establish the concept of credibility they possess.

An example of this is the judiciary. This institution has a low level of credibility because the media, for some participants, represent the central and most relevant source of information through which they develop a view of the judiciary as having low credibility.

Institutional actions and practices are in several occasions decodified by the public through the media. Likewise, on occasion, the media do not remain apart from the validation of these actions and practices. Media valuation of companies' actions and practices has an impact, to a higher or lower degree, on public opinion perceptions and on the definition of the degree of institutional credibility ascribed to an institution.

This situation shows the role of the media as a factor that influences public decodification of institutional actions operating within the milestone of values where credibility holds up and is consistent with the data referred to in Carroll and McCombs (2003).

References

Canel, M. J., Llamas, J. P., & Rey, F. (1996). El primer nivel del efecto agenda setting en la información local: Los "problemas más importantes" de la ciudad de Pamplona [The first level of the agenda-setting effect in local information: The "Most important problems" of the city of Pamplona]. *Comunicación y Sociedad, 9,* 17–38.

Carroll, C. E., & McCombs, M E. (2003). Agenda-setting effects of business news on the public's images and opinions about major corporations. *Corporate Reputation Review,* 6(1), 36–46.

Casermeiro De Pereson, A. (2004). *Los medios en las elecciones: Agenda setting en la ciudad de Buenos Aires* [Media in elections: agenda-setting role of the news media in the city of Buenos Aires]. Buenos Aires, Argentina: Editorial de la Universidad Católica Argentina (EDUCA).

Centro de Estudios de la Opinión Pública (CEOP). (2005a). *Systematic trackings on institutional credibility (1998–2005): Quantitative investigation including door-to-door personal interviews in Buenos Aires metropolitan area and the provinces of Cordoba, Rosario, Mendoza, Neuquen-Cippolleti area and Tucuman.*

Centro de Estudios de la Opinión Pública (CEOP). (2005b). *Systematic trackings on satisfaction and credibility jointly with the National Government (1997–2005): Quantitative investigations with door-to-door personal interviews in Buenos Aires metropolitan area, Cordoba, Rosario, Neuquen-Cippolletti area and Tucuman.*

Fombrun, C. J., Gardberg, N. A., & Sever, J. M. (2000). The Reputation Quotient: A multi-stakeholder measure of corporate reputation. *Journal of Brand Management, 7*(4), 241–255.

IPSOS Group. (2004). *Los argentinos DC 2004. Después del Corralito...De Cara al 2004* [The Argentines DC 2004. After the "Corralito"... Towards 2004]. IPSOS: Buenos Aires; Based on studies EGM 2003 and IPSOS BUS. Unpublished research report ceded by IPSOS, Buenos Aires, Argentina.

Latinobarómetro. (2004). *Annual survey on political, economic and social scenarios in Latin America: Quantitative research with personal door-to-door interviews in 18 countries of Latin America.* Retrieved from http://www.latinobarometro.org

McCombs, M. (2004). *Setting the agenda: The mass media and public opinion.* Cambridge, UK: Polity Press.

McCombs, M., López-Escobar, E., Llamas, J. P., & Rey Lennon, F. (1997). Candidate image in Spanish elections: Second level agenda-setting effects. *Journalism & Mass Communication Quarterly, 74*(4), 703–717.

McCombs, M., López-Escobar, E., Llamas, J. P., & Rey Lennon, F. (1998). Two levels of agenda setting in the 1995 Spanish election. *Political Communication, 15*(2), 225–238.

Monteiro, R. (2006). *La agenda setting en la televisión: Teorías, perspectivas y estudio de caso.* Río Cuarto, Argentina: Universidad Nacional de Río Cuarto.

Rey Lennon, F. (2000). The agenda-setting role of the news media in national elections. In *Public opinion in the nineties and the new millennium* (pp. 21–27). Canberra, Australia: WAPOR & The School of Professional Communication, University of Canberra, Australia. (Original work published 1998)

Rey Lennon, F., & Bartoli Piñero, J. (2007). *Reflexiones sobre el management de la comunicación* [Thoughts about the management of communication]. Buenos Aires, Argentina: La crujía.

Soler, P. (1997). *La investigación cualitativa en marketing y publicidad* [Qualitative research in marketing and advertising]. Barcelona, Spain: Paidós.

Stempel, G. H. III. (1991, Fall). Where people really get most of their news. *Newspaper Research Journal, 11*, 2–9.

16 Corporate Reputation and the News Media in Brazil

Ana Luisa de Castro Almeida,
Dário Arantes Nunes, and Leandro L. Batista

This chapter examines how the Brazilian media influence the public's perception of corporations. Here, as in most countries, agenda-setting studies have focused primarily on political matters. Approaches to the agenda-setting phenomenon as it relates to organizations are rare, which emphasizes the importance of this study. To put the subject in context, we will first present an overview of Brazil's economic, social, and political aspects.

Brazil belongs to a group of emergent or developing countries. It is a country with a consolidated democratic regime and it is categorized as "free" by Freedom House, an independent and nongovernmental organization which supports the worldwide expansion of freedom.

Nevertheless, the country is characterized by great social contrasts. Structural deficiencies keep it from developing in an accelerated way when compared to other emergent countries, and a major reason for this is the problem of serious infrastructural problems in terms of transport.

Brazil has recently achieved oil self-sufficiency, however, and has a strong and diversified industrial section with large companies that export raw materials, agricultural products, manufactured goods, and even products of high technological value such as automobiles and planes. From a social point of view, it is one the worst countries in terms of income distribution. Of 126 countries for which information is available, Brazil is ranked as having the 10th greatest income inequity. This factor contributed to Brazil's 69th ranking according to the Human Development Index (HDI) in 2004, even though it is the 14th largest economy in the world. Brazil is ranked 66th of 125 countries on the 2006 Global Competitiveness Index (GCI)[1]. This derives from Brazil having a significant budget deficit as compared to other countries. High levels of government debt and an elevated interest rate have caused heavy bank costs, which negatively affects private sector investments, and has contributed to Brazil's low economic growth in the last few years.

In regard to the perception of corruption, Brazil is ranked as 70th on the Corruption Perceptions Index (2006),[2] according to a survey administered by the NGO Transparency International involving 163 countries. Only taking into consideration the 154 countries present in the index in the past 2 years, Brazil has lost 5 places in relation to the study in 2005, going from 61st to 66th. This is mostly due to corruption scandals involving members of the government of the president Luiz Inácio "Lula" and the National Congress. It is in this context that the media finds itself.

In Brazil, freedom of speech is a reality, even though the press's freedom is sometimes curtailed because of civil and criminal lawsuits against journalists.

Corporate Reputation in Brazil

Corporate reputation has been increasingly attracting the attention of researchers all over the world, Brazil included. In 2005, the Reputation Institute was launched in Brazil in partnership with the Pontifícia Universidade Católica de Minas Gerais (PUC Minas), aiming to broaden the generation and dissemination of knowledge on reputation. In the academic field, there are some studies about corporate image and corporate reputation which will be grouped here, according to Berens and Van Riel's (2004) classification of corporate reputation literature, in three conceptual streams: social expectations, corporate personality traits associations, and trust associations. Amongst others, the following Brazilian studies are highlighted.

Social Expectations Perspective

Schuler's study (2004) is discussed: It is about the development of a research method to assess an organization's image from the perspective of a specified group, through organizational communication activities to build a positive image. Almeida's study (2005), which was the first in Brazil to analyze the relation between projected image and reputation, and to use measuring techniques applied in international studies, such as the Reputation Quotient (RQ), perceived external prestige (PEP), projected identity (APOI), organizational identification (OID), organizational citizenship behavior (OCB), and the study by Carrieri, Almeida, and Fonseca (2004) about organizational image.

Corporate Personality Traits Associations

Here we can highlight Thomaz's (2003) study of the influence that culture, identity, image, and communication have on corporate reputation; the research by Brito, Campos, Ledur, and Thomaz (2005) on the relation between corporate reputation and performance; and the study by Brito, Thomaz, Brito, and Artur (2004) which relates corporate reputation as a strategic resource.

Trust Associations

The Annual Trust Barometer, a study administered in the country by Edelman,[3] goes along with this perspective.

The definition by Fombrun and Rindova (1998) about corporate reputation is the most commonly used one: "corporate reputation is a collective representation of a company's past actions and results that describes the company's ability to deliver valued outcomes to multiple stakeholders."

The Agenda-Setting Theory in Brazil

Recent studies about agenda-setting theory published in Brazil focus on level 1; most published articles aim at identifying which political themes are present in the mass media during election periods (Colling, 2000) or in specific political situations such as the impeachment of the governor of Santa Catarina, a southern state in Brazil (Golembiewski, 2000). There is also a study of the political field that discusses the relation between media content and content of the Free Electoral Program,[4] a differential aspect of the Brazilian electoral system (Miguel, 2004).

Still in level 1, some authors observe the effects of agenda-setting theory outside the political content, considering, for example, social topics within soap operas (Pereira, 2000); studying the effects of media in determining public policies from an anthropological point of view (Ferreira, 2002); and to turn to the present work, on how the association agenda of design companies is influenced by the content of stories published in the media (Reyes, 2002).

Theoretical aspects of agenda setting have also been published in Brazilian academic literature, such as the relation between agenda setting and reception (Barros Filho, 2003); the relation with framing (Colling, 2002); and the theoretical relation produced by agenda setting of advertising material and news content of communication media (Batista, 2005).

Some publications that can be found in English analyze agenda setting in Brazil using different focuses, such as the relation between companies and politics (Scheineder, 1998), ideological aspects of Brazilian news (Schiff, 1996), the development of policies related to the environment (Carvalho, 2001), and the effect of political influence on editorial content and readers' letters in a newspaper (Frota e Souza, 2005).

Business and News Media in Brazil

It seems that no research on testing the agenda-setting hypothesis from a corporate perspective has been developed in Brazil in recent years. However, some works deal with the effects of the second-level affective dimension of agenda setting, or the valence of the organization (Silva, 1997), focusing on the capacity the company possesses to influence the media into reporting the construction of a new General Motors plant in Brazil; still at the second level, it is possible to find at least one master's thesis (e.g. Schneider, 2001) that focuses on the effects of agenda setting from the observation of telecommunication companies' publicity content.

Case Study: Corporate Reputation in Brazil

There are already surveys in Brazil that assess the reputation of companies. A survey that has already been consolidated, "The Most Admired Companies in Brazil," has been presented by Interscience for 8 years, in partnership with the Carta Capital publication.[5] The methodology is similar to the one used by *Fortune* magazine in the United States. Over the eight annual issues of the survey, there has been an increase in the valuation of national companies and growing relevance of social and environmental responsibility projects (Almeida, 2005). In the last two issues, seven companies within the 10 most admired were Brazilian, such as Natura, which for the second consecutive time, took first place.

Another important survey to contribute to the discussion of corporate reputation is the "Best Companies to Work For" ranking survey, which has been conducted since 1997 by the *Exame* and *Voce S/A* publications.[6] The survey, which is being reformulated this year, assesses data with 70% weight relative to the "employee's view of the company," such as identity, satisfaction and motivation, leadership, learning and development; data with a weight of 25% relative to "what a company offers to its employees," such as salary and benefits, professional career, education, health, concern about worker's integrity, social and environmental responsibility; and data with a 5% weight relative to the "visit to preclassified companies." In 2006, 502 companies in various industries took part.

There are international organizations that already work in markets such as the United States, Europe, and Asia and they are now directing their survey activities toward Brazil, such as Hill and Knowlton, which has been developing a survey since 1997 called *Corporate Reputation Watch*,[7] with the objective of assessing the level of importance and understanding that executives give to issues related to how companies' reputations are built and managed. This survey was conducted in Brazil for the first time in 2003 and we have referred to some of its results here. For 72% of the Brazilian respondents, a company's reputation has become more important than it was 5 years ago, a percentage quite a bit higher than the 60% in other regions around the world. When questioned about what the greatest threats to a company's reputation are, the answers varied: unethical behavior by the company, problems with products and services, consumer complaints, and negative stories in the media were the main answers (Almeida, 2005). Another important survey was done for the first time in 2006 to assess the reputation of the 20 largest national companies—The Global RepTrak™ Pulse 2006—conducted by the Reputation Institute. It was the first of a series of annual studies of the corporate reputations of the largest companies in 25 countries, including Brazil. An increase of managers' concern regarding the importance of corporate reputation and ways in which it can be managed can be noted, considering that recent international surveys indicate that reputation is number one in the ranking of the most challenging threats to a business.

Media Systems in Brazil

The framework proposed by Sriramesh and Verčič (2003) will be used to describe the media system in Brazil. The framework basically leads to an analysis of the mass media along three dimensions: media control, media outreach, and media access.

Media Control

Sriramesh and Verčič (2003, p. 13) point out that in order to keep an effective relationship with the media, public relations professionals should understand who controls the media organizations in the country and whether such control affects editorial content. For that purpose, the authors suggest research on the Freedom House Web site. According to that NGO, in 2006 freedom of speech in Brazil was categorized as "partly free." This categorization was based on an analysis of the country's legal environment, political influence, and the economic environment. The 1998 Constitution provides for freedom of speech and of the press and these rights are usually respected in practice. However, the broadcasting services operate under the old telecommunications code of 1962 and the press law has been in place since its 1967 imposition by the military dictatorship.

As per the 2006 Freedom House assessment, press freedom continues to be attacked by means of civil and criminal lawsuits, a method that is frequently used by politicians, public officials, and businesspeople as a tool of intimidation against journalists and the news media. Aside from this obstruction, Brazilian journalists are usually able to report the news freely, including coverage of cases of corruption and irregularities involving the main public authorities.

The media market in Brazil, South America's largest, is vigorous, dynamic, and diversified. However, media ownership is highly concentrated, particularly within the broadcast sector. The Globo organization, the largest media conglomerate in Brazil, boasts a hegemonic position, possessing the largest primary television network, radio stations, and press media in the form of newspapers, magazines, and cable TV distribution.

The media system in Brazil was started in 1922 with the launch of radio in Rio de Janeiro, then the country's capital. The Brazilian media system had a fast evolution due to its organization in the form of societies or clubs which allowed its independence from advertising revenue; the support came from listeners' contributions and the contents were mainly devoted to education and information (Guareschi & Biz, 2005).

In 1932, the government decreed that the exploitation of the mass media should be exclusively Brazilian property, controlled by the state and private capital (Lima, 2001). Due to this new regulation, there was a search for the monetary incentive of advertising, which provoked a fast expansion of radio, with the creation of several broadcast organizations, around 1950. It was also in this year that television broadcasting was inaugurated in Brazil, following the North American model of commercial exploitation. Brazilian television was inaugurated in São Paulo, the country's commercial and industrial center. Early television already possessed the same characteristics observed in this market today; that is, the formation of media conglomerates. The first Brazilian television station was part of the Diários Associados (Associated Diaries), a group that owned several regional newspapers and radio stations and that belonged to a senator of the republic who was Brazilian ambassador in London, and therefore a politician. This initiative lead to the creation of new television broadcast companies in São Paulo and Rio de Janeiro. The first TV company outside the Rio-São Paulo axis was TV Gaúcha in Porto Alegre, Rio Grande do Sul (Guareschi & Biz, 2005), one of Brazil's most important states.

The largest development of the telecommunications industry in Brazil happened during the period of the military dictatorship, mainly in its beginning in

1964 with the construction of transmission towers, implantation of telephone direct dialing systems, and communication satellites. This made possible the development of extensive television systems that reached practically the whole country; the prominent point in this endeavor was direct TV transmission of the 1970 Soccer World Cup in Mexico (Guareschi & Biz, 2005).

The adopted model and the new regulations of the media system in Brazil led to great ownership concentration. According to Lima (2001) in the Brazilian media system we can observe four types of communication systems:

1. Horizontal concentration: a few groups control the cable and broadcast television systems;
2. Vertical concentration: several channels of broadcast TV export programs to other countries, with high financial gains;
3. Crossed property: amplification of the monopoly through ownership of other communication organizations such as magazines, newspapers, radios, cable television, and Internet providers; and
4. Crossed monopolies: where there is regional reproduction of the national monopolies.

These monopoly systems can be observed by the concentration of TV broadcasting stations in six networks: Globo, SBT, Record, Bandeirantes, Rede TV!, and CNT. In 1998, these stations already owned 79% of Brazilian broadcasting stations (263 of 332). These same networks possessed 53 of the 94 private channels (the government's concession). Other great owners of TV channels are linked to religious groups: Universal Church (five TV stations), Catholic Church (three TV stations), and Assembly of God (one TV station).

Rede Globo dominates more than 50% of the TV audience, followed by SBT with 23%, and the other networks below 10%. In financial terms (total advertising budget was over U.S.$3 billion). Distribution follows audience numbers: Rede Globo (53%), followed by SBT (20%), and the others below 10%, according to Lima (2001).

Azevedo (2006) states that in Brazil there is a historical association between media ownership and the elite, which is mainly the case with the big newspapers. Legislation passed to keep ownership of the mass media out of the hands of non-Brazilian groups facilitated the formation of family monopolies. Lima (2001) identifies eight large groups that control radio and TV in Brazil. Three of these groups are at a national level:

1. Marinho (Rede Globo) with 32 TV and 20 radio stations, along with cable TV services, TV content providers, newspapers, magazines, portals, Web sites, and Internet providers;
2. Saad (Bandeirantes) with 12 TV and 21 radio stations; and
3. Abravanel (SBT) with 10 TV stations.

In regional terms, it is possible to identify other powerful families who control mass media, namely the Sirotsky family (RBS-south) with 20 TV and 20 radio stations. Three other families control other media systems, mainly including newspapers, magazines, Internet portals and Web sites, and cable TV: Civita (Group Abril), Mesquita (Group O Estado de São Paulo), and Frias (Grupo Folha). Emissoras e Diários Associados, founded by Assis Chateaubriand, which owns 12 newspapers, six television stations, and news agencies, Internet providers, and video producers is also very significant. This group has a unique organizational feature: it is a cooperative of 22 shareholders who hold the majority of the companies' shares, which cannot be transferred, negotiated, or inherited. About 90% of the Brazilian media is controlled by only 15 family groups (Lima, 2001).

The radio and TV concessions follow the traditional concentration of political forces. There is a lack of current data, but a study in 1996 (Bayma, 2001, cited in Guareschi & Biz, 2005) identified 13 political parties as dividing these concessions, with an ownership concentration (77%) in four major parties: the Liberal Front Party (PFL; 34%), a party that in the past was associated with the military government; the Party of the Brazilian Democratic Movement (PMDB; 18%); the Brazilian Labor Party (PTB; 16%); and the Brazilian Social Democracy Party (PSDB; 9%). All of these parties can be considered center right. The other 23% are divided in a fairly balanced proportion (varying from 0.5 % to 4 %) among nine other parties.

Media Outreach

Media outreach can be assessed by the average number of newspaper buyers and by the audience for TV and radio programs. In Brazil, media outreach is limited due to illiteracy and socioeconomic discrepancies.

According to Associação Nacional de Jornais (ANJ), the average access to a newspaper by the adult population in 2006 was only 45.3 copies per 1,000 inhabitants, a lower number as compared to developed countries and even some emergent countries such as Chile and South Africa. The average number of daily newspapers sold in 2006 was around 7.23 million, which represented an increase of 6.5% from the previous year. The newspapers reached 48% of adults, 52% men, 44% women, and 38% of the heads of families.

A significant part of the Brazilian population has a low income, and, according to ANJ, it is a typical example of the relationship between economic performance and newspaper sales. In 2001, 2002, and 2003, Brazil's GNP rose by only a small amount, which had a negative impact on newspaper circulation. From 2004 on, the economic indicators improved and the newspaper sector benefited. Brazilians started to buy more newspapers when their incomes improved. In line with the previous years' accomplishments, the newspaper industry focused its efforts on reaching low income consumers and launched low cost newspapers.

In a survey carried out by ANJ, newspapers were appraised as having high credibility (above that of the Catholic Church), being just below medical doctors. Radio and television are widely distributed; they were available in 2004 in 87.7% and 89.8% of Brazilian households respectively, according to Lima (2006).

Media Access

The large organizations have privileged access to the media to spread their message, mainly via the specialized economic and business media. At these companies, the press–investor relations department is usually well-structured, enabling easy access to the media. Middle-sized and small companies use the services of public relations providers to act as intermediaries. Despite that, it is important to point out that a given message may not be given much space in newspapers, which reserve prominence for news that has a strong impact on public opinion.

Organizational Newsworthiness

Theoretically, any subject matter can be presented in the media. However, Barros Filho (1993) states that analysis of the informational media shows that certain types of story are considered newsworthy. For Barros Filho (1993), novelty and the ability to hold the audience's attention are the main elements to make a story newsworthy.

When we look at corporate news, a content analysis of the communication media in Brazil indicates that global processes and corporate mergers and acquisitions arouse a lot interest from the media. Also, corporate social projects that emphasize sustainable development, as well as the specific programs, policies, and guidelines of corporate governance are themes that are considered worthy of media coverage.

Media space is always limited, and corporate press offices must consider this when trying to place stories that relate to their corporation, because any story must hold the attention of the public.

Public Relations in Brazil

The public relations profession was launched 100 years ago in Brazil, with the creation of the public relations department of the Canadian energy company the Light and Power Co[8] which was active in the United States, England, and Canada (França, 2003; Kunsch, 2006). But until the 1950s, public relations was not widely used (Wey, 1986).

The 1960s and 1970s were marked by the military regimen, with the suppression of constitutional and civil rights, restriction of individual freedom, and strong censorship of communication media. It was within this context that the profession was regulated (law number 5.377, in 1967), a fact that is considered by some authors to be evolutionary in the defense of professional space, yet is questioned by others such as Kunsch (2003), França (2003), and Ferrari (2003), who point out the lack of a theoretical base and professional practices that could better make possible a consistent definition of public relations.

The political context limited the evolution of activities within the public relations sector, which found itself facing closed doors and in response adopted a low profile. In the governmental sector, the main form of communication was through political propaganda (França, 2003; Kunsch, 1997, 2003).

There has been a suspicion that the public relations profession attempts to deceive public opinion with distorted information or manipulation and buying of media space, without acknowledging that the space has been purchased. The period of the dictatorship when the government controlled the press and companies were afraid to attract government attention marked a period of questioning and lack of definition and positioning of the public relations profession.

Within the academy, the first course started in 1967, at the Escola de Comunicação e Artes da Universidade de São Paulo (ECA/USP), created by one of the main researchers in the area, Professor Cândido Teobaldo de Souza Andrade (Kunsch, 2006). At that time, the first public relations consultants were created.

The 1980s marks the beginning of the country's gradual redemocratization process, with the public fighting for its rights and the organization of social movements. On the economic front, the early 21st century is marked by a major crisis with high inflation and a recession. In communication, the first studies to adopt an integrated communication policy were developed, which made public relations professionals responsible for planning communication (Kunsch, 1986). The way organizations understand and work with public relations, press, and propaganda activities began to change. According to Kunsch (2003), there was also an increase in the volume of scientific production about organizational communication and an increase in the number of communication consultancy companies.

Academic studies and discussions in the 1980s brought new perspectives and a critical view of the public relations area, although multiple concepts of what constitutes public relations still prevail (Andrade, 1983). A prominent work in the critical literature was the book by Peruzzo (1986), which, by recognizing the contradictions of capitalism, leads us into reflecting on the impossibility of the public relations professional's search for harmonious relations because the interests involved are often adversarial.

The 1990s, which was marked by technological advances, globalization, access to information, and mergers of media companies, determined new ways of relationship and new expectations for the diverse social actors. This context amplifies the demand for and behavior of communication professionals, and reinforces the perspective of integrated communication. In the conceptual approach of public relations, various authors highlight the role of the professional as manager of the relationships between the organization and its stakeholders, such as Kunsch (2003), Oliveira (2002), Ferrari (2003), and França (2003).

Today in Brazil, two institutions that encourage academic production are prominent: the Sociedade Brasileira de Estudos Interdisciplinares da Comunicação—Intercom and the COMPÓS. The Intercom is a scientific nonprofit association founded in 1977, integrated into international communication science networks such as the Asociación Latinoamericana de Investigadores de la Comunicación (ALAIC), International Association for Mass Communication Research (IAMCR), International Federation of Mass Communication Associations (IFCA), and Federação Lusófona de Ciências da Comunicação (Lusocom).

The Associação Nacional dos Programas de Pós-Graduação em Comunicação (COMPÓS) was founded in 1991 in Belo Horizonte to give master's and doctoral degrees. Both institutions possess as main goals to strengthen and qualify professionals and defend the theoretical, cultural, scientific, and technological development of the field of communication. In the professional field, Associação Brasileira de Comunicação Empresarial (ABERJE) was founded in 1967 to bring together professionals and companies regarding organizational communication.

As for the public relations industry, according to an article[9] by the Associação Brasileira das Agências de Comunicação (ABRACOM), there are now more than 1,000 communication agencies with regular operations in Brazil. Broadening a little more the criteria for what is considered a regular operation; if we consider all professionals as independent companies that are intermittently active in this area, this number could double, going to 2,000 agencies. Income from public relations activity is estimated at R$30 million per year. For Eduardo Ribeiro (2006), a specialist on the public relations industry, this number of agencies in Brazil is excessive given the market for their services and may lead to mergers and acquisitions.

Research Methodology

Content Analysis   The aim of the research is to assess the three hypotheses of agenda setting and their possible influence on the reputation of two large Brazilian organizations. One of them is a large regional company that generates, transmits, and distributes energy, which we designate Alpha company; the other is a large, transnational steelmaking company designated Beta company. Both companies are listed on the New York, Madrid, and São Paulo stock exchanges. A case study will be presented that is based on the content analysis of news stories about the companies, published in two of the largest newspapers in the country, during 2005.

Choice of News Media   According to surveys by the Annual Trust Barometer Edelman (2006), the Brazilian people differ from those in other countries by having a high level of trust in the media, 56% against 30% in the United States and Europe, and 45% in Canada. Other data show that the newspaper is the preferred channel for Brazilians who want to keep reliably informed about a story (29%), followed by the Internet (26%), TV (12%), and radio (2%). This survey reinforces the choice of newspapers as the ideal subject for research.

Media Selection   Two media have been selected: *Valor Econômico*, the most influential economic newspaper, with a daily average of 65,000 copies, and *Estado de Minas*, a large regional newspaper, with a daily average of 83,500 copies .

The newspaper *Valor Econômico* is published by two of the largest media conglomerates in Brazil: the Grupo Globo and the Grupo Folha. The target audience is executives and the majority of readers are men (84%), aged over 41 years (52%), with higher education (college or more) (83%), and wealthy (85%).

O *Estado de Minas* is a regional newspaper, the largest in Minas Gerais, one of the most important states in Brazil.

Researches about Reputation   The Global RepTrak Pulse is a survey methodology developed by the Reputation Institute that ranks companies according to their reputations. In this study, the overall reputation of companies is measured based on the esteem, feeling, trust, and admiration the general public has toward them.

The first of a series of planned annual rankings was conducted in 2006 across 25 countries in Europe, Asia, the Americas, and Africa. The RepTrak Pulse 2006 was conducted online using Web based questionnaires. The largest local companies within each country were measured according to their total revenue. Among other criteria, the companies had to be minimally familiar to the general public in order to be included in the study.

In Brazil, 20 companies were evaluated with a total of 3,139 respondents. Each respondent has a chance to comment on the reasons that led them to rate the companies the way they did. These comments are then categorized according to the RepTrak[10] model in products/services, innovation, workplace, governance, citizenship, leadership, and performance. This categorization helps identify what drives the company's reputation. All ratings are standardized, which allows comparisons across countries and industries.

Data Analysis

Information from Media   The media news was classified and analyzed with the objective of assessing the three hypotheses of agenda setting, which are:

Media Visibility: (1) The story was announced only in the newspaper of regional circulation; (2) the story was announced in the newspaper of national circulation; (3) the story was announced in both newspapers.

Content (Cognitive): Classification according to the seven dimensions of the RepTrak model: products and services, workplace, leadership, citizenship, governance, innovation, and performance.

Citations: To calculate the percent of citations for each dimension of the RepTrak model, we applied weights that consider the importance of each dimension for corporate reputation.

Organizational image (evaluative): News content was classified as (1) favorable, (2) unfavorable, and (3) neutral. Still within hypothesis 3, the news was also analyzed and classified according to their tonality: 1 – tonality more emotional than informational or 2 – tonality more informational than emotional.

Results

Hypothesis 1, Level 1 of Agenda Setting—Visibility in the Media   According to Table 16.1, as seen below, the regional newspaper *Estado de Minas* published, in 2005, around 353 news stories about the company Alpha, and the national newspaper *Valor Econômico* published 109 news stories about this same company—57 news stories were published simultaneously in both newspapers—which demonstrates the high visibility of the company in the media.

Table 16.1 Alpha Company

Reputation Dimension	Favorable News	Quot. X	% RepTrak™	Unfavorable News	Neutral news	Emotional News	Informational News	EM Newspaper	VE Newspaper	EM+VE Newspaper
Products & Services	121	25,73	50.65%	33	24	54	86	121	19	10
Workplace	5	0.65	1.28%	1	0	1	5	5	1	0
Leadership	10	1.8	3.54%	0	0	3	7	7	3	0
Citizenship	117	13.31	26.20%	6	5	27	105	132	0	0
Governance	19	2.09	4.11%	4	3	4	22	16	10	3
Innovation	2	0.2	0.39%	0	0	0	2	1	1	0
Performance	83	7.02	13.82%	25	4	5	141	71	75	44
Total	357	50,80	100%	69	36	94	368	353	109	57
Total %	77%			15%	8%	20%	80%			

Source: Media RepTrak™ adaptation – Reputation Institute

Table 16.2 Beta Company

Reputation Dimension	Favorable News	Quot. X	% RepTrak™	Unfavorable News	Neutral news	Emotional News	Informational News	EM Newspaper	VE Newspaper	EM+VE Newspaper
Products & Services	14	4.34	14.47%	4	0	2	16	6	12	3
Workplace	5	0.65	2.17%	1	0	2	4	4	2	0
Leadership	40	7.2	24.00%	0	1	12	29	29	12	1
Citizenship	67	7.37	24.57%	1	0	10	58	61	8	1
Governance	38	4.18	13.93%	35	5	24	54	44	34	16
Innovation	2	0.2	0.67%	0	0	1	1	2	0	0
Performance	101	6.06	20.20%	18	9	9	119	37	90	37
Total	267	30	100%	59	15	60	281	183	158	58
Total %	78%			17%	5%	18%	82%			

Source: Media RepTrak™ adaptation — Reputation Institute

The RepTrak Pulse 2006 survey classified the company Alpha in ninth place in reputation, amongst the 20 largest Brazilian companies. This company obtained 66.5 points and is 8.4 points below the first in the ranking which obtained 74.9 points.

In regard to company Beta, according to Table 16.2, as seen below, the newspaper *Estado de Minas* published in 2005 around 183 news stories, and *Valor Econômico* published 158 news stories on this same company—58 news stories were published simultaneously in both newspapers. These values demonstrate that both company Alpha and company Beta have got good visibility in the media.

The RepTrak Pulse 2006 survey classified the company Beta as being in eighth place in reputation amongst the 20 largest Brazilian companies. This company obtained 67.3 points and is 7.6 points below the first in the ranking which scored 74.9 points.

The results above found for the two companies confirm Hypothesis 1. This reinforces the confirmation by Carroll and McCombs (2003) that the amount of news coverage that a company receives in the news media is positively related to the public's awareness of the company (Carroll & McCombs, 2003, p. 39).

Hypothesis 2: Level 2 of Agenda Setting—Content (Cognitive)   Figures 16.1 and 16.2 below demonstrate the values that were found on the RepTrak Pulse 2006 survey, realized in 2006 for the seven reputation dimensions of the companies Alpha and Beta, respectively, in comparison to the analysis of the favorable news published in the newspapers *Estado de Minas* and *Valor Econômico*.

When comparing the results found in the news published in the media and the results found in RepTrak Pulse 2006, relative to the companies Alpha and Beta, we can conclude the following:

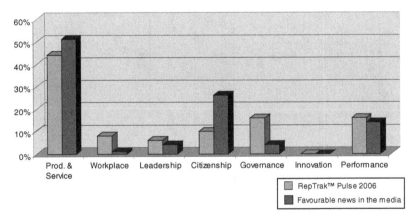

Figure 16.1 Alpha company. *Notes.* Comparison between the values for the seven dimensions of reputation in the RepTrak™ Pulse 2006 survey – Reputation Institute, with the analysis of favorable news announced in the media – Company Alpha.

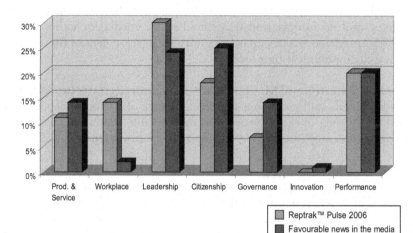

Figure 16.2 Beta company. *Notes.* Comparison between the values for the seven dimensions of reputation in the RepTrak™ Pulse 2006 survey – Reputation Institute, with the analysis of favorable news announced in the media – Company Beta.

- The dimension Products and Services had the highest score on the number of news stories published about company Alpha in the media, and the RepTrak Pulse 2006 survey indicates that this is the most important dimension according to the general public's evaluation of the company.
- In regard to the dimension Citizenship, both of the companies had good news coverage. However, the RepTrak Pulse 2006 survey presented lower scores than those found in the news analysis, which means that even though both companies were announcing their actions of social-environmental responsibility and citizenship, they did not obtain the same level of recognition from the general public.
- The company Alpha obtained little visibility on the dimension Leadership in the media and also in the perception of the general public. Company Beta obtained a high score in media coverage, with the president of the company being cited repeatedly, with pictures and interviews, which also led to a positive perception, by the general public, of the company's leadership, as the score on the RepTrak Pulse indicates.
- As for the dimension Governance, for the Alpha company the RepTrak Pulse 2006 survey identified a higher perception by the general public in relation to this dimension, and for the Beta company, the opposite was identified.
- In regard to the dimension Workplace, we found that, usually, the media is not open to information about this theme. This is a theme the press offices need to announce better.
- The dimension Performance reveals a direct relation between the news coverage and the general public's perception, confirming an alignment for both companies between what is being published about the companies and the general public's perception.

- The dimension Innovation was not assessed in the RepTrak Pulse 2006 survey and no information was found in the media for either company, which also demonstrates an opportunity for development of this dimension through communication processes.

According to Carroll and McCombs (2003), organized efforts to communicate a corporate agenda will result in a significant degree of correspondence between the attribute Agenda of the company and news media (p. 42). We can say then, considering both companies, that these findings confirm Hypothesis 2.

Hypothesis 3, 2nd Level of Agenda Setting: Media Favorability (Image)   From the point of view of media favorability, in relation to company Alpha, 77% of the news is favorable, 8% is neutral, and 15% is not favorable. As for company Beta, 78% of the news is favorable, 5% is neutral, and 17% is not favorable, which demonstrates great favorability on the part of the media regarding news coverage about these two companies.

By observing the news tonality, we can notice that for company Alpha, 80% of the news is more informative than emotional and 20% is more emotional than informative, whereas for company Beta, 82% of the news is more informative than emotional and 18% is more emotional than informative. The influence of the media agenda over the companies' agenda increases favorable and more emotional than informative news.

The high percent of media favorability is identified in the high reputation values from both companies, measured by the RepTrak Pulse. These results confirm Hypothesis 3.

Discussion

This case study suggests that agenda-setting influences the perception of the public about the reputation of great organizations. Theorists in reputation also state that organizations with a strong reputation have more favorable media coverage, indicating that reputation influences the media. Therefore, we can say that media and corporate reputation can be mutually influenced. This demonstrates the strategic importance of communication areas in the companies, more specifically press office areas. It is also important to underline that in periods of crisis, the faster dissemination of negative news through global media must be reason for great concern by the executives responsible for managing reputation risks, according to a report published by the Economist Intelligence Unit,[11] the result of a survey in October 2005 with the participation of 269 senior risk managers.

This situation leads us to conclude that the communication media exert influence in terms of positively reinforcing a strong reputation, and, on the other hand, these same media have a negative influence when crises threaten a company's reputation. The media agenda setting in relation to the business world has been influenced by global processes which have led to the merging and acquisition of companies.

One of the limitations of this study lies in the limited number of communication media analyzed, which may not correspond to an information mean derived from the whole media.

Conclusion

Despite the limitations identified above, this study makes a contribution to a clearer understanding of the influence of the media over the public's opinion of organizations, more specifically about the influence of agenda setting on the reputation of companies in Brazil. Positive media coverage has a strong influence on a company's reputation, so corporate communication must be sharply focused when it is defining newsworthy themes to be included in the agenda.

Notes

1. The Global Competitiveness Index (GCI) 2006 Report. Retrieved November 12, 2006, from http://www.weforum.org/pdf/Global_Competitiveness_Reports/Reports/gcr_2006/gcr2006_rankings.pdf
2. The Corruption Perceptions Index 2006. Retrieved November 12, 2006, from www.transparency.org/publications/publications/annual_reports/annual_report_2006
3. Edelman is the world's largest independent public relations firm, with 20,000 employees and 45 offices around the world.
4. Broadcast time on television and radio that has been granted to political parties.
5. *Carta Capital* is a information magazine from Brazil in and established in 1994.
6 *Exame* is the most influent and respected magazine in business and economy in the Brazil. It was established in 1967. *VocêSA* is a magazine that focuses on professional careers in the Brazil.
7. Corporate Reputation Watch is a Hill & Knowlton's Annual Global Survey of Senior Executive Opinions on Corporate Reputation Management conducted in cooperation with the Economist Intelligence Unit.
8. Known today as AES Eletropaulo
9. The article was retrieved Dec. 10, 2006, from http://www.abracom.org.br/descricao.asp?id=1744.
10. The RepTrak™ model consists of 23 attributes divided into seven dimensions, which are used in the analysis of a company's reputation by the Reputation Institute (Products/Services, Innovation, Workplace, Governance, Citizenship, Leadership, and Performance).
11. The Economist Intelligence Unit provides a constant flow of analysis and forecasts on more than 200 countries and six key industries.

References

Almeida, A. L. C. (2005). *A influência da identidade projetada na reputação organizacional* [The influence of the projected identity on organizational reputation]. Unpublished doctoral dissertation, Universidade Federal de Minas Gerais, Faculdade de Ciências Econômicas, Belo Horizonte, Brazil.

Andrade, C. Teobaldo de Souza (1983). *Para entender relações públicas* [To understand public relations]. São Paulo, Brazil: Loyola.

Azevedo, F. A. (2006). Mídia e democracia no Brasil: Relações entre o sistema de mídia e o sistema político [Media and democracy in Brazil: Relationship between the media system and the politics system]. *Opinião Pública, 12*(1), 88–113.

Barros Filho, C. (2003). *Ética na Comunicação* [Ethic on communication] (4th ed.). São Paulo, Brazil: Summus.

Batista, L. L. (2005). Efeitos da teoria do agenda-setting na percepção do público de atributos típicos e não-típicos de uma catgoria de produtos [Effects of the Agenda-setting theory in the public perception of the typical and untypical attributes of a category of product]. *Revista da ALAIC, 2*(3), 64–71.

Bayma, I. F. C. (2001). A concentração da propriedade dos meios de comunicação e o coronelismo eletrônico do Brasil [The concentration of the media ownership and the electronic colonialism of Brazil]. Brasília: Partido dos Trabalhadores/Assessoria Técnica. Retrieved from http://www.pt.org.br

Berens, G. A. J. M., & Van Riel, C. B. M. (2004). Corporate associations in the academic literature: Three main streams of thought in the reputation measurement literature. *Corporate Reputation Review, 7*(3), 161–178.

Brito, E. P. Z., Campos, L. A., Brito, L. A., Thomaz, J. C., & Carlos, J. (2005). Reputação corporativa e desempenho: Uma análise empírica no setor bancário [Corporate reputation and performance: a empiric analysis in the bank industry]. *Encontro da ANPAD, Brasilia:Anais do XXIX EnANPAD, 1*(1), 1–10.

Brito, E. P. Z., Thomaz, J. C., & Brito, L. A. L.(2004). Corporate reputation as a strategic resource. *Curitiva. 28*(1), 240.

Carrieri, A., Almeida, A. L. C., & Fonseca, E. (2004). *Imagem organizacional: Um estudo de caso sobre a Puc Minas* [Organizational image: a case study about Puc Minas]. Paper presented at the 27th Anais Congresso Brasileiro de Ciências da Comunicação, Pontifical Catholic University of Rio Grande do Sul, Porto Alegre, Brazil.

Carroll, C. E., & McCombs M. E. (2003). Agenda-setting effects of business news on the public's images and opinions about major corporations. *Corporate Reputation Review, 6* (1)36–46.

Carvalho, G. (2001). Metallurgical development in the Caraja's area: A case study of the evolution of environmental policy formation in Brazil. *Society & Natural Resources, 14*(2), 127–143.

Colling, L. (2000). *Agendamento, enquadramento e silêncio no jornal nacional nas eleições presidenciais de 1998* [Agenda-setting, framing and silence in the Jornal Nacional during the presidential elections of 1998]. Unpublished master's thesis). Universidade Federal da Bahia, Brazil.

Edelman. (2006). www.edelman.jp/img/news/FullSupplement.pdf

Ferrari, M. A. (2003). *Relações públicas e sua função estratégica* [Public relations and its strategic role]. Paper presented at the 26th Congresso Brasileiro de Ciências da Comunicação, Belo Horizonte.

Ferreira, G. M. (2002). Paradigmas do campo comunicacional relacionados com a antropologia [Communicational field paradigms related with anthropology]. *Contra-campo, 7,* 141–156.

Fombrun, C. J., & Rindova, V (1998). Reputation management in global 1000 firms: A benchmarking study. *Corporate Reputation Review, 1*(3), 205–212.

França, F. (2003). *Subsídios para o estudo do conceito de relações públicas no Brasil* [Subsidies for the study of the public relation concept in Brazil: communication & society]. Comunicação & Sociedade. São Bernardo do Campo, Brazil: Póscom-Umesp.

Frota, M. H., & Souza, D. N. (2005, May). *Mass media and empowerment in Brazil:* The loss of *innocence.* Proceedings of the Association Business Communication 7th European Convention.

GolembiewskI, C. (2000). *Impeachment na mídia: O caso de Paulo Afonso em Santa Catarina* [Impeachment in the media: Paulo Afonso case in Santa Catarina]. Tese de Mestrado, Brazil: PUC/RS.

Guareschi P., & Biz, O. (2005). *Mídia, educação e cidadania: Tudo o que você deve saber sobre mídia* [Media, education and citizenship: all you need to know about media]. Petrópolis, RJ: Editora Vozes Brazil.

Kunsch, M. M. K. (1986). *Comunicação e educação: Caminhos cruzados* [Communication and education: cross ways]. São Paulo, Brazil: Loyola.

Kunsch, M. M. K. (1997). *Relações públicas e modernidade: Novos paradigmas na comunicação organizacional* [Public relation and modernity: New paradigms at the organizational communication]. São Paulo, Brazil: Summus.

Kunsch, M. M. K. (2003). *Planejamento de relações públicas na comunicação integrada* [Public relations planning at the integrated communication] (4th ed.). São Paulo, Brazil: Summus.

Kunsch, W. L. (2006). *De Lee a Bernays, de Lobo a Andrade: A arte e a ciência das relações públicas em seu primeiro centenário (1906–2006)* [From Lee to Bernays, from Lobo to Andrade: the art and the science of the public relation in its first centenary (1906–2006)]. Paper presented at the sixth Encontro dos Núcleos de Pesquisa da Intercom, Brasilia.

Lima, V. A. (2001). *Mídia, teoria e política* [Media, theory and politics]. São Paulo, Brazil: Editora Fundação Perseu Abramo.

Lima, V. A. (2006). *Mídia: Crise política e poder no Brasil* [Media: politics crisis and power in Brazil]. São Paulo, Brazil: Editora Fundação Perseu Abramo.

Miguel, L. F. (2004). Discursos cruzados: Telenoticiários, HPEG e a construção da agenda eleitoral [Cross speeches: TV news, HPEG and the construction of electoral agenda]. *Sociologias, 11,* 238–258.

Oliveira, I. de L. (2002). *Dimensão estratégica da comunicação organizacional no contexto contemporâneo: um paradigma de interação comunicacional dialógica* [Strategic dimension of the organizational communication at the contemporary context: a paradigm of dialogic communication interaction]. Unpublished doctoral dissertation, Universidade Federal do Rio de Janeiro, Escola de Comunicação, Rio de Janeiro.

Pereira, B. M. S. (2000). *Mas como, o MST na telenovela? Aproximações à dimensão socio-política da telenovela O Rei do Gado* [But how: the MST on the soap opera? Approaches to social-politics dimension of the soap opera *O Rei do Gado*]. Tese de Mestrado, Brazil: UFBA.

Peruzzo, C. M. K. (1986). *Relações públicas no modo de produção capitalista* [Public relations at the capitalist production way] (2nd ed., Vol. 1). São Paulo, Brazil: Summus.

Reyes, M. L. V. (2002). *Design Hoje: sobre o que se fala: Agenda Brasil 2000* [Design today: what you said about: Agenda Brasil 2000]. Unpublished master's thesis, Pontifical Catholic University of Rio Grande do Sul, Porto Alegre, Brazil.

Ribeiro, E. (2006). *O caminho das agências de comunicação* [The way of communication agencies]. Retrieved from http://www.abracom.org.br

Scheineder, B. R. (1998). Organized business politics in democratic Brazil. *Journal of Interamerican Studies and World Affairs, 39*(4), 95–127.

Schneider, E. de N. (2001). *Telefonia vs. Telet: Agenda-setting através da publicidade* [Telephony vs. Telet: Agenda-setting throughout the publicity]. Unpublished master's thesis, Pontifical Catholic University of Rio Grande do Sul, Porto Alegre, Brazil.

Schiff, F. (1996). The dominant ideology and Brazilian tabloids: News content in class-targeted newspapers. *Sociological Perspectives, 39*(1), 175–206.

Schuler, M. (2004). Management of the organizational image: a method for organizational image configuration. *Corporate Reputation Review, 7*(1), 37–53.

Silva, M.C.V.G. (1997, November). General Motors e meio ambiente [General Motors and the environment]. *Famecos, 7*(2), 67–73.

Sriramesh, K., & Verčič, D. (2003). *The global public relation handbook: Theory, research and practice.* Mahwah, NJ: Erlbaum.

Thomaz, J. C. (2003). *Reputação corporativa de organizações hospitalares: Influências da cultura, da identidade, da imagem e da comunicação corporativas* [Corporate Reputation of hospital organizations: influences of culture, identity, image and corporate communication]. Unpublished master's thesis, Administração de Empresas, Universidade Presbiteriana Mackenzie, São Paulo, Brazil.

Wey, H. (1986). *O processo de relações públicas* [The public relations process] (2nd. ed.). São Paulo, Brazil: Summus.

17 Corporate Reputation and the News Media in Chile

Magdalena Browne and Martin Kunc

Chilean companies function in a modern, globalized economy, and as a result they are increasingly concerned about managing corporate reputation. Since 2000, a modern transport infrastructure, advanced logistics, and world-class telecommunications services have helped to eliminate the differences between Chile and the rest of the emerging world. Simultaneously, Chile has successfully opened markets to foreign investors. Since 1990, Chile has developed an expanding network of free trade agreements with, amongst others, Mexico, China, the European Union, the United States, and South Korea. These agreements have not only increased the distribution of Chilean goods in foreign markets, but they have also led to dynamic cultural and social exchanges between these countries and Chile.

At the cultural and societal level, Tironi and Cavallo (2004) suggested that Chile achieved the proper environment for the development of strategic communications when, as a result of the return of democracy, a degree of individualism along with personal freedom became possible again.

Despite the tremendous changes in the Chilean economic and social environment, conglomerates continue to be the predominant form of corporate structure in Chile (Lefort & Walker, 1999) and one of the three leading entities that exert the highest level of power in Chile after the news media and ministries related to economic affairs (Programa de las Naciones Unidas para el Desarrollo Humano [PNUD], 2004). One of the many reasons for the development of conglomerates in Chile is related to the level of competition among economic groups, which facilitates the need to control large numbers of assets to avoid high transaction costs (Khanna & Palepu, 2000).

However, this situation has changed since 2006. Tironi (2006) suggests that it was as a result of a rupture directly related to the decline of conglomerates' power, and consequently corporate thinking in Chile has been motivated by a more in-depth analysis of the news media by the economic and political elites. News media have been transformed into a relevant channel which represents individuals in the public space and have acquired major influence over public opinion.

This sophisticated news media system and the return of democratic rule have shaped a setting that is conducive to powerful advocacy groups. These groups emphasize communicating their concerns and beliefs through mass media, aiming to create agendas to which corporations and governments must respond. Consequently, these new forces, in combination with a changing media and social dynamic, have forced companies to become more transparent with their stakeholders (Ferreira, 2003; Sriramesh & Verčič, 2003).

This new dynamic sees Chilean corporations increasingly focused on building and maintaining their reputation and responding to new demands characterized by more freedom, global business, a new media role, and more active stakeholders. This chapter examines two Chilean companies, which had received consistently favorable reputations, but whose rankings recently dropped, and two Chilean companies that significantly and rapidly rose to the top of the reputation rankings.

Overview of Corporate Reputation in Chile

Corporate Reputation as a Local Discipline

The history of public relations in Chile has always been closely linked to the evolution of journalism (Sriramesh & Verčič, 2003). The requirement for a 5-year university education as a minimal qualification for a job as a journalist has shaped their active participation in communications management in public and private organizations; the majority of public relations positions are held by journalists. Ferreira (2003) has suggested that public relations failed to achieve the prestige of journalism in organizations' communications departments due to the delayed recognition of public relations at the university level by the Ministry of Education. Thus, Ferreira (2003) concluded that the strategic role of public relations in Chile was never exercised by professionals who were specifically trained for that work.

Once the corporate landscape became more complex due to the democratization of Chilean society, professionalization of the media, and globalization of the economy, the field developed a more professional approach to corporate reputation management. As the activity of strategic communication agencies has boomed in recent years, the interest of practitioners and scholars has increased as well. Many articles related to corporate public relations activity have been published in Chile, mostly by the School of Communications at Pontificia Universidad Católica, but no studies have been published concerning the effect of strategic communication agencies or news media on corporate reputation. Turner (2005) suggests that strategic communication agencies exist via their ability to liaise between their clients, corporations, and the news media without being explicitly accepted by journalists. He believes both media and public opinion should demand more transparent behavior from strategic communications companies because the activities of these firms are increasing, and commercial entities increasingly put pressure on the news media as they push to control news content. Correa and Alvarez (2005) also presented a similar study about the evaluation of lobbyist activity and its reflection in newspaper content.

Corporate Reputation as a Local Industry

The national power of Chilean corporate strategic communication firms has risen to become one of the top 20 most powerful institutions in the country according to the United Nations Development Program (PNUD, 2004). According to *PR Week*, of the approximately 50 consulting firms in communication and public relations, which are located mostly in Santiago, Chile's capital, the top six consulting firms' revenues approach U.S.$10 million per year in the early 2000s (Muñoz Vázquez, 2006).

As strategic communications became a key driver of industry in Chile, innumerable agencies have emerged in the last decade. Many well-known international agencies have opened offices in Chile, including Hill & Knowlton Captiva and WPP Burson-Marsteller. However, local strategic communication firms have shown vigorous growth in the industry. Some of those most recognized in the market are Tironi (2003), Extend Comunicaciones, Nexo, ICC Crisis, and Feedback Comunicaciones. One key aspect of the Chilean strategic communication industry is that many of the largest consulting firms have either been absorbed into or were originally developed by advertising agencies.

The Chilean Press

The relevance of news depends on the nature of the media organization that transmits it. News content becomes biased toward developing loyal consumers rather than defending editorial values. Therefore, traditional editorial style based on news values has been replaced by policies that concern the targeted consumers. Though more than 80% of the Chilean population watches television for local and international news, a public opinion poll showed that 86% of the population considered newspapers as better sources of information than television or radio (Marin & Cordero, 2005). The percentage of people that recognize newspapers as a source of quality news is higher than the percentage of people that actually read them: only 23% of Chileans read newspapers daily (Marin & Cordero, 2005; Porath, 2000). Most readers of print media are from the upper and middle classes and opinion leaders from political and business elites (Marin & Cordero, 2005).

A readership analysis indicates that most readers from Santiago, Chile's political and economic capital, read two main newspapers from the two leading newspapers groups: El Mercurio and COPESA. El Mercurio publishes a newspaper with the same name, while COPESA publishes *La Tercera*.

El Mercurio is a traditional Chilean newspaper with the highest weekly circulation; it is considered a "serious" newspaper with a conservative even elitist ideology. The newspaper, which is widely read by the political class and very influential on the center right, contains a highly regarded economics section. The same company also publishes *Las Ultimas Noticias,* a tabloid oriented toward a lower-middle class readership, which has acquired some education, and *La Segunda,* a traditional afternoon newspaper in Santiago that emphasizes political issues (Porath, 2000). Puente and Mujica (2004) found that business news is the fourth most published topic in *El Mercurio* though it only takes up 8% of the total space devoted to news.

La Tercera, the main newspaper owned by editorial group COPESA, is a tabloid with high national readership, especially amongst the middle class and it competes with *El Mercurio*, especially for the political elite audience (Porath, 2000). The editorial content is primarily concerned with investigative journalism and places special emphasis on political news.

News Value and Organizational Newsworthiness

Puente and Mujica (2004) found the main Chilean news value to be: unexpected or novel stories that were socially challenging, related to something familiar to readers, directly experienced, or with high impact images. However, deviances from norms are usually not sanctioned by Chilean society. The mostly conservative country strongly rejects sudden change, punishing deviancy in every aspect of society. This trend may explain the low levels of respect in the Chilean news media for deviance from what is socially acceptable. The Chilean tendency to avoid conflict is reflected in media analysis results. Editorial content has not traditionally given space to deviation from the norm or social change (Puente & Mujica, 2004).

While there are no studies of the use of press releases by journalists until 2006, Gronemeyer (2003) found that their use is widespread in articles. However, none of the copy from a press release would be seen on the first page of a story and reference to the source of a news story was rare. The characteristics of press release usage led Gronemeyer to conclude that there is a deliberate process of concealment of news sources in the Chilean media.

Agenda-Setting Theory Application

While studies debate the role of strategic communication in corporate reputation, scholars from journalism school have focused research efforts on the transformations that media, especially television, is generating in the agenda-setting process, mainly in the political arena. Porath (2000) explored the role of media in the 1999 presidential campaign and found that the culture of the country, the strength of political parties, and the relationship between media and political parties were important determinants of what is acceptable for news media agenda setters.

Marín and Cordero (2005) presented an opposite study, suggesting that the media are independent from the political elite but connected to public opinion. The media's shift in loyalty led to the establishment of a public agenda independent from the sources of traditional power in Chilean society and closer to individuals and social problems. However, the results were strongly influenced by the prominence of television as a source of information for Chileans.

Finally, Dusaillant (2005) analyzed the Chilean media content for one month during a presidential campaign. He concluded that the media, in general, transmitted a "neutral, if not positive image, of the candidates," which in his opinion constitutes a framing criterion contrary to what is observed in other countries.

Case Study: Corporate Reputation Systems at Work in Chile

Exploring the Relationship of News Media and Corporate Reputation in the Chilean Context

Carroll and McCombs (2003) suggested a number of hypotheses explaining the relationship between corporate news and corporate public image. Their first hypothesis explained that the amount of news coverage a firm receives from the news media is positively related to the public's awareness of the firm. However, Carroll and McCombs (2003) also mentioned a number of contingent conditions relevant to agenda-setting effects on corporate reputation. In the case of Chile, some of these contingencies may be stronger influences than media coverage on corporate reputation.

Schultz, Mouritsen, and Gabrielsen (2001) concluded that large firms' reputations are stable and remain high in the long term, especially in small countries like Chile. They attributed the origin of a stable reputation to the greater public awareness of large firms because they are more visible in the business community to the responding population. Corporate reputation is not solely an outcome of media coverage; it is the process of collective representation of a company's stakeholders. Thus, stakeholders not only consider news media coverage, but also the historical accumulation of facts that constitute a previously observed identity (Melewar, 2003), the effects of other communication forms like advertising, the behavior of personnel (Alessandri & Alessandri, 2004), and in the case of retail companies, the product or service they offer (Cravens, Goad, & Ramamoorti, 2003).

Ownership is another determinant of corporate reputation in Chile. After analyzing four cases of unsuccessful retail internationalization in the Chilean market, Bianchi and Ostale (2006) found that these retail firms defied local institutional pressures from consumers, suppliers, competitors, retail executives, and the business community. The management of these firms did not embed themselves in the broader social network that affects legitimacy, failing to recognize that the Chilean business community is a very relevant social actor and social network relationships are highly valued. Therefore, we propose that the presence of Chilean corporations in reputation rankings should be stable in the long term, independent of small changes in their media coverage (Hypothesis 1).

In regard to the second-level agenda setting, Carroll and McCombs (2003) suggested a second hypothesis that the amount of news coverage devoted to particular attributes of a firm is positively related to the proportion of the public that defines the firm by those attributes.

Nonetheless, individuals have difficulty remembering firm-specific details over time, thus many impressions get lost in general beliefs of how the company performs especially when its size draws higher attention from business periodicals (Schultz et al., 2001). Since corporate reputation rankings are multi-dimensional, this study hypothesizes no differences between media attention toward certain dimensions and its reflection on the valuation that respondents assign to a certain company in a certain dimension in Chile (Hypothesis 2).

Hypothesis 3, proposed by Carroll and McCombs (2003), implies that more positive media coverage of a particular attribute will positively impact the perception of the public about this particular attribute. Conversely, the more negative media coverage regarding a particular attribute, the more negatively members of the public will perceive that attribute.

The reputation of Chilean corporations should be stable in the long term unless major external or internal events and company activities, such as an industry disaster or unethical corporate behavior undermine their reputation and decrease its rank (Greyser, 2003; Schultz et al., 2001). These significant events, which deviate from the norm, are usually sanctioned by Chilean society, especially when magnified by media attention. Accordingly, this study hypothesizes that decreases in a company's corporate reputation ranking are positively related to increasing negative media coverage about a particular company attribute (Hypothesis 3).

Chilean Corporate Reputation Indexes

Aside from several well-known international reputation indexes such as those of *Fortune* magazine and the Reputation Institute, many Chilean rankings exist that are highly anticipated by the business elite because they justify the strategic communication programs developed by them. Six rankings related to corporate image and reputation are published yearly by Chilean media. Table 17.1 summarizes the four most important corporate rankings.

Published since 2002, the corporate reputation ranking codeveloped by Hill & Knowlton Captiva and *La Tercera* is one of the few rankings that captures consumer opinion, namely 3,500 citizens of Santiago. Despite its importance, this ranking varies yearly, perhaps reflecting unstable parameters or even the fluctuating conceptualization of corporate reputation among Chilean public opinion.

Since 2006 the Reputation Institute, based on Gardberg and Fombrum's (2002) project on global reputation indicators, has included Chile, publishing its rankings in the economics section of *El Mercurio*. Over 1,550 consumers are contacted via the Internet, which causes citizens in lower socioeconomic groups (C3 and D) to be underrepresented.

Since 1999, PricewaterhouseCoopers has developed an annual ranking based on executives' opinions, creating "the most admired companies of Chile" (2006). The ranking itself, published in the economic newspaper *Diario Financiero*, does not suggest companies for evaluation, but instead allows executives to propose names for the final list, which is generally composed of 10 firms.

Adimark (2006), a well-known survey firm, developed a ranking focused on information-oriented citizens, in particular, 105 executives from the most important Chilean companies. Executives respond to a Web based survey. Since 1995, this ranking has measured the perceptions of key executives with respect to the most admired companies operating in Chile. Given the high level of the respondents' knowledge, this study hypothesized that ranking changes only occur due to important changes in a corporation's reputation made possible by strategic communication programs or corporate activities that captured the long-term attention of news media due to their effect on society. This ranking is the one that has been published over the longest time in Chile, and it is not only highly visible among informed people, but also stabilized in terms of the dimensions for the respondents.

Table 17.1 Most Important Rankings on Corporate Reputation in Chile

Ranking	Corporate Reputation	Method	Main Dimensions	Ranking size	Top 5 firms (in 2006)
Company	Hill & Knowlton –Captiva	• Pre-selection of 25 firms based on mentions (500 people) • Addition of 12 more firms from the same industries as those selected and good reputation • Telephonic surveys to 3700 consumers in Santiago randomly selected and adjusted to the socio-economic distribution • Each respondent evaluates two firms randomly selected from the 37 firms in six dimensions.	• Emotional • Financial Performance • Social Responsibility • Work environment • Leadership and management • Product and services	25 firms	1. Coca-Cola 2. Metro 3. Nestle 4. Soprole 5. Sony
Year of creation	2002				
Published in	La Tercera				
Company	Reputation Institute	• Survey to over 1550 consumers in Santiago • Self managed survey via web	• Products and services • Innovation • Workplace • Governance • Citizenship • Leadership • Performance	70 firms	1. Nestle 2. Carozzi 3. Nokia 4. Soprole 5. Iansa
Ranking	RepTrack				
Year of creation	2006				
Published in	El Mercurio				

(Continued)

Table 17.1 Continued

Ranking	Corporate Reputation	Method	Main Dimensions	Ranking size	Top 5 firms (in 2006)
Company	Pricewaterhouse Coppers	• There is no pre selection of the firms, rather a free nomination. • Web survey applied via email to 3000 executives	• Business Strategy • Financial solvency • Innovation capacity • Product and service quality	10 firms	1. Bco Santander - Santiago
Ranking	The most admired firms	• Respondents evaluate nine aspects with a grade from 1 to 7	• Marketing attractiveness • Corporate image		2. CMPC 3. Coca Cola
Year of creation	1999	• Methodology similar to FT ranking	• Workforce and executives quality		4. CCU
Published in	Diario Financiero		• Corporate governance • Social responsibility		5. BCI
Company	Adimark	• Survey to 105 businessmen and top executives from the most important firms in Chile	• Seriousness and solvency • Environment • Balance work and family	15 firms	1. Lan 2. Cencosud 3. Unilever
Ranking	The most respected firms	• Self-managed surveys	• Probity and transparency • Education and training		4. Bco Santader - Santiago
Year of creation	1995	• Based on number of mentions per category	• Social support • Women working opportunities		5. CMPC
Published in	La Segunda		• Attractiveness to Professionals • Innovative capacity and technology • Consumer satisfaction • Marketing practices		

Case Studies

Three hypotheses were examined, applying a content analysis of four case studies about the evolution of the corporate reputation ranking selected, Adimark/*La Segunda*'s "the most respected firms," from 2002 to 2006. Specifically, we examined the coverage of the two main newspapers, *La Tercera* and *El Mercurio*, 4 months before the published ranking (see Table 17.2 for a detailed explanation of the content analysis method employed).

Case Study 1: A Chilean Holding Concentrated Mainly in Pulp and Paper Manufacturing   Established in 1920, this holding has been a pioneer in pulp and paper manufacturing in Chile. The holding maintains strong ties to the Chilean business community. The company, with strong brands in disposable diapers, toilet paper products, napkins, and paper towels followed a strong internationalization process by purchasing local companies and installing others in Latin American Southern Cone countries.

The company, part of one of the biggest Chilean conglomerates, has been in the top three of the ranking in 3 of the last 5 years. In 2006, the company fell to fifth position after a series of environmental issues of another key company in the same industry. Content analysis results demonstrated that this company has a stable minimal public profile, averaging nine articles per period, and at least two per month. When compared to cases 2 and 3, this company has hardly any media presence. Although low in terms of presence, the media coverage is positive and focused on business and management issues. Therefore, this case may

Table 17.2 Media Topics for Each Case Measured in Number of Appearances

	2002	2003	2004	2005	2006
Case Study 1	3	16	9	9	10
Environmental issues	2	0	0	1	0
Context	1	2	0	0	1
Corporate Governance	0	0	0	4	1
Business and Management	0	14	9	4	8
Case Study 2	5	19	23	138	104
Environmental issues	0	0	1	79	58
Context	0	0	2	1	9
Corporate Governance	0	1	2	30	7
Business and Management	5	18	18	28	30
Case Study 3	1	13	40	58	29
Environmental issues	0	0	0	0	0
Context	0	0	1	1	3
Corporate Governance	0	0	0	5	1
Business and Management	1	13	39	52	25
Case Study 4	0	1	2	5	2
Environmental issues	0	0	0	0	0
Context	0	0	1	0	1
Corporate Governance	0	0	0	3	0
Business and Management	0	1	1	2	2

Note: Appearing in February, March, April, and May of each year.

Table 17.3 Tone for Each Case

	2002	2003	2004	2005	2006
Case Study 1	3	16	9	9	10
Negative	0	1	0	0	2
Neutral	3	5	1	3	5
Positive	0	10	8	6	3
Case Study 2	5	19	23	138	104
Negative	0	3	3	42	37
Neutral	1	5	3	48	33
Positive	4	11	17	48	34
Case Study 3	1	13	40	58	29
Negative	0	1	2	8	3
Neutral	1	7	11	20	10
Positive	0	5	27	529	16
Case Study 4	0	1	2	5	2
Negative	0	0	0	2	0
Neutral	0	1	1	0	0
Positive	0	0	1	3	2

Note: Appearing in February, March, April, and May of each year.

show how corporate reputation can be built from opinion leaders, independent of media coverage, and could be stable and positive due to others factors such as ownership, age, and size.

These results might have been different if other stakeholders' opinions were also considered. As seen in other indexes, which include all socioeconomic segments, case 1 is not at the top of these rankings. Hence, media and advertising may be an important determinant of the mass audience's perceptions than are the beliefs of opinion leaders.

Case Study 2: A Chilean Holding with Interests in Energy and Natural Resources   This holding, owned by one of the three wealthiest businessmen in Chile, has investments concentrated in two large areas of specialization: energy and natural resources. In the energy field, the holding is prominent in the distribution of liquid fuels, liquefied petroleum gas, and natural gas, sectors that are strongly linked with Chilean growth and development. In natural resources, the holding is active in forestry, commercial fishing, and mining industries in which the country enjoys clear-cut advantages in comparison with other countries.

In 1987 the company expanded and by 1991 had become Chile's largest and most modern market pulp mill. A year later, the company commenced the construction of a market pulp mill located in Valdivia. The project, one of the largest in Chile, called for an investment of $1.2 billion and enabled the company to significantly increase pulp production, thus turning it into one of the largest pulp companies in the world. Unfortunately, this project unleashed a number of problems, mainly environmental issues, which were extensively covered by the Chilean media and involved many different actors.

Though it held the top reputation ranking from 2002 to 2005, the company fell to ninth position in 2006, its lowest position in many years. In contrast to case 1, this company received almost permanent coverage due to continuing interest in environmental issues from local advocacy groups.

The results imply that the negative exposure of case 2 may be related to a decrease in its reputation among opinion leaders, reflected in the fall in the company's corporate reputation the following year. However, the results obtained from the content analysis of case 2, revealed important positive coverage related to business and management issues. Therefore, case 2 can be described as having a "dual image," a combination of hypotheses 2 and 3, stating that positive or negative consideration of a company in a certain dimension depends on media coverage and its favorability. However, negative media coverage of a certain dimension does not automatically imply a full deterioration of the image of the corporation. Indeed, the highest fall in the corporation reputation ranking used is in the environmental dimension although the company remains a leader in financial related topics, one of the dimensions that boosted its ranking. It is for this reason perhaps that the company continued to be in the top 10 most admired firms in the selected index.

Case Study 3: A Chilean Holding Focused on Retail In 1960, this company became the first self-service food retailer in Chile. In 1976, the company began a revolution in the retail industry by developing the first supermarket in Chile, followed by a similar one in Argentina a few years later. A pioneer developer of shopping centers in Chile and Argentina, the company has grown strongly since 2006 by opening new stores and acquiring large supermarket and department store chains in Chile and Argentina. In 2004 the company's shares were amongst those most traded on the Chilean stock exchange.

In 2002 the company was listed in the top 10 most admired companies, climbed to the sixth position in 2003, and maintained this position until 2006 when it climbed to second place. The results of the content analysis show an increasing prominence in the news, as the company grew in size and relevance through bold acquisitions and the trading of its shares. Consequently, the media increased their coverage of the company, especially when it was in the process of acquiring another company, with a breaking point in 2004 when it became a public company, one whose activities are reflected almost daily in the media.

Case Study 4: A Foreign Global Brand Management Corporation Only one foreign company among the top 10 firms in the corporate reputation ranking appeared before 2006. With 400 brands spanning 14 categories of home, personal care, and foods products, the company is visible in almost every aspect of people's lives in most countries. Despite its omnipresence globally, it has maintained a low profile among the business community in Chile until 2006 when it was listed as one of the top five most recognized firms.

While the media coverage of this foreign company as a corporation appeared to be minimal, the media influenced respondents who were top executives from Chilean companies because the global corporation chose Santiago as its headquarters for Latin America. Additionally, this study found a similar degree of editorial coverage of the corporation that was not included in the results because they were published after the chosen time period.

Discussion and Conclusions

The analysis of Hypotheses 1, 2, and 3 was only exploratory and preliminary. While content analysis was used to illustrate media coverage, a direct relationship between media coverage and people's perceptions could not be statistically determined as traditional agenda-setting methods suggest. Nonetheless, useful observations that suggested the direction of further research were found.

The exploratory analysis from the four case studies suggests that corporate reputation is a complex, multifaceted concept, not only for large corporations, but also for small firms because of the contingent factors enumerated in Carroll and McCombs (2003) such as ownership, size, and the level of relationship with consumers (direct or indirect). In contrast to what has been observed in political contexts, contingent factors seem to be more important than the immediate role of the media in highlighting corporate activities. We suggest that the media are more concerned with highlighting negative consequences of corporate activities that challenge societal norms and traditions (case study 2) rather than enhancing the reputation of a specific firm. Only when a firm grows in relevance to society does media attention seem to increase, and only after receiving media attention, does corporate reputation grow (case study 3). The relative effect of media attention is influenced by the recurrence of its observations about the firm, "one [item of] news is not enough to change the reputation of a company" (Tironi & Cavallo, 2004). Consequently, Hypothesis 1 may be valid when a company is visible enough to become newsworthy; and a company is newsworthy when it is relevant to society because of its size, ownership, or its strategic communications plan.

Firms that do not conform to societal norms (e.g., case studies 2 and 4) are more prone to be exposed by the media and their corporate reputation will be more sensitive to media coverage, especially negative coverage, than firms embedded in the tradition of the business community. Though unable to be empirically tested, we observed from the four cases that media attention was focused on the dimension that deviated from the norm, and theoretically this element is very salient in the determination of corporate reputation (Hypothesis 2).

The third hypothesis appears to be valid considering case studies 2 and 3 but for opposite reasons. While the media concentrated on negative aspects of corporate activities in case study 2, the media seemed to be very positive about everything from the company in case study 3.

From this analysis, some caveats can be suggested about researching the effect of news media on corporate reputation. First, the proposed method strongly affects the examination of news media's influence on corporate reputation. In this case, a corporate reputation ranking defined mostly by highly informed people was chosen because of the low level of readership of newspapers among the Chilean population. The low level of readership indicates that corporate reputation rankings based mostly on consumers can be affected by factors other than news media, such as advertising and brand positioning. Thus, corporate rankings based on consumers vary yearly due to factors other than media visibility. In small countries such as Chile, contingent factors can have a greater effect than the power of the news media on corporate reputation, especially in countries strongly based on traditions. The power of the news media is at its height only in situations where an industry disaster or an ethical lapse by a company has occurred, as in case study 2 (Grayser, 2003; Schultz et al., 2001). Lastly, firms that are directly connected to consumers, such as retailers, have higher chances of being perceived as newsworthy by the media. Therefore, companies accrue more media attention and thus more opportunity to develop a positive reputation if, like the company in case study 3, they expand.

References

Adimark. (2006, July 31). *The most respected firms.* Diario la Segunda, Business Section, pp. 4, 6, 18, 30–32, 36, 38.

Alessandri, S. W., & Alessandri, T. (2004). Promoting and protecting corporate identity: The importance of organizational and industry context. *Corporate Reputation Review, 7,* 252–268.

Bianchi, C., & Ostale, E. (2006). Lessons learned from unsuccessful internationalization attempts: Examples of multinational retailers in Chile. *Journal of Business Research, 59,* 140–147.

Carroll, C., & McCombs, M. (2003). Agenda-setting effects of business news on the public's images and opinions about major corporations. *Corporate Reputation Review, 6,* 36–46.

Correa, E., & Alvarez, L. (2005). El lobby y la prensa en Chile: Relaciones positivas [Lobby and press in Chile: Positive Relations]. *Cuadernos de Información—Facultad de Comunicaciones, Pontificia Universidad Católica de Chile, 18,* 72–78.

Cravens, K., Goad, O. E., & Ramamoorti, S. (2003). The Reputation Index: Measuring and managing corporate reputation. *European Management Journal, 21,* 201–220.

Dussaillant, P. (2005). Medios y elecciones: La elección presidencial de 1999 [Media and elections: The 1999 presidential election]. *Cimas/Centro de Estudios Bicentenario.*

Ferreira, M. A. (2003). Public relations in Chile: Searching for identity amid imported models. In K. Sriramesh & D. Verčič (Eds.), *The global public relations handbook: Theory, research and practice* (pp. 378–398). Mahwah, NJ: Erlbaum.

Gardberg, N., & Fombrun, C. J. (2002). The global reputation quotient project: First steps towards a cross-nationally valid measure of corporate reputation. *Corporate Reputation Review, 4,* 303–307.

Greyser, S. (2003). *Revealing the corporation: Perspectives on identity, image, reputation, corporate branding and corporate-level marketing anthology.* London: Routledge.

Gronemeyer M. E. (2004). Estudio sobre el uso de los comunicados de prensa: La iniciativa del periodista puesta a prueba [A study of the use of press releases: The journalist initiative put to the test]. *Cuadernos de Información—Facultad de Comunicaciones, Pontificia Universidad Católica de Chile,* 16–17.

Hill & Knowlton Captiva. (2006, December). Corporate reputation. *Diario La Tercera,* Business Section, p. 59.

Khanna, T., & Palepu, K. (2000). The future of business groups in emerging markets: Long-run evidence from Chile. *Academy of Management Journal, 43,* 268–285.

Lefort, F., & Walker, E. (1999). Ownership and capital structure of Chilean conglomerates: Facts and hypotheses for governance. *Revista Abate, 3,* 3–27.

Marín, C., & Cordero, R. (2005). Los medios masivos y las transformaciones en la esfera pública en Chile [Mass media and the transformations in the public life in Chile]. *Persona y Sociedad, 29,* 233–258.

Melewar, T. C. (2003). Determinants of the corporate identity construct: A review of the literature. *Journal of Marketing Communications, 9,* 195–220.

Muñoz Vázquez, M. (2006). El mercado de la comunicación corporativa en Chile [The corporate communication market in Chile]. Retrieved from http://www.losrecursoshumanos.com/comunicación-corporativa-chile.htm

Porath, W. (2000). La agenda de la prensa nacional durante la campaña presidencial 1999 [The national press agenda during 1999 presidential campaign] (Working paper). Centro de Estudios de la Realidad Contemporánea/Instituto de Estudios Mediales, Pontificia Universidad Católica de Chile.

PricewaterhouseCoopers. (2006, October 31). The most admired firms. *Diario Financiero,* Special Section, p. 4.

Programa de las Naciones Unidas para el Desarrollo Humano (PNUD). (2004). *Desarrollo humano en Chile: El poder: ¿para qué y para quién?* [Human Development in Chile: The power: what is for and for whom?]. Santiago, Chile: Author.

Puente, S., & Mujica, C. (2004). ¿Qué es noticia (en Chile)? [What is news (in Chile)?] *Cuadernos de Información—Facultad de Comunicaciones, Pontificia Universidad Católica de Chile, 16–17,* 86–100.

Schultz, M., Mouritsen, J., & Gabrielsen, G. (2001). Sticky reputation: Analyzing a ranking system. *Corporate Reputation Review, 4,* 24–41.

Sriramesh, K., & Verčič, D. (Eds.). (2003). *The global public relations handbook: Theory, research and practice.* Mahwah, NJ: Erlbaum.

Tironi, E. (2003). *Comunicación estratégica, por qué surge...y Hacia dónde va* [Strategic Communication, why it began and where it is going]. Retrieved from http://www.eugeniotironi.cl/inicio/vermas_detalle.php?id_documento=38

Tironi, E. (2006). *La cuarta ruptura: Reflexiones sobre comunidad, participación y liderazgo en el Chile de hoy* [The fourth rupture: Reflections about community, participation and leadership in the actual Chile]. Retrieved from http://www.eugeniotironi.cl/inicio/vermas_detalle.php?id_documento=41

Tironi, E., & Cavallo, A. (2004). *Comunicación estratégica: Vivir en un mundo de señales* [Strategic communication: Living in a world of signals]. Santiago, Chile: Aguilar.

Turner, G. (2005). Medios y empresas de relaciones públicas: ¿Cuánto vale ser noticia? [Media and public relations firms: How much does it cost to be news?]. *Cuadernos de Información–Facultad de Comunicaciones de la Pontificia Universidad Católica de Chile, 18,* 64–71.

18 Corporate Reputation and the News Media in China

LiFeng Deng

In the summer of 2006, the UK *Mail on Sunday* carried a report entitled "iPod City," disclosing that laborers in some Chinese iPod factories owned by Foxconn (富士康) work long hours for low pay and live in "slave" conditions. Shortly after this, another report appeared in *China Business News* (CBN), further disclosing the poor working and living conditions of Foxconn's workers. Foxconn, which had kept its distance from the media before, immediately announced that it would sue two journalists from CBN for "damaging its reputation," demanding a compensation of RMB30 million, an amount many times more than a journalist could make in a lifetime in China. Later, under fire from Chinese academics, as well as from the Chinese and foreign press, for attacking freedom of the press, and under pressure from its contractor, Apple, Foxconn withdrew the charges and reached a compromise with CBN. Foxconn's reputation, however, was severely affected by the crisis. Foxconn attempted to improve its reputation through a series of image-promoting activities in the Chinese media, but the results were negligible.

The Foxconn crisis of 2006 is but one example of the increasingly tense interactions between the commercial news media and corporations in China. The relationship between the news media and corporations in China has undergone huge changes since the media were pushed into the market. Revenues from advertising have become the main source of the media's income, so they are under increasing pressure to attract audiences and enlarge market share. To attract audiences, the media have expanded their role as a watchdog, focusing on investigative reporting. In the Foxconn–CBN case, however, a media organization was attacked for its negative coverage and was even forced to apologize. This not only reflects the environment of press freedom in China, it also shows that the Chinese news media are increasingly dependent on corporations and are forced to cooperate with them. At the same time, corporations fear the media's power. They resent and attack the media's critical reporting but dare not offend powerful media, especially the whole press circle. The Foxconn case is a good example of this.

Chinese news media and corporations have not yet found an effective way to communicate with each other. Over the last 5 years in mainland China, many lawsuits have been launched against the media's critical reporting, and journalists have lost in some cases. Compared with Western countries, it is rare to see the media's critical reporting have a powerful effect. Even so, because China's corporations often lack the ability to deal with crises, it is difficult for them to cope with critical reporting, and some have even been bankrupted due to news media criticism. The 2001 Guan Shengyuan (冠生园) case is an example. The Guan Shengyuan Company in Nanjing used moldy filling to produce moon cakes for the Mid-Autumn Festival and was exposed by China's Central Television (CCTV). The old and famous brand was completely ruined. In cases like this one, the media can not only ruin corporate reputation, but even end the life of a company.

The early agenda-setting studies were done mainly in the field of political communication, but in recent years studies have expanded into such new areas as corporate reputation, education, sports, and organized religion (McCombs, 2005). Do the agenda-setting effects of the mass media on the reputation and image of corporations have the same results as in political communication? Aiming to answer this question, Carroll and McCombs (2003, 2006) have suggested that agenda-setting theory can be applied to corporate reputation, and have put forward the following three hypotheses:

Hypothesis 1. The amount of news coverage that a firm receives in the news media is positively related to the public's awareness of the firm.

Hypothesis 2. The amount of news coverage devoted to particular attributes of a firm is positively related to the proportion of the public who define the firm by those attributes.

Hypothesis 3. The more positive that media coverage is for a particular attribute, the more positively will members of the public perceive that attribute. Conversely, the more negative media coverage is for a particular attribute, the more negatively will members of the public perceive that attribute.

These three hypotheses are the starting points of the present study. We first offer a description of corporation reputation ranking in China and a review of how the agenda-setting theory was introduced. Next, we test the above three hypotheses in China's context through a combination of public opinion polls and news contents analyses, taking into consideration the Chinese media system, news values, and practices of public relations. Finally, through quantitative analysis of the public awareness of multinational companies in China, corporations' involvement in corporate social responsibility (CSR) activities, and the public's general appreciation of multinational corporate reputation, we attempt to analyze the agenda-setting effects of news media on corporate reputation in China.

Our analysis of corporate reputation and the news media focuses on mainland China. Due to huge differences in political environment, mainland China differs greatly from Hong Kong, Macau, and Taiwan. The latter three areas have a capitalist system and a more Westernized political–economic environment than the mainland. Moreover, they have also maintained a more intact Confucian tradition (Chan, 1996). These historical and cultural differences have resulted in the relationship between the media and corporations in these three regions being very different from that on the mainland. This difference is also reflected in the

Global Competitive Index: in the most recent edition, released in 2006, China ranks 54, Hong Kong 7, and Taiwan 13. Bearing these differences in mind, the present study focuses on mainland China.

Literature Review: Corporate Reputation in China

Chinese proverbs express the negative and positive attitudes Chinese hold about sales promotion. "Ring one's own bell" ("Wang Po Mai Gua, Zi Mai Zi Kua") embodies a positive attitude; however, the dominant attitude is mirrored in "Good wine needs no peddling, the aroma will sell it" ("Hao Jiu Bu Pa Xiang Zi Shen"), which conveys a conservative idea about corporate reputation. The concept of corporate reputation derives not from the Chinese context but from the Western, especially American, context; that is, most of the literature about corporate reputation is not developed from Chinese commercial practices but from foreign ones. In October 2009, a search of the China Periodical Net—the largest Chinese-language academic database based in mainland China, covering almost 30 years from 1979 to 2009—yielded only 243 academic articles having the words *corporate reputation* in the title. Of these, the first, Zhu's "Building up Corporate Reputation," was published in 1984, and 228 were published after 2000 (see Figure 18.1). Most of these articles have the same theme: calling for a higher level of attention to corporate reputation management. More than 95% of these articles are general introductions and summaries of American or Western literature in this area.

It should be noted that the terms for *reputation* (*Sheng Yu*, 声誉) and *credit* (*Xin Yu*, 信誉) are distinct in Chinese. In most cases, these two concepts are confused—for instance, the word *reputation* in *Reputation Institute* is translated into Chinese as *Sheng Yu* (reputation), while in *Reputation Institute in China*, the branch organization established in March 2006, it is translated into *Xin Yu*

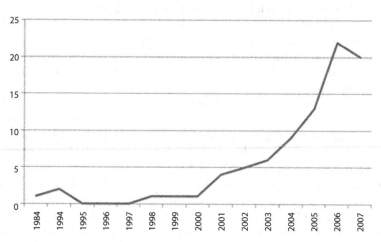

Figure 18.1 The number of Chinese academic papers in the CNKI database with "Qiye Shengyu" (corporate reputation) in the title

(credit). Actually, *Xin Yu* (信誉)and *Sheng Yu* (声誉) have different implications in Chinese. Bai Yongxiu and Xu Hong (2001) have noted that the former (credit) is a process value, which means being honest and keeping promises. In economic terms, it is in flux. Whether one has *Xin Yu* depends on how well one's promises match one's behaviors. In contrast, *Sheng Yu* (reputation) is a state value, which is the sum of the commercial behaviors of a corporation, its social behaviors, and those of its staff. The term *Xin Yu* has nothing to do with social status and wealth. Whether discussing an ordinary citizen or a multinational company, as long as words and conduct cohere, both have the same amount of *Xin Yu* (信誉). *Sheng Yu* (声誉), in contrast, has a close relationship with social status, prestige, and wealth; that is, those who are prestigious and wealthy often have more *Sheng Yu* than those who are less prestigious and wealthy, though both may have the same amount of *Xin Yu*. Finally, *Sheng Yu* involves a judgment about ethics, while *Xin Yu* does not. In a Chinese context, even a thief can have *Xin Yu* (credit), but it is impossible for him to have good *Sheng Yu* (reputation).

Agenda-Setting Theory

Agenda-setting theory, included in the translations of American communication theory textbooks, was first introduced to China in the 1980s, but not until the mid-1990s did a systematic introduction appear, when Guo Zhenzhi translated and wrote several articles about agenda-setting theory (1997, 1999).

Though Guo Zhenzhi did not move on to test the agenda-setting effects of news media in the Chinese context, her work stimulated other scholars' interest in testing the theory. Employing the classic research method of agenda-setting theory—a combination of public opinion survey and content analysis—Zhang Guoliang, professor of journalism at Fudan University in Shanghai, chaired a survey of agenda-setting effects in China and together with his associates published several journal articles (Zhang Guoliang & Li Benqian, 2002b, 2003). The contribution of this research lies in its reproduction of the American experience in the Chinese context, proving the agenda-setting theory's effects in China.

More recent research involved case studies on the content analysis of news media, focusing on the formation of various media agendas instead of their influence on the public. The reason for this is twofold: funding was insufficient to support public opinion research, and international academic interest at that time had shifted from testing agenda-setting effects to investigating the formation of the media agenda. Nie Yi (2005) has noted that research of this kind constitutes the majority of the agenda-setting research in China. Examples include "Who Set the Agenda of Today's China? Reconstructing News Events of the Party-Organ Newspapers in BBS" (Li Xiguang & Qin Xuan, 2001) and "Setting the News Agenda: Journalists, Corporations, and Unidentified Sources in Auto News" (Jiang Zhigao, 2004). In the first article, the author discovered that the Internet has eroded the traditional authoritarian position of the Party-state newspapers, though these newspapers have always attempted to convince the public of the correctness of the Party line. If people no longer trust domestic media, they will turn to international media, and as a result, Western media may eventually set the agenda for the public in China. The second article is the only one in China to apply agenda-setting theory to the analysis of business reports. The author employed content analysis to examine the news sources used by three major Chinese business newspapers for reports on the automotive industry over a 6-month period. The author came to the conclusion that news sources exercise different influences on the news agenda. Journalists, heads of automobile companies, and unidentified news sources were found to be the dominant influences on the news media. Heads of automobile companies, secondary to journalists, constitute 92% of all the sources used.

Overall, agenda-setting research in mainland China is still at an early stage of theoretical introduction and discussion. Cases studies based on the classic agenda-setting method are needed. Research on agenda-setting theory in terms of political communication, as well as of business communication, is still scarce.

Business and the News Media

The rapid transition of China to a market economy in the 1990s led to the rise of the business news media. The business news pages and business reports soon evolved into business newspapers and special television channels. Business news and its reporters became distinct from the journalism community at large. This phenomenon deserves special attention. As an emerging field, business journalism is increasingly important and has already been institutionalized as a popular major in the universities. Meanwhile, business reporters—whether young graduates or those who changed from other beats—are caught between media sycophancy and objective reporting.

The relationship between business and the transitional news media has gained little attention from Chinese academia. One reason for this is that media bribery is rampant and people in China are too accustomed to it to call it into question. Overall, there is a lack of research on news production, especially on the black box operations existing in the business reports and public relations. Rational, constructive, and systematic research is urgently needed.

The present study is not quantitative but is rather a systematic study based on the relevant literature and qualitative data. In light of the social culture and media environment in China, and based on the work of Carroll and McCombs (2003), the present study proposes three hypotheses about the agenda-setting influences of the news media on corporate image and reputation.

Carroll and McCombs have noted that audiences' attention and the media visibility of corporations' names are the first reflection of agenda-setting effects:

> Before analyzing how the public thinks about a firm, we need to determine that the public, or a sub-segment such as a stakeholder group, even thinks about the firm at all. This early stage in the communication process, attention, is the initial focus of agenda-setting theory, which objects are even on the agenda. In agenda-setting terms, the "top of mind" name recall that the public has for a particular firm should correspond to the firm's media visibility. (p. 39)

In addition, the quantitative research carried out by Zhang Guoliang and Li Benqian (2002a, 2003) found a high correlation between the mass media agenda and the public agenda at the macrolevel, but a rather low correlation at the microlevel. What correlation exists between the frequency of news media reports and the public recognition of corporations? This is the first hypothesis the present study explores.

Hypothesis 1. The more media coverage a firm receives, the higher the degree of public recognition that firm gets. Takeshita (1997) noted that "agenda-setting research has had a kind of issue-centered bias—that is, the great majority of agenda-setting studies published thus far chose to adopt the same concept of an agenda of general issues as the original McCombs and Shaw study did" (McCombs, Shaw, & Weaver, 1997, p. 20). Influenced by this tradition of agenda-setting research, most research in this field is studying "the shell of the topic" instead of "the substance of an issue" (Takeshita, 1997, p. 20). The research chaired by Zhang Guoliang (2002b, 2003) has the issue-centered bias. And Jiang Zhigao's research (2004) on automobile coverage by business news media discovered that the automobile giants constitute a key source of business news and exercise great influence on the media agenda. Therefore, the second hypothesis is formulated in terms of the relationship between the attributes of a corporation and the public understanding of those attributes.

Hypothesis 2. The more an attribute of a firm is emphasized by the news media, the more likely the public is to use that attribute to define the firm. Given that China's media credibility has been under discussion in the business and academic community since the media reform started in the late 1970s and that cash for news coverage has come to symbolize corruption in the media industry, it is important to test whether the attitude agenda of Chinese media, which used to represent solely the Party-state, has retained credibility and a dominant influence over the public.

Hypothesis 3. The more positively a firm is covered by the news media, the more positively that firm is perceived by the public; and the more negatively a firm is covered by the news media, the more negatively that firm is perceived by the public.

Case Study

Corporate Reputation in China

Corporate reputation rating is a new concept in China. There was no corporate reputation ranking until 2001, when the *Economic Observer*, a leading business press headquartered in Beijing, issued a "most admired companies in China" list, inspired by *Fortune*'s "most admired companies in the United States" list. Even the standards used were modeled after *Fortune*'s study. Currently, four Chinese newspapers sponsored corporate reputation rankings: the *Economic Observer*, *China News Weekly*, *China Business News*, and *Capital Weekly*. These newspapers are the key actors in economic journalism in China.

What is common among these corporate reputation rankings is the presence of multinationals or joint-venture companies, while some key state-owned enterprises are nearly absent from them. The Chinese practice differs greatly from that in European and American rankings in this regard. This is shown by comparing the "most admired companies in China" list released by the *Economic Observer in 2007*, with the "top 500 Chinese companies" list, consisting mainly of state-owned companies, jointly released by the United Association of Chinese Enterprises and the Association of Chinese Entrepreneurs in 2008. The top 15 Chinese companies in the latter list are absent in the former (see Table 18.1).

From the existing corporate rankings in China, some observations can be made. First, the influence of multinational companies in China is extraordinary. These companies are playing a key role in transforming various aspects of Chinese society and the economy. The organizing agents in charge of corporate rankings pay great attention to this point. This is evidenced by the fact that transnational companies enjoy a conspicuous status in various types of rankings.

Second, with the support of consultant companies, these corporate reputation rankings seem to be procedurally fair, but the public has been skeptical about their credibility. For instance, though the selection procedure adopted by the *Economic Observer* in its "most admired companies in China" list is regarded as the most standardized, the criteria used in the selection has not been consistent through its 5 years.

Third, the rankings bear the clear marks of public relations involvement. The news media conducting these rankings do not hesitate to admit that this is their second most important revenue source next to advertising. In an intensely

Table 18.1 "Top 500 Chinese Companies" List in 2008 and "Most Admired Companies in China" List in 2007

	"Top 500 Chinese Companies" List in 2008		The "Most Admired Companies in China" List in 2007
Rank	Company names	Rank	Company names
1	China Petroleum and Chemical Co.	1	Lenovo Group
2	State Grid Corporation of China	2	China Merchants Bank
3	China National Petroleum Corporation	3	Huawei Technology
4	Industrial and Commercial Bank of China	4	Vanke
5	China Mobile Communication Co.	5	Phoenix Satellite Television
6	China Life Insurance (Group) Co.	6	ZTE Corporation
7	Construction Bank of China	7	Sina.com
8	Bank of China	8	Mengniu
9	Agriculture Bank of China	9	IBM (China)
10	China Southern Power Grid Co., LTD.	10	H&P
11	Sinochem Corporation	11	General Motors (Shanghai)
12	Baosteel Group	12	Microsoft China
13	China Telecom	13	Alibaba.com
14	China FAW Group Corporation	14	Tsingtao Brewery Group
15	Foxconn	15	Cisco China

competitive advertising market, economic newspapers, especially latecomers such as the *Economic Observer*, are keen to find new revenue sources. Corporate reputation rankings have become an important source of revenue. Thus, it is not surprising that the advertising clients of the *Economic Observer* and its partner *Phoenix Television* constitute 80% of the companies listed in the "most admired companies in China" in its 2004 and 2005 rankings.

Media Structure

Public relations as a profession was first brought to China in the 1980s. At that time it offered three major services: public affairs, ceremonial activities, and media publicity. After 20 years of development, the services of public relations companies have become more professional. Investment relations, crisis communication, staff relations, and sports marketing, as well as corporate citizenship, are all included as new professional offerings. Nevertheless, media relations management is still the core business of most companies' services. Hence, media relations management appears especially important in China. Regarding media system analysis, Sriramesh and Verčič (2003) proposed an analysis framework that divides media systems into three aspects: media control, media outreach, and media access. We will first analyze media structure in China, and then apply this media system analysis framework to the media situation in China.

The current media structure in China began with the founding of the People's Republic of China in 1949. In the late 1970s, with the "open-up" policy initiated by Deng Xiaoping, Chinese media began its own reform as well. Since 1992, China's media has begun a rapid commercialization process. Numerous newly launched market-oriented media, which are affiliated with different levels of Party press groups, have dramatically transformed the structure of the Chinese media. As of 2008, China had 49 press corporations, 1,943 newspapers, 9,549 magazines, 287 TV stations, and 1,993 broadcasting stations.

At this point, China has two systems of media: the Party-state media and the market-oriented media. The Party-state media are divided into party organs for the Party and government, such as the *People's Daily* and the local Party newspapers in every province and city, and the targeted media for specific social groups, such as *The China Youth Daily, The Chinese Women's Report,* the *Worker's Daily,* the *Legal Daily,* and so on. The market-oriented newspapers can also be divided into two categories: mass-appeal metropolitan newspapers, and the economic and financial press. The market-oriented metropolitan newspapers are usually the offspring of the local Party-state media; that is, they have a close "mother–child" relationship with a particular Party-state media group, and editorial policy, human resources, financial affairs, and so forth, are all handled directly by the Party-state media group. The economic and finance press belong to the responsible departments. In reality, however, the "responsible departments" usually have no involvement in editorial policy, human resources, and financial affairs. Compared to the Party-state media, the two categories of market-oriented newspaper both have apolitical and nonideological characteristics.

Table 18.2 Media Structure in China (selected newspapers)

Party Organs	Market-Oriented Media	
	Offspring Press Affiliated with the Party Organs	Media Affiliated the Responsible Departments
People's Daily	Beijing Times (affiliated with People's Daily)	China Business (weekly)
Guangming Daily	Beijing News (affiliated with Guangming Daily)	China Business News (daily)
Nanfang Daily	Nanfang Metro News (affiliated with Nanfang Daily)	Nanfang Weekend (weekly)
Economic Daily		Beijing Youth News (daily)

With the advent of the new millennium, new trends have arisen in the Chinese media industry. Party-state media groups at the provincial level that are geographically located in different cities have begun joint ventures to launch new market-oriented press. *Beijing News* is one, begun in 2003 by the *Guangming Daily* in Beijing and the *Guangzhou Daily* in Guangzhou. One year later, *China Business News* was launched in Shanghai and its main investors included the Shanghai Media Group (SMG), the Beijing Youth Daily Press Group, and the Guangzhou Daily Press Group. This kind of cross-regional and cross-sectional media is a totally new phenomenon in China. It has further diversified the media structure of China and has far-reaching implications, especially as compared to the former regional-based media model where media entities were usually founded by the local- or regional-level Party commission.

Media Outreach

According to United Nations Development Program statistics, the literacy rate of Chinese adults was 90.9% in 2002. By 2008, China's broadcasting coverage rate reached 95.96%, with TV coverage rate reaching 96.95%. Out of 349 million families in China, 126 million families had cable TV. According to the *China Statistical Data Collection of Press and Publication* published by the General Administration of Press and Publication of China (GAPP) in 2004, of the top 20 highest circulation newspapers, all were the offspring of Party-state media groups except two: the *People's Daily* and *Economic Daily*, the organs of the Chinese Communist Party and the State Council of China, respectively. The highest circulation newspaper in China was the Xinhua agency's *Reference News (Can Kao Xiao Xi)*, reaching 2.53 million, while the *People's Daily* reached 1.773 million and was ranked second.

In the new millennium, the Internet continued its fast-paced development. According to data released by the Chinese Internet Information center (CNNIC) in June 2009, the number of Chinese Internet users reached 338 million, accounting for 26% of the population. The CNNIC's report shows that typical Chinese Internet users are male and unmarried, and most are below the age of 35. Of those who had graduated from college or university, 91.5% were Internet users.

The majority of the Internet-using community, therefore, is made up of people who have received a good education and are middle class. Dramatic gaps in Internet usage exist between urban and rural areas and between eastern coastal and western inland areas, and the gap between urban areas and rural areas is still increasing. There are 788,400 Web sites in China; among them, accounts with the domain name ".CN" account for 43.3%, accounts with the domain ".com" account for 44.7%, accounts with the domain ".net" account for 9.4%, and accounts with the domain ".org" account for 2.5%.

According to the GAPP's statistics, there were 1,943 newspapers in 2008, including 224 national newspapers and 826 provincial newspapers. The provincial Party organs and the metropolitan newspapers affiliated with the Party organs are both considered regional newspapers. Although there are more than 200 national newspapers in China, only a few big Party organs have nationwide influence, such as *The People's Daily, Guangming Daily, China Youth Daily*. In addition, since the late 1990s, the economic and financial press, such as *China Business, Economic Observer*, and *21st Century Business Herald*, has influenced the major cities in the country. To take *China Business* as an example, 70% of its circulation centers on the 11 metropolitan areas, mainly eastern coastal cities such as Beijing, Shanghai, and Guangzhou. Its circulation in Beijing, Shanghai, and Guangzhou accounts for 40% of its total circulation. The circulation breakdown is very similar to that of other economic publications in China.

Media Access

In terms of media access, two main powers control the source of news: the government and corporations. In charge of the official media, the government is always the principal reportage; that is, news about government leaders' routine activities, conferences, and the government's achievements (*San Men,* 三门). This news usually came from the government bureaucracy (*Gong Men,* 宫门); the media administration departments (*Ya Men,* 衙门); and the the judiciary, the police, and the military (*Yuan Men,* 辕门) (Li Liangrong, 2006). After the media reform and commercialization, Chinese media revenues changed from government subsidies to advertising, and the penetration of corporate power into the media became a hot topic in Chinese news media circles. Since the reform, unlike in Western countries, there is no clear-cut separation between the editorial department and the advertisement department. As a result, at the very beginning of the reform, media bribery emerged. In 2003, in a very influential Chinese journalism trade journal, an article by a reporter appeared with the title, "Is Being a Journalist Still a Respected Profession?" (Hu Tingmei, 2004). According to an assessment by the U.S. Institute of Public Relations (IPR) of the tendency of journalists in 66 countries to accept "cash for coverage," China is the country where this is most likely to occur (the International Bribery for Media Coverage Index, 2003). Cui Yongyuan, a well-known TV host on CCTV, once said that "if it [CCTV] is a public TV station, it is the worst one in the world; if it is commercial, it is the least commercial one in the world"—which seems to support the IPR's ranking.

Media Control

In the 1990s, economic weaning, pushed by the Party impelled the economic independence of Chinese news media, but failed to free the news media of Party-state control, which has in fact become tighter and more sophisticated. In the mid-1990s, with government support and encouragement, the country's media began to form conglomerates, and the main goal of this reform, besides integrating resources and enhancing the media's overall economic health, was to make it easier for the Party-state to strengthen its control. As Hong (1998) points out, "In China, news outlets at all levels are expected to promote policies and priorities set at the top, and the Party and government officials remain chief arbiters of how 'news' is defined" (p. 45).

Many researchers have focused on government control of China's news media (Chen, 1996; Chen & Culbertson, 2003), but since commercialization, corporate control is increasingly significant. At present, advertising is the main revenue source for most Chinese news media; even the CCP's party organ, the *People's Daily*, is defined by the Party as "an institution operated as a business." Operating the news as a business means that news production will inevitably be constrained by external factors such as advertisers, market competition, and so on. According to the findings of Chin-chuan Lee and his colleagues (2006), based on a case study of a party organ press group (Shenzhen Daily Press Corporation), the Party-state media reform changed it into "Party Publicity Inc.": the original internal propaganda function of the Party's commission. However, the penetration of corporate power into the Chinese media is not limited to news production. Although it is not legal for industrial capital to invest in the news sector, the indirect investment by corporations is a well-known "secret" in China. The principle shareholder of *Economic Observer* is the Shandong Sanlian Corporation, a privately owned enterprise in Shandong province whose main business is as a household electric appliance chain store and real estate company. Many Chinese corporations consider investment in news media as another profit source. It is safe to say that with the penetration of industrial capital into the Chinese news media, private economic interests are a rising power that influences news production in many different ways, from information subsidies to cross-ownership.

News Values

According to a widely used Chinese textbook, *Introduction to Journalism Theories* (Tong Bin, 2000), news value is based upon the following: reality, importance, prominence, interest, and humanity. These news value standards were introduced from West, and Chinese media have adapted this news value system to accommodate China's news practice. Take prominence as an example: in China, if an important government official is participating in activity, it is often considered as a notable activity; therefore, some unremarkable activities attract media coverage by having important officials present. This is parallel to multinational corporations' PR activities, such as having the CEO visit China and meet with Chinese top leadership or provincial leaders, since this will generally be reported in the mainstream Chinese media.

The two media systems—the Party-state media and the market-oriented media—create two sets of news value standards in China. The Party-state media's function is publicity, so its news production process emphasizes social mobilization to implement the Party's policies; it is really "propaganda value," not "news value." Moreover, the Party organ is forbidden to expose news disadvantageous to the Party and government; as Mao Zedong put it, "*Xin wen* (新闻, the news), *Jiu Wen* (旧闻, the delayed news), *Bu Wen* (不闻, the censored news)" (Mao Zedong, 1983).

With the market-oriented media, news values introduced by Western media are more likely to be practiced. The Chinese financial press often models itself after its counterparts in the United States or Britain in news judgment and in selection of topics. For example, when a report titled "China Price" appeared in the American *Business Week* in March 2005, one of China's financial newspapers translated it into Chinese and published it together with other related articles. Later, other Chinese economic and financial press published a series of lengthy reports on this topic. The Chinese financial press also clones its Western counterparts' column offering, page layout styles, and so on. The *Economic Observer* even uses pink newsprint paper like that used by the British *Financial Times* since its publication in 1893.

During its founding in the 1950s, the People's Republic of China modeled its journalism after the former Soviet Union and built up the Party journalism tradition, which still has influence today. Since the 1980s, this model has changed to mirror that of the United States. The Americanization of news values among Chinese market-oriented media may be the tip of the iceberg of the Chinese media's Americanization.

Organizational Newsworthiness

In China, the common practice of the news media is to be, not the watchdog, but the songbird, reporting achievements rather than problems. In past decades, an unprecedented amount of favorable coverage by all levels of news media has been published regarding foreign direct investment (FDI) in China. This was partly because the GDP was the most important criterion the central government used in checking up on local officials. As mouthpiece for the local government, the local Party-state media were usually in the same boat with local officials, trying to promote investment projects. For instance, in 2006, the officials in Nanchang, capital of Jiangxi province in central China, had successfully attracted Wal-Mart to open a store, and this was featured as the local officials' achievement in improving the local business and investment environment.

Historically, newsworthiness in China has been closely linked with the Party's policies, and thus the media agenda of "hard news" is usually dominated by government policies rather than by the audience's interests. News media are often tools used by the government to punish corrupt officials and misguided corporations, or to praise honest officials and those companies actively implementing the Party's economic policies. *Focus Interview* (焦点访谈), a well-known prime-time TV program on CCTV launched in 1994, is an example of this kind of new genre. Another good example is the PRC's Cleaner Production Promotion Act of 2002, Article 17 of which states that "environmental protection bureaus can publish in mass media a list of the polluting companies." The news media had long been used to criticize some companies and to reward others; here, public shame was being wielded as a tool to get companies to improve their environmental performance and link that to company reputation (Guo Peiyuan, 2005).

Public Relations

Much like *corporate reputation*, *public relations* is a modern term from abroad. It was not until the 1980s that public relations emerged as a profession in China. But the practice of public relations has a very long history in China (Chen, 1994). The emperor of the Tang dynasty, Tang Taizong (A.D. 599–649) famously compared his subjects to water and his kingdom to a boat: "The water that bears the boat is the same that swallows it up," suggesting that the building and maintaining of good relations with subjects was viewed seriously even in imperial times in China.

After it was brought to China from Western countries, public relations as a new profession was first popular in southern parts of China, such as Shenzhen and Zhuhai, where special economic zones were being set up. In these economic zones, dozens of newly founded joint-venture hotels began to adopt Western style management, and then set up public relations departments. Later, public relations spread from the south to the north, from the eastern coastal areas to the central, western inland areas. By the end of 2008, China had more than 1,500 public relations companies, with a total annual revenue of more than RMB14 billion, and employing about 20,000 professionals.

Although the profession of public relations was well known among the Chinese people, legitimacy was not conferred until 1999, when the "public relations profession" was listed in the *PRC Grand Classification of Occupations* published by the Ministry of Labor and Social Security, marking official recognition of the profession by the Chinese government.

The public relations industry developed rapidly during the 1980s. After the Tiananmen Square Incident in 1989, however, the process of reform and opening up was temporary halted, and the public relations industry was restrained as a "Western ideology." China went back to the way of reform after Deng Xiaoping's 1992 tour of southern China, and the public relations industry was revived again. Recently, however, public relations has increasingly been linked with official corruption and business bribery, and many in business believe "public relations" is a synonym for bribery.

Nevertheless, such associations with the term cannot overshadow its important role in the rapid economic development in China, and the government soon came to realize this. The industry has boomed, with an annual growth rate of more than 30% over the past 5 years (CIPRA, 2009). In May 2005, the Chinese government engaged Patton Boggs, a famous American public relations company, to take charge of communicating with the U.S. Congress on behalf of the Chinese embassy. From this we can see a great change taking place in the government's attitude toward the public relations industry. In fact, during the 2003 SARS outbreak, government press meetings were routinized, and the Foreign Ministry promoted this as a new institution to the other 66 ministries and many lower level government entities—and in China, the government's action is often seen as setting the direction for the rest of society.

Since China entered the World Trade Organization, foreign PR companies have been permitted to set up branches in China, and major international companies, such as APCO, Burson-Marsteller, Edelman, Fleishman Link, and Hill & Knowlton have set up their own or joint-venture PR companies. In 2008, CIPRA ranked the top 10 PR companies, which included Burson-Marsteller, Fleishman Hillard, Hill & Knowlton, Ketchum Newscan, Ogilvy PR, Ruder-Finn, and Weber Shandwick.

Currently, the local PR markets are mainly focused in Beijing, Shanghai, Guangzhou, and Chengdu, which occupy 70% of the market share. A 2008 survey conducted by CIPRA within its 90 membership companies revealed that many companies have established branches nationwide. Public relations education in Chinese universities in China is still far from perfect, and the more than 30% annual growth rate has challenged PR companies to find qualified employees. According to CIPRA's data, in 2008, employees in this industry had to work more than 46 hours each week (CIPRA, 2009).

The rapid development in the PR industry has had prominent influence on the news media's agenda setting. More and more Chinese companies have started hiring PR agencies for their products promotion and corporate branding. Media relations management is still a core service for many PR firms in China. Partly due to PR firms' efforts, most Chinese news media have "a list of the protected" compiled by the advertising department and shared with the editorial department. Companies listed usually get more favorable coverage than others and are subject to less critical reporting. To understand the media's agenda setting effects in China, therefore, requires an awareness of the role of PR firms.

Research Methodology

The present research was based on the data collected for a corporate reputation ranking project, "the most influential multinational corporations in China in 2004." Along with this project, the Beijing Horizon Research and Consultancy Group (BHRCG) conducted a public opinion poll with 1,252 respondents. BHCRG completed the survey in October 2004, in Beijing, Shanghai, Guangzhou, Wuhan, Chengdu, Shenyang, and Xi'an, and in each city the sample number was at least 170. The survey method was multistage random sampling.

In addition, another database for news content analysis and news articles was selected from the *People's Daily* and *Economic Daily* one year before the survey conducted by BHRCG. By comparing the findings from these two databases, we tried to test the three assumptions about the first- and second-level agenda-setting effects proposed by Carroll and McCombs (2003).

Choice of News Media

The *People's Daily* and *Economic Daily* were chosen for content analysis for the following reasons: First, both have high prestige in China and are authoritative outlets for news and policies toward multinational corporations in China and thus both often become the agenda builders for other domestic news media in China. Second, both have large circulations and considerable influence on readers and have almost no competitors in terms of circulation and social influence. Third, both have complete newspaper archive databases so content analysis is practical.

The present study analyzed the *People's Daily* from March 1, 2002, to December 31, 2003, and *Economic Daily* from October 1, 2002, to October 31, 2004. This period of *Economic Daily* was chosen because it was 2 years before BHCRG finished its public opinion survey, and the period up to December 2003 of the *People's Daily* was chosen because its archive database only extended through December 31, 2003.

Public Opinion Polls

The BHCRG survey results yielded the overall multinational corporate reputation ranking, as well as the overall awareness of multinational companies, their involvement in corporate social responsibility (CSR) activities, and Chinese corporate reputation rankings.

Based on the database of news content analysis, the number of news articles for each multinational company in the two newspapers was determined, along with their involvement in CSR activities reported by both newspapers and the corporate reputation rankings.

Comparing the data from the two databases, first, the first-level agenda-setting effect was analyzed, namely the relationship between the overall top-of-mind name recall of multinational companies and numbers of articles about them in both newspapers. Second, the two dimensions of the second-level agenda-setting effect, known as attributes agenda-setting effects, including substantive and evaluative effects, were analyzed. "Substantive effects" here refers to the relationship of the salience of multinational companies' involvement in CSR activities on the

Table 18.3 Descriptions of the Conceptions in the Survey for "The Most Influential Multinational Corporations in China in 2004"

Items	Descriptions
Overall awareness of multinational companies	The top-of-mind awareness by the public
Public awareness of multinational companies' attribute	Awareness of involvement in CSR activities in areas such as education, health, philanthropy, environment protection, etc.
	Corporate reputation rankings. The public's general appreciation for the multinational companies

Table 18.4 Top-of-Mind Awareness of Multinational Companies and Number of News Articles

Rank	Top-of-Mind Awareness of Multinational Company		Number of News Articles in People's Daily (200210-200312)	Number of News Articles in Economic Daily (200210-200410)	Media Agenda (Total)
1	McDonald's	106	38	129	167
2	Coca Cola	77	33	160	193
3	Motorola	50	64	279	343
4	Amway	41	25	49	74
5	Microsoft	37	67	314	381
6	Simons	31	55	214	269
7	Sony	30	57	293	350
8	Samsung	28	101	342	443
9	P&G	27	14	69	83
10	Nokia	26	53	206	259
11	Toshiba	24	21	164	185
12	Panasonic	23	51	273	324
13	AIA	19	7	50	57
14	Carrefour	18	36	174	210
15	BMW	17	26	250	276
16	Nestle	16	13	74	87
17	Colgate	16	3	11	14
18	Volkswagen	16	143	446	589
19	Pepsi	14	7	50	57
20	Adidas	13	14	23	37

two newspapers and the salience of this attribute on the public agenda. "Evaluative effects" refer to the relationship of the number of news articles with the overall positive, neutral, or negative tone, and the extent of the public's general appreciation for each multinational company.

Results

Hypothesis 1. Top-of-mind awareness of multinational companies and the number of news articles: The data failed to support the first hypothesis. Two explanations are possible. First, the public top-of-mind awareness of multinational companies may not have depended mainly on reports from media but rather on experience as consumers and on advertising. The data showed that companies with a high top-of-mind name recall usually invested heavily in advertising, but these companies were not often written about in the media. The cause of high top-of-mind awareness for multinational companies might differ from that of a political candidate. The public's awareness of multinational companies did not arise wholly from media reports, even mainly not from news reports.

Table 18.5 Correlation between Top-of-Mind Awareness of Multinational Companies and Number of News Articles

		Agenda of People's Daily	Agenda of Economic Daily	Media Agenda
Public agenda	Pearson Correlation	0.08	0.04	0.05
	Sig. (2-tailed)	0.73	0.85	0.82
	N	21	21	21

Table 18.6 Awareness of Involvement in CSR Activities and the Number of News Articles

Rank	Awareness of Involvement in CSR Activities		Number of News Articles in People's Daily (200210-200312)	Number of News Articles in Economics Daily (200210-200410)	Media Agenda (Total)
1	Coca Cola	64	3	10	13
2	McDonald's	54	3	4	7
3	Amway	37	8	11	19
4	P&G	32	3	4	7
5	Microsoft	27	3	2	5
6	Toshiba	22	3	3	6
7	Panasonic	20	2	3	5
8	Johnson & Johnson	19	1	5	6
9	Pepsi	17	1	3	4
10	Carrefour	17	1	1	2
11	Nike	16	0	3	3
12	Sony	16	2	0	2
13	Reno	15	0	0	0
14	Samsung	15	1	3	4
15	Motorola	15	1	4	5
16	Simons	14	3	1	4
17	Nestle	14	2	2	4
18	Metro	13	0	0	0
19	Sharp	12	0	0	0
20	Nokia	12	3	1	4
21	Colgate	12	1	0	1
22	Volkswagen	12	0	1	1
23	AIA	11	0	0	0
24	BMW	11	0	0	0

Table 18.7 Correlation between Awareness of Involvement in CSR Activities and Number of News Articles

		People's Daily	Economic Daily	Media Agenda
Public Agenda	Pearson Correlation	0.56**	0.76**	0.74**
	Sig. (2-tailed)	0	0	0
	N	24	24	24

Note. ** Correlation is significant at the 0.01 level (2-tailed).

Table 18.8 General Corporate Appreciation Rankings and Number of News Articles

Rank	General Corporate Appreciation Rankings by the Public		Number of News Articles in People's Daily (200210–200312)			Number of News Articles in Economics Daily (200210–200410)			Media Agenda (Total)		
	Companies	Frequency	Positive	Neutral	Negative	Positive	Neutral	Negative	Positive	Neutral	Negative
1	McDonald's	86	2	35	1	15	143	2	17	178	3
2	Coca Cola	57	4	28	1	15	144	1	19	172	2
3	Amway	43	10	15	2	17	32	0	27	47	2
4	Simons	41	7	48	0	15	194	7	22	242	7
5	P&G	36	3	11	0	5	64	0	8	75	0
6	Toshiba	35	4	18	0	13	164	0	17	182	0
7	Motorola	33	9	55	0	12	266	1	21	321	1
8	Nokia	32	12	41	0	18	188	0	30	229	0
9	Samsung	27	6	94	1	23	319	0	29	413	1
10	Microsoft	26	7	60	0	15	311	3	22	371	3
11	Panasonic	22	8	43	0	16	257	0	24	300	0
12	Pepsi	21	2	5	0	2	48	0	4	53	0
13	Colgate	19	1	2	0	2	9	0	3	11	0
14	Carrefour	17	2	34	0	2	170	4	4	204	4
15	AIA	17	0	7	0	4	36	0	4	43	0
16	Switzerland Banking Co.	16	0	11	0	2	37	0	2	48	0
17	Hitachi	16	2	22	0	5	127	0	7	149	0
18	Volkswagen	15	7	136	0	20	426	0	27	562	0
19	Sony	14	6	52	0	12	281	0	18	333	0
20	BMW	13	3	23	0	7	243	0	10	266	0
21	Nestle	13	2	11	0	3	75	0	5	86	0

Table 18.9 Correlation

		Positive Reporting	Neutral Reporting	Negative Reporting
Public Agenda	Pearson Correlation	0.34	-0.09	0.45*
	Sig. (2-tailed)	0.13	0.71	0.04
	N	21	21	21

Note. * Correlation is significant at the 0.05 level (2-tailed).

Second, while doing content analysis the author found a correlation between the number of news articles about some companies and the amount of advertisements from the same companies. In other words, the more advertising a company did, the more news coverage it got from the media.

Hypothesis 2. Awareness of involvement in CSR activities and the number of news articles: The data supported the second hypothesis. Here there were also two explanations. First, compared with multinational companies, Chinese companies were not active in CSR activities except in the case of natural disasters such as floods; otherwise, the public seldom saw Chinese companies doing CSR projects. Multinational companies' CSR activities were therefore of special interest to Chinese media and resulted in more news coverage. Meanwhile, the public increased their awareness of multinational companies in comparison with that of Chinese companies. Second, regarding corporations' involvement in CSR activities, differentiating products and services from advertising, the public relied much more on the information provided by media. Therefore, the number of news articles had a direct effect on public awareness and appreciation of a company's attributes.

Hypothesis 3. The general corporate appreciation rankings and the number of news articles: The data failed to support the third hypothesis. After more than 10 years of commercialization reform in the media industry, "cash for coverage" became worse. Even journalists from the high-prestige state-owned Xinhua News Agency were involved in several scandals of media bribery; thus, the public has taken a "read between the lines" approach toward the news and become cynical toward news reports. Negative articles definitely resulted in negative impressions of companies, but positive articles did not necessarily guarantee positive impressions. Consequently, corporate reputations declined along with media's credibility.

Discussion

The commercialization reform of the news media allowed the Chinese media to become more independent. These changes brought about two contrary results: on the one hand, the news media have become the partner for corporate reputation building, while on the other, to succeed in competition and enhance social credibility or to help to implement the Party's policy, news media have used critical reporting to destroy corporate reputation, especially for corporations involved in unfair competition, environmental pollution, and lack of social accountability, such as Foxconn, mentioned at the beginning of this chapter.

Will the structural transformation of Chinese news media lead the media to become "songbirds" who mainly cover corporate success and achievements in China, or to become the croaking crows who disclose the dark side of corporate activities? The answer is still unclear. Because of corporate penetration of the media, to survive the current grueling competition many one-time crows have already become songbirds. The 2006 Foxconn scandal that ended with *China Business News* apologizing to Foxconn is a striking case, but we cannot foretell the future of China's business news media from this one event.

Different companies' visibility in the Chinese news media depends to a great extent on three factors: the degree of their involvement in China's economy, the amount of investment in advertising, and the degree to which their corporate strategy aligns with the Party's policy. For example, if a multinational company has a joint venture with a local Chinese company its media exposure rate will be much higher than one that does not. The German auto company Volkswagen, for example, has a joint venture with companies in Changchun and Shanghai and has done so for more than 20 years. Therefore, media coverage of Volkswagen in China is much higher than that for other multinational automobile companies. Likewise, companies whose strategy aligns well with the Party's policy—such as Chery, Geely, Lenovo, Huawei, and Zhongxing, all known as innovative "national companies" that enjoy celebrity status in China—have more opportunities to be covered by the Chinese mainstream media, the Party-state media, and the influential market-oriented economic press. In sharp contrast, news coverage of the giant state-owned enterprises and monopolies that shape China's economic destiny and employ advertising, is relatively limited. For those companies that advertise more in the news media, the coverage rate is usually much higher, something especially evident in the newly established financial press and metropolitan newspapers. As Shoemaker and Reese (1996) noted, since advertising income was crucial to the survival of the commercial media, the bigger the advertiser, the more muscle it had. The advertiser often told the media what to think and how the content should be changed.

Finally, public relations firms in China have become increasingly sophisticated and were already one of the main actors influencing news production; thus their role in creating corporate reputation and image has become more and more evident. Recently the notion of "corporate citizenship" in the public relations field has become popular in China. The mainland companies, especially those exporting their products abroad, have gradually recognized the Social Accountability 8000 (SA8000) certificate. Whereas in August 2002, there were 34 companies holding SA8000 certificates, by October 2004, that number had reached 57. Although corporate social responsibility is currently popular primarily among big businesses with a Western management style, it has nevertheless had a great influence on local firms.

Generally speaking, in China's news media, American and European companies have better corporate images than those originating in Japan and Taiwan. If the poor image of Japanese companies in China can be attributed to the tension of Sino-Japan relations and to anti-Japanese sentiment among Chinese due to Japan's stance on its invasion during World War II, what about the Taiwanese companies? Most of them are original equipment manufacturers (OEM) and pay little attention to their brand management and social responsibility in mainland China; as a result Taiwanese companies have the worst reputation on the mainland. Foxconn, for instance, is seen as a typical Taiwanese company.

The limitations of this study lie in these two areas: (a) How does the public construct its overall recognition of a company as well as its appreciation of corporate image and reputation? Answering this question will require in-depth interviews and focus-group interviews. (b) At the moment, there are structural differences among Chinese media's approach to the corporations. The Party-state media usually take a stance of economic nationalism, while the market-oriented media take a laissez-faire stance; why do these editorial policies differ? This also remains to be explored.

Conclusions

Based on an analysis of the Chinese news media and its coverage of corporations' reputations, as well as an analysis of other factors, such as the media system, media values, concept of newsworthiness, and public relations, the present study concludes the following:

1. The evaluation of corporate reputation in China is still in its infancy and has low public credibility.
2. The state media system and the market media system, developed out of the Chinese media reform of the past 30 years, have developed two attitudes toward corporations, a complimentary one and a critical one.
3. Western news values have been adjusted to China's local situation after they have been introduced to China, but there is an obvious American mark on the news values of the Chinese media.
4. The news values of the Chinese media in a large degree depend on whether they are compatible with the Party-state's economic policies; if so, they are rewarded by the Party-state.
5. Due to the perceived connection between the public relations and government corruption, as well as corporate bribery, the public relations industry has a mixed reputation in China and has gone through ups and downs in its over 20 years of development there. Now public relations companies and the techniques they use have become increasingly sophisticated, and they have become one of the main powers influencing the agendas of the Chinese news media, which means that they are having increasing effects on corporate image and corporate reputation in China.

References

Bai, Y., & Xu, H. (2001). On market order and corporate reputation. *Fujian Forum Journal, 6*, 109–130.

Carroll, C. E., & McCombs, M. (2003). Agenda-setting effects of business news on the public's images and opinions about major corporations. *Corporate Reputation Review, 6*(1), 36–46.

Carroll, C. E., & McCombs, M. (2006). Agenda-setting effects of business news on the public's images and opinions about major corporations. *Journal of Journalism and Communications, 1*, 107–117.

Chan, J. M. (1996). Television development in greater China: Structure, exports, and market formation. In J. Sinclair, E. Jacka, & S. Cunningham. (Eds.), *New patterns in global television: Peripheral vision* (pp. 126–160). Oxford, UK: Oxford University Press.

Chen, N. (1994). Public relations education in the People's Republic of China. *The Journalism Educator, 49*(1), 14–22.

Chen, N. (1996). Public relations in China. In H. Culbertson & N. Chen (Eds.), *International public relations: A comparative analysis* (pp. 121–154). Mahwah, NJ: Erlbaum.

Chen, N., & Culbertson, H. M. (2003). Public relations in mainland China: An adolescent with growing pains. In K. Sriramesh & D. Verčič (Eds.), *The global public relations handbook: Theory, research, and practice* (pp. 187–211). Mahwah, NJ: Erlbaum.

China International Public Relations Association (CIPRA). (2009). *Annual report*. Beijing, PRC: Author.

Chin-Chuan, L. (Ed.). (2003). *Chinese media, global context*. New York: Routledge Curzon.

Chin-Chuan, L., Zhou, H., & Yu, H. (2006). "Chinese Party Publicity Inc." conglomerated: The case of the Shenzhen Press Group. *Media, Culture & Society, 28*(4), 581–602

Guo, P. (2005). *Corporate environmental reporting and disclosure in China, corporate social responsibility Asia*. Retrieved from http://www.csr-asia.com/upload/environmentalreporting.pdf

Guo, Z. (1997). On the agenda-setting role of mass media. *Guo Ji Xin Wen Jie* [Journal of International Communication], *3*, 18–25. (In Chinese)

Guo, Z. (1999). The agenda-setting role of the mass communication. *Xinwen Daxue* [Journalism Quarterly], *2*, 32–36. (in Chinese)

Hong, J. (1998). *The internationalization of television in China: The evolution of ideology, society, and media since the reform*. Westport, CT: Praeger.

Hu, T. (2004). Is journalism still a respected occupation? *Xin Wen Ji Zhe* [Journalist], *11*, 4–5. (In Chinese)

International Bribery for Media Coverage Index. (2003). *A composite index by country of variables related to the likelihood of the existence of "cash for news coverage."* (Commissioned by the Institute for Public Relations [USA], The International Public Relations Association [UK], and Sponsored by Hürriyet, a Member of Dogan Media Group [Turkey]).

Jiang, Z. (2004). Setting the news agenda: Journalists, corporations, and unidentified sources in auto news. *Xin Wen Yu Chuan Bo Yan Jiu* [Journalism and Communication], *1*, 50–55. (In Chinese)

Li, L. (2006). From unity to diversity: The restructuring and transformation in media industries in China. *Journalism Quarterly, 2*, 1–10.

Li, X., & Qin, X. (2001). Who set the agenda of today's China? Reconstructing news events of the party-organ newspapers in BBS. *Journal and Communication, 3,* 55–62.

Mao, Z. (1983). *Selected works on news work by Mao Zedong.* Beijing, PRC: Xinhua. (In Chinese)

McCombs, M. E. (2005). A look at agenda-setting: Past, present and future. *Journalism Studies, 6*(4), 543–557.

McCombs, M. E., Shaw, D. L., & Weaver, D. H. (1997). *Communication and democracy: Exploring the intellectual frontiers in agenda-setting.* Mahwah, NJ: Erlbaum.

Nie, Yi (2005). *Reflections on the agenda-setting research in China* (Unpublished master's thesis). School of Journalism and Communication, Wuhan University, PRC. (In Chinese)

Shoemaker, P. J., & Reese, S. D. (1996). *Mediating the message: Theories of influences on mass media content.* White Plains, NY: Longman.

Sriramesh, K., & D. Verčič (2003). *The global public relations handbook: Theory, research, and practice.* Mahwah, NJ: Erlbaum.

Takeshita, T. (1997). Exploring the media's roles in defining reality: From issue-agenda setting to attribute-agenda setting. In M. E. McCombs, D. L. Shaw, & D. H. Weaver (Eds.), *Communication and democracy: Exploring the intellectual frontiers in agenda-setting theory* (pp. 15–27). Mahwah, NJ: Erlbaum.

Tong, B. (2000). *Introduction to journalism theories.* Beijing, PRC: Renming University of China Press. (In Chinese)

World Economic Forum. (2006). Global Competitive Index. Geneva, Switzerland: Author.

Zhang, G., & Li, B. (2002a, June). *Chinese audience and the agenda setting role of mass media in China.* Paper presented at the 2nd China Communication Studies Forum, Shanghai, PRC. (In Chinese)

Zhang, G., & Li, B. (2002b). Public agenda: An empirical research on the relationship between the media agenda and the real world. *Modern Communication, 1.* (In Chinese)

Zhang, G., & Li, B. (2003). Research on the public agenda and the agenda-setting effects of the mass media in China. *Fudan Journal* [Social Science Journal], 1. (In Chinese)

Zhu L. (1984). Building up corporate reputation. *Fujian Luntan (She Ke Jiao Yu Ban),* 7, 59–60.

19 Corporate Reputation and the News Media in Egypt

Kevin L. Keenan

As a country whose entire economy was nationalized for much of the second half of the 20th century, and where many important industries remain under government control, the concept of corporate reputation is rather different in Egypt than in most of the developed world. Historic and cultural factors unique to the systems of commerce and communications in Egypt call for consideration of corporate reputation, and the influence of the mass media on establishing and maintaining reputations, from somewhat different perspectives than might be used in the West.

This chapter will examine particular aspects of the situation in Egypt relevant to corporate reputation and the relationships between organizations, the news media, and public relations activities that can impact corporate reputation. It provides a review of literature that has dealt with the topic directly or indirectly, offers points of reference for understanding Egyptian practices and outcomes, and presents ideas for conducting empirical research looking at media content and public opinion data.

Review of the Literature: Corporate Reputation

Without presenting a full history of Egypt, it is important in discussing the status of the public relations profession and notions of corporate reputation, to point out that modern corporate entities have really only existed in Egypt since the 1970s. Prior to that, and beginning with the Revolution of 1952 in which the government of Gamal Abdel Nasser seized the holdings of foreign corporations, Egypt was entirely nationalized, with all business and economic functions handled by the government (Vatikiotis, 1991). Thus, with no corporations, there was no such thing as corporate reputation.

Even after Nasser's death in 1970, and through the administrations of Egyptian presidents Anwar Sadat (1970–1981) and Hosni Mubarak (1981–present), emergence from the nationalist period and a mentality of government control and toward openness has been a struggle. While *free markets* and *privatization* have been popular buzzwords over the past 20 years of so, only very recently has much progress in that direction actually been made. Finally, though, in the first decade of the 21st century, there are indications that policies favorable to private business are taking hold and evidence of corporate success in certain fields (Omran,

2004). It would seem, then, that corporate reputation is something that Egyptian businesspeople and academics will give increased attention to in coming years.

Agenda-Setting Theory

The theory of media agenda setting, used by Carroll and McCombs (2003) to examine how news coverage may affect an organization's corporate image, is an area familiar to most communication scholars in Egypt, though it has not been applied to that topic. Instead, the limited agenda-setting work done there has used the traditional political issue framework for relating the amount of attention an object receives in the news media to its prominence on the public agenda. In all cases, the focus has been on what the literature would call first-level effects involving the placement of an issue or object on the agenda, rather than delving into second- and third-level effects looking at attributes of the object that are characteristic of much contemporary agenda-setting research elsewhere (Takeshita, 2006).

Egyptian agenda-setting studies include English-language theses showing both print (Ghabour, 1990) and broadcast (Goueli, 1993) media content affecting the importance audiences assign to an issue. Research in Arabic, the official language of Egypt, consists of a doctoral dissertation analyzing television news content and public opinion data to confirm the basic agenda-setting hypothesis for foreign news topics (Khalek, 2005) and separate dissertations that find agenda-setting effects on environmental (Eissa, 1999), children's (Dawaba, 2005), and gender issues (Rizk, 1999; Othman, 2002).

Business and the News Media

The relationship between business and the media, and the coverage of business topics by the media, has received limited attention from researchers in Egypt. One reason for this is likely the relative paucity of business news traditionally reported by the Egyptian media. With the recent introduction of satellite stations devoted to Arab business and financial news ("Satellite Station," 2003), this may change in the near future.

Among the few studies that have considered research questions in the realm of business and media in Egypt, Alfaiz (2002) used in-depth interviews with upper-level management personnel to investigate the importance of media reports on their decision-making processes. Findings showed CNN as an especially influential source of information for businesspeople and the single most important media outlet in the interviewees' own estimation.

Keenan and Shoreh (2000) conducted a content analysis of Egyptian news coverage of the advertising industry over the 20-year period from 1978 to 1997. They found that the media tended to present the advertising business in a negative light and to stress practices/attributes such as deception, advertising's harmful effects on children, and cultural inappropriateness. The authors raise the possibility of this coverage being causally related to Egyptian attitudes toward advertising and call for audience studies to provide data for evaluating agenda setting or other hypotheses linking media content and public perceptions about the advertising industry.

Hypotheses

Despite the scarcity of literature on corporate reputation in Egypt from which to build testable agenda-setting research hypotheses, there exists what might be thought of as a "universal" literature laying out propositions about how media can affect the way a company is viewed by its publics (Carroll & McCombs, 2003). There are also recent examples of primary research into these basic propositions (Kiousis, Popescu, & Mitrook, 2007; see also various chapters in the present book) that might serve as comparative benchmarks for considering how media coverage is related to corporate reputation in Egypt.

Accordingly, the following three hypotheses, adopted from Carroll and McCombs (2003), should be examined as programs of research are developed and interest in the topic grows. The first of these involves basic, first-level agenda setting, and proposes that media visibility is positively related to audience awareness of a company.

Hypothesis 1. The more news coverage a firm receives in Egyptian media, the higher it will rank in Egyptian public awareness. The second hypothesis addresses the notion of substantive attributes and second-level agenda setting. This involves the amount of media attention given to particular attributes or characteristics of an organization having an effect on how likely the audience is to think of the organization in terms of those attributes.

Hypothesis 2. The more Egyptian news coverage stresses a given attribute of a firm, the more likely the Egyptian public is to define the firm by that attribute. Beyond the amount of attention given to an attribute, the third hypothesis considers whether it is reported on in positive or negative terms. Getting at the idea of third-level agenda setting and evaluative attributes, this hypothesis holds that positive media attention to an attribute will result in positive audience perceptions of the attribute and that negative attention will lead to negative perceptions.

Hypothesis 3. The more positive or negative the news coverage of an attribute of a firm in the Egyptian media, the more positive or negative the Egyptian public is likely to consider that attribute.

Case Study: Corporate Reputation in Egypt

While little has been written specifically on corporate reputation in Egypt, and scholarly research on the topic is completely lacking, there should be substantial interest as local, regional, and multinational firms establish a presence in what was until recently a government-controlled economy. On most levels, these firms are starting from scratch in trying to build corporate reputations in Egypt.

Certain Egyptian companies, associated with successful brands, might be thought to have made progress toward favorable reputations on the basis of their popularity. In a consumer survey conducted in 19 Middle Eastern countries ("The Top," 2006), brand rankings were constructed based on responses to questions about brand familiarity, relevance, trust, and recommendation. No Egyptian brands were in the top 30, but four ranked between 33 and 40, including the Melody television channels, a privately held group of music video stations; Fayrouz soft drinks, recently acquired by Heineken International after several years as part of the Egyptian firm Al-Ahram Beverages, and until 1997 a government owned enterprise; Two Apples "shisha" tobacco, produced by the Egyptian company Al Nakhla Tobacco, and Orascom Construction, one of the largest construction companies in the Middle East.

Considering brand and corporate reputation from a regional perspective, looking at the Arab Middle East as a whole instead of, or in addition to considering Egypt alone, may make some sense. As Zahrana (1995) has pointed out, Arab nations have more in common with each other than they do with Western cultures. Vujnovic and Kruckeberg (2005) have made a similar point and suggest that wholly different strategies and forms of communication are called for in Arab countries.

Though not designed to address questions of corporate reputation, and in fact never using the term, two Egyptian studies may have implications for investigating the phenomenon there. In a field experiment dealing with "country-of-origin" effects of advertising copy, Al-Kadi and Keenan (2004) found that the association of a brand or product with the United States had positive implications for perceived quality, but negative ones for purchase intention and overall attitude toward the brand among Egyptian consumers. Survey research by Mobarak (2004), looking at Egyptian attitudes about Al Hurra, the U.S. government's Arabic language television network, showed that respondents who know of the network's U.S. government ties had more negative feelings toward it than those who did not. To relate the findings of these studies in the language of agenda-setting research and corporate reputation, it might be posited that the reporting of the country a corporation is based in or identified with is the kind of substantive attribute that second-level agenda setting is based on, and that at least in the case of U.S. corporations in recent years, that it can be something of an unfavorable evaluative attribute which could lead to third-level agenda-setting effects in Egypt.

Media Systems

Sriramesh and Verčič (2009) stress the important interplay between public relations and the mass media and the need for rethinking the traditional media systems approach to studying media environments, given changes in world conditions over the 50 years since it was first stated by Siebert, Peterson, and Schramm (1956). They have proposed a framework consisting of three key factors for evaluating a country's mass media. Those are media control, media outreach, and media access.

By media control, Sriramesh and Vercic are referring to whether the news media in a country are owned directly or indirectly by the government, or if they are part of the private sector. In Egypt, the trend toward privatization in certain industries has not really included the media, which have been state-owned or state controlled since the time of Nasser (Keenan, 2009). Recent years have seen some loosening of government authority, with a few small advertiser supported media outlets being permitted. But strict government censorship and indirect government controls that include licensing procedures, managing the supply of printing materials, and a government owned distribution system prevent any Egyptian media from being truly independent. The major print and broadcast media all remain government owned.

Beyond the borders and absolute control of the government, new media such as the Internet and satellite television are penetrating the Egyptian market and offer opportunities to reach certain publics there with messages and methods not available through traditional media. As a whole, though, the media system in Egypt remains an example of what Rugh (2004) has labeled the "mobilization" model of control, in which the government oversees all aspects of the media, from news gathering and staffing through production, distribution, advertising, and enforcement of rigid censorship procedures.

The concept of media outreach (Sriramesh & Verčič, 2009) deals with how wide an audience is exposed to a country's media. In Egypt, problems of illiteracy, poverty, and isolation restrict the reach of certain media. While the major newspapers are available throughout the country, the fact that barely half the population is literate severely reduces the likely audience for messages placed there (Keenan, 2009). Outside of the major population centers of Cairo and Alexandria, many Egyptians are only able to afford the most basic electronic media, diminishing the effectiveness of satellite television, Internet communication, and other new media options. The dispersion of the population in remote areas beyond the Nile Valley makes media outreach inefficient and problematic for some purposes that public relations practitioners should recognize.

Media access involves factors permitting or restricting access to the media by organizations and other groups. Accessibility is a serious matter in Egypt, with practices and problems not common in most other countries. As discussed earlier, the Egyptian media are government controlled. With such an arrangement there are obvious access issues, where those affiliated with or favored by the government have special advantages in gaining access to or favorable positions within the media (Keenan, 2009).

Perhaps even more troubling than the issue of government control, and beyond the usual system of media gatekeepers, it is common in Egypt for the media to demand payment or require the purchase of advertising for those seeking media access through news releases or other means. In a study measuring what they call the "cash for news coverage" phenomenon, Kruckeberg and Tsetsura (2003) found that Egypt was among the very worst countries in terms of conditions leading to media seeking compensation for allowing access, ranking 61 out of the 66 evaluated. Their findings are consistent with the general atmosphere of corruption in Egypt and the conclusions reached by others about the lack of business ethics in the country and the region (Izraeli, 1997).

Given these points about media control, media outreach, and media access, businesses seeking to make use of the Egyptian media for purposes of corporate reputation should recognize the special circumstances they face. As the three research hypotheses suggested earlier indicate, there are reasons to feel that the media can influence corporate reputation in Egypt, but idiosyncrasies of the Egyptian media system must be taken into account in considering exactly how the process might work.

News Values

Just as the ownership, audience, and accessibility of Egyptian media are somewhat unique, so are their seeming news values. Not entirely surprisingly, given the level of government control, but still quite extreme, is the dominance of news dealing with the executive branch of Egypt's government. Front page headlines of the major newspapers and lead television news stories consistently report on the daily activities of the President or of his wife, a format which Berenger (2006) has called protocol news.

Egyptian media also share certain values with the media of other Arab countries. Among these is the tendency to underreport or leave out information that would be included in news stories in other parts of the world. As one Middle Eastern journalist/editor phrases it, "Ours is a system of denial. We commit sins of omission, not commission" (Khazen, 1999, p. 87).

Organizational Newsworthiness

Where business news is concerned, no research has looked at the specifics of who or what gets covered in Egypt. It is likely that some of the points raised by Khazen (1999) in his essay on Arab news values in general apply to news about business organizations in particular. These might include the practice of underreporting, as cited above, and the equating of news with scandal, which Khazen also says is a feature of the Arab press. If the circumstance of news coverage being synonymous with scandal holds in Egypt, newsworthiness may not be an altogether desirable thing for corporations.

Larter (2006) has claimed that Egyptian CEOs have historically avoided media attention. Listing case histories of businesspeople burned by the media, he explains that common thinking has usually been that keeping a low profile is the best strategy for minimizing negative media coverage. A senior consultant for Hill & Knowlton Egypt, Larter goes on to suggest that especially in a country like Egypt, where morals and values are given special importance, it might make better sense for business leaders to seek out the media and to actually solicit coverage.

Public Relations

While the term *public relations* is familiar to most Egyptians, and many organizational structures include a department or section with the title of "public relations," the meanings and functions assigned to PR are generally more limited in Egypt than in more developed countries. Since the first efforts at privatizing the economy in the late 20th century, *public relations* has been a popular buzzword among businesses and advocates of reduced government control. The fact is, though, that much of what has passed as public relations might more accurately be considered marketing support or customer relations (Keenan, 2009).

As is true in other parts of the Arab world, the Egyptian conception of public relations emphasizes external over internal publics, tends not to value research or two-way approaches to communication strategy, considers public relations subservient to sales, and lacks both qualified practitioners and understanding management (Kirat, 2005).

With some exceptions, Egyptian public relations professionals accept these conditions and practices such as the payment to media for publicity opportunities and placements. There is also a lack of respect for public relations among most Egyptian reporters and editors. Even with their own situations being heavily restricted by government control of the media, journalists generally have little use for their public relations brethren, complaining that they are rarely authorized to provide the kind of information reporters want (Lussier, 2002), and that Egyptian PR practitioners lack even basic news release writing skills (Bakr, 2006).

Given such a background, the public relations industry in Egypt might seem to have little to offer organizations seeking corporate reputation assistance. Certainly those interested in building positive reputations should be aware of these factors involving Egyptian public relations. There may be reason to think certain things are changing, though, and more sophisticated public relations approaches may be developing.

If privatization continues and as more multinational companies are attracted to Egypt, it is likely that the public relations industry will have to adapt or be replaced by more modern thinking and practices. The International Public Relations Association held their annual conference in Egypt in both 2002 and 2006, and it should be hoped that almost by osmosis, the presence of industry leaders and experts has an influence on their local counterparts. There is also an increased presence of international public relations firms in Cairo, with Brodeur Worldwide, Fortune Promoseven, Hill & Knowlton, and Weber Shandwick all setting up offices in recent years and both local and multinational advertising agencies taking on more involved public relations assignments.

The public relations industry, then, is not likely to be a major hindrance, nor a particularly effective facilitator of media effects on corporate reputation in Egypt. The hypotheses listed earlier and the research proposed for addressing the topic do not deal with public relations practices as central variables, though it is useful and even essential to recognize the role of the profession in preparing and implementing the kind of information and tools from which media coverage is likely to result. That is, it is important to consider both media agenda building and agenda setting as processes that may affect corporate reputation.

In Conclusion

The concept of corporate reputation and the role of the mass media in establishing and influencing how a corporation is perceived are clearly areas calling for study in Egypt. Building from the propositions and research models of Carroll and McCombs (2003), and taking into account circumstances and characteristics unique to Egypt, an understanding of the topic should benefit existent organizations and those just entering the country as the transition to a more private economy continues. Scholars from the fields of communication, management, and other areas are likely to have interests in and contributions to offer investigations of corporate reputation and the news media in Egypt through detailed content analyses, public opinion polling, theory building, and consultation with business and public relations professionals. To supplement findings such as those described in other chapters of this volume, research in Egypt can add to a broader, global knowledge of the subject.

References

Al-Kadi, T., & Keenan, K. (2004). *Country of origin considerations for advertising in the Middle East: An examination of consumer ethnocentrism, animosity, and pan-Arabism effects.* Paper presented to International Management Development Association Conference, Maastricht, Netherlands.

Alfaiz, J. (2002). *The effect of CNN on media and business decision-makers in Egypt.* (Unpublished master's thesis). The American University in Cairo, Egypt.

Bakr, A. (2006, January). PR industry growing, but still learning. *Business Monthly: The Journal of the American Chamber of Commerce in Egypt, 22*, 23.

Berenger, R. (2006). Media in the Middle East and North Africa. In T. McPhail (Ed.), *Global communication theories, stakeholders, and trends* (pp. 192–225). Malden, MA: Blackwell.

Carroll, C. E., & McCombs, M. (2003). Agenda-setting effects of business news on the public's images and opinions about major corporations. *Corporate Reputation Review, 6*(1), 36–46.

Dawaba, I. E. (2005). *The role of television talk shows and awareness advertisements in setting public agendas towards children's issues* (Unpublished doctoral dissertation). Cairo University, Egypt. (in Arabic)

Eissa, R. (1999). *Egyptian journalism and agenda-setting of environmental issues* (Unpublished doctoral dissertation). Cairo University, Egypt. (in Arabic)

Ghabour, A. (1990). *The agenda-setting function of Egyptian newspapers* (Unpublished master's thesis). The American University in Cairo, Egypt.

Goueli, S. A. (1993). *Agenda-setting and local issues on Egyptian regional television broadcasting* (Unpublished master's thesis). The American University in Cairo, Egypt.

Izraeli, D. (1997). Business ethics in the Middle East. *Journal of Business Ethics, 16*, 1555–1560.

Keenan, K. L. (2009). Public relations in Egypt: Practices, obstacles, and potentials. In K. Sriramesh & D. Verčič (Eds.), *The global public relations handbook: Theory, research, and practice* (pp. 362–380). New York: Routledge.

Keenan, K. L., & Shoreh, B. (2000). How advertising is covered in the Egyptian press: A longitudinal examination of content. *International Journal of Advertising, 19*(2), 245–257.

Khalek, S. M. A. (2005). *Foreign news agendas of television news programs and their effects on public agendas* (Unpublished doctoral dissertation). Cairo University, Egypt. (in Arabic)

Khazen, J. (1999). Censorship and state control of the press in the Arab world. *Harvard International Journal of Press Politics, 4*(3), 87–92.

Kiousis, S., Popescu, C., & Mitrook, M. (2007). Understanding influence on corporate reputation: An examination of public relations efforts, media coverage, public opinion, and financial performance from an agenda-building and agenda-setting perspective. *Journal of Public Relations Research, 19*(2), 147–165.

Kirat, M. (2005). Public relations practice in the Arab world: A critical assessment. *Public Relations Review, 31*(3), 323–332.

Kruckeberg, D., & Tsetsura, K. (2003). *A composite index by country of variables related to the likelihood of the existence of "cash for news coverage."* Gainesville, FL: Institute for Public Relations/International Public Relations Association.

Larter, C. (2006, June). Stepping into the spotlight. *Business Monthly: The Journal of the American Chamber of Commerce in Egypt, 22,* 66.

Lussier, A. M. (2002, August). The wages of spin. *Business Monthly: The Journal of the American Chamber of Commerce in Egypt, 18,* 38–45.

Mobarak, R. A. (2004). International broadcasting to the Middle East: A case study of Al Hurra network. *Global Media Journal, 3*(5), article number 16. Retrieved from http://lass.calumet.purdue.edu/cca/gmj/fa04/graduatefa04/gmj-fa04grad-mobarak.htm

Omran, M. (2004). Performance consequences of privatizing Egyptian state-owned enterprises: The effect of post-privatization ownership structure on firm performance. *Multinational Finance Journal, 8*(1&2), 73–114.

Othman, S. M. (2002). *The Nile news channel and agenda-setting among women viewers* (Unpublished doctoral dissertation). Cairo University, Egypt. (in Arabic)

Rizk, A. S. (1999). *Female journalists as agenda-setters for Egyptian women on women's issues* (Unpublished doctoral dissertation). Cairo University, Egypt. (in Arabic)

Rugh, W. A. (2004). *Arab mass media: Newspapers, radio, and television in Arab politics.* Westport, CT: Praeger.

Satellite station to state dearth of Arabic business news. (2003, August). *Business Monthly: The Journal of the American Chamber of Commerce in Egypt, 19,* 15.

Siebert, F. S., Peterson, T., & Schramm, W. (1956). *Four theories of the press.* Urbana: University of Illinois Press.

Sriramesh, K., & Verčič, D. (2009). A theoretical framework for global public relations research and practice. In K. Sriramesh & D. Verčič (Eds.), *The global public relations handbook: Theory, research, and practice* (pp. 1–19). New York: Routledge.

Takeshita, T. (2006). Current critical problems in agenda-setting research. *International Journal of Public Opinion Research, 18*(3), 275–296.

The top 40 Arab brands. (2006, October 18). *Forbes.* Retrieved from http://www.forbes.com/2006/10/17/top-arab-brands-biz_cz_fas_1018toparabbrands.html

Vatikiotis, P. J. (1991). *The history of modern Egypt: From Mohamed Ali to Mubarak.* London: Weidenfeld & Nicolson.

Vujnovic, M., & Kruckeberg, D. (2005). Imperative for an Arab model of public relations as a framework for diplomatic, corporate and nongovernmental organization relationships. *Public Relations Review, 31*(3), 338–343.

Zaharna, R. S. (1995). Understanding cultural preferences of Arab communication patterns. *Public Relations Review, 21*(3), 241–255.

20 Corporate Reputation and the News Media in Russia

Katja Koikkalainen

This chapter examines how the news media in Russia are linked with the public's perceptions of companies. The focus is on how corporations are presented in the news media, and these results of content analysis are compared with surveys and polls of corporate reputation and listings of corporations' economic performance. During 2006 and 2007, Russia was among the countries with the highest economic growth rate (Sutela, 2009), but in 2008 it was hit by a financial crisis; however, despite the crisis, in 2008 the real GDP growth rate was still 5.6% (World Economic Forum, 2009).

In a report by the World Economic Forum, Russia was rated 109th in the enabling trade index and 96th as a business environment in 2009. The report analyzes institutions, policies, and services enabling trade and sees need for improvement for Russia in all the categories. The main area of concern is the restricted access to markets (World Economic Forum, 2009).

The Russian state has increased its ownership in big business during the last few years but it has not involved itself with small- and medium-sized companies (Liuhto & Vahtra, 2009, p. 2). The private sector formed some 65% of GDP in mid-2008 (European Bank for Reconstruction and Development [EBRD], 2008). Of all the companies registered, most are small scale and big business has a dominant role. The revenues of the leading 100 enterprises produced almost 60% of Russia's GDP in 2007 (Liuhto & Vahtra, 2009, pp. 2–3). A large part of privately owned business is under the ownership of major financial–industrial groups: five leading groups control more than half of the total turnover of the top 100 companies. These groups are Alfa Group (oil and gas, banking, insurance, media etc.); Basic Element (energy, manufacturing, financial services, etc.); Interros (metals, banking, media, etc.); Sistema (service-based and high-tech industries, telecommunications); and Severstal Group (steel, mining, machinery). The concentration rate has been high during the last few years, and the financial crisis has meant more ownership consolidation: private assets have been transferred to fewer hands and the state has intensified its ownership of industrial assets (Liuhto & Vahtra, 2009).

The oil and gas sector continues to drive the Russian economy, and steel and mining is the second largest sector. Twelve of the 100 largest companies are in the oil and gas industry, and these are responsible for almost 40% of the aggregate turnover of the top 100 companies. The largest companies in the oil and gas sector are Gazprom, Lukoil, and Rosneft, of which Gazprom and Rosneft are majority state owned and Lukoil is privately owned. The metal sector is largely in private ownership (including, for example, the three leading companies, Norilsk Nickel, Severstal, and RusAl) (Liuhto & Vahtra, 2009, pp. 5–8; see also RA Expert, 2008).

Large companies have received good corporate reputation ratings. In the list of the world's most reputable companies, the largest Russian bank, Sberbank, was the leading Russian company in 2007 and 2009, while in 2008 it was the Lukoil oil company, and in 2006 the Magnitogorsk Iron & Steel Works took this position (Reputation Institute, 2009). In a rating published by Interbrand Zintzmeyer & Lux AG together with *Business Week Rossiya*, the highest rated Russian brands in 2007 were Beeline (telecom operator), MTS (telecom operator), Baltika (beer company), Lukoil and Rosneft (RBC, 2007).

Corporate Reputation in Russia

Corporate reputation has been relatively widely discussed in the Russian media and at various seminars and conferences over the last few years, and in addition to books translated from English there are some Russian textbooks on the topic (e.g., Buksha, 2007). Company owners, scholars, and analysts are increasingly asking whether a good reputation affects corporate financial results (Tsvetkova, 2007). In times of financial crisis, companies seek ways to make the best of reduced PR budgets without detracting from their reputation (Bezgodova, 2009). There seem to be comparatively few English-language publications on reputation of Russian coporations. However, there is a study that suggests that in Russia, domestic media have little power when it comes to pressuring companies that are misbehaving, while foreign media can have an impact (Dyck, Volchkova, & Zingales, 2008). According to Dyck et al. this is mainly due to the lack of credible domestic media outlets and unsophisticated public opinion.

Use of Agenda-Setting Theory in Russia

Agenda-setting theory seems not to be a widely researched area in Russia. Some Russian textbooks review agenda-setting theory on the basis of Anglo-American literature (Dyakova & Trakhtenberg, 1999). However, even though the term *agenda setting* is not widely used, studies on the theme have been published under different headings in different disciplines; a Russian term, *povestka dnya*, is sometimes used in media studies (see, e.g., Yasaveyev, 2009 and published proceedings of a conference, *Zhurnalistika v 2008 godu*, 2009) and political studies (Lebedeva, 2007). The Russian term can refer to many kinds of analyses of media content and studies of the role of media in society. Also the term *role of media* is used in this context. The political impact of the media has been a central topic for media scholars. There are several studies, for example, on the role of the media in electoral campaigns, and some of this research has been published in English (e.g., Goldfain, 2000; Koltsova, 2006; Oates, 2006; Raskin, 2002; White & McAllister, 2006).

When it comes to corporate reputation, media visibility and top-of-mind awareness has been studied mainly in media and marketing research, including studies on PR. On the Russian Internet, the most often mentioned brands are media brands like news agencies RIA novosti, Regnum, Itar-Tass, and Interfaks and other media outlets like RBC, *Vedomosti, Izvestiya,* and NTV. Half of the top 20 brands were from the media sector in 2008; other companies in the top 20 include Gazprom (gas company), Windows (ICT), Microsoft (ICT), VTB (bank), Intel (ICT), MTS (telecom), Google (ICT), Finam (finances), Apple (ICT), and Lukoil (oil company) ("Top 100 samykh upominayemykh brendov runeta," 2009). One way to look at the visibility of companies is to review the advertising. The leading advertisers in the first quarter of 2008 on Russian television and in the print media were international companies that make cars or other consumer products: Mercury, Volkswagen, Ford Motor Co., Procter & Gamble, Unilever, L'Oreal, Mars-Russia, Colgate-Palmolive, Danone ("Rynok menyayetsya—lidery ostayutsya," 2008).

In media studies, one of the recent studies on the impact of positive media coverage on the image of corporations included a study of the role of media in the formation of the image of banks (Firsova, 2009). In her study, Firsova (2009) found that in most of the analyzed quality newspapers and magazines the image of banks was negative or cautious, and the mass publications mention the banking sector less extensively than do business publications. In this context, it is worth noticing that trust in banks is low in Russia. According to a poll by the Russian public opinion research center VCIOM, only one in four Russians has got savings in a bank and over half of them are afraid of losing their savings (VCIOM, 2008).

Case Study: Corporate Reputation Landscape in Russia

Public opinion polls on corporate reputation in Russia have been published over the past few years. For example, in 2007 the most reputable industrial companies were national telecom operator Rostelekom, aircraft manufacturer Sukhoy, and refrigerator manufacturer Indesit. In the category of service and consumer oriented companies, the winners were mobile operator MTS, airline Aeroflot, and mobile operator Vimpelcom. Of the companies that are operating in raw materials and the steel industry, gas company Gazprom, oil company Lukoil, and steel company Severstal were the most reputable; in the banking and financing sector, Vneshtorgbank, Sberbank, and Alfa were the leaders (VCIOM, 2007). In 2008, amongst banks Sberbank was regarded as having the best reputation (ROMIR, 2009).

In the Russian media, issues of corporate reputation are handled mainly in business publications and specialized publications on marketing and PR. The number of stories on this topic has risen steadily during the last few years.

Ekspert, a weekly business magazine, has published ratings of corporate reputation at least five times; the latest one available on the Internet is from 2003 (Shmarov & Polunin, 2003). When it comes to corporate reputation in Russian regions, some studies have been published by *Ekspert* as well (e.g., Ekspert-Ural, 2005).

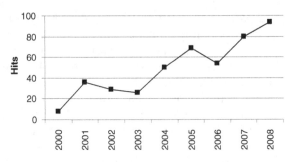

Figure 20.1 The term "corporate reputation" in Russian mass media. Publications including the term "corporate reputation" (korporativnaya reputatsiya) in Russian mass media. *Source:* Integrum database (includes a large variety of sources: most of the central and regional printed publications, news agencies, TV and radio monitoring, and internet media).

Media System

The Russian media underwent an enormous transformation after the collapse of the Soviet Union. The centralized media structure changed to a regionalized and localized model with only television remaining as a national medium, replacing the central position of national newspapers (Pietiläinen, 2009). However, an understanding of the overall media is complicated by the mixture of old and new with quite dissimilar media performance and practices on the national and regional levels and in different media sectors (Vartanova, 2009, p. 286). The Russian media model could be described as a combination of politically or state-controlled and market-driven mass media (Becker, 2004; Pietiläinen, 2009; Vartanova, 2009). The state has a strong position, especially in television.

The political situation in the country significantly influences the media industry. Vartanova and Smirnov (2009) note that "competition in the political arena determines the order for the mass media services, especially during the preelection period" (p. 118). This means for one thing that there is investment in the media from big nonmedia investors. Because the media business is young, it faces many problems that include limited transparency, close connections between media and other economic sectors, the weakness of the technical infrastructure, shortage of high-quality content, and insufficient professional staff (Vartanova & Smirnov, 2009, p. 119). However, the wants and needs of advertisers and audiences are increasingly shaping the structure of the media market which may minimize the traditional impact of politics (Vartanova, 2009, p. 283). In spite of their shortcomings, the trust in media is good. According to a monthly nationwide poll by Russian public opinion research center VCIOM, 51% of Russians in the summer of 2009 fully approved of the functioning of the media while 29% disapproved (VCIOM, 2009). In the poll, trust in the army was slightly higher than trust in the media while law enforcement agencies, political parties, and the judicial system were less trusted than the media.

During the years of rapid economic growth in the early 2000s, advertising contributed to the expansion of the media market and diversification of media products. Advertising revenues have made media less dependent on state structures and regional authoritarian regimes and in this way reduced political influence on the media. Nonetheless, the qualitative diversity of media is decreasing since competition promotes commercially profitable content and formats (Vartanova, 2009, pp. 295–296). The financial crisis that began in 2008 has had consequences also in the media industry. The availability of credit has decreased, advertising income has declined, the volume of printed products has shrunk, consumer sales are down, and media companies are optimizing their development strategies and financial and personnel policies (FAMPK, 2009, p. 7).

In the dynamically developing print media market, a large number of new newspapers and magazines appear annually, published by both Russian and foreign investors. The trend is toward consolidation of publishing houses or media holdings. There are almost 60,000 registered media outlets in the country but not all of them are really functional. So, the supply of printed media is diverse while the average audiences are relatively small. The average reader spends 18 minutes a day on reading newspapers and magazines, and about 21% of Russians say that they do not read newspapers at all (Vartanova & Smirnov, 2009).

Television is the largest and most developed segment of the media industry. There are approximately 200 national and regional television channels and 500 cable television operators. Despite the variety of channels, two state channels (Pervyy kanal and Rossiya) attract almost half the television audience and half of the advertising budgets. This is mainly due to their accessibility: between 95 and 99% of people have access to them. Also the regional television market is growing. The change to a digital format is planned for 2017 (Vartanova & Smirnov, 2009).

When it comes to media consumption, the increase of Internet penetration has changed media usage. Today, one Russian in five is using the Internet (Vartanova & Smirnov, 2009, p. 118). Especially in large cities, where the Internet is most widely available, and among young people it has challenged and even become a substitute for the print media because of the collapse of the newspaper distribution system and the public's distrust of the political dailies (Vartanova, 2009, p. 296).

Despite the preceding description, there is a wide selection of Russian news media, although not all of it is accessible to all. This affects also the degree to which the news media may affect organizations' top-of-mind awareness and image. According to an all-Russian survey, the most important source for both regional and national economics news is television, followed by the print media, which is a more important news source on regional economics issues than on national economics ("Social distinctions in contemporary Russia," 2007).

News Values

Several studies show that Russian media practices have become Westernized over the last several decades, and the change has been faster and more extensive in the nonpolitical media (Pietiläinen, 2009). The arrival of foreign formats and practices has been most visible in entertainment television, radio programming, magazines, and the business press (Koikkalainen, 2009a; Pietiläinen, 2009; Rulyova, 2009).

The change in journalism includes the introduction of the professional news format of the inverted pyramid. However, its generalization has not been as rapid in Russia as in, for example, Estonia (Pietiläinen, 2009). The contemporary media field also reveals the existence of traditional Russian features like "replacement of information with opinions, self-censorship and the large role of the state in the public space" (Vartanova, 2009, p. 297). Russian journalists still value the old traditions of presenting ideas clearly to their audience and believe their function is to help develop the public's intellectual and cultural interests (Pasti & Pietiläinen, 2008, pp. 120–121). At the same time, rapid responses to current news and sound facts are of central importance to them (Pasti, 2009). Russian journalists who write for the leading business publications seem to appreciate fact-based news journalism that discusses all the relevant aspects of an event. They also emphasize the higher levels of professionalism in business journalism, compared with other Russian media (Koikkalainen, 2009b).

Public Relations

The use of the concept of public relations is relatively new in Russia. However, the field has developed rapidly after the collapse of Soviet Union in 1991 and today the public relations industry is an important sector. The practice of marketing, advertising, and public relations has been strongly influenced by Western practitioners (McElreath, Chen, Azarova, & Shadrova, 2001, p. 668).

There is little difference between journalists' and PR practitioners' education; for example, at the Moscow State University both disciplines are taught in the journalism faculty. The proximity to journalism is evident also in Russian public relations theory. A business-type orientation predominant in business and technical universities is also favored. Since education programs started earlier in Moscow and St. Petersburg and in the European metaregion than in other parts of Russia, the public relations profession has developed at a different rate in different places (Tsetsura, 2003).

According to Tsetsura (2003, p. 306), many Russian advertising agencies offer public relations services and only a few agencies exclusively practice public relations, and those that do mainly work in political public relations. In Russian companies, especially at the regional level, public relations is often focused on a positive publicity model rather than on strategic public relations because the managers or stakeholders have no clear understanding of the nature of public relations. This means that there is a focus on the technical side of PR like organizing events and writing press releases. One reason behind this practice is the lack of economic development that limits financial resources (Tsetsura, 2003, p. 309).

There is discussion among Russian practitioners and scholars about "white PR" and "black PR." The divide is based on ethical reasoning: black PR is associated with manipulative technologies (used especially during electoral campaigns) while white PR refers to the Western kind of ethical practices. This discussion reflects the underdeveloped state of ethical regulation and self-regulation (Tsetsura, 2003, p. 306). Another widespread practice in Russia is *zakazukha*, hidden advertisement that is favorable to an organization and written by a journalist for a fee. This practice is forbidden by law but remains in use because of poor law enforcement (Tsetsura, 2003, p. 311).

Research Methodology

Content Analysis

The main aim of the content analysis in this study is to examine the impact of media visibility on organizational prominence and top-of-mind awareness in Russia. The impact of media favorability on the public's organizational images is examined comparing the results of the content analysis with secondary survey data and listings.

The content analysis gives information on companies, mentioned on the front pages of two leading Russian business papers. The front pages were chosen for the analysis because of their function as a window to the newspaper content (Barnhurst & Nerone, 2001, p. 190). In this study, the main interest lies in the area of operation of the most visible companies, their origin (Russian vs. international), and company size (large vs. small companies). The data were collected in the context of a wider research setting of the changes in outlook and content of the leading Russian business newspapers *Kommersant* and *Vedomosti* (reported in Koikkalainen, 2009b).

In the sample, one week from every year from the year 1990 is included in the study, altogether 134 front pages (94 from *Kommersant* in 1990–2007, 40 from *Vedomosti* in 2000–2007). The sample week is week 13, and the material was mostly collected in the Russian state library and the newspaper archive at the faculty of journalism, Moscow State University.

For the quantitative content analysis, a coding scheme was applied from which data on actors were used for this study. Data on up to the three first mentioned actors[1] in every first page unit (story, news item, or other block, including text or picture) was collected, including the following information: the name of the actor, the actor's identifying group (politics, administration, business, culture, etc.), the type of actor (person; group; named/anonymous representative of an institution/corporation; or an institution/corporation), and gender. For this study, the data were used to find the percentage of actors from the business sector. The next step was to identify the number of corporations that were operating in different sectors of the economy, and to discover the companies that were most often mentioned.

Choice of News Media and Their Place in the Russian Media System

In Russia, the business press was "reestablished" after the collapse of the Soviet Union. During the 1990s and in the early 2000s numerous launches have occurred in this field because the rising health of the economy has contributed to the growing demand for economics and business information (Koikkalainen, 2007).

The analysis focuses on two quality general financial and business dailies. Of these, *Kommersant* ("Businessman") was founded in 1989, and *Vedomosti*

("Gazette") in 1999. *Kommersant* today resembles a general quality newspaper more than a specialized financial daily, but it was the first financially oriented newspaper in the new Russia, and in many ways it led the way for other business publications, which makes it still today an important publication for the business community. The print run of *Kommersant* has been between 100,000 and 130,000 in recent years. The founding father of the paper was journalist Vladimir Yakovlev, who sold the publication to oligarch Boris Berezovsky in 1999. From Berezovsky, ownership of the publishing house Kommersant passed to Badri Patarkatsishvili and then to Alisher Usmanov in 2006 (Koikkalainen, 2009b).

Vedomosti has also gained a stable position and is regarded with respect in the financial newspaper market. The print run of *Vedomosti* has grown steadily and was 73,000 in 2008. *Vedomosti* was founded by a foreign-owned publishing house, Independent Media, together with the *Financial Times* and the *Wall Street Journal*. So, it represents a more straightforward borrowing of an international model of a financial daily. In 2005, Independent Media was sold to Sanoma Magazines, which is owned by the Finnish Sanoma Corporation (Koikkalainen, 2009b).

According to a survey by the Russian association of managers (AMR, 2004), *Kommersant* and *Vedomosti* are the most popular business papers[2] in the country, followed by *Izvestiya, Gazeta,* and *Rossiyskaya gazeta*. Respondents wanted their reading to be trustworthy, informative, impartial, and topical. At the same time, the readers valued *Kommersant*'s style, which was to express an opinion while at the same time presenting objective reports. *Kommersant* and *Vedomosti* have been described as the most influential newspapers in Russia according to the citing frequency in other media outlets and other barometers ("Reyting vliyatel'nosti rossiyskikh SMI," 2008; "Samye tsitiruyemye izdaniya," 2008; "Samye vliyatel'nye SMI 2008 goda dlya rossiyskogo biznesa," 2008).

Kommersant and *Vedomosti* are at the top of the Russian business daily press. Other central publications include quality weekly and monthly magazines like *Den'gi* ("Money"), *Ekspert* ("Expert"), *Forbes,* and *Profil* ("Profile"). Also a weekly newspaper *Ekonomika i zhizn* ("Economics and Life") from Soviet times is still published after reorientation. In the Russian regions, a variety of business publications, mainly weeklies, has emerged. Among the best known publications outside Moscow is a St. Petersburg daily *Delovoy Peterburg* (St. Petersburg Business). In addition to the print media, there are Internet services, news agencies, and TV and radio channels and programs devoted to economics and business news (Koikkalainen, 2009b).

Even if there is a great variety of business publications, the market is scattered and readership numbers remain comparatively low. For example, *Kommersant* has got approximately the same circulation in a country with over 140 million inhabitants as the Swedish business daily *Dagens Industri* in a country with 9 million people. Possible explanations can be found in audience profiles: In Russia, readers are mainly managers and specialists with higher than average income while in the Nordic countries the audience is more heterogeneous and includes, for example, small investors (Koikkalainen, 2007). Other reasons for comparatively low circulation in Russia could include a poor delivery system and the different needs of audiences in different locations.

Data Analysis

In the data analysis, 2,532 units from the *Kommersant* and *Vedomosti* front pages were classified and from these 4,116 actors were identified. The reliability of the data collection was verified using recoding for a part of the sample (Koikkalainen, 2009b, p. 130). Among the three most visible actors in front page stories those from the business sector amount to on average 25% in *Kommersant* and 52% in *Vedomosti*.

In the following, the outcome is discussed using time periods that were defined according to trend changes in the content of the newspapers. The periods are the years 1990 to 1992, 1993 to 1996, 2000 to 2003, and 2004 to 2007. During the first period, *Kommersant* was informative on politics and economics. The next period, years 1993 to 1996 has an emphasis on financial news. During the years 1997 to 1999, *Kommersant* shifted its content toward general news; it leaned more toward political news than in earlier years. Years 2000 to 2003 presented a period when both *Kommersant* and *Vedomosti* gave more attention to international news and consumer business. During the years 2004 to 2007 both papers kept this line, and *Vedomosti* emphasized corporate business even more than it

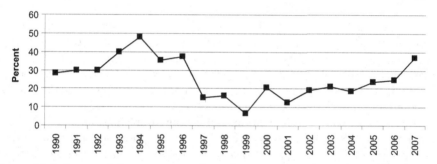

Figure 20.2 Amount of corporate and market actors in *Kommersant* front pages, percentage

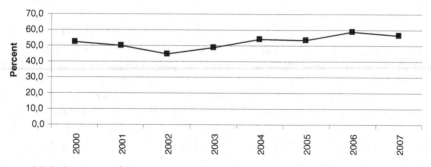

Figure 20.3 Amount of corporate and market actors in *Vedomosti* front pages, percentage

had done in earlier periods. Also in *Kommersant*, the amount of corporate issues discussed on the front pages increased (Koikkalainen, 2009b).

Results

Hypothesis 1. Media Visibility

According to the content analysis, the institutional and corporate actors together with actors with a political background prevailed in *Kommersant*'s front pages in the early 1990s. Then, the grip of corporations and market actors strengthened for some years and diminished again toward the end of the 1990s. In the early 2000s, actors from corporations were again on the rise in *Kommersant*. In *Vedomosti*, in its turn, the representatives of corporations and other market-oriented actors prevailed from the beginning, and were among the three most visible actors in front page stories. Banking and energy issues have been at the center of attention during the whole sample period in both publications. The number of different companies that were mentioned in the front pages, has risen toward the end of the research period, and, in this way, made the news landscape more diverse.

During the years 1990 to 1992, *Kommersant* seldom published news on a specific corporation. There were stories that referred to banks, experts, stock exchanges, the telecommunications sector, and so on, where the focus was on a current sector of the economy but not on individual corporations.

In the period 1993 to 1996, the news on corporations started to blossom in *Kommersant*. Still, there were a lot of stories on the front pages that referred to whole sectors of the economy. The most often mentioned companies included the oil company Lukoil, bank Menatep, beer company Baltika, car manufacturer Avtovaz, insurance company Ingosstrakh, gas company Surgutneftegaz, and foreign companies Hewlett-Packard and Merrill Lynch. The above mentioned companies got from two to seven mentions during the sample period.

In 1997 to 1999, the visibility of individual corporations again shrank in *Kommersant*. Only oil company Rosneft was mentioned twice among the three most visible actors in front page stories; no other corporation got two or more mentions in the sample.

In 2000 to 2003, the change in *Kommersant* from the previous period was clearly toward business reporting. Again, there were a lot of stories on the banking sector and many stories also on the energy sector and airlines. The companies most often mentioned in the sample were telecom operator MTS, airline Aeroflot, U.S. based company Halliburton, gas company Gazprom, energy company RAO UES Russia, credit company Transkredit, and diamond company Alrosa; all these got a minimum of three mentions. In *Vedomosti*, there were a lot of stories on banking and the energy sector and also on telecommunications in 2000 to 2003. The most often mentioned corporations were Gazprom, Aeroflot, Yukos, RAO UES, Fiat, Mercury, Microsoft, Rosneft, and Sberbank, all having at least three mentions.

In 2004 to 2007, the focus in *Kommersant* was still on the banking and energy sectors. As during previous periods, banks were often handled as a group, and there were many individual banks as actors, but only the central bank of Russia got many mentions. The most often mentioned companies in the sample included Gazprom, Yukos, Microsoft, RAO UES, Vneshtorgbank, Lukoil, bank Renessans, bank Russkiy standart, Sibneft, Telenor, Video International, and Vimpelcom. Also in *Vedomosti*, there was an emphasis on banks and energy during the same period. The most often mentioned corporations included Gazprom, Alfa bank, RAO UES, Russkiy standart, Sberbank, and Surgutneftegaz.

Hypothesis 2. The Impact of Media Favorability on Organizational Image

There is a correlation between the corporations mentioned on the front pages of *Kommersant* and *Vedomosti* and the top listings of Russian corporations. For example, the most often mentioned companies in 1993 to 1996 included Lukoil, Menatep, Baltika, Avtovaz, Ingosstrakh and Surgutneftegaz. Of these, Lukoil was the second largest company in terms of sales in 2007 (RA Expert, 2008), and Surgutneftegaz the seventh. Baltika can be found at number 47, and Ingosstrakh at 88. In 2004 to 2007, both *Kommersant* and *Vedomosti* had many stories on Gazprom, RAO UES, and Russkiy standart, having places 1, 5, and 60 in the top list of enterprises by sales.

Some of the most visible companies in the *Kommersant* and *Vedomosti* front pages succeeded also in the survey on corporate reputation by *Ekspert* magazine (Shmarov & Polunin, 2003). In this rating by *Ekspert*, Alfa was cited as the most reputable bank, Ingosstrakh in the category of insurance companies, MTS was the winner in telecom operators, and Yukos in the energy sector. Similarly, in the VCIOM poll from 2007 the most reputable companies were mainly the same ones that prevailed on the front pages of *Kommersant* and *Vedomosti*.

Discussion

The results of the content analysis show that in the leading Russian daily business publications *Kommersant* and *Vedomosti* the large companies are the most visible. The most often mentioned companies on the front pages are usually among the top 100 companies by sales and among the most reputable in polls and surveys.

The visibility of foreign companies increased during the 1990s and the early 2000s. International companies that made their way to the front pages of *Kommersant* and *Vedomosti* were mostly well-known international brands, including companies like Hewlett-Packard, Merrill Lynch, Halliburton, and Microsoft. Usually, the stories on these companies were tied with their operations in Russia or a major international news item.

The results show that in these central publications, only large companies, domestic or foreign, can really make it to the front page news. Important sectors in national economics are best covered. In a large country, only the largest companies can get coverage in the main news in federal television and publications while medium- and small-sized enterprises are mostly left for regional or local media.

The main limitation of the research setting was that it was mostly concentrated on first level agenda setting, on media visibility, and top-of-mind awareness. The levels of substantive agenda setting and affective agenda setting were discussed on the basis of comparisons between the content analysis data and secondary data on listings or surveys. In addition, the research was limited to front page stories and, moreover, to the three first mentioned actors in every news item or story. However, the validity of the results rises thanks to the relatively long time span and the large amount of analyzed elements that make it possible to keep track of the trend changes.

Conclusions

The main contribution of this study is as an analysis of organizational newsworthiness in the Russian business press. The study uses primary empirical data, collected from two leading Russian business newspapers and not previously published in English. Moreover, the comparisons with secondary data on corporate reputation and other listings on corporations bring valuable new information on the interrelationship between news media and corporate reputation in Russia.

Since agenda-setting theory has not been widely applied in Russia, there are many areas to cover in further research. Further research is needed to provide a better understanding, for example, of how media coverage can affect the public's organizational images of corporations in Russia and what the relationship is between the public relations industry and news practices.

Notes

1. The "actor" is here defined as a person, group, institution, or other subject that has an active role in the sentence level. For example, if the story starts "The president opened the seminar," the "president" is classified as an actor in the story.
2. The survey included both financial and business newspapers and general newspapers with a financial section.

References

AMR. (2004). Reyting kachestva i popul'yarnosti delovykh pechatnykh SMI Rossii [Rating of the quality and popularity of business publications in Russia]. Assosiatsiya menedzherov Rossii. Retrieved from http://www.amr.ru/pdf/reyting_SMI.pdf

Barnhurst, K. G., & Nerone, J. (2001). *The form of news: A history.* New York: Guildford Press.

Becker, J. (2004). Lessons from Russia: A neo-authoritarian media system. *European Journal of Communication, 19*(2), 139–163.

Bezgodova, O. (2009). Upravleniye reputatsionnymi riskami v usloviyah minimizatsii PR-byudzheta [Managing the risks to reputation when PR budgets are minimal]. *Industrial'nyy i b2b marketing, 2,* 106–114.

Buksha, K. S. (2007). *Upravleniye delovoy reputatsiey: Rossiyskaya i zarubezhnaya PR-praktika* [Managing the corporate reputation: Russian and foreign PR-practices]. Kiev, Ukraine: Williams.

Dyck, A., Volchkova, N., & Zingales, L. (2008). The corporate governance role of the media: Evidence from Russia. *Journal of Finance, 63*(1), 1093–1135.

Dyakova, E. G., & Trakhtenberg, A. D. (1999). *Massovaya kommunikatsiya i problema konstruirovaniya real'nosti: analiz osnovnykh teoreticheskikh podkhodov* [Mass communications and the problem of constructing reality: Analysis of main theoretical approaches]. Yekaterinburg, Russia: YrO RAN. Retrieved from http://www.visiology. fatal.ru/texts/mass-communication.htm

Ekspert-Ural (2005, November 28). Mnogolikaya reputatsiya [Many-sided reputation]. *Ekspert-Ural*. Retrieved from http://www.expert-ural.com/1-198-2266/.

European Bank for Reconstruction and Development (EBRD). (2008). *Transition report 2008*. Retrieved from http://www.ebrd.com/pubs/econo/tr08.htm

FAPMK (2009). *Rossiyskiy rynok periodicheskoy pechati. Sostoyaniye, tendentsii i perspektivy razvitiya* [Russian periodical press market: Situation, trends and prospects]. Federal'noye agentstvo po pechati i massovym kommunikatsiyam. Retrieved from http://www.gipp.ru/zip/27801_Rospechat_Press_2009.pdf

Firsova, N. S. (2009). Rol' sredstv massovoy informatsii v formirovanii obraza banka [The role of media in the formation of the image of a bank]. In E. L. Vartanova & Ya. N. Zasurskiy (Eds.), *Zhurnalistika v 2008 godu: obshchestvennaya povestka dnya i kommunikativnye praktiki SMI* [Journalism in year 2008: Social agenda and communications practices in media] (pp. 460–461). Moscow, Russia: Moskovskiy gosudarsrvennyy universitet imeni M. V. Lomonosova.

Goldfain, E. (2000). *The power of "The fourth power"*. Paper presented at the Agenda Setting 2000 Conference, Leipzig, Germany. Retrieved from http://www.agendasetting.com/2000material.php?item=3

Koikkalainen, K. (2007). Business media in Nordic countries and Russia: Global trends, local contents. In E. L. Vartanova (Ed.), *Media and change* (pp. 180–190). Moscow, Russia: Media Mir & Faculty of Journalism, Moscow State University.

Koikkalainen, K. (2009a). The local and the international in Russian business journalism: Structures and practices. In B. Beumers, S. Hutchings, & N. Rulyova (Eds.), *Globalisation, freedom and the media after communism* (pp. 71–85). New York: Routledge.

Koikkalainen, K. (2009b). *Talousjournalismin tiennäyttäjät Venäjällä: Kansainväliset vaikutteet ja paikalliset erityispiirteet Kommersant- ja Vedomosti-sanomalehdissä* [The innovators of the business press in Russia: International influences and local features in the newspapers *Kommersant* and *Vedomosti*]. Tampere, Finland: Tampere University Press.

Koltsova, O. (2006). *News media and power in Russia*. New York: Routledge.

Lebedeva, I. K. (2007). Metody analiza dokumentov kak osnova prikladnogo analiza formirovaniya informatsionnoy povestki dnya [Methods of document analysis as the basis for applied analysis of the formation of information agenda]. *Analitik, 2*. Retrieved from http://analyst.gospolitika.ru/nomera/a5/03_IK_Lebedeva_2007_11.pdf.

Liuhto, K., & Vahtra, P. (2009). *Who governs the Russian economy? A cross-section of Russia's largest corporations*. Turku School of Economics, Turku, Finland. Retrieved from http://www.tse.fi/pei

McElreath, M., Chen, N., Azarova, L., & Shadrova, V. (2001). The development of public relations in China, Russia, and the United States. In R. L. Heath (Ed.), *Handbook of public relations* (pp. 665–673). Thousand Oaks, CA: Sage.

Oates, S. (2006). Where's the party? Television and election campaigns in Russia. In K. Voltmer (Ed.), *Mass media and political communication in new democracies* (pp. 152–167). New York: Routledge.

Pasti, S. (2009, March 28–30). *Stable journalists in a stable epoch: Initial results of the survey of Russian journalists 2008*. Paper presented at the British Association for Slavonic and East European Studies (BASEES) Conference, Cambridge, UK.

Pasti, S., & Pietiläinen, J. (2008). Journalists in the Russian regions: How different generations view their professional roles. In S. White (Ed.), *Media, culture and society in Putin's Russia* (pp. 109–132). Houndmills, UK: Palgrave Macmillan.

Pietiläinen, J. (2009, June). *Russian media transition or transformation in comparison with Central Eastern European countries.* Paper presented at the Beyond East and West Conference, Budapest, Hungary.

RA Expert. (2008). *Reyting "Ekspert—400: Krupneyshiye,"* 2008 [Rating "Ekspert —400: The largest," 2008]. Retrieved from http://www.raexpert.ru/ratings/expert400/2008/.

Raskin, A. (2002). Television: Medium to elect the president. In K. Nordenstreng, E. Vartanova, & Y. Zassoursky (Eds.), *Russian media challenge* (2nd ed., pp. 93–114). Helsinki, Finland: Kikimora.

RBC. (2007). Top 40 rossiyskikh brendov [Top 40 Russian brands]. Retrieved from http://rating.rbc.ru/article.shtml?2007/11/01/31695543

Reyting vliyatel'nosti rossiyskikh SMI [Rating of the influence of Russian media]. (2008). *Novosti SMI, 12,* 38–39.

Reputation Institute. (2009). *R I hall of fame.* Retrieved from http://www.reputationinstitute.com/knowledge-center/hall-of-fame#r

ROMIR. (2009). *Reyting delovoy reputatsii rossiyskikh bankov: Sberbank zanimayet pervoye mesto* [Rating of corporate reputation of Russian banks: Sberbank in first place]. Retrieved from http://rumetrika.rambler.ru/publ/article_show.html?article=3665

Rulyova, N. (2009). Domesticating the Western format on Russian TV: Subversive glocalisation in the game show Pole chudes [The field of miracles]. In B. Beumers, S. Hutchings, & N. Rulyova (Eds.), *Globalisation, freedom and the media after communism* (pp. 121–140). New York: Routledge.

Rynok menyayetsya—lidery ostayutsya [The market changes—The leaders stay]. (2008). *Novosti SMI, 8,* p. 29.

Samye tsitiruyemye izdaniya [The most cited publications]. (2008). *Novosti SMI, 22,* 57.

Samye vliyatel'nye SMI 2008 goda dlya rossiyskogo biznesa [The most influential media in 2008 for Russian business]. (2008). *Novosti SMI, 23,* 48–49.

Shmarov, A., & Polunin, Y. (2003, October 13). Reputatsiya: kak eto delayetsya v Rossii [Reputation: How it is made in Russia]. *Ekspert, 38.* Retrieved from http://www.expert.ru/printissues/expert/2003/38/document75404/

Social distinctions in contemporary Russia. (2007). Material from a survey. Russian Academy of Sciences, Institute of Sociology [data collection].

Sutela, P. (2009). Talouspolitiikan haasteet kriisin jälkeen [The challenges of economic policy after the crisis]. In I. Korhonen, J. Rautava, H. Simola, L. Solanko, & P. Sutela. *BOFIT Online 2009 No. 5: Venäjä kriisin kourissa* [Russia in the hands of crisis] (pp. 26–28). Retrieved from www.bof.fi/bofit. (In Finnish)

TOP 100 samykh upominayemykh brendov runeta [TOP 100 of the most often mentioned brands on the Russian Internet]. (2009). *Novosti SMI, 5,* 48–49.

Tsetsura, K. (2003). The development of public relations in Russia: A geopolitical approach. In K. Sriramesh & D. Verčič (Eds.), *The global public relations handbook: Theory, research and practice* (pp. 301–318). Mahwah, NJ: Erlbaum.

Tsvetkova, A. B. (2007). Rol' korporativnoy reputatsii v formirovanii uspeshnosti kompanii na rynke [The role of corporate reputation in the formation of the success of a company in the market]. *Reklama: Teoriya i praktika, 5.*

Vartanova, E. (2009). Russian media: Market and technology as driving forces of change. In E. Vartanova, H. Nieminen, & M.-M. Salminen (Eds.), *Perspectives to the media* in Russia: "Western" interests and Russian developments (pp. 283–300). Helsinki, Finland: Aleksanteri Institute.

Vartanova, E., & Smirnov, S. (2009). A brief review of the condition of the media market in Russia: The general situation. In E. Vartanova, H. Nieminen, & M.-M. Salminen (Eds.), *Perspectives on the media in Russia: "Western" interests and Russian developments* (pp. 117–144). Helsinki, Finland: Aleksanteri Institute.

VCIOM. (2007, August 20). *Reyting delovoy reputatsii rossiyskikh kompaniy* [Rating of corporate reputation of Russian companies]. Press release. Retrieved from http://wciom.ru/arkhiv/tematicheskii-arkhiv/item/single/8633.html?no_cache=1&cHash=a7b3850b01.

VCIOM. (2008). *Lyudi i banki: Informirovannost' rastet, doveriye—padayet* [People and the banks: Information rising, trust dropping]. Press release. Retrieved from http://wciom.ru/arkhiv/tematicheskii-arkhiv/item/single/11030.html?no_cache=1&cHash=3a9df97d2e

VCIOM. (2009, June). *Reyting obshchestvennykh institutov* [Rating of social institutions]. Retrieved from http://wciom.ru/novosti/reitingi/reiting-obshchestvennykh-institutov.html.

White, S., & McAllister, I. (2006). Politics and the media in post-communist Russia. In K. Voltmer (Ed.), *Mass media and political communication in new democracies* (pp. 210–227). New York: Routledge.

World Economic Forum. (2009). *The global enabling trade report*. Retrieved from http://www.weforum.org/en/index.htm

Zhurnalistika v 2008 godu: obshchestvennaya povestka dnya i kommunikativnye praktiki SMI [Journalism in year 2008: social agenda and communications practices in media]. (2009). Moscow, Russia: Moskovskiy gosudarstvennyy universitet imeni M. V. Lomonosova.

Yasaveyev, I. G. (2009). Konstruirovaniye "povestki dnya": Sotsial'nye problemy rossiyskogo obshchestva v novostyakh federal'nykh telekanalov [Construction of "daily agenda": Social problems of Russian society in federal television news]. *Upravleniye obshchestvennymi i ekonomicheskimi sistemami, 1*. Retrieved from http://www.bali.ostu.ru/umc/arhiv/2007/1/Yisaveev.pdf

21 Corporate Reputation and the News Media in South Korea

Heewon Cha and Sung-Un Yang

Since 2000, the concept of corporate reputation has been increasingly studied in South Korea from various perspectives, such as business, marketing, public relations, and advertising. Business researchers have primarily focused on corporate performance, while marketing and advertising research has centered on customers' purchasing intentions, corporate advertisement, and corporate social responsibility. In the field of public relations, there have been about 20 published research papers on topics that include: organization-public relationships; corporate social responsibility; crisis communications; media visibility; news coverage credibility; public relations performance, responsibility, and asset value; CEO reputation and reputation's relationship to national image; and reputation measurement indices.

Main Trends in the Conceptualization of Corporate Reputation

Most previous studies have been based on the definitions of corporate reputation developed by Fombrun and Shanley (1990), Fombrun (1996), Fombrun and Rindova (2000), Fombrun and Van Riel (2003), and Bromley (1993, 2000, 2002). Previous research has focused on the following factors: (a) shared perceptions about the results of corporate performance (e.g., products and outcomes); (b) overall perceptions or cognitive representations that combine various kinds of information used by multiple stakeholders; (c) cumulative evaluations by stakeholders of the company's past performance; (d) substantial behavioral attributes that also include stakeholders' expectations about future performance of the company (Han & Kim, 2005; Han, Kim, & Mun, 2005; Han & Ryu, 2004); (e) collective representations of corporate performance that multiple constituents of the company share over time (Yang & Yang, 2003); (f) overall favorability of the company based on various measures of corporate performance; (g) strategic assets that provide competitive advantage over other companies (Park, Kang, & Lee,, 2005; J.C. Shin, Song, Hong, & Kang, 2004; Yoon & Cho, 2005); (h) collective corporate attributes that can be estimated on the basis of the company's past performance or stakeholder-related trust (Park, 2000); and (i) corporate identity or collective beliefs about the company (Kang & Jo, 2003).

To summarize, these measures of corporate reputation all include "various aspects of corporate performance," "evaluations of corporate performance that have been accumulated over time," "stakeholders' overall perceptions," and "overall favorability and trustworthiness." These aspects of corporate reputation have also been highlighted in the non-Korean literature.

Reputation Measurement

South Korean researchers have used existing reputation measurement systems and modified them according to their research topics. Most South Korean studies on reputation measurement have been based on Fombrun and Gardberg's (2000) Reputation Quotient (RQ) or *Fortune* magazine's measurement system. For example, to measure corporate reputation, Noh et al. (2003) focused on such dimensions as management quality, transparency, financial soundness, prospects for future growth, corporate social responsibility, product quality, employee care, customer service, environmental responsibility, and globalization. The exception is Cha's (2004) previous research that focused on developing a reputation measurement system to fit the South Korean context. Based on the results of a public survey and in-depth interviews with experts, Cha proposed three dimensions of corporate reputation measurement: corporate identity, management strategy, and corporate communication. According to Cha, the unique aspect of South Korean companies is that the dimension of corporate identity is composed of subdimensions, such as corporate philosophy, organizational culture, CEO leadership, and corporate social responsibility. These subdimensions reflect the overall South Korean corporate culture that has recently emphasized corporate philosophy, management ethics and transparency, social responsibility, and the corporate contribution to national economy.

Agenda-Setting Theory

Overview

Agenda-setting research has been ongoing in South Korea since the 1980s; in the 2000s, focusing on second- level agenda-setting and priming effects, South Korean researchers have been conducting research in political communication, online journalism, and public issue areas. Those studies have been regularly published in major South Korean journals, such as the *Korean Journal of Journalism and Communication Studies* ("Un-ron Hak-bo"), *Journal of Communication and Information* ("Un-ron Jung-bo Hak-bo"), *Korean Journal of Broadcasting* ("Han-kuk Bang-song Hak-bo"), *Korean Advertising Research* ("Gwang-go Yeon-gu"), *The Korean Journal of Advertising* ("Gwan-go Hak Yeon-gu"), and *The Korean Journal of Public Relations Research* ("Hong-bo Hak Yeon-gu"). Most recently, agenda-setting research in South Korea has expanded to new areas such as advertising and public relations research.

Research Areas

More specifically, regarding agenda-setting theory, South Korean researchers have studied second-level agenda-setting effects in political campaigns or public issues (Ban, 2004; Ban, Choi, & Shin, 2004a, 2004b; G. Lee, 2006) and priming effects regarding politicians or policy evaluations (G. H. Lee, 2002; Rlee, 2001; Song, Kim, & Cho, 2005). Additionally, researchers have studied agenda-setting effects on issues of social conflict, such as "media coverage of the nuclear waste storage facility in Wido" (Ban et al., 2004a), "media coverage of real-estate issues" (Choi & Ban, 2006), and "media coverage of risks caused by GMO food" (Song et al., 2005).

Recently, agenda-setting effects in the area of new media—including such topics as the Internet, online newspapers, and Web site campaigns—have been increasingly studied (S. T. Kim & Lee, 2006; Ku, 2002; Yoon & Shim, 2003). Also, D. G. Lee and Lee (2005) compared agenda-setting effects between traditional media and the Internet.

However, agenda-setting effects in business-related topics have not yet been widely studied in South Korea. Exceptions are corporate/public advertising campaign research (Chung, 1995; Kim, 2001; Kwon, 1997, 2002) and a few studies on the relationship between media reputation and corporate reputation (Cha, 2004; J. H. Shin, Park, & Cameron, 2006; Yang & Grunig, 2005).

To summarize, most agenda-setting effects have been studied in terms of first-level effects in political, social, and business-related areas; some studies have examined second level agenda-setting effects and priming effects. Additionally, a few researchers have found significant relationships between issue framing and the news recipients' opinions, attitudes, and evaluations of the information.

Business and the News Media

In South Korea, research on the relationship between business and media has focused on, (a) public relations professionals as news sources and (b) media–practitioner relations (Lee, 1996; J. H. Lee, 2004; Oh, 2000; Park, Cho, & Hong, 2001; Shin, 2000; H. C. Shin & Kim, 2003). The research suggests that South Korean journalists are prone to being influenced by personal relationships with public relations professionals and corporate requests. Therefore, gatekeeping, a coorientation model, and contingency theory have been popular theoretical frames used to guide research on business and the news media.

Recently, as more studies have focused on corporate reputation, public relations research has increasingly dealt with the relationships between corporations and the news media; studies of the visibility of companies in the media (Cha, 2004; Yang, 2004); negative media coverage during crisis situations (Jo, 2005; Yoon & Cho, 2005); news coverage related to CEO image, and credibility of media coverage (E. K. Han & Kim, 2005). Key theoretical frames include corporate reputation, agenda setting, CEO image, corporate social responsibility, and crisis management. Additionally, other corporate reputation research has focused on such diverse topics as the effects of organization–public relationships or corporate social responsibility on corporate reputation (E. K. Han et al., 2005; Hwang, 2004; C. H. Kim & Oh, 2003; S. K. Yang & Yang, 2003; Yoon & Suh, 2003) and the effects of corporate reputation on customers' supportive purchasing intentions, attitudes toward brands, and other corporate outcomes (E. K. Han & Ryu, 2004; Hwang, 2004; Park, 2000; J. H. Park, Kang, & Lee, 2005).

According to research on the relationship between businesses and the news media, the news media influence corporate reputation in terms of (a) quality of journalist–PR professional relationships from the perspective of *PR professionals as information subsidies*, and (b) favorable corporate media coverage (e.g., positive news, social responsibility, crisis-related coverage) on the basis of *media agenda-setting effects*. More specifically, to summarize the findings of previous studies, corporate visibility and corporate issue salience in the media resulted in a higher level of public awareness about the companies overall (i.e., agenda setting at the first level), some of the corporate issues extensively covered by the media (i.e., substantive agenda setting at the second level), and favorable corporate reputation (i.e., affective agenda setting at the second level). Therefore, we propose the following hypotheses based on the previous research regarding the news media agenda-setting effects on corporate reputation:

Hypothesis 1. The amount of news coverage that a firm receives in the news media is positively related to the public's awareness of the firm.

Hypothesis 2. The amount of news coverage devoted to particular attributes of a firm is positively related to the proportion of the public that defines the firm by those attributes.

Hypothesis 3. The more positive that media coverage is for a particular attribute, the more positively will members of the public perceive that attribute.

Also, in testing the media's agenda-setting effect on corporate reputation, we want to examine additional variables that affect corporate reputation. Scheufele (2000) has suggested that the media's agenda-setting effect can be significantly moderated by some variables such as demographic, social, and psychological variables. Likewise, South Korean scholars also have found some variables to be crucial in examining the media's agenda-setting effect (e.g., Cha, 2004; Jo & Kim, 2004; Yang, 2004; Yoon & Shim, 2003). Such research findings indicate that when the media's agenda-setting effect is examined in research, it should *be controlled for by other important variables* (i.e., the variables related to the public's characteristics) or *be included as a moderator* for more accurate analyses. For this reason, we explore the effects of some additional variables on corporate reputation and control for the media agenda-setting effects of those additional variables in data analyses.

RQ1: What are the additional variables other than agenda-setting variables that significantly influence corporate reputation? And what are the effects of media agenda-setting when controlled for by such additional variables?

Case Study

Corporate Reputation in South Korea[1]

Since 2000, *Fortune* magazine, the Reputation Institute, and major public relations agencies have increasingly discussed the importance of corporate reputation. Following this American trend, many South Korean news media have highlighted their keen interest in corporate reputation, and some of them have even released *Fortune*-type reputation measurement results, such as "Most Admired Companies in South Korea" and "Reputation Rankings among South Korean Companies." The criteria used to calculate the results of such ranking systems have been inconsistent; however, in general, they include shareholders' value, employee value, customer value (i.e., product quality and customer service), and environmental and social responsibility.

In particular, the dimension of *social responsibility* has recently emerged as a main focus. Like global trends in reputation measurement systems, South Korean systems have emphasized corporate responsibility toward society and the environment. Since the time when social issues related to companies' management ethics became controversial in South Korea, financial soundness and clean corporate image have been emphasized.

According to the results of major corporate reputation surveys, for example, Samsung Electronics and Yuhan-Kimberly were first in "The 30 Most Admired South Korean Companies in 2005," a survey jointly conducted by Dong-A Ilbo and Korea IBM BCS. The second-place winners were Posco, Samsung Fire Insurance, and Hyundai Motors. The third-place winners were Busan Bank, LG Electronics, Kyobo Life Insurance, Amore Pacific, and LG Chemical. This survey was conducted on the basis of five dimensions of attributes of 60 major South Korean companies since 2004. Another example of a reputation survey includes a survey conducted by KMA Consulting called "Most Admired South Korean Companies" since 2004.

The results of these *Fortune*-type reputation surveys have been very similar across different surveys. This might be because these surveys are valid and reliable based on evaluations made by multiple stakeholders, such as customers, journalists, financial analysts, and so forth. Very often, the top 10 best companies have been almost identical, including South Korean domestic conglomerates Samsung Electronics, Hyundai Motors, Posco, Yuhan-Kimberly, LG Electronics, SK Telecom, Samsung Life Insurance, and CJ. It is very interesting that multinational companies have not been ranked among the most admired companies in these surveys, suggesting that marketing outcomes are differentiated from the criteria used to evaluate admired companies. Rather, Posco and Yuhan-Kimberly have been ranked most favorably, indicating that, when South Koreans evaluate admired companies, they typically value domestic companies that perform good "corporate citizenship."

Additionally, these survey findings indicate that regional companies are not greatly admired, perhaps because they lack visibility amongst the survey respondents. Most of the top-ranked companies are conglomerates and may have relatively higher visibility than small regional companies. Another reason is that these small regional companies do not retain competitive advantages in financial outcomes over conglomerates such as Samsung or Hyundai. By industry sector, telecommunications, automobile, insurance, and food companies have often been ranked amongst the top companies in reputation surveys. Finally, banks have recently been included in the ranking now that banks have recovered public trust due to changes in the industry, such as mergers and acquisitions. Thus, we believe that, based on the results of such reputation surveys, political, social, and economic issues and trends in South Korean society affect the concept of corporate reputation.

Media Systems

According to the Korea Research Foundation's (KRF) report in 2006, media systems in South Korea consist of national/regional newspapers, national/regional broadcasting companies, new media (cable TV, satellite TV, and satellite DMB), and the Internet (Internet newspapers and portal news). In 2005, new media alone had advertising sales exceeding ₩1 trillion. Since then, traditional media have struggled to compete; for example, traditional media have tried to reflect the audience's media use patterns so as to establish the "one-source and multiuses" (i.e., convergence in media use) in their media systems.

The Internet has recently emerged as the key medium in South Korea, thanks greatly to the Internet portal sites, which had up to 22,390,000 users (out of a population of some 48 million) in 2006. Given the trend of decreasing TV watching and newspaper subscription, such a large number of portal site users is remarkable. Additionally, due to the downturn in the national economy, traditional media have suffered financial problems. However, it has been increasingly discussed whether new media are trustworthy sources compared to traditional media.

Since lawmakers passed the Newspapers Law and the Media-Mediation Law in 2005, there have been great efforts to preserve the diversity of news media as well as to develop newspapers from various aspects. Consequently, over 400 Internet newspapers have been officially registered; a national subsidy of ₩100 million has been allotted to foster such efforts and the establishment of a telecommunication convergence body has been widely discussed. This body would manage changes in media systems due to the emergence of new media. To media users, the emergence of new media has not been entirely positive. Media users have been bombarded with information, the credibility of which has often been very questionable. Public relations professionals also have relied on new media to provide direct and indirect information to the public (often on a 24/7 basis); consequently, the public has less credible information.

Media Outreach   South Korea has excellent media outreach. Since 2005, the number of satellite Digital Multimedia Broadcasting (DMB) service subscribers has exceeded 600,000. More than 14 million households subscribe to cable TV, increasing the market share to 42% (KRF, 2006). After the Newspaper Law was amended in 2005, the competition between traditional newspapers and Internet-based newspapers increased drastically. South Korea has one of the strongest Internet user bases in the world: The total number of Internet users is the sixth largest in the world, and the total time spent on the Internet is the third longest in the world.

Media Access   According to the KRF report, the key information sources used by South Koreans include TV, newspapers, and the Internet. For example, 41% of the survey respondents said they read newspapers every day, and 78% said they watch TV news every day. In terms of daily media use, the average person spends 37 minutes reading newspapers, 2 hours and 44 minutes watching TV, and 77 minutes on the Internet. Interestingly, the KRF report noted that Internet use has increased every year. The survey respondents considered TV to be the most credible medium in South Korea. This might be because newspapers and the Internet are privately owned and are often easily swayed by political forces or biases.

Media Control   The interests of the government, media owners, political and economic stakeholders, and the public have affected media control in South Korea. The government has encouraged competition in the media industry through such measures as passing the amended Newspapers Law and Media-Mediation Law in 2005, granting permission for ground wave DMB to provide daytime broadcasting, and launching satellite/ground wave DMB service. For this reason, media owners have increasingly become key players in media control in South Korea.

Such changes in the media environment have influenced corporate public relations practices. Due to the increasing diversity of information sources, public relations professionals have widely utilized new media to manage corporate reputation. Corporate communication professionals have focused on publicity for products and services, sports promotion, events for marketing public relations, corporate CEO impression management in the media, corporate issue/crisis management, and corporate reputation management by increasing media coverage on corporate philanthropy activities.

News Values

The newsworthiness model suggested by Shoemaker and her colleagues predicts that the prominence of a story will increase with the newsworthiness of the event involved (e.g., Shoemaker, 1996; Shoemaker & Cohen, 2006; Shoemaker, Danielian, & Brendlinger, 1991). The model proposes two indicators of newsworthiness: deviance and social significance.

According to the KRF report in 2004, South Korean journalists selected the following criteria as the most important in determining newsworthiness: the quality of the news source, the news desk's influence, audience surveys, competing media decisions, and the relative importance of the news. The quality of the news source is related to organizational legitimacy or power. South Korean journalists have often regarded conglomerates with economic power or governmental organizations with political power as credible news sources. Consequently, systematic corporate/governmental public relations tactics—to nurture relations with journalists—result in "creating news" for and by such powerful organizations, therefore setting the public's agenda for the sake of those organizations.

Son and Lee's (1999) Korea Press Foundation report compared the news values of South Korean TV news with those of the BBC and NBC (see Table 21.1). They found that TV news values in South Korean media emphasize negativity, fame, and novelty and downplay the values of influence, utility, conflict, and

Table 21.1 Components of TV News Values and Response Frequency

Categories	South Korean TV		BBC		NBC	
	Frequency[b]	Response[c]	Frequency	Response	Frequency	Response
Timeliness	29.2	53.9	26.6	56.2	31.7	68.8
Fame	9.5	17.7	7.4	15.7	3.6	7.8
Proximity[a]	0.7	1.2	3.2	6.7	N/A	N/A
Influence	9	16.7	11.7	24.7	17.3	37.5
Conflict	9.5	17.5	13.8	29.2	16.5	35.9
Visual interest	8.2	15.1	6.9	14.6	5.8	12.5
Human interest	4.4	8.1	11.7	24.7	3.6	7.8
Novelty	5.8	10.7	3.2	6.7	3.6	7.8
Negativity	21.3	39.4	11.7	24.7	14.4	31.8
Utility	2.6	4.7	3.7	7.9	3.6	7.8
Total	100	185	100	211.2	100	217.2

Note. [a]Proximity was examined only in international coverage. [b]Frequency is the percentage of the given category over the entire categories. [c]Response rate is the percentage of selection of the given category over the entire TV news stories coded by the researchers.

timeliness. Therefore, South Korean TV news tends to reflect only the negative aspects of social reality while focusing too much on "visual sensation."

Organizational Newsworthiness

According to Cha (2004), the most frequently covered corporate attributes in South Korean newspapers include *management/marketing, human resource/ management, social philanthropy,* and *corporate issue-related* attributes. A poll revealed that the public tends to focus on additional corporate attributes, such as CEO quality and management ethics, to form its opinion of companies. This suggests that public relations professionals should expect increasing media coverage of attributes related to "management ethics," due to the media's social surveillance efforts. Also, by applying Shoemaker's concept of "social significance," South Korean public relations professionals can develop organizational newsworthiness when they focus on news events that are related to "socially significant" entities, such as a new products, global management outcomes of companies, organizational news stories on global events (e.g., World Cup, Olympic, elections), and corporate social responsibility (CSR) activities.

Public Relations in South Korea

Many public relations theories, such as excellence theory (Grunig, Grunig, & Dozier, 2002), have been widely discussed from both positive/descriptive and normative aspects of South Korean public relations practice. However, there have been few studies on how societal and cultural constraints have shaped public relations practice in South Korea.

Before attempting to determine the ideal model of South Korean public relations practice, one must note the societal/cultural differences between the United States and South Korea. South Korean public relations development was initiated when "Chaebols" (Korean-style conglomerates) began to develop a public relations department to lessen or neutralize negative public opinion about their "cozy/under-the-table" relationships with the political arena and their monopoly of economic stakes. Thus, this early stage of South Korean public relations development evolved around publicity (i.e., media relations). At that time, there was no development of ethical and professional public relations in South Korea.

According to Kim and Cha (2002), public relations practice in South Korea is largely divided into two conflicting and opposing trends. One stream includes *nonprofessional* public relations activities that stem from cultural traditions such as "networking" and "personal communication." The other stream encompasses *professional* public relations activities, including "public-oriented public relations" and "consulting public relations." Kim and Cha argue that the latter is more suitable in today's globalized environment, though, until recently, the former dominated South Korean public relations practices.

An example of the once rampant "unprofessional" public relations activities is "networking-oriented public relations," in which practitioners' utilize their networks and "Jeong" (i.e., emotional tie cultivated by personal relationships) based on the Confucian culture that emphasizes the context of human relations. In addition to Confucian tradition, several decades of military dictatorship have led to many negative aspects in South Korean public relations, such as "authoritarian public relations," which is influenced by the government authorities, "under-the-table" public relations, and gender discrimination among practitioners.

Nevertheless, according to Kim and Cha (2002), as societal conditions in South Korea have changed, professional public relations practice has emerged. The most significant influencing factors include the inflow of multinational companies, public relations needs for specialization in venture companies, changes in CEOs' worldview regarding the function of public relations in symmetrical communications, and the development of new media and the emergence of "netizens" (i.e., citizens who participate in online communications). Following such societal trends, the new mode of professional public relations has been named variously: (a) "scientific public relations," which is tailored to each member of the target audience based on scientific research processes; (b) "consulting public relations," which highlights a consulting role for public relations professionals for corporate management; (c) "social-responsibility public relations," which improves corporate reputation through quality community/social relations; and (d) "partner public relations," which maintains a quality, symbiotic relationship with journalists rather than "under-the-table" media relations.

Rhee (2002) applied the excellence theory (L. Grunig et al., 2002) and found evidence of professional Korean public relations. According to Rhee, cultural collectivism and Confucianism are key dimensions of public relations in South Korea.

Additionally, Berkowitz and Lee (2004) found that unique aspects of public relations in South Korea include "jeong" and "face" between public relations professionals—and between journalists and public relations professionals. Like-wise, regarding professionals' interpersonal relationships, Jo and Kim (2004) also noted that cultivating quality interpersonal relationships is a key criterion for becoming a competent public relations professional in South Korea.

Research Methodology

This research concerns: (a) media reputation (i.e., media visibility and issue prominence) and (b) corporate reputation. To study media reputation, we examined the amount and the content of media coverage, media reputation, and issue prominence. To study the public's perceptions of corporate reputation (i.e., second-level agenda setting and evaluations of companies), we conducted a public opinion poll.

Content Analysis

Choice of News Media

News Media and Company Selection Criteria We conducted a content analysis of five major companies based on media coverage from the three major newspapers[2] in South Korea ("Cho-sun Ilbo," "Dong-a Ilbo," and "Jung-ang Ilbo") between January and September 2005. The five companies studied were selected on the basis of reputation surveys and the amount of media coverage.

Sampling Procedure To sample the news articles, we used online versions of those newspapers—www.kinds.or.kr (for "Cho-sun Ilbo" and "Dong-a Ilbo") and www.joins.com (for "Jung-ang Ilbo")—along with a thorough investigation of news article figures and pictures from the print versions. There was a total of 6,252 news articles. To avoid sampling bias across the five companies studied, we applied systematic random sampling to yield a similar ratio of sampled articles from the population for each of the five companies studied (see Table 21.2).

Intercoder Reliability To assess intercoder reliability, four social-science graduate students read the coding frame three times and coded 40 randomly selected articles out of 1,554 sampled articles. The results yielded 98% agreement of the coding.

Table 21.2 The Ratio between the Population and the Sample

	The Population	*The Sample*	*The Ratio (%)*
Samsung Electronics	2,394	590	24.6
Hyundai Motors	963	240	24.9
LG Electronics	1,409	354	25.1
SK Telecom	808	201	24.9
Posco	678	170	26.4
Total	6,252	1,554	25

Coding Units and Coded Variables   The coding unit is each of the sampled news articles. The coded variables are *formatting* information and *content* information about news articles. First, the formatting information includes: (a) the name of the news media; (b) the length of the article; (c) the position of the article (i.e., front-page coverage or not, the actual position in the newspaper); (d) the use of figures, graphs, pictures, or just text; (e) the use of company names in the headlines; (f) the extent of the use of company names in each news article (full, partial, or simple); and (g) coverage valence (negative, neutral, or positive).

Second, the content information is used to measure second-level agenda-setting effects, which include: (a) management (e.g., management outcomes, market prospect, new business, etc.); (b) marketing (e.g., brand, new product, event/promotion, etc.); (c) human resources (e.g., corporate culture, employee care, employee benefit, human resource management, etc.); (d) management ethics; (e) corporate communication (e.g., public relations, advertising, etc.); (f) CEO; and (g) corporate social responsibility activities.

Public Opinion Polls

We sampled about 400 residents in Seoul, South Korea. This public opinion poll was conducted 3 to 4 months after the content analysis had been completed. The sampling strategy was multistage/random quota sampling. First, based on the 2000 Census, age and sex quotas were decided. Second, based on the population of Seoul, the sample was decided through multistate random clusters: to six first-level clusters and then to three to five second-level clusters that were randomly selected at both stages sequentially. Trained research assistants collected the data over 3 weeks in November 2005, in one-on-one personal interviews.

There were two survey questionnaires. To avoid respondent fatigue due to a lengthy questionnaire, the researchers intentionally selected only three companies for each version of the questionnaire. Questionnaire 1 covered Samsung Electronics, SK Telecom, and Posco; Questionnaire 2 covered Hyundai Motors, LG Electronics, and Samsung Electronics. Therefore, in total, we collected 387 questionnaires about Samsung Electronics and 190 questionnaires about each of the other four companies studied. Regarding the sex of the survey respondents, there were 174 male and 213 female respondents. Over 87% of the respondents reported an education level equal to or greater than college.

The survey content consisted of the following areas: unaided and aided awareness of companies studied; evaluations of corporate attributes and companies; company-related information and involvement; issue-related information and involvement; media credibility; and demographic information.

Data Analysis

To analyze the results, we used the SPSS program to perform a correlation analysis, a factor analysis, and a multiple regression analysis. First, to assess media reputation, we decided weights for *media visibility* on the basis of Media Link and the Reputation Institute; the Media Reputation Index (MRI) was calculated as the product of media visibility and the valence of media coverage. We did not give differential weights to the media since we only focused on three newspapers in this research.

Media Reputation Index (MRI) = $\sum$M1i X M2j

M1*i*: 1) position, 2) picture, 3) figure/graph, 4) company name mentioned in the headline, & 5) company name was exclusively mentioned (sum will range from 0 to 5)

M2*j*: positive (+2), neutral (+1), or negative (-1)

The public's perceptions of corporate attributes refers to the extent to which the public values certain corporate attributes; *the public's evaluations of corporate attributes* means the given company's fit to certain corporate attributes. To measure the public's perceptions of corporate attributes, we asked the participants to rate the following: "How important do you think each of the following attributes is for each of the following companies?" on a 5-point scale, with 1 being "not important at all" and 5 being "very important." Also, to get corporate evaluations, we asked, "How well do you think each of the following companies fits the described corporate attributes?" on a 5-point scale. The corporate attributes used in the survey were from the content analysis. In total, 13 corporate attributes were used; for example, "this company demonstrates sound financial outcomes," "this company is outstanding for its social responsibility," "this company offers quality products and services," "the CEO of this company maintains clear vision and philosophy," and so forth.

To measure *corporate reputation*, we used the 20 items whose factor loadings were high from Cha's (2004) previous reputation measurement instrument. We used 5-point scales for these 20 items. After conducting an exploratory factor analysis, we identified four factors with the items that retained factor loadings equal to or greater than .5; all four factors explained between about 50 and 70% of the variance in the total items. Reliabilities for each of the four factors were greater than .80 in alpha. The four factors of corporate reputation include (a) management/leadership (five items), (b) social responsibility (four items), (c) brand/marketing (six items), and (d) corporate communications (five items). We used the mean score of those four factors as the index of corporate reputation of the companies studied.

To test research hypotheses, we analyzed correlations between (a) the valence of media coverage, (b) media visibility, and (c) media reputation—the variables examined in the content analysis, and (d) public's awareness of companies, (e) the public's perceptions of corporate attributes, and (f) corporate reputation—the variables from the survey. Also, we conducted a hierarchical multiple regression to examine the predictors of media agenda setting effects.

Results

Hypothesis 1: Media Visibility

Table 21.3 shows that the amount of media coverage for the companies studied was largest for Samsung Electronics (590 cases), followed by LG Electronics (354

Table 21.3 Media Coverage and Public Awareness of Companies

Companies	Media Coverage		Public Awareness	
	Coverage Frequency	Coverage Percentage	Coverage Frequency	Coverage Percentage
Samsung Electronics	590	38	375	32.1
LG Electronics	354	22.8	210	18
Hyundai Motors	239	15.4	181	15.5
SK Telecom	201	12.9	141	12.1
Posco	170	10.9	67	5.7
Total	1554	100	974	83.4

cases), Hyundai Motors (239 cases), SK Telecom (201 cases), and Posco (170 cases). Interestingly, we found an identical rank order between the amount of media coverage and the public's awareness of the five companies studied. The public's awareness was measured by top of mind (TOM) frequency for each company. Also, in terms of percentage, the amount of media coverage and the public's awareness were very close.

Hypothesis 2: Organizational News Topics

The following five types of substantive attributes mainly appeared in the media coverage (see Table 21.4): management/marketing (1,034 cases); human resources (235 cases); social responsibility (113 cases); CEO qualities (59 cases); and corporate issues (105 cases). We subdivided the five types of corporate attributes into 13 attributes (see Table 21.4).

Overall, according to Table 21.5, there existed significant correlations between the amount of media coverage of corporate attributes and the public's perceptions of them, suggesting that, when the public evaluates corporations, the salient attributes are those covered by the media, especially in areas involving management outcomes, brand/new products, human resources, and social responsibility. However, based on the results of this research, it is noteworthy that the public perceived some attributes as important (such as CEO characteristics, management ethics, and corporate issues) that were not salient in media coverage. This might be because such attributes were considered to be related to "management outcomes."

Second, the pattern of frequencies of corporate characteristics attributed to each of the companies studied was very similar to the pattern of media coverage. Samsung Electronics had substantial media coverage on management/marketing—especially management outcomes/company growth, human resource, brand/new products—and social philanthropic activities. Likewise, LG Electronics had media coverage on management outcomes, company growth, brand, and human resources, along with corporate issues (relatively more than other companies studied). In the case of Hyundai Motors, media coverage was mainly

Table 21.4 Detailed Frequencies of Media Coverage and the Public's Evaluations of Corporate Attributes by Categories

Corporate Attributes		Media Coverage (Frequency)						Public Evaluations of Corporate Attributes					
		Total	SE[c]	H	L	SK	P	Total	SE	H	L	SK	P
A[a]	Mgmt./Marketing	1034	398	246	139	143	108	4.05	4.21	3.58	3.49	3.86	3.69
	HR	235	96	59	30	21	29	4.05	4.03	3.45	3.41	3.68	3.82
	CSR	113	54	19	8	17	15	4.05	3.48	3.12	3.07	3.22	3.47
	CEO	59	20	15	13	5	6	4.23	4.17	3.38	3.5	3.45	3.6
	Corporate Issues	105	18	15	48	15	9	4	3.84	3.31	3.31	3.48	3.56
Total		1554	590	354	239	201	170						
B[a]	New Products	147	61	35	20	28	3	4.29	4.31	3.8	3.61	3.93	3.6
	Brand	163	45	52	28	26	12	4.37	4.36	3.73	3.75	3.9	3.96
	Prospect	194	78	51	16	24	25	4.19	4.21	3.54	3.45	3.84	3.63
	Mgmt. Outcomes	234	97	54	47	20	16	4.27	4.51	3.61	3.79	4.1	3.95
	Event/promotion	28	12	9	4	2	1	3.4	3.65	3.33	3.15	3.4	3.25
	New business	64	18	9	15	15	7	3.9	4.01	3.37	3.37	3.63	3.44
	Ad	16	8	2	0	6	0	3.94	4.4	3.7	3.32	4.23	4.01
	Employee Benefit	9	5	2	0	0	2	3.94	3.92	3.37	3.3	3.65	3.82
	HR	178	77	48	18	7	17	4.17	4.14	3.54	3.53	3.71	3.82
	Mgmt. Ethics	10	3	1	4	1	1	4.1	3.03	3.11	2.94	3.03	3.55
	CSR	113	54	8	19	17	15	4.05	3.48	3.12	3.07	3.22	3.47
	CEO	59	20	18	15	5	6	4.23	4.17	3.38	3.5	3.45	3.6
	Corporate issues	105	18	48	15	15	9	4	3.84	3.31	3.31	3.48	3.56
Total[b]		1320	296	332	201	166	114						

Note. [a]A = Overall categories; B = Specific categories. [b]Since the category of "other" was excluded, the total number in the category B is less than the total number in the category A. [c]SE = Samsung Electronics, H = Hyundai Motors, L = LG Electronics, SK = SK Telecom, and P = Posco.

Table 21.5 Correlations between the Amount of Media
Coverage on Company Attributes and the Public's
Perceptions of Corporate Attributes

Companies	Correlation Coefficient
Total	.62*
Samsung Electronics	.49†
LG Electronics	.52†
Hyndai Motors	.73*
SK Telecom	0.44
Posco	0.16

Note. †p < .10. *p < .05.

about management outcomes, brand/new products, human resources, and social
philanthropic activities. Interestingly, this company had relatively more coverage
of management outcomes than did the other companies studied. SK Telecom had
relatively less media coverage on human resource than others did. Finally, since
Posco does not deal with customers directly, its corporate attributes concerned
company prospects, management outcomes, human resources, and social
philanthropy rather than marketing areas such as new products or brands.

Regarding the relationship between the amount of media coverage of company attributes and the public's perceptions of corporate attributes (see Table
21.5), the correlation in the case of Hyundai Motors was statistically significant
($r = .73$, $p < .05$). For Samsung Electronics and LG Electronics, the correlations
were close to significance: $r = .49$, $p < .10$ for Samsung Electronics, $r = .52$, $p <$
.10 for LG Electronics. For these three companies, high correlations were found
in the corporate attributes that experienced extensive media coverage, such as
management outcomes, new products/brands, human resources, and so forth.
This indicates that significant second-level substantive agenda setting existed in
the relationship between the amount of media coverage on corporate attributes
and the public's perceptions of corporate attributes.

Hypothesis 3: Corporate Reputation and Valence

This hypothesis was to test the valence of media coverage on corporate reputation. To this end, we tested the relation between the Media Reputation Index
(MRI) and the Corporate Reputation Index (CRI), as shown in Table 21.6. The
results indicate that Samsung Electronics had the highest score, at 873, on the
descriptive analyses of MRI. LG Electronics scored 536; Hyundai Motors, 312;
SK Telecom, 225; and Posco, 214. This rank order is very close to the rank order
of public awareness. However, the results show that the rank order of MRI was
not strongly related to the rank order of corporate reputation, suggesting that
second-level affective agenda-setting effect was not supported by the data. In
the case of CRI, the companies that had the lowest MRI score, SK Telecom and
Posco, were ranked only after Samsung Electronics, the top company among the
five in terms of CRI.

Table 21.6 Media Reputation and Corporate Reputation

Companies[a]	Coverage	Media Visibility	Media Reputation Index (MRI)	Public's Awareness of Companies[c]	Corporate Reputation Index[b]
SE	590	762	873	375	3.97
H	354	476	536	210	3.42
L	239	285	312	181	3.4
SK	201	217	225	141	3.64
P	170	181	214	67	3.67

Note. [a]Multiple response scale. [b]Mean scores of five-point scales. [c]SE = Samsung Electronics, H = Hyundai Motors, L = LG Electronics, SK = SK Telecom, and P = Posco.

On the basis of such findings, we concluded that media reputation might not be a direct predictor of corporate reputation. Scheufele (2000) has suggested that the media's agenda-setting effect can be significantly moderated by some variables, such as the public's demographic, social, and psychological variables. Likewise, South Korean scholars also have found some crucial variables in examining the media's agenda-setting effect (e.g., Cha, 2004; Yang, 2004; Yoon & Shim, 2003). According to them, when researchers examine the media's agenda-setting effect, it should *be controlled for by other important variables* (i.e., the variables related to the public's characteristics) or *be included as a mediator* for more accurate examination. For this reason, we included microlevel predictors (i.e., the public's characteristics) to be controlled for in examining the media's agenda-setting effect on corporate reputation.

RQ: Predictors of Corporate Reputation: Microlevel Predictors

For this study, we analyzed the effects of some microlevel predictors of corporate reputation: (a) customer/public variables; (b) media variables; (b) information source and knowledge; and (d) corporate involvement and trust variables. We ran hierarchical regression analyses to examine the effects of such predictors on corporate reputation.

For all five companies, significant predictors were customer/audience variables, corporate familiarity and knowledge variables, and corporate involvement and trust variables. However, media variables (i.e., "news media as the key information source about the companies studied" and "news media as a trustworthy source of the information about the companies studied") turned out to be insignificant predictors of corporate reputation (see Table 21.7). Interestingly, for those companies that often engage in more "indirect" communication with the public, such as Hyundai Motors and Posco, indirect information level and corporate involvement had strong effects on corporate reputation as measured by the composite of the four dimensions (i.e., marketing, management leadership, corporate communication, and corporate social responsibility).

As Table 21.7 shows, significant predictors of corporate reputation differed widely depending on each company's characteristics and emerging issues.

Table 21.7 Predictors of Corporate Reputation: Hierarchical Regressions

Predictor Variables		Samsung E[a]	LG E	Hyundai M	SK T	Posco
		(t score)	(t score)	(t score)	(t score)	(t score)
Block 1	Intercept	9.33***	7.51***	7.46***	6.40***	8.78***
	Sex	1.66†	0.53	0.63	-0.02	-0.21
	Age	3.40***	2.06*	1.15	4.06***	3.80***
	Education	0.79	0.03	1.80†	-2.45*	-1.95*
	Income	1.800†	-0.85	-1.6	1.73ᵃ	1.52
Block 2	Key Info. Source[b]	0.58	1.98*	1.89†	-2.25*	0.09
	Trusted source[c]	0.42	-0.48	-0.79	1.98*	0.6
Block 3	Media info.	2.57*	0.84	-0.54	1.71†	1.44
	Direct info.	3.01**	1.2	0.55	0.53	-1.18
	Indirect info.	0.03	0.32	2.35*	0.03	0.01
	Knowledge	2.04*	1.89†	1.58	1.65	1.49
Block 4	Info. search	1.53	2.87**	3.31***	2.75**	1.64
	Involvement	2.44*	0.72	1.54	1.1	2.24*
	Org-public trust	6.76***	5.99***	3.93***	5.58***	5.74***
F		22.69	15.37	11.15	14.45	11.85
R^2		.46***	.54***	.46***	.53***	.48***
R^2 change (Model A)		.06***	0.01	.05*	.12***	.13***
R^2 change (Model B)		.01†	0.01	0.01	.03*	0.02
R^2 change (Model C)		.25***	.34***	.24***	.19***	.15***
R^2 change (Model D)		.14***	.16***	.16***	.18***	.18***

Note. †$p < .10$. *$p < .05$. **$p < .01$. ***$p < .001$. ᵃSamsung E = Samsung Electronics, LG E = LG Electronics, Hyundai M = Hyundai Motors, SK T = SK Telecom. [b]News media as the key information source about the companies studied. [c]News media as a trustworthy source of the information about the companies studied.

Nonetheless, the effect of relational trust was the strongest predictor of corporate reputation among all five companies studied, suggesting that organization–public relational outcomes is the key predictor of corporate reputation, as Yang and Yang (2003) and Yang and J. Grunig (2005) also found.

Discussion

The purpose of this chapter was to review South Korean literature on the effects of the news media on corporate reputation, to explain the South Korean context of public relations practice, and to explore the media's agenda-setting effect using empirical research; that is, triangulation of content analysis of the news media and public poll data.

Corporate reputation and the media's agenda-setting effect have emerged as key research topics in South Korean public relations literature. Furthermore, South Korean researchers have increasingly studied "media reputation" in examining the media's agenda-setting effect on corporate reputation at the first and/or second level of agenda-setting.

In describing the South Korean context of public relations practice, we have highlighted the emergence and the implications of new technologies and the new media environment for public relations in South Korea. Especially, in South Korea, the Internet is one of the most effective delivery tools of communication content to the audience. We noted significant effects of new formats of broadcasting media in public relations (i.e., broadcasting media that have increasingly transformed to be digitalized, boundless, and timeless, such as the integration of satellite/ground wave DMB service).

During such changes in the media environment, South Korean practitioners have transitioned from being traditionally defined publicity makers to communication consultants/strategists that perform strategic and two-way communications. Also, it should be noted that Western theories, such as the Excellence theory, can be applicable to public relations in South Korea but should be applied differently due to the South Korean social/cultural context. Many South Korean researchers have found that South Korean public relations professionals are still influenced by social and historical constraints that have shaped their social roles as public relations professionals (e.g., those who deal with the "toxic sludge" of unethical behaviors of their companies) and by cultural aspects such as collectivism or Confucianism that highlight "jeong" (emotional ties cultivated by personal relationships) or "face" between fellow professionals or journalists.

Finally, a content analysis and a public poll support the first- and second-level substantive agenda setting effect of the news media. Regarding first-level agenda setting, we found identical rank orders between the amount of media coverage and the public's awareness of the five companies studied.

Second, regarding second-level, substantive agenda setting, there existed a significant relationship between the amount of media coverage on corporate attributes and the public's perceptions of corporate attributes, especially in the corporate attributes that received the most extensive media coverage.

However, regarding second-level affective agenda setting effect, we found that the media's agenda setting was not very influential in predicting corporate reputation. Rather, the public's relational trust and involvement with the companies studied turned out to be consistently significant predictors of corporate reputation for the five companies studied.

Therefore, the findings of the study suggested that, in South Korea, media reputation contributes to enhancement of the public's awareness and the public's evaluation of corporate attributes; however, media reputation might not have a significant, direct influence on the formation of corporate reputation. Past results of reputation surveys in South Korea support this finding, suggesting that well-ranked companies are transparent about their operation at every level and cultivate relational outcomes (such as relational trust) to establish the loyalty base of the public. Therefore, we note that the effect of the news media's agenda setting on corporate reputation is partially supported in the South Korean context. That is, public relations professionals should delve into factors that foster quality relationships with the public, such as professionalism, ethical corporate behaviors, and social responsibility, in order to manage corporate reputation indirectly.

Regarding media relations, public relations professionals need to focus on making media coverage of "corporate citizenship" (Fombrun & Van Riel, 2003) visible in the media. By doing so, first-level agenda setting or second-level substantive agenda setting can create second-level affective agenda setting on corporate reputation. The public's awareness of corporate performance matters is a prerequisite of favorable corporate reputation but cannot be equated with excellent corporate reputation unless "quality communications" help the public to cultivate trust with companies, even for nonmarket areas. On this point, as we noted earlier, the new trends in South Korean public relations practice are very encouraging: to be professional, scientific, two-way oriented, and socially responsible.

We propose that future research examine significant moderators and mediators of corporate reputation and integrate them with variables related to the media's agenda-setting effect. By taking an integrative and systematic approach, we believe that the media's role in corporate reputation will be much clearer than in simple bivariate analyses of media reputation and corporate reputation.

Notes

1. This case study is from part of an earlier research article (Cha, 2006), with reconstruction of the data.
2. According to *Sisa Journal*, one of the prime current-issue magazines in South Korea, those three newspapers have been nominated as the most influential South Korean newspapers for three consecutive years from 2002 to 2004.

References

Ban, H. (2004). Analysis of political candidate attributes: second-level agenda setting theory. *Korean Journal of Journalism & Communication Studies, 48*(4), 175–198.

Ban, H., Choi, W. S., & Shin, S. H. (2004a). News attributes and the second-level agenda setting study: Coverage of the nuclear waste storage facility in Wido. *Journal of Communication and Information, 25*, 65–104.

Ban, H., Choi, W. S., & Shin, S. H. (2004b). The voters' decision and priming effects: A case study of the 17th general election in Korea. *Korean Journal of Broadcasting, 18*(4), 398–443.

Berkowitz, D., & Lee, J. (2004). Media relations in Korea: Cheong between journalist and public relations practitioner. *Public Relations Review, 30*, 431–437.

Bromley, D. B. (1993). *Reputation, image, and impression management.* Chichester, UK: Wiley.

Bromley, D. B. (2000). Psychological aspects of corporate identity, image, and reputation. *Corporate Reputation Review, 3*(3), 240–252.

Bromley, D. B. (2002). Comparing corporate reputations: League tables, quotients, benchmarks, or case studies? *Corporate Reputation Review, 5*(1), 35–50.

Cha, H. W. (2004). Agenda-setting effects of mass media on corporate reputations by public involvement and media credibility. *Korean Journal of Journalism and Communication Studies, 48*(6), 274–304.

Cha, H. W. (2006). The effects of media reputation and issue reputation on corporate reputation by issue attribute. *Korean Journal of Journalism and Communication Studies, 50*(5), 297–324.

Chang, M. S. (1995). A research on agenda-setting roles of corporate advertising. *The Korean Journal of Advertising, 6,* 7–34.

Choi, W. S., & Ban, H. (2006). The study of agenda-setting effect model on the public opinion and behavior: Coverage of bubble real estate prices and government polices. *Korean Journal of Journalism & Communication Studies, 50*(1), 406–436.

Fombrun, C. J. (1996). *Reputation: Realizing value from the corporate image.* Boston: Harvard Business School Press.

Fombrun, C. J., & Gardberg, N. A. (2000). Who's tops in corporate reputation? *Corporate Reputation Review, 3*(1), 309–317.

Fombrun, C. J., & Rindova, V. P. (2000). The road to transparency: Reputation management at Royal Dutch Shell. In M. Schultz, M. J. Hatch, & M. H. Larsen (Eds.), *The expressive organization: Linking identity, reputation, and the corporate brand* (pp. 77–96). Oxford, UK: Oxford University Press.

Fombrun, C., & Shanley, M. (1990). What's in a name? Reputation building and corporate strategy. *The Academy of Management Journal, 33*(2), 233–258.

Fombrun, C. J., & Van Riel, C. B. M. (1997). The reputational landscape. *Corporate Reputation Review, 1,* 5–13.

Fombrun, C. J., & Van Riel, C. B. M. (2003). *Fame and fortune: How successful companies build winning reputations.* Upper Saddle River, NJ: Pearson Education.

Grunig, L. A., Grunig, J. E., & Dozier, D. M. (2002). *Excellent public relations and effective organizations: A study of communication management in three countries.* Mahwah, NJ: Erlbaum.

Han, E. K., & Kim, Y. (2005). A study on the effect of the trust in contents of the press on the relationship between corporate PR and reputation. *The Korean Journal of Advertising, 16*(1), 183–202.

Han, E. K., Kim, Y. H., & Moon, H. J. (2005). A study on the effect model of the corporate reputation and the CEO reputation: with focus on Samsung and SK. *The Korean Journal of Advertising, 16*(2), 125–144.

Han, E. K., & Ryu, J. H. (2004). A study on corporate reputation factors to influence the purchasing intention of consumers: Based on Korean and Japanese dairy products companies. *Gwang-go Yeon-gu, 65,* 127–146.

Hwang, B. I. (2004). The effects of corporate expertise, trustworthiness, social responsibility on corporate reputation and customer's relationship retention intention. *The Korean Journal of Advertising, 15*(5), 361–378.

Iyenger, S., & Kinder, D. R. (1987). *News that matters: Television and American opinion.* Chicago, IL: University of Chicago Press.

Jo, J. Y. (2005). A study of response strategy to negative news coverage for reputation management. *The Korean Journal of Advertising, 16*(4), 257–275.

Jo, S., & Kim, Y. (2004). Media or personal relations? Exploring media relations dimensions in South Korea. *Journalism and Mass Communication Quarterly, 81*(2), 292–306.

Jo, S. S., & Kim, Y. J. (2004). A comparative study of online journalism in relation to agenda-setting function. *Korean Journal of Journalism & Communication Studies, 48*(3), 302–330.

Kang, M. H., & Jo, J. Y. (2003). Localism & relationship: A review of local broadcasting companies' cultural events. *The Korean Journal of Public Relations Research, 7*(2), 43–68.

Kim, B. H. (2001). Agenda-setting effects of corporate advertising: A case study of United Technologies Corporation (UTC) (Korean) *Journal of Advertising Research, 50,* 7–36.

Kim, C. H., & Oh, M. Y. (2003). Relationships between organization-public relationships and image: Interaction between behavioral relationships and symbolic relationships. *Korean Journal of Journalism & Communication Studies, 47*(2), 78–108.

Kim, S. T., & Lee, Y. H. (2006). New function of internet mediated agenda-setting: Agenda-rippling and reversed agenda-setting. *Korean Journal of Journalism and Communication studies, 50*(3), 175–205.

Kim, Y., & Cha, H. (2002). The emerging conflict between tradition and changes: Exploring the Korea-style public relations. *Korean Journal of Journalism and Communication Studies, 46*(5), 5–42.

Korea Press Foundation (2006). *Korean media yearbook 2006.* Seoul, South Korea.

Ku, G. (2002). The impact of website campaigning on traditional news media and public agenda: Based on agenda-setting. *Korean Journal of Journalism and Communication Studies, 46*(4), 46–77.

Kwon, J. (2002). Positioning the social problems carried on PSA (public service advertising). *The Korean Journal of Advertising, 8*(2), 67–86.

Kwon, J. R. (1997). Agenda-setting effects of public service announcement: An experimental study. *The Korean Journal of Advertising, 8,* 67–86.

Lee, C. H., & Cha, H. W. (2005). A study on reputation as corporate asset. *Journal of Communication and Information, 30,* 1–74.

Lee, D. G., & Lee, K. Y. (2005). Inter-media agenda setting between online and offline News media. *Korean Journal of Broadcasting, 19*(3), 7–20.

Lee, G. (2006). Agenda setting and priming effects of online media: Experiment on online media's role of salience transfer and evaluative dimension building. *Korean Journal of Journalism and Communication Studies, 50*(3), 367–393.

Lee, G. H. (2002). Negative emotion, cynicism, and efficacy: Political effect of media framing. *Korean Journal of Journalism and Communication Studies, 46*(3), 252–290.

Lee, J. H. (2004). A study of analyzing the factors affecting the media relationship: Focusing on the evaluation by PR practitioners. *Korean Journal of Journalism and Communication Studies, 48*(3), 248–274.

Lee, Y-S. (1996). *A study on PR practitioners' roles and professionalism in Korea: Based on mutual evaluation between PR professionals in companies, agencies, and the press.* Unpublished master's thesis, Yonsei University, Seoul, South Korea.

Oh, C. W. (2000). The influence of public relations on journalism: A system-theory approach to an examination of the effects of press release and the journalists' assessment of press release. *Korean Journal of Journalism and Communication Studies, 44*(4), 120–171.

Park, D. S., Cho, Y. H., & Hong, J. H. (2001). A qualitative study of news source-reporter relations: On the problems of beat reporting system. *Korean Journal of Journalism & Communication Studies, 45*(5), 367–398.

Park, J. H., Kang, S. R., & Lee, E. S. (2005). A study on the effect of partner's reputation, alliance type and commitment on the performance of venture firms. *Jung-so Gi-yep Yeon-gu, 27*(2), 109–141.

Park, J. M. (2000). An analysis on the relations among consumer brands, brand advertising and corporate reputation in consumer's purchase intentions. (Korean) *Journal of Advertising Research, 49,* 77–108.

Rhee, Y. (2002). Global public relations: A cross-cultural study of the excellence theory in South Korea. *Journal of Public Relations Research, 14*(3), 159–184.

Rlee, J. W. (2001). Impacts of news frames in the coverage of conflicting issues on individual interpretation and opinion. *Korean Journal of Journalism & Communication Studies, 46*(1), 441–484.

Rho, B. H., Lim, C. U., & Hwang, K. J. (2004). A field survey research on Korean firm's reputation. *Sogang Journal of Business, 15,* 29–44.

Scheufele. A. D. (2000). Agenda-setting, priming, and framing revisited: Another look at cognitive effects of political communication. *Mass Communication and Society, 3*(2&3), 297–316.

Shin, H. C., & Kim, M. H. (2003). A comparative study of PR practitioners and journalists' perceptions on media relations. *Korean Advertising Research, 6*(1), 81–120.

Shin, J. C., Song, C. S., Hong, S. T., & Kang, M. S. (2004). A study on the determinants of the SMEs' internet marketing intention. *Korean Research on Middle-sized Firms, 26*(2), 145–170.

Shin, J-H. (2000). *PR practitioners' and journalists' informal relations: Perceptions and cross-perceptions.* Unpublished master's thesis, Sogang University, Seoul, South Korea.

Shin, J. H., Park, J., & Cameron, G. T. (2006). Contingent factors: Modeling generic public relations practice in South Korea. *Public Relations Review, 32*(2), 184–185.

Shoemaker, P. J. (1996). Hard-wired for news: Using biological and cultural evolution to explain the news. *Journal of Communication, 46*(3), 32-47.

Shoemaker, P. J., & Cohen, A. (2006). *News around the world: Practitioners, content and the public.* New York: Routledge.

Shoemaker, P. J., Danielian, L. H., & Brendlinger, N. (1991). Deviant acts, risky business, and U.S. interests: The newsworthiness of world events. *Journalism Quarterly, 68*(4), 781–795.

Son, S-H., & Lee, C-H. (1999). *TV journalism and news value: A content analysis of Korean, English, American TV news.* Korea Press Foundation, Seoul, South Korea.

Song, H. R., Kim, W. J., & Cho, H. M. (2005). A study on audience's awareness about the media reports of science technology risk: focused on the genetically modified organism (GMO) case. *Korean Journal of Journalism and Communication Studies, 49*(3), 105–130.

Yang, S. K., & Yang, S. U. (2003). The moderating effect of level of involvement between organization–public relationships and organizational reputation. *Journal of Communication and Information, 21,* 114–147.

Yang, S. U. (2004). *The effects of organization-public relationships, organizational visibility, and media coverage in reputation formation.* Paper presented at the Public Relations Society of America (PRSA) International Conference, New York City.

Yang, S. U., & Grunig, J. E. (2005). Decomposing organizational reputation: the effects of organization-public relationship outcomes on cognitive representations of organizations and evaluations of organizational performance. *Journal of Communication Management, 9*(4), 305–325.

Yoon, K., & Cho, J. S. (2005). The effect of a crisis caused by a negative media publicity on corporate reputation: The role of corporate social responsibility activities. *The Korean Journal of Public Relations Research, 9*(2), 196–220

Yoon, K., & Suh, S. h. (2003). The influence of corporate advertising and social respon-sibility activities on corporate image and brand attitudes. *Gwang-go Yeon-gu, 61,* 47–72.

Yoon, T. I., & Shim, J. C. (2003). Agenda-setting effects of controversial websites. *Korean Journal of Journalism & Communication Studies, 47*(6), 194–220.

22 Corporate Reputation and the News Media in Turkey

Serra Görpe and Erkan Yüksel

This chapter examines how the news media in Turkey affect public perceptions of corporations. We survey the definition of corporate reputation in the Turkish context and the progress of agenda-setting theory studies in the country. The first agenda-setting study in Turkey was completed for a master's thesis by Çelebi in 1990, and only a few studies have been carried out since then. There are few agenda-setting studies applied to public relations in Turkey. This chapter summarizes corporate reputation rankings in Turkey and then presents original research on first-level agenda setting in Turkey, using *Capital* magazine's "Most Admired Companies" for the reputation data and 18 daily Turkish newspapers for media data. The chapter also surveys Turkey's media system and highlights issues relating to media ownership, and its effects. Public relations' history, development, and education is reviewed with a focus on current research findings and data provided for and from international associations. In Turkey, the lack of regular public opinion polls, corporate reputation public opinion polls, and especially the lack of comparative data extending back over several decades, limit the comprehensiveness of research in these areas.

Turkey has borders with Georgia, Armenia, Nakhichevan, and Iran on the east; Bulgaria and Greece on the west; and Iraq and Syria on the south. Turkey is the only Islamic country that is secular, both in its Constitution and in practice. With the foundation of the Republic in 1923, religion and state affairs were separated, and laws were formulated according to secular principles. On the Global Competitiveness Index rankings released by the World Economic Forum (2006), Turkey ranked 59th of 125 countries, up from 71st in 2005. According to the report, among middle-income countries, Turkey showed one of the highest rates of dynamism (Claros-Lopez). Turkey was ranked 53rd among 131 countries in the Global Competitiveness Report of 2007–2008 (World Economic Forum, 2008).

Review of the Literature: Public Relations in Turkey

As is the case in many countries, the public relations profession has been affected by the culture and developments in Turkey, a country combining Western and Eastern cultures. As Verčič, Grunig, and Grunig (1996) have noted, the general principles of excellent public relations can be practiced if contextual variables are identified. Factors that shape public relations practices are the political–economic system, activism, the level of development (including the development of public relations as a profession), the media system, and the overall culture.

Turkey's culture is characterized by extremes of and wealth, low individualism, strong avoidance of uncertainty, and moderate feminism. Schwartz (cited in Ararat & Göcenoğlu, 2006) noted that Turkey ranked above average in conservatism, hierarchy, and harmony, which supports Hofstede's (2003) findings. A more recent study, "Global Leadership and Organizational Behavior Effectiveness Research Program" (GLOBE; 2004), which surveyed 62 cultures, showed that group collectivism and inequality in terms of power are the two predominant characteristics of Turkish culture.

To analyze the history of public relations in Turkey, one must consider the societal structure during the era of the Republic (the 1950s), the effects of the 1961 Constitution, and the 1980s and 1990s. All these transitional periods have influenced the practice of public relations (Kazancı, 2002). Coups d'état in Turkey's history, and today its market economy and its relations with the European Union all affect the PR profession.

The practice of modern public relations in Turkey first emerged under the leadership of the government in the 1960s, but with the multinational companies' entrance into the Turkish market, public relations efforts shifted from the public sector to the private sector. The first public relations practitioners were mostly former journalists.

The public relations profession had its roots in the professional world, but by the 1990s it was flourishing in the academy as well. Public relations instruction in Turkey first began in 1966, in the Journalism and Public Relations Vocational School, which is part of the Political Science Faculty of Ankara University. Although journalism and public relations education were taught together, by 1992, public relations institutions became faculties that taught public relations under separate divisions within departments of communication (Görpe, 2006–2007). In Turkey, there are now 32 communication faculties, including private and public universities (http://www.iletisimfakulteleri.gen.tr/fakulteler.asp).

Although Turkey does not have a long history of public relations as either a profession or an academic field, Turkish public relations has been represented by practitioners at international associations such as the International Public Relations Association (IPRA), the European Public Relations Confederation (CERP), and the Global Alliance for Public Relations and Communications Management (Görpe, 2006–2007). Betül Mardin served as the first Turkish President of International Public Relations Association (IPRA) in 1995, and Ceyda Aydede was elected President in 2003 (Özden & Saran, 2004). Mardin is the winner of the Public Relations Society of America's 2005 Atlas Award for Lifetime Achievement in International Public Relations.

Turkey's public relations association, Halkla İlişkiler Derneği (HİD), was founded in 1972 by 13 practitioners. In February 2005, HİD officially changed its status and name to the Turkish Public Relations Association (TÜHİD), thus representing the profession in Turkey. During the first period, which lasted until the 2000s, the TÜHİD worked mostly for the acknowledgment of public relations in Turkish society. The second period has been highlighted by revisions in the structure of the association, including revision of its mission, vision, and ethics, as well as the achievement of close networking with international associations.

In addition to the national association, there is the Public Relations Consultancies Association (HDD), founded by Turkish IPRA members. There is also the Communications Consultancy Companies Association (IDA/ICCO Turkey), founded by 11 communications consultancy firms in order to expand the public relations and communications consultancy sector and raise service standards. They have been officially active since September 2004, but as the former PRCI/ICCO Turkey, they made important contributions such as the rewriting of ICCO bylaws (Görpe, 2006–2007). By the end of 2008, there were 16 members of the association.

Turkey was ranked 21st in a study commissioned by the Institute of Public Relations (IPR), the International Public Relations Association (IPRA), and sponsored by the *Hürriyet* newspaper in Turkey, a member of the Doğan Group, that was conducted in 2003 (IPRA, 2003). By June 2008, the IPRA had 38 active members in Turkey, 28 of whom are women. It is tied with China as the fifth largest IPRA group, behind Britain, the United States, Saudi Arabia, and Nigeria (IPRA Secretariat, personal communication June 17,2008). All these data are indicators of Turkey's growth, determination, and involvement.

A study conducted by the PRCI/ICCO Turkey in 2002 on the perception of the public relations industry, provided data from the media, public relations consultancies, and in-house professionals. Corporate reputation, research/evaluation, and media relations were seen as the three top areas that would be among the most important to the business world in the short term. Public relations consultancies also believed that corporate social responsability will be an accelerating trend. (personal communication, Halkla İlişkiler Sektörü Nasıl Algılanıyor, February 6, 2003) The top five services provided by public relations consultancies were media relations, employee communications, crisis communications, issues management, sponsorship, and corporate social responsibility (Strateji/GfK, personal communication, November 18, 2002).

A study completed in August 2006 joinly sponsored by the TÜHİD and IDA/ICCO Turkey, yielded comprehensive findings on the perception of the public relations profession. The study surveyed communication professionals from the corporate side, CEOs/general managers, communication consultancy agencies, and the media. More than 90% indicated that the contribution of corporate communication activities to business objectives is high. Communication consultancies agreed with this statement the most. CEOs/general managers, communication consultancies, and communication managers all agreed that the most effective communication service currently is corporate reputation management. In the future, according to all respondents corporate reputation management will still be the most effective tool; other areas of predicted growth in the near future were online communications, sponsorship, corporate social responsibility, and direct marketing (GfK Türkiye, September 2006).

The IDA/ICCO Turkey Country Report presented on October 4, 2006 in Delhi showed that the total annualized fee income from its members in 2005 was US$17,117,954. Factors seen as inhibiting growth were Turkey's internal political situation, the election medium, uncertainity about the EU process, the external political situation, the economic reflection of these political issues, lack of economic stability, and insufficent foreign investment. Factors seen as assisting growth were the EU accession process, the success of privatization, the importance given to CSR projects, the rise of new sectors, and increased awareness and demands from communications consultancies. According to the report, industry market sectors with the best growth prospects are construction, fast moving consumer goods (FMCG), energy, and health. Textiles, retail clothing, automotive, banking, and IT were among the industry market sectors with the worst growth prospects in 2007. The unemployment level was decreasing slightly, and there was difficulty finding qualified employees. The estimated proportion of members' fee income derived from international business was 40 to 42%, which was expected to increase in 2007.

Corporate Reputation in Turkey

Since the mid-1980s both public relations professionals and academics have tried to redefine public relations and have claimed that current public relations practices fail to encompass the wide range of responsibilities implicit in public relations. In the 1990s, two terms became popular: *reputation management* and *perception management.* "Reputation and perception are considered as two important dimensions of public relations and you cannot do without either of them," says Salim Kadıbeşegil, a pioneer in reputation management development in Turkey who authored the first book on reputation management in Turkish in 2006.

Although Kadıbeşegil sees reputation management as different from public relations and claims that it should not be left in the hands of such practitioners, some public relations professionals disagree. Reputation management terminology became popular when public relations was seen as insufficient to achieve desired outcomes. *Public relations* became an overused term, and when it was used it was focused narrowly on short-term results as a marketing tool or in terms of media relations. Reputation management was seen as more relevant, although some Turkish public relations professionals think that they are also managing reputation. The picture is blurred, but the concept of reputation management has become more familiar with Turkish professionals since 1999.

Necla Zarakol, president of the Zarakol Communication Agency, defines reputation management as an institution's efforts to position itself on the mental map of its stakeholders in the desired manner and to coordinate its communication activities in the light of that positioning (Zarakol, 2006). Meriç Renkver, managing partner of Etica Communication Consultancy, says that reputation is the product of public relations (Renkver, 2006). According to Betül Mardin, sometimes called the "mother" of public relations in Turkey, "Increasing interest in reputation and the risks these corporations were witnessing made them listen—at long last—to their communication directors and/or consultants" (Mardin, 2005, p. 6).

Haluk Gürgen, professor of public relations, says that the problem with reputation management is that it needs more research on reputation processes (personal interview, September 19, 2006). Gürgen adds that very few people

Table 22.1 Graduate Work on "Corporate Reputation"

Title	Author/Year	Type	Institution	Year
Corporate image, corporate reputation and a study about how automobile producers are perceived by their costomers	Çeşminaz Didem Bilgin (2004)	Master	Istanbul University	2004
The management of corporate reputation and an application in Turkey	Şengül Ebru (2004)	Master	Istanbul University	2004
Corporate reputation for competitive advantage	Sinan Yılmaz (2004)	Master	Karaelmas University	2004
The role of corporate image and corporate reputation on customer loyalty: An investigation in a financial institution	Seda Süer (2005)	Master	Dokuz Eylül University	2005
The internal and external shareholders Perceptions regarding corporate reputation in educational organizations	Turgut Karaköse (2006)	Dissertation	Fırat University	2006
Corporate reputation and the case of Anadolu University	Erkan Altıntaş (2005)	Master	Anadolu University	2005
Corporate reputation management and one application	Duygu Akmehnet (2006)	Master	Marmara University	2006
The Impact of Art Sponsorship On Corporate Reputation	Selçuk Tavlak (2007)	Master	Marmara University	2007
The reputation management in political marketing as a sort of political communication	Duygu Kotan (2005)	Master	Marmara University	2005
Public relations and reputation management in organizational culture: An example of Aegean and the Mediterranean region tourism organization	Murat Usta (2006)	Master	Dokuz Eylül University	2006
Lobbying in the United States: Reputation management of Turkey	Memnune Alev Pak (1994)	Master	Bilkent University	1994

in the academic field are working on this topic. Public relations academics are instead approaching the topic through corporate communication courses or books. A search of master theses and doctoral dissertations with the key words *reputation, corporate reputation,* and *reputation management* shows that 11 graduate studies were produced, all of them between the years 2004 and 2007.

Business and the News Media

The business and media relationship in Turkey became significant in the 1980s as businesspeople began to own newspapers and private television and radio stations. Monopoly ownership of the Turkish press was the topic dominating discussion during those years. Before this period, business and media relationships existed at the news level but not the organizational level. In the 1990s and 2000s, the ownership pattern of the Turkish media changed, and the country's largest newspapers came to be owned by the largest developing media groups. In the early years of journalism in Turkey, journalists were the owners of the newspapers. Today media groups have large holdings that own several newspapers, magazines, radio, and television stations as well as other businesses such as travel and marketing.

Bank owners also had large holdings in the Turkish media, and, with the crisis in the banking system in the early 2000s, many banks had to sell their investments and some lost control of their media groups. The governmental banking control system, Tasarruf Mevduatı Sigorta Fonu (TMSF), took over the investigation of these banks and their companies, including their media companies. For a brief period, the government became the biggest media group in Turkey, after which the media companies were sold to new owners. A report on media ownership patterns in Turkey prepared by *MediaCat* magazine (2008) is summarized in Table 22.2.

According to Barış (2006), the media landscape of Turkey is unstable. The owners of the media can change from one day to the next, and the media support or oppose certain interest groups or the government, depending on the economic and political interests of the owners. For this reason, she notes, any information about the media in Turkey can rapidly become outdated.

The monopolization of media ownership raises doubts as to the objectivity and independence of journalists and the quality of journalism in Turkey. It is not unusual to hear claims that certain news stories were deliberately ignored or exaggerated to protect the interests of cross-media groups. Media power has also been used by private broadcasters to promote their owners' interests (Barış, 2006).

News Values

News values determine how much prominence a news story is given by the media. No specific study describes the prominence of the Turkish media's news values, but there are articles and books that include discussion of news values in Turkey (Girgin, 2000; Tokgöz, 2000; Yüksel & Gürcan, 2005). So, despite comparatively light coverage, several news values can be identified (Yüksel & Gürcan, 2005, pp. 58–60):

Table 22.2 Media Ownership Pattern in Turkey

	TV	News-paper	Radio	Maga-zine	Distri-bution C.	Digital	News Agency
Albayrak Group	1	1					
Avrupa, Amerika Holding Company	4		4				
Bagimsiz Gazeteciler Yayincilik		1		5			
Baskent University	1		1				
Canwest Medya Turkiye			4				
Ciner Group	2		1	11			
Cumhuriyet Vakfi (Foundation)		1					
Calik Holding Company	1	6	1	11	1		
Cukurova Group	23	3	2	8		1	
Dogan Holding	26	8	3	27	1	1	1
Dogus Group	5		4	7			
Dunya Group		1		10			
Feza Gazatecilik (Journalism)		2		2			
Goktug Elektronik Yayincilik	1						
Ihlas Holding	1	1	1	9			1
Koza Ipek Holding		1					
MHP	1						
MNG Group	1						1
News Corporation	2						
Property International	1	2					
Samanyolu Yayincilik	3		3				
TMSF	1		1				
Termikel Group	1						
Yasam Televizyon Yayincilik	1						
Yeni Dunya Iletisim	4		2				

Timeliness

Timeliness refers to the answer to the question, "when?" Recent events have higher news value than those that are less recent. News must be new, instantaneous, and current.

Nearness or Proximity

Nearness or proximity refers to the answer to the question, "where?" Events that happen in close proximity have higher news value. For a local newspaper, events happening in the city come before events that happen in other cities.

Importance

Importance refers to how important the event is for the audience, city, country, or people. Events with the most relevance or meaning to a given audience, city, country, or individuals have higher news value.

Impact/Effective Interest

Impact and effective interest refers to the fact that an event is not of interest to everybody. Therefore, it is important for news to attract as many people as possible who will be interested in it. More interested people mean more news value for the event.

Bizarreness/Unexpectedness

This concept refers to the idea that news must be interesting. A classic example of this is the dog-bites-man story vs. man-bites-dog story. Man-bites-dog is more bizarre and therefore has more news value.

Organizational Newsworthiness

There has been no specific research in Turkey into news values as they relate to business news. Yüksel's (1999) study shows that the content of the business pages in the main daily newspapers has changed from period to period parallel with the country's economic development. The results of a content analysis establish a list of news issues. Banking sector issues head the list, followed by privatization; relationships with the European Community; legal agreements and new applications; money market or financial issues; unions, associations, and organizations; the national treasury; investments and enterprises; the stock exchange market; company presentation or introduction; taxation; the automotive sector; social security; new products; imports; computers; air transportation; tourism and travel; labor unions; and insurance.

Agenda-Setting Theory

Agenda-setting theory has mainly been used to understand the relationship between the real world indicators and media coverage, as well as to understand the role of media content on public perceptions in Turkey. Several studies that use the term *agenda setting* investigate mainly media agenda setting and real world indicators. Table 22.3 lists agenda-setting studies and their hypotheses.

Table 22.3 Agenda-Setting Studies in Turkey

Dissertation Thesis	Research	Hypothesis
Atabek (1997)	Model of agenda-setting and the realities of inflation, traffic, and social security issues and the comparison of media and public agenda	First level agenda setting, and real world indicators
İrvan (1997)	Foreign Policy and Press: Analysis of the foreign news in Turkish press with the angle of agenda setting hypothesis	First level agenda setting
Yüksel (1999)	The relationship between economy pages' agenda and policy agenda in Turkey: An agenda setting study on privatization issue	Intermedia agenda setting, media agenda setting, policy agenda setting and real world indicators (Published as a book by Anadolu University in 2000)
Turan (2004)	Agenda-setting processes of evening television news bulletins in Turkey	Public opinion, and opinions of news directors and editors on the agenda-setting role of the television news bulletins.
Terkan (2005)	The relationship between the press and the policy	Press agenda and the policy agenda relationship.
Master Thesis	*Research*	*Hypothesis*
Çelebi (1990)	Discourse Analysis: A Critical Approach to the newspapers' news making and agenda setting functions	Partly media agenda setting
Hazar (1996)	Effects of mass communication and agenda-setting as a social functions	First level agenda setting
Zengin (2000)	Effects of national newspapers' policies on Turkey's agenda	Media agenda setting
Tosun (2001)	Agenda-setting and the case of PR activities of Ministry of Justice	Media agenda setting
Şimşek (2002)	An applied research on the agenda setting effects of Internet web sites	Media agenda setting
Abrak (2006)	A news analysis of the process of Turkey's membership to EU under the light of agenda setting model	Media agenda setting
Uçak (2007)	The agenda setting role of the press under the context of agenda and news relationship	Media agenda setting

(*Continued*)

Table 22.3 Continued

Articles	Research	Hypothesis
Akdemir (1991)	Agenda-setting process on environment pollution and Turkish Press: Cases on Halic and Gokova	Media agenda setting
Alpkaya and Çelebi (1994)	Agenda-setting in the Media: Case for Hurriyet Newspaper in 1994	Media agenda setting
Güz (1996)	Agenda-setting in Turkish Press	First level agenda setting
Symposium Papers	*Research*	*Hypothesis*
McCombs & Yüksel (2001)	The Economic Privatization Issue in Turkey: A Four-Part Investigation of Agenda Setting Theory	Intermedia agenda setting, attribute agenda setting, media agenda, policy agenda and real world indicators,
Yüksel (2003)	A Second Level Agenda Setting Study in Turkish Parlimentary Elections	Second Level Agenda Setting
McCombs & Yüksel (2004)	The Agenda Setting Capacity of the National Security Council and the Education Reform Issue in Turkey	Media agenda setting and the role of National Security Council
Pelenk & Gül (2004)	Examining the Role of Agenda Setting in Public Relations Process as an Issue: A Case Study	Media agenda setting and Public Relations
Gül (2005)	A Media Agenda-Setting Research: The Mardin Kızıltepe Event	Media agenda setting
Tandaçgüneş & Yalın (2005)	Agenda Setting Theory and Proactive PR: A Research About World AIDS Week	Media agenda setting and Public Relations
Görpe & Yüksel (2007)	Media Content and Corporate Reputation Survey 2006 in Turkey: A First Level Agenda-Setting Study	Media agenda setting and Public Relations

Most of the research on agenda-setting theory in Turkey has been published in Turkish (Yüksel, 2008), and few of the studies have applied agenda-setting theory to the public relations field. Pelenk and Gül's (2004) paper "Examining the Role of Agenda Setting in the Public Relations Process as an Issue: A Case Study" deals with the Türkiye Eğitim Gönüllüleri Vakfı (TEGV; English Educational Volunteers of Turkey) case and its media agenda-setting role. The research finds that TEGV is effectively an agenda setter, but the research does not deal with the reputation of TEGV. The second study, by Tandaçgüneş and Yalın (2005), "Agenda-Setting Theory and Proactive PR: A Study of World AIDS Week" does not look at the reputation of the NGO, but compares periods when activities were coordinated by a public relations consultancy with those when they were not. One master's thesis by Tosun (2001) looks at agenda setting and public relations activities at the Ministry of Justice.

Case Study

The Corporate Reputation Landscape in Turkey

In Turkey, the first corporate reputation study was initiated by the Koç Group in 1999. They wrote the famous *Green Book* on the subject. In addition to visionary corporations such as the Koç Group, others came to understand the importance of reputation management more when they encountered crises or saw world-wide scandals reported in the media. In an interview, Kadıbeşegil claims that currently 50 corporations are conducting regular research on their corporate reputation, but what is of equal importance is what will be done with the results of these studies.

Capital monthly magazine, which belongs to the Hürriyet magazine group, conducted the first "Most Admired Companies" study in 1999. This study is an adaption of the research done by *Fortune* magazine in the United States and the *Financial Times* in Britain; the respondents of the *Capital* study are top level managers (Yağcı, 2006).

The research is being revised yearly in terms of criteria, content, and industries included. For example, the first study used 10 criteria and 23 different sectors (En Beğenilen Şirketler, 2006).

The 2002 study was based on 18 criteria, each of which can potentially gene-rate admiration for a company on a scale of 1 to 10: The criteria included, the most admired company and reasons for that choice, the top three most admired companies in the industry and reasons for those choices, evaluation of the most admired company in the industry with each attribute (Dörtok, 2006).

Analysis of the results of the four studies (2001, 2002, 2003, and 2004) reve-aled three criteria that make a Turkish corporation reputable: being customer-oriented; providing quality services or products; and quality of management.

The Arçelik company, a manufacturer of household appliances, ranked first during each of these years (Büyük, 2006). Ten to 15 corporations always ranked among the top 20 and the top-ranked company in seven industries has not chan-ged; a similar result is found in the other three industries included in the study in the last years. The second and third place rankings have been shared among four corporations: Vestel, Turkcell, the Koç Group, and the Sabancı Group. Main-taining a rank among the top 20 was not that easy: Coca Cola, the Eczacıbaşı Group, Garanti Bank, Microsoft, Procter and Gamble, Unilever, and Ülker were ranked on all four lists, though their specific ranks differed from year to year.

The sixth "Most Admired Companies" of Turkey studied over 500 compa-nies, 1,350 professionals, and 30 industries (Büyük, 2006). An additional crite-rion was added to the previously used criteria: "a corporation's contribution to the community with its investments." Turkcell, Arçelik, and the Koç Group were the three most admired companies in this regard. In some industries, the same company received the highest ranking in 2004 and 2005 (Büyük, 2006).

Salim Kadıbeşegil is a consultant for that annual study, and it is carried out with a research firm. Traditionally, the "Most Admired Companies" research starts in June, and the results are reported in December.

Research Methodology

As seen from the literature review, *reputation management* is a novel term that has replaced *public relations* in certain situations, but few academic studies have been conducted in that field in Turkey. This study analyzes the corporate reputation rankings in Turkey and then presents original research on first-level agenda setting in Turkey, using *Capital* magazine's "Most Admired Companies" for the reputation data and 18 daily Turkish newspapers for media data.

Public Opinion Polls

There are few corporate reputation public opinion polls in Turkey. The one that *Capital* magazine performs asks questions of top-level people in corporations and various sectors. The results of these annual studies are also used by academics for research.

The questions regarding the most admired company were asked by *Capital* magazine and Gfk Research during the period of September to October 2004. The public saw the Sabancı Group as the most reputable and most accountable to the public due to its social responsibility. The public rated Arçelik as second most reputable due to its products and services. The public and the leaders had different views as to the most admired corporations, though there were some similarities in the overall lists of the public and the leaders. For example, the leaders rated Arçelik as number 1 and Sabancı Holding as number 5.

Capital magazine's corporate social responsibility research, which has been carried out for 2 years, is designed to discover what the public thinks about companies that are socially responsible. For example, the study examines the effectiveness of CSR in Turkey, and the relationship between corporations and their CSR practices. The Sabancı Group, the Koç Group, and Arçelik were named as the three corporations for which people most wanted to work. The top five companies seen as most successful in CSR were the Sabancı Group (39.2%), the Koç Group (24.3%), Turkcell (9.9%), Arçelik (6.7%), and the Eczacıbaşı Group (5.5%). When compared with the previous study, the major difference was that the public is more sensitive to CSR practices. The Sabancı Group was seen as the most succesful in almost every subcategory of CSR, and the public wants these efforts to be communicated to them (Büyük, 2006).

Reputation Data

The present study bases itself on data from *Capital* magazine's research for the "Most Admired Companies." Because of its good positioning and comprehensiveness in surveying both the professionals and the public this survey is a reputation indicator—indeed, a benchmark study thatwas carried out over a period of 6 years. The present study employs two types of data: one obtained from the media, and the other, the reputation data, from the annual reputation surveys of *Capital* magazine. The study is based on the "Most Admired Companies of Turkey" published in the December 2005 issue of *Capital* magazine. The results of the poll conducted with 1,350 top managers in Turkey showed the most admired companies in 30 different sectors according to 19 criteria. The present study looked at the most admired corporations in five different sectors: fuel oil, petroleum, and energy; cement; banking; white goods; and automotive. The reputation data resulted from the surveys of 2004 and 2005.

Choice of News Media

The present study analyzed data from Turkish print media. Media data were gathered by content analysis of 18 different national daily newspapers in Turkey: *Akşam, Cumhuriyet, Dünden Bugüne Tercüman, Dünya, Gözcü, Halka ve Olaylara Tercüman, Hürriyet, Milliyet, Posta, Radikal, Referans, Sabah, Star, Takvim, Türkiye, Vatan, Yeni Şafak,* and *Zaman*. The data were gathered from these dailies using the PRnet online search engine. A keyword search of the names of the corporations listed as the "Most Admired Companies' of *Capital* magazine for the years 2004 and 2005, was performed using this search engine. The total number of published articles about these corporations over a one-year period was evaluated as indicating the importance of the corporations in the media agenda.

As of January 2005, there were 34 daily national newspapers, including two sports newspapers, in Turkey. The total average daily sales of these 34 newspapers were 4,867,863. Ten of these newspapers have combined sales of less than 50,000 copies. The newspapers selling more than 50,000 copies have a combined total of 4,775,849 daily average sales (Report of YAYSAT, 2005).

The 18 newspapers selected for the media data analysis comprise more than 80% of the total sales of newspapers in Turkey, totaling 3,980,208 copies. This media analysis is the largest in Turkey, and for the first time it covers many newspapers with different owners and which circulate through a wide population

Data Analysis

The data gathered from *Capital* magazine's December 2005 issue lists the most admired companies of 2004 and 2005 in different sectors. Table 22.4 summarizes the findings of 2004, including the names of the corporations according to five sectors chosen and media data. The number of articles that appeared about these corporations and the coverage rank of these corporations in the newspapers were analyzed for the present study.

Table 22.5 lists the names of the top three most reputable companies according to the five sectors they operate in, and also includes the findings of content analysis about these corporations in year 2005.

Table 23.4 Findings of the Year 2004

2004	Capital Reputation List	Corporations	Number of Articles	Coverage Rank
Energy	1	Shell	662	1
	2	BP	573	2
	3	Ak Enerji	322	3
Cement	1	Akçansa	169	1
	2	Çimsa	111	2
	3	Adana Çimento/Nuh Çimento	94/63	3
Banking	1	Garanti	1,816	2
	2	Akbank	2,906	1
	3	Denizbank	838	3
White Goods	1	Arçelik	1,722	2
	2	Vestel	2,400	1
	3	Tefal	78	3
Automotive	1	Ford Otosan	2,567	2
	2	Toyota	1,592	3
	3	Oyak Renault	2,919	1

Results

The current study evaluated the following hypotheses:

Hypothesis 1

The amount of news coverage that a firm receives in the news media is positively related to the public's awareness of the firm. In other words, the research focuses only on visibility, not on second-level agenda setting. Particular attributes of the firm reported in the media, such as products and services, or social responsibility, have not been analyzed, nor were the media's favorable or unfavorable attitudes (evaluative attributes) taken into consideration; these will be considered in the discussion and conclusions section at the end of this chapter.

The findings show that in Turkey the most admired corporations of 2004 and 2005, in five different sectors, have different rankings in the Turkish press. We can approach the findings from different angles, but in any case, it is clear that there is a relationship between visibility in the media and the ranking of the corporations, and that in some sectors the relationship is stronger than others.

When we compare the news coverage of sectors, the automotive sector is the one that receives the most coverage from the Turkish media. This is followed closely by banking and white goods. In 2005, the Yapı Kredi Bank ranked third both in visibility and reputation. Both the cement and energy sectors have less

Table 23.5 Findings of the Year 2005

2005	Capital Reputation List	Corporations	Number of Articles	Coverage Rank
Energy	1	Shell	1,647	1
	2	BP	844	3
	3	Zorlu Enerji	1,000	2
Cement	1	Akçansa	356	1
	2	Çimsa	258	2
	3	Nuh Çimento	134	3
Banking	1	Garanti	2,644	2
	2	İş Bankası	3,085	1
	3	TEB/	493/	3
		Yapı Kredi	2,122	
White Goods	1	Arçelik	1,694	2
	2	Vestel	3,792	1
	3	Bosh	436	3
Automotive	1	Ford Otosan	2,681	2
	2	Toyota	1,676	3
	3	Oyak Renault	2,951	1

visibility in the media compared to the other sectors analyzed, and when we compare 2004 media with 2005 media, the number of articles in these two sectors increased. Another general finding which is true for all these sectors is that the media covered more stories about them in 2005.

In 2004, the rank of the the top three most admired corporations in the energy and cement sectors is the same rank as the number of articles published about them. In 2005, this was true only for the cement sector, but Zorlu Enerji, with 1,000 articles in the media, was the third most reputable in the energy sector, while it ranked second in visibility.

The list of most admired corporations in the banking and white goods sectors differs slightly from their ranking on the most admired corporations list and visibility list. In 2004, Akbank was the focus of more articles but was ranked second on the most reputable company list. In 2005, though Garanti Bank was ranked first in reputation, an increase of articles that year allowed three other banks to join the list. Of those, İşbankası had the most articles published in this sector and was ranked second. Yapı Kredi Bank, which was ranked third on the *Capital* list along with TEB, had very good visibility in the media as compared to TEB, which was featured in only 493 news articles. In white goods, Arçelik maintained its second-place rank in the most reputable companies list for 2 years, but Vestel, which had the most visibility in the media for those 2 years, was also ranked second. In the automotive sector, the reputation rankings of the corporations did not change in 2004 and 2005, and in both years, the company ranked third on the admired list, Oyak Renault, was ranked first in media coverage. Vestel from the white goods sector, with media coverage of almost 4,000 articles in 2005, had the highest media coverage of all companies tracked.

The results showed no consistent relationship between the most admired corporations and the number of articles published about them in most sectors, but in some sectors, such as the energy and cement sectors, there was a strong relationship.

Discussion and Conclusions

This study has messages for the players in the communications industry and the academic world, while at the same time it leaves the researchers with unanswered questions that need to be studied in terms of agenda setting, especially second-level agenda setting and corporate reputation. The paucity of traditional agenda-setting studies in Turkey may be due to the difficulty of access to the newspaper archives and the lack of regular public opinion surveys. The data are incomplete, especially since research that compares present data with past data seems almost impossible to conduct. One key question for academics has been how to determine the reliability of findings reported by various sources and whose data to take as a parameter for further research.

From the perspective of public relations or reputation management in Turkey, this shows that the field is missing data with which to demonstrate its contribution to companies' reputations, since heretofore not a single study had even looked into such basic issues as the agenda-setting effects of business news and the public's images of different companies. A series of studies that examine the agenda-setting effects of news on the public's perception of corporations will, in fact, make the public relations industry more accountable to themselves and to clients. Second-level agenda setting, which requires more in-depth analysis, has a lot to contribute to public relations' self-evaluation. The influence of news releases on the content of Turkish news media, the influence of advertising expenses, the sectors' coverage in the media in general, the effects of being a local company versus an international one, the attributes of companies emphasized, the tone of this emphasis (favorable, unfavorable), the age and size of a corporation, the number of business segments in which it is operating, its issue ownership (e.g., social responsibility), whether it has a crisis situation—these are only some of the things requiring investigation and collaboration among scholars of related disciplines and professionals as well. Funding is one of the major keys to accomplishing these research goals.

If we divide the major partners in communication into academics, consultants, clients, professionals, and the media, then this initial study, which combines corporations in the news and corporate reputation, may be an opportunity for all parties in the system to look at their roles in a more systematic and comprehensive way.

The founder of the Koç Group has expressed the importance of reputation in these words: "It is very difficult to win reputation, but very easy to lose it. It takes time to repair the reputation lost. Therefore, my advice to all of my friends in the group is that that they should sacrifice whatever they can today so as not to lose the reputation of today" (Yağcı, 2006).

Bibliography

Abrak, E. (2006). *Gündem belirleme modeli ışığında Türkiye'nin Avrupa Birliğine giriş sürecinin haber analizi* [A news analysis of the process of Turkey's membership in the EU in the light of an agenda setting model]. Unpublished master's thesis. Kocaeli University, Institute of Social Sciences, Kocaeli, Turkey.

Akdemir, S. (1991). Çevre sorunlarina ilişkin gündem oluşturma süreci ve Türk basını: Haliç ve Gökova Örneği [Agenda-setting process of environment problems and Turkish Press: Example of Halic and Gokova]. *Kurgu, 9*, 149–194.

Alpkaya, F., & Çelebi, A. (1995). Medya'da gündem oluşturma: Hürriyet 1994 örneği [Agenda-setting in the media: Example of Hurriyet 1994]. *Toplum ve Bilim, 65*, 122–156.

Ararat, M., & Göceneoğlu, C. (2006). Drivers for sustainable corporate responsibility. Retrieved from http://info.worldbank.org/etools/mdfdb/docs/wp_UJRCS.pdf

Atabek, N. (1997). *Gündem belirleme modeli ve enflasyon, trafik ve sosyal güvenlik konularindaki gerçeklerle medya ve kamu gündemlerinin karşilaştirilmasi* [Model of agenda-setting and the realities of inflation, traffic and social security issues and the comparison of media and public agenda]. Unpublished doctoral dissertation, Anadolu University, Institute of Social Sciences, Eskişehir, Turkey.

Barış R. (2006). Media landscape Turkey. Retrieved from http://www.ejc.nl/jr/emland/turkey.html

Büyük, S. S. (2003, December 1). Türkiye'nin en beğenilen şirketleri [The most admired corporations of Turkey]. Retrieved from http://www.capital.com.tr/haber.aspx?HBR_KOD=624

Büyük, S. S. (2004, December 1). İtibar liginde 4 yılın analizi [Analysis of 4 year reputation league]. Retrieved from http://www.capital.com.tr/haber.aspx?HBR_KOD=1729

Büyük, S. S. (2005, December 1). İtibar zirvesinde büyük mücadele [Big struggle on reputation summit]. Retrieved from http://www.capital.com.tr/haber.aspx?HBR_KOD=3221

Büyük, S. S. (2006, December 1). En beğenilenler ligi'nde zirveye Koç [Koç on the most admired league is at the top]. Retrieved from http://www.capital.com.tr/haber.aspx?HBR_KOD=3868

Carroll, C. E., & McCombs, M. E. (2003). Agenda-setting effects of business news on the public's images and opinions about major corporations. *Corporate Reputation Review, 6*(1), 36–46.

Çelebi, A. (1990). Söylem çözümlemesi: gazetelerin "haber" oluşturma ve "gündem" belirleme işlevlerine eleştirel bir yaklaşım [Discourse analysis: A critical approach to newspapers' news making and agenda setting function]. Unpublished master's thesis, Ankara University, Institute of Social Sciences, Ankara, Turkey.

Culberston, H. M., & Chen, N. (1996). *International public relations: A comparative analysis*. Mahwah., NJ: Erlbaum.

Dörtok, A. (Winter 2006). A managerial look at the interaction between internal communication and corporate reputation. *Corporate Reputation Review, 8*(4), 322–338.

En beğenilen şirketler [The most admired corporations]. (n.d.). Retrieved from http://arsiv.hurriyetim.com.tr/hur/turk/99/12/03/ekonomi/02eko.htm

Fombrun, C., & Van Riel, C. (1997). The reputational landscape. *Corporate Reputation Review,* 1(1–2), 5–13.

Gfk Türkiye. (2006, September 20). İş dünyasinin sponsorluk projelerine bakişi [The evaluation of sponsorships by the business world]. GfK Türkiye–Arya Sponsorship and Communication Ad Hoc Research, http://www.aryasponsorluk.com.tr/sponsorluk_hakkinda_arastirmalar.html

Gfk Türkiye. (2006, September 20). TÜHİD-IDA iletişim hizmetleri algilama araştirmasi raporu [TÜHİD-IDA *Report of communication services perception research*].

Girgin, A. (2000). *Yazılı basinda haber ve habercilik etik'i* [News in press and news ethics]. İstanbul, Turkey: İnkılap.

Global competitiveness ındex rankings and 2005 comparisons. (n.d.).Retrieved from http://www.weforum.org/pdf/Global_Competitiveness_Reports/Reports/gcr_2006/gcr2006_rankings.pdf

Global competitiveness report 2007–2008. (n.d.). Retrieved from http://www.gcr.weforum.org

Global leadership and organizational behavior effectiveness research program. (n.d.). Retrieved from http://info.worldbank.org/etools/mdfdb/docs/wp_UJRCS.pdf

Görpe, S. (2006–2007). Structured PR education reaps rewards. *Hollis Europe* (17th ed.). pp. 290–291.

Görpe, S. (2007). Women and the news: Europe, Egypt and the Middle East, and Africa. In P. Poindexter, S. Meraz, & A. Schmitz Weiss (Eds.), *Women, men, and news divided and disconnected in the news media landscape* (pp. 175–212). New York: Routledge.

Görpe, S., & Yüksel, E. (2007, May 16–18). A media content and corporate reputation survey 2006 in Turkey: A first level agenda-setting study. In *Fifth international symposium: Communication in the millennium* (pp. 124–136). Eskisehir, Turkey: Anadolu University Publications.

Gül, A. A. (2005). A media agenda-setting research: Mardin Kızıltepe event. In *Third international symposium: Communication in the millennium: A dialogue between Turkish and American scholars*. Eskisehir, Turkey: Anadolu University Publications.

Güz, N. (1999). Türk basınında gündem oluşturma [Agenda-setting in the Turkish media]. *Yeni Türkiye, 12,* 982–996.

Halkla İlişkiler Sektörü Nasıl Algılanıyor? [How is public relations sector perceived?]. (2003, February 6). Retrieved from http://turk.internet.com/haber/yaziyaz.php3?yaziid=65007.

Hazar, Ç. M. (1996). *Kitle iletişiminin etkileri ve sosyolojik işlevlerinden gündem kurma* [Effects of mass communication and one of its sociological functions, agenda-setting]. Unpublished master's thesis,. Hacettepe University, Institute of Social Sciences, Ankara, Turkey.

Hofstede, G. (2003). *Cultures and organizations*. London: Profile Books.

IDA/ICCO. (2006, October 4). *Turkey country report.* Presented at ICCO Board Meeting, New Delhi, India. http://www.iletisimfakulteleri.gen.tr/fakulteler.asp; http://www.ida.org.tr/index.asp?dil=en

International Public Relations Association (IPRA). (2003). Retrieved from http://instituteforpr.org/index.php/IPR/research_single/index_of_bribery.

İrvan, S. (1997). *Dış politika ve basin: Türk basinindaki diş politika haberlerinin gündem belirleme yaklaşimi açisindan çözümlenmesi* [Foreign Policy and press: An agenda-setting analysis of foreign policy news in Turkish press]. Unpublished doctoral dissertation, Ankara University, Institute of Social Sciences, Ankara, Turkey.

Kadıbeşegil, S. (2006). *İtibar Yönetimi* [Reputation management]. İstanbul, Turkey: MediaCat.

Kadıbeşegil, S. (2006, September 3). İtibar, algilama yönetimi ya da "repuception." [Reputation, perception management or repuception]. Retrieved from http://www.orsa. com.trcgi-bin/asp/print.asp?lang=TR&id=111&menuid=&type=nor

Kazancı, M. (2002). *Kamuda ve özel kesimde halkla ilişkiler* [Public relations in the public and private sector] (4th ed.). Ankara, Turkey: Turhan.

Kazancı, M. (2006). Osmanlı'da halkla ilişkiler [Public relations in the Ottomon Empire]. *Selçuk Üniversitesi İletişim Dergisi, 4*(3), 5–20.

Kruckeberg, D., & Tsetsura, K. (n.d.). An international index of bribery for news coverage' commissioned by the Institute for PR, the IPRA. Sponsored by *Hürriyet*, a member of Doğan Media Group. Retrieved January 8, 2007, from   http://institute-forpr.org/index.php/IPR/research_single/index_of_bribery/

Kunczik, M. (1997). *Images of nations and international public relations*. Mahwah., NJ: Erlbaum.

Lopez-Claros, A. (n.d.). World Economic Forum, Executive summary. Retrieved from http://www.weforum.org/pdf/Global_Competitiveness_Reports/Reports/gcr_2006/ gcr2006_summary.pdf

Mardin B. (2005). *Do as the Romans do: The Romans are going global*. 2005 Atlas Award Lecture on International Public Relations, Istanbul, Turkey.

May May, M., & Kleinnijenhuis, J. (2006a). Issue news and corporate reputation: Applying the theories of agenda setting and issue ownership in the field of business communication. *Journal of Communication, 56*, 543–559.

May May, M., & Kleinnijenhuis, J. (2006b). News and corporate reputation: Empirical findings from the Netherlands. *Public Relations Review, 32*, 341–348.

McCombs, M. E.,& Yüksel, E. (2004). The agenda-setting capacity of the national security council and the education reform issue in Turkey. In *Second international symposium communication in the millennium: A dialogue between Turkish and American scholars* (pp. 381–391). İstanbul, Turkey: İstanbul University Publications.

MediaCat. (2008). Retrieved from http://www.mediacatonline.com/tr/news/details. asp?ID=5702&hl=medya%20sahipliği

MediaScape Reports. (2000). Türkiye'de medya [Media in Turkey] 1,2. Center for Communication Research, Ankara University. Ankara. Retrieved from http://ilaum. ankara.edu.tr/yazi.php?yad=2362

Medya Takımadaları: Türkiye medya sahipliği haritası [Media archipelago: Turish media ownership map]. Retrieved from http://www.mediacatonline.com/tr/news/details. asp?ID=5702&hl=medya%20sahipliği

Özden, Z., & Saran, M. (2004). Turkey. In B. Van Ruler & D. Verčič (Eds.). *Public relations and communication management in Europe: A nation-by-nation introduction to public relations theory and practice* (pp. 441–459). Berlin, Germany: Mouton de Gruyter.

Özgen, M. (2000). *Türkiye'de basinin gelişimi ve sorunu* [Problem and development of Turkish press in Turkey]. İstanbul, Turkey: Istanbul University, Faculty of Communication Publication.

Pelenk, A., & Gül, Ö. (2004). Examining the role of agenda setting in public relations process as an issue: A case study. In *2nd International symposium: Communication in the millennium A dialogue between Turkish and American scholars* (pp. 803–814). İstanbul, Turkey: İstanbul University Publications.

Renkver, M. (2006, January). Halkla İlişkilerde Sonuç İtibardır [Result is reputation in public relations] [Special issue]. *MediaCat, 11.*

Sriramesh, K., & Verčič, D. (Eds.). (2003). *The global public relations handbook: Theory, research and practice.* Mahwah, NJ: Erlbaum.

Şimşek, S. (2002). *İnternet sitelerindeki haberlerin gündem belirlemedeki etkileri üzerine uygulamalı bir çalışma* [An applied research on the agenda setting effects of Internet Web sites]. Unpublished master's thesis. Selçuk University, Institute of Social Sciences, Konya, Turkey.

Tandaçgünes N., & Yalın, D. (2005, August 21–26). *Agenda setting theory and proactive PR: A research about World AIDS Week.* Paper presented at the International Forum for Social Sciences and Health (IFSSH) World Congress 2005, "Health Challenges of the Third Millennium," Yeditepe University, İstanbul, Turkey.

Terkan, B. (2005). *Türkiye'de basın ve siyaset ilişkisi: Basın gündemi ve siyasal gündemin karşılaştırılmasına yönelik bir gündem belirleme çalışması* [The relationship between the press and the policy: An agenda setting study of press agenda and policy agenda relationship]. Unpublished doctoral dissertation, Selçuk University, Institute of Social Sciences, Konya, Turkey.

Tokgöz, O. (2000). *Temel Gazetecilik* [Basic journalism]. (4th ed.) İstanbul, Turkey: Imge

Tosun, Ş. M. (2001). *Gündem belirleme ve örnek olay Adalet Bakanlığı'nın halkla ilişkiler çalışmaları* [Agenda-setting and the case of PR activities of Ministry of Justice]. Unpublished master's thesis, İstanbul University, Institute of Social Sciences, İstanbul, Turkey.

Turan, E. (2004). *Türkiye'de televizyon ana haber bültenlerinde gündem oluşturma süreçleri* [Agenda-setting processes of evening television news bulletins in Turkey]. Unpublished doctoral dissertation, İstanbul University, Institute of Social Sciences, İstanbul, Turkey.

Turkish General Staff Portal, History. Retrieved from http://www.tsk.mil.tr/eng/genel_konular/tarihce.htm

The Turkish Higher Education System.Retrieved from http://tez2.yok.gov.tr/

Uçak, O. (2007). Gündem haber ilişkisi bağlamında Türkiye'de basının gündem belirlemedeki rolü [The agenda setting role of the press under the context of agenda and news relationship]. Unpublished master's thesis, Marmara University, Institute of Social Sciences, İstanbul, Turkey.

Verčič, D., Grunig, L. A., & Grunig, J. E. (1996). Global and specific principles of public relations: Evidence from Slovenia. In H. M.Culberston & N. Chen (Eds.), *International public relations: A comparative* analysis (pp. 31–64). Mahwah., NJ: Erlbaum.

World Economic Forum. (2006). Global competitiveness reports. Retrieved from http://www.weforum.org/pdf/Global_Competitiveness_Reports/Reports/gcr_2006/gcr2006_rankings.pdf.

World Economic Forum. (2008). Retrieved from http://www.gcr.weforum.org

Yağcı, A. (2006, February 1) Beğeni Şampiyonu Dentaş'ın Öyküsü [The story of admiration champion Dentas]. *Capital.* Retrieved from http://www.capital.com.tr/haber.aspx?HBR_KOD=2901

YAYSAT, Report of. (2005). YAYSAT tarafından dağıtılan gazetelerin aylık olarak günlük ortalama net satışları. [The average daily sales of newspapers distributed by YAYSAT, on a monthly basis. Retrieved from http://www.dorduncukuvvetmedya.com/arastirma/2005GAZETESATIS.htm

Yüksel, E. (1999). *Türkiye'de ekonomi basını gündemi ve siyasal gündem ilişkisi: özelleştirme örneğinde bir gündem belirleme çalışması* [The relationship between economy pages' agenda and policy agenda in Turkey: An agenda-setting study on privatization issue]. Unpublished doctoral dissertation, Anadolu University, Institute of Social Sciences, Eskişehir, Turkey.

Yüksel, E. (2003). A second level agenda setting study in Turkish parliamentary elections. In *First international symposium communication in the millennium* (pp. 345–355). Eskişehir, Turkey: Anadolu University Publications.

Yüksel, E. (2004). *Medya güvenlik kurulu* [Media security council]. Eskişehir, Turkey: Anadolu University Publications.

Yüksel E. (2008). Türkiye'deki gündem belirleme araştırmaları [Agenda-setting studies in Turkey]. In C. Yaşin (Ed.), *Gündem belirleme kuram ve araştırmaları* [Agenda-setting theory and researches] (pp. 153–181). Ankara, Turkey: Yargı

Yüksel, E., & Gürcan, H. İ. (2005). *Haber toplama ve yazma* [News gathering and writing]. Konya, Turkey: Tablet.

Yüksel, E., & McCombs, M. E. (2001). The economic privatization issue in Turkey. A four-part investigation of agenda-setting theory. In *First International communication symposium* (pp. 148–161). Eskisehir, Turkey: Anadolu University Publications.

Zarakol, N. (2006, January). Halkla ilişkiler itibari somutlaştiriyor [Public relations legitimizes reputation]. [Special issue]. *MediaCat, 10.*

Zengin, A. (2000). Ulusal gazetelerin yayın politikalarının Türkiye gündemine etkileri [Effects of natinonal newspapers' policies on Turkey's agenda]. Unpublished master's thesis, Ege University, Institute of Social Sciences, İzmir, Turkey.

23 Corporate Reputation and the News Media in Nigeria

Olusanmi C. Amujo, Olutayo Otubanjo, Beatrice Laninhun, and Daniel I. Adejo

Nigerian corporate reputation literature has been on the increase recently, with the majority of theories focusing on the planning, management, and measurement aspects of corporate reputation. There is only limited evidence, however, to suggest that the meaning of corporate reputation has been actively and thoroughly addressed in Nigerian business corporate and marketing communications literature. A textual review reveals that the concept of corporate reputation lacks consensual definition and has mostly been addressed passively by Nigerian authors.

Corporate reputation plays a vital role in the realization of organizational goals and objectives, so image audits are regularly conducted in Nigeria. The results of some of these investigations are widely publicized by the local media. For example, PricewaterhouseCoopers, in conjunction with Business Day Media Limited, commissioned Nigeria's "Most Respected Company and CEO" survey. The survey results, based purely on the opinions of Nigerian company CEOs, were presented at an awards ceremony in 2006 in Lagos, Nigeria. In the company category, Nestlé Nigeria Plc. emerged as Nigeria's most respected company of 2006, while Cadbury Nigeria Plc. won in 2005. In the CEO category, Mr. Bunmi Oni of Cadbury Nigeria Plc was the most respected CEO of 2006.

Second-Level Agenda Setting

Second-level agenda-setting theory (Carroll & McCombs, 2003; McCombs & Ghanem, 2001; McCombs, Lopez-Escobar, & Llamas, 2000) has gained significant currency in business research. For instance, Carroll and McCombs (2003) assert that while first-level agenda setting is concerned with the saliency of objects such as public issues, political candidates, or companies, second-level agenda setting is concerned with the salience of the attributes of those objects. Additionally, Carroll and McCombs (2003) added that the media do more than present an agenda of objects; they describe each of the objects. By media description of agenda of objects, they mean that the media articulate the attributes and traits of specific objects on the media agenda. It must be stressed that corporate reputation represents a judgment about a company's attributes (Gray & Balmer, 1998). It reflects behavior exhibited day in and day out through hundreds of small decisions (Vergin & Qoronfleh, 1998). The media provide a vehicle through which a company's and a CEO's attributes are communicated to the stakeholders.

To test the salience of second-level agenda setting, this study conducted a content analysis of news stories published by the *Financial Standard* newspaper from July 2004 to December 2005 and held semistructured interviews with investors and consumers in Lagos, the commercial and industrial capital of Nigeria.

The Nature of Nigerian Media Systems

In Nigeria, there is both public (federal and state) and private ownership of media organizations, and there is one federal radio network, Federal Radio Corporation of Nigeria (FRCN), which has 37 individual FM stations. In addition, there are 40 state-owned stations, 17 private stations, and the Voice of Nigeria (VON). The federal government owns one television network, the Nigerian Television Authority (NTA), that maintains 97 stations. On the other hand, there are 32 state-owned stations and 14 private stations. There are three direct-to-home stations, 35 cable stations, and two direct satellite stations. So far as the print media are concerned, there are over 90 titles published in Nigeria, including dailies, weeklies, sports, and business papers. Additionally, there are over 40 magazine titles, and 124 outdoor firms manage almost 21, 000 billboards across Nigeria (Mediafacts, 2006).

Access to Media

Research findings reveal that billboards (89%) have the highest penetration among the Nigerian populace, followed by radio (67%) and television (62%). Newspapers (25%) and magazines (13%) have the lowest penetration rate. Results are presented in the Table 23.1.

Media Control

In the early 2000s, two main regulatory bodies control the Nigerian media. The National Broadcasting Commission (NBC) is empowered by legislative acts 38 and 55 of the National Assembly to license, monitor, regulate, and conduct research in broadcasting in Nigeria; it has established and disseminates a

Table 23.1 Penetration of Media Vehicles

	Population	*Percent*
Total population	66,532,359,000	100
TV	41,093,303,00	62
Radio	44,887,210,00	67
Newspaper	16,348,116,00	25
Magazine	8,859,204,00	13
Billboard	59,105,901,00	89

Source: Media Planning Services (MPS)/All Media and Products Survey (AMPS) 2005, cited in Mediafacts, 2006, p. 13.

national broadcasting code and sets standards with regard to the contents and quality of broadcast materials (NBC, 2004). The Nigerian Press Council (NPC) regulates journalism practices in Nigeria and is expected to perform roles similar to those of the NBC. Apart from these regulatory bodies, the media also self-censor. Via house policies, the media control content to suit their owners or sponsors (advertisers). Self-censorship oftentimes erodes courage, initiative, and objectivity.

Financial Standard, July 2004 to December 2005

Given the high level of Nigerian consciousness concerning stock market investment across all industries, this study scrutinized articles published between July 2004 and December 2005 from the weekly *Financial Standard*. Arguably, public awareness of the Central Bank of Nigeria's (CBN) N25 billion ($208,333,333.33) bank recapitalization policy was due to coverage in the *Financial Standard*. The bank's recapitalization induced many companies to look to the stock market to raise funds. The *Financial Standard* presents news authoritatively and its extensive in-depth coverage of business, economics, and financial issues and events, is paralleled by no other publications. Furthermore, its audiences cut across critical business and financial strata of society, which puts the weekly at an advantage.

Methodological Approach and Data Analysis

This study used both quantitative and qualitative content analysis techniques supported by semistructured interviews to test how, if at all, second-level agenda setting of the media affects stakeholders of for-profit corporations within the Nigerian business community.

Content Analysis

A quantitative content analysis was performed on news stories published by the *Financial Standard* between July 2004 and December 2005 on four critical industries in the Nigerian economy: banking, telecommunication, manufacturing, and aviation. Second, a qualitative content analysis was applied to the semistructured interviews that were carried out with some consumers/investors to test the effects of saliency of the second-level agenda setting. These consumers/investors were exposed to the news stories published by the *Financial Standard* between July 2004 and December 2005 in Nigeria.

Finally, a quantitative classification was made of the new stories that were utilized, dividing the stories into distinct categories with positive and negative reputational attributes. In order to determine the positive or negative tone of each story, the writer's use of positive or negative adjectives, phrases, and sentences to commend or rebuke the activities of the corporation or the particular industry were examined.

Semistructured Interviews

Semistructured interviews were conducted with 30 consumers/investors between the ages of 25 and 36 within the Lagos metropolis. The interviewees were all university graduates and employed professionals; respondents were conversant with prevailing Nigerian socioeconomic issues. Most often bought and read Nigerian business newspapers, especially the *Financial Standard,* and listened to financial news on the radio and television. The interview transcripts were inductively analyzed using qualitative content analysis in order to give added rich and thick description to the data (Geertz, 1973; Huberman & Miles, 1998; Merriam, 1998).

The semistructured interviews were conducted with a fairly open framework that allowed for focused, conversational, two-way communication between the interviewers and the interviewees. The results, typically rich with detail and insights into participants' experiences of the world, "may be epistemologically in harmony with the reader's experience" and thus more meaningful (Stake, 1978).

Interview Guide

Initially, participants were asked if the *Financial Standard's* news stories influenced their formation of reputation attributes for certain Nigerian corporations. Subsequently, participants were asked to describe the influence of *Financial Standard* news stories on their stock market investment and consumer goods buying decisions. The interview guide then focused on the effects of media news exposure on respondents' formation of reputation attributes of some corporations and on their investment decision making as it concerned purchase of stocks, consumer products, and services in Nigeria.

Procedures

The interview structure allowed a follow-up on issues the participants raised and modifications of the questions based on the respondents' answers. This open-ended format was adopted because the study's principal objective was to capture the participants' view of the media's influence on corporate reputation in their business world. Interviews were arranged with the participants at locations of their choice.

Data Analysis

The authors first transcribed the results of the interviews verbatim, then read and reread the transcripts in order to capture any overarching themes. Subsequently a qualitative content analysis was conducted (Graneheim & Lundman, 2004; Hsieh & Shannon, 2005), which inductively analyzed the interview transcripts for meaning units, which Tesch (1990, p. 116) defines as "a segment of text that is comprehensible by itself and contains one idea, episode, or piece of information." The authors discussed their interpretations and called the meaning units as codes in accordance with Graneheim and Lundman (2004). Codes were taken directly from the text as they captured the key thoughts or concepts expressed by the respondents. Subsequently, the codes were grouped into subcategories and categories. Moreover, the authors formulated themes from the underlying meaning of the categories.

Evidence of Second-Level Agenda-Setting Effects of Business News in Nigeria

The following four research questions were analyzed to test the evidence of second-level agenda-setting effects on stakeholders' perception of reputations of Nigerian corporations and industries.

Research Question 1

Does the amount of news coverage received by a corporation positively connect to the public awareness of the corporation?

The saliency of media agenda-setting effects on corporate business, as proved by Carroll and McCombs (2003), has corollary effects on stakeholders' perception of corporate reputation attributes of some profit-making Nigerian corporations. For example Table 23.2 shows the frequency distribution of 305 news stories and 46 advertisements, making a total of 351 news items on the mandatory N25 billion recapitalization reform policy in the banking industry, which was ordered by the Central Bank of Nigeria, began in July 2004, and continued until December 31, 2005. Moreover, close scrutiny of the news stories and advertisements called for a classification system according to positive and negative categories (Table 23.3). A total of 334 positive news items (95.14% of total news items) and 17 negative news items (4.83% of total news items) in Table 23.3 were published about the banks that participated in the consolidation exercise. Finally, Table 23.4 contains the results of the semistructured interview content analysis.

Table 23.2 Frequency of News Stories Published by the *Financial Standard* on the Central Bank of Nigeria's N25 Billion Recapitalization Policy by Banks between July 2004 and December 2005

	Full Page	Half Page	Quarter Page	Small Page	Total	Percentage (%)
Front page stories	2	16	3	9	30	8.54
Middle page stories						
Inside page stories	30	59	78	87	254	72.36
Back page stories	6	3	5		14	3.98
Adverts	12	19	15		46	13.10
Editorial		7			7	1.99
Total	50	104	101	96	351	

Table 23.3 Classification of New Stories and Advertisements Published by Nigerian Banks on the N25 Billion Recapitalization Policy

	Number of Positive News Stories	Percentage (%)	Number of Negative News Stories	Percentage (%)
Front page stories	29	8.26	1	0.28
Middle page stories	0		0	
Inside page stories	241	68.66	13	3.70
Back page stories	11	3.13	3	0.85
Adverts	46	13.10	0	
Editorial	7	1.99	0	
Total	334	95.14	17	4.83

Table 23.4 Content Analysis of Semi-Structured Interview with Stock Market Investors in Nigeria

Meaning Unit	Code	Categories	Sub-Categories	Theme
The management of corporate resources	Good management style Good resource allocation High organizational capabilities	Management efficiency	Management	Efficient
Maintaining good business relations with stakeholders	Timely and open information Effective message delivery Delivering on promises	Relationship management	Relationship	Trustworthy
Investing in the community and people	Good community involvement Open administrative system Humane employment policies	Social responsibility	Social responsibility	Ethical
Profitable management of the corporate business	High business breakthroughs Increase market share value High return on investment	Business efficiency	Business success	Profitable
Evidence of friendly service management	Innovative quality customer care Timely management of complaints Good service delivery system	Service quality	Service experience	Delightsome

Interestingly, 28 respondents (93%) confirmed that the *Financial Standard* news stories they read about excellent management efficiency, relationship management, social responsibility, business efficiency, and quality service delivery of the involved banks influenced their positive perception of their reputation attributes and invariably persuaded them to buy shares in the stock market. However, two respondents (7%) held a contrary view. Thus, the overwhelming majority of respondents confirmed the saliency of second-level agenda-setting theory on the reputations of 25 banks that recapitalized out of about 95 banks before December 31, 2005. It must be underscored that the N25 billion recapitalization of banks enjoyed unprecedented positive media publicity, compelling attention and high public awareness among the citizenry in Nigeria. Furthermore, it generated high levels of discussion, heated arguments, seminars, workshops, comments, and editorials across the country. Some of the 25 banks that raised equity in the capital market were oversubscribed due to public awareness generated by the media reports. For example, Zenith Bank Plc went to the stock market to raise N10.6 billion, but ended up with oversubscription of N48.5 billion; Guarantee Trust Bank went to the stock market to raise N10.5 billion, but eventually was oversubscribed with N21.20 billion; Intercontinental Bank Plc went to the capital market to raise N30.6 billion, but received an oversubscription of N97.7 billion.

Research Question 2

Does the amount of news coverage dedicated to specific attributes of a corporation positively connect to the proportion of the public that defines the corporation by these attributes? (See Table 23.5, Table 23.6, and Table 23.7.)

From the debut of Global System of Mobile (GSM) in Nigeria in 2001, the new licensed telecommunication corporations have enjoyed high positive media coverage with few negative criticisms. Prior to the inception of GSM in Nigeria, the reputation of the national carrier, Nigeria Telecommunication company (NITEL), had ebbed beyond redemption owing to poor service delivery, dropped calls, network congestion, unavailability of telephone lines, poor infrastructure, poor management, and gross negligence from the government. The advent of

Table 23.5 Frequency of News Stories Published by the *Financial Standard* Newspaper on the Telecommunication Industry in Nigeria between July 2004 and December 2005

	Full Page	Half Page	Quarter Page	Small	Total	Percentage (%)
Front page stories	3	2			5	1.79
Middle page stories			4	11	15	5.37
Inside page stories	20	35	46	95	196	70.25
Back page stories						
Adverts	50	10	3		63	22.58
Editorial						
Total	73	47	53	106	279	

Table 23.6 Classification of News Stories According to Positive and Negative Reputational Attributes

	Number of Positive News Stories	Percentage (%)	Number of Negative News Stories	Percentage (%)
Front page stories	5	1.79	0	
Middle page stories	12	4.30	3	1.07
nside page stories	180	64.51	16	5.73
Back page stories	0		0	
Adverts	63	22.58	0	
Editorial	0		0	
Total	260	93.18	19	6.80

Table 23.7 Content Analysis of Semi-Structured Interview with Consumers of the Telecommunication Industry

Meaning Unit	Code	Categories	Sub-Categories	Theme
There is efficient management of human and material resources	Quality management style Efficient resource allocation Availability of good competencies	Efficient management	Good management	Efficient
Optimal communication flow with stakeholder groups	Regular information dissemination Reliable message delivery system Responsive of feedback mechanism	Effective communication	Communication	Trustworthy
Healthy board culture with policy safeguards and processes.	Corporate philanthropy Corporate accountability Transparency and reporting system	Corporate governance	Openness	Accountable
Efficient financial and business management planning	High return on investment Network expansion and capacity building High cash flow and financial management	Business success	Financial success	Profitable
Responsive customer services for enhancing customer loyalty	Interactive customer care Timely complaints resolution Need improvement on service delivery	Service management	Service delivery	Fair

GSM operators such as MTN, Econet (now Celtel), and M-Tel initiated updates to wireless operators such as Starcom, Retel, Multilink, Intercellular, Cellcom, and MTS First Wireless to provide telecommunication services, changing the poor reputation of the Nigerian telephone system. The media, agog with news stories, continually extolled the management skills of MTN and others, customer care, network expansion, and efficiency.

A careful examination by the authors of mounting media coverage of large telecommunication companies in the *Financial Standard* during the given period yielded 216 news stories and 63 advertisements, equaling a total of 279 news items. The news items were further analyzed, then classified into positive and negative categories based on the positive or negative adjectives, phrases, and sentences used by the journalists or contributors in the stories. The authors discovered that a total of 260 positive news items (93%) specifically extolled the attributes of these companies, while 19 negative news items (7%) criticized some of the specific attributes of the above listed telecommunication companies during the period under review.

The data from the semistructured interviews were then analyzed. A total of 24 respondents confirmed that the news stories they read in the *Financial Standard* concerning specific attributes of the listed corporations such as efficiency, trustworthiness, accountability and transparency, profitability, and adequate service delivery influenced their positive perception of their reputation attributes, which positively connected to the way they defined the corporation by these attributes. However, six respondents alleged that the dropped calls associated with the corporation needed to be fixed. Nevertheless, the overwhelming number of respondents attested to the potential confirmatory relationship of second-level agenda-setting effects on corporate reputation in Nigeria. For instance, an attempt by the Lagos State Government to promulgate telecommunication acts to regulate the increasing installation of masts, towers, and base stations and to impose tariffs and charges on these installations received resounding public condemnation. In response to the public's outcry, the Lagos State Government backed down on the proposed legislation.

Research Question 3

Is more positive media coverage for a specific attribute going to lead the public to perceive that attribute in more positive terms? (See Table 23.8, Table 23.9, and Table 23.10.)

The saliency of second-level agenda-setting effects on reputation management of manufacturing companies has been confirmed in Nigeria. After careful scrutiny and analysis of news stories and advertisements published by the *Financial Standard* during the given period, 286 news stories and 38 advertisements concerning specific Nigerian manufacturing companies were discovered. A total of 299 news items were classified as positive (92%), while 25 news items were deemed negative (8%). After scrutinizing the semistructured interviews, 26 respondents (87%) confirmed that the news stories they read in the *Financial Standard* concerning specific attributes of the above mentioned corporations,

Table 23.8 Frequency of News and Photo Stories Published by the *Financial Standard* on the Manufacturing Iindustry in Nigeria between July 2004 and December 2005

	Full Page	Half Page	Quarter Page	Small	Total	Percentage (%)
Front page stories		4		1	5	1.54
Middle page stories						
Inside page stories	19	21	27	203	270	83.33
Back page stories	11				11	3.39
Adverts	27	8	2	1	38	11.72
Editorial						
Total	57	33	29	205	324	

most especially their collective determination to survive in the face of an inclement business environment in Nigeria, influenced their definition of the critical attributes concerning the given corporation. On the other hand, the remaining four respondents (13%) believed that these corporations had not performed anything extraordinary. The identification of "determination to survive" by these corporations, among other favorable reputational attributes, was considered a unique attribute by 26 respondents of the 30 respondents interviewed. The Nigerian media, including the *Financial Standard*, have constantly maintained nationalist posturing about the country's economic development: they rarely bring to public awareness the problems that plague the manufacturing industry. Interestingly, the media have been criticizing the government and the financial industry, which they believe should provide an adequate environment and funding for manufacturing industries, allowing for an industrialized Nigeria. Such criticisms include misrule and corruption by the military and political class; difficulty for manufacturing companies in accessing bank loan facilities; double taxation (sales tax) by some state governments; underutilization of capacity; closure of some industrial complexes due to inadequate funds to purchase raw materials

Table 23. 9 Classification of News Stories According to Positive and Negative Reputational Attributes

	Number of Positive News Stories	Percentage (%)	Number of Negative News Stories	Percentage (%)
Front page stories	5	1.50	0	
Middle page stories	0		0	
Inside page stories	247	76.23	23	7.09
Back page stories	9	2.77	2	0.61
Adverts	38	11.72	0	
Editorial	0		0	
Total	299	92.22	25	7.70

Table 23.10 Content Analysis of Semi-Structured Interviews with the Consumers of Manufacturing Industry

Meaning Unit	Code	Categories	Sub-Categories	Theme
There are indices of high level business success and effective management	High turnover of investment Good return on equity Sustained cash flow system Regular payment of dividends/bonus	Business performance	Performance	Profitable
The industry is witnessing increase in expansion, diversification and distribution	Large distribution and service outlets Increased customer base and patronage Effective resource sourcing and management Sustained production level	Business expansion	Expansion	Determined
More organized service delivery and customer relationship	Quality service delivery Listening and timely resolution of complaints High service automation and customer care	Service quality	Services	Pleasing
Presence of information dissemination and feedback system	Clarity and simplicity of information Regular and timely message Balanced and true messages Listening to suggestions and consultation	Effective communication	Communication	Credible
Better brand innovation and marketing system	Effective brand innovation and extension Diversified brand portfolio Enhanced brand management and distribution	Brand management	Branding	Distinctive

from Europe, the United States, or Asia; the high cost of power generation arising from incessant power outages; high bank interest rates; high cost of salaries; and overhead and distribution expenditures. Therefore, it is worth mentioning the corporations that brave these odds and continue producing while hundreds of their competitors have folded.

Research Question 4

Will more negative media coverage for a specific attribute lead to more negative perceptions of that attribute on the part of the general public? (See Table 23.11, Table 23.12, and Table 23.13.)

The Nigerian aviation sector has been bedeviled by malaise and constant mishaps in the last few years, receiving increasingly frequent attacks from the media. From July 2004 to December 2005, the aviation industry had several ghastly crashes that claimed Nigerian lives. For example, there was the Bellview airline crash in which 111 passengers and six crew members were killed in October 2005; and the Sosoliso airline disaster in December 2005 that resulted in 103 deaths, most of the dead being school children (Edeaghe, Esosa, & Idiodi, 2006; Olusesan & Osakwe, 2005), and these were just two of many horrible crashes during this period.

Of the news analyzed from the *Financial Standard* between July 2004 and December 2005, 169 news stories and 10 advertisements regarding the national aviation industry were catalogued. After classifying each news story as positive or negative, only 12 positive news items, 8 of which were advertisements, were sympathetic to the aviation industry, whereas 169 negative news items (93%) made scathing criticisms and uncomplimentary remarks about the reputational attributes of the aviation industry. Of the interviewed respondents, all 30 confirmed that the negative news stories they read in the *Financial Standard* concerning specific attributes of the aviation industry resulting from its constant crashes, potentially influenced their perception and description of the attributes of the industry as corrupt, inefficient, unsafe, unfriendly, and administratively incompetent. Thus, the above analysis confirms the potential of second-level agenda-setting effects of business news in influencing the perception of reputational attributes of corporations and the aviation sector in the Nigerian business environment.

It is instructive to state that the incessant air crashes that characterized the aviation industry in the last few years have eroded its credibility and reputation among Nigerians. Many citizens called for the resignation of the Minister for Aviation and for an investigation into the crashes and activities of the industry.

Table 23.11 Frequency of News Stories Published by the *Financial Standard* Newspaper on the Aviation Industry in Nigeria between July 2004 and December 2005

	Full Page	Half Page	Quarter Page	Small	Total	Percentage (%)
Front page stories			2	1	3	1.67
Middle page stories						
Inside page stories	6	4	59	96	165	92.17
Back page stories						
Adverts	2	8			10	5.58
Editorial		1			1	0.55
Total	8	13	61	97	179	

Table 23.12 Classification of News Stories According to Positive and Negative Reputational Attributes

	Number of Positive News Stories	Percentage (%)	Number of Negative News Stories	Percentage (%)
Front page stories	0		3	1.67
Middle page stories	0		0	
Inside page stories	4	2.23	161	89.94
Back page stories	0		0	
Adverts	8	4.46	2	1.11
Editorial	0		1	0.55
Total	12	6.69	167	93.29

Table 23.13 Content Analysis of Semi-Structured Interview with the Consumers of Aviation Industry in Nigeria

Meaning Unit	Code	Categories	Sub-Categories	Theme
There is high mismanagement of resources in the industry	Bad resource allocation High corrupt practices Lack of maintenance culture Management inefficiency	Bad management	Bad management	Inefficient
There is clear evidence of bad handling of customers	Dereliction of duties Poor listening and delay complaints mgt Aloofness and nonchalant attitude Tight bureaucratic system	Poor customer relation	Customer relation	Unfriendly
Risk management process and safety system	Bad risk assessment and management Frequency of mishaps Poor rescue operation capability	Poor safety management	Poor safety	Unsafe
The service culture in the industry is very poor	Negligence and regular service failure Constant breakdowns of facilities Slow response to complaints Poor attitude to and bad quality of repair	Services failure	Services failure	Incompetent

Conclusion

This study was meant to expand upon the literature on the agenda-setting effects of business news on stakeholders' perceptions of profit-led business organizations in Nigeria. Thus, four agenda-setting research questions with regard to business news coverage and stakeholders' perceptions of profit-led business organizations in Nigeria were drawn and tested using content analysis of news stories published by the *Financial Standard* newspaper between July 2004 and December 2005. The results of the content analysis were supported by data from a semistructured interview conducted to explore the possibility of second-level agenda-setting effects on four critical Nigerian industries.

Four major findings emerged from this study. The first finding confirmed Carroll and McCombs's (2003) theory that the amount of news coverage received by a corporation connects positively to the public's awareness of the corporation. This indicates that there is a strong corollary effect on stakeholders' perception of corporate reputation attributes of some profit-making corporations in Nigeria's business environment. The second finding emerging from this study supported the Carroll and McCombs (2003) argument that the amount of news coverage dedicated to specific attributes of business organizations in Nigeria is connected to the proportion of the public who define the corporation by these attributes. Third, this study confirmed the Carroll and McCombs (2003) finding that the more the media cover a specific attribute from a positive perspective, the more positively the general public will perceive this attribute. Therefore, the outcome of this investigation indicated that the saliency of second-level agenda-setting effects has a confirmatory potential relationship to reputation management of manufacturing companies in Nigeria. The fourth finding from this study relates to how more positive media coverage for a specific attribute triggers greater positive perception of the specific attribute among the general public. The outcome of this study confirmed Carroll and McCombs's (2003) belief that the more negative media coverage is for a specific attribute, the more negative will be the general public's perception of that attribute.

The findings from this study support all aspects of Carroll and McCombs's (2003) work, implying that the nature of corporate reputation in Nigeria is similar and fundamentally connected to U.S. management of this entity. One can reasonably argue that based on the outcome of this study, corporate reputation theories as examined in much of Western literature can be applied to reputation studies in Nigeria. These studies should provide a foundation for the development of corporate reputation theory in Nigeria. Likewise, in practice, the outcome of this study implies that managers and consultants charged with the responsibility of managing corporate reputation in Nigeria and in the United States can learn much from each other. For instance, because of the similar nature of reputation practices in Nigeria and the United States, some Nigerian reputation management firms are now affiliated with public relations firms in the United States. This bilateral relationship implies that while Nigerian firms learn from their American counterparts in the areas of training, American firms can obtain useful market data from Nigerian reputation management firms.

References

Carroll, C. E., & McCombs, M. E. (2003). Agenda-setting effects of business news on the public's images and opinions about major corporations. *Corporate Reputation Review, 6*(1), 36–46

Edeaghe, H., Esosa, O., & Idiodi, H. (2006). Comparative analysis of the Bellview and Sosoliso air crashes in Nigeria: Matters arising. *The Internet Journal of Rescue and Disaster Medicine, 5*(2). Retrieved from http://www.ispub.com/ostia/index.php?xmlP rinter=true&xmlFilePath=journals/ijrdm/vol5n2/aircrash.xml

Financial Standard. (August 2004–December 2005). Lagos, Nigeria.

Geertz, C. (1973). Thick description: Toward an interpretive theory of culture. In *The interpretation of cultures: Selected essays* (pp. 3–30). New York: Basic Books.

Gray, E. R., & Balmer, J. M. T. (1998). Managing corporate image and corporate reputation. *Long Range Planning, 31*(5), 695–702.

Hsieh, H.-F., & Shannon, S. E. (2005). Three approaches to qualitative content analysis. *Qualitative Health Research, 15,* 1277–1288.

Huberman, A. M., & Miles, M. B. (1998). Data management and analysis methods. In N. K. Denzin & Y. S. Lincoln (Eds.), *Collecting and interpreting qualitative methods* (pp. 286–323). Thousand Oaks, CA: Sage.

McCombs, M., & Ghanem, S. I. (2001). *The convergence of agenda setting and framing.* In S. D. Reese, O. H Gandy, Jr., & A. E. Grant (Eds.), *Framing public life: Perspectives on media and our understanding of social world* (pp. 67–81). Mahwah, NJ: Erlbaum.

McCombs, M., Lopez-Escobar, E., & Llamas, J. P. (2000). Setting the agenda of attributes in the 1996 Spanish general election. *Journal of Communication, 50*(2), 77–92.

Mediafacts. (2006). The media overview in Nigeria. In *Revised Nigeria-West Africa MediaFacts Book 2006.* Retrieved from http://www.mediareachomd.com/Media-FactBook2006.pdf

Media Rights Agenda Year 2000. (2000). *Annual report.* Lagos, Nigeria: Author.

Merriam, S. B. (1998). *Qualitative research and case study applications in education.* San Francisco, CA: Jossey-Bass

National Broadcasting Commission (NBC). (2004). *This is NBC: A handbook.* Abuja, Nigeria: Author.

Olusesan, R., & Osakwe, V. (2005, December). Sosoliso plane crash: An air disaster too many. *Libération Afrique,* pp. 1–3. Retrieved from http://www.liberationafrique.org

Stake, R. E. (1978, February). The case study method in social inquiry. *Educational Researcher, 7*(2), 5–8.

Tesch, R. (1990). *Qualitative research analyses types and software tools.* New York: Falmer Press.

Vergin, R. C., & Qoronfleh, M. W. (1998, January–February). Corporate reputation and the stock market. *Business Horizons,* 19–26.

24 Corporate Reputation and the News Media in Slovenia

Klement Podnar and Dejan Verčič

Slovenia is a constitutional democracy with a division of powers between the executive, legislative, and judicial branches. It is a small but open economy with a GDP of €33 billion. In 2006, Slovenia's GDP per capita was €19,200, which is 77% of the average per capita income of the enlarged EU, placing Slovenia 16th among the 25 member states (in the top spot is Luxemburg with twice the average and on the bottom Latvia with 41% of the average). The annual growth rate of Slovenia's economy in 2006 was 5.2%. Services contribute 63%, industry 35%, and agriculture 2% to the GDP. It is a member of the European Union and NATO, and its currency is the Euro.

Slovenia, as a small and young country, is interesting because of high media penetration; with less than 2 million inhabitants it has more than 1,200 different media entities. Media include five national TV channels (one public TV station with two channels and one commercial TV station with three channels), over 80 radio stations of which 6 have national coverage, nearly 1,000 print media, but only eight main daily newspapers, three of which are very influential in terms of forming public opinion regarding politics and business. The 2008 Freedom House (2008) report on media freedom places Slovenia at 46th place (of 195 listed), together with Spain, Surinam, Trinidad and Tobago, and Vanatu.

As has been documented elsewhere (Verčič, 2003, 2004), Slovenia has a highly concentrated media market in which four big media companies control 90% of the daily newspaper market, and the two largest TV companies control around 90% of their market. Media outreach is very high, but media access "can be said to be general, yet mediated by corporativist structures" (Verčič, 2003, p. 296).

This chapter examines how coverage in the Slovenian media affects the public's perceptions of companies' reputations. First, a brief overview of corporate reputation and agenda-setting theory research in Slovenia is provided, including an overview of the main news media in Slovenia. Second, the methodology, the data, and the results of our analysis are described. This chapter ends with suggestions for further research.

Literature Review: Public Relations and Corporate Reputation in Slovenia

The history of strategic communication in the Slovenian language has been documented since the early Middle Ages. The origins of corporate communication that also served reputational needs can be found in the 19th century, but in its contemporary forms public relations and communication management in Slovenia have been professionalized only since the mid-1990s. This process is well documented by Ašanin Gole and Verčič (2000), Gruban, Verčič, and Zavrl (1994), Grunig, Grunig, and Verčič (1998), and Verčič (2002).

There are some traces of empirical and theoretical work about image and reputation to be found in Slovenia (see Podnar, 2005) but we can say that the evolution of the concept has been similar to other parts of the world. In the early 1970s, psychologists conducted preliminary researches into product influence on company image and cosmetic companies' images (Košak, 1972). Several years later (1989) an unknown author wrote about the field of public relations and its role in building company reputation in a Slovenian marketing magazine for professionals. A year later Ilic (1990) reported the results of research by the Broullard Communication Agency from New York, examining the correlation between communication and reputation. He wrote that "it is common knowledge that a good reputation can be a company's greatest treasure" (Ilic, 1990, p. 19).

A few years later authors discussed the image of a newly born country, Slovenia. One of them was Repovš who later wrote a book about corporate visual identity. In his book Repovš (1995) defines image as a perception of a company created by an individual (p. 16). Reputation became quite an important topic in the same year when Kline conducted the first Slovenian corporate reputation research of Slovenian companies. Those were the foundations for the yearly reputation measurements conducted ever since. Kline (1997, 1999, pp. 28–29) notes a clear difference between the meaning of corporate image and the meaning of reputation. He argues that the image of a company can be constructed by an individual who has merely heard of a company, whereas reputation is formed by an individual's personal experience with a company. Reputation, according to Kline, can be thus defined as an estimated image. In addition to the basic reputation research, Kline has managed to examine closely the influence of financial success on corporate reputation. Jančič (1999) on the other hand, at that time introduced a theoretical review of image understanding and made a distinction between identity and image.

Gruban (1995) focuses on the relation between image and reputation. He follows Grunig in claiming that the semantically more appropriate term *reputation* should be substituted for the term *image*. Two years later Gruban and Verčič (1997) introduced a model, a so-called Pristop's reputation diamond, based on the idea that organizations too must take care of their good name and existence (Gruban & Verčič, 1997, p. 9).

Verčič (2000) argues that in today's public relations theory the concept of reputation follows the fate of the term *image* which has been overused so much that it has become denotatively vacant: it can stand for anything.

Podnar (1999), on the other hand, deals with the question of relations and proportions among corporate identity, image, and reputation. He introduces a framework for researching and managing corporate identity in which he acknowledges Fombrun's definition of reputation and Kline's definition of image. Podnar (2000b) also argues that only corporate identity and communications can be directly managed by an organization, but image and reputation, on the other hand, cannot be. They are both within the domain of individuals or the public (receivers). In his case study research (Podnar, 2001) based on the biggest Slovenian oil company, Podnar found that a good reputation in itself does not ensure the successful introduction of a new brand in the case of brand extension if the product or the brand does not match the company's identity; and he introduces the notion of branch identity. In his research about corporate identity in Slovenia Podnar (2005) argues that among Slovenian companies, image and reputation formation is considered as one of the main benefits managers expect from a strong corporate identity.

Agenda-Setting Theory Research in Slovenia

Agenda-setting theory has been translated in Slovenia as "prednostno tematiziranje" (Splichal, 1999), which in descriptive terms means "media topics prioritizing." Agenda setting is a familiar concept in Slovenia and has been since the early days (mid-70s), and is a part of the curriculum in communication and journalism university programs. However, limited theoretical and empirical research using this theory has been conducted. In his seminal book on public opinion, Splichal (1997) argues that there is a certain degree of congruity between how much weight mass media gives to a certain topic and what the public believes is important. The view of public opinion as a form of social control, for example, is based on the assumption that there is a direct casual link between media content and public behaviors and attitudes. Splichal (1999) examines three topics which are fundamental to contemporary media democratization discourse: the principle of publicity, information subsidies, and media agenda setting. Splichal uses agenda-setting theory to resonate the significance of mass media for the political system in the context of public opinion formation and expression. He argues that mass media help determine and demonstrate the limits of legitimate public debate in society. Similarly, Erjavec (2000), following agenda-setting theory, argues that mass media are pervasive in contemporary society and they influence the public's awareness of political and social reality. In her article she addresses the question of knowledge and skills that are essential for being a citizen in a media age and concludes that media literacy is an essential part of political socialization. Pušnik (2004) uses agenda-setting theory when she examines how journalists define and select relevant/newsworthy topics and help to construct the "collective memory of Slovenians" and the process of forming a national community. She concludes that instead of promoting democratic practices and citizens' abilities to make informed decisions based on a clear understanding of events and of knowing different opinions, news reports become a tool for reproducing hegemonic state-building formations. Oblak (2000) has written one of the most extensive articles on Slovenia in which agenda-setting theory formation and development is presented. In her empirical analysis she questions a direct link between the quantity of reporting of certain issues in the media and the perceived importance of these issues in public and vice versa as is suggested by agenda-setting theory. She focuses on the question of which issues were prominent in newspapers regarding joining the EU and how often the arguments pro and con were biased. Based on the results of her study, she rejects the hypothesis of direct causal media effect on the audience.

It is clear that in Slovenia agenda-setting theory has been solely applied to media studies and mass communication studies. Although authors use agenda-setting theory for their reasoning regarding the power of media they have a rather critical approach. Agenda-setting theory is also very popular among students writing their bachelor's theses.

According to our literature review, in Slovenia there is no study which would apply agenda-setting theory in a business context. One of the reasons why empirical studies using agenda-setting theory are not performed frequently is that conducting this kind of research is much more expensive than surveys grounded in other theories, such as the uses and gratification approach or the discursive approach. Agenda-setting theory requires content analysis of both media and public opinion research.

Although there are several research agencies that provide media analysis reports with quantitative and qualitative data for companies, such as the number of appearances of a particular company, the size, time, context, shape and contents, evaluation of a company's image in the media, creation of journalist lists, which help in managing relations with the media, there are no publicly available reports on this matter.

This chapter is the first attempt to empirically investigate agenda-setting properties in the Slovenian business environment by exploring the influence of the Slovenian media in the generation of corporate reputation. The purpose is to find out whether there is a positive relation between media visibility of the firm and its reputation. As argued by Fombrun and Shanley (1990), publics construct reputations from a variety of available information about companies' activities, the media being an important source of such information. The amount of information in the business press and mass media can bias the public's construction of companies' reputations (Fombrun & Shanley, 1990). Thus, our hypothesis is worded as follows: The greater a company's media visibility, the better its reputation will be.

Case Study

Institution of the first communication management consultancy, Pristop, in the early 1990s institutionalized media monitoring and analysis systems in Slovenia, initially by introducing a clipping service, Kliping. From being a department of Pristop through becoming an independent limited liability company in 2005, Kliping in 2007 consolidated the industry in Central and South Eastern Europe by merging with the largest Croatian provider of media monitoring and analysis systems and annexing more such companies from Bosnia and Herzegovina, Macedonia, Montenegro, and Serbia to form a new company MCA GRUPA, one of the largest providers of such services in Europe. Its Slovenian branch currently serves over 350 clients, mainly from the corporate sector, and is a member of the World Association of Media Monitoring Agencies (FIBEP) and the Association for Measurement and Evaluation of Communication (AMEC). Besides Kliping, three other media monitoring companies operate in Slovenia: Press clipping, Doseg, and Genion.

The public opinion polls in Slovenia are well known and established, but they do not perform corporate reputation rankings. There are several research agencies (Valicon, GfK, Mediana, Aragon, Spem) which offer ad hoc nonstandardized reputation and image surveys that are performed for individual subscribers only. In fact there are only two standardized reputation rankings in Slovenia, the first of which, RM Plus specializes in the banking sector and makes an annual report. The second, Kline & Partner covers companies from all branches and for more than 10 years has annually polled a representative sample of the Slovenian population as well as researching among specific groups of stakeholders such as managers. It is interesting that Slovenian companies prevail and can be found in all the top positions in terms of Slovenian reputation rankings. Those corporations are also the dominant players in the domestic market (Mercator, Petrol, Merkur, Mobitel), and some of them are also the biggest Slovenian exporters (Krka, Lek, Gorenje, Revoz). There is also a very high correlation between the most successful (by income and profit) and the most reputable companies.

Research Methodology

In order to verify our thesis we decided to combine the data from two different databases. As media visibility data we have used a list of the top 100 companies that were mentioned most frequently in the main Slovenian media in 2006, which covers 98% of all business related news in Slovenia, including: print media (*Finance, Kapital, Manager, Marketing Magazin, Podjetnik, Delo, Demokracija, Dnevnik, Jana, Lady, Mag, Mladina, Primorske novice, Slovenske novice, Direkt, Večer, Direkt, Žurnal, Dobro jutro*); Radio Slovenia (with three main information programs); national TV (RTV SLOVENIJA) and commercial TV (POP TV); and the most popular Web news portal in Slovenia, www.24ur.com. The content analysis database was provided by Pristop's clipping service Kliping.

As the second variable we used the rankings of the top 100 most reputable Slovenian companies in 2006. Rankings are based on the mean score for each company evaluated on a scale from 1 (not reputable) to 5 (highly reputable). This research was conducted by the Kline & Partner agency on a representative sample of Slovenian general and business publics. This is the only annual measurement of corporate reputation available in Slovenia.

For the purpose of our study we used the frequency of media exposure for each company and its reputational standing on the list of the 100 most reputable companies, evaluated both by general and business public. In our analysis both variables were correlated using the Pearson's correlation coefficient.

Results

The results show that the company with the highest media coverage was mentioned 5,291 times in various media in 2006 whereas the company with the lowest media coverage was mentioned only 26 times. The first 10 companies are also among the biggest Slovenian companies by income. Table 24.1 shows the first 10 and the last 10 companies by media coverage. It can be seen that there is a big gap in media coverage between the two extremes. There are also quite big differences in the reputational rankings when the first and last 10 companies on the list are compared.

The results of the correlation analysis show that media coverage and reputation rankings among the general and business publics in 2006 are quite highly correlated and that there is almost no difference between the correlations (see Table 24.2).

The correlation coefficient between the media coverage and reputation rankings among the general public is 0.460 and the correlation coefficient between

Table 24.1 The First Ten and the Last Ten Companies by Media Coverage in 2006

Company	Media Coverage (No. of Publications)	Rep. Rankings (General Public)	Rep. Rankings (Business Public)
Mercator	5,291	3	4
NLB	2,972	30	31
Petrol	2,933	4	5
Krka	2,593	1	1
Istrabenz	2,438	15	12
Delo	2,144	35	n/a
Gorenje	2,136	2	2
Pivovarna Laško	2,124	8	11
Telekom Slovenije	2,110	18	18
Luka Koper	1,988	38	23
Sava Tires	79	62	15
Gorenjski tisk	62	96	88
Svea	56	64	60
Color	48	60	64
Pomurske mlekarne	46	51	86
Grawe	42	99	91
Eta Cerkno	35	81	68
Pliva Ljubljana	35	69	95
Zdravilišče Rogaška	30	31	66
Merkur zavarovalnica	26	85	87

Table 24.2 The Correlations between the Media Coverage and Reputational Rankings of Slovenian Companies in 2006

	Media Coverage	Rep. Rankings (General Public)
Media coverage	—	
Rep. rankings (general public)	0.460**	—
Rep. rankings	0.456**	0.778**
(business public)	0	0

** Significant at the 0.01 level

the media coverage and the business public is 0.456. Both are significant at a 0.01 level. As can also be seen from the results, the correlation between the reputational rankings of general and business publics is also very high indicating that there are almost no differences in evaluation of companies between the two different publics.

Conclusion

In this chapter we tried to make a preliminary empirical link between two important concepts related to public relations research: the agenda setting and the reputation. Both concepts are fairly underresearched in Slovenia and their link has never been investigated before.

The research and work on corporate reputation among Slovenian scholars became salient in the 1990s. At that time concepts such as corporate identity, image, and reputation caught the attention of Slovenian scholars. They examined them theoretically and empirically—in the late 1990s the first measurements of reputation among Slovenian companies were made. As is the case elsewhere, the notion of reputation in Slovenia was also closely linked to public relations theory and practice and with media coverage. Contrary to the concept of reputation, the theory of agenda setting has been well known in Slovenia since the 1970s; however, only limited theoretical and empirical research using this theory has been conducted.

It has been said previously by Fombrun and Shanley (1990) that reputation can also be interpreted as the outcome of different processes—media exposure included—where companies signal their characteristics to different stakeholders. Hence, in our research we proposed that media coverage should be closely related to reputations. Our results confirm this thesis; the results of correlations between media coverage and reputational rankings are fairly high. Interestingly, our results are quite different from the results obtained by Fombrun and Shanley (1990) who tested a similar hypothesis. The link between media exposure and reputations proved to be negative in their case. Some differences can be assigned to different measures and methodology, but we can also anticipate that Slovenian media are in most cases relatively nonnegative toward the companies and that media seem to be one of the most important sources of information for the general as well as the business public in Slovenia.

Our study has several limitations. Some of them are due to the data obtained from the secondary sources which lack the exact methodological explanations. One of the limitations is that we did not explore in detail the relation between positive and negative or nonpositive media coverage and reputation. Another concern is that our research is based only on the one-year results. As is clear from the literature, reputation is something that is usually built over a longer period, hence a longitudinal analysis of the relation between the two variables would be beneficial.

References

Anonymous. (1989). Javni odnosi [Public relations]. *MM*, July, 10.

Ašanin Gole, P., & Verčič, D. (Eds.). (2000). *Teorija in praksa slovenskih odnosov z javnostmi* [Slovenian public relations theory and practice]. Ljubljana, Slovenia: Slovensko društvo za odnose z javnostmi [Public Relations Society of Slovenia].

Erjavec, K. (2000). Medijska pismenost kot pogoj uspešne politične socializacije [Media literacy as a condition for successful political socialization]. *Teorija in praksa, 27*(4), 672–685.

Fombrun, C., & Shanley, M. (1990). What's in a name? Reputation building and corporate strategy. *Academy of Management Journal, 33*(2), 233–258.

Freedom House. (2008). Report retrieved from http://www.freedomhouse.org/uploads/fop08/FOTP2008_WorldRankings.pdf

Gruban, B. (1995). *Odnosi z javnostmi in komunikacijski management* [Public relations and communication management]. Ljubljana, Slovenia: CISEF.

Gruban, B., & Verčič, D., & Zavri, F. (Eds.). (1997). *F. Pristop k odnosom z javnostmi* [Entering public relations]. Ljubljana, Slovenia: Pristop.

Gruban, B., Verčič, D., & Zavrl F. (1994). *Odnosi z javnostmi v Sloveniji: raziskovalno poročilo 1994* [Public relations in Slovenia: research report 1994]. Ljubljana, Slovenia: Pristop.

Grunig, L. A., Grunig, J. E., & Verčič, D. (1998). Are the IABC's excellence principles generic? Comparing Slovenia and the United States, the United Kingdom, and Canada. *Journal of Communication Management, 2*(4), 335–356.

Ilič, M. (1990, February). Ugled korporacije [Corporate reputation]. *MM, 90*, 19.

Jančič, Z. (1999). *Celostni marketing.* Ljubljana, Slovenia: FDV.

Kline, M. (1997). *Vpliv finančne uspešnosti podjetja na njegov ugled* [Relation between profit and corporate reputation]. Paper presented at the Slovenian marketing conference (DMS), Lipica, Slovenia.

Kline, M. (1999). Kaj se skriva za imenom podjetja [What is hiden behind the corporate name]. *MM*, 219–220.

Košak, G. (1972). Praktični primer preučevanja image—a določene firme s tehniko semantičnega diferenciala [Measuring corporate image with a semantic differential]. *Psihološke razsprave* (pp. 441–445). Ljubljana: Drusštvo psihologov Slovenije.

Oblak, T. (2000). Problematizacija modela "prednostnega tematiziranja": Primer analize medijskega poročanja o vstopanju Slovenije [Critical view on agenda-setting theory: Media reporting in the case of Slovenia joining the EU]. *Teorija in praksa, 37*(1), 96–115.

Podnar, K. (1999). Conception of corporate identity (Working Paper, No. 1999/7). Glasgow, Scotland: University of Strathclyde, International Center for Corporate Identity Studies.

Podnar, K. (2000a). Korporativna identiteta, imidž in ugled. Vregov zbornik [Corporate identity, image and reputation]. *Javnost, 7,* Suppl., 173–181.

Podnar, K. (2000b). Razumevanje koncepta korporativne identitete—meje novonastajajočega raziskovalnega polja [Understanding corporate identity — limitations of newly arisen research field]. *Akad. MM, 4*(6), 67–76.

Podnar, K. (2001). Velik ugled še ne pomeni konkurenčne prednosti: Študija primera dveh slovenskih farmacevtskih podjetij [The high reputation doesn't mean competitive advantage: Case study of two Slovenian pharmaceutical companies]. In P. Hvala (Ed.), *Zbornik prispevkov 6. marketinške konference* (pp. 129–138). Ljubljana: Društvo za marketing Slovenije & Finance.

Podnar, K. (2005). Corporate identity in Slovenia. *Corporate Communication: An International Journal, 10*(1), 69–82.

Pušnik, M. (2004). Novičarsko upravljanje z javnim mnenjem [News politics of public opinion}. *Teorija in praksa, 41*(3–4), 678–689.

Repovš, J. (1995). *Celostna grafična podoba* [Holistic visual identity]. Ljubljana, Slovenia: Studio Marketing.

Splichal, S. (1997). *Javno mnenje: Teoretski razvoj in spori v 20. stoletju* [Public Opinion: Theorethical development and disputes in 20th century]. Ljubljana, Slovenia: Fakulteta za družbene vede.

Splichal, S. (1999). Ownership, regulation and socialisation: Rethinking the principles of democratic media. *Javnost/Public, 6*(2), 5–24.

Verčič, D. (2000). Ugled—modna muha odnosov z javnostmi: Pripisovanje pomena podjetju kot blagovni znamki [Ascribing meanings to companies as brands]. In N. Serajnik & K. Podnar (Eds), *Slovenska konferenca za odnose z javnostmi. Zbornik referatov* [Slovenian public relations conference. Proceedings] (pp. 52–59). Ljubljana, Slovenia: Public Relations Society of Slovenia.

Verčič, D. (2002). Public relations research and education in Slovenia. In S. Averbeck & S. Wehmeier (Eds.), *Kommunikationswissenschaft und public relations in Osteuropa: Arbeitsberichte* (pp. 157–173). Leipzig, Germany: Leipziger Universitätsverlag.

Verčič, D. (2003). Public relations in a corporativist country: The case of Slovenia. In K. Sriramesh & D. Verčič (Eds.), *The global public relations handbook: Theory, research, and practice* (pp. 281–300). Mahwah, NJ: Erlbaum.

Verčič, D. (2004). Slovenia. In B. Van Ruler & D. Verčič (Eds.), *Public relations and communication management in Europe: A nation-by-nation introduction to public relations theory and practice* (pp. 375–386). Berlin, Germany: Mouton de Gruyter.

25 Corporate Reputation and the News Media in the United Arab Emirates

Timothy Walters

While today's leaders in the United Arab Emirates may use more sophisticated public relations techniques, they have continued what was begun by their forebears. The story of how today's leaders have succeeded in spreading the message of a user friendly economic environment offers great lessons for other such societies about managing the development metaphor.

Because of the hurly burly development in the United Arab Emirates, some of the facts in this paper will have changed in the months between writing and publication. New buildings will have risen, new initiatives will have begun, and the Emirates of Abu Dhabi and Dubai and the five outlying smaller Emirates will have created new businesses with accompanying public relations programs. Even as this time goes by the gist of the story will remain the same.

As the 2002 Arab Human Development Report (Fergany, 2002) suggested, this story is full of contradictions. It covers a time during which the economic news coming from the region was written in superlatives. Yet, buried beneath the hyperbole was a grim reality—many Gulf countries faced a daunting and uncertain future. Those that did not modernize their economies, reduce subsidies to their citizens, create real jobs, and get their ecological housing in order would find the not-so-distant future especially bleak (Quinn, Walters, & Whiteoak, 2003).

Because Saudi Arabia and Kuwait have been victims of misspent windfalls, and because Bahrain, Oman, and Qatar are playing catch-up, the United Arab Emirates has become the economic leader in the Gulf Cooperation Council. During the last 3½ decades, the UAE was transformed from seven small, impoverished desert principalities of frond-topped huts to a modern state with towering skyscrapers. To his credit, much of this was due to the simple, clear agenda set by the late President His Highness Sheikh Zayed bin Sultan Al Nahyan, who led the country from its formation in 1971 until his death in November 2004. Under his tutelage, the UAE developed a diversified economy with one of the world's highest mean standards of living. Many of the UAE's petrodollars have been used to build its infrastructure, broaden its economy, and build its reputation.

From the early days when fundamental choices were made, the United Arab Emirates has been utterly transformed. Fifty years ago, when the grandparents of today's college students were young adults, the country had no electrical grid, indoor plumbing, telephone system, public hospital, or modern school. As late as 1950, Dubai was a city of huts and unpaved streets. In 1970, literacy rates hovered just above 20%. Only a fraction of the mothers of today's college students graduated from high school, and that fraction was just slightly higher for the fathers. As recently as 1992, Dubai's Sheikh Zayed Road—now lined with glass-and-steel towers—was desert as far as the eye could see from the lone skyscraper, the 39-story Dubai World Trade Center. Today that skyscraper is dwarfed by its near neighbor, the 56-story Emirates Tower and the view from the top includes dozens of skyscrapers (Walters, Walters, & Quinn, 2005). In the future the world's tallest building, the 200-story Burj Dubai, will loom over all.

Modern high-speed highways now cross a landscape that just one generation ago was only rutted roads. Modern ports, including those that house container facilities and dry docks, now dot the coastline. Dubai International Airport has estimated that more than 22 million passengers would pass through its concourses in 2006, and that 60 million would do so in 2010 (Dubai International Airport, 2005). Abu Dhabi's airport is currently undergoing an AED25 billion redevelopment and expects to handle 20 million passengers by 2010 (Abu Dhabi International Ariport, n.d.).

Along with spectacular developments, the United Arab Emirates (particularly Dubai) has carefully cultivated its reputation as a visitor friendly, safe, modern, and reasonable Arabic/Islamic state. Some visitors are from neighboring Arab states who come for an Islamic friendly vacation or for something different from their own country's monotonic, monotonous landscape. Others are snowbirds from Europe with deep pockets, seeking the warm sunshine, white-sand beaches, and second homes. Still others are "temporary workers" who come seeking employment in the Middle Eastern version of El Dorado.

Corporate Reputation

Much like the line from Al Capp's Li'l Abner, "What's good for General Bull-moose is good for everybody," what is good for this economy is seen as good for the newly developing country (Walters, Kradagic, & Walters, 2006). In creating this economy, the United Arab Emirates was striving to become the Singapore of the Middle East. To date, much of that story has been the story of the Emirate of Dubai. This is so for several reasons. Dubai was the first of the seven Emirates to create a modern airport, has developed an airline with a global reach, and has the country's most widely circulated English-language newspaper, the *Gulf News*.

When then crown prince of Dubai Sheikh Mohammed Bin Rashid Al Maktoum manned a booth at Comdex 2000 in Las Vegas designed to attract techies and their businesses to Dubai Internet City, one glib observer noted that the royal was trying to, "pull a Bugsy Siegel in the middle of the Dubai desert," while building a technological city instead of casinos (Gartner, 2000). Much of this plan has been brought to fruition.

Dubai has become a kaleidoscope of modernistic skyscrapers and master-planned communities as the vision of the master architect Sheikh Mohammed unfolds before his eyes. Dubai is cultivating itself as a luxury brand destination, and Dubai Holding, the government investment branch, has developed into the engine of this growth. In becoming this investment manager, the company has developed, "an investment empire where the sun never sets" (7Days, 2006, pp. 16–17). Under the umbrella of Dubai Holding, the empire now includes Dubai Investment Group, Jumeriah Hotels, Istithmar, Emaar, Dubai International Capital, Dubai Ports International, Dubai Islamic Bank, Dubai Ports World, and Dubai Financial, among others. Other government entities include Emirates Airlines, one of the world's fastest growing and most profitable airlines and the flagship of transportation and promotion in Dubai.

Some seasoned observers valued the brand name Dubai at $24 billion in 2004. But they also suggested that the city and Emirate must move beyond merely leveraging its strategic location and newly built infrastructure to become something more than the vocabulary of big and bigger. That something more includes developing intangibles because many potential competitors exist in the surrounding Gulf Cooperation Council countries. Thus, the country must fortify its educational backbone, create a more humane climate in the labor market, establish a meritocracy, and develop better human resource management (Varughese, 2005). To date, the most visible thing Emirati authorities have done is ban the importation of child camel jockeys from India and Pakistan. Even so, the motive may have been less about humane treatment of children and more about not being the punch line of a telling joke. Discussions about replacing the term *migrant workers* with *temporary workers*, which is discussed as window dressing in a Human Rights Watch report that criticizes labor conditions demonstrated that those controlling the country sometimes would rather distract than honestly tackle problems head on (Al Baik, n.d.). Occasionally, they don't even bother to distract; ministries have been known to refuse to comment about a problem or toss reporters out of their offices. Corporate reputation programs in the UAE were crafted in different ways for different audiences because of the inherent differences between Arabic and English. For the most part, Arabic is a lyrical, almost musical language that deals with a vision in a holistic way. It is the sum of the parts that matters. English is a more direct bottom-line language that gets to the point, in which the individual parts are essential in and of themselves. This difference seems grounded in inherent differences in where language comes from and how it is processed in the brain. In Western languages, reading and writing go from left to right, and exercise the brain's left hemisphere, the alphabetic mind. Arabic reads right to left and exercises the right brain, the "thousand pictures side" (Pink, 2005, pp. 18–19).

Thus, while the Burj Dubai (the world's tallest building) might be sold to an Arabic audience as the most, "prestigious square kilometer on earth," offering breathing views, it was sold to English language audiences as cost per square foot or as convenient to shopping. This linguistic perspective was in sync with the 2006 Economist Intelligence Unit survey in which 145 senior executives said that cultural and linguistic adaptation were critical for success here (GMR online, 2006). Academic study also supports this opinion, suggesting that inherent cultural differences in message construction between Arabic and English mean that repetition versus simplicity, imagery versus accuracy, exaggeration versus understanding, words versus action, and vagueness versus specificity must be understood if effective communication is to take place (Zaharna, 1995).

Business and the News Media

United Arab Emirates studies of the relationship between business and the news media are relatively new and largely unscientific. Walters, Bhatti, Fakhreddine, Gulovsen, and Hassall's (2006) pioneering, 1,115-respondent systematic study of news and news values has examined the relationship of the media to its various target audiences in the Emirates. These audiences, which reflect the nature of this divided society, include nationals, expat Arabs, Indians, other Asians (Pakistanis), and native English speakers. Among other things the study found: (a) respondents turned to media that used their native language and supported their native culture; (b) news was ranked as important based on its cultural proximity, meaning that the closer a story was to a respondent's cultural or linguistic background, the more important that respondent deemed the story to be; (c) Indians, other Asians, and native English speakers tended to get their information from newspapers; (d) Al Jazeera was the overwhelming source of news and business information for nationals and expat Arabs alike; and (e) native English speakers turned Westward toward home for news, as they also did for business information, which they found largely on the Internet.

Both native English speakers and English-as-a-second-language residents turn first to newspapers for cultural, linguistic, and practical reasons. Pragmatically speaking, the wide use of English as the language of commerce translates into English-language media enterprises such as the *Gulf News* and *Khaleej Times*, which cater to disparate bands of English readers from the subcontinent as well as from the British Isles, Australia, the United States, and Canada.

In the United Arab Emirates, neither nationals nor expat Arabs are much interested in business news. In a recent survey of media usage habits only about 14% of nationals and 16% of expat Arabs judged regional business news as extremely important; only 14% of nationals and 18% of expat Arabs viewed international business as extremely important; and only 19% of nationals and 15% of expat Arabs viewed the stock market as extremely important. Of national English speakers only about 22% viewed regional business news as extremely important; 37% viewed international business as extremely important; and 24% viewed the stock market as extremely important. The top information sources for business news for nationals were Al Jazeera and UAE TV; for expat Arabs it was Al Jazeera or Arabic language dailies; and for native English speakers it was English-language daily newspapers and the Internet (Walters, Bhatti, et al., 2006).

Although the government monopoly Internet service provider Etisalat's official figures suggest a techno-savvy, broadly wired, Internet-informed society, the reality in 2006 was different. In a comprehensive survey of actual media usage, about 63% of nationals reported having access to the Internet at home, but only about 16% of national respondents reported using the Internet on a daily basis. This percentage is much less than that of college-age Emiratis, of whom more than 90% use the Net daily (Walters, Quinn, & Walters, 2005). It is also much less than the about 60% of native English speakers who use the Internet daily, many turning to the Net for news from home and to manage their finances long distance (Walters, Bhatti, et al., 2006).

The UAE governments in their various incarnations own, license, or otherwise permit all media, and thus have the final say about what is read, seen, or heard. Because of their large-scale presence, temporary workers are carefully catered to by the media. The free-to-air media mix includes radio stations such as Radio 4; Ajman broadcasts in Hindi; HUM FM broadcasts in Hindi/Urdu; Al Khaleejiya has news/talk/music in Hindi; al Quran broadcasts religious programming; and City 101.6, broadcasts Arabic pop (RadioStationWorld, 2006). Pay-to-play television packages feature stations from across the Arabic-speaking world. Packages appeal to several language groups from India, the Philippines, and the United States and Western Europe. Packages are available from about AED58 to upwards of AED500 monthly.

The landscape has exploded so quickly that Arab Advisors, a Jordan based media consultancy group, has estimated that the total number of free-to-air satellite (FTA) channels broadcasting on Arab sat and Nile sat had reached 263 by October 2006. This meant, according to their figures, that the number of FTA channels on these services had jumped by 163 between January 2004 and October 2006 (Arab Advisors, 2006).

An interpretation of the communication climate is complicated by the presence of a "new" generation of nationals represented by the age group 20 to 29. They have become the "bulge" in the python for the United Arab Emirates. They are the leading edge of a groundbreaking generation of highly trained citizens, many of whom have been educated in an English-speaking environment. Having been exposed to new consumer ideas and brands via advertising and programming, these young people are among the first to harvest the many benefits of a marketplace economy. What appears clear is that this group is more media savvy, more media oriented, and more brand aware than either their parents or grandparents.

Media usage patterns of population groups in the United Arab Emirates have implications for local governmental policy makers, advertisers, and interested observers. Above all else, the patterns reflect a media-related "cultural distance," particularly with sources of news (see Hofstede, 2004.) Anecdotal evidence suggests that story frame, source credibility, and "brand name" (a surrogate for positive reputation attributes in this context) are essential. This same anecdotal evidence suggests that UAE audiences are exceptionally adroit about differentiating between and among information sources, picking up subtle body language and other nonverbal clues (Gladwell, 2005). Even those who may not be fluent in Arabic are able to differentiate the who, what, when, and where of the news presenters.

The data also speak to the difficulty of coordinating any standardized communications campaign. Although the glocal strategy seems the best option for social, political, and commercial purposes in the UAE, the data suggest that policy makers and interested observers must take the long-term view about strategy and tactics and about what information types best achieve their ends.

Corporate Reputation in the United Arab Emirates

The corporate reputation landscape in the United Arab Emirates reflects the country's segregated economic, political, and linguistic landscape. Because of a more welcoming economic and social environment than their Gulf Cooperation Council (GCC) neighbors, the United Arab Emirates, particularly Dubai, has become home to dozens of transnational corporations such as Microsoft, Siemens, and Reuters, which are among the hundreds of companies calling Dubai Media City or Dubai Internet City home. (For a complete list, see http://www. dubaimediacity.com/ or http://www.dubaiinternetcity.com/.) These companies have corporate images, brand identities, and reputations upon which Dubai has capitalized in developing the Emirate's public face.

Reputation building efforts of national companies move outward from a center tent pole. As Emirati-based corporations build and manage reputations, they proceed from Emirate, to nation, to Gulf, to region, and then to continents of concern. Leading the pack in the United Arab Emirates has been the Emirate of Dubai, which has capitalized on a systematic public relations program. This process means that a company such as the government-run Emirates Airlines labored to build its reputation in the Emirate of Dubai first, then the entire United Arab Emirates, then Gulf Cooperation Council countries, then the 22 members of the Arabic League, and then to locations where the airline opens new routes. Whenever Emirates Airlines opens a new route, it spends much time, energy, and effort developing its reputation among the populations who live where these flights land, emphasizing comfort, luxury, safety, and ease. With 80 worldwide destinations in scattered places, such as New York, Paris, Beijing, Shanghai, Hong Kong, Lahore, and Sydney, the airline now proudly serves as the stalking horse of the Dubai brand name.

Whatever else can be said, hyperbole and superlatives have become a way of life in the country. Ventures are regularly described not in terms of excellence but in P.T. Barnum's vocabulary of the "biggest," "tallest," or "newest." The only thing missing from the process is a sign saying this way to the egress, which is unlikely to appear until visitors' pockets have been drained of cash.

The term *world class* has been bandied about so often that it has lost meaning. Master-planned communities sprout up everywhere the royals will allow. During 2004 and 2005, the rapid-fire announcements of Dubailand, Health City, the Dubai International Financial Center (DIFC), Burj Dubai, and Falcon City waxed lyrical in local newspapers. Today, these have been joined by the world's longest hotel strip, a 31-hotel, U.S.$27 billion, 10 km project on superhighway E311, labeled Bawadi, a Bedu word meaning roughly "place where you live in the desert."

Local media (which the several governments either directly influence or control) have used hyperbole about these developments that borrow liberally from the iconography of other lands. Then Dubai Crown Prince General, now ruler, Sheikh Mohammad bin Rashid Al Maktoum, was said to have topped "his previous visionary initiatives" with the AED18.5 billion Dubailand theme park, "the Middle East answer to Disneyland." To be built on 2 billion square feet of land, Dubailand has been projected to attract 15 million more people a year to the area (AME Info).

Falcon City of Wonders at Dubailand, which will replicate the "wonders of the world," was described as an ambitious AED5.5 billion project. "Shaped like a falcon, the city features structures based on ancient and modern wonders of the world," including the Pyramids, the Hanging Gardens of Babylon, the Eiffel Tower, the Taj Mahal, the Great Wall of China, the Leaning Tower of Pisa, and the Lighthouse at Alexandria, in which you can live, shop, and play. Dubai, of course, will do them better. "These structures," according to reports, "will be larger than the originals" (Jacob, 2005). The AED6.7 billion Healthcare City has been called "world's first health care free zone" and includes internationally known brand health care providers such as Harvard Medical School and the Mayo Clinic (Dubai Healthcare City). Such initiatives, the leaders say, help make Dubai a leading hub in the new global economy.

Topping this off is a building designed to rival the Colossus of Rhodes. According to the *Gulf News*, "passengers flying into Dubai's planned Jebli Ali airport should not be alarmed when greeted by the imposing figure of a 140-metre tall human figure. The structure will be...a 35-story [structure] designed to resemble a man dressed in traditional Gulf Arab dress..." (Ditcham, 2007).

Articles in the business section of the *Gulf News* and the *Khaleej Times* speak about the hub metaphor as if working from the same talking-points memo. Tim Clark, president of Emirates Airlines, contends that Dubai is the center of new wealth in the world. We are the crossroads for the emerging economies of West Africa and East Africa, for the embrace of capitalism in Russia and Eastern Europe, for India, for North East and South East Asia, and for China (*Khaleej Times*, 2006a). The *Gulf News*, in describing Dubai as the destination of choice in the Gulf, has said that Dubai has successfully separated politics from business and has become a center of opportunity in which dreams can come true (Kalaf, 2006, p. 39). And the Dubai Department of Tourism and Commerce Marketing is busily putting Dubai on the world stage by participating in 28 overseas travel industry exhibits, thus creating better awareness of Dubai as a destination (2006).

Governments regularly cultivate reporters. Not to be outdone by the ruler of Dubai, a few years ago President His Highness Sheikh Khalifa Bin Zayed Al Nayhan sponsored a 50-member UAE Journalists' Association group on a Hadj trip to Saudi Arabia. "The grant," according to the Gulf News, was "part of Sheikh Khalifa's ongoing material and moral support to journalists based on his appreciation of the role they play for the UAE" (Gulf News, 2006b). Or maybe this was because he did not want to be outdone by Sheikh Mohammed of Dubai who donated AED5 million to the UAE Journalists Association. These funds were to be used to help the association meet its social and humanitarian commitments, which included paying back loans granted to 60 members (Wakalat Anba'a al-Emarat, WAM, 2006).

News Values

Newsworthiness in the United Arab Emirates is the product of the society's form, which is pyramidal in shape and sharply divided by culture, language, and income. Because most non-Emirati populations have not yet been (nor will they ever be) assimilated, they exist on virtual islands in the stream of information that flows around the Arabian Peninsula, adapting to the workplace, but living segregated lives. Many share Islam in common with UAE nationals, and may watch or hear the same Imam preaching on Friday, but most migrants do not share much else with their reluctant hosts. Many transport artifacts of their culture with them (Appadurai, 1991).

Separateness includes school as well, because government-run K-12 schools are almost exclusively for nationals; so, too, are national universities. Non-Emiratis must bring their educational systems with them, leave their children back home, or send them home. Exclusion is instrumental in generating real boundaries because children often serve as agents of acculturation, bringing home from school not just backpacks, but the norms, history, and traditions of their adopted country (Ewen, 1992). This inculcation of values does not happen in the United Arab Emirates, except in the way that consumers transport common lifestyle symbols and corporate reputation inherent in brand names from the marketplace to home.

The consequence of the multifaceted Emirati "separateness" is that expatriate communities often exist in physically distinct neighborhoods or in walled, inwardly turned enclaves within neighborhoods. Though a pidginized English has become the "lingua Anglo" of public interaction and of business, each group has retained its own distinct language, culture, and identity for use in the home and for interacting with friends.

Because the United Arab Emirates remains a separated society in which people maintain their particular cultural identity, newsworthiness is directly related to that cultural identity. When looking at issues of the day, different cultural groups rank issues in starkly different orders. Nationals and expat Arabs are concerned with different things and, as noted above, they look at different media as well.

Organizational Newsworthiness

A great pride and terrific boosterism fill the United Arab Emirates today, as a new vision of society is being formed in the Arabian Desert. As a product of this pride and because the media frequently view their role as cheerleaders, the media are full of positive stories about business development. When asked why the newspaper does not typically include negative coverage, the editor of the Dubai-based *Gulf News* responded that the paper did not want to embarrass a business owner or force that business to close its doors. Words such as *bigger, better, more,* and *higher* are sprinkled upon business pages of all newspapers, emphasizing the positive. After the first page, business sections are mostly filled with stories with a byline, sans name, but with the appellation "by a Staff Reporter." This is a euphemism for a story that has been printed verbatim from a press release. This euphemism is meaningful because from the moment of creation all ministry and government releases are, by legal definition, newsworthy. The law requires that all ministry and government releases be printed or broadcast or otherwise used, and reporters rarely edit these materials in any way. And, many of the "public enterprises" are actually government-run entities in disguise as Emiratis are masters of the shell game.

Cultural imperatives mean that the front pages of Arabic and English language newspapers usually feature a four-color photograph of a Sheikh above the fold. (Except for war causalities, there are usually no women on the front page.) The caption always identifies the most important Sheikh using his full title, wherever he appears in the picture. The mere structure of the name suggests power. Not only does the mention of a Sheikha or Sheikh imply authority, but a knowledgeable reader understands that bin (son of) or bint (daughter of) also conveys something of consequence. Someone reading the caption which includes the name "His Highness Sheikh Hamdan bin Mohammed bin Rashid Al Maktoum" understands that this is the very young son of the current ruler of Dubai who is, in turn, the son of Sheikh Rashid, one of the country's founders.

A caption rarely identifies people from left, right, or center; it identifies the most important person no matter where he is. The assumption is that the reader knows who the principal person is. Sheikh Mohammed is typically identified as High Highness Sheikh Mohammed Bin Rashid Al Maktoum, Vice President and Prime Minister of the UAE and Ruler of Dubai. Sheikh Khalifa is typically identified as His Highness Sheikh Khalifa Bin Zayed Al Nayhan President of the UAE and Ruler of Abu Dhabi. If you are unfortunate enough to be standing next to the most important royal, the likelihood is that you will remain unidentified, even if you are the president of a major corporation or any other VIP. One story on a Bill Clinton speech was accompanied by a picture not of the ex-president, but of a rapt male royal sitting in a velvet-covered chair at the front of the audience.

A typical caption front page caption reads: "President His Highness Sheikh Khalifa Bin Zayed Al Nayhan yesterday received a message from Iranian President Mahmoud Abhadinejad dealing with bilateral relations and issues of mutual concern. The message was handed to Sheikh Nayhan by Sadiq Mahsouli, adviser to the Iranian President" (*Gulf News*, 2006b)

Because the ruling family and their extended kinfolk often mix politics with business, their pictures and stories not only appear on the front page or at the top of the newscast, but in the business news as well. Besides capitalizing on the attention-getting power of the ruling families, business news is filled with stories of the impending opening of mega projects, celebrity attendance at meetings, another memorandum of understanding, and the most recent top brand to come to the country. Mega projects are described as bigger than or taller than or the largest on planet earth, business stories wax prosaic about celebrities such as Bill Clinton, Richard Branson, and Cherie Blair, and assorted well-known economic gurus such as Tom Peters and Edward de Bono, and are breathless when the latest LV product is announced or the newest BMW 7 series is unveiled. Whether it is luring an ex-president with a six-figure honorarium, a professional golfer with a seven-figure appearance fee, or using a helipad for a tennis match, Emiratis know how to turn the spotlight on themselves.

Today a couple of women have become feature players in the news. One is Princess Haya bint Al-Hussein, the young, pretty wife of Sheikh Mohammed of Dubai, who maintains her own Web site listing her achievements (see http://www.princesshaya. net/). The second is Sheikha Lubna Al Qasimi the niece of the ruler of Sharjah, who is the Minister for Economy and Planning of the United Arab Emirates.

Method

This study used data derived from key word searches in both the *Gulf News*, the local English language newspaper of record, and Google. Because of the general absence of published public opinion about business, these figures have been used as gross measures of public awareness, corporate attributes, and public perception of that attribute. Key words included *Dubai* and *power outage, water shortage, Dubai expensive, apartment rental, property prices increase,* and *traffic congestion.*

The Dubai Shopping Festival, the wildly popular annual event, held each spring, has continued growing since its inception. Mean visitors per day have grown from about 40,000 to about 100,000 and total spending has increased as well. It has grown from about AED1340 in 1996 to about AED2002 per person in 2005. Despite these rosy figures, spending, adjusted for inflation, actually declined during the period from 2001 to 2006 as inflation has escalated from 5% to upwards of 14% per annum (see Table 25.1) .

Even as visitors continued arriving in record numbers, Emirate Airlines customer satisfaction has slipped. From a ranking of first in the airline of the year category in 2001, Emirates slipped to number 2 in 2004, and then to number 3 in 2005. And, though the airport reports double digit growth of transit passengers, the growth in the number of visitors actually staying in Dubai's hotels has dropped as well (see Table 25.2).

Table 25.1 Dubai Shopping Festival 2001–2005

	2001	2002	2003	2004	2005
Visitors	2.55	2.68	2.92	3.1	3.3
Days	31	31	32	32	32
Visitors per day	0.08	0.09	0.09	0.1	0.1
Dirhams per person	1.76	1.72	1.75	1.87	2.02

Source: Gulf news, 23 November, page 26.

Table 25.2 Growth in Number of Visitors Staying in Hotels in Dubai

Year	Growth
2001	5.88%
2002	31.94%
2003	4.84%
2004	8.43%
2005	12.96%
2006	3.28%

Source: Gulf News, 12 January 2007, page 32.

Table 25.3 Property Appreciation

Year	Rate of annual appreciation	Sold out/Not sold out
2002	46.5	Sold out
2003	45	Sold out
2004	36.7	25% units remaining
2005	19	25% units remaining
2006	13.6	More than 25% remaining

Source: Gulf News, 12 November 2007, page 43.

This decline in the growth of visitors to hotels has been accompanied by a slowdown in the rate of appreciation in property values. The annual appreciation rate declined precipitously during the period from 2002 to 2006. Damac, a leading government property developer, listed the following figures (see Table 25.3).

While property appreciation figures and hotel growth rates look robust at first glance, the data suggest that bits and pieces of the Dubai brand name are suffering with the exploding growth. There has been an increase in the number of stories about problems such as power outages, water shortages, Dubai becoming an expensive place to life, apartment rental prices jumping, property prices increasing, and traffic congestion becoming worse, and the appreciation of property values has slowed drastically. Indeed, Pearson correlations for news story counts of property appreciation and water shortages, Dubai becoming expensive, apartment rental prices jumping, property prices increasing, and traffic congestion are all negative, highly correlated, and significant at $p = .02$. With respect to news story counts in the *Gulf News* power outages, water shortages, Dubai becoming an expensive place to life, apartment rental prices jumping, property prices increasing, and traffic congestion becoming worse were negative, highly correlated, and significant at $p = .02$. And, although traffic has grown at the Dubai International Airport, not only has that rate of growth slowed down, but problems with customer service reflected in the lowering of Emirates Airlines overall ranking with Skytrax are highly correlated with the numbers of passengers coming through the airport and venturing into the city. This correlation is highly correlated, negative, and significant at $p = .05$.

Discussion

As the bad news has spread, the economic engine and reputation of Dubai seem poised to slow down. While the newspaper business pages remain chock full of happy talk, the changing times terms are clearly reflected in real estate advertisements in the newspaper. Where once developers would have required large down payments and cash, master developer Dubai Properties is now offering a development called Skycourts (www.skycourts.ae) for a down payment of 5% (*Gulf News*, 2006c, p. 56). Other Emirates are now capitalizing on the mess that Dubai is making. Ras Al Khaimah is advertising Yasmin Village as "an oasis where your life, your family, and your investment can really flourish" while pointing to Dubai as "an overdeveloped property market..." (*Gulf News*, 2006c, p. 47).

The finger pointing at Dubai as an overdeveloped and overhyped market seems all the more valid because Dubai jumped from 73rd to 25th and Abu Dhabi from 64th to 30th on Mercer's list of the world's most expensive cities (infoplease, n.d.). Whether and how Dubai and the UAE recover is a serious question. The answer to this question will determine whether the city and country make a hard or soft landing when the bills come due.

References

Abu Dhabi International Airport. (n.d.). Retrieved from http://www.airport-technology. com/projects/abu_dhabi/

Al Baik, D. (n.d.). Ministry failed to meet us: Watchdog. Retrieved from http://archive. gulfnews.com/articles/06/11/13/10082301.html

AME Info. (2006). Superbrand status for Dubai International Airport. Retrieved from http://www.ameinfo.com/89066.htm

Appadurai, A. (1991). *Modernity at large: Cultural dimensions of globalization.* Minneapolis: University of Minnesota Press.

Arab Advisors. (2006). *Satellite TV in the Arab world 2006.* Amman, Jordan:. ART. Retrieved from http://www.art-tv.net/

Ditcham, R. (2006, October 25). Nakheel unfazed by project delay. Business section. *Gulf News*, p. 1.

Ditcham, R. (2007, January 10). Dubai's man mountain unveiled. Retrieved from http:// archive.gulfnews.com/articles/07/01/10/10095732.html

Dubai Department of Tourism and Commerce Marketing. (2006, October 18). Putting Dubai on the world stage. *Gulf News.* Retrieved from http://uaeinteract.com/news/ default.asp?ID=20#22477

Dubai Healthcare City. (n.d.). Home. Retrieved from http://www.dhcc.ae/en/Default. aspx?type=1&id=5

Dubai International Airport. Retrieved from http://www.dubaiairport.com/DIA/%20 English/Home

Dubai Internet City. Partners. Retrieved from http://www.dubaiinternetcity.com/ partner_directory/

Ewen, S. (1992). *Channels of desire: Mass images and the shaping of America.* Minneapolis: University of Minnesota Press.

Fergany, N. (2002). *Arab Human Development Report.* Retrieved March 6, 2010 from http://www.fimam.org/Informe%20PNUD%202002CompleteEnglish.pdf

Gartner, J. (2000, November 14). It's Sheik to be techie. *Wired.* Retrieved from http:// www.wired.com/news/business/0,1367,40167,00.html

Gladwell, M. (2005). *Blink: The power of thinking without thinking.* Boston, MA: Little, Brown.

GMR. (2006). News analysis: Truly "glocal" or lost in the translation? Retrieved from http://www.grm-online.com/article_display.aspx?articleid=632

Gulf News. (2006a, November 9). Polls, p. 47. Retrieved from http://www.gulf-news. com/polls/results/previous.html

Gulf News. (2006b, November 29). Khalifa receives Ahmadinejad message. *Gulf News*, p. 1.

Gulf News. (2006c, December 1). p. 56.

Infoplease. (n.d.). Retrieved from http://www.infoplease.com

Hofstede, G. (2004). *Culture and organizations: Software of the mind.* New York: McGraw-Hill.

Kalaf, R. (2006, October 7). The destination of choice. *Gulf News,* p. 39.

Khaleej Times. (2006a). UAE's Ambition to achieve economic super status.

Khaleej Times. (2006b, October 25). Palm Jumeriah slips behind schedule. *Business Times, International,* p. 33.

Khalifa to sponsor Hadj trip of 50 journalists. (2006, November 29). *Gulf News,* p. 7.

Pink, D. H. (2005). *A whole new mind.* New York: Riverhead Books.

Quinn, S., Walters, T., & Whiteoak, J. (2003). A tale of three (media) cities. *Australian Studies in Journalism, 12,* 121–149.

RadioStationWorld. (2008). *United Arab Emirates radio stations.* Retrieved March 6, 2010, from http://radiostationworld. com/Locations/United_Arab_Emirates/radio_ websites.asp

7 Days. (2006, October 23). An investment empire where the sun never sets, pp. 16–17.

UAE media. Media and information. Retrieved from http://uae.gov.ae/Government/ media.htm

Varughese, S. (2005, June 27). Dubai—mirage? Retrieved from http://www.brandchan-nel.com/print_page.asp?ar_id =238&section=profile

Walters, T., Bhatti, T., Fakhreddine, J., Gulovsen, B., & Hassall. P. J. (2006, August 2-4). *Determinants of cross cultural media usage patterns.* Paper presented at the International and Intercultural Communication Association, San Antonio, Texas.

Walters, T., Kadragic, A., & Walters. L. (2006, September). Miracle or mirage: Is development sustainable in the United Arab Emirates? *MERIA, 10*(3), Article 6/10. Retrieved from http://meria.idc.ac.il/journal/2006/issue3/jv10no3a6.html

Walters, T., Walters, L., & Quinn. (2005). Media life among gen zeds. *International Journal of Cultural Studies, 8*(1), 65–86.

Wakalat Anba'a al-Emarat (WAM). (n.d.). Retrieved from http://www.wam.org.ae/serv-let/Satellite?c=Page&cid=1135099399988&pagename=WAM%2FPage%2FW-T-P-AboutUs

Wakalat Anba'a al-Emarat (WAM). (2006, October 18). Mohammed donates Dh5m to journalists. Retrieved December 2, 2006, from http://www.wam.org.ae/servlet/ Satellite?c=WamLocEnews&cid=1159347530646&pagename=WAM%2FWamLocE news%2FW-T-LEN-FullNews

Zaharna, R. S. (1995). Understanding cultural preferences of Arab communications patterns. *Public Relations Review, 21*(3), 241–255.

Part IV
Summary and Conclusions

26 The State of Agenda-Setting Research on Corporate Reputation and the News Media around the Globe

Conclusions, Cautions, and Contingent Conditions

Craig E. Carroll

It is difficult for a final chapter to do justice to the broad spectrum of research produced for the present volume. There is no single set of directions for research that can be uniformly advanced. The state of research, the media landscape, and the level of progress in each country's state of the art suggests an uneven playing field that thwarts any attempt to make a grand statement that can be applied across all the chapters. This chapter reviews the existing state of the research literature prior to the writing of each chapter, the top-level findings of each chapter related to first- and second-level agenda setting applied to organizations, and discusses cautions and a host of contingent factors affecting the relationship between news media agenda setting and corporate reputation.

State of the Literature in Frontier, Developed, and Emerging Markets

Each chapter examined the state of research about the influence of the news media on corporate reputation for their individual country. One aspect of the research was to document the degree to which agenda-setting theory had been addressed in their country's mass communication theory and research. In addition, researchers were asked to identify origins and sources of influence on the concept of corporate reputation. In most cases, the authors were the first to examine agenda-setting theory as it was applied to organizations (e.g., Carroll & McCombs, 2003) in their countries.

Agenda-Setting Theory

Each country studied varies in the degree of penetration that agenda-setting theory has made. In Europe, the agenda-setting concept has seen the most application, particularly in the Netherlands and Spain. In the Netherlands, the agenda-setting concept has been developed in both political communication studies (De Vreese, 2003; De Vreese & Boomgaarden, 2006; Kleinnijenhuis & Rietberg, 1995; Peter, 2003) and in corporate contexts (Meijer 2005; Meijer & Kleinnijenhuis, 2006). In Spain, scholars have offered notable advances on and contributions to agenda-setting theory. McCombs and Evatt's (1995) pioneering piece on second-level agenda setting was published in the scholarly Spanish journal *Comunicación y Sociedad*. Moreover, some of the initial research empirically examining attribute agenda setting, published in the *Journal of Communication, Political Communication*, and *Journalism and Mass Communication Quarterly*, focused on data from Spanish elections. In Italy, numerous empirical applications of the agenda-setting framework to political campaigns have been published in journals such as *Comunicazione Politica*. In Norway, several researchers have written about the agenda-setting hypothesis (e.g., Mathiesen, 1993; Waldahl, 1999), though few empirical studies have been conducted. In Turkey and Greece, agenda-setting studies are just now starting to emerge. One explanation for this is the number of scholars trained in the United States who return to their home countries bringing agenda-setting theory with them, where, as Görpe and Yüksel (chapter 22 this volume) and Goutzamani, Zyglidopoulos, and Bantimaroudis (chapter 6 this volume) have noted, the scholarly field of media studies is relatively young and underdeveloped. Another source of influence is the annual "Communication in the New Millennium" conference co-sponsored by the University of Texas at Austin and various universities in Turkey which rotates between the U.S. and Turkey each year.

Asian agenda-setting research varies widely due to the disparate political structures across the region. South Korea leads the way with ongoing research since the 1980s. In Japan, Takeshita's (1983) research has played a key role in the transmission of agenda-setting theory through his translation of seminal works into Japanese. Similarly, in China, Guo Zhenzi (1997, 1999, cited in chapter 18) wrote and translated several articles on agenda-setting theory, though he has not applied agenda-setting effects of the news media to Chinese contexts.

Focal research on agenda setting in Africa and the Middle East occurs primarily in Egypt, where Keenan (chapter 19 this volume) found agenda-setting studies that included English-language theses showing both print (Ghabour, 1990, cited in chapter 19) and broadcast (Goueli, 1993, cited in chapter 19) media content affecting the importance audiences assign to issues. He also found research in Arabic—a doctoral dissertation analyzing broadcast news content and public opinion data that confirmed the basic agenda-setting hypothesis for foreign news topics (Khalek, 2005, cited in chapter 19). Other Egyptian dissertations found agenda-setting effects in a variety of contexts, such as the environment, children's issues, and gender issues.

In South America, one of our authors from Argentina was a part of the original studies in Spain and was also a pioneer of agenda-setting theory in Latin America (Rey Lennon, 2000, 2007, cited in chapter 15). Outside of Rey Lennon's research, our research teams only turned up two studies exploring agenda setting applied to organizations. In Brazil, Almeida, Nunes, and Batista (chapter 16 this volume) identified one master's thesis (Schneider, 2001, cited in chapter 16) on the effects of agenda setting, which focused on the publicity content of telecommunication companies. Another study in Argentina examined how the content of stories published in the media influenced the agenda of design companies (Reyes, 2002, cited in chapter 16).

Our research also determined that mass communication textbooks imported from the U.S. shape mass communication theory and research in many countries. Due to this, most studies in languages other than English are general introductions or summaries of U.S. or Western literature on the topic of agenda-setting theory; little empirical work has been carried out, with the exception of the studies noted.

In sum, there is a range of variation in how much agenda-setting theory has permeated mass communication scholarship around the world. Future research on agenda-setting theory should examine how the theory as applied to organizations offers unique formulations that may be of use in agenda setting's original domain—political communication, public issues, and election studies.

Corporate Reputation

Our research on corporate reputation in these different countries revealed several points of origin for current thought. One source of influence has been the corporate reputation ratings and rankings themselves, since *Fortune* magazine's rankings have influenced the development of rankings in other publications, including those of the *Financial Times, Asian Business*, and the *Far Eastern Economic Review* (Fombrun, 1998).

Nevertheless, most of the authors in the present volume have confirmed that the prevailing source of influence is the work of Fombrun and Van Riel (Fombrun, 1996; Fombrun & Van Riel, 1997; Van Riel & Fombrun, 2006; Van Riel, Stroeker, & Maathuis, 1998). Authors tend to frame the topic of corporate reputation in terms current in English-language journals, primarily those in the U.S. tradition. Other schools of thought concerning corporate reputation do exist—Schwaiger's (2004) research in Germany, for instance, and Eisenegger's (2005) in Switzerland represent original local contributions to the field of reputation studies, and Luoma-aho, Uskali, Heinonen, and Ainamo (chapter 3 this volume) have noted that the original work on reputation in Finland was published in Finnish (Karvonen, 1997, 1999, 2000, cited in chapter 13). Moreover, in Russia, there is a scholarly journal, *Reputalogy,* devoted to the study of reputation. These schools of thought, however, have not yet reached the same degree of influence and global reach as Fombrun's and Van Riel's work, most likely due to boundaries imposed by translation.

Thus, while varying definitions and traditions of corporate reputation exist, the prevailing definition, which has also shaped the studies in this volume, has been that of Fombrun and Van Riel (Fombrun, 1996; Fombrun & Van Riel, 1997). Future research should examine the degree to which alternate definitions of corporate reputation shape the way the relationship between corporate reputation and news media effects are conceptualized, measured, and evaluated.

Applying Agenda-Setting Theory to Corporate Reputation

Carroll and McCombs (2003) were the first to develop propositions applying agenda-setting theory to the study of organizations and corporate reputation.

The present collection of research studies revealed that scholarship around the globe is in various states of readiness for the importation and consideration of agenda-setting theory as it applies to organizations and corporate reputation.

Most of the scholars in this volume confirm that their studies are the first in their native countries to take agenda-setting theory and apply it to corporate reputation. These include the chapters on Denmark, France, Greece, Italy, Finland, and Japan. The Netherlands was the only country found to have previous research on agenda setting applied to reputation prior to the development of the present project: Meijer's (2004) doctoral dissertation was the first study in the Netherlands that applied agenda-setting theory to business; the data from the study were used in the chapter in this volume. During the time in which this project was brought to completion, new explorations of agenda setting applied to corporate reputation have been made in China (Jiang Zhigao, 2004, cited in chapter 18), Germany (Einwiller, Carroll, & Korn, 2010), South Korea (Cha, 2006), Spain (Capriotti, 2007), and Russia (Tsetsura & Chernov, 2009).

Other scholars in this volume laid groundwork for future research by reviewing the existing literature on corporate reputation and the news media in their native countries. The authors of the chapters on Norway and Egypt, for instance, provide fertile ground for other scholars who are doing research. Similarly, the qualitative research performed by Amujo, Otubanjo, Laninhun, and Adejo In Nigeria (chapter 23 this volume) and by Rey Lennon & Peña in Argentina (chapter 15 this volume) should open the door for exciting studies in the future.

Future research should begin exploring ways that global comparative evaluations can be made across countries, particularly in the conceptualization of the key concepts of reputation dimensions and media salience, in research design issues, and perhaps even in data sources or organizations studied.

Summary of Empirical Findings

Each chapter examined the theoretical propositions set forth by Carroll and McCombs (2003) as applied to their native countries.

First-Level Agenda Setting Applied to Organizations in Developed, Emerging, and Frontier Markets

The research found support for the hypothesis of agenda setting applied to organizations at the first level in many of the developed countries but in only one of the emerging markets. In Denmark, Kjaer and Morsing (chapter 2 this volume) found that the 10 firms highest on the Danish media agenda were among the 15 best known firms in the *Berlingske Nyhedsmagasin*'s (BNY) annual image ranking, while the 10 least-known firms were among those receiving the least media coverage. In Finland, Luoma-aho, et al. (chapter 3 this volume) observed similar results for the larger firms in their study, but not for the smaller firms; the top 25 most reported companies received six or more mentions in the five media outlets studied. In France, Davidson and Chazaud (chapter 4 this volume) found that the agenda-setting relationship was stronger within the business press than within the mainstream press. In Norway, Ihlen and Brønn (chapter 10 this volume) found examples of support for the first level of agenda setting: when news coverage about Ikea nearly doubled between 2003 and 2005, the company went from being unlisted in the top 20 most visible firms to ranking number one just one year later. Since then, the firm has remained in the top five. In Spain, Arrese and Baigorri (chapter 11 this volume) found an agenda-setting relationship overall, but it was stronger for publicly-traded companies than for private companies. In the United States, Carroll (chapter 14 this volume) found a direct correspondence between the prominence of firms in the first phase of the Annual RQ 2000 and the volume of news reports published on the front page, the front page of the business section, and the opinion pages of *The New York Times*. In South Korea, Cha and Yang (chapter 21 this volume) found an identical rank order for the amount of news coverage and the public's awareness of the five firms studied.

In addition, support was found for agenda setting applied to organizations in some of the emerging markets. In Russia, Koikkalainen (chapter 20 this volume) examined media visibility over 17 years. Her research determined that in one newspaper, the *Vedomosti*, the number of firms receiving prominent news coverage increased over the years of the study. She noted, however, that only the largest companies were featured on the front pages of the papers; small- to medium-sized enterprises were mostly featured in regional or local media that fell outside of her analysis. In Brazil, Almeida et al. (chapter 16 this volume) found support for the first level of agenda setting when they applied it to the two firms they investigated.

No support for the first level of agenda setting applied to organizations was found in Greece, Italy, or Japan. In Greece, Goutzamani, Zyglidopoulos, and Bantimaroudis (chapter 6 this volume) found that the companies with the best reputations had less news coverage than other companies, but also that these favorite companies had higher levels of negative news coverage. This surprising finding is consistent with the experimental evidence of Kiousis, Bantimaroudis, and Ban (1999), who found a political candidate's negative attribute salience produced a higher public salience. Dalpiaz and Ravasi (chapter 7 this volume) found no relationship between media coverage and reputation in Italy, and suggested this was due to the media selection. They studied newspaper reports, but TV and radio have larger Italian audiences and newspaper readership is declining in Italy as it is elsewhere. In Japan, Ishii and Takeshita (chapter 8 this volume) found results similar to those of Dalpiaz and Ravasi (chapter 7): company news had no relationship with prominence, but advertising expenditures did.

On the whole, support for agenda setting at the first level varied widely within regions. Future research should investigate the first level of agenda setting as media convergence continues to unfold.

Second-Level Agenda Setting Applied to Organizations in Frontier, Developed, and Emerging Markets

Cognitive Dimensions   Support for the agenda-setting hypothesis applied to cognitive attributes was not as strong and in some cases was inconclusive. In

Norway, Ihlen and Brønn (chapter 10 this volume) found some support for the second level through their literature review, citing a study that focused on the impact of Norway's hosting of the 1994 Winter Olympic Games. The strongest case was made in the Netherlands, in which Meijer (chapter 9) examined a much smaller number of organizations across a few industries in the Netherlands and found support for second-level agenda setting by television on all eight of the organizations studied and by print media for six of the eight. In Switzerland, Eisenegger, Schranz, and Schneider (chapter 13 this volume) found that a company's involvement in issues that are intensively and emotionally discussed in the media had a strong influence on change in a firm's corporate reputation. Using data from the beginning of the economic crisis, Eisenegger et al. found that small regional banks in particular enjoyed a reputation boost because their business models, in contrast to those of the large banks, were deemed to be sustainable and less subject to risks.

Mixed results occurred for many of the other countries. In Finland, Luoma-aho et al. (chapter 3 this volume) observed that about half of their news stories were about stock price and that the content of the stories was factual, mostly affected by news criteria, and included little about the attributes of their corporate reputations. Details about executives, employees, products, and services were present in some of the bigger stories, but Luoma-aho et al. (chapter 3) noted that their appearance was more list-like, providing background information, rather than central to the story. In Italy, Dalpiaz and Ravasi (chapter 7 this volume) found that only two firms in their study had enough news coverage about different reputation attributes to allow them to study the firms in more depth. In their study, most of the articles and media associations focused on business and financial topics rather than on social dimensions of reputation such as corporate social responsibility (CSR) activities. Dalpiaz and Ravasi observed that part of the relationship between media associations and corporate associations may relate to the degree of personal experience consumers have with the company. If attributes are directly observable, then the media will play a smaller role; if attributes are less readily observable, the media will play a greater role (Einwiller, Carroll, & Korn, 2010). In Japan, Ishii and Takeshita (chapter 8 this volume) focused on only one attribute: research and development activity. They noted that hundreds of new products are released each year, but only a select number achieve news coverage. In South Korea, Cha and Yang (chapter 21 this volume) found a significant relationship between the amount of news coverage on corporate attributes and the public's perceptions of those attributes. In China, Deng found support for cognitive attribute agenda setting (chapter 18 this volume). He examined CSR news reports and the public's CSR associations and found that Chinese companies were not as active as multinational companies. In Argentina, Rey Lennon and Peña (chapter 15) found that 58.7% of the news coverage was devoted to small- and medium-sized enterprises, with only 19.3% discussing large multinational corporations. Most of the large-scale news about larger corporations focused on management or on national policies applicable to them.

Affective Dimension Support for agenda setting at the second-level affective dimension also varied. Support was found in Denmark, Finland, Italy, Switzerland, and the United States. In Denmark, Kjaer and Morsing (chapter 2) found a positive correlation between the share of positive and neutral coverage of a firm and its overall image ranking. In Italy, Dalpiaz and Ravasi (chapter 7) tested the hypothesis with two different dependent variables: the first was the percentage of the public nominating the firm as having a favorable reputation; the second used a three-item measure of trust, admiration, and respect from the Annual RQ that has been termed "overall emotional appeal" (Fombrun, Gardberg, & Sever, 2000). In both cases, they found that positive news articles did correlate with firms having favorable images. In the United States, Carroll (chapter 14) used the same three-item measure and found a direct correspondence between media favorability and firms' levels of public esteem.

Other interesting findings from different countries include the following. In Argentina, Rey Lennon and Peña (chapter 15) found that 66% of the tone of the news coverage for small- and medium-sized enterprises was positive, in contrast to coverage of large multinationals, most of which was negative. In Finland, Luoma-aho et al. (chapter 3) also observed that 40% of the company mentions were neutral and noted that the foreign firms in their study received slightly more negative coverage in stories than did Finnish firms.

No support for agenda setting applied to image was found in Japan, China, and South Korea. In Japan, Ishii and Takeshita (chapter 8) found no support for companies' image in the press being related to the public's preferences. In China, Deng (chapter 18) attributed that lack of support as related to the issue of "cash for coverage," which arose during the period of his investigation: several journalists from the state-owned Xinhua News Agency were involved in media bribery scandals, increasing public cynicism about the news media. Thus, Deng found that while negative news coverage resulted in negative impressions, positive news coverage did not necessarily lead to positive impressions due to a lack of trust in the media. In South Korea, however, Cha and Yang (chapter 21) found that media associations were more important in determining the public's perceptions than the direct effect of the firms they studied.

Cautions and Contingent Conditions

Though it is not an actual limitation, one caution should be set forth here: although globally, as discussed in the introduction to this volume, interest in business news is on the rise, this rising interest is not evenly distributed across countries. For instance, a recent survey carried out in the European Union found that, while levels of interest in business news in Sweden and Finland were higher than 40%, the average level for the 27 countries of the EU was 28%, and in Spain (as noted by Arrese and Baigorri, chapter 11 this volume), the figure was only 18% (Eurobarometer, 2007, cited in chapter 11). Similarly, in a recent survey of media usage in the United Arab Emirates, among nationals and expat Arabs those who had a high interest in national, regional, and international business news ranged from 14% to 19%, while among nationals who were English speakers, only about 22% felt regional business news was extremely important, and only 24% felt the stock market was extremely important, although the figure rose to 37% for international business news (Walters, Bhatti, Fakhreddine, Gulovsen, & Hassall, 2006).

It should also be noted that most of the research exhibits an urban bias (Pratt & Manheim, 1988). In developing countries, for instance, the media reach a relatively small, homogenous segment of the total population which is "educated, fairly affluent, middle class citizens" (Sriramesh & Verčič, 2009, p. 19). Other forms of media are often used by those who are living in poverty and who are illiterate, including docudramas, skits, and plays in rural communities, such as in India. Future research within developing and emerging countries should investigate corporate reputation in these contexts. Is corporate reputation even a relevant topic or concern for these populations?

The studies in this volume identified numerous practical challenges in empirically applying agenda-setting theory to corporate reputation. The most basic is the expense of gathering enough primary data to be statistically valid for examining the relationship between corporate reputation and the news media. Most research, for now, will have to rely on combining original media analysis with secondary analyses of published public opinion polls. The sample size required is also a major challenge. It is relatively easy to get 100 to 200 respondents to fill out surveys about their perceptions of companies, but getting a sample size large enough for comparative work among companies is more difficult, and obtaining a sample size large enough to conduct multiple regression or other multivariate analyses is challenging indeed. With few exceptions, the samples available in our current research would not be large enough to conduct studies for using such techniques.

The issue is further complicated by the need for longitudinal data in order to address the issue of reverse causality—the degree to which firms' existing reputations make them newsworthy and the degree to which the media self-monitor their reports as a way of maintaining source relations with organizations. It is possible to conduct these studies, thanks largely to the efforts of the Reputation Institute, but most studies involve the release of only top-level, aggregated analysis at the organizational level rather than the individual level required for initial data exploration.

The contributors to this volume have helped to advance our understanding of the power of media effects on corporate reputation. They also point to contingent conditions (e.g., Cancel, Cameron, Sallot, & Mitrook, 1997) we need to consider to advance our understanding about the antecedents, contents, and consequences of media coverage for corporate reputation. These areas are explored below in more detail. They include *country characteristics,* such as size of the country and trust in the news media and other institutions; the *influence of global media systems,* including the nature of media control, media access, and reach; the *multiple reputations* of transnational corporations operating in multiple countries; and a variety of *organizational characteristics,* such as the degree of retail presence, organizational demographics, and the degree of corporate communications involvement. These can be considered some of the contingent factors affecting the relationship between media agenda setting and corporate reputation, and they deserve further attention.

Country Characteristics

The contributors to this volume come from widely differing countries and they discussed how some of the physical and cultural characteristics of their countries impact the relationship between media agenda setting and corporate reputation. Future comparative research should examine how the size of the country affects the importance of the news media as a source for corporate reputation information and the degree to which the news media impact reputation. In addition, future research should examine countries' placements in various rankings as it relates to confidence in institutions, particularly trust in the news media and in big business.

Size of the Country   Many contributors to this volume have noted that their country's size affected the media environment and the extent of influence the media could have on reputation. Denmark's small size and subsequent potential for word-of-mouth communication creates a ripe environment for influencing those perceptions. Kjaer and Morsing (chapter 2 this volume) noted that Denmark is a tightly networked society where companies seek negotiation and consensus rather than conflicts between employer and employee organizations, and thus the public's perceptions of companies are often built on experience and firsthand knowledge of the company (Kristensen, 1999, cited in chapter 2). Finland, too, is a relatively small country for both business and media; Luoma-aho et al. (chapter 3 this volume) speculated that the news media's effects are less visible than in larger countries where diffusion of news occurs directly via social contact. In Chile, Browne and Kunc (chapter 17 this volume) suggested that contingent factors can be stronger than the power of news media in their effects on corporate reputation, especially in countries strongly based on traditions. They noted that in Chile, the power of news media is at its height only in situations where an industry disaster or a company's ethical lapse has occurred. They proposed that the presence of Chilean corporations in reputation rankings is likely to be stable in the long term, independent of small changes in their media coverage.

Trust in the News Media   The countries also varied in terms of the degree of trust that their citizens placed in the news media. In Finland, Luoma-aho et al. (chapter 3 this volume) noted that more than 80% of the Finns trust the veracity of the news in their newspapers either very much or most of the time. In Russia, 51% of Russians fully approve of the functioning of media while 29% do not (VCIOM, 2009, cited in chapter 20); trust in the Russian army was slightly higher than trust in the media, while law enforcement agencies, political parties, and the judicial system all lagged behind the media. In Argentina, a survey carried out by ANJ found the newspapers had a high credibility (above that of the Catholic Church), being ranked just below medical doctors. The Edelman Annual Trust

Barometer 2006 revealed that 56% of Brazilian respondents trusted the media, compared to only 30% of U.S. respondents.

Trust in Companies   Countries also vary in the degree of trust their citizens place in business, corporations, and other organizations. Dalpiaz and Ravasi (chapter 7 this volume) noted that in 2006, the mass media were the least trusted institution in Italy, while the 10 most trusted organizations in the country were all multinational companies and NGOs. Finland is transparent and noncorrupt, prompting some to describe the country's climate for corporate activity as "open" (Luoma-aho, 2005, cited in chapter 3 this volume). A 2007 survey measuring confidence in French companies (TNS-Sofres, 2007, cited in chapter 4 this volume) found that, in comparison to 1993, confidence in corporations had not collapsed but rather had risen. In contrast, Arrese and Baigorri noted (chapter 11 this volume) that in Spain there has historically and culturally been a mistrust of companies and businesspeople; they contend that this mistrust extends to economic activities in general.

Media Systems Characteristics

The countries represented in this volume differ greatly in their national media environments. For instance, the news media in Finland are dominated by one major newspaper (cf. Ainamo, 2003, cited in chapter 3), whereas Turkey has 18 different national daily newspapers. This is true even of countries in the same region: for example, due to dramatic differences in political environment, the media systems in mainland China differ greatly from those in Hong Kong, Macau, and Taiwan. Significant divergences can exist even within one country—Switzerland, for instance, has a heterogeneous media environment, with regions of the country divided between French, German, and Italian media systems.

Newspapers are often chosen for research on the media and corporate reputation because radio and TV programs rarely report on focal companies, and because previous studies have shown that newspapers have stronger agenda-setting effects (Takeshita, 1983). According to a study of the main free-on-air TV channels in Spain, for instance, business and economic issues took up just 3% of the news programs in prime time. Most readers of the printed press stem from the upper and middle classes and include opinion leaders from political and business elites (Marín & Cordero, 2005). Future research should examine the degree to which media control and media reach affect corporate reputation. It would also be valuable to examine how media bias, particularly related to preference for tone, particular styles of writing, and topics influence the relationship between news media agenda setting and corporate reputation.

Media Control   The contributors to this volume illustrate the dramatic differences between countries in terms of media ownership and control. For instance, Dalpiaz and Ravasi (chapter 7 this volume) point out that in Italy, the ownership structure of both print and TV media is highly concentrated in the hands of privately held industrial conglomerates that attempt to influence politics. In Argentina, in contrast, numerous foreign enterprises have direct investments in the local media, including the Telefónica Group (Spain), Hi Prime (Australia), Cisneros (Venezuela), Globo (Brazil), Televisa (Mexico), and Rupert Murdoch's News Corp. (Australia). As Deng noted (chapter 18 this volume), China has developed a hybrid system with a state media system and a market media system, resulting in two different attitudes toward corporations, one favorable and one critical.

Media Reach   Our contributors reported widely different levels of different kinds of media penetration in their countries. The Finnish news media is politically a rather homogenous entity compared to the media in other European countries (Ojala & Uskali, 2005, cited in chapter 3 this volume). Finland is interesting, however, in that it is the leading country in Europe in aggregate newspaper circulation relative to the population (Jyrkiäinen & Savisaari, 2003, cited in chapter 3). Newspapers daily reach more than 80% of Finns. High rates are also reported in Norway and in Japan, where newspapers reach 65% of the population. In the Netherlands, De Bakker and Scholten (2003) estimated that national newspapers reach approximately 64% of households. In Brazil, newspapers are read by 48% of adults. The ratio of daily newspaper copies per 2000 inhabitants in 1996 was 590 for Norway, 445 for Sweden, and 331 for Britain, while it was only 153 for Greece (Papatheodorou & Machin, 2003, cited in chapter 6). In 2006, Germans spent an average of 28 minutes each day reading the newspaper (Media Perspektiven, 2006, cited in chapter 5). In Russia, the average reader spends 18 minutes a day reading newspapers and magazines, although 21% of Russians say they read no newspapers at all (Vartanova & Smirnov, 2009, cited in chapter 20). In Nigeria, newspapers (25%) and magazines (13%) maintain a low penetration rate. Similarly, only 23% of Chileans read newspapers daily, and only 21% of Argentines (Porath, 2000, cited in chapter 17 this volume).

For the vast majority of the population of the countries discussed in this volume, television and radio are the main sources of information. The average Spaniard spends about 3½ hours a day watching television, and almost 2 hours listening to the radio (Arrese & Baigorri, chapter 11 this volume). In Italy, radio audience has increased in recent times: in 2005, about 72% of the Italian population aged 11 and older listened to the radio each day (Dalpiaz & Ravasi, chapter 7 this volume). On average, the French spend more time listening to the radio and watching television than reading print media (Davidson & Chazaud, chapter 4 this volume). In Brazil, radio and television were present in 2004 in 87.7% and 89.8% of households, respectively, according to Lima (2006, cited in chapter 16 this volume). In Egypt, Alfaiz (2002, cited in chapter 19 this volume) used in-depth interviews with upper-level management personnel to investigate the importance of media reports on their decision-making processes and found that CNN was an especially influential source of information for businesspeople and the single most important media outlet. Hence, it may be that the public's awareness of firms varies less with press articles than with news broadcast on TV, radio, or the Internet.

The Internet is one of the most effective tools by which communication content can be delivered to an audience, especially in South Korea (Cha & Yang, chapter 21 this volume). In the United Arab Emirates (UAS), Al Jazeera was the overwhelming source of news and business information for nationals and expat Arabs alike. In contrast, native English speakers who lived in the UAE turned westward toward home for news, as they also did for business information, which they found largely on the Internet (Walters et al., cited in chapter 25 this volume). The results from Japan (Ishii & Takeshita, chapter 8 this volume), which included Internet discussion boards, suggest that, in addition to the major news media, small media, including magazines, books, and the Internet, occupy a position of influence. The low diversity of news reports in major media may be balanced by such small media. Future studies need to consider the effects of these smaller media.

Media Bias and Tone   This volume has presented some interesting findings related to tone, some of which probably spring from cultural characteristics of the media or the national environment in individual countries; these elements deserve to be carefully disentangled in future research. For instance, Einwiller, Bentele, and Landmeier (chapter 5 this volume) noted that, in comparison to citizens of other countries, Germans are rather critical toward corporations and reticent about giving positive appraisals, following to the German adage that "not grumping is sufficiently praising" (Wiedmann, 2007, cited in chapter 5). In Norway, Ihlen and Brønn (chapter 10 this volume) found that business news coverage was more negative than positive, whereas in Finland, Luoma-aho et al. (chapter 3 this volume) found that the media covered most Finnish businesses only in a positive light. In Greece, the media openly displayed partisan affiliations, using colorful and excessive language that would be deemed unacceptable by journalists in many other countries (Zaharopoulos & Paraschos, 1993, cited in chapter 6 this volume). In Italy, similarly, the distinction between tabloid press (devoted to soft news) and elite press (focused on hard news) does not exist (Murialdi, 1984 cited in chapter 7 this volume).

Certainly, tone matters. In Greece, only negative reputation, when correlated with newspaper coverage, yielded positive relationships with the public's top-of-mind awareness of firms (Goutzamani, et al., chapter 6 this volume). A recent study in Sweden of Skandia, which showed how negative visibility in media coverage significantly decreased its reputation, supports these results (Jonsson, Greve, & Fujiwara-Greve, 2007, cited in chapter 12 this volume). Similarly, in Switzerland, Eisenegger et al. (chapter 13 this volume) found that being associated with a negative issue was significantly more important in explaining the change in corporate reputation than the positive effect. In contrast, in Italy, Dalpiaz and Ravasi (chapter 7 this volume) found that the tone of news reports had no correlation with the firms' change in reputation.

Related to tone is the degree to which the news media believe they can challenge the status quo of business or take on companies in cases of social irresponsibility. In China, Deng (chapter 18 this volume) noted that a media organization was attacked for its negative coverage and was even forced to apologize. This not only reflects the environment of press freedom in China, it also shows that Chinese news media are increasingly dependent on corporations and are forced to cooperate with them. At the same time, corporations fear the media's power. They resent and attack the media's critical reporting but dare not offend powerful media, especially the whole press circle. Deng (chapter 18) pointed to the 2006 Foxconn scandal, which ended with China Business News apologizing to Foxconn, as a striking example.

Closely related to tone is the matter of style, which Davidson and Chazaud (chapter 4 this volume) discussed in relation to the French media. Previous comparative content analyses of French and American news have shown that French news provides a wider diversity of viewpoints than what is found in the United States (Benson & Hallin, 2005, cited in chapter 4). Less concerned with the content of the news, French journalism enjoys delivering news with stylistic excellence and critical argumentation (Neveu, 2004, cited in chapter 4). Such characteristics must be kept in mind when examining the media systems of different countries.

Media Topics   The topics of media reputation deserve more research in the future, similar to what Shoemaker and Cohen (2006) accomplished with their international investigation of news topics. Nevertheless, some significant findings from the present volume deserve to be highlighted. In Egypt, Keenan (chapter 19 this volume) observed a tendency to underreport or omit information that would be included in news stories in other parts of the world. As one Middle Eastern journalist/editor put it, "Ours is a system of denial. We commit sins of omission, not commission" (Khazen, 1999, p. 87, cited chapter 19). In Italy, qualitative comparison between media associations and corporate associations seems to indicate that the influence of the media may be stronger when respondents do not have a direct experience of the company and its products (Dalpiaz & Ravasi, chapter 7 this volume). Einwiller, Carroll, and Korn (2010) found similar results in Germany. This topic needs to be investigated in other cultures.

According to Cha (2004, cited in chapter 21), the most frequently covered corporate attributes in South Korean newspapers included management/marketing, human resource/management, social philanthropy, and corporate issue-related attributes. In this study, a poll revealed that the public tended to focus on other corporate attributes, such as CEO quality and management ethics, to form its opinion of companies. The public perceived some attributes as important (such as CEO characteristics, management ethics, and corporate issues) that were not salient in media coverage, perhaps because such attributes were considered by the public to be related to "management outcomes." In Spain, Arrese and Baigorri (chapter 11 this volume) found as regards the second level of agenda setting, the substantive agenda, a great predominance of economic issues and attributes (95.7% of the news) compared with the social issues and attributes of businesses (4.3%). In Switzerland, there is an increasing focus on corporate scandals and personalities (Eisenegger & Imhof, 2008; Schranz, 2007, both cited in chapter 13 this volume). In Sweden, the labor market and consumerism receive minor attention on the business news pages, and news about business and companies dominate (Bjur, 2006; Kjaer, Erkama, & Grafström, 2007, cited in chapter 12 this volume). Much of today's Swedish business news is of a popular nature and focuses on individuals, scandals, and even gossip from the corporate world. Photographs and other types of graphics are frequently used and have become important features of business journalism (Kjaer et al., 2007, cited in chapter 12 this volume), a development that has been described as "business" becoming "show business" (Petrelius, 2002; Petrelius & Karlberg, 2006, both cited in chapter 12 this volume).

Multinational Companies across Geographical Borders

An interesting dimension that emerged in the studies in this volume was the degree to which specific multinational corporations appeared in studies across countries. This theme emerged in three ways: corporate icons operating in their home country, firms operating as multinationals in other countries, and the degree to which countries may exhibit an anticountry bias against multinationals from other nations. Future comparative research examining these dimensions could produce significant results.

Corporate Icons in Their Home Country   Countries vary in their preference for their home companies. For instance, Keenan (chapter 19 this volume) reported that not a single Egyptian company appeared in the top 30 rankings within the study he examined. Similarly, Dalpiaz and Ravasi (chapter 7 this volume) reported that the Italian companies were not among the highest ranked in Italy. In both cases, companies with the best reputation were those based outside of the country. These results were certainly atypical. More common was the tendency to favor national corporate icons. As Kjaer and Morsing (chapter 2 this volume) write, describing Denmark,

> These types of companies are overrepresented in the media in relation to their importance. What characterizes all these firms is that they are "local heroes." AP Møller is the Danish firm to invest in, Danske Bank is the firm that handles the Danes' money, TDC is responsible for the Danes' telecommunication, and Carlsberg for the Danes' beer consumption. All four firms are "Danish," and international companies highly present in the Danish corporate landscape.

The same was true of the majority of the most visible companies in Sweden—they have a local heritage, even though the current ownership may be more international.

Foreign MNCs   Moreover, Davidson and Chazaud (chapter 4 this volume) noted that many French elites consider American corporations, especially those operating in cultural industries, to be a threat to French cultural integrity. Scholars have noted that the roots of Franco-American animosity stem from both countries' universalist ambitions to shape the world in their own image

(Bourdieu, 1992; Hoffman, 2000, both cited in chapter 4 this volume). In Egypt, somewhat similarly, Al-Kadi and Keenan (2004, cited in chapter 19 this volume) found that the association of a brand or product with the United States had positive implications for perceived quality, but negative ones for purchase intention and overall attitude toward the brand among Egyptian consumers.

Anticountry Bias   The United States is not the only country facing a negative bias in the press of other countries. In China's news media, American and European companies have better corporate images than those originating in Japan and Taiwan. If the poor image of Japanese companies in China can be attributed to the tension of Sino-Japanese relations and to anti-Japanese sentiment among the Chinese due to Japan's stance on its invasion during World War II, what about the Taiwanese companies? Most of them are original equipment manufacturers' (OEM) factories and pay little attention to their brand management and social responsibility in mainland China; as a result Taiwanese companies have the worst reputation on the mainland. In Argentina, Rey Lennon and Peña (chapter 15 this volume) noted that only 27.2% of the coverage of non-Argentinean companies was framed positively compared to coverage of local firms.

In sum, the most common tendency was for national reputation listings to focus mainly on companies with their global headquarters located within the nation's boundaries. Indeed, the global reputation rankings published by the Reputation Institute make this a requirement. With the exception of the unusual findings noted above (namely, in Italy, where the companies with the best reputations are non-Italian, or in Egypt, where U.S. brands had positive reputations that did not translate into sales), most countries favor their own brands.

Organizational Characteristics

The contributors to this volume discuss a wide range of organizational characteristics that impact the relationship between media agenda setting and corporate reputation. Three organizational issues apply across countries and studies included in this volume, namely the degree of retail presence, organizational demographics, and the degree of corporate communications involvement. Organizational size was the organizational demographic most often examined, but every chapter was not able to examine organizational demographics (such as age, size, and industry), at least not in a quantitative, multivariate way. Future research needs to consider these factors in greater detail.

Retail Presence   Another theme that emerged frequently from the data, whether in qualitative or quantitative terms, was the role that firms' retail presence had on their reputations and degree of visibility in the media. Regarding corporate reputation in France, Davidson and Chazaud (chapter 4 this volume) noted that companies having a direct retail presence under the company name were more salient in the French public's mind than companies that had no retail presence. They argued that firms with a direct retail relationship with their consumers, through which they can convey an image independent of the press, can bypass, to an extent, the media agenda-setting process. In Spain, Arrese and Baigorri (chapter 11 this volume) also noted three companies with significantly small media coverage compared to their high reputation. These three companies worked hard on detail sales, and their reputation, and the prestige of their business model, has been built from a direct and intense contact with millions of clients on the point of sale. Similarly, in Chile, Browne and Kunc (chapter 17 this volume) noted that firms directly connected to consumers, such as retailers, had higher chances of being perceived as newsworthy by the media. Studies on different countries vary as to whether corporate reputation has been applied to business entities only or to other organizational forms as well. In Finland, Luoma-aho's (2005, 2007) research, for instance, has been applied to public organizations. Similarly, in Switzerland, Eisenegger, Schranz, and Schneider's (chapter 13 this volume) formulation of reputation can also be applied to a variety of organizational forms. The studies by Rey Lennon and Peña (chapter 15 this volume) and Meijer (chapter 9 this volume) used this opportunity to do comparative work across organizational forms.

Organizational Size   Reputation studies that only included domestic brands revealed interesting variations having to do with company size. Generally speaking, the larger, more established firms had better reputations, or at least, were more familiar. In Italy, Dalpiaz and Ravasi (chapter 7 this volume) found that organizational size had a positive effect on top-of-mind awareness. Moreover, small- to medium-sized enterprises (SMEs) generally lack news values (i.e., newsworthiness). Indeed, in Finland, Luoma-aho et al. (chapter 3 this volume) noted that smaller corporations with good reputations (e.g., Marimekko, Technopolis) were rarely the focus of news stories on their own but rather were usually introduced within other stories as examples of good image or brand management. In Russia, Koikkalainen (chapter 20 this volume) noticed that only the largest companies were featured on the front pages of the papers; SMEs were usually featured in regional or local media that fell outside of her analysis. In Denmark, Kjaer and Langer (2003, cited in chapter 2 this volume) found that newspapers prioritized companies based on financial assets in terms of stock value (publicly-traded firms were clearly prioritized) and number of employees.

But that was not true in every country. Switzerland had the greatest degree of variation. Eisenegger et al.'s (chapter 13 this volume) study included large Swiss multinationals (UBS, Credit Suisse, Nestlé, Novartis, Roche, ABB, Swiss Re, Zurich Insurance); companies owned partially or wholly by the state (SBB, Post, Swisscom, cantonal banks); and even cooperatives with strong social commitments (Migros, Co-op, and Raiffeisenbanks). Eisenegger et al. noted that the types of company found regularly in the front ranks of all these studies were the cooperatives with strong social commitments. In Argentina, Rey Lennon and Peña (chapter 15 this volume) found that *Clarín*, the country's main newspaper, covered SMEs differently from the larger entities studied: in their content analysis, 66% of the news about SMEs was framed positively, as opposed to only 30.8% of the news about large national companies.

Corporate Communications Involvement A third major organizational characteristic was the degree of corporate communications involvement. This dealt with two closely connected topics: advertising vs. news and cash for news coverage. In regard to distinguishing advertising from news, the countries differed dramatically. In some cases, advertising expenditures were found to be related to corporate reputation—for instance, in the United States (Carroll, chapter 14), Italy (Dalpiaz & Ravasi, chapter 7), and Japan (Ishii & Takeshita, chapter 8). In other cases, advertising was related to the volume of news reports about the firms as in China (Deng, chapter 18), although this was not a reflection of advertising in the media itself. In most countries, advertising data were not available. Nevertheless, some contributors noted anecdotally what they perceived to be the influence of advertising on news content. In Finland, Luoma-aho et al. (chapter 3) noted the clearly delineated boundaries between news and advertising contents published in newspapers. They also noted how newspaper subscriptions account for media revenue rather than a dependence upon advertising revenue. Other scholars outside of this volume have noted the blurring of boundaries between news and advertising contents. Future research needs to explore this phenomenon in more detail, both locally and across geographical boundaries.

Corporations have access to the media via advertising as well as via reporting based on press releases. With the increased pressures of real-time media, corporate press releases have gained power as a source for news. Most of the research on media relations and journalist-source relations has been done in the United States and South Korea. A study on "cash for news coverage" ranked countries as to the difficulty of news sources being able to bribe journalists in order to publish news: near the top were Denmark, Finland, Germany, Sweden, Switzerland, and Germany (Kruckeberg & Tsetsura, 2003). The United States was slightly above Italy and Spain, while the United Arab Emirates, Nigeria, Egypt, and China were among the lowest ranked. The interaction of corporate communications, whether in the form of advertising, press releases, or actual bribery, is yet another complex component of the interaction between the media and corporations that needs further study.

Summary

This volume has produced a wealth of research that is valuable for its additions to our knowledge of the media's agenda-setting effects as they apply to corporate reputation in different countries around the globe, as well as for the pathways it opens for new and fruitful scholarship. Research on the content and effects of the news media on corporate reputation is essential because, in a world in which the mass media's presence is ever more pervasive, relationships between organizations and the public have become increasingly mediatized and mediated, and are likely to become even more so in the future. There is, thus, a vital need for more coordinated, comparative research on the antecedents, contents, and consequences of the news media's agenda-setting function and its relation to corporate reputation across international borders. It is hoped that this compilation will be a useful starting point for further efforts to develop coordinated and comparative research on corporate reputation and the news media—research that can serve as a window on the intricate web of relationships between the media, organizations, and the individual in an ever more complex and interconnected world.

References

Cancel, A. E., Cameron, G. T., Sallot, L. M., & Mitrook, M. A. (1997). It depends: A contingency theory of accommodation in public relations. *Journal of Public Relations Research, 9*(1), 31–63.

Capriotti, P. (2007). Economic and social roles of companies in the mass media: The impact media visibility has on businesses' being recognized as economic and social actors. *Business & Society, 20*(10), 1–16.

Carroll, C. E., & McCombs, M. E. (2003). Agenda-setting effects of business news on the public's images and opinions about major corporations. *Corporate Reputation Review, 6*(1), 36–46.

Cha, H. (2006). The effects of media reputation and issue reputation on corporate reputation by issue attribute. *Korean Journal of Journalism & Communication Studies, 50*(5), 297–324.

Edelman. (2006). Annual Trust Barometer. New York, NY.

Einwiller, S., Carroll, C. E., & Korn, K. (2010). Under what conditions do the news media influence corporate reputation? The roles of media systems dependency and need for orientation. *Corporate Reputation Review, 12*(4), 299–315.

Eisenegger, M. (2005). *Reputation in der Mediengesellschaft: Konstitution, issues monitoring, issues management.* Wiesbaden, Germany: VS Verlag für Sozialwissenschaften.

Fombrun, C. J. (1996). *Reputation: Realizing value from the corporate image.* Boston, MA: Harvard Business School Press.

Fombrun, C. J. (1998). Indices of corporate reputation: An analysis of media rankings and social monitors' ratings. *Corporate Reputation Review, 1*(4), 327–340.

Fombrun, C. J., Gardberg, N. A., & Sever, J. M. (2000). The Reputation Quotient: A multi-stakeholder measure of corporate reputation. *Journal of Brand Management, 7*(4), 241–255.

Fombrun, C. J., & Van Riel, C. B. M. (1997). The reputational landscape. *Corporate Reputation Review, 1*(1/2), 5–13.

Luoma-aho, V. (2005). Faith-holders as social capital of Finnish public organizations. *Studies in Humanities 42,* University of Jyväskylä. Retrieved from http://urn.fi/URN:ISBN:951-39-2262-6

Kiousis, S., Bantimaroudis, P., & Ban, H. (1999). Candidate image attributes: Experiments on the substantive dimension of second-level agenda setting. *Communication Research, 26*(4), 414–428.

Kleinnijenhuis, J., & Rietberg, E. M. (1995). Parties, media, the public and the economy: Patterns of societal agenda-setting. *European Journal of Political Research, 28*(1), 95–118.

Kruckeberg, D., & Tsetsura, K. (2003). *A composite Iidex by country of variables related to the likelihood of the existence of 'cash for news coverage.'* Gainesville, FL: Institute for Public Relations.

Luoma-aho, V. (2007). Neutral reputation and public sector organizations. *Corporate Reputation Review, 10*(2), 124–143.

Marín, C., & Cordero, R. (2005). Los medios masivos y las transformaciones en la esfera pública en Chile. *Persona y Sociedad, 29*, 233–258.

Mathiesen, T. (1993). *Makt og medier: En innføring i mediesosiologi* (2nd ed.). Oslo, Norway: Pax.

McCombs, M. E., & Evatt, D. S. (1995). Los temas y los aspectos: Explorando una nueva dimension de la agenda-setting [Objects and attributes: Exploring a new dimension of agenda-setting]. *Communicacion y Sociedad, 8*(1), 7–32.

Meijer, M. M. (2004). *Does success breed success? Effects of news advertising on corporate reputation.* Unpublished doctoral dissertation, Vrije Universitiet, Amsterdam, The Netherlands.

Meijer, M. M. (2005). *Does success breed success? Effects of news advertising on corporate reputation.* Amsterdam, The Netherlands: Aksant.

Meijer, M. M., & Kleinnijenhuis, J. (2006). Issue news and corporate reputation: Applying the theories of agenda setting and issue ownership in the field of business communication. *Journal of Communication, 56*(3), 543–559.

Peter, J. (2003). Country characteristics as contingent conditions of agenda setting: The moderating influence of polarized elite opinion. *Communication Research, 30*(6), 683–712.

Pratt, C. B., & Manheim, J. B. (1988). Communication research and development policy: Agenda dynamics in an African setting. *The Journal of Communication, 38*(3), 75–95.

Schwaiger, M. (2004). Components and parameters of corporate reputation—An empirical study. *Schmalenbach Business Review, 56*(1), 46–71.

Shoemaker, P. J., & Cohen, A. A. (2006). *News around the world: Content, practitioners, and the public.* New York, NY: Routledge.

Sriramesh, K., & Verčič, D. (2009). *The global public relations handbook: Theory, research, and practice.* New York, NY: Routledge.

Takeshita, T. (1983). Media gidai-settei kasetsu no jisshoteki-kento [An empirical examination of the media agenda-setting hypothesis]. *Todai Shimbun-Kenkyujo Kiyo, 31*, 101–143.

Tsetsura, K., & Chernov, G. (2009). Constructing corporate reputation in the Russian media. *Russian Journal of Communication, 2*(1–2), 46–65.

Van Riel, C. B. M., & Fombrun, C. J. (2006). *Essentials of corporate communication.* London: Routledge.

Van Riel, C. B. M., Stroeker, N. E., & Maathuis, O. J. M. (1998). Measuring corporate images. *Corporate Reputation Review, 1*(4), 313–326.

Vreese, C.H. de (2003). *Framing Europe: Television news and European integration.* Amsterdam, The Netherlands: Aksant.

Vreese, C. H. de, & Boomgaarden, H. G. (2006). Media effects on public opinion about the enlargement of the European Union. *Journal of Common Market Studies, 44*(2), 419–436.

Waldahl, R. (1999). *Mediepåvirkning* [The media's influence] (2nd ed.). Oslo, Norway: Ad Notam Gyldendal.

Walters, T. N., Bhatti, T., Fakhreddine, J., Gulovsen, B., & Hassall, P. J. (2006). *Determinants of cross cultural media usage patterns.* Paper presented at the International and Intercultural Communication Association, San Antonio, Texas.

Contributors

Daniel I. Adejo (M.A., University of Ibadan, Nigeria, 1996) worked as the Communications Liaison Executive, China Ocean Shipping Company (COSCO), Lagos before joining First Bank of Nigeria Plc in 1999. Adejo works in the Communication and Culture Unit, Human Capital Management, First Bank of Nigeria Plc and edits the FirstBank's newsletter. He is an Associate of the Nigerian Institute of Public Relations.

Antti Ainamo (Ph.D., Helsinki School of Economics HSE, 1996) is Professor in Department of Sociology at the University of Turku. Co-editor of *Handbook of Product and Service Development in Communication and Information Technology* (Kluwer/Springer), his research is published also in *Journal of Marketing Management, Innovation Journalism, Human Relations, Scandinavian Economic History Review, Research in the Sociology of Organizations, Organization Science, and Business Strategy Review.*

Ana Luisa de Castro Almeida (Ph.D., the Universidade Federal de Minas Gerais –UFMG/Erasmus University, 2005) is Communication and Business Professor at Pontificia Universidade Católica de Minas Gerais and Fundação Dom Cabral. Her work on reputation management has appeared in books in Brazil, including *Integrated Management of Intangible Assets* (2009), *Handbook of Corporate Communications* (2009) and the *Handbook of Public Relations* (2009). She serves on the editorial board of *Corporate Reputation Review.*

Olusanmi C. Amujo (M.A., University of Ibadan, Nigeria, 1996) is a Corporate Marketing Scholar. His research has been published in *NIPR Public Relations Journal* and *NIPRNews, Corporate Communication, Corporate Reputation Review, Journal of Product and Brand Management,* and *Journal of Communication Management.* He serves on the editorial boards of *NIPR Public Relations Journal, NIPRNews,* and *The Chronicle.*

Ángel Arrese (Ph.D., University of Navarra, 1994) is Assistant Dean for Research and Professor of Marketing and Economic and Business Journalism in the School of Communication at the University of Navarra (Spain). He is the author of four books, including *Economía, medios y ciudadanía* (2008), and he coedited with

Alan Albarran *Time and Media Markets* (2003). He has been editor of *Comunicación y Sociedad*, the leading communication journal in Spanish language, and a member of the Editorial Board of the *Journal of Media Economics* and *The Journal of Media Business Studies*.

Manuel Baigorri (Ph.D. University of Navarra, 2010 candidate) is Assistant Professor in the School of Communication at the University of Navarra (Spain). His research focuses on business journalism. He has interned as a reporter for *BusinessWeek* magazine in Chicago and Hong Kong.

Philemon Bantimaroudis (Ph.D., University of Texas at Austin, 1999) is Assistant Professor of Mass Media and Culture in the Department of Cultural Technology and Communication at the University of the Aegean. His research has been published in various journals such as *Communication Research, Mass Communication and Society, Harvard International Journal of Press/Politics, Journal of Media and Religion, and Media War & Conflict*. He serves on the editorial boards of *Museology* and the *Open Communication Journal*.

Leandro L. Batista (Ph.D., University of North Carolina at Chapel Hill, 1996) is Assistant Professor in the *Escola de Comunicações e Artes* at the University of São Paulo, Brazil. His research has been published in Brazilian journals and addresses the cognitive effects of advertising and propaganda, risk communication and use of stereotypes in advertising. He serves on the editorial boards of several Brazilian journals.

Günter Bentele is Professor for Public Relations at the University of Leipzig, Germany, where he holds the chair for public relations. He served as president of the German Association for Communication and Media Studies from 1995–1998 and as president of EUPRERA, the European organization for PR Education and Research, in 2004. He is a prolific author and editor and has written more than 280 scientific articles in the fields of public relations, communication theory, journalism, and semiotics.

Peggy Simcic Brønn (D.B.A., Henley Management College, UK) is Associate Professor at the Norwegian School of Management in Oslo, where she is also Associate Dean of the school's bachelor's program in Public Relations. She is published in several international journals, including *Journal of Communication Management, Journal of Business Ethics, Corporate Reputation Review, Public Relations Review* and *European Journal of Marketing*. She serves on the editorial boards of *Journal of Communication Management and Corporate Reputation Review*.

Magdalena Browne (M.Sc., London School of Economics, 2004) is Professor of the faculties of Communication of Universidad Católica and Universidad Adolfo Ibáñez, in Chile. Along with her academic work, Magdalena is managing director of TIRONI Asociados, a communication consulting firm, where she oversees research and planning in strategic communication and public relations for local and global corporations.

Craig E. Carroll (Ph.D., University of Texas at Austin, 2004) is Assistant Professor in the School of Journalism and Mass Communication at the University of North Carolina at Chapel Hill. His research has been published in *Communication Research, Corporate Reputation Review, Journalism & Communication Monographs* [Chinese], *Journal of Organizational Change Management, Management Learning, Public Relations Journal*, and *Public Relations Review*. He serves on the editorial boards of *Corporate Communications, Corporate Reputation Review, Journal of Communication, Journal of Public Relations Research*, and *Public Relations Review*.

Heewon Cha (Ph.D., Ewha Womans University, 2001) is Assistant Professor in the Department of Media Studies at Ewha Womans University, South Korea. Her professional experience includes 5 years at KorCom PorterNovelli and in the marketing research field at A.C. Nielson (Korea) Limited. She has won professional and academic awards for Korean Corporate Reputation Index from Korea Public Relations Association, and she received a presidential medal for her contribution in 2005. Her articles have been published in *Journal of Public Relations Research*, and in the Korean publications *Journal of Journalism & Communication Studies, Advertising Research*, and *Journal of Communication & Information*. She has served on the editorial boards of the Korean journals *Journalism & Communication Studies* and *Journal of Public Relations Research*.

Nicolas Chazaud (Ph.D, University of Montpellier, 2008) is Social Media Expert at LexisNexis Analytics, a Paris-based unit of LexisNexis specializing in web analysis. He has presented his research outputs at the Reputation Institute Conferences and at the annual International Communication Association conferences. He regularly teaches corporate reputation and social media impact at various business schools.

Elena Dalpiaz is a Ph.D candidate in management at Bocconi University in Milan, Italy. Her research interests are in organizational change processes that involve the hybridization of different institutional logics and in the use of cultural resources for strategy development and implementation.

Roei Davidson (Ph.D., University of Michigan, 2007) is Lecturer in the Department of Communication at the University of Haifa, Israel. His research has been published in the *Journal of Communication, International Journal of Public Opinion Research* and *International Journal of Communication*. His current research focuses on the comparative study of political and economic communication.

LiFeng Deng (Ph.D., Tsinghua University, China) is Assistant Professor in the School of Communication and Design at Sun Yat-Sen University, Guangzhou, China. His articles in Chinese have appeared in Chinese academic journals, including *Journalism and Communication, Journalism Quarterly,* and *Journal of International Communication.* He has worked for Beijing Horizon Research and Consultancy Group, a marketing research and consulting firm in China, as a senior communication expert.

Sabine Einwiller (Ph.D., University of St. Gallen, Switzerland, 2003) is a Professor in the Department of Communication at the Johannes Gutenberg-University Mainz, Germany. Before completing her Ph.D., she gained practical experience as a corporate communications officer in the chemical industry. Her research been published in such journals as the *Journal of the Academy of Marketing Science, Journal of Consumer Psychology, Corporate Reputation Review, Journal of Applied Social Psychology,* and *Personality and Social Psychology Bulletin.* She serves on the editorial board of *Corporate Communications: An International Journal.*

Mark Eisenegger (Ph.D., University of Zurich, 2004) is a Senior Lecturer and Director at the Research Centre for the Public Sphere and Society (fög) at the University of Zurich, Switzerland. He has published in *Studies in Communications Sciences,* and *Relation–Journal for Communication Research* and has edited and published several books on public relations and reputation Management in German. He serves as head of the European Centre for Reputation Studies (ECRS) and as Chair of the Cross-National Research Collaboration Taskforce of ICA's Public Relations Division.

Magnus Fredriksson (Ph.D., University of Gothenburg, 2008) is Lecturer at the Department of Journalism and Mass Communication at the University of Gothenburg, Sweden, and former director of the program in Communication Management at the University West. He is co-editor of *Public Relations and Social Theory,* and he has co-authored two books on trust and corporate communications. Fredriksson has written for two Government Commission Reports and served as chronicler for the Swedish Public Relations Association.

Serra Görpe (Ph.D. İstanbul University, 1999) is Professor in the School of Communication, Public Relations and Advertising Department of İstanbul University. She has authored and edited works in Turkish. She serves as the editorial board of the *Revista Transilvana de Ştiinte ale Comunicari.* She is Vice-President of European Public Relations Confederation (CERP), Board Member of Turkish Public Relations Association (TÜHİD), and Council Member of International Public Relations Association (IPRA) from Turkey.

Eva Goutzamani is a Ph.D. candidate at the department of strategy and entrepreneurship at Athens University of Business & Economics in Greece. Her research has been published in the local national press and she served as co-editor at their special edition issues on reputation. Goutzamani is the managing partner of Reputation Lab, a consulting firm specializing in reputation audits in Greek and international markets.

Maria Grafström (Ph.D., Uppsala University, 2006) is a Researcher and Lecturer at the Department of Business Studies at Uppsala University and visiting scholar at the Centre for Advanced Studies in Leadership at Stockholm School of Economics. Her research has been published in both national and international books on topics such as business journalism, news production, corporate communication, and corporate social responsibility.

Jouni Heinonen (M.Soc.Sc., University of Helsinki, 1993) is the Managing Director of Reputation Management Consultancy Pohjoisranta in Finland. He has published two books and numerous articles in Finnish.

Øyvind Ihlen (Dr.Art., University of Oslo, 2004) is Professor of Communication and Management at BI the Norwegian School of Management. He has written and co-written five books. His award-winning research has appeared in numerous anthologies and in journals such as *Journal of Public Relations Research, Journal of Public Affairs, International Journal of Strategic Communication, International Journal of Organizational Analysis, Nordicom Review, Rhetorica Scandinavica,* and *Business Strategy and the Environment.* Ihlen serves on the editorial boards of six international journals.

Kenichi Ishii (Ph.D. in Policy and Planning Sciences, University of Tsukuba, 2000) is Associate Professor of Graduate School of Systems and Information Engineering at the University of Tsukuba in Japan. His research has been published in the *Journal of Communication, Journal of Broadcasting & Electronic Media, CyberPsychology & Behavior, Gazette, Telecommunications Policy, Telematics and Informatics,* and *Journal of International Consumer Marketing.* He has authored several books on communication and media in Japanese.

Kevin L. Keenan (Ph.D., University of Georgia, 1990) is Associate Professor of Journalism and Mass Communication, and Director of Graduate Studies, at the American University in Cairo, Egypt. His work has been published in *International Journal of Advertising, Journal of Advertising Education, Journal of Media and Religion, Journalism and Mass Communication Quarterly,* and *Proceedings of the American Academy of Advertising.* He serves on the editorial boards of *Journalism and Communication Monographs* and *Public Relations Review.*

Peter Kjaer (Ph.D., Stockholm University 1996) is Associate Professor in the Department of Organization at Copenhagen Business School in Denmark. His research has been published in *Journal of Economic Issues, Scandinavian Journal of Management, Business History and Journal of Health Organization and Management.* Kjaer has served as Director of Center for Health Management at Copenhagen Business School and is currently Head of the Department of Organization.

Katja Koikkalainen (Ph.D., University of Tampere, 2009) is a Researcher at the Aleksanteri Institute, the Finnish Centre for Russian and Eastern European Studies, affiliated with the University of Helsinki, Finland. Her research has been published in the journals *Europe-Asia Studies, Futura* [Finnish], *Tiedotustutkimus* [Finnish], and *Medialmanakh* [Russian] and as book chapters in *Media, Culture and Society in Putin's Russia* and *Globalisation, Freedom and the Media after Communism.*

Martin Kunc (Ph.D., London Business School, 2005) is Assistant Professor in Warwick Business School at the University of Warwick. His research has been published in *Strategic Management Journal, Management Decision,* and *International Journal of Learning and Intellectual Capital.*

Christine Landmeier (M.A., Johannes Gutenberg-University Mainz, 2007) is a Doctoral Research Assistant in the Department of Communication at the Johannes Gutenberg-University Mainz, Germany. Her article on the tabloidization of the German Quality Press between 1982 and 2006 appears in the book series of the Media Symposium. Landmeier's research interests are in the area of corporate communication lie in employee communication and crisis management.

Beatrice Laninhun (Ph.D., University of Ibadan, Nigeria, 1987) is a Senior Lecturer in the Department of Communication and Language Arts, University of Ibadan, Nigeria. Her research has been published in *Legon Journal of the Humanities, NIPR Public Relations Journal,* and *Castalia.* She has published book chapters on interpersonal and group communication, and communication for development. Laninhun serves as Head of the Department Communication and Language Arts.

Vilma Luoma-aho (Ph.D., University of Jyvaskyla, Finland, 2005) is Researcher at the Department of Communication at JYU, Finland. She has authored book chapters on social capital, reputation, and stakeholder relations, and co-edited the volume *Public Organizations in Communication Society.* Her research has been published in *Corporate Reputation Review, Business History, Public Relations Review,* and *International Journal of Public Sector Management.*

May-May Meijer (Ph.D., Free University of Amsterdam, 2004) worked as Assistant Professor at the Centre for the Study of Philanthropy at the Free University of Amsterdam. Her dissertation on the effects of news on corporate reputation has been published in the United States and the Netherlands. She has published in international journals, including the *Journal of Communication, Public Relations Review, Business & Society,* and the *International Journal of Nonprofit and Voluntary Sector Marketing.* She has also worked as a PR consultant for Shahrzad News.

Mette Morsing (Ph.D., Copenhagen Business School, 1993) is Professor and Director of Copenhagen Business School Center for Corporate Social Responsibility. Morsing has published her work in such journals as *Human Relations, Corporate Reputation Review, Corporate Governance, Harvard-Deusto Business Review,* and *Business Ethics: a European Review.* Her latest books in English are *Media, Organization and Identity; Corporate Communication: Convention, Complexity and Critique;* and *Corporate Social Responsibility.* Morsing is a member of a number of Nordic/European committees and boards on issues of CSR.

Dário Arantes Nunes (M.Sc., the Pontifícia Universidade Católica de Minas Gerais, 2007) is Communication and Business Professor in the Instituto de Educação Continuada at the Pontifícia Universidade Católica de Minas Gerais. His research has been published in the Revista Brasileira de Comunicação Organizacional e Relações Públicas–Organicom and in the academic journal of the Associação Nacional de Pós-Graduação e Pesquisa em Administração–AnPAD.

Olutayo Otubanjo (Ph.D., Brunel University London, 2008) is Assistant Professor of Marketing at Lagos Business School. His work has appeared in such journals as *Corporate Communications: an International Journal, Management Decisions,* and *Journal of Product & Brand Management,* and in edited volumes on branding. His research interests include corporate identity and reputation, corporate communications, and corporate branding.

Gonzalo Diego Peña (Master of Public Opinion Research, Fundación Banco Patricios, 1998) is Academic Coordinator of the Masters in Market Research, Media and Opinion (UCES), Professor in UCES University, Universidad Católica Argentina (UCA), and Senior Management Business School (ADEN). Peña is author of Intelligent Integration International Markets. Peña is a speaker at International Congress of ESOMAR, and ABEP SAIMO and author of scholarly articles and news for media and universities. Peña also serves as Director of OH! PANEL, specializing in online market research.

Klement Podnar (Ph.D., University of Ljubljana, 2004) is Associate Professor at the Faculty of Social Sciences at the University of Ljubljana in Slovenia. His research has been published in *European Journal of Marketing, Journal of Public Policy & Marketing, Corporate Communication, Journal of Communication Management, Corporate Reputation Review,* and *Journal of Marketing Communications.* Podnar serves as the Head of Marketing Communication and Public Relations Department at the University of Ljubljana.

Davide Ravasi (Ph.D., Bocconi University, 1999) is Associate Professor of Management at the Management Department of Bocconi University in Italy. His work has been published in the *Academy of Management Journal, Journal of Management Studies, Journal of Business Venturing, Industrial and Corporate Change, Long Range Planning,* and *Corporate Reputation Review,* among others. He serves on the editorial boards of the *Academy of Management Review,*

Journal of Management Studies, Corporate Reputation Review, and the *Journal of Management and Governance.*

Federico Rey Lennon (Ph.D., University of Navarra, 1996) is a University Professor in the Institute of Communication at the Argentine Catholic University. His research has been published in such journals as *Journalism & Mass Communications Quarterly, Political Communication, Comunicación y Sociedad, Signos Universitarios,* and *Chasqui.* He serves on the editorial boards of *Cronia* and *Ecos de la Comunicación.* He is author of several books, including *Reflexiones sobre el management de la comunicación.* He serves on the Board of the Public Relations Council of the Argentine Republic. He is founder and CEO of Rey Lennon & Partners, a PR firm.

Jörg Schneider (M.A., Philipps-University Marburg, 1999) is Scientific Assistant at the Research Centre for the Public Sphere and Society (fög) at the University of Zürich, Switzerland. His interests focus on reputation analytics and methods of empirical social research. He does consulting in the area of reputation management for public and private corporations.

Mario Schranz (Ph.D., University of Zurich, 2007) is a Senior Lecturer and Director at the Research Centre for the Public Sphere and Society (fög) at the University of Zürich, Switzerland. He has published articles in the fields of Corporate Social Responsibility, Public Relations, and Reputation.

Toshio Takeshita (Ph.D., University of Tsukuba, 1998) is Professor in the School of Political Science & Economics at Meiji University in Tokyo, Japan. He is the author of *The Agenda-Setting Function of the Media* (in Japanese), and he has contributed chapters to *Media and Politics in Japan, Communication and Democracy, The Handbook of Election News Coverage around the World,* and *Political Communication in Asia.*

Turo Uskali (Ph.D., University of Jyväskylä, 2003) is Senior Research Scholar in the Department of Communication at the University of Jyväskylä, Finland, where he heads the Information Business Research group, and Global Innovation Journalism research project. He has authored or co-authored four books about the evolution of global journalism and the changes in media industries in Finnish. He serves as a Member of Scientific Committee for Helsingin Sanomat Foundation.

Dejan Verčič (Ph.D., London School of Economics, 2000) is a founding partner in Pristop, a communication management consultancy based in Ljubljana, Slovenia, and Associate Professor at the University of Ljubljana. He has published in *Communication Yearbook, Journal of Communication Management, Journal of Political Marketing,* and *Journal of Public Relations Research.* He serves on the editorial boards of *Journal of Communication Management, Journal of Public Affairs,* and *Public Relations Review.* He organizes BledCom, an annual international Public Relations Research Symposium, and served as President of the European Public Relations Education and Research Association (EUPRERA).

Timothy Walters (Ph.D., University of Texas at Austin) is Head of the Department of Mass Communication, at the American University of Sharja in the United Arab Emirates. He has published in *Public Relations* Review and is a member of the editorial board of *Public Relations Review.*

Sung-Un Yang (University of Maryland, 2005) is Assistant Professor of Public Relations at S. I. Newhouse School of Public Communications, Syracuse University, with a joint appointment in the Public Diplomacy program. He serves on the editorial boards of *Communication Research, Journal of Public Relations Research*, and *Communication Quarterly.* Dr. Yang is the author of *Reputation Management for Organizations*, and has authored or coauthored 22 referred publications in *Journal of Public Relations Research, Public Relations Review, Corporate Reputation Review*, and *Journal of Communication Management*, among others.

Erkan Yüksel (Ph.D., Anadolu University, 1999) is Associate Professor in the Faculty of Communication Sciences at Anadolu University in Turkey. He is author of numerous works in Turkish, including *Media Security Council, Agenda-Setting Power of the Media, Privatization Issue in Press and Policy Agenda, Earthquake in the Press, News Gathering and Writing* (with H. İ. Gürcan), *Handbook of Journalism* (with H. İ. Gürcan), and editor of the book *Secrets of Magic Mirror.* He is co-founder and co-chair of the annual international symposium Communication in the Millennium.

Stelios C. Zyglidopoulos (Ph.D., McGill University, 2000) is a University Lecturer of Strategic Management in the Judge Business School at the University of Cambridge and Director of Management Studies and Fellow of Homerton College. His research has been published in the *Journal of Management Studies*, the *British Journal of Management*, the *Journal of Business Ethics,* and *Business &Society*, among others. He serves on the editorial boards of *Corporate Reputation Review, Business & Society*, and *Organization Studies.* He co-authored the volume *Charting Corporate Corruption: Agency, Structure and Escalation.*

Index

Printed in the United States
by Baker & Taylor Publisher Services